Pattern
and
Growth
in
Personality

Pattern and Growth in Personality

By GORDON W. ALLPORT

Harvard University

HOLT, RINEHART AND WINSTON
New York • Chicago • San Francisco
Toronto • London

May, 1964

Copyright 1937, © 1961

by Holt, Rinehart and Winston, Inc.

Library of Congress Catalog Card Number: 61-15283

20348-0311

Printed in the United States of America

TO MY STUDENTS

I have made a ceaseless effort

not to ridicule, not to bewail,

nor to scorn human actions,

but to understand them.

—SPINOZA

Preface

ALTHOUGH in one sense this volume is a revision of my book, *Personality: a Psychological Interpretation* (1937), in another sense it is wholly new.

Like the earlier volume, it offers a survey of the most important fruits of personological research. It likewise supplies coordinating theory to knit together the results of this research. The outlook, scope, and emphasis are not greatly changed.

At the same time, the present volume is distinctly different. Only a few sentences and paragraphs are reprinted verbatim. The investigations cited are, for the most part, of recent date. Unlike its predecessor, the present book is intended for college students who have little or no background in psychology.

The earlier edition took up cudgels in behalf of a psychology of the normal and integrated person. Most existing schools of thought seemed inadequate, whether they favored stimulus-response, psychoanalysis, differential psychology, typology, or factor-analysis. To a considerable extent the inadequacies still exist, and are again pointed out.

Yet in the interval much welcome progress has occurred. Many recent writers have joined me in arguing that psychology should not be content with studying an artificial man, but should describe and explain a real one. In recent years several new movements have had a beneficial impact—among them existentialism, phenomenology, client-centered therapy, and so-called ego-psychology.

Thanks to these developments, and to new investigations, and also to my own critics, I have, I hope, improved my exposition. New chapters deal with cultural factors in personality, with cognition, with the self. I have revised my argument for functional autonomy. So much has happened in the fields of learning, assessment, and in "person perception" that totally fresh accounts of these topics have been prepared.

The basic problem remains unchanged. This problem, as I see it, is to discover the proper balance between uniform factors and individual morphogenic factors in personality. Let me explain what I mean by referring to the science of biology. Molecular biology shows increasingly that life-substances are identical across species. The building blocks of life—vegetable and animal—turn out to be strikingly uniform in terms of nucleic acids, protein molecules, and enzymatic reactions. Yet a sparrow differs from a pine tree, a man from a sparrow, and one man is very unlike another. The challenge of morphogenesis (accounting for pattern) waxes more and more acute as we discover the commonalities in life.

It is so with psychology. The more we search out, and discover, what is uniform in human nature, the more urgent it becomes to account for uniqueness in the form and pattern of the whole. Just as morphogenic biology lags behind analytic and molecular biology, so too does morphogenic psychology lag behind analytic and molecular psychology. One important purpose of this volume is to call attention to this gap and to possible ways of closing it.

Our emphasis, therefore, is upon the inner organization of motives, traits, and personal style. In spite of lively attacks from critics, I persist in my belief that patterned individuality should be, and can be, a datum for the science of personality. This conviction leads me to resist the reduction of personality to commonalities found in all men.

It leads me likewise to resist the current fashion in social science that would reduce personality to a matter of roles, to interpersonal relations, to incidents within the sociocultural system. Important as culture and society are, they should not be allowed to eclipse the internal coherent system that is the essence of personality. It is true, of course, that personality is fashioned in, and expresses itself in, a social milieu. Yet it is also a self-contained system, and as such merits study in its own right.

In one additional respect this book departs from current trends. It is lukewarm toward models that render personality in terms of giant computing machines, mathematical and statistical constructs, and other simulations. There is no objection to the use of such models for explorative research. Damage is done only when devotees claim that their approach yields accounts "more fundamental" than does an empirical-humanistic approach. Statistics, for example, can provide valuable tools for symbolizing sound arguments; but if an argument is basically unsound (or lacking), statistical elaboration does nothing but enhance the confusion.

Notwithstanding these reservations I hope and believe that the reader will find in these pages a comprehensive and reasonably eclectic account of scientific studies of personality. At the present time we have no right to close off, or discourage, any avenue of approach to the investigation of human nature. Narrow dogmatism is out of place. At the same time it is legitimate for an author to test the contributions he reports from some systematic point of view. Do these contributions, we ask, have clear relevance to personality conceived as *a patterned and growing system?*

I am fully aware that the weakest area of empirical research to date is the one that this volume especially favors, viz., studies of the concrete pattern, the internal order, of a single personality. Much that we have to say on this topic remains in the realm of program. And yet this is not altogether true. In most chapters we are able to point to research developments that focus upon internal pattern and growth, dealing thereby with human life in the concrete, which is the only way human life is lived.

All books on the psychology of personality are at the same time books on the philosophy of the person. It could not be otherwise. A writer who decides that one theory of learning, or of motivation, is better than another is thereby endorsing one view of the nature of man at the expense of other views. In most psychological texts, however, the philosophy is hidden. Only a sophisticated reader can detect it. In this regard the present volume is more candid. It invites the reader to note the philosophical consequences of endorsing one psychological interpretation rather than another. My own view is that, taken in the large, the evidence before us does not depict man as a reactive robot. It points rather to a conception of man as a being with unique potential for growth. Most of the potentialities of man are never realized, and until we understand them better than we do they will not be called forth.

The beginnings of this book lay in investigations undertaken forty years ago. Ever since that time it has been in the process of writing or revising. The edition of 1937 was in general well received, and perhaps helped to define the psychological science of personality. Following its publication many special topics claimed my attention. The result was a series of books properly regarded as supplements to the original volume: *The Use of Personal Documents in Psychological Science* (1942), *The Individual and His Religion* (1950), *The Nature of Prejudice* (1954), *Becoming: Basic Considerations for a Psychology of Personality* (1955). In addition there were many related papers, some of which are reprinted in a volume of essays, *Personality and Social Encounter* (1960). In the present text I have tried to restate in simplified fashion the gist of all these writings, in the light of contemporary psychological research and theory.

The material has been presented many times to my classes. Through their interest in and their discussion of and participation in experiments, students have contributed to its present form and content more than they know. I therefore dedicate the volume to them, and also to students in all lands who in the future may seek to solve the riddles of human personality.

For specific aid in preparing the present volume I wish to thank Ada L. Allport, Katherine F. Bruner, James H. Laue, Carl C. Seltzer, Doris C. Simpson, Harold E. Allport, Renato Tagiuri, and Luberta H. McCabe. Especially deep is my indebtedness to Theodore Newcomb, who helpfully read the entire manuscript and gave valuable criticism, and to Eleanor D. Sprague, whose advice and practical aid were at all times indispensable.

Cambridge, Massachusetts   G.W.A.
July 1, 1961

Table of Contents

Preface   ix

PART   I.   AN APPROACH TO PERSONALITY

CHAPTER

1. Psychology and Individuality   3
2. Personality, Character, Temperament   22
3. Insights from the Past   36

PART   II.   DEVELOPMENT OF PERSONALITY

CHAPTER

4. Foundations of Personality   57
5. Principles of Learning   83
6. The Evolving Sense of Self   110
7. The Unconscious Stratum   139
8. Culture, Situation, Role   165
9. The Development of Motives   196
10. The Transformation of Motives   219
11. Cognition and Personality   258
12. The Mature Personality   275

PART   III.   STRUCTURE OF PERSONALITY

CHAPTER

13. Search for Elements   311
14. The Theory of Common Traits   332

15. Personal Dispositions   357
16. The Unity of Personality   376

PART IV. ASSESSMENT OF PERSONALITY
CHAPTER
17. A Survey of Methods   395
18. A Survey of Methods (Cont.)   422
19. Expressive Behavior   460

PART V. UNDERSTANDING PERSONALITY
CHAPTER
20. Person Perception   497
21. The Nature of Understanding   523
22. The Person in Psychology   549

Index of Subjects   575

Index of Names   585

PART I AN APPROACH TO Personality

CHAPTER 1

Psychology
and Individuality

INHERITANCE • BIOCHEMICAL INDIVIDUALITY • PATTERNED IN-
DIVIDUALITY • SCIENCE AND UNIQUENESS: THE DILEMMA •
THE MEANING OF "LAW" • PROPOSED SOLUTIONS • THREE
SETS OF NORMS • DIFFERENTIAL PSYCHOLOGY • TYPES • CLIN-
ICAL PSYCHOLOGY • SUMMARY

LET us start by comparing two statements: (1) "What an
interesting personality Walter has." (2) "What an interesting thing
personality is."

In the first statement I exclude Sam, Jim, and Ruth; I am calling
attention to the unique psychological pattern that marks Walter as
an individual. In the second statement I mean to include Walter,
Sam, Jim, Ruth, and everyone else in the world.

The two statements are poles apart in their coverage: one man
and billions of men. But both statements are equally true. The term
personality refers both to mind-in-particular and to mind-in-general.
If we wish to study personality at all we must be ready to shift our
attention rapidly from the particular to the general, from the concrete person to the abstract person, and back again. This shuttling is
helpful. What we learn from Walter helps us to know man-in-gen-

eral; and what we know about man-in-general is in part applicable
to Walter.

The pages of this book contain many instances of shuttling. Our
purpose is to discover general principles of the development, organization, and expression of personality, even while we emphasize the
fact that *the outstanding characteristic of man is his individuality.*
He is a unique creation of the forces of nature. There was never a
person just like him, and there never will be again. Remember the
fingerprint; even it is unique.

All sciences, including psychology, tend to neglect this paramount
fact of individuality for reasons that we shall soon examine. In daily
life, on the other hand, we are in no danger of forgetting that individuality is the supreme mark of human nature. All during our waking life, and even in our dreams, we recognize and deal with people
as separate, distinct, and unique individuals. We know they are
born and die at definite times and throughout their life span manifest their own special pattern of physical and mental traits. In view
of the uniqueness of each person's inheritance and environment it
could not be otherwise.

Inheritance

Nature's method of sexual reproduction guarantees superla-
tively novel genetic equipment for every mortal that is born. Theoretically half of one's inheritance comes from the mother and half
from the father. Think first of the uniqueness of the mating. One
particular male from a billion plus in the world mates with one particular female from a billion plus. No other combination would
produce this particular double source of inheritance.

Now in the human germ cells are 46 chromosomes. Each cell is
packed with about 30,000 genes. One or more genes are required for
an inherited trait. At a certain stage in development the germ cells
undergo "reduction fission" and come out with only 23 chromosomes,
thus discarding many possibilities for inheritance because chromosomes possess different combinations of various genes. A further
hazard—an enormous one—concerns the chance that one particular
sperm (of all the 300,000,000 deposited in the vagina during sexual
intercourse), containing its own peculiar gene variants, will unite
with a given ovum to result in the conception of a new life. It is

preposterous to suppose that any two individuals on earth (except only identical twins formed from the same ovum and same sperm) can have a common pattern of inheritance. The number of possible combinations of human genes with their possible mutations Dobzhansky estimates as "vastly greater than the number of atoms in the entire universe. Obviously only an infinitesimal fraction of the possible gene combinations are, or ever can be, realized anywhere in the world. . . . Every human being is, then, the carrier of a unique genotype."[1]

From these impressive facts we conclude that no two human beings (with the possible exception of identical twins) have even the potentiality of developing alike, especially when to all these genetic differences we add the differences that will occur in the environments and experiences of each mortal person.

Yet—and here we are shuttling—we dare not forget that genes create for all representatives of *Homo sapiens* certain gross features in common. They all have upright postures, possess two eyes and ears, hands and legs, and are bilaterally symmetrical (more or less). They have the same chemical elements in the body, and a capacity for feeling and thinking, for speaking, imagining, remembering, reproducing. Exceptions are rare.

Biochemical Individuality

The glands of internal secretion, we know, have a profound effect on temperament, on the course of growth, on motivation. The variation in their weight and size, even within *normal* limits, is vast. Williams gives us the following examples:[2]

pituitary	weight varies from 350 to 1,100 mg.
thyroid	weight varies from 8 to 50 gm.
parathyroids	weight varies from 50 to 300 mg.; number of lobes vary 2–12.

[1] T. Dobzhansky, *The biological basis of human freedom* (New York: Columbia Univ. Press, 1956), p. 56. Dunn and Dobzhansky add: "A biologist must assert the absolute uniqueness of every human individual. The same assertion translated into metaphysical and political terms is fundamental for both ethics and democracy." L. C. Dunn and T. Dobzhansky, *Heredity, race and society* (New York: Penguin, 1946), p. 46. See also C. J. Herrick, *The evolution of human nature* (Austin: Univ. of Texas Press), 1956, p. 115.
[2] R. J. Williams, *Biochemical individuality* (New York: Wiley, 1956).

testes	weight varies from 10 to 45 gm.
ovaries	weight varies from 2 to 10 gm.; contain (at birth) 30,000–400,000 ova.
adrenals	weight varies from 7 to 20 gm. 10-fold variation in thickness of cortex.

The factor of severalfold variation is not confined to glands. The metabolic rates of individuals range widely, so too their reaction to drugs, their consumption of water, their need for potassium, sodium, calcium, iodine, and amino acids. Their vitamin requirements show a severalfold variation; on the same diet one sailor will develop scurvy due to deficiency in vitamin C, and another will not. Susceptibility to diseases varies widely, so too the effects of oxygen deprivation, and ability to taste various substances. In one experiment the amount of mercuric chloride necessary to produce skin irritation was tested. Out of 35 subjects, 1 showed skin irritation when a solution of 1 part per 100,000 was used; 5 more responded to 10 parts; 11 more to 30 parts; 4 failed to respond to any of the concentrations tested.[3]

The morphology of the nervous system is no less variable. Many people have three sets of splanchnic nerves instead of the more usual two; the patterns of facial nerves are about as different as the river systems on different continents. About 15 percent of people have no direct pyramidal nerve tracts in the spinal cord. Some individuals have the sciatic nerve so embedded that it is well protected, whereas in others it is relatively exposed. Both the gross and the microscopic anatomy of the brain reveal vast differences. After reviewing the subject, Lashley writes, "Even the limited evidence at hand, however, shows that individuals start life with brains differing enormously in structure; unlike in number, size and arrangement of neurons, as well as in grosser features."[4]

For a period of twelve years Dearborn and Rothney measured annually the growth rates of over 3,000 children. Although all the children *did* grow, and although most showed a preadolescent spurt

[3] *Ibid.,* p. 110.
[4] K. S. Lashley, Structural variation in the nervous system in relation to behavior *Psychol. Rev.,* 1947, **54**, 325–334.

in rate of growth, still the indices differed so greatly from child to child that the authors conclude that "no two cases have been found to have exactly the same developmental pattern."[5]

With such a range of genetic and structural and biochemical variability we must expect temperament and motivation, indeed every known psychological function, to vary widely. Some people seem fated to find life a bitter burden; to others it will be as heady as champagne. The personal forms of intelligence will range all over the human landscape, and so too the strength and direction of different motives. Well-known studies of sexuality show a variation in the intensity and expression of the sex drive that surprises those who have thought that uniformity prevails in this area of motivation.[6]

Think for a moment of the implications of this wide-ranging individuality for therapy—whether it be surgical, medical, or psychological. The therapist cannot successfully follow mere rules of thumb. No one is normal (in the sense of average) in more than a few attributes. It is certainly safe to say that no one is average in *all* his endocrine, anatomical, neural, cortical, and motivational capacities.

After considering the problem we are discussing, Goethe exclaimed, "Nature seems to have staked everything on individuality."[7]

Patterned Individuality

Thus every person deviates in thousands of ways from the hypothetical average man. But his individuality is not the sum of all these separate deviations. This is a point of extreme importance—and unless it is understood the reader will fail to grasp the burden of this book.

Take lungs for a moment—yours and mine. There is no living relation between your lungs and my lungs, nor between your cortical metabolism and mine. But my lungs do influence *my* cortical metabolism and so do yours. My potassium need interacts with my sodium need. These chemical needs may be *compared* with yours, but they have no organic *functioning relation* to yours. It is my heredity, my

[5] W. F. Dearborn and J. W. M. Rothney, *Predicting the child's development* (Cambridge, Mass.: Sci-Art, 1941).

[6] A. C. Kinsey, *et al.*, *Sexual behavior in the human male* (Philadelphia: Saunders, 1948); A. C. Kinsey, *et al.*, *Sexual behavior in the human female* (Philadelphia: Saunders, 1953).

[7] The statement *Sie scheint alles auf Individualität angelegt zu haben* appears in the fragment entitled *Die Natur.*

early experience, my temperament, brain capacity, emotions, motives, pulse rate, memory, cultural history, and imagination that are bound together in one individual functioning; they comprise one system, made up of various subsystems.

Unfortunately science studies chiefly my pulse rate in comparison with yours, my emotions as different from yours, my height as deviant from the norm; it seldom studies my height, pulse, emotions as an interacting *pattern*.

I object strongly, therefore, to a point of view that is current in psychology. Eysenck states it as follows: *To the scientist, the unique individual is simply the point of intersection of a number of quantitative variables.*[8]

What does this statement mean? It means that the scientist is not interested in the mutual interdependence of part-systems within the whole system of personality. He is interested only in separate dimensions whereby he can compare many persons. He is interested in hearts (yours and mine) or in lungs (yours and mine) but not in the mutual interaction of my heart with my lungs, or your heart with your lungs. He is interested in some trait (e.g., introversion)—yours and mine; but is not interested in the manner in which your introversion interacts with your other traits, with your values, and with your life plans. The scientist, according to this view, then, isn't interested in the personality system at all, but only in common dimensions. The person is left as mere "point of intersection" with no internal structure, coherence, or animation. I cannot agree with this view.

Science and Uniqueness: The Dilemma

It is easy, however, to see that a quandary confronts us. The individual, whatever else he may be, is an internally consistent and unique organization of bodily and mental processes. But since he is unique, science finds him an embarrassment. Science, it is said, deals only with broad, preferably universal, laws. Thus science is a *nomothetic* discipline. Individuality cannot be studied by science, but

[8] H. J. Eysenck, *The scientific study of personality* (New York: Macmillan, 1952), p. 18. It is difficult to see how the author can reconcile this conception of the individual with his own definition of personality as "the more or less stable and enduring organization of a person's character, temperament, intellect, and physique, which determines his unique adjustment to the environment." *The structure of human personality* (London: Methuen, 1953), p. 2.

only by history, art, or biography whose methods are not nomothetic (seeking universal laws), but *idiographic*.[9] Even the medieval scholastics perceived the issue, and declared *scientia non est individuorum*.

If we accept this dogma concerning the scope and limitations of science we shall have to abandon the person as a person. But we are not yet discouraged. That the individual is a system of patterned uniqueness is a fact. That science likes universals and not particulars is also a fact. Yet personality itself is a universal phenomenon though it is found only in individual forms. Since it is a universal phenomenon science must study it; but it cannot study it correctly unless it looks into the individuality of patterning! Such is the dilemma.

Can we not say, as some scientists do, that a particular is what it is by virtue of the fact that it is a complex combination of universals? Even if we disregard the fact that the phrase "complex combination" begs the whole question, the statement itself is misleading. It says that all men are composed of the same qualities (universals) but that their combination makes for uniqueness. Let us take just two universals and see how it works out:

Individual	Quality A Intelligence	Quality B Dominance
John	90 percentile	10 percentile
Henry	10 percentile	90 percentile

Here we are told that John is a very bright fellow but quite submissive; Henry is dull but dominant. So far so good. But may not Quality A interact with Quality B so that a new unit is formed? May not John be a brilliant follower, Henry a stupid aggressor? And the flavor of their conduct will be further altered by their other qualities, so that the emergent pattern is not predictable from the universals. A molecule of water and of peroxide have the same universals

---

9 These terms were originally established by W. Windelband, but are now fairly widespread in their usage. See his *Geschichte und Naturwissenschaft* (3d ed.; Strassburg: Heitz, 1904). See also R. Eisler, *Wörterbuch der philosophischen Begriffe* (Berlin: Mittler, 1904), p. 512.

The reader's attention is called to the spelling of *idiographic*. Its origin lies in the Greek ιδιος (meaning one's own). The same root is found in *idiom, idiosyncrasy*. It should not be confused with *ideographic*, which, like *ideology*, derives from ιδέα—idea (that which is seen, a semblance). The term *nomothetic* is from νομοθετικός—nomothetikos (the giving or enacting of laws).

—hydrogen and oxygen; they differ only quantitatively (H_2O and H_2O_2), but a small quantitative difference leads to totally unlike products. Try them on your hair and see.

The problem of individuality, then, is not how John's intelligence or dominance compares with these same qualities abstracted from other people, but how John's intelligence is related to his dominance, to his values, to his conscience, and to everything else in his personality. It is the "inside system" that baffles a conventional science of universals.

The Meaning of "Law"

The reason conventional science is baffled is that it cannot see how the internal organization of the particular can fit into its nomothetic search for general laws. But several thoughts are of possible help here.

In the first place, it is a universally true statement, and therefore a law, that the personal patterns of individuality are unique. The psychology of personality would do well to acknowledge this as its *first* law.

In the second place, we can look hopefully to many general principles of biology and dynamic psychology for those processes that bring about uniqueness. The general principles of genetics, for example, are laws that tell us how uniqueness occurs.

In the third place, the behavior of every individual is lawful in its own right. We do not have to understand every life in order to discover the lawful regularities in one life. If you have an intimate friend, you may know very well why he behaves as he does, and be able to predict and partially to control his behavior in the future, just because you know the lawful regularities in his life. You do not need a knowledge of human nature in general in order to do so.

This last point is important, for it raises the question of statistical (actuarial) regularities versus the lawful regularities of an individual person. Nomothetic science, as we have said, tends to favor the former and to neglect the latter. Its measures of statistical significance are geared to a large population of people, not to the single case.

Suppose a group of a hundred delinquents in a prison hear the warden say these words: "Your life in prison is a preparation for your return to society." And suppose, as seems likely, ninety-nine of the jailbirds silently laugh at the bromide and promptly forget it. Statistical psychologists would say that it is a law that this pious exhortation will have no effect. And in a sense they are right.

But suppose that for one man the words happen to "ring a bell" and set him on the road to genuine reformation. What will the statistician say? That it is "due to chance," or that this event is not "statistically significant"? Such a reply would be absurd. The fact of the matter is that an important causal relation exists in this case. It may be a rare (even a unique) happening, but it is entirely lawful—an inevitable event considering the internal pattern of the person to whom the words appeal.

And so we conclude that we must not be browbeaten by narrow definitions of "law," or, for that matter, by narrow definitions of science. It is the duty of science to illuminate what *is*, not merely what is convenient, or what is traditional. Long before the method of natural science attained its commanding position with psychology paddling in its wake, there was an ancient meaning of *scientia*. It prescribed no method, set no limits; it signified simply *knowledge*.

Proposed Solutions

As might be expected, many perceptive writers have noted this dilemma of science-uniqueness. The most obvious solution, of course, is to declare that generality belongs to science, individuality to art. This proposal says in effect: let us acknowledge the limitations of science. It can never by its very nature do justice to the intact individual—only drama, poetry, biography can do so. Science is ruthless in its exclusion of particularities. Hence science is at best merely "an accessory to wisdom."[10] Such a solution appeals to many scientists and probably to all humanists.

This proposal, however, is a counsel of despair. Psychology is a young discipline and ideally should develop mastery of both abstract and concrete phenomena. It is premature to freeze it into an exclu-

[10] H. A. Murray, *et al., Explorations in personality* (New York: Oxford, 1938), p. 716. See also G. W. Allport, Personality a problem for science or for art? *Personality and social encounter* (Boston: Beacon, 1960), Chap. 1.

sively nomothetic way of thinking. We should keep the individual within the science.

Such was the view of Samuel Bailey who a century ago criticized psychology for paying attention almost entirely to what is "common to mankind," and for dealing with individual character "only incidentally and briefly—too briefly for the importance of the subject."[11]

Another solution is to declare for two separate and distinct psychologies—one devoted to the nomothetic and one to the idiographic position. The latter, of course, would work hand in hand with history, biography, literature, and perhaps be indistinguishable from them. Many German writers have favored this view, assigning nomothetic psychology to the natural sciences (*Naturwissenschaften*) and idiographic psychology to the mental-cultural sciences (*Geisteswissenschaften*). The former is a psychology of "elements," the latter a psychology of "structure." The former uses the method of analysis and causal explanation, the latter uses the method of "understanding" (*Verstehen*). "We *explain* nature (by analysis and law)," they say, "but we *understand* people" (in their patterned individuality).[12]

My own position regarding this proposed solution can be briefly stated. The separation of psychology into two opposed branches is too sharp. I agree with the French psychiatrist Azam, who many years ago wrote that the science of character "cannot proceed by generalities, as does psychology, nor by individualities, as does art. It occupies an intermediate position."[13] There is no reason why we should not learn from every generalization about human nature that we can. At the same time we need to be alert for concepts and methods that enable us to understand patterned individuality. As we have seen,

11 S. Bailey, *Letters on the philosophy of the human mind* (London: Longmans, Green, 1855–1958), II, 265.

12 This point of view is presented by E. Spranger, *Types of men* (Transl. by P. Pigors; Halle: Niemeyer, 1928).

Essentially the same distinction is upheld by Bergson. He contrasts sharply the method of analysis by which we freeze certain elementary relationships and disregard the flow or continuity of life, with the method of "intuition" which enables us to bind the related aspects of a person into a sense of their continuous development. H. Bergson, *Introduction to metaphysic* (New York: Putnam, 1912). We shall return to this problem in Chapter 21.

13 E. Azam. *Le caractère dans la santé et dans la maladie* (Paris: Alcan, 1887), p. vi.

the individual represents lawful order in nature. We should use *all* avenues of approach in the developing science of the psychology of personality.

We have not yet covered all the proposed solutions to the dilemma of science-uniqueness. Let us look more closely at some additional suggestions.

Three Sets of Norms

How do we know a person? Partly we do so by comparing his characteristics with three sets of standards (norms). Kluckhohn and Murray put the matter in the following way:[14]

Every man is in certain respects:

a. like all other men (universal norms)
b. like some other men (group norms)
c. like no other men (idiosyncratic norms)

This statement is true and helpful—up to a point. We shall soon consider one pitfall that it contains for the unwary. It is, however, true that the psychology of personality utilizes all these norms as Figure 1 indicates.

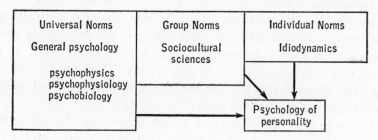

Figure 1. Three Sets of Norms Utilized in the Psychology of Personality

Universal Norms. When we say that a person is tall, or quick, or energetic, or cheerful, or that he has an intelligence quotient of 110, we are comparing him with the general population of human beings we have known (or measured). Sam, we note, is at average, or above or below average in some attribute. So far so good. In a sense

14 C. Kluckhohn, H. A. Murray, and D. M. Schneider, *Personality in nature, society, and culture* (New York: Knopf, 1953), p. 53.

Sam's personality is a matter of conformity with, or deviation from, the average human being.

Group Norms. Strictly speaking, universal norms are hard to come by. If Sam is an American we are more likely to judge him in comparison with other Americans than in comparison with English-men or Chinese. If Sam's IQ is 110, we really mean that he is slightly above average for the group that has been tested with a certain test, presumably American nationals. But this distinction need not trouble us: we merely note in passing that the universal norms shade into group norms.

Group norms are especially important when we say that Sam is a typical something-or-other: a typical businessman, a typical hard-shell Baptist, an egghead, a manic-depressive type, a sporting type, or a typical Southerner. Such statements mean that Sam has a cluster of qualities that do not differ very much from the majority of members in the group to which he belongs or with which he is being com-pared. Or, vice versa, we may say that Sam is a deviant within his own group: he is *not* a typical doctor or farmer. We might say, "It is hard to believe that he is a schoolteacher." But whether he is like or unlike others in his group we use group norms in order to assess his nature.

Individual Norms. After we become acquainted with Sam we set up our own expectations regarding him. His own traits, his per-sonal pattern of interests, the organization of his personality consti-tute a standard for judgment. If an act fits our expectation we say, "How characteristic of him"; if not, we say "How unlike him," or "He isn't himself today." To the study of this personal pattern Rosenzweig has applied the term *idiodynamics.*[15]

We note that universal and group norms are the concern of nomothetic science. Individual norms lead us back again to the con-ception of idiographic science. Our argument here is, as indicated in Figure 1, that the psychology of personality cannot proceed by gen-eralities alone, nor by individualities alone, but "occupies an inter-mediate position."

Although we accept the formula of three sets of norms, we should guard against one pitfall. This approach might mistakenly imply that the individual as such is only a handful of residual, and perhaps

15 S. Rosenzweig, The place of the individual and of idiodynamics in psychology: a dialogue, *J. indiv. Psychol.,* 1958, **14,** 3–21.

negligible, idiosyncrasies, a leftover when we have accounted for most of his behavior in terms of universal or group norms. The facts are otherwise. Sam, to be sure, has many attributes characteristic of the human species, and many that resemble his cultural fellows: *but he weaves them all into a unique idiomatic system*. His personality does not contain three systems, but only one. Individuality is not the residual ragbag left over after the nomothetic sciences have had their say. The organization of the individual life is first, last, and all the time a primary fact of human nature.

Differential Psychology

Differential psychology is another name for the psychology of individual differences. It grew up at the beginning of this century and still flourishes.[16] In fact, many psychologists would consider this movement as coextensive with the psychology of personality.

Suppose a thousand people have taken tests for acuity of hearing, for mechanical intelligence, for dominance, for neurotic tendency, for interest in science (or other measurable dimensions). It is helpful to know where Sam or Jane stands in relation to the *group norms* thus obtained.

When we know their scores we can plot them on a profile (or psychograph). Figure 2 illustrates the procedure in the case of Sam for the variables we have listed above.

Among the virtues of this approach is that it focuses attention

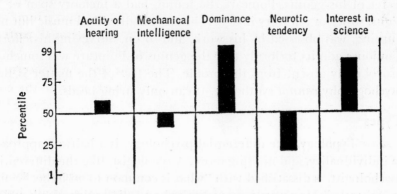

Figure 2.   Illustrative Profile for Sam

16 An important pioneer volume was W. Stern, *Die differentielle Psychologie* (3d ed.; Leipzig: Barth, 1921). A modern representative is A. Anastasi, *Differential psychology* (3d ed.; New York: Macmillan, 1958).

upon Sam in relation to the population at large. There will be few, if any, profiles exactly like Sam's. With its aid we can counsel and advise him; we can hire him for some job if his scores fit our requirements. We spot his strengths and weaknesses. A profile brings us near, but not very near, to our goal of individuality.

The method has marked limitations. For one thing we learn nothing about Sam that has not previously been chosen by the investigator for testing. Sam may have some cardinal personal trait that is not tapped at all—perhaps he is first and foremost a surgeon by taste and in skill, a fact which the battery of tests overlooks.

Another principal limitation is the fact that a profile tells us nothing about the *organization* of the qualities in question. How does Sam's dominance interact with his interest in science? What is the pattern that results from having a high interest in science but not a strong mechanical intelligence to support it? Does this opposition make him a conflicted and unhappy person, or a contented clerical assistant to some engineer? Of all profiles we may say, "The traits are there but the organization is lacking."

When differential psychology was young, a French experimentalist, Toulouse, tried the method of psychography with the famous mathematician Henri Poincaré. He said he was not satisfied with universal norms, since they expressed only what is "common to an imbecile and to an Aristotle."[17] Therefore he tested Poincaré to determine his deviations from the average in order to discover the secret of his genius. Poincaré, he found, had a memory span of 11 digits, superior auditory imagery; he slept badly, liked music but not hunting, was obsessed by his work, and so on. Surveying his efforts, Toulouse admits forlornly that the genius of Poincaré was somehow provokingly absent from the profile. The fact of the matter is that psychography *cannot* synthesize. It can only string beads.

Types

Typology, like differential psychology, is a halfway approach to individuality, and nothing more. A typologist, like the differential psychologist, is dissatisfied with "what is common to an imbecile and to Aristotle." He wants a more limited and discerning classification of human nature.

Type doctrines, however, say nothing more than that certain people resemble other people *in some respect*. One may correctly

[17] E. Toulouse, *Henri Poincaré* (Paris: Flammarion, 1910).

say that there are four types of people: those who (1) use a convex toothbrush, (2) use one that is concave, (3) use a straight one, (4) use none at all—plus, of course, the mixed type that uses sometimes one or another shape. This is a valid typology if one is interested in tooth-brushes. Similarly, there are people who are extraverts, who are introverts, and who are both. This too is a valid typology, if one is interested in extraversion and introversion. But suppose that you are interested both in toothbrushes used in brushing teeth and in extraversion. The scheme breaks down because not all users of one kind of brush are introverts. Our friend Sam, who is *one* person, would have to be classified into *two* types.

There are so many *respects* by which we can classify people, physical and mental, that we shall soon find that we have located Sam in hundreds of possible types, and again have lost his internal unique pattern of organization.

Of course many type doctrines work for inclusiveness and breadth. Let's name a few at random. We say a person is a liberal, or a narcissist, that he is cerebrotonic, an authoritarian, a beatnik, that he has a market-place personality, is Apollonian, other-directed, that he belongs to the anal type, or the oral type, or the genital type. These and countless other proposals have been made hoping for a broad and valid categorization of human beings. Each points to a cluster (syndrome) of attributes that usually (but not always) hang together.

But whether the basis for classification is broad or narrow, types always fall short of depicting the whole individual. Figure 3 shows the dilemma.

Sam fits the authoritarian type, as do other individuals, A, B, C, and D. But he can also be classed with O, P, Q and R, if we look at him in respect to the Freudian syndrome of "oral" traits. Each classification is correct, but Sam as an individual is almost untouched. His qualities have been related to similar qualities in other individuals, and have not been related within the organic field of his own nature to one another. How does his orality interact with his authoritarianism? We do not know. And many regions of his life are unaccounted for. Typologies are convenient and seductive, but none has ever been invented to account for the total individual.

Before leaving the subject we should call attention to one special form of type doctrine. Some writers advocate the use of *ideal types*. This conception escapes our criticism, for it is not intended to cover real persons. Ideal types are not arrived at by the exact study of

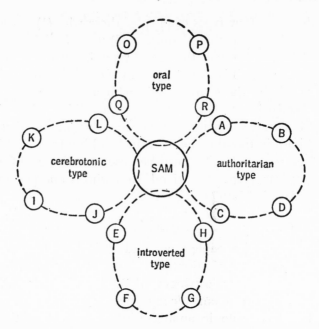

Figure 3. Typology *versus* Individuality [Dotted ellipses signify types; solid circles, individuals].

concrete people. They are derived by rational, not by *empirical* methods. Ideal types are, in Spranger's term, mere "schemata of comprehensibility."[18] Thus we can depict a "typical" Italian, an American businessman, a John Bull, a Christian, or an ideally consistent theoretical, esthetic, or political personage, without assuming that any perfect representative of the type actually exists. Such schemes for comprehension have their uses, perhaps especially in the study of "national character." Some people, of course, do, to varying degrees, approach the ideal type. And this fact may be helpful to us when we come to the assessment of personality. But ideal types are invented in the armchair, not in the laboratory.

Clinical Psychology

Many psychologists today are in "clinical work." They serve in hospitals, social agencies, schools, prisons, industrial plants, churches, and the armed forces. Their work is called "clinical" because, like physicians, they deal always with single individuals, hoping to bring about better adjustment and improved mental health. Al-

18 Spranger, *op. cit.*, note 12 above.

Meehl, for example, reviewed over a score of research investigations using both actuarial data (scores on scales obtained by the method of differential psychology) and idiographic ("intuitive") predictions of behavior. In about half the studies the two methods were approximately equal in success; in the other half the actuarial (nomothetic) mode of prediction was superior.[20]

There are now available tests and scales that have enjoyed some success in predicting success or failure in college, in forecasting delinquency, even in predicting happiness in marriage. Take an example from delinquency. Among boys who have a history of truancy, a rejective family life, and other deficiencies, it may safely be said that 85 percent will come into conflict with the police. Such an actuarial prediction reminds us of the success of safety councils in forecasting the number of traffic deaths that will occur over a holiday week end. Insurance companies are masters at such statistical prediction.

But there is a fallacy here. To say that 85 in 100 boys having such and such a background will become delinquent is not to say that Jimmy, who has this background, has 85 in 100 chances of being delinquent. Not at all. Jimmy, as an individual, either will or will not become delinquent. There is no 85 percent chance about him. Only a complete knowledge of Jimmy will enable us to predict for sure. The fact that clinicians using an "intuitive" method may fail in their prediction is beside the point. If we knew Jimmy and his environment fully we should be able to improve upon statistical forecasting, which applies only to groups of people and not to individuals.

The point at issue was once expressed by Sherlock Holmes, who said to his friend Dr. Watson: "While the individual man is an insoluble puzzle, in the aggregate he becomes a mathematical certainty. You can never foretell what any one man will do, but you can say with precision what an average number will be up to. Individuals vary but percentages remain constant."

[20] P. E. Meehl, *Clinical vs. statistical prediction* (Minneapolis: Univ. of Minnesota Press, 1954).

though the clinical psychologist needs training in general, phys
logical, experimental, and social psychology—all dealing with univ
sal or with group norms—his primary focus is upon the speci
person who sits before him.

Would it not seem, therefore, that the solution to our dilemma o
uniqueness is simple? Is not the clinical psychologist an idiographi
specialist, in contrast to all other kinds of psychologists who are
nomothetic? Partly this is true, but the situation is more complex.
Many clinical psychologists do not advance beyond the stage of differential psychology. They give tests and plot the scores on a profile,
and the individual as such is forsaken. He is reduced to a mere heap
of percentiles. If the clinical psychologist is working in a mental hospital he may hand over his findings to a psychiatrist, who tries to fit
them into the clinical picture, to put the pieces together to see what
the patient's internal systems and capacities are really like.

The process of weighting the fragmentary scores, of confronting
one bit of evidence with another, and finally of synthesizing what
one knows in order to discover the personal pattern is exceedingly
complex. Unfortunately we do not yet know how we accomplish the
task as well as we do. Suppose you wish to select a roommate or a
wife or a husband, or simply to pick out a suitable birthday gift for
your mother. Your knowledge of mankind in general will not help
you very much, or even your knowledge of group norms.

It is precisely here that "scientific" psychologists have much
trouble. They would like to think that idiographic understanding is
no better than results achieved by following actuarial data (i.e., universal or group norms).[19]

[19] Vehement antagonism against the idiographic (purely clinical) position is expressed
by many writers, among them W. Seeman and E. Galanter, Objectivity in systematic
and "idiodynamic" psychology, *Psychol. Rev.*, 1952, **59**, 285–289; G. W. Lundberg,
Case-studies vs. statistical methods—an issue based on misunderstanding, *Sociometry*,
1941, **4**, 379–383; H. J. Eysenck, The science of personality: nomothetic! *Psychol. Rev.*,
1954, **61**, 339–342; T. R. Sarbin, R. Taft, and D. E. Bailey, *Clinical inference and
cognitive theory* (New York: Holt, Rinehart and Winston, 1960).

These (and other writers) are frankly scandalized by the issue I here dare to raise.
To them it seems self-evident that the prevailing epistemological theory in psychology is
sacrosanct. General laws leading to inferences (aided by statistics) account for all our
knowledge of individual people. These writers are stanch defenders of Anglo-American
tradition of associationism and empiricism. Although I do not doubt that knowledge
of this order exists and is of great importance when applied to the single case, I also
hold that it leads to rough and routine coding, not to genuine acquaintance with individual personalities. The sad truth is that psychologists are not conspicuously successful as judges of personality. The trouble may lie in their one-sided view of the nature
of human knowledge. The problem is complex, and further discussion of it will be
deferred to Chapter 21.

The true goal of clinical psychology is not to predict the aggregate, but to foretell "what any one man will do." In reaching this ideal, actuarial prediction may sometimes help, universal and group norms are useful, but they do not go the whole distance.

Our conclusion is that the dilemma of uniqueness haunts the house of clinical psychology. Up to now the methods of differential psychology have prevailed. Deviations from universal or group norms are the clinician's primary tool for the study of individuals. Yet many clinicians feel that living human beings cannot be known exclusively through statistical laws. The person is more than "a point of intersection" of these laws. He is a lawful pattern in and of himself. New methods and new theories will be required before the dilemma is solved. We shall return to this problem in later chapters.

Summary

Individuality is a prime characteristic of human nature. To develop a science of personality we must accept this fact. But it is easier to construct an artificial man out of universal and group norms than to deal adequately and scientifically with a real man.

To be sure, general and social psychology are the root and stem upon which the psychology of personality grows. We need laws of learning, of perception, of cognition, and we need a knowledge of culture and society in order to account for the development and growth of the individual. But we need also a special point of view in order to bring these general principles to converge upon the individuality of pattern that comprises personality.

The psychology of personality is not exclusively nomothetic, nor exclusively idiographic. It seeks an equilibrium between the two extremes. If in this chapter our bias is toward the idiographic emphasis we are merely trying to redress the present one-sidedness of psychology. Many elementary textbooks in psychology offer a concluding chapter entitled "Personality." The gesture toward adequacy is commendable. But often we find that the picture of personality offered is that of an uncemented mosaic of elements and test scores, or of fragmentary processes, never vitally interrelated. Such a lifeless picture is jarring to one who feels that the individuality of man, the future-pointed thrust of his living, and the systematic interlacing of his key qualities, are the central features of his personality.

CHAPTER 2

Personality, Character, Temperament

EXTERNAL EFFECT • ORIGINS OF THE TERM "PERSONALITY" • INTERNAL STRUCTURE • THE POSITIVIST VIEW • A DEFINITION FOR THIS BOOK • A PHILOSOPHICAL OBJECTION • CHARACTER • TEMPERAMENT • SUMMARY

E VERYONE, it seems, knows what personality is, but no one can precisely describe it: hundreds of definitions are available. Broadly speaking, they fall into three classes which we shall call *external effect, internal structure,* and *positivist* definitions. We shall discuss the first briefly and then, after examining the origins of the term, the last two.[1]

External Effect

We say of one acquaintance, "He lacks personality," and of another, "She has a great deal of personality." We mean, of course,

[1] Since the student of personality is not primarily concerned with etymological and historical issues, the problem of definition is condensed in the present chapter to an irreducible minimum. The reader who is interested in a fuller account can consult my *Personality: a psychological interpretation* (New York: Holt, Rinehart and Winston, 1937), Chap. 2.

that our acquaintance makes, or fails to make, an impact on other people. Often a form for recommendation will ask us to rate an applicant on "personality." Usually what is wanted is an estimate of the applicant's social effectiveness or appeal.

One investigator set himself the task of determining what qualities make for a high rating on "personality" among women teachers. A teacher with "lots of personality," it turns out, is one who seems to others to display eight attractive qualities: "She is interesting in conversation, is competent, has wide interests, is intelligent, athletic, a good sport, and is both sincere and adaptable."[2]

Thus the popular conception of personality refers to a certain cluster of traits that is socially pleasing and effective. Advertisers who claim to help you "develop personality" aim to strengthen this cluster with their offerings of instruction in public speaking, in posture, in dancing, in conversation; even their cosmetic aids make this claim. A certain lipstick or a modish dress is said to "confer personality." In this case personality is not even skin-deep.

We cannot accept the proposition that one person has "more" or "less" personality than another. Those who lack charm are, in a psychological sense, as richly endowed as those who possess it, and are every bit as interesting to science.

Somewhat more sophisticated, but still in the same vein, are definitions offered by certain psychologists who likewise take a social or "outer" view of personality.[3] Personality is

the sum-total of the effect made by an individual upon society.

habits or action which successfully influence other people.

responses made by others to the individual as a stimulus.

what others think of you.

There is one point in favor of these "external effect" definitions. It is only through the judgments of us made by other people that

---

[2] E. G. Flemming, The "halo" around "personality," *Teachers College Record*, 1942, 43, 1–6.
[3] These and other "biosocial" (outer) definitions are listed in *Personality: a psychological interpretation*, pp. 39–43.

our personalities are known at all. Unless we *affect* people how can we be known? This is true, but what if we affect different people in different ways? Do we then have many personalities? May it not rather be that one judge may have a correct impression of us, and others a wrong impression? If so, we must have something inside our skins that constitutes our "true" nature (variable though this may be). Definitions in terms of external effects confuse personality with *reputation;* and one may have many reputations.

And what about the solitary hermit, or the feral child (living among wolves), or Robinson Crusoe before the advent of his man Friday? Do these isolates lack personality because they have no effect on others? Our own view is that such exceptional creatures have personal qualities that are no less fascinating than those of men living in human society. A TV actor may have an impact on millions of people, but may have a less complex personality than a recluse dwelling in attic obscurity.

Of course the impression we make on others, and their response to us are important factors in the development of our personalities. These are matters to which we shall turn in later chapters. But it would only befuddle our minds to confuse the external effects of personality with the internal structure itself.

Origins of the Term "Personality"

The word *personality* and its root *person* have long held fascination for students of language. Max Müller, for example, becomes enthusiastic over their abstractness and wide serviceability:

> Let us take such a word as *person.* Nothing could be more abstract. It is neither male nor female, neither young nor old. As a noun it is hardly more than what *to be* is as a verb. In French it may even come to mean nobody. For if we ask our concièrge at Paris whether anybody has called us during our absence, he will reply, "Personne, monsieur," which means, "Not a soul, sir."
>
> But this word *persona* has rolled along with wonderful bounds, striking right and left, suggesting new thoughts, stirring up clouds of controversy, and occupying to the present day a prominent place in all discussions on theology and philosophy, though few only of those who use it know how it came to be there.[4]

4 F. M. Müller, *Biographies of words* (New York: Longmans, Green, 1888), p. 32.

The terms *personality* in English, *personnalité* in French, and *Persönlichkeit* in German closely resemble the *personalitas* of medieval Latin. In classical Latin *persona* alone was used. All scholars agree that this word originally meant *mask*. (This fact can give some comfort to those who prefer to define personality in terms of external effect. Appearance, not inner organization, receives the emphasis.) But *persona*, even in ancient times, came to mean other things, including the player behind the mask, i.e., his true assemblage of inner and personal qualities. It also came to mean an important person (whence *personage, parson*). The term was also used to designate the three persons of the Trinity. And whether these *personae* were three masks of one God or three co-equal persons became a theological dispute of long duration. Perhaps the most famous definition of *persona* was given by Boethius in the sixth century: *Persona est substantia individua rationalis naturae*—a person is an individual substance of a rational nature.

And so we see that the term bounded along even in classical Latin with various meanings. Some of them anticipated the "external effect" definitions of the present day, some of them the "internal structure" definitions.

Internal Structure

Most philosophers and psychologists (except for the modern positivists whom we shall soon consider) prefer to define personality as an objective entity, as something that is "really there." They grant that the person is open to the world around him, is affected by it and affects it at every step. Yet a personality has its own life-history and its own existence; it is not to be confused with society nor with the perceptions that other people have of it. Thus William Stern, who was both a philosopher and a psychologist, speaks of personality as a "multiform dynamic unity." He adds that no one ever fully achieves a perfect unity but always has this as his aim.[5]

Some writers add a note of "value" to this type of definition. Personality is something to be prized. Thus Goethe speaks of personality as the one thing in the world that has "supreme value." And Kant's moral philosophy is based on the same conviction. Everything in life can be used by men as a means to some end—save only person-

5 W. Stern, *Die menschliche Persönlichkeit* (Leipzig: Barth, 1923), pp. 4, 20.

ality. No one may exploit another. The integrity of personality must be forever respected. Judeo-Christian ethics initiated this line of thought.

Although Western psychologists likewise customarily place high value on the integrity of personality (because it is, after all, the creed of democracy), their definitions are less exalted. They drop out any attempt at evaluation, and give a simple descriptive statement. A typical example is the following. Personality is

the sum-total of all the biological innate dispositions, impulses, tendencies, appetites, and instincts of the individual, and the acquired dispositions and tendencies—acquired by experience.[6]

Although this definition regards personality as an accessible datum for study, it fails to stress the integration of structure of the many listed component parts. It is representative of what we may call omnibus or "ragbag" definitions of personality. More "structural" is the following definition:

Personality is the entire mental organization of a human being at any stage of his development. It embraces every phase of human character: intellect, temperament, skill, morality, and every attitude that has been built up in the course of one's life.[7]

Also the following:

Personality is the organized aggregate of psychological processes and states pertaining to the individual.[8]

Some definitions stress the subjective cognitive factor that makes for internal organization, saying that personality is

a unified scheme of experience, an organization of values that are consistent with one another.[9]

My own definition will likewise be in terms of internal structure. (Some writers would call definitions of this type "essentialist.") But first we must examine a contrasting approach.

[6] M. Prince, *The unconscious* (2d ed., rev.; New York: Macmillan, 1924), p. 532.

[7] H. C. Warren and L. Carmichael, *Elements of human psychology* (Rev. ed.; Boston: Houghton Mifflin, 1930), p. 333.

[8] R. Linton, *The cultural background of personality* (New York: Appleton-Century-Crofts, 1945), p. 84.

[9] P. Lecky, *Self-consistency: a theory of personality* (New York: Island, 1945), p. 90.

The Positivist View

Some contemporary psychologists object strenuously to essentialist definitions. They argue that "internal structure" is inaccessible to science. We cannot know the "multiform dynamic unity" that is "really there." Inner structure, if it exists at all, simply cannot be studied directly.

What we know about personality is merely our "operations." If we administer a personality test and obtain such and such a score—these are our operations, i.e., our method. From the positivist point of view, therefore, inner personality is a myth, "a mere construct tied together by a proper name." The best we can do is to make guesses about it—"conceptualize" it. The conceptualization must not go beyond the scientific methods we use.

An example of such an operational definition is the following. Personality is

the most adequate conceptualization of a person's behavior in all its detail that the scientist can give at a moment of time.[10]

Here we note a resemblance to "external effect" definitions. Personality is not what one has, but is someone else's perception, in this case, the scientist's. In other words, personality is a "construct," something thought about but not actually existing "out there."

To press the point still further, there are psychologists who say we should never employ the concept of personality at all. If we knew enough about the "stimulus" and the "response" (so-called S-R psychology) we would not have to bother our heads with any "intervening variable," like personality. This is the view of extreme positivistic behaviorism. Only outer, visible, manipulable operations are tolerated. Personality as such evaporates in a mist of method.

Although such is the goal of some psychologists, it is questionable whether they are following the lead of the elder sciences. Does an astronomer who studies Arcturus think of the star as a construct tied together by a name? Hardly; to him it is a celestial body, truly existing, and possessing a composition and structure that he will try scientifically to comprehend. When a biologist dissects a plant he

10 D. McClelland, *Personality* (New York: Sloane, 1951), p. 69. The problem under discussion is considered by C. S. Hall and G. Lindzey, *Theories of personality* (New York: Wiley, 1954), p. 9.

does not believe that the plant's structure and physiology reside only in his manipulations.

Personality is even more difficult to study than stars or plants, but the situation is the same. No psychologist and no layman ever fully understands any single personality, not even his own, but this fact does not negate the existence of the personality. Like the astronomer or the biologist we *try* to comprehend an existent fact of nature. We should adapt our methods so far as we can to the object, and not define the object in terms of our faulty methods.

A Definition for This Book

There is, of course, no such thing as a correct or incorrect definition. Terms can only be defined in ways that are useful for a given purpose. For the purposes of the present volume we require a definition of personality that is "essentialist." We shall treat personality as a unit "out there," possessing internal structure in its own right. All phrasings are full of pitfalls, but for better or for worse our definition follows:

> PERSONALITY IS THE DYNAMIC ORGANIZATION WITHIN THE INDIVIDUAL OF THOSE PSYCHOPHYSICAL SYSTEMS THAT DE-TERMINE HIS CHARACTERISTIC BEHAVIOR AND THOUGHT.

We may now examine briefly the key concepts in this definition:

Dynamic organization. We have seen that omnibus or ragbag definitions are not adequate. The central problem of psychology is mental organization (the forming of patterns or hierarchies of ideas and habits that dynamically direct activity). Integration and other organizational processes are necessary to account for the development and structure of personality. Hence "organization" must appear in the definition. The term implies also the reciprocal process of *disorganization,* especially in those abnormal personalities that are marked by progressive disintegration.

Psychophysical. This term reminds us that personality is neither exclusively mental nor exclusively neural (physical). Its organization entails the functioning of both "mind" and "body" in some inextricable unity.

Systems. A system (any system) is a complex of elements in mutual interaction. A habit is a system, so too a sentiment, a trait, a concept, a style of behaving. These systems are latent in the organism even when not active. Systems are our "potential for activity."[11]

Determine. Personality *is* something and *does* something. The latent psychophysical systems, when called into action, either motivate or direct specific activity and thought. All the systems that comprise personality are to be regarded as *determining tendencies.* They exert a directive influence upon all the adjustive and expressive acts by which the personality comes to be known.

Characteristic. All behavior and thought are characteristic of the person, and, as argued in Chapter 1, they are unique to him. Even the acts and concepts that we apparently "share" with others are at bottom individual and idiomatic. It is true that some acts and concepts are more idiosyncratic than others, but none can be found that lacks the personal flavor. In a sense, therefore, it is redundant to employ the term *characteristic* in our definition. Yet redundancy is not necessarily a bad thing; it helps to drive a point home.

Behavior and thought. These two terms are a blanket to designate anything whatsoever an individual may do. Chiefly what he does is to adjust to his environment. But it would be unwise to define personality only in terms of adjustment. We not only adjust to our environment but we reflect on it. Also, we strive to master it, and sometimes succeed. Behavior and thought, therefore, make both for survival and for growth. They are modes of adjustment and outreach elicited by the environmental situation we are in, always selected and directed by the psychophysical systems that comprise our personality.

The question may be asked whether, by this definition, animals have personality. The answer is a guarded "Yes." Animals no doubt have rudimentary forms of inherited and learned psychophysical systems that lead to characteristic (unique) activity. (We know nothing about their thought.) But this concession does not carry us very far. The psychophysical individuality of lower animals is exceedingly

11 R. R. Sears defines personality as "the potential for activity" in A theoretical framework for personality and social behavior, *Amer. Psychologist,* 1951, **6**, 476–483. The aphorism has much to commend it. But its weakness lies in its failure to admit the necessary criterion of organization. A neurone has a potential for activity, but we cannot consider such a structure in isolation as having personality.

primitive and cannot serve as a helpful prototype of human personality. We venture to assert that the difference between any two species of subhuman vertebrates is not as great as the difference between any one human being and another. The enormous complexity of the human brain, in contrast to the simpler brains of other vertebrates, would seem to warrant this assertion.

A Philosophical Objection

One term in our definition has as yet received no comment— the term *individual*. Some philosophers would say that we commit the unpardonable sin of begging the whole question. Who is this "individual" in whom personality resides? Are we not secretly admitting an organizer—a "self"? Do we not have on our hands an unexplained entity that somehow creates a unity of personality?

This objection comes especially from personalistic philosophers who feel that some continuing, unified agent is implied (or needed) by all definitions of personality. One such philosopher, Bertocci, would modify our definition as follows:

A self's personality is that self's dynamic organization of its own unique psychophysical wants and abilities which renders adjustments to its environment unique.[12]

That there is a pressing problem of relating *self* to *personality* we hasten to admit. We shall return to this puzzling issue in Chapter 6. But for the moment it is enough to say that the objection misrepresents our use of the term *individual*. When we say that the dynamic organization lies within the individual, we mean merely that it lies within the organism, i.e., "within the skin." It is our way of denying that personality is merely a matter of "external effect."

As for the concept of *self*, we see no need to include it in our definition. One's self is surely an important (no doubt the most important) psychophysical system within personality, as we shall later show. For the time being, however, the problem need not detain us.

Character

No less fascinating than the term *personality* is the term *character*. The two are often used interchangeably, although the first

12 P. A. Bertocci, Personality. In P. L. Harriman (Ed.), *Encyclopedia of psychology* (New York: Philosophical Library, 1946), p. 458.

is of Latin derivation, the second of Greek. χαραχτήρ means engraving. It is the mark of a man—his pattern of traits or his life-style. The most famous user of the term in ancient Greece was Theophrastus, a pupil of Aristotle. He wrote many perceptive character sketches, of which thirty survive. In Chapter 3 we shall examine his interesting method.

Today, as we have said, the two terms are often used synonymously. European psychologists, however, seem to have a preference for *character,* while American psychologists favor *personality.* There is an interesting reason for the difference. *Persona* originally meant mask; χαραχτήρ, engraving. The former term suggests appearance, visible behavior, surface quality; the latter suggests deep (perhaps inborn), fixed, and basic structure. Now American psychology has a preference for environmentalism; its behavioristic leaning leads it to stress outer movement, visible action. European psychology, on the other hand, tends to stress what is inborn in the nature of man, what is deeply etched and relatively unchanging. Freud, for example, speaks often of character-structure but seldom of personality. In Europe the term *characterology* is commonly used, but seldom in America. American psychologists have produced a great many books entitled *Personality* but few entitled *Character.* Thus the ancient difference in flavor of the two terms seems to account for present-day regional preferences.[13]

The term *character* has acquired a special connotation beyond its original meaning of engraving. When we say a man is of "good character" we are referring to his moral excellence. (If we say he has a "good personality" we mean merely that he is socially effective—the popular usage we discussed early in this chapter.) Thus whenever we speak of character we are likely to imply a moral standard and make a judgment of value. This complication worries those psychologists who wish to keep the actual structure and functioning of personality free from judgments of moral acceptability. It is largely for this reason that the present book favors the term *personality.* (The astute reader may say, "Your emphasis on internal structure corresponds well to what the ancient Greeks meant by character." And so it does,

---

[13] For a fuller discussion of the differences, see G. W. Allport, European and American theories of personality. In H. P. David and H. von Bracken (Eds.), *Perspectives in personality theory* (New York: Basic Books, 1957), Chap. 1.

but it is the later accretions of value-judgment that make us hesitate to use it.)

Now one may, of course, make a judgment of value concerning a personality as a whole, or concerning any part of a personality: "He is a noble fellow." "She has many endearing qualities." In both cases we are saying that the person in question has traits which, when viewed by some outside social or moral standards, are desirable. The raw psychological fact is that the person's qualities are simply what they are. Some observers (and some cultures) may find them noble and endearing; others may not. For this reason—and to be consistent with our own definition—we prefer to define *character* as *personality evaluated;* and *personality,* if you will, as *character devaluated.*

The term *characteristic* is a bird of another feather. We have employed it in our definition of personality, for fortunately it has escaped the value-aura of the parent word. It has no reference to moral judgment. Since it stands close to the original meaning of character we shall find it useful. It will serve to cover habits, traits, attitudes, and interests—any graven mark of individuality. It is a curious fact that "characteristic" should have kept its primitive meaning, whereas its root-form has gathered much ethical moss.

Before we leave the matter we should refer to one additional usage of the term *character.* Some psychologists regard it as a special part of personality. Thus one defines it as "the degree of ethically effective organization of all the forces of the individual." Another as "an enduring psychophysical disposition to inhibit impulses in accordance with a regulative principle." A certain amount of research has been published under the title *Studies in Character* or *Dimensions of Character.*[14] Such reports deal with investigations of children's honesty, self-control, thoughtfulness of others, religious loyalty.

Now the fact that a child or an adult has moral ideals, conscience, and religious beliefs is very important for a study of his personality, since they are features of his internal structure. It is also important to know whether a person has a "disposition to inhibit impulses in accordance with a regulative principle." But all these trends are

14 The first definition cited is from W. S. Taylor, Character and abnormal psychology, *J. abnorm. soc. Psychol.,* 1926, **21,** 86. The second is from A. A. Roback, *The psychology of character* (New York: Harcourt, Brace, 1927), p. 450. The series of *Studies in Character* are summarized in H. Hartshorne, M. A. May, and F. K. Shuttleworth, *Studies in the organization of character* (New York: Macmillan, 1930). See also E. M. Ligon, *Dimensions of character* (New York: Macmillan, 1956).

within the *personality*. The fact that they are perceived and judged favorably does not alter the case. And so we prefer not to consider character as some special region of the personality. We can stand on our simple definition of character as *personality evaluated*. Ethical theory is an important branch of philosophy, but it should not be confused with the psychology of personality.

Temperament

From ancient times down to the present comes the doctrine that a person's temperament is determined largely by the "humors" (glandular secretions) of the body. The term *temperament* came into English in the Middle Ages along with the doctrine of the four humors (Chapter 3). It meant then, and still means, a "constitution or habit of mind, especially depending upon or connected with physical constitution." Research on the subject of temperament today often goes under the name of "constitutional psychology."

Temperament, like *intelligence* and *physique,* might be said to designate a class of "raw material" from which personality is fashioned. All three factors lean heavily upon gene-determination, and are therefore the aspects of personality that are most dependent on heredity. Temperament refers to the chemical climate or "internal weather" in which personality evolves. The more anchored a disposition is in native constitutional soil the more likely it is to be spoken of as temperament. "Her native temperament is gay." "He has a slow and sluggish temperament."

A few authors, particularly in Great Britain, sometimes use the term as equivalent to personality—as when they say "temperament tests" rather than "tests of personality." But this usage is exceptional and decreasing. And some authors who are writing on the limited topic of temperament mistakenly use broader terms, as in the following book titles: *Glands regulating personality, Physique and character, Biological foundations of personality*. In all these cases "temperament" would fit the subject matter of the book more precisely.

In order to make needed advances in the study of temperament we require much more research in human genetics, biochemistry, neurology, endocrinology, and physical anthropology. We know that personality is largely conditioned by temperament, but we do not know the precise sources of temperament itself.

What does temperament include? No clear answer is possible. When we say that a person is easily startled, has powerful or weak sex urges, has a "frightful temper"; when we say that someone is by nature slow-moving and lethargic, that another is excitable, energetic, or has a "sour disposition," we are describing temperament. There have been various attempts to analyze out basic dimensions of temperament with the aid of psychological tests, but as yet no final agreement is reached.

It does seem probable that a primary factor relates to *drive and vigor* or its opposite, *apathy*. Constitutions high in drive and vigor may have high metabolic rates and strong thyroid functioning.[15] But our knowledge of the physical basis is not yet secure, nor do we know how many additional dimensions we need for the purpose of classifying major forms of temperament.[16]

Lacking more precise knowledge of the subject we offer the following definition as fairly representing current psychological usage, and as serving adequately the purposes of this book.

Temperament refers to the characteristic phenomena of an individual's emotional nature, including his susceptibility to emotional stimulation, his customary strength and speed of response, the quality of his prevailing mood, and all peculiarities of fluctuation and intensity in mood, these phenomena being regarded as dependent upon constitutional make-up, and therefore largely hereditary in origin.

This definition is not meant to imply that temperament is unchanged from birth to death. Like physique and intelligence, temperament may be altered (within limits) by medical, surgical, and nutritional influences as well as in the course of learning and life-experience. Temperament may alter as personality evolves. Yet the fact remains that in our endowment from birth onward there are constitutional, chemical, metabolic, neural levels that establish for

[15] See C. J. Adcock, The differentiation of temperament from personality, *J. gen. Psychol.*, 1957, **57**, 103–112.

[16] A useful survey of the present stage of knowledge is contained in S. Diamond, *Personality and temperament* (New York: Harper, 1957), Chaps. 7 and 8. Diamond is of the opinion that animal research and factorial analyses of human temperament "contain repeated assurances of the importance of dispositions to *affiliative, aggressive, fearful,* and *controlled* (or impulsive) behavior" (p. 171). The numerous authors he cites use, of course, varying terms, but Diamond believes that their labels point to the same basic dimensions of temperament. My criticism would be that his labels suggest traits of personality rather than constitutional dispositions (true temperament), but there may be underlying physiological dispositions to support this, or some similar, classification of trends in temperament. Continued research is needed.

us a characteristic stock in trade. Alteration is possible but not unlimited.

Summary

Voltaire once wrote, "If you would converse with me, you must first define your terms." Especially do highly abstract words such as *personality, character,* and *temperament* call for definition in order to make conversation profitable.

My own definition of personality is "essentialist." Personality is what a person "really is," regardless of the way other people perceive his qualities or the methods by which we study them. Our perceptions and our methods may be in error, just as an astronomer may fall short in studying the constitution of a star. But the star is still there, a challenging object for study. My definition does not, of course, deny that a person is variable over time or that his behavior may change from situation to situation. It says simply that the person has an internal structure and range of characteristics (variable, to be sure, but ascertainable), and it is this structure that we hope to study.

Character is a term we can largely dispense with since it refers (by our definition) to the evaluation of personality. *Characteristic,* on the other hand, keeps its original meaning of engraving (a uniquely etched feature), and is therefore useful for our purposes.

Temperament, like intelligence and physique, refers to "raw materials" out of which personality is fashioned. One's temperamental endowment is not unchangeable though it sets limits upon the development of personality. The next chapter bears further on the subject of temperament.

CHAPTER 3

Insights from
the Past

THE FOUR TEMPERAMENTS • PHYSIOGNOMY • LITERARY CHAR-
ACTEROLOGY • PHRENOLOGY • THE LATER NINETEENTH CEN-
TURY • GALTON AND EXPERIMENTATION • SUMMARY

W E are not interested here in a museum of antiquities and oddities. Man's efforts throughout the ages to formulate a science, or pre-science, of human personality have led often enough into blind alleys and absurdities. Yet it is likewise true that past centuries have yielded their gems of insight. There are important lessons we cannot afford to overlook. In this chapter we shall consider a few instructive approaches from former times, pointing to their relevance for present-day research and theory.

The Four Temperaments

The most ancient psychological theory of which we have any record is at the same time the theory that has had the greatest influence down through the centuries. In some respects it still stands close to the spirit and findings of modern science.

The theory starts with the ancient Greek belief, ascribed to

Empedocles in the fifth century B.C., that all of nature is composed of four elements: *air, earth, fire,* and *water.* The second stage in the theory was soon added by Hippocrates, the "father of medicine," who claimed that this formula for nature as a whole (the macrocosm) must be reflected in man's own make-up (the microcosm). Long before the days of endocrinology he decided that these elements are represented in the human body in the form of four "humors" (cf. hormones). If one humor predominated in the body we would expect to find a corresponding predominance of some one temperament. The doctrine was further formulated by the Roman physician Galen in the second century A.D. Galen saw the humors as the root not only of temperament but of diseases. Too much of yellow bile might cause fever; too much black bile, depression and decline.

Cosmic Elements	Their Properties	Corresponding Humors	Corresponding Temperaments
Empedocles, cir. 450 B.C.		Hippocrates, cir. 400 B.C. Galen, cir. A.D. 150	
Air	warm and moist	blood	sanguine
Earth	cold and dry	black bile	melancholic
Fire	warm and dry	yellow bile	choleric
Water	cold and moist	phlegm	phlegmatic

Although modern science has shown that the hormonal substances of the body are more numerous and complex than the ancients knew, still the happy guess that temperament, the emotional groundwork of personality, is conditioned by body chemistry has been increasingly borne out in modern research.

In addition to the lucky guess about body chemistry there is another, and still stronger, reason for the long and tenacious life of this theory. (Some modern writers, Pavlov among them, claim that the four-part typology of the ancients cannot be improved upon.)[1] The four patterns described by the theory fit neatly into almost any modern dimensional scheme for classifying temperament.

It is true that the names of the temperaments have a qualitative flavor: choleric means *irascible,* sanguine *hopeful,* melancholic *sad,* phlegmatic *apathetic.* But these qualitative colorings, we soon dis-

[1] See W. Sargant, *Battle for the mind* (New York: Doubleday, 1957).

cover, are congruent with a logical and quantitative view of the possible dimensions of temperament.

Suppose that a writer thinks of temperament as varying in terms of the *speed* and *intensity* of emotional arousal, as Wundt did. Figure 4A shows that we have no difficulty locating the ancient quartet according to this logical dimension.

Suppose that a theorist proposes that *breadth* and *depth* are the fundamental dimensions of temperament. Again the four are a good fit, Figure 4B.

Or suppose that one wishes to emphasize *excitability* and *affect*, the fit is still excellent, Figure 4C.

Still another plausible dimensional scheme views the temperaments in terms of *high* versus *low activity* and a tendency to *approach* or *withdraw*, as in Figure 4D.[2]

Virtually all the ingredients of temperament mentioned in our definition (page 34) can be fitted to some one of these dimensional schemes, accommodating the four humoral types along the way.

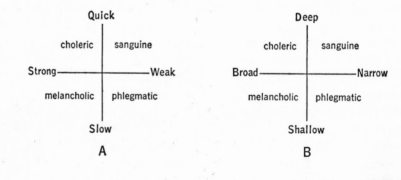

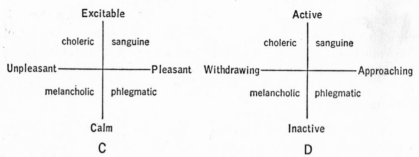

Figure 4. The Four Temperaments Fitted to Various Dimensions of Emotional Response

[2] Cf. S. Diamond, *Personality and temperament* (New York: Harper, 1957), p. 129.

Little wonder that countless writers have made satisfied use of the four temperaments. The doctrine is as elastic as the platform of a political party. One may see in it what one wants to see. Its versatility helps explain its colossal influence and longevity. Following Galen, both Western and Islamic medicine were written almost exclusively in terms of this theory. *Quattuor humores regnant in nostro corpore* sang an eleventh-century medical poem. Until Harvey discovered the circulation of the blood in the seventeenth century, Galenian medicine was supreme.[3]

Throughout the centuries the fine arts have produced famous sculptures, friezes, portraits celebrating the four types. Burton's *Anatomy of Melancholy* was based on the doctrine, as were many other works of literature. The theory was put to all manner of uses. It accounted for the pathology of the body, for the individuality of man, even for the stages of life: youth being *sanguine,* manhood *choleric,* later maturity *melancholic,* senility *phlegmatic.* Among psychological writers who have made extensive use of the fourfold division of temperament are Kant, Wundt, Höffding, Herbart, Külpe, Ebbinghaus, Klages, Pavlov. Many recent textbooks give it a favorable nod.

Should we not say of so robust a theory that there must be something to it? Yes, its merit lies both in its recognition of body chemistry and in its flexibility, fitting, as it does, several logical dimensions of analysis.

At the same time, like all typologies, we find that it fails to cover individuality of pattern. Our phlegmatic friends, we know, have choleric moments, and our sanguine friends may show threads of melancholy. The facts of biochemical individuality make it difficult to accept any typology for any concrete person.

Interestingly enough we find a turning away from the four-part scheme today in favor of a three-part scheme. The tripartite classification (identified with the names of Kretschmer and Sheldon) is described in Chapter 4.

Physiognomy

Physiognomy is the art (and potential science) of discovering characteristics of personality—particularly of temperament—from out-

---

[3] The medical history of the doctrine is well told by C. S. Sherrington, *Man on his nature* (2d ed.; New York: Doubleday, 1953). See also J. R. Irwin, Galen on the temperaments, *J. gen. Psychol.,* 1947, **36**, 45–64.

ward appearance, but especially from the configuration, cast, or expression of the face. The oldest treatise on the subject is entitled *Physiognomonica,* and is attributed to Aristotle.[4] Ancient though it is, it makes reference to systems of physiognomic character reading practiced in the still more distant past. We may overlook its proposal that if a man resembles an animal he must partake of the animal's qualities: a man who looks like a fox must be sly. More valuable are three assertions, all of which find support in modern research and theory:

(1) Although judgments may be based on any mobile feature, the most revealing are *facial expression, movements,* and *gestures.* (2) "It is silly to rely on a single sign; you will have more confidence in your conclusions when you find several signs all pointing one way." In Chapter 19 we shall return to the error of "monosymptomatic" diagnosis from expressive acts. (3) Most valuable of all is the suggestion that bone structure, body texture, and the like (constitution) reveal what is innate and relatively unchanging (temperament), whereas muscular structure and movement reveal acquired features of personality. The latter are more to be trusted, although the former are also important.

Let us examine this last proposition by looking at some very old physiognomic representations of the four temperaments. Most people (over 80 percent) correctly identify the types depicted in Figure 5. Number 1 looks like the traditional love-sick poet who is by reputation *melancholic.* Similar associations attach to the others: Number 2 appears to be a fighter, clearly endowed with *choler;* Number 3 is sleepy, flaccid, and *phlegmatic;* Number 4, because of the suggestion of vacuous optimism, is *sanguine.* These judgments are based on physiognomic cues. It is from our experience in observing bony and muscular structure that we develop these stereotypes.

What are the cues we employ? The drawings, we note, depend for their effect upon both bony and muscular structure. The slenderness and delicate texture of the *melancholic* type is given by nature, but the downcast eyes and vertical furrows in the brow reflect acquired habits of withdrawal and unpleasant thought. Similarly, the *choleric* face betrays natural vigor and strength of physique (tem-

---

[4] This treatise, covering only 24 pages, is translated by T. Loveday and E. S. Forster and appears in the *Opuscula,* Vol. VI, of the *Works of Aristotle* (W. D. Ross, Ed.; Oxford: Clarendon, 1903).

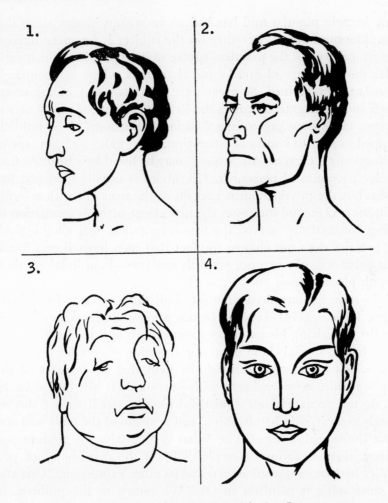

Figure 5. Physiognomic Representations of the Four Temperaments

perament) plus acquired habits of open-eyed responsiveness to the environment and a heavy seaming due to intense emotional feeling. The *phlegmatic* face is lethargic in build, inattentive in habit; the lines on the face are due to fat rather than to feeling. The *sanguine* face is normal enough in bony structure, but is not marked by lines indicating deep or lasting emotional experience. As the ancient Greek document says, we gain important cues from both constitutional build and from habitual muscular sets.

With the Aristotelian revival in the thirteenth century, physiognomy became popular and has had an unbroken history since that time. The quantity of literature on the subject is far more striking than its quality, for the practical nature of its appeal brought it early under the patronage of quacks and charlatans, where unfortunately it has largely remained. So great were its abuses that in the seventeenth and eighteenth centuries the British Parliament passed acts to sentence all persons pretending skill in physiognomy to be publicly whipped or sent to houses of correction. Even today a cheap type of physiognomy is current. An "expert" may be hired by a business firm to solve problems of personnel. His advice is usually filed and forgotten, but the physiognomist goes on to the next job with a lordly fee in his pocket, and impresses the new client with his reputation of having "successfully" served the first corporation. But all this shadowy practice does not change the fact that men have always found some assistance—of a sort not yet fully understood—in judging others through physiognomic cues.

The most famous physiognomist of all times was a Swiss, Johann Kaspar Lavater (1741–1801).[5] He was a vigorous propagandist and moralist, practicing his art upon street crowds and in churches. His system has no special claim upon our attention, except for one point upon which he strongly insisted: he held that all features of the body are ultimately consistent with one another. Mirthful eyes, he says, do not occur without a mirthful mouth, and if we are shrewd enough to see it, gait, handwriting, and postures of the body will also reflect the mirthful disposition. What is suggestive for modern psychology, then, is Lavater's emphasis upon the consistency of personality both in its inward aspects and its outer expression: "One and the same spirit is manifest in all." We return to the problem in Chapter 19.

Literary Characterology

Dipping again into ancient Greece, we find the earliest literary depictions of personality. In Chapter 2 we mentioned the "Characters" written by Theophrastus, a pupil of Aristotle. Sometimes Aristotle's own portrait of *The Magnanimous Man* is credited with inventing the style.

[5] His chief work, *Physiognomische Fragmente zur Beförderung der Menschenkenntniss und Menschenliebe,* issued in 1783–1787 in three volumes, has many times been republished. Still earlier editions of this work appeared in 1772 and 1775 under different titles.

A successful "Character" is a brief description of some common type of human being that can be recognized and appreciated by readers of any age in any land as a simplified but essentially correct image. The thirty extant Characters of Theophrastus follow a rigid style of composition. Each commences with a brief definition of the dominant trait, and continues with typical instances of the operation of this trait. (The numerous imitators of Theophrastus throughout the ages depart in varying degrees from this rigid formalism.) It is a peculiarity of Theophrastus' Characters that all thirty represent vicious or at least unpleasant types. Whether he found the good man too dull to write about, or whether many of his sketches have been lost we cannot say. The following example demonstrates his style. Though written over two thousand years ago it is applicable to some of our acquaintances today.

The Penurious Man

Penuriousness is economy carried beyond all measure. A Penurious Man is one who goes to a debtor to ask for his half-obol interest before the end of the month. At a dinner where expenses are shared, he counts the number of cups each person drinks, and he makes a smaller libation to Artemis than anyone. If someone has made a good bargain on his account and presents him with the bill he says it is too much.

When his servant breaks a pot or a plate, he deducts the value from his food. If his wife drops a copper, he moves furniture, beds, chests and hunts in the curtains. If he has something to sell he puts such a price on it that the buyer has no profit. He forbids anyone to pick a fig in his garden, to walk on his land, to pick up an olive or a date. Every day he goes to see that the boundary marks of his property have not been moved. He will destrain on a debtor and exact compound interest. When he entertains the members of his deme, he is careful to serve very small pieces of meat to them. If he goes marketing, he returns without having bought anything. He forbids his wife to lend anything—neither salt nor lamp-wick nor cinnamon nor marjoram nor meal nor garlands nor cakes for sacrifices. "All these trifles," he says, "mount up in a year." To sum up, the coffers of the penurious men are moldy and the keys rust; they wear cloaks which hardly reach the thigh; a very little oil-bottle supplies them for anointing; they have hair cut short and do not put on their shoes until midday; and when they take their cloak to the fuller they urge him to use plenty of earth so that it will not be spotted so soon.[6]

[6] Reproduced, with permission, from R. Aldington (Ed. and Transl.), *A book of characters* (New York: E. P. Dutton, 1925). Other translations are by R. C. Jebb, *The characters of Theophrastus,* 1909; C. E. Bennett and W. A. Hammond, *The characters of Theophrastus,* 1902; F. Howell, *The characters of Theophrastus,* 1824. (The last two have physiognomical sketches.)

In all ages and in all lands there have been penurious men. The skill of Theophrastus consists in his selection of vivid types, in his choice of illustrative incident, and in his economy of expression.

Although he does not explicitly say so, Theophrastus is propounding an important theory of personality; indeed, he foreshadows the argument to be presented in Chapters 14 and 15. To him penuriousness is a dominant trait of some people, a dynamic and directive force, a true mainspring of conduct. It is stable, predictable, self-consistent, and compulsive. In the case of the penurious man nineteen samples of conduct all exemplify a master trait.

Whether he is at business or at home, whether he is entertaining his friends or making his toilet, whether he deals with his wife, his servants, friends, debtors, neighbors, or deity, the man is driven by his trait of penuriousness. It is safe to predict that in new situations he will react in the same way. Note well: the man does not have merely a "habit" of wearing his tunic short, and another habit of examining the boundary marks of his property. Each activity is but one manifestation of a central motive.

In a sense Theophrastus is depicting an "ideal type" (page 17). Such utter consistency is hardly ever encountered in real life. And yet all persons do have central traits and personal styles. It is this insight that we may safely adopt, even though we reject the exaggeration.

The list of imitators of Theophrastus is long, including such famous writers as Ben Jonson, John Donne, Samuel Johnson, George Eliot. The seventeenth-century French author, Jean de La Bruyère changed the method somewhat, shifting from types to portraits. In the case of Giton, to select one example, he depicts an individual style of life, a consistent pattern of traits, and not merely a single cardinal disposition.

Giton

Giton has a fresh complexion, a full face and bulging cheeks, a fixed and assured gaze, broad shoulders, a projecting stomach, a firm and deliberate tread. He speaks with confidence; he makes those who converse with him repeat what they have said and he only moderately enjoys what is said. He unfolds an ample handkerchief and blows his nose noisily; he spits to a great distance and sneezes very loudly. He sleeps by day, he sleeps by night; he snores in company. At table and in walking he occupies more room than anyone else. He takes the center and walks with his equals; he stops and they stop; he walks on and they walk on; all regulate themselves by him; he is not interrupted, he is listened to as long as he likes to talk; his opinion is accepted, the rumors he spreads are believed. If he sits down you will see him settle into an armchair, cross his legs, frown, pull his hat over his eyes and see no one, or lift it up again and show his brow from pride and audacity. He is cheerful, a hearty laugher, impatient, presumptuous, quick to anger, irreligious, politic, mysterious about current affairs; he believes he has talents and wit. He is rich.[7]

An American imitator, Stark Young, has kept particularly close to Theophrastus by titling his book of sketches *Encaustics,* an admirable translation of χαρακτήρ.

Since literature and psychology provide the two more important methods for the study of personality, the comparison between them is instructive. Dramatists, biographers, novelists have special abilities, but the psychologist inclines to be skeptical of their work.

> Says the literary man: "It seems clear to me that psychology is merely saying what literature has always said, only it is saying it less artfully."
>
> The psychologist replies, "Less artfully perhaps but more exactly."
>
> "More exactly perhaps, but less truly; a portrait in oils may be more true than a photograph, for the portrait throws significant features into relief; whereas the photograph presents equally the irrelevant and relevant. Art is selective; exact science is merely photographic."

And this argument may go on endlessly. Literature has only one way of "proving" its case. A portrait must hang together, must be a plausible, if selective, unity. In commenting on a character of Thackeray's, G. K. Chesterton once remarked, "She *drank,* but Thackeray didn't know it." The quip reflects the demand that all good characterizations must have the virtue of "self-confrontation." Given one set of facts about a person, other relevant facts must follow. No one requires that we validate Hamlet scientifically. This mighty portrait validates itself, and so too does any successful characterization. When all lines of evidence "hang together" we speak of self-confrontation.

Psychology has not learned to use the method of self-confronta-

[7] Aldington, *op. cit.*

tion. To do so would require further development of the idiographic approach. As yet we have few techniques for discovering the way in which one part-system in a personality relates to other part-systems. Nomothetic approaches, as we have seen, run the risk of losing the vital pattern of individuality. And yet the psychologist is right in chiding literature for its lack of safeguards. Biographers are in special trouble. Two accounts of a given life may diverge widely. Each biographer achieves self-confrontation in his portrait, but the confrontations may not correspond. A psychologist would feel the need for outer checks on the reliability of his interpretation.[8]

The effects of literature are gained by skillful selection and exaggeration. The *petits faits vrais* are made prominent, inconvenient inconsistencies are discarded. The psychologist, by contrast, is permitted no artistic accentuation. *Exaggeration apropos* is not allowed. The literary writer strives to be entertaining, to communicate his own images, to express his own biases. The psychologist is permitted only to discover and record, and must work hard to exclude his biases. He cannot measure his success simply by the reader's applause.

Free from the bondage of science, the literary writer can be reckless in ascribing causes. One of his characters may have "menial blood in his veins," another "a weak chin." A hand may possess "a wonderfully cruel greed," and a blond head may "radiate fickleness." Such undisciplined metaphors give cadence and inspire a bland credulity. But no psychologist could write thus without being torn limb from limb by his professional colleagues.

Psychology will not supplant literature, nor will the scorn of artists hinder the growth of psychology. The two methods are distinct and complementary.[9] If psychology today "is discovering only what literature has always said" it is nevertheless giving precision to ancient truths. Less enjoyable, it is more disciplined; less subtle, it is more verifiable; less artful, it is more exact.

[8] Cf. J. A. Garraty, The interrelations of psychology and biography, *Psychol. Bull.*, 1954, 51, 569–582. See also G. W. Allport, *The use of personal documents in psychological science* (New York: Soc. Sci. Res. Council, Bull. No. 49, 1942).

[9] A fuller comparison of literary and psychological methods is in my collection of essays, *Personality and social encounter* (Boston: Beacon, 1960), Chap. 1.

Few psychologists have attempted to correlate the insights of literature and the insights of psychology. One important effort in this direction is H. Cantril and C. H. Bumstead, *Reflections on the human venture* (New York: New York Univ. Press, 1960).

Phrenology

Lacking an adequate science of personality, people have always been a prey to fortunetellers, numerologists, palmists, phrenologists, astrologers, and other questionable experts who have a prefabricated scheme for telling you what you are like or how your prospective employee (or fiancé) will turn out. Quackery and superstition flourish. But the slums of psychology need not detain us. The kernel of truth that lies in some, but not all, popular schemes of "character reading" may in time be rescued by the scientific approach. Some indications will be given in Chapter 19.

Here let us consider one movement that was enormously popular a century ago and has only slowly faded out of favor. First promulgated by Franz Joseph Gall (1758–1828), phrenology or, as he preferred to call it, organology or cranioscopy, swept the world. Like all popular systems it had its disreputable side, being a lucrative racket for its promoters, who operated in business offices, lyceums, clubs, churches, and even universities.[10] But phrenology has another, less familiar, but more significant side. It began with an honest attempt to discover the radical units composing human personality.

Gall was a serious-minded and critical theorist. He was also a forerunner of differential psychology. His argument ran approximately as follows: Mind and body are in some way related. We must therefore expect the inner structure of personality to have outward

[10] The popularity of phrenology immediately commenced with Gall's first lectures in 1796. It spread rapidly through the enterprising salesmanship of Gall's assistant, Johann Gaspar Spurzheim (1776–1832), who, however, separated from his master in 1815, and wrote many independent works, lecturing widely in England and on the Continent. Spurzheim, who came to America in 1832, lectured to large audiences and was well received at Harvard. He died in Boston.

Gall's chief work appeared in four volumes between 1810 and 1819, and was entitled, *Anatomie et physiologie du système nerveux en général, et du cerveau en particulier, avec observations sur la possibilité de reconnoître plusieurs dispositions intellectuelles et morales de l'homme et des animaux par la configuration de leur têtes.* In 1822–1825 Gall published a revised edition in six volumes under the title, *Sur les fonctions du cerveau.* The corresponding American edition, *On the functions of the brain,* was published in 1835.

The name "phrenology" was invented by Dr. Thomas Forster and was adopted by Spurzheim in 1815. Gall himself never used the term, but referred to his doctrine as "organology," "cranioscopy," or, more often, as "the physiology of the brain."

Interesting and discriminating accounts are those of E. G. Boring, *A history of experimental psychology* (New York: Appleton-Century-Crofts, 1929), Chap. 3; M. Bentley, The psychological antecedents of phrenology, *Psychol. Monogr.,* 1916, No. 92; C. Blondel, *La psychophysiologie de Gall* (Paris: Alcan, 1913); McQ. De Grange, *The science of individuality* (Lyon: Bascou, 1923); H. D. Spoerl, Faculties *versus* traits; the solution of Franz Joseph Gall, *Charact. & Pers.,* 1936, 4, 216–231.

manifestations. Since the brain is the most important "organ of the mind" we can look for diagnostic signs in the shape of the brain-casing, the cranium. Now this pathway into "bumpology" was Gall's supreme blunder. It is, unfortunately, the only aspect of his doctrine that is remembered.

More important was Gall's search for the "primitive" units comprising personality. He criticized severely the psychology of his time, which was based on the assumptions of "faculties"—although he too adopted the term *faculty* to designate his twenty-seven primitive units. The faculties he objected to were such universal mental functions as *perception, will, desire, understanding, imagination.* "Every man except an idiot," he says, "enjoys all these faculties. Yet all men have not the same intellectual or moral character." What we need, he added, is a classification of primitive powers, traits, and capacities that will account for *individual differences* in personality.

Gall's search, though not very successful, resembles closely the attempts of psychological science today to find out what "primary mental abilities" or what "source traits" form the best scheme for comparing one person with another (cf. Chapter 13).

Gall's list includes a mixture of qualities such as *self-esteem, good nature, firmness, mechanical aptitude, wit,* none of which appear among the universal faculties of his predecessors (Christian Wolff, Thomas Reid, Dugald Stewart, and others). Yet it must be admitted that his total list of characterological variables is not wholly unlike the traditional lists of universal faculties. But, in contrast to his predecessors, Gall was a strict empiricist, studying people intently, examining their skulls, and trying, in good scientific spirit, to write an inductive science of personality.

Neither his list of primitive units nor his cranioscopy has survived modern criticism, but the fact remains that Gall, for all his errors, was a serious and influential seeker, and in a way one of the founders of differential psychology and of psychophysiology. How unlike his theory of brain localization is to a modern view is seen in Figure 6.

The Later Nineteenth Century

Shortly after Gall's time John Stuart Mill proposed the formation of "an exact science of human nature."[11] It was to be

11 J. S. Mill, *System of logic* (New York: Harper, 1846), Bk. VI, Chap. 5.

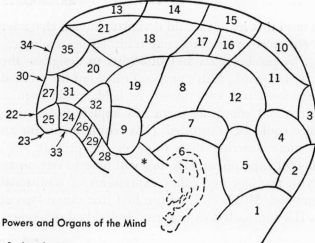

Powers and Organs of the Mind

1. Amativeness
2. Philoprogenitiveness
3. Inhabitiveness
4. Adhesiveness
5. Combativeness
6. Destructiveness
7. Secretiveness
8. Acquisitiveness
9. Constructiveness
10. Self-esteem
11. Love of approbation
12. Cautiousness
13. Benevolence
14. Veneration
15. Firmness
16. Conscientiousness
17. Hope
18. Marvellousness
19. Ideality
20. Mirthfulness or gayness
21. Imitation
22. Individuality
23. Configuration
24. Size
25. Weight and resistance
26. Colouring
27. Locality
28. Calculation
29. Order
30. Eventuality
31. Time
32. Melody
33. Language
34. Comparison
35. Causality

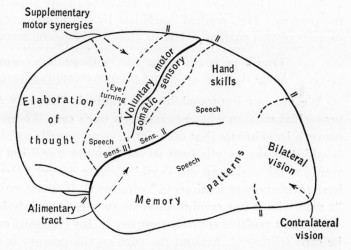

Figure 6. Two Views of Brain Localization: Nineteenth and Twentieth Century. The phrenological chart was employed by G. Spurzheim in *Phrenology, or the doctrine of the mind* (London: Treuttel, Wurtz, and Richter, 1825. The summary of major functional regions of the human cortex is taken from W. Penfield and T. Rasmussen, *The cerebral cortex of man*, p. 221. Copyright 1950 by The Macmillan Company and used with their permission.

called *ethology,* a term that he felt would designate human character in a broad sense. (In recent years this same term has been adopted, less appropriately, by psychologists and biologists to designate the science of instinctive behavior.) Mill's proposal ruled out the method of experimentation; for a true experiment, he held, would require bringing up children and educating them in complete isolation so that every influence could be controlled. (His requirements for an experiment were more exacting than those of the present day!) Lacking the method of experiment, ethology will have to rely on an analysis of proverbs, maxims, and other expressions of traditional wisdom. By this method, Mill hoped, we can find true causal laws of human character. His approach does not stress individual differences as did Gall's.

Mill is important for personality study chiefly because of his influence on Alexander Shand, who late in the nineteenth century launched the doctrine of *sentiments.*[12] Shand follows Mill's advice and uses proverbial wisdom as his data (or "premises for deduction"). His "basic law" is that "every sentiment tends to form a type of character of its own." He then presents 144 special laws dealing with the impact of various sentiments on behavior and thought. Thus one law reads: "Hope tends always to make the future appear better than the present." He "verified" each law by the wisdom of the ages. In support of this particular law he cites Shakespeare, among others:

> True hope is swift, and flies with swallow's wings;
> Kings it makes gods, and meaner creatures kings.

We are not impressed by this method. One may choose from proverbial wisdom whatever supports one's case. There is scarcely a proverb in existence that does not have an equally valid opposite. It is said, "As the twig is bent so inclines the tree," but also that "a young monk makes an old devil." Goethe wrote, "The weak often have revolutionary sentiments," whereas G. B. Shaw maintained that "a man who is not revolutionary by twenty is an inferior."

Shand's positive contribution lies in his recognition of the unit he calls *sentiment.* Around the turn of the century it was adopted enthusiastically by McDougall.[13] All men, McDougall held, start life with a uniform set of instincts (or "propensities"). These include an

[12] A. F. Shand, Character and the emotions, *Mind,* new ser., 1896, 5, 203–226. Also, *Foundations of character* (London: Macmillan, 1914).
[13] W. McDougall, *Introduction to social psychology* (Boston: Luce, 1908). Also, Organization of the affective life: a critical survey, *Acta psychologica,* 1937, 2, 233–346.

instinct of flight, gregariousness, parental activity, self-abasement, self-assertion, and the like. But in the course of development these instincts become attached to certain objects. Thus the parental instinct in one person becomes attached to his own family, in another to helpless children or sick people, in another to pet poodles. These people accordingly develop differing sentiments. Thus, religion, patriotism, awe, hostility, and thousands of other sentiments arise, each with its own coloring in individual cases. The theory allows for an endless variety of individuality. The structural unit is the sentiment. Some of these are major and some minor parts of a personality. Ordinarily all are organized under one master sentiment, the sentiment of "self-regard," which takes the form of a self-conscious devotion to certain selected ideals and holds the minor sentiments in a more or less orderly array according to the nature of this master sentiment. Although McDougall's underlying theory of instincts is not widely accepted today, the concept of sentiment—and it may be used without the doctrine of instinct—is decidedly useful. Some writers believe that it gives us the most suitable of all possible units for the analysis of personality.[14]

One additional British writer should be mentioned, Alexander Bain, who in 1862 published *On the Study of Character.* This volume ties together two of the trends we have described. It includes Bain's original translation of the *Characters* written by Theophrastus. It also takes its origin from Mill's proposal for an "ethology," although Bain wishes to bring this proposal "more in accordance with the present state of our knowledge of the human constitution." What he accomplished, however, is chiefly a restatement of a very old theory: that man's nature is composed of three primary faculties: *emotion, volition,* and *intellect.* This same tripartite division of the human soul was proposed by Plato, and it is found in much psychological writing, even today.

Bain added something to the doctrine. He proposed (following Herbert Spencer) that a given man has a certain amount of "energy." If it habitually flows through emotional channels, it is not available for intellectual activities; or similarly, if a person is strongly "volitional" he cannot be equally "emotional" or "intellectual." "Human nature being limited, if one's vitality runs very much to the active organs, less will go to other parts." And so, it turns out, that this flow

14 For example, H. A. Murray and C. D. Morgan, A clinical study of sentiments, *Genet. Psychol. Monogr.,* 1945, **32**, 3–311.

of energy (like a steam boiler with valves) results in a type doctrine: men tend to be *mental* (intellectual), *motor* (volitional) or *vital* (emotional and sensuous). It becomes easy to popularize such a conception, and even today we often hear about these three "ultimate" types of character.

One feature of Bain's theory merits special attention. He makes much of the direction of flow of man's psychic energy. Like a steam boiler, man has a certain load or pressure, and where this energy goes depends on what valves are habitually open. It is a short step from this hydraulic metaphor to the more modern theories of psychoanalysis. The libido or id, according to Freud, is "filled with energy." It may be bottled up (by repression), it may escape in indirect ways (sublimation, displacement). In Freudian theory (Chapter 7) both sexuality and aggression behave very much like high-pressure forces, and their channeling is the principal problem of man's life. Other dynamic psychologists also speak in terms of "energy" and its direction, drainage, canalization, or other utilization. And so we may, in a sense, regard Bain as one of the founders of modern dynamic psychology.

Galton and Experimentation

During the nineteenth century the literature of characterology was rich in observation and hypothesis, but no writer prior to 1884 proposed to apply the newly developed experimental method to the study of personality. The rapidly growing interest in experimental psychology, which in 1879 materialized in the first psychological laboratory at Leipzig, was not at first concerned with personality. Interest in individual differences was beginning to appear, but not so much for its own sake as to show the ranges in which nomothetic functions operate (for example, reaction time).

It was Sir Francis Galton (1822–1911), the pioneer in so many psychometric fields, who first proposed that the standards of experimentation be applied directly to the study of personal forms of behavior: "The character which shapes our conduct is a definite and durable 'something,' and therefore . . . it is reasonable to attempt to measure it."[15] One method of measurement advocated by him was the *rating* of complex qualities. Schoolmasters, for example, have

[15] F. Galton, Measurement of character, *Fortnightly Rev.*, 1884, **42,** 179–185.

enviable opportunity to count the frequency and estimate the intensity of their pupils' responses of fear, anger, loyalty, and ambition. Norms should be established for the development of personality at successive ages. The method of correlation, indispensable in modern studies of personality, originated with Galton. These are all scientific contributions of great worth. But Galton's proposal to employ actual experiment is striking indeed.

Observation, he argues, is a slow process, especially while waiting for critical episodes of life to appear. But "emergencies need not be waited for; they can be extemporized; traps, as it were, can be laid." He gives the following example:

> Thus when two persons have an "inclination" to one another, they visibly incline or slope together when sitting side by side, as at a dinner table, and they then throw the stress of their weight on the near legs of their chairs. It does not require much ingenuity to arrange a pressure gauge with an index and dial to indicate changes in stress, but it is difficult to devise an arrangement that shall fulfill the threefold condition of being effective, not attracting notice, and being applicable to ordinary furniture. I made some rude experiments, but being busy with other matters, have not carried them on, as I had hoped.[16]

This amusing, but nonetheless reasonable, proposal marks the beginning of experimentation in the field of personality. The special problem with which it is concerned, expressive movement, is only now commencing to employ instruments of measurement analogous to the device Galton proposes. Handwriting pressure, gait, facial expression have yielded to more or less precise measurement. Unconscious inclination of the body—the topic that intrigued Galton—has been ingeniously measured by Hull through the simple expedient of attaching unnoticed threads to one's collar which, in turn, register body sway on a kymograph—a simpler device than Galton's![17]

Although experimentation is only one method of scientific approach to personality (cf. Chapters 17 and 18), it is an important method, and we trace its origins without interruption back to Galton.

Summary

Out of the long and varied past this chapter has selected only a few doctrines that have some special significance for the contempo-

16 *Ibid.*, p. 184.
17 C. L. Hull, *Hypnosis and suggestibility* (New York: Appleton-Century-Crofts, 1933).

rary study of personality. In a few cases ancient and persistent blunders have concerned us, but for the most part positive contributions have been recorded.

Humoral psychology, the oldest of all doctrines of human nature, owes its longevity partly to its undisputed claim that there is a correspondence between the chemistry of the body and emotional makeup; partly to its anticipation of later dimensional analyses of temperament.

Physiognomy, too, claims that a relationship exists between temperament and skeletal and muscular structure, especially of the face. Lavater held that all expressive features are consistent with one another—a hypothesis important to test with modern methods.

Theophrastus claimed that small everyday acts of a man are remarkably congruent with one another. He sought the *dominant trait* that conferred unity upon behavior in many situations. Many imitators extended the method of character-writing. So artful are their productions, as well as those of fiction, drama, biography, that psychology, by contrast, seems clumsy and inept. But clumsy exactness is a wholesome antidote to undisciplined felicity. Either alone is one-sided; but taken together the two approaches provide a well-rounded equipment for a student of personality.

Phrenology stresses the parallel between man's personal qualities and his cranial structure. The parallel is certainly not what Gall thought it to be. Yet in seeking the primitive units of personality Gall was anticipating both the later discipline of differential psychology and also the modern search for primary dimensions in personality analysis.

In proposing ethology as an exact science of human nature Mill saw clearly the interdependence of psychology, literature, and common sense. Shand and McDougall, with their useful concept of *sentiment,* were the primary fruits of Mill's effort. Bain anticipated the dynamic flow of energy into various channels of personal expression. His hydraulic metaphor is a clear anticipation of Freud's later theories.

The era of experimentation, rating, measurement, correlation was ushered in by Galton. Mill declared experimentation in the field of personality to be impossible, but it is not Mill's view but, rather, Galton's that has prevailed.

PART II DEVELOPMENT OF Personality

CHAPTER 4

Foundations of Personality

PHYSIQUE AND TEMPERAMENT • INTELLIGENCE • INHERITANCE
• THE BIOLOGICAL VIEW OF PERSONALITY • PERSONALITY IN
THE FIRST YEAR • PREDICTING DEVELOPMENT • SUMMARY

A newborn babe can scarcely be said to have personality (because it lacks a characteristic organization of psychophysical systems—page 28). But we can safely say that personality begins at birth; and we may also say that the infant has a *potential* personality: certain capacities and characteristics are almost bound to develop. But on the whole it seems wisest to regard a newborn infant as a "psychological thing" rather than as a person.

We have already suggested that *physique, temperament,* and *intelligence* may helpfully be regarded as the "raw materials" of personality, even though they undergo maturation slowly over the years. We speak of them as raw materials because they depend heavily (though not exclusively) on what is "given" by inheritance. Of these three, *physique* is most visibly tied to heredity in a complex way, but there is strong evidence for regarding the foundations of *temperament* and of *intelligence* as likewise genetically determined. Once more, it is necessary to warn the reader that we are not denying that

57

all three factors can be affected during the course of life by nutrition, by health and disease, and by learning—within limits.

Physique and Temperament

In the last chapter we saw that even the ancient Greeks were convinced that a person's body form must give us important clues to his temperament. The course of reasoning is simple, and in principle is still acceptable to modern science.

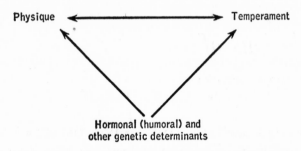

Figure 7. Derivation of Physique and Temperament from One Common Source

Figure 7 presents the elementary logic of the claim. If the glands and other biochemical agencies regulate growth, and if they have some bearing upon the "internal weather" of the emotional and activity levels, then from physique we ought to be able to infer temperament, and vice versa.

Let us take a rather striking example. There is no contemporary record of the physical appearance of Jesus. The first known "portraits" are in the catacombs of Rome, and date from the second or third centuries A.D. Why, then, from early times has the Christ-figure been portrayed in art as slender rather than muscular or fat? A roly-poly or athletic Christus would somehow seem inappropriate. But why? Is it not because the capacity for inwardness, for withdrawal from the world, for "introversion" is normally found in elongated, slender physiques?

The conviction that this tie exists has persisted throughout the ages. Julius Caesar, we recall from our Shakespeare, preferred around him men who were fat and amiable, "such as sleep o' nights." He distrusted Cassius because of his "lean and hungry look; he thinks too much."[1] It is no accident that Falstaff is portrayed as both fat and good-natured. That there is some basis in fact for this traditional physiognomic belief is supported by modern science. A large number of confirmatory studies could be cited.

• Recent credit goes to the German psychiatrist Kretschmer, who studied classes of mental disease.[2] His finding was that disorders of mood and emotion (e.g., manic-depressive psychosis) tended to be found more often among people with roly-poly (pyknic) physiques; whereas disorders of thought-life (extreme introversion; schizophrenia) were associated with slender (asthenic) physiques. But Kretschmer had no sure way of measuring physique and overlooked the factor of age; schizophrenia tends to strike earlier in life than manic-depressive disorder, and at a time when physical build tends to be slender.

A more exact method was invented by Sheldon.[3] For one thing, he devised a scheme to determine what proportion of each of three body types (somatotypes) a given person has. By measuring various lengths, diameters, and ratios, we can give each individual a score (from 1 to 7) on each of three body builds:

> the *endomorphic* (Kretschmer's pyknic) having large digestive viscera and other body cavities, a "roundish" build, but relatively weak in bony and muscular development; the *mesomorphic* (athletic) having large bones and muscles and a "squarish" build; the *ectomorphic* (asthenic) having long, slender extremities but small body cavities and lacking in muscular development—a "linear" build.

If we place scores 1–7 against each type in this same order we give to each individual three marks: the first for the amount of endomorphy in his constitution, the second and third for the amounts of

1 *Julius Caesar,* Act I, Sc. 2.
2 E. Kretschmer, *Physique and character* (transl.; London: Routledge & Kegan Paul, 1925).
3 W. H. Sheldon, S. S. Stevens, and W. B. Tucker, *The varieties of human physique* (New York: Harper, 1940); W. H. Sheldon and S. S. Stevens, *The varieties of temperament* (New York: Harper, 1942); W. H. Sheldon, C. W. Dupertuis, and E. McDermott, *Atlas of men* (New York: Harper, 1954).

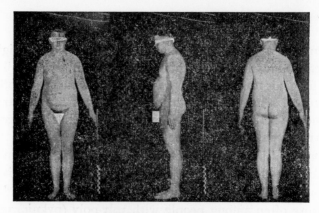

EXTREME ENDOMORPH

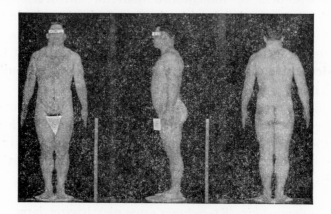

DOMINANT MESOMORPH

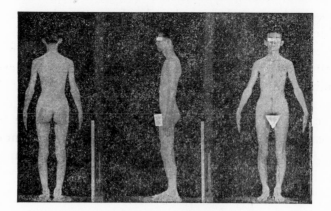

EXTREME ECTOMORPH

Figure 8. Basic Somatotypes According to Sheldon

mesomorphy and ectomorphy respectively. Many combinations of scores are possible, though not all are found. Obviously a 7–7–7 or a 1–1–1 would be an impossibility. There are, however, many average physiques with scores at, or close to, 4–4–4.

In addition to this basic analysis Sheldon thinks it important to look for certain special features of body build. For example, a male can be scored for physical resemblance to the female physique, and a woman scored for "maleness." This dimension he calls *gyanandromorphy*. Likewise, different regions of the body may show different somatotypes—an endomorphic torso could be attached to ectomorphic legs. Such irregular physiques are called *dysplastic*. In all Sheldon holds that we can distinguish more than 70 types of constitutional build.

So much for physique. How about temperament? The theory holds that each major somatotype corresponds closely to a basic temperament pattern, as follows:

the *viscerotonic* (normally associated with endomorphic build): relaxation, love of comfort, slow reaction, love of eating, sociability, amiability, complacency, deep sleep, need people when troubled.

the *somatotonic* (normally associated with mesomorphic build): assertiveness, love of physical adventure, energetic, need for exercise, love of dominating, of risk and chance, directness of manner, courage, general noisiness, need for action when troubled.

the *cerebrotonic* (normally associated with ectomorphic build): restraint in posture and movement, rapid reactions, overintense, anxious, secretive, inhibited, poor sleep, introverted in thought, need solitude when troubled.

In the original investigation Sheldon claimed a very high degree of association between the temperament and body types. (The coefficients of correlation were over .80).[4] Subsequent studies have indi-

4 The coefficient of correlation is a measure we shall frequently need to use. It expresses the relationship between two sets of measures (in this case between scores on body build and on temperament). Perfect correlation, or correspondence, gives a coefficient (symbolized as *r* or *rho*) of 1.00. The absence of any relationship gives a coefficient of .00. Negative coefficients ranging from —1.00 to .00 indicate an inverse relationship,

cated that this claim is excessive. A few investigations find no significant correlation, though many find a moderate correspondence in the
expected direction.[5] On balance we conclude that there is something
in Sheldon's formulation (a fact which merely confirms our traditional belief in this physiognomic parallel).

The Gluecks report a careful study of the theory in the area of
juvenile delinquency. The physiques of 500 delinquent boys tended
toward mesomorphy at least twice as often as did the physiques of
500 matched nondelinquent boys.[6]

This finding raises an important question. Does the high *assertiveness* that, by Sheldon's theory, accompanies mesomorphy predis-
pose boys to delinquency? That is to say, does the innate physical-
temperament syndrome lead to delinquency? Or, on the other
hand, is the delinquency a matter chiefly of bad home conditions,
and the predominance of mesomorphy among delinquents due
simply to the fact that some boys are stronger and more vigorous,
leading them to more conspicuous conflicts with the law?

Pressing this issue still further, we ask whether the fundamental
association between body build and temperament is itself an inborn
correlation or due to life experiences. Take a boy markedly ectomorphic in physique and more frail than his fellows. He is not good
at sports, and finds himself licked in fist fights. What, then, does he
do? May he not develop a nature that is tense, secretive, inhibited,
introverted? Like Cassius may he not "think too much"? The fat
child, like the thin, learns that the playground gives the rewards to
the mesomorph, not to him. We cannot prove that it is only such
life-experience that accounts for the correspondence between body
build and temperament, but it probably plays some part. The opposite interpretation is supported by one study that finds seven-year-
old children (who have scarcely rubbed shoulders with the rougher
world) already displaying the pattern of characteristics that Sheldon

---

i.e., a tendency for one score in a pair to be high while the other is low. A rough
guide to the significance of coefficients follows.

.90—.99—outstandingly high
.75—.89—high
.50—.74—positive
.20—.49—appreciable but low
.00—.19—ordinarily of no significance

[5] A thoughtful report on validation studies is contained in S. Diamond, *Personality and
temperament* (New York: Harper, 1957), Chap. 7. See also H. Winthrop, Attitude consistency and body type, *J. Pers.*, 1957, 25, 372–382.
[6] S. Glueck and E. Glueck, *Physique and delinquency* (New York: Harper, 1956).

describes. Ectomorphs at this age seem more anxious, more submissive, more restless, and more meticulous than other body types.[7]

To conclude, we cannot doubt the fact that bodily constitution and temperament have some close relationship. They are paired raw materials from which we fashion in part our personalities through learning. The sciences of genetics, of biochemistry, and of anthropological and psychological measurement have not advanced enough to tell us precisely what parallels exist. Yet the doctrine of somatotypes in relation to temperament gives us a promising, if still imperfect, guide.

Intelligence

It is necessary to include intelligence among the raw materials of personality, because intelligence is in some way closely related to the central nervous system, and the central nervous system is as much a matter of native endowment as is the neuroglandular system underlying body build and temperament.

No one can say in how many ways at the start of life one human nervous system may differ from another. There are wide variations in the number of brain cells existing: in their arrangement, metabolism, conductivity, connectibility, and general availability for use (cf. page 6). When the combinations are favorable, a person is endowed with high intelligence; when unfavorable, with low; and when conditions are mixed, the results are intermediate.

Intelligence is difficult to define. Most writers point to it as the innate potential of a person for making appropriate judgments, for profiting from experience, or for meeting adequately new problems and conditions of life. Certainly there is something that distinguishes an idiot from a genius, and this factor we call "general intelligence" (sometimes labeled "g"). There seems to be likewise "special" intelligences. Even a generally stupid person can have limited regions of special ability (*idiot savant*), and many geniuses are virtual imbeciles in some respects. One near genius has no sense of direction and can scarcely leave home without becoming hopelessly lost. One otherwise feeble-minded boy is a "whiz" with machinery.

How do we know that intellectual capacity, whether general or special, leans heavily on native endowment? There are many lines

[7] M. A. Davidson, R. G. McInnes, and R. W. Parnell, The distribution of personality traits in seven-year-old children: a combined psychological, psychiatric and somatotype study, *Brit. J. educ. Psychol.*, 1957, **27**, 48–61.

of evidence. The study of family histories show that genius or near genius will crop up frequently in one line, whereas in another dullness and feeble-mindedness are the rule. (Of course in this case home environments as well as heredity may be a factor.) It is clear from animal research that "bright" and "dull" lines of rats can be produced within a few generations by selective breeding.[8] Animal and human inheritance is probably similar in this regard. Studies of identical twins (having presumably identical heredity) show a correlation of intelligence around .90; whereas the intelligence of siblings (some similarity in heredity) correlates around .50, a child and one parent, around .30; and unrelated children, .00.[9] Another line of evidence comes from the study of a given child from early years to later years. Ordinarily, it seems, a bright child makes a bright adult, though there are exceptions. This problem of the "constancy of the intelligence quotient" has been worked on extensively.

One study, to give a single example, measured the same children year after year from the age of three to twelve. The intelligence measured at three was not a very good predictor of intelligence at twelve ($r = .46$); but all correlations from the age of six to twelve were .73 or higher. Between the measures of IQ at eleven and twelve the agreement was .93. The authors found that 62 percent of their children changed as much as 15 IQ points between the ages of three and ten. And so we conclude intellectual ability is relatively constant, but not completely so.

An interesting feature of this study is its search for reasons why some children gained or lost ground in their IQ's. Those who gained turned out to be children having a certain pattern of personality traits: independence, self-initiation, competitiveness (a cluster making for high achievement). Children with the opposite qualities lost ground. Their IQ's at the age of twelve were lower than at younger ages.[10]

This study demonstrates that intelligence is not determined exclusively by the texture of central nerve tissue. Motives and traits

[8] R. C. Tryon, Genetic difference in maze-learning ability in rats, *Yearb. nat. Soc. Stud. Educ.*, 1940, 39, 111–119.

[9] H. H. Newman, F. N. Freeman, and K. J. Holzinger, *Twins: a study of heredity and environment* (Chicago: Univ. of Chicago Press, 1937).

[10] L. W. Sontag, C. T. Baker, and V. L. Nelson, Mental growth and personality development: a longitudinal study, *Monogr. Soc. Res. Child Develpm.*, 1958, **23**, No. 68.

alter the product. And, further, we can be sure that treatment at home, stimulation in the environment, rewards and punishments cooperate in giving one child a higher level of functioning than another.[11]

Centering for a moment on the relations between personality and IQ, we can be sure that they interact, but apparently there is no standard pattern. Surveying 200 relevant studies, Lorge fails to find any uniform relation between measures of intelligence and measures of emotional and personal traits.[12] This means that bright (or dull) people have an equally good chance of being introverted, anxious, dominant, sociable, neurotic, or anything else.

Although there are no uniform correspondences between intelligence and personality, there are nonetheless many subtle relations between them. To use one's "innate potential" to good effect certainly requires a push from other regions of the personality.

In a follow-up study of 750 highly gifted children, twenty years after they were first tested, Terman and Oden found that some were markedly successful, others unsuccessful in their careers. Both groups are known to be high in "g." What, then, is the difference? Two features are distinguishing. Members of the successful group are more "interested in their work"; they are also judged by their associates to be more persevering, more self-confident, and better integrated in their goals.[13] Thus for efficient intellectual functioning (whatever the IQ), qualities of personality are needed.

Here, then, is a point of considerable importance: *a person's pattern of intelligence is idiographic,* basically unique, partly because of his never-repeated inheritance and partly because intelligence is blended inextricably with the total personality. When we say this we are not denying that for certain purposes a gross measure of "g" may be useful. But measures of "g" or even of "special abilities" do not show the uniqueness of the blend.

11 For a particularly discerning study of the factors entering into the determination and modification of intelligence see P. E. Vernon, The psychology of intelligence and G, *Bull. Brit. psychol. Soc.,* 1955, No. 26, pp. 1–14.
12 I. Lorge, Intelligence and personality as revealed in questionnaires and inventories, *Yearb. nat. Soc. Stud. Educ.,* 1940, 39, 275–281.
13 L. M. Terman and M. H. Oden, *The gifted child grows up* (Stanford, Calif.: Stanford Univ. Press, 1947).

Case of Peter, a sixteen-year-old farm boy. He does not do well in school, especially in reading, languages, and spelling; his scores on "verbal" intelligence are low. On "mechanical" intelligence tests he stands high, and successfully tinkers with all his father's farm equipment. But to divide his abilities according to this familiar nomothetic scheme (verbal versus mechanical intelligence) does not do justice to the peculiar patterning that is characteristic of Peter. He has a special interest in postage stamps, and has no difficulty with the language, history, or other "verbal" material so long as it is relevant to postage stamps. Further, he is peculiarly gifted in "social intelligence." Not that he is sympathetic and helpful, for he is not. But he can "size up" people, giving first impressions that adults at first reject but later find to be valid. He does this with a curious characteristic cynicism—with understanding but not with sympathy. And we may add that his acuity does not extend at all to understanding his own parents. If one knows Peter all these curious ceilings and troughs in his intelligence make sense and are congruent; but his abilities elude coarse methods of measurement, and the pattern as a whole defies direct comparison with other people.

Case of Professor Lowe. Here "verbal" ability is high—in spots. He lectures fluently on psychology—at least on his own brand of mathematical and measurement psychology. When it comes to other areas of psychology he has a blind spot. For example, he cannot seem to comprehend what is meant by "dynamic psychology," but confuses it with his own favored outlook on measurement. He does good amateur cabinetmaking but cannot drive a car without bumping fenders and alarming all pedestrians. He is meticulous in his writing and editing, but manages to antagonize many people in his human relationships. He is surprised when they take exception to his insulting comments— which he did not intend as insulting but whose impact he was unable to estimate in advance. He plays chess well but is a dub at bridge. He can mend broken electrical equipment but not motors.

What we find in real people, then, is a *personalistic* patterning of intelligence, closely meshed with interests, traits, and outlook on life. It is sometimes useful to know the level of "g" (IQ) or the scores on special skills (e.g., verbal, mechanical), or to have a profile of "primary abilities" (language, number, spatial thinking, mechanical principles, dexterity, perception, learning, reasoning).[14] But however finely we subdivide intellectual functions we never reach the personal pattern. In general, psychology has scarcely touched the riddle of the personal organization of intelligence. Each of us is flexible in some encounters, rigid in others. We have areas of creativeness, but are pedestrian and conformist in others. Our skills are spotty: we can play by ear but not by note, or vice versa; we can dance a rhumba but not a waltz. Of only one thing we can be sure: *intelligence moves in channels that correspond fairly closely to interests,* though which is cause and which effect we cannot clearly say.

Eminence in a given profession is not due to intelligence alone. Dr. Roe studied outstanding scientists. Although their performance on intelligence tests tended to be high (but not always), their scores could be matched or exceeded by thousands of noneminent mortals. What, then, made them distinguished? Sustained devotion to, and interest in, their work is an important factor. Also, with fair frequency the men felt that early feelings of inferiority provided them with initial incentive. Most had had some successful experience in creative research as young students in college. Although no two patterns are precisely alike, we can safely conclude that both intelligence and personality factors combine to make for eminence.[15]

Inheritance

Human beings in common with all other living creatures are subject to the laws of heredity. What these laws are, and to what degree they determine physique, temperament, intelligence, and personality, we are just beginning to learn. The process is infinitely subtle. In so lowly a creature as the fruit fly (drosophila) as many as fifty genes may determine the usual red color of the eye. Jennings writes,

By changing any one of the fifty genes of the fruit fly that take part in producing the eye color, the color is altered; eyes of another color are produced; or there is no pigment in the eye; or it is structurally im-

---

14 This listing of primary mental abilities is taken from E. B. Greene, *Measurements of human behavior* (Rev. ed.; New York: Odyssey, 1952), pp. 257 ff.
15 Anne Roe, *The making of a scientist* (New York: Dodd, Mead, 1953).

perfect. The same situation is found for all characteristics, in the fruit fly or in ourselves.[16]

And when we come to human heredity, and especially to personality with its complex traits of laziness, ambition, courage, we can only agree with Charles Darwin who exclaimed, "The whole subject of inheritance is wonderful."

The most important point of scientific agreement is that no feature or quality is exclusively hereditary, and none is exclusively environmental in origin. One cannot even say that blue eyes are inherited but a coat of tan is acquired, for nutrition in childhood may affect eye color, and tan would not occur at all unless pigments in the skin were prepared by nature to respond to the sun's rays. We cannot even say that a dog's bark is inherited but his response to his name is learned. Reared in isolation, a dog may fail to bark; and unless an inherent teachability exists no dog will learn to come when called.[17] Everyone, then, seems to agree that the following equation is valid: *Personality*—or any of its subsystems, such as habit, trait, sentiment $= f$ *(heredity)* x *(environment)*. The two causal factors are not added together, but are related as multiplier and multiplicand. If either were zero there could be no personality.

Even though we agree that no feature of personality is devoid of both hereditary and environmental influence, the persistent question arises: *How much* of this or that characteristic is due to genetic determination and how much to environmental influence? It seems clear, for example, that it is easier for a dog to learn to bark than to respond to his name. Likewise, as we have suggested, it seems that a person's innate neural and glandular equipment contribute more to his intelligence, temperament, and physique than they do to his vocabulary, ideology, or cultural conformity. In short, some of the content of personality is more, and some less, subject to environmental influence and learning. We learn certain attitudes and cultural practices more easily than others do simply because we have genetic bents that enable us to do so. One helpful suggestion, therefore, is that *ease of learning* provides a fair definition of heredity. No

[16] H. S. Jennings, *The biological basis of human nature* (New York: Norton, 1930), p. 17. A recent survey of genetics in relation to psychological topics is J. L. Fuller and W. R. Thompson, *Behavior genetics* (New York: Wiley, 1960).

[17] T. H. Howells, The obsolete dogmas of heredity, *Psychol. Rev.*, 1945, 52, 23–34.

activity is devoid of some learning, but when the learning is very easy we suspect an assist is coming from native endowment.[18]

Let us take the example of *handedness*. In any large group of people, ask the question, "How many of you consider yourself to be left-handed?" Almost without fail about 10 percent will raise their hands. This group has found it much, much more easy to learn to favor the left hand than the right (in spite of all environmental pressure to the contrary). There is no doubt that inheritance is almost entirely responsible.

If 10 percent are incorrigibly left-handed may we not infer that 10 percent are incorrigibly right-handed (due to the structure of the brain)? These people would resist all efforts to make them conform to the habits of a left-handed culture—if there were such a culture.

What shall we say about the remaining 80 percent of right-handers? These presumably are individuals who by nature are potentially ambidextrous. The brain structure permits them to favor either hand. But culture is right-handed.[19] Therefore the parent and society teach the child to favor his right hand.

If this analysis is correct we may say that inheritance is the major determinant of handedness in 20 percent of the population; environmental learning, in 80 percent.

The illustration is useful in pointing out that one person may owe a given trait primarily to inheritance, another person primarily to learning. One person may be reclusive and retiring chiefly because of his temperament, another because of conflict with his environment. One may be irritable chiefly for genetic reasons; another, because of overstimulation and frustrations in his life-experience.

Our knowledge of genetic determination comes chiefly from three sources: (1) animal studies, (2) a comparison of the qualities of people having varying degrees of hereditary closeness (identical twins,

18 *Ibid.*
19 Why all known cultures are right-handed is a question we cannot answer. One theory holds that the heart on the left needs protection. Primitive warriors, for example, held their shields over the heart, leaving the right hand free for skilled movements. There is, of course, the opposite possibility: in the human race as a whole the left brain hemisphere is ordinarily dominant, making it easier for most people to favor the right hand. If this should be the case, our present analysis is, of course, erroneous.

siblings, parent-child comparisons), and (3) a study of identical twins separated in early life and reared apart.

From animal studies we learn that we can breed strains to produce in successive generations variations in size, greater or lesser intelligence, anxiety, wildness or tameness, aggressiveness, quickness of reaction, and even temperature preference.[20] This information alone convinces us that features of physique, intelligence, and temperament do tend to "run in families." But we knew this already.

Turning to studies of human kinship we find that nature has given us a special kind of aid. Identical twins are the product of the same sperm cell and the same ovum. For this reason their genetic equipment is much more alike than that found in fraternal twins or in ordinary siblings.[21] From the point of view of genetic similarity the following order holds:

> identical twins
> { siblings
> { one parent-child
> unrelated individuals

Many studies show that the closeness of correlation of intelligence measures follows this order precisely. So close is the relation that one student of determinants of intelligence claims that genes are "four or five times" as important as environment when it is uniform.[22]

Resemblances in many other characteristics have been studied.[23] Summing up the results as best we can, we may reach the following conclusion. Family members are most alike in physique; next most

20 C. S. Hall, The genetics of behavior. In S. S. Stevens (Ed.), *Handbook of experimental psychology* (New York: Wiley, 1951), pp. 304–329.

21 We dare not assert, however, that identical twins have absolute identity of inheritance. Williams writes: "No two human beings possess the same genes. Even in identical twins, although the genes are theoretically identical initially, they occur in such large numbers and the possibility of somatic mutations is sufficient (minor mutations may be very common) that the metabolism in fully developed 'identical' twins is likely not to be identical in every respect." R. Williams, *Biochemical individuality* (New York: Wiley, 1956), p. 11.

22 E. L. Thorndike, Heredity and envorinment, *Eugenical News*, 1944, **29**, 39–45.

23 Representative sources are the following: M. N. Crook, Intra-family relationships in personality test performance, *Psychol. Rec.*, 1937, **1**, 479–502; Newman, Freeman, Holzinger, *op. cit.* (Note 9 above); H. J. Eysenck and D. B. Prell, The inheritance of neuroticism: an experimental study, *J. ment. Sci.*, 1951, **97**, 441–465; Anne Anastasi, *Differential psychology* (3d ed.; New York: Macmillan, 1958), Chap. 9.

alike in measured abilities (intelligence, reaction time, motor skills, sensory discriminations). They are somewhat similar in emotional characteristics, qualities of temperament, of mood, and of neuroticism; but they seem to be less alike (though still similar) in attitudes, beliefs, values, and interests. In all these attributes identical twins are most alike, but especially in physique.

All studies of family resemblances face the question whether similar home training may not be partly responsible for the results. Brothers and sisters receive approximately the same kind of treatment. Identical twins are often dressed alike and treated in the same way. In later life identicals often win attention and rewards by cultivating their similarity. Von Bracken finds that as a rule identical twins like to deny any difference between them. "Which of you can run the faster?" asks the stranger. "Oh, we are equal. You know we are identical twins," is a common reply. Fraternal twins, on the other hand, are often thrown into keen competition with one another.[24]

And so to disentangle the influence of the genes from that of the environment is difficult indeed. The only known method is to find cases of identical twins who have been separated early in life and who have grown up in contrasting environments. If the genes are all-powerful we would expect close resemblances even if the course of education and life-experience were markedly different. Unfortunately, only a few pairs of identical twins separated in this way have been traced for study. In these few cases it turns out that the separated twins still resemble each other almost perfectly in anatomical characteristics. In diseases and in glandular disorders there are some striking similarities. Intelligence tests give mixed evidence; in most cases the resemblance is high, but in a few cases differing amounts of education make an appreciable difference. In personality there are persistent resemblances but not to a degree that gives all credit to genes.[25] The results, so far as they go, seem to confirm our claim that inheritance plays a larger role in fashioning the "raw materials" of personality than in fashioning the developed personality itself.

One final warning is in order. Inheritance may account for differences in personality within a family as well as for resemblances. Since every personal genotype is unique (page 4 f.) we must expect

24 H. von Bracken, Mutual intimacy in twins, *Charact. & Pers.*, 1934, **2**, 293–309.
25 Newman, Freeman, Holzinger, *op. cit.*; also B. S. Burks and A. Roe, Studies of identical twins reared apart, *Psychol. Monogr.*, 1949, **63**, No. 5. See also J. Shields, Twins brought up apart, *Eug. Rev.*, 1958, **45**, 213–246.

this to be so. The genes of one child may make for an easygoing temperament; those of his brother, for a tense and rigid approach to life. Consider the following conversation between two brothers. It shows how differently they react to their common home life, particularly to their father.

"My father," said Ora, "was a sloppy, lazy, booze-hoisting old bum, and my mother didn't know much besides cooking, and she was too busy to give me much attention, and the kids I knew were a bunch of foul-mouthed loafers that used to hang around the hoboes up near the water tank, and I never had a chance to get any formal schooling, and I got thrown on my own as just a brat. So naturally I've become a sort of vagabond that can't be bored by thinking about his 'debts' to a lot of little shop-keeping lice, and I suppose I'm inclined to be lazy, and not too scrupulous about the dames and the liquor. But my early rearing did have one swell result. Brought up so unconventionally, I'll always be an anti-Puritan. I'll never deny the joys of the flesh and the sanctity of Beauty."

"And my father," said Myron, "was pretty easygoing and always did like drinking and swapping stories with the Boys, and my mother was hard-driven taking care of us, and I heard a lot of filth from the hoboes up near the water tank. Maybe just sort of as a reaction I've become almost too much of a crank about paying debts, and fussing over my work, and being scared of liquor and women. But my rearing did have one swell result. Just by way of contrast, it made me a good, sound, old-fashioned New England Puritan."[26]

The same fire that melts the butter hardens the egg.

The Biological View of Personality

The human being, like other organisms, has a biological nature. The bodily system is composed of fluids, bones, skin, of muscular, connective, and neural tissue. The functioning of these materials, separately or in combination, is the *physiology* of the organism.

Now most psychologists would say that there is no psychological process (and no personality) without some corresponding physiological process (the theory of "psychophysical parallelism"). Some say that the two types of process are only two aspects of the same underlying organismic process ("double aspect" theory). Only a few would hold that mental functions and bodily functions are of wholly

[26] S. Lewis, *Work of art* (New York: Doubleday, 1934), pp. 310 ff. Reprinted by permission.

different genre, and that they may affect one another but are not always tied together ("interactionist" theory).

No one knows for sure which theory is correct, but there is plenty of evidence that the interdependence between "mind" and "body" is close. When the brain is injured or when small portions of it are removed, there is some disturbance in personality—though often less than one might expect. A generation ago attention was focused on the close parallel between the glands of internal secretion and certain parallel functions of personality (better, *temperament*). Nowadays there is lively interest in the electrical rhythms of the brain as possible substrata of personality differences among people.[27] Many writers urge us to keep personality theory abreast of progress in anatomy, neurology, and physiology.[28]

A contrasting point of view holds that the biological sciences cannot tell us enough about the complex psychological functioning to be helpful. Better to examine only *behavior,* and not try constantly to interpret behavior in terms of the hidden, and often speculative, facts of nerve tissue and/or physiological functioning.[29]

My own view of the matter is that the *psychological* study of personality is considerably more advanced than is the *biological* study of personality. (I say this in all modesty, for in psychology we still stumble at thresholds.) We know that heredity is important but have little knowledge of the underlying mechanics of genetics. We know something about the laws of learning but little about the neurology of learning. We can study traits, attitudes, philosophies of life without knowing their neural and physiological equivalents.

We have faith that sometime in the distant future well-proved facts concerning personality will be found to interlock with well-proved facts of human biology. Until that time we believe that the "psychological model" is on the whole the safest guide to follow in constructing the science of human personality. Some day the "biological model" may catch up.

27 See W. C. Walter, *The living brain* (New York: Norton, 1953). Also, D. B. Lindsley, Electroencephalography. In J. McV. Hunt (Ed.), *Personality and behavior disorders* (New York: Ronald, 1944), Chap. 33.

28 For example, D. O. Hebb, The role of neurological ideas in psychology. In D. Krech and G. S. Klein (Eds.), *Theoretical models and personality theory* (Durham, N.C.: Duke Univ. Press, 1952), pp. 39–55. The volume contains other discussions of biological and psychological models.

29 B. F. Skinner, *The behavior of organisms: an experimental analysis* (New York: Appleton-Century-Crofts, 1938).

Biological science, though it is not as helpful in detail as we could wish, contains a basic point of view of profound relevance to the theory of personality—the evolutionary point of view. Just as organisms take on the form of some *species,* each of which represents a successful mode of survival in the evolutionary struggle, so too do individuals within the human species attain *personality* as the form of survival most suitable to their particular needs within a particular environmental framework. Thus my personality is the unique *modus vivendi* that I have arrived at in my own peculiar struggle for survival. *Personality* is to the individual what *species* is to all living phyla.

To state the theory more fully: the personality of an individual is the mode of adjustment or survival that results from the interaction of his organic needs with an environment both friendly and hostile to these needs, through the intermediation of a plastic and modifiable central nervous system.[30]

According to this view the organic needs arise in the glands and viscera of the body involving primarily the autonomic (vegetative) nervous system. These needs encounter potential satisfaction or danger or obstacles in the environment. The central nervous system then brings about some type of learned or unlearned adjustment, usually satisfying the needs. Personality is thus an executive whose function it is to guarantee survival. The autonomic nervous system and the environment are "tyrants" and the personality is a kind of habitual trouble shooter. Figure 9 represents this view.

In its broad outlines this biological theory of personality is acceptable. Personality does represent the mode of survival that the individual has consciously or unconsciously worked out for himself. Not all his adjustments are successful, and some of his traits may be harmful, but they can be explained as abortive *attempts* to find suitable patterns for living in a complex interplay of forces.

The scheme, however, is oversimplified. Not all our strong cravings arise in the bodily tissue. Many of them are intellectual (e.g., *curiosity*) or spiritual (e.g., *ideals*). Nor is it true that our personalities are simply servants of the two tyrants. Often we control and

[30] An early but still standard presentation of the biological point of view is E. J. Kempf, The autonomic functions and the personality, *Nerv. & ment. Dis. Monogr. Ser.,* 1921, No. 28.

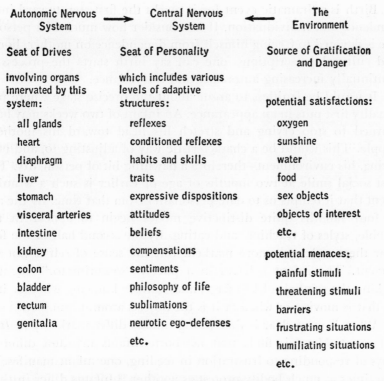

Autonomic Nervous System →	Central Nervous System ←	The Environment
Seat of Drives	**Seat of Personality**	**Source of Gratification and Danger**
involving organs innervated by this system:	which includes various levels of adaptive structures:	potential satisfactions:
all glands	reflexes	oxygen
heart	conditioned reflexes	sunshine
diaphragm	habits and skills	water
liver	traits	food
stomach	expressive dispositions	sex objects
visceral arteries	attitudes	objects of interest
intestine	beliefs	etc.
kidney	compensations	potential menaces:
colon	sentiments	painful stimuli
bladder	philosophy of life	threatening stimuli
rectum	sublimations	barriers
genitalia	neurotic ego-defenses	frustrating situations
	etc.	humiliating situations
		etc.

Figure 9. Biological Theory of Personality

master them. Nor can we say that the subsystems that comprise personality lie only in the central nervous system. Everything that we know about neural organization indicates that both nervous systems are involved in the patterning of personality.

On the whole, the simple biological view of personality is better when applied to early infancy than to adult years.

Personality in the First Year

The infant is not greatly different from a fetus. Independent breathing is his principal achievement. Otherwise he is far more like a fetus than like the child he will become. For this reason we cannot look for signs of personality in the newborn. He is equipped with many potentialities or, better, *ranges* of potentialities, by his genes. But he has not yet developed "characteristic modes of thought and behavior."

Birth is a dramatic event for it marks the first step toward independence and individuation. If we consider how much of a person's life is devoted to freeing himself from dependence on mother, home, and cultural prescriptions, one can say birth starts the process of continually increasing autonomy and self-reliance.

It would be fruitless to argue about the precise stage where personality first puts in an appearance. An infant of two weeks may have learned to stop crying and stretch his head toward his mother's nipple. This would be a characteristic way of adjusting to, and mastering, his environment—therefore a dawning bit of personality. The first social smile at two months of age or earlier is such a winning event that it tempts us to date personality from that time. By the age of four months quite distinctive modes begin to appear in the babble, styles of reaching, and eating. By the second half of the first year these styles are more marked. But the sense of self is not yet present. The infant behaves in a purely "sensorimotor" manner, lacking the symbols of language, and scarcely knowing whether it is he that is moving or whether it is the objects around him.[31]

What is most clear is that young infants differ markedly in *temperament*. Marquis finds that newborn infants manifest different ways of responding to frustration in feeding, one infant manifesting five times as much bodily protest as another.[32] Infants differ in their crying, in their manner of sucking, in their responsiveness to startling and frustrating stimuli, in their readiness to smile and to laugh, in their general level of energy and vigor, and in many other ways that express temperament.[33]

Stone and Church give a summary picture:

Some people are presto, some andante, some largo. Some are staccato, some legato. Some babies drain their bottles in a single rush, others remain unhurried and even indifferent during a feeding. Some babies can hardly wait to become mobile, others seem content to stay comfortably in one place. Even though there is probably an hereditary basis for tempo, parents and their children do not always move at the same pace, any more than they necessarily match in other hereditary traits. And a fast-

---

[31] Cf. D. E. Berlyne, Recent developments in Piaget's work, *Brit. J. educ. Psychol.*, 1957, 27, 1–12.

[32] D. Marquis, A study of frustration in newborn infants, *J. exper. Psychol.*, 1943, 32, 123–138.

[33] For a review of some relevant studies, see S. Diamond, *Personality and temperament* (New York: Harper, 1957), pp. 96–105.

moving mother paired with a slow-moving child, or vice versa, can spell mutual frustration, exasperation, and conflict.[34]

How important is the first year? If it is true that "as the twig is bent, the tree's inclined," we should expect the initial slanting of the infant to have important long-range effects on his later personality. Such evidence as we have on the matter seems at first sight to be contradictory, though not irreconcilable.

The negative evidence comes from studies that test the long-range effects of *specific* child-handling practices. Following the Freudian position, some psychologists would say that to attain a secure, nonneurotic later personality the infant should enjoy (a) breast feeding, (b) a prolonged period of nursing, (c) gradual weaning, (d) a self-demand nursing schedule, (e) easy and late bowel and bladder training, (f) freedom from restraint, (g) freedom from punishment, (h) "secure" sleeping, e.g., sleeping with the mother. To test these specific hypotheses Sewell compared the personalities of children at the age of six who did and who did not have these experiences during the first year of life. The results were negative.[35] The one positive finding had to do with sleeping with the mother. Infants who during the first year of life slept with the mother showed poorer adjustment scores and poorer family relationships than did other children—a finding in opposition to the original hypothesis.

Hence, so far as this evidence can guide us, it seems to make no difference for later personality development whether the young infant is bottle- or breast-fed, whether the nursing is scheduled or on demand, whether weaning is abrupt or gradual, or what methods of bowel training may be used. It seems safe to conclude that during the first year of life the infant is so plastic and resilient that no point-for-point correspondences are built up between specific modes of training and later traits.

On the positive side we come to studies that deal not with specific and detailed practices but with a much broader factor that we might call "style of mothering." A child who in the first year of life is removed from his mother and finds no good mother-substitute

[34] L. J. Stone and J. Church, *Childhood and adolescence* (New York: Random House, 1957), p. 61.
[35] W. H. Sewell, Infant training and the personality of the child, *Amer. J. Sociol.*, 1952, 58, 150–159. Several surveys report similarly negative results. See H. Orlansky, Infant care and personality, *Psychol. Bull.*, 1949, 46, 1–48; A. R. Lindsmith and A. L. Strauss, Critique of culture-personality writings, *Amer. Sociol. Rev.*, 1950, 15, 587–600.

seems to be adversely affected—even for a long period of time, possibly permanently. Goldfarb studied two groups of children who had been separated from their mothers in the first months of life. Half of these children had from the time of separation received good foster home care; the others had lived in an institution. When studied more than ten years later there was an important difference. Not only were the intellectual abilities of the institutional children lower; they seemed relatively deficient in emotional control and in social adjustment.[36] Essentially the same retarding and injurious effects of lack of adequate mothering—"hospitalism" it is sometimes called—have been noted by other investigators.[37] Such evidence has led Erikson to hold that the first and most important crisis of life is the development of trust.[38] Trust, says the dictionary, is "the assured reliance on another's integrity." Unless a child, a wholly dependent creature, can trust in a mothering individual, his start in life is poor indeed.

A child need not be institutionalized in order to lack adequate mothering. Some women reject their babies. Every service they give is grudging and their tone of voice and physical movements are such as to alarm rather than evoke trust in the child.[39]

To sum up, the child in the first year of life is more plastic, more resilient, and more vegetative than he will be at any later stage of life. He has no concept of himself, no lasting memories, and no firm anchorage of habits. For these reasons we may say that what happens to him in a detailed way—what sights surround him, how he is fed, leave relatively little impress. In a sense the first year is the least important year for personality, assuming that serious injuries to health do not occur.

At the same time, roots are being formed, particularly the taproot of trust. Our best evidence to date seems to show that an ade-

[36] W. Goldfarb, The effects of early institutional care on adolescent personality, *J. exper. Educ.*, 1943, **12**, 106–129.
[37] See R. A. Spitz and K. M. Wolf, Anaclitic depression. In A. Freud, *et al.* (Eds.), *The psychoanalytic study of the child* (New York: Int. Univ. Press, 1946), II, 313–342. Also J. Bowlby, *Maternal care and mental health, Bull. World Hlth Organization,* 1951, **3**, No. 3. This last-named author believes that the effects of maternal deprivation are greatest in the first three years of life, less important (though still serious) from three to five, and still less significant in middle and later childhood.
[38] E. H. Erikson, *Childhood and society* (New York: Norton, 1955), Chap. 8.
[39] Cf. D. M. Levy and A. Hess, Problems in determining maternal attitudes toward newborn infants, *Psychiat.*, 1952, **15**, 273–286.

quate amount of mothering (regardless of specific practices) is an essential factor in establishing a normal course of psychological growth.

It has been said that personality progresses from *dependency* in childhood, through growing *independence* in adolescence to *dependability* in adulthood.[40] The problem of the first year of life is to establish dependency on firm and natural foundations. If this need is met, then in Maslow's terms, the child is in far better position in later years to enter the stage of "self-actualization."[41] If it is not met, the whole life may manifest greediness, possessiveness, and similar efforts to obtain the condition of loving dependence that the individual was at first denied. In place of trust, the life is built on mistrust. There is some evidence that children lacking basic trust in early life are prone to develop in later childhood a suspiciousness of nature, including prejudice against minority groups.[42]

Predicting Development

One of the aims of science is prediction. Can we foretell by careful study of the infant years what the later personality will be? If heredity and early learning are important we should expect to have some success, although no one, of course, can foresee all the environmental influences that lie ahead.

In one experiment more than thirty infants were studied at some time between the ages of two and eight months. Many predictions were made concerning their probable style of behaving at the age of five years. Safeguards were strict: one psychologist made the initial study, a different psychologist made the study at age five, and still others judged the correspondence of the two reports.

By way of illustration we take a small excerpt from the case of Roddie.

Prediction (made at five months): "I do not expect Roddie to be a strikingly masculine little boy, although this does not imply

40 O. H. Mowrer and C. Kluckhohn, A dynamic theory of personality. In J. McV. Hunt (Ed.), *Personality and the behavior disorders* (New York: Ronald, 1944), pp. 69–135.
41 A. H. Maslow, *Motivation and personality* (New York: Harper, 1954).
42 Cf. G. W. Allport, *The nature of prejudice* (Cambridge, Mass.: Addison-Wesley, 1954), Chap. 18.

an anticipation of 'sissyness.' Rather I imagine that he will go through the cowboy and soldier stages, will be interested in machinery, etc., just like other boys. But his stance, motion, and demeanor may not have the aggressive masculine quality observed in many five-year-olds."

Outcome (at age of five years): "He occasionally displayed a masculine swagger and verbal bravado. He also participated in the common interests of boys such as Hopalong Cassidy, Superman, and fishing trips with his father. Yet a 'soft' quality in his behavior was commented upon by all observers . . . he did not assertively behave as though he felt himself to be strong . . . (as did most boys in our sample)."

Not all predictions for Roddie were equally accurate. Thus, *prediction:* "I expect Roddie to be precocious in speech development"; *outcome:* "Earned low average scores on vocabulary and verbal comprehension."

By this method—and scored conservatively—about two thirds of all predictions were correct or predominantly correct; one third were false or mostly false. Generally speaking it was the broad and lasting temperamental dispositions that could be spotted. Roddie, for example, was seen correctly to be a high-strung, hyperactive, sensitive child at both five months and at five years of age. What was not predictable were the type of inner control, personal attachments, the self-image he would later learn and which would inevitably affect his personality.[43]

Once more we see that temperament, motility, and, to some extent, intelligence seem to be lasting endowments, but what pattern they will weave with environmental influences cannot be known in advance.

How about predictions over a longer span of time? Here, too, we discover that success, though far from perfect, is greater than chance.

Shirley wrote personality sketches of nineteen children during the first two years of their life. Fifteen years later, Neilon was able to locate sixteen of these children, tested them again, and, without any reference to the original sketches, wrote new de-

[43] Adapted from S. Escalona and G. M. Heider, *Prediction and outcome* (New York: Basic Books, 1959). The case of Roddie is described on pp. 221–232.

scriptions of their personalities. The question arose, Can outside judges match the originals with the later sketches? In other words, is a young person identifiably the same at the ages of two and seventeen? The judges had far greater than chance success, especially with girls. They were able to match nearly all of the girls' sketches at seventeen with those at two, but in one case there was complete failure. Apparently although some children undergo great change, the average consistency is considerable.[44]

From this and similar evidence we conclude that the pattern of later personality is to some extent discernible in infancy.[45] The predictive process is elusive and not wholly dependable. Consistency is not perfect. For one thing, the child in infancy lacks firm memories and has no sense of self or self-image to guide his development. Freud asserts that when these and other capacities develop, by the age of three, then the guidelines for later development are firmly established. The character structure is determined by the age of three. My own view is less fatalistic. Directions may change drastically in later childhood, in adolescence or in adulthood. But that the child, to some extent, is father of the man we cannot completely deny.

Summary

Through many centuries men have believed that body build reflects innate temperament. Science is at last learning how to establish the parallels that exist. Somatotyping is a method that holds some promise.

Not only physique and temperament but intelligence, too, comprise the raw materials of personality that later training and experience will fashion into a fully developed personality. On the broad average, intellectual capacity runs in families, though we must not forget that genetic endowment accounts for dissimilarities as well as for similarities within the family. Psychologists unfortunately tend to overlook the personalistic patterning of abilities that for each in-

44 M. Shirley, *The first two years:* Vol. III, *Personality manifestations* (Minneapolis: Univ. of Minn. Press, 1933); P. Neilon, Shirley's babies after 15 years, *J. genet. Psychol.,* 1948, **73,** 175–186.
45 Reliable longitudinal studies of personality development are not numerous and are difficult to carry through. A partial bibliography of existing studies is A. A. Stone and G. C. Onqué, *Longitudinal studies of child personality* (Cambridge, Mass.: Harvard Univ. Press, 1959).

dividual blend uniquely his native endowment and his acquired interests and traits.

A geneticist once said, "Human personality is 100 percent genetic," meaning that no feature or act is without some genetic influence. He was right. But equally correct is the statement, "Human personality is 100 percent environmental," meaning that surrounding influences and learning enter into every feature and act. Researches, however, help us to decide that genetic influences weigh heavily in the endowments of physique, temperament, intelligence.

Although there is certainly a biological substratum of personality, it seems that at the present stage of scientific progress it is more helpful on the whole to study the phenomena of personality from a *psychological* than from a biological point of view. We can, however, adopt as roughly applicable the biological theory of evolution, and regard personality as the formula an individual has evolved to assure his survival and mastery within the framework of his existence.

Personality, defined as the distinctive organization of adjustment patterns, is not formed at birth, but may be said to begin at birth. In the first year of life specific forms of training and learning seem less decisive than the style of trustful relationship that the child establishes with his mother.

Research shows that some broad predictions can be made in infancy concerning the style of personality that will develop. The success of these predictions is not great enough to justify the belief that personality is firmly fixed in the early years. The process of becoming continues one's whole life through.

CHAPTER 5

Principles of Learning

CONTRASTING VIEWS OF MOTIVATION • THE QUASI-MECHANI-
CAL VIEW • CRITIQUE OF QUASI-MECHANICAL MOTIVATION •
QUASI-MECHANICAL FACTORS IN LEARNING • DIFFERENTIA-
TION AND INTEGRATION • COGNITIVE (ORGANIZATIONAL) LEARN-
ING • PARTICIPATION (BIOGRAPHICAL LEARNING) • SUMMARY

INHERITANCE, as we have seen, exerts a universal influence
in shaping personality—particularly in the regions of physique, basic
abilities, and temperament. And yet, considering the course of development as a whole, we are tempted to say that *learning* is a factor
of still greater importance. Perhaps it is unprofitable to estimate the
proportions in this way. A florist never asks "how much" of his prize
chrysanthemum is due to seed and "how much" to soil and cultivation. Be that as it may, it is clearly a fact that compared with all
other organisms, man is extremely modifiable. The raw materials he
inherits can be molded in a vast number of ways.

Think for a moment of how many *kinds* of learning take place
in the course of life. We learn to walk, talk, and dance; to drive
automobiles, swim, and play the piano; to spell, write, and read; we
memorize facts, phone numbers, and poems. We learn what to eat,

what to fear, what to shun, and what objects to desire sexually. We acquire morals, values, and interests. We come to embrace religions, beliefs, ideologies. We develop preferences, prejudices, and manners. We learn new concepts, meanings, and conformities; also foreign languages. We learn new motives, ambitions, and hopes. We learn signs, cues, and symbols. Gradually we acquire our own traits and trends of personality, and evolve a guiding personal conscience and a more or less comprehensive philosophy of life. We even learn how to learn.

Before undertaking to review some of the main principles of learning, two important statements must be made.

1. The array of things learned is so vast that we ought not to expect any simple theory of learning to suffice. No problem in psychology has inspired so much experimental research as learning. Much has been discovered. Yet if we were to criticize the output to date we should say that current theories tend to be one-sided and narrow. They lack the sweep required to embrace the many forms of learning that occur.

2. Theories of learning (like much else in psychology) rest on the investigator's conception of the *nature of man*. In other words, every learning theorist is a philosopher, though he may not know it. To put the matter more concretely, psychologists who investigate (and theorize about) learning start with some preconceived view of the nature of human motivation. This issue (*the philosophy of motivation*) is so important that we must now examine it directly, and return again to the problem in Chapters 9 and 10.

Contrasting Views of Motivation

From the window of a farmhouse I see an old barn, weathered, disintegrating, and unable to repair itself, gradually collapsing. Beside the barn are sturdy, ever-expanding growths of bamboo, raspberry bushes, and wild cherry. They are marching over the hayfield and at the same time competing with each other for the rich earth and for space to expand.

Inanimate nature obeys the second law of thermodynamics. Lifeless matter decreases in its degree of organization, becoming more and more random, run-down. *Entropy* the process is called. Rocks erode, the sun loses its heat, barns collapse.

By contrast life is inherently synthetic. From substances both organic and inorganic it manufactures new organic compounds of bewildering variety. The key of the process is *organization*, the opposite of entropic disorganization. The organizing capacity of life is not confined to its chemical syntheses. Organisms *adapt, reproduce, invent,* and *grow* in a manner unknown to inanimate nature. This creativity is more marked among animals than among plants, and most marked of all among human beings. Whatever else personality may be, it is the crowning example of the principle of expanding organization. It is an open and growing system.

Philosophers of science are perplexed by this double channeling in nature. As soon as an organism dies its body starts immediately to disintegrate under the impact of weather and bacteria, which it successfully resisted and turned to its own use during life. The living person continually synthesizes foodstuffs, oxygen, bacterial action, past experience, present needs, and images of the future. By so doing he not only survives as an independent being but develops and grows in such a way as to become ever more characteristic of what he is. The bamboo and the wild cherry are stubbornly fulfilling the destiny of their kind. Human personality is doing more: it is advancing toward the fulfillment of plans and hopes. *Self-actualization* is the term often employed. Philosophers of science call this aspect of growth *teleological,* meaning that it is marked by an advance toward goals.

At the same time all manner of mechanical determinants act on living organisms. If we scorch our hand in a flame the resulting burn is mechanically caused, though the process of self-repair that immediately sets in is not. Like inanimate nature, living beings are subject to the effects of heat, moisture, gravity, and (most sensitively) radiation; yet our organizing powers are normally such as to preserve us from their fatal effects. We invent air conditioning, build shelters, elevators, and discover antidotes to poisons.

In philosophical terms we must allow for both *mechanical determinism* and *teleology*. One student of the subject, after examining the evidence, concludes: "Nothing more remains but to admit that the riddle surpasses us and to conclude that the contrast of mechanism with teleology is the very foundation of the order of nature, which must ever be regarded from two complementary points of view."[1]

[1] L. J. Henderson, *The order of nature* (Cambridge, Mass.: Harvard Univ. Press, 1917), p. 209.

At the same time—and here we are gradually approaching the problem of motivation—philosophers and scientists are restive in the face of such contradictory principles. Is it not possible, they ask, to find one common type of law? They wish to achieve a "unity of science" rather than two separate kinds of science, or two violently contrasting sets of principles for any one life-science to handle.

Now the earliest triumphs of science dealt only with inanimate nature. Even today natural science is far out in front of the life-sciences, including the science of personality. It is easy, therefore, to understand why the concept of mechanical determinism is popular. And it is easy to understand why many psychologists think that personality theory would do well to confine itself to conceptions *as mechanical as possible*.

Thus—and now we come at last to motivation—research in and theory of personality, especially in America, have evolved various sets of quasi-mechanical concepts. We name them *quasi,* for they are not wholly mechanical. No psychologist can completely fit human conduct to measures of centimeters-grams-seconds; nor to the functions found in biochemistry, in electronics, and in "thinking machines," although attempts of this order are often made.

Quasi-mechanical theories try so far as possible to discover simple *pushes* capable of explaining human conduct. They try to empty the organism of inner teleological forces (such as instincts, attitudes, intentions, purposes). This type of "empty organism" approach we call stimulus-response psychology. *S* (stimulus) and *R* (response) are on the outer fringes of the person. As such they seem free from teleological flavor.

The Quasi-mechanical View

Most of the research supporting the S-R approach comes from work with animals, chiefly rats. Rats to be sure, like any living creature, display organization, but they are relatively simple animals, and one hopes that by studying them, instead of human beings, one may discover how alleged teleology can be reduced to a more mechanical type of causation. The argument proceeds essentially as follows.

Drive. Suppose one's stomach is empty: it sags, and thus creates a "deficit stimulus" which impels the organism to make restless movements. The fact that hunger is also caused by chemical deficiencies in the blood stream complicates but does not alter the essential picture. A drive—any drive—is defined as a "tissue change" that sets up nervous activity until the equilibrium of the tissue is restored. Hunger and thirst, oxygen lack, and a craving for sugar or salt are examples of "deficit" stimulation. Other drives, such as urination, defecation, and perhaps fatigue and sexual cravings may be viewed as "excess" stimulations arising from the pressure of waste or secretions within the body. Since a great deal that a person does is clearly impelled by these and other "tissue changes" we must admit that we have here a simple and compelling beginning for a theory of motivation. Let it be noted that in order to keep as close as possible to mechanical causation we are not here speaking of "instincts." With a few exceptions, drives at the start of life seem to lead only to random, restless, or mechanically reflex action. The newborn infant, to be sure, seems to suck automatically, to breathe freely (after the first slap), and to eliminate automatically. But none of this activity is as "purposive" as instincts are usually thought to be. That is to say, there are no clearly set goals such as would exist if we assumed an instinct of mating, of self-preservation, of escape, or of gregariousness.

Tension-Reduction. Pursuing the quasi-mechanical view one step further, S-R psychologists seek a law that will define the over-all operation of drive. Since all drives clearly arise from some disequilibrium in tissues (excess or deficit stimulation) it seems clear to these psychologists that drive motivation is always a process of reducing tension. And if man, like all other animals, has no essential motives other than drives, it follows that *all motivation is a pressure toward tension-reduction.*

If you ask how all motivation can result in drive-reduction, the answer is that *learning* (to which we shall soon turn) is responsible. Learning provides us with habitual strategies that relieve our tensions. Learning also accounts for the fact that not all our motives seem to be based on primitive tissue needs. Thus if you say that one of your main motives in life is to make your aged parents comfortable, the explanation is given that this motive is simply a learned and complex extension of your earlier desire for food. If you say that you are intent on learning a profession, again the motive is explained in terms of satisfying food, sex, fatigue, or other drives.

The theory of tension-reduction has interesting historical antecedents. In ancient Greece the Epicureans held that all man does in life is to try to *avoid pain* (tension). If we are wise we try to diminish our desires so as to have a minimum of tension to reduce. Some philosophers stated the matter in a more cheerful way, saying that tension-reduction brings pleasure, and therefore all man's motives are to be summed up as *pleasure-seeking*. Throughout the centuries philosophers and psychologists have insisted, as did Jeremy Bentham, that "pain and pleasure are our sovereign masters." The view is called *psychological hedonism*.

The modern S-R psychologist does not speak of pleasure and pain, simply because these are words describing conscious states; and the S-R psychologist feels that a good mechanical theory ought not use the language of "mind." There is no "mind" in mechanical process: hence "tension-reduction" is the preferred term for modern hedonism.

Some psychologists, less extreme in their views, are worried about so simple a formula. They point out that the quickest way to reduce tension is to commit suicide. Yet most people try to stay alive at all costs, thus maintaining and increasing their desires. To live at all is to have tension. Kluckhohn and Murray suggest a compromise. Men do not really seek a tensionless state, but rather seek the *process* of reducing tension. We like the activity involved in solving our problems, in seeking rest, in eating, in sexual pursuit, in working—because though not tensionless, such activities lead us away from want and strain.[2]

Homeostasis. Another favored, and related, conception is borrowed from physiology. The capacity of the body to keep its chemical composition, its temperature, its state of health at a proper level is intricate and awe-inspiring. Some psychologists, borrowing the concept, say that homeostasis is also the basic law of human motivation. We tend to persist in being what we are in a "steady state." We maintain the tonus and tensions necessary to life. We desire balance, equilibrium, preservation of our being.[3] This picture of motivation is obviously somewhat more teleological than tension-reduction. Life

[2] C. Kluckhohn, H. A. Murray, and D. M. Schneider, *Personality in nature, society, and culture* (Rev. ed.; New York: Knopf, 1953), p. 36.
[3] R. Stagner, Homeostasis as a unifying concept in personality theory, *Psychol. Rev.*, 1951, **58**, 5–17.

has a tendency to preserve itself and repair itself; it is not merely something goaded by excess or deficit stimulation. Yet homeostasis is a stay-put conception. It is static, unprogressive, allowing inadequately for either change or growth. The picture is one of a semi-closed system, not of a system fully open to the world, capable of expanding and becoming more than it is.[4]

Critique of Quasi-mechanical Motivation

Opponents of these views say that they account for only a small part of the desires, aspirations, hopes, and yearnings of the human person. They say it is impossible to reduce elaborate adult motives to a drive-basis. Drives exist, yes, and for the most part they do tend to push the organism to seek relief from tension. But they are only the primitive, and animal-like, part of human motivation. They have a basic protective function, making for safety but not for growth and development.

This criticism is explicitly developed by Maslow, who distinguishes between safety motivation and growth motivation in both children and adults. Safety comes first. Before he can grow in a psychological sense the child must have reached a stage where he can trust his parents and his environment to provide the basic satisfactions of nourishment, comfort, safety. If he does not successfully pass this stage he grows up as an anxious, apprehensive person who is always fixated on the satisfaction of his immediate drives. In mental hospitals (but also in ordinary life) we meet people who seem to have no capacity for growth but are centered entirely on their vegetative life—on the satisfaction of their segmental (drive) cravings.

On the other hand, a child who has a basic relation of trust with his environment is a child who reaches out to the world in wonder and interest. He is literally delighted with all that he finds: shells on the beach, stories he hears, new skills that he acquires. He is free

---

[4] For a fuller discussion and criticism of homeostasis see G. W. Allport, The open system in personality theory. In *Personality and social encounter* (Boston: Beacon, 1960), Chap. 3. See also Chapter 22 of the present volume.

Recent studies of the "reticular activating system" in the brain stem of mammals indicate that there is a nervous mechanism to maintain continuous, spontaneous activity during the waking state. The organism cannot help being active; it need not wait to be goaded by stimuli nor to re-establish a disturbed equilibrium. The waking organism is always "on the go." See M. Arnold, *Emotion and personality* (New York: Columbia Univ. Press, 1960), I, 223.

from fear, free from constant protective needs, entering greedily into the process of becoming.[5]

The healthy child and adult are continually building up tensions, in the form of new interests, and are going way beyond the basic, safety level of homeostasis. New experiences, which most of us crave, cannot be put in terms of tension-reduction, nor can our desire to acquire knowledge for its own sake, to create works of beauty and usefulness, nor to give and receive love, for love involves all manner of responsibilities and strains. Nor can the sense of duty—doing the best one can throughout one's life—be logically reduced to drive psychology. The history of the Arctic explorer, Roald Amundsen, shows us the difficulty of basing a theory of motivation wholly upon drives or homeostasis.

> In his autobiography he tells how from the age of fifteen he had one dominant passion—to become a polar explorer. The obstacles seemed insurmountable, but the interest and striving persisted. When he experienced success he did not relax with tensions reduced. He raised his level of aspiration to accord with his commitment. Having sailed the Northwest Passage, he embarked on the painful project that led to the discovery of the South Pole. Having discovered the South Pole, he planned for years, against extreme discouragement, to fly over the North Pole, a task he finally accomplished. His commitment never wavered until in the end he lost his life attempting to rescue a less gifted explorer, Nobile, from death in the Arctic. Not only did he maintain one style of life without ceasing, but this central motive enabled him to resist many temptations to diminish segmental tensions created by fatigue, hunger, ridicule, and danger.[6]

Quasi-mechanical views give us a picture of goads, pushes, drives. What is conspicuously missing is the forward or future thrust that seems always to mark mature motivation.

In spite of these severe criticisms we must accept the importance of drives as motivating factors throughout life. Klineberg rightly calls them "absolutely dependable motives"—found in all men and

---

5 A. H. Maslow, *Motivation and personality* (New York: Harper, 1954).
6 Drawn from R. Amundsen, *My life as an explorer* (New York: Doubleday, 1928).

in all cultures.[7] Although drives cannot account for all later motivation, they are with us all our life, and in infancy they completely dominate the motivational scene.

Drives, then, form the *starting point* for our theory of development. Not only are they themselves quasi-mechanical in nature; they are, especially in early life, acted upon (modified and controlled) by quasi-mechanical principles of learning.

Quasi-mechanical Factors in Learning

Learning is the modification of psychological characteristics resulting from experience. The quasi-mechanical theorist, as we have said, starts with drives. His next step is to look for an explanation of the way drives change during lifetime, so far as they do, and of the way movements become more expert so that the drives may be satisfied.

At once the mechanical model runs into some difficulty. Why an organism should learn at all is a problem. Inanimate nature doesn't learn, nor does it have drives. Snow is blown into drifts and ice will crack rocks, but the forces of change are wholly external and there is no organization of their effects into a continuing system. Hence even a mechanical theory of personality must make the assumption that life-processes are, after all, not wholly mechanical.

So far as they go, several quasi-mechanical principles are acceptable and important. We shall review these briefly.

Registration of Traces and Imprinting. A mechanical theory, like any theory, must assume that the nervous tissue is capable of retaining some faint copy of the original experience. All impressions linger—some a short time (such as the afterimage in the eye), some all one's life long (such as an intense emotional shock, due to accident, illness, or bereavement). In fact, it is safe to assume that nothing that impresses the nervous tissue at all is ever totally lost. Some trace is left that makes later excitation by a similar stimulus more probable. And even when individual experiences are gradually fused

[7] O. Klineberg, *Social psychology* (Rev. ed.; New York: Holt, Rinehart and Winston, 1954).

into habits and attitudes, so that no one single memory predominates, still the result of the imprint is there.

Some recent research suggests that *first* imprinting may be of major importance. A baby gosling, for example, may follow any object that first meets its eyes after hatching. Usually the object is the mother goose, but if the object happens to be a human being, then the human form is what the gosling will follow.[8]

Whether anything quite so primitive occurs in the learning of human infants we cannot say. It is conceivable that the infant's mother, as well as other features of its environment, becomes imprinted in such a way that the baby early comes to "identify" with the mother, and also comes to regard its familiar environment as a safe and desirable frame of life. It may also be that at certain "critical phases" the child becomes susceptible to new forms of imprinting.

For the present, we can only suggest that the first and basic law of learning is that impressions remain in some form as nervous traces. As imprinting continues, the result is a richer and richer store of material to be organized and utilized. The process by which impressions are absorbed into existing systems of experience is called *assimilation.*

Conditioning. The burned child avoids the flame. This familiar proverb sums up the principle of conditioning. The flicker of a flame at first attracts the infant, but once he is burned, the sight of the flame will cause avoidance. The law of the conditioned reflex may be stated as follows: Whenever a stimulus has a motor outlet, any stimulus occurring simultaneously will tend to acquire the same motor outlet; after sufficient repetition (sometimes one occasion is enough) the second stimulus alone will suffice to produce a discharge in that motor outlet. Withdrawal from intense heat is an unconditioned (inborn) reflex; withdrawal from the *sight* of the flame is a conditioned reflex.

A bold S-R psychologist might say that conditioning is the only (or almost the only) principle of learning that we need. Drive plus conditioning, he might argue, accounts for all of personality. We give an example of how the combination might work.

[8] K. Z. Lorenz, Comparative behaviourology. *Proc. of WHO Study Group on Psychological Development of the Child* (J. M. Tanner and B. Inhelder, Eds.; New York: Int. Univ. Press, 1957), I, 108–131. Also, for an introduction to modern "ethology," see K. Lorenz, *King Solomon's ring* (New York: Crowell, 1952).

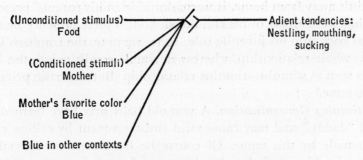

Figure 10. Development of a Taste through Conditioning

Suppose that a woman decorates her room in blue, is fond of blue dresses, plants many blue flowers in her garden. She has a strong general preference for blue. The developmental story in terms of conditioning might be told as in Figure 10. Originally food caused approaching (adient) response. This is an inborn, unconditioned reflex. The mother is a "stimulus occurring simultaneously"; so by the law the mother arouses approaching behavior (i.e., acquires the same "motor outlet" as did the food). In due time other things associated with the mother (e.g., her preference for blue) become second-order conditionings. The mother is perhaps now dead, but blue in any context still causes our hypothetical lady to "approach." Some such history of conditioning could be invoked to explain an adult's liking for pictures, vocations, churches, foods, races of people, philosophical or moral doctrines.

Although the law has considerable validity, it applies most clearly to animals and infants. Adults make trouble for it by selecting, rejecting, avoiding, or assisting the conditioning process according to their own desires and by following other, perhaps contradictory, principles of learning. No one is at the mercy of all the host of possible stimuli that might theoretically condition an ongoing drive-response. For example, the mother in our illustration might always have worn eyeglasses, but this feature has acquired no conditioning power.

A variant of the conditioning doctrine should have special mention. *Reintegration* tells us that some small part of an original experience, now occurring, can reactivate the whole original experience. The photograph of a friend can arouse all manner of memories and sentiments. The smell of a certain flower can cause us to relive a whole chapter of our childhood. A college student, who behaves as an adult away from home, is uncomfortable in his parents' presence, for they were a part of his childhood, and in their presence he feels forced back into his juvenile role. Here, we note, the emphasis is on a part-whole relationship, whereas in simple conditioning, the linkage is seen as stimulus-stimulus relationship. But the basic principle is the same.[9]

Stimulus Generalization. A year-old baby may have learned the word "daddy," and may cause mild embarrassment by calling every adult male by this name. Of course he has some very special responses for his own father, but his store of words is small at this age —perhaps five or six. Hence he uses them overtime. At eighteen months one child called his toy dog "toodle-oo" but he also called the wart on an old lady's face "toodle-oo." Speaking pseudo-mechanically we may say that the stimulus to a response becomes generalized; many different objects are treated as if they were one. A child frightened by a dog may shy away from cats, rabbits, hens, and animals in general. A cruel farmhand locked a small boy in a room with a fox. The boy was terrified. In later years he forgot (repressed) the incident, but for a long time he was seized with uncontrollable alarm if the doors of the room he was in were closed. His claustrophobia was cured only when the original memory was recovered and put in perspective with the aid of a psychiatrist.

Adults, too, behave according to stimulus generalization. We learn that toadstools are poisonous, and so we avoid all fungi in the woods, including edible mushrooms. We know that weeds are not good to eat (a false bit of "knowledge") and so avoid them all, even those that are nourishing. We may once have had an unpleasant experience with a Chinese, or a Jew, or a Negro. On the basis of this slender evidence we may acquire prejudice against a whole ethnic group.

Correct stimulus-generalization is a good thing. We could not possibly live if we had to learn a separate adjustment to every book, flower, food, person—to every possible stimulus in our life-space. But *incorrect* categorizing (treating too coarse a group of stimuli as

[9] Aristotle first noted the associative link between parts and wholes (subordinates reactivate superordinates). Later the principle became the major law of learning in the writings of Sir William Hamilton and H. L. Hollingworth. Recently it has been used as the chief explanatory principle in a book on personality theory: R. W. Leeper and P. Madison, *Toward understanding human personalities* (New York: Appleton-Century-Crofts, 1959).

alike) is responsible for race prejudice, for false classifications, and for most errors of reasoning.

We shall see in Chapters 14 and 15 that the concept of stimulus-generalization is important for an understanding of the traits that compose personality. The very structure of our personalities is determined by whatever ranges of stimuli we hold to be "equivalent."

Reinforcement. Figure 10 shows that classical conditioning is entirely a principle of *afferent* modification, that is to say, it deals only with the extension of cues or stimuli that come to evoke a given response.

But how about the response itself? The lady whose passion for blue is indicated in the diagram does not as an adult mouth, suck, or nestle when blue bobs up in her horizon. Rather, she buys clothing, papers her room, gazes with rapture at the sky—all to express her love of blue. How does she come to make these adaptive, adult acts?

The principle of *reinforcement* (formerly called the law of effect) says, in brief, that in the beginning an infant's drives cause it to make all sorts of wiggly and audible responses (random movements). Now, in time, some of his actions or cries are "rewarded." Thus, if he reaches correctly for his nursing bottle he can get it to his mouth and satisfy the hunger drive. This correct (adaptive) act is thus "reinforced." Success stamps it in (hedonists would say "pleasure" stamps it in).

Let us continue the illustration. Reaching for the bottle proves to be more often rewarded than merely whining or crying. Later, going to the refrigerator for the carton of milk is "stamped in" as a successful way to satisfy the drive. Also, the child learns that asking politely is good strategy—usually more successful than demanding. Later still he discovers that in most human relationships a tactful approach pays off. The diplomat learns that flowery and indirect language usually accomplishes more for his purposes than do rougher tactics. And so it goes: we learn those ways of acting that successfully reduce tension.

Here obviously is an intriguing law of immensely wide applicability. It is so widely useful that we find "reinforcement" hailed as the primary, if not the sole, law of learning. Since it "explains" efferent modification (changing actions) it can be used together with conditioning (afferent modification) to make a whole system of S-R learning theory.[10]

There are many weaknesses as well as merits in this formulation. Certainly we learn to make the "right" movements in talking, riding a bicycle, selling merchandise, on the basis of reward. But the theory does not explain why we so often change or vary a previously successful response and take risks. A man who generally wins at chess when he uses the king's pawn opening will nevertheless try new and novel gambits. According to the strict law of reinforcement he should not do so. In his well-known poem "If," Rudyard Kipling speaks of success and failure as "twin impostors." His point is that true maturity leads us to do things for reasons that are not mechanically enslaved to the principle of reward and punishment.

Frequency, Primacy, and Recency. Before we leave the listing of quasi-mechanical principles we should mention three additional familiar principles. *Frequency* tells us that "practice makes perfect"— the oftener any connection is made, the stronger it becomes. *Primacy* tells us that, other things being equal, the first in a series of impressions is likely to be powerful (cf. imprinting). We recall the first line of a poem or a hymn much better than later lines. Our early childhood experiences are often indelibly impressed upon us. The principle of *recency,* though opposite to primacy, seems also to hold broadly. We recall this morning's breakfast better than a breakfast we ate a week ago. These are all useful principles though we find many exceptions to them.

Comment. Already we see that learning is a complex subject— and our account is by no means complete. While we do not want to multiply principles needlessly, we shall be doomed to failure if we rest the case of personality development solely on the quasi-mechanical principles here described. They have a true but limited utility.

It is important to note that none of these quasi-mechanical principles makes any use whatever of an "active intellect." Rather, they refer to properties of the nervous system that are supposed to come into play automatically when properly goaded. They overlook such factors as a person's deliberate intent to learn, his effort, his striving, and his ability to perceive the fitness or appropriateness of an act for his purposes. There are no planning and no guiding self-image to

[10] The work of Clark Hull and of the so-called Yale School of learning theory is of this order.

steer and intensify the learning. Such factors are not allowed for, and yet they are of prime importance in the learning process.

But before turning to these additional principles of learning let us depict the consequences of learning (any form of learning) for the structure of personality.

Differentiation and Integration

The course of nature, said Goethe, is to divide what is united, and to unite what is divided. He was expressing well the two aspects of all growth. The process of development may be viewed in part as the progressive *differentiation* of structure and of behavior; and in part as the progressive *integration* of behavior and structure.

Differentiation. Lewin points out that the child, to a greater extent than the adult, is a dynamical unity. The infant acts first with its whole body and only gradually acquires the ability to execute part actions.[11] At first the child is capable only of mass movement, gross retractions or outreaching, or else random twisting and squirming of the whole body. Gradually from this amorphous matrix finer activities emerge. Vocal habits, reaching, handedness become differentiated; later, working, spending, saving, collecting, and skills and interests of all sorts emerge from the original global whole. We may represent this progressive differentiation of regions after the manner of Lewin in Figure 11. The boundaries between the functional systems are weak in infancy (if one drive is aroused the child is aroused "all over"); likewise the barrier between the child and his environment is less firm, leaving him a prey to all manner of environmental stimuli that later in life he will be able to disregard. The weakness

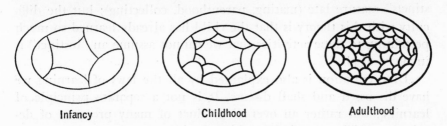

Infancy   Childhood   Adulthood

Figure 11. Differentiation of Functional Systems

11 K. Lewin, Environmental forces in child behavior and development. In C. C. Murchison (Ed.), *Handbook of child psychology* (1st ed.; Worcester, Mass.: Clark Univ. Press, 1931), Chap. 4.

of this barrier prevents the development of sharp self-consciousness in the first year or two of life. The young child cannot distinguish himself from his surroundings.

A good example of differentiation comes from the infant's emotional life. At birth it is impossible to distinguish different systems of emotion; there is only a diffuse distress-excitement. By the end of the first year, as Figure 12 shows, the child still has far fewer emotional systems than does an adult, but he does express differentially anger, fear, distress, delight, and affection.

Although the principle of differentiation is especially clear in early childhood, much of the progressive change in later life shows the same course. All knowledge can be viewed as a matter of making finer and finer distinctions. We first approach the subject of psychology, let us say, and find it a great confused blur. The process of learning the subject is one of breaking it up into constituent topics, laws, concepts, theories. The child who first tries to "make a boat" is all thumbs; he simply cannot execute the necessary separate movements to handle saw, hammer, and nails. The later precision of the boat builder, the surgeon, the pianist, involves finer and ever-finer differentiations.

In part differentiation is explained by *maturation*. Maturation means ripening without learning. It is clear that the nervous capacities of the child are not complete: his brain is not fully equipped with a myelin sheath. His glandular development is incomplete. Not until puberty is there maturation of the sexual glands. We see maturation when certain motor coordinations appear: creeping, walking, climbing, babbling, laughing—none of which is possible at birth. Some authors (McDougall, for example) say that some "instincts" mature late (mating, parenthood, collecting); but the difficulty with this theory is that the child has already learned so much pertaining to these activities that we cannot assume an "instinct" is involved at all.

Differentiation is also explained by all the laws of learning we have discussed and shall discuss. It is not a separate principle of learning, but rather an over-all product of many processes of development. The same is true of integration.

Integration. The significance of the concept of integration is best understood by referring to the cell theory in biology. The initial fact is that the human body contains trillions of cells, over nine billion

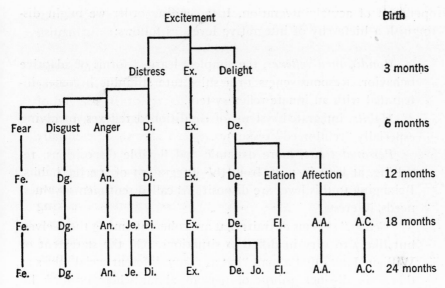

Figure 12. Differentiation of Infant's Emotional Life

KEY: A.A. = affection for adults. A.C. = affection for children. An. = anger. De. = delight. Dg. = disgust. Di. = distress. El. = elation. Ex. = excitement. Fe. = fear. Je. = jealousy. Jo. = joy (from K. M. B. Bridges, Emotional development in early infancy, *Child Develpm.*, 1932, 3, 340).

of which are found in the brain. Somehow out of this astronomic array of single bits a relatively unified personality is constructed. Separate nerve cells function together in such a way as to lose their independence. From the many there emerges the one; the motto of integration is *e pluribus unum*. We hasten to add that personality is never completely unified (see Chapter 16), but the trend of integration is toward this goal.

Integration suggests a hierarchical organization of personality. The simplest possible integration would be of two nerve cells (one sensory and one motor) functioning together as a simple reflex arc. Whether or not there are any reflexes involving as few as two neurones is not known. C. S. Sherrington, the physiologist who above all others is responsible for the concept of integration, regards this limiting case of integration as a "convenient though improbable abstraction." Similarly, at the opposite extreme, the completely integrated personality is also a convenient though improbable abstraction. But between these limiting cases there is ample room for the operation of actual integration. In ascending order we might distinguish a hierarchy of integrative levels as follows:

Conditioned reflexes, the simplest learned forms of adaptive behavior. Responsiveness to a substitute stimulus becomes integrated with an innate reflex system.

Habits, integrated systems of conditioned reflexes, involving especially "reinforced" responses.

Personal traits, more dynamic and flexible dispositions, resulting, at least in part, from the integration of specific habits. Belonging to this level are dispositions called sentiments, values, needs, interests.

"Selves," systems of traits that are coherent among themselves, but likely to vary in different situations. (Cf. the statement of William James that a man "has as many different social selves as there are distinct *groups* of persons about whose opinion he cares.") An extreme example would be the case of "multiple personality" as represented in Robert Louis Stevenson's fictional story of Dr. Jekyll and Mr. Hyde.

Personality, the progressive but never complete integration of all systems that deal with an individual's characteristic adjustments to his various environments.

The integrative theory of personality can be suggested, somewhat imperfectly, in the diagram in Figure 13.

We should not speak of the infant as well integrated, in spite of the totality of his response. Through differentiation he must first learn specific and skilled adjustments, separate words, single conditioned responses. Later he can "put together" what he has learned into his own preferred patterns of adjustment, forming characteristic habits and traits, and later still dispositions to play certain roles in certain surroundings (called in the diagram "Selves").

We do not imply that older people have achieved perfect, or even extensive integration. Although unity is an ideal (Chapter 16), still in actual life an adult is to some extent a mere bundle of conditioned reflexes, habits, traits, "selves" that often war with one another. Relative to the infant, however, the adult shows broader systems of integration. An infant is a homogeneous biological system, but an

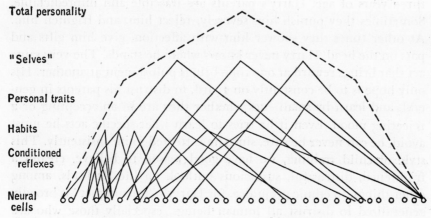

Figure 13. Schematic Representation of Integration

adult is more of a psychologically differentiated and integrated system.

Cognitive (Organizational) Learning

Integration and differentiation are the consequences of intricate learning processes. While such quasi-mechanical principles as conditioning and reinforcement may account for some learning, they do not account fully for the strikingly rich changes which experience produces in the growth of personality. The elementary principles we have described offer little more than a starting point—and are more applicable to animal and infant learning than to adult human learning. As Razran has said, the quasi-mechanical processes apply to the "unknowing" level of learning.[12] They leave out the role of conscious weighing, understanding, intention, and ego-relevance.

We have already called attention to the diversity of things that must be learned by the developing personality, including skills, knowledge, attitudes, interests, traits, hopes and fears, hates and loves, a sense of humor, a conscience, culture.[13] It is not likely that any single theory of learning will suffice. And so we continue our task of listing additional needed principles.

Learning Sets. Consider two young children, Harry and Joe, each

[12] G. Razran, Conditioning and perception, *Psychol. Rev.*, 1955, **62**, 83–95.
[13] Cf. also J. J. Gibson, The implications of learning theory for social psychology. In J. G. Miller (Ed.), *Experiments in social process* (New York: McGraw-Hill, 1950), Chap. 8.

three years of age. Harry's parents are irascible and unpredictable. Sometimes they punish him severely, reject him, and frighten him. At other times they shower him with affection, give him gifts and pats on the head. Harry never knows where he stands. The very same act that brings reward at one time brings punishment at another. His only hope is to be constantly on guard, to distrust his parents in general, and learn by small cues whether they are in an accepting or a rejecting mood. Even if he tries to learn what specific acts he must avoid, he can never be sure, since he is treated so inconsistently. This style of child training, we have good reason to believe, creates a frightened, distrustful, suspicious outlook on life. It leads, among other things, to ethnic prejudice, for Harry's "learning set" is broadly generalized to distrust all human beings, especially those who are unfamiliar to him.[14] Young Harry will probably become anti-Jewish, anti-Negro, anti-most-everything.

Joe, by contrast, has parents who are affectionate and entirely consistent in their rewards and punishments. Even when they punish him they do not withdraw their love. He knows that however badly he may behave he is accepted. He grows up therefore with a basic trust. He generalizes from his experience at home. People are assumed to be decent and trustworthy. He develops no social alarm, no generalized hostility, no prejudice.

We use this example to show how certain broad postures of learning may influence the whole course of development. Trust and distrust are basic attitudes affecting the child's learning about human relationships.

Many additional learning sets could be identified. One child develops early hostility toward mathematics. He cannot and will not learn it, and his schoolwork is adversely affected for this reason. Another child early forms a strongly favorable set toward a medical career. Throughout his youth, indeed throughout his life, he absorbs greedily all medical knowledge that comes his way. He may be obtuse to art, hobbies, and religion, but not to medical matters. In this area of learning he is a sponge.

Besides such long-range sets there are short-range intentions to learn. Quasi-mechanical theories fail to recognize that very little conditioning or rewarding is effective after infancy unless the child

---

14 For a fuller discussion of the two styles of child training described here see D. P. Ausubel, Ego-development and the learning process, *Child Develpm.*, 1949, **20**, 173–190.

or adult *wants* to learn. Even repeated experiences are unlikely to register unless one desires them to. You may look up a given phone number fifty times in the directory and still not remember it; but if you put your mind to the task of memorizing it—then it sticks.

Insight. To introduce this important principle we take a few elementary instances from early life.

A little girl of thirteen months, not yet able to walk, had a habit of pulling herself to a standing position by the kitchen range and turning on the gas. Because of the danger the mother sharply slapped the offending hand every time, hard enough to cause crying. Now the quasi-mechanical principles of conditioning and reinforcement would say that the child would soon learn to withdraw from the tempting gas cock. Not at all! The baby persisted in the misdemeanor. What she did learn, however, was to hold out her hand to be slapped after each transgression.

In this case the child saw some vague connection between her misdeed and the slap. She put two and two together, but not with the result intended by the mother. (Of course in many cases the conditioning slap works as intended—but not always.)

Another simple example, this one from the parents' diary of little Andrew:

9 months. A. watches intently father smoking his pipe. When father offers A. the pipe (properly cleaned), A. puts the stem into his mouth and *blows* vigorously.

According to quasi-mechanical principles Andrew should have *sucked* the stem (as he would a nipple or pacifier). But Andrew was trying to imitate the father by blowing out the smoke. He was deliberately attempting to re-create the situation *as understood* by him. He could not, of course, know that smoking required sucking as well as blowing. Again from Andrew's history:

14 months. A. always objects to having his nose wiped; but he takes handkerchief out of his mother's apron pocket, puts it to his own nose and snuffles.

20 months. The doctor gave A. discomfort by depressing his tongue with a spatula while examining his throat, causing A. to cry, squirm, and reject the object. Fifteen minutes later, left to himself, A. picks up the spatula and puts it down his throat just as the doctor had done.

In these instances we see Andrew deliberately reinstating situations that caused annoyance and pain. According to the principles of reinforcement and conditioning he should not have done so. Here we see at work a desire to comprehend, to reproduce a structure of events that has been previously experienced. Andrew was trying to execute a *meaningful* act.

Insight has been defined as the process of forming a mental structure that corresponds to some outside structure in nature. When we suddenly see how the parts of a Chinese puzzle fit together, we have insight. It has sometimes been labeled as the "ah ha" type of learning.

Our last three examples have dealt with insightful imitation. We do not imply that all imitation illustrates learning by insight. There are cases where quasi-mechanical principles apply. Thus a child of two may laugh when he hears adults laugh but without knowing the reason. This is clearly a simple conditioned response type of imitation. Or a younger child may learn that by doing as his older brother does he finds many rewards (the hidden candy, the kiss from the home-coming daddy), and so by reinforcement he develops a "set to imitate."[15] On the other hand, some imitation is not due to conditioning or reinforcement but is deliberate copying of others' acts in order to solve problems; it is insightful, not blind. Our conclusion is that "imitation" is not itself a separate principle of learning, but is a mirroring type of behavior, different forms of which reflect different kinds of learning.[16]

Identification. A special form of imitation is emotional identification. A child of nine asks his father, "Daddy, what are *we?*" Are we, he is asking, Republicans, Democrats, Presbyterians, Methodists, Scotch-Irish, American Yankee? Every child regards himself as automatically belonging to the same group as his parents. He is identifying with his parents, and under this broad, emotionally toned, learning set he acquires many of his attitudes, values, and forms of reasoning. Freud held that identification is almost the only principle of learning that we need in order to explain the development of personality. While much that we do, think, say, and feel is affected

15 Cf. N. E. Miller and J. Dollard, *Social learning and imitation* (New Haven, Conn.: Yale Univ. Press, 1941).
16 For a fuller analysis of the forms of imitation see G. W. Allport, Historical background of modern social psychology. In G. Lindzey (Ed.), *Handbook of social psychology* (Cambridge, Mass.: Addison-Wesley, 1954), Chap. 1.

by identification, we cannot place as much weight on this factor as does Freud.

Identification works in subtle ways. A young boy's imagination is fired by the exploits of a baseball hero. This hero is a kind of ego-ideal for the lad. He would like to have the prowess and status and adult prerogatives of his hero. In his fantasies he may feel that he is this hero. Under this broad learning set, he is therefore attentive to every detail: to his hero's manner of speech, to the neckties he wears, to his posture and gait. All these and other tokens of prowess the boy imitates. He cannot have the whole of his hero's status but he will take what parts he can.

Subsidiation. Much learning seems to be chiefly a matter of rounding out, of filling in some incomplete structure. In Bartlett's terms, we are almost always making an "effort after meaning." Learning is a matter of completing what is incomplete. Gestalt psychologists speak of "closure tendency." Jung refers to "the constellating power of a complex." Thorndike maintains that "belongingness" is a central principle of learning. Whatever term we use (and here I suggest that *subsidiation* expresses the idea fairly well) we call attention to the active, organizing property of all cognition. We are saying in effect that thought-processes to some extent contain their own motivation: they insist on forming firmer structures, on completing unfinished business, on putting bits and pieces of experiences into systems of meaning. We shall assume the existence of the principle of subsidiation as we now discuss our final set of learning principles.

Participation (Biographical Learning)

Attention and Intent to Learn. To common sense nothing is more obvious than the fact that learning requires concentration, effort, sustained attention, or absorbing interest. If these conditions are present in sufficient degree we can learn almost anything. If they are not present, very little learning takes place, and this little is called "incidental learning." According to a theory developed by Köhler and Wallach, when attention is concentrated on an object, the underlying electronic cortical process will be intensified.[17] Such intensification leads to clear perception and to retention.

[17] W. Köhler and H. Wallach, Figural after-effects. *Proc. Amer. phil. Soc.*, 1944, **88**, 269–357.

Attention is so obviously required for learning that we might venture as the first and most important law that the individual will learn what he is "set" to learn, "set" being considered as participation through the centering of attention, effort, or interest on the acquisition of skills or knowledge.

Levels of Participation. We may distinguish two levels of attention and concentration. The first of these we may call *task-involvement,* meaning that the individual is actively doing something about the object of his attention.

A classic experiment by Gates on learning at school shows that children may learn twice as much if they spend more time in reciting than in passive study.[18] The present author asked several hundred college students to recall some memory of their grammar school days. The great majority recalled a recitation, game, or event in which they themselves were actively participating. Few reported incidents where they were passive, such, for example, as merely listening, seeing, reading. Razran shows that the establishment of so simple a form of learning as the conditioned reflex is speeded up if the subject himself *does* something in the experiment (such as turning the switch that starts the conditioning buzzer).[19]

Summing up such evidence as this, and adding new evidence of their own, Haggard and Rose formulate the *law of participation:* "When an individual takes an active role in a learning situation (a) he tends to acquire the response-to-be-learned more rapidly, and (b) this response tends to be more stably formed, than when he remains passive."[20]

Why does such task-involved *doing* bring about more rapid and more stable learning? In doing, there is a more complete neurophysiological involvement. Passivity means that there is *impression* on the nervous system, but no *expression;* sensory and cortical nerves are involved but few motor nerves and muscles. The whole sensorimotor circuit is required for building firm traces and systematized habits. (This, of course, is the reason why the project and laboratory methods of teaching are usually to be preferred over the lecture

[18] A. I. Gates, Recitation as a factor in memorizing, *Arch. Psychol.,* 1917, **6,** No. 40.
[19] G. Razran, Attitudinal control of human conditioning, *J. Psychol.,* 1936, **2,** 327–337. Also, The dominance-contiguity theory of the acquisition of classical conditioning, *Psychol. Bull.,* 1957, **54,** 1–46.
[20] E. A. Haggard and R. J. Rose, Some effects of mental set and active participation on the conditioning of the auto-kinetic phenomenon, *J. exper. Psychol.,* 1944, **34,** 45–59.

method.) Croce, the Italian philosopher, insists that unless we engage in some form of *expression* we cannot *know*. Sometimes a student will say to his teacher, "Well, I know the answer, but I cannot express it." Croce would say, "Sorry, my lad, but unless you can express it, you don't know it."

But there is a still deeper level of participation which we may call *ego-involvement*. Two children may participate equally in taking piano lessons or in studying geography; that is to say, they spend an equal amount of time at the task, make the same movements, and give a superficially similar performance. They are task-involved to the same extent. But they may not be equally "ego-involved." The participation of one child may be at the circumference of his personality, so to say; of the other, at its center. To one child the activity is important; to the other it is not.

We are obviously speaking now of *interest*. In this chapter we have encountered various principles that claim to be "the most important" law of learning; but the case for interest is strongest of all. Interest is participation with the deepest levels of motivation.

Personal Relevance. The point is so important that we venture to restate it. After the age of infancy, we encounter partially formed interest systems. These systems distinguish the central and "warm" portions of personality from portions that are on the rim of one's being. The child is developing a sense of "self" and his interests fit into the self-system. An eight-year-old boy who finds himself interested in moths and butterflies will absorb much relevant knowledge, and for the time being learn less from his schoolroom tasks. A teen-age girl learns more about cinema and TV stars than about her high school history. We learn most from ego-involved experiences; they have more personal relevance and therefore more staying power. Borrowing a term from Razran, we may call this process of acquisition "biographical learning."[21] Whatever is ego-relevant is absorbed and retained.

Comment. For convenience we have separated our descriptions of learning principles to an unwarranted degree. We should try to think of them as operating simultaneously—difficult though it is to do so. Perhaps in animal learning it is possible to demonstrate pure conditioning and reinforcement. But in human learning, such an effort is doomed to failure. To explain how a person develops an

21 G. Razran, Conditioning and perception. See note 12.

interest in surgery, a liberal political outlook, a prejudice, or a religious sentiment certainly requires many, if not all, principles of learning working in concert.

Summary

How personality develops is basically a problem in the psychology of learning. But our theory of learning is tied to our view of the nature of man. Specifically, if we think of man as a thing, pushed and pulled by external forces (or even "half think" of him in this way) we seek for quasi-mechanical principles of learning. We embrace a stimulus-response view that puts as much emphasis as possible on simple physiological forces (drives) and on elementary processes of nerve tissue. As a result we try to explain the development of personality largely in terms of traces, conditioning, reintegration, stimulus generalization, reinforcement, frequency, primacy, and recency. These are all valid principles—up to a point. They seem by and large more applicable to the learning process as we find it in animals and in infants than in the more advanced stages of personality development.

It is helpful to view the growing individual as progressing in both differentiation and integration. Learning brings about both types of structural change, and leads to an organization marked by the articulation of finer systems (differentiation) and by the hierarchical arrangements of these systems within the total personality (integration).

In order to account for these systems we need principles of learning that are "cognitive" as well as S-R in type. Among these principles we discover the signal importance of learning sets, of insight, of identification (and other forms of imitation), and finally of subsidiation.

In general, however, S-R principles seem too external to the growing life, and cognitive principles seem (for the most part) too intellectualistic. We need to place additional emphasis on the fact that participation is basic to learning. Participation may occur at the simple level of attentiveness; at the level of motor doing (task-involvement); and at the most significant level of all—ego-involvement and personal relevance. This "biographical learning" leads us in the next chapter to a discussion of selfhood—which is the basis of all personal relevance.

The issue we have raised in this chapter has to do with the problem of *organization*. Whatever else personality may be, it has the properties of a system (wherein all parts are mutually related). Quasi-mechanical views of learning stress fragmentary acquisition. They do not allow adequately for coherence and self-relevance. Hence we must accept additional principles to account more fully for pattern and organization within the total personality system.

CHAPTER 6

The Evolving Sense of Self

EARLY INFANCY • BODILY SELF • SELF-IDENTITY • SELF-ESTEEM • THE EARLY SELF: SUMMARY • FOUR TO SIX • SIX TO TWELVE • ADOLESCENCE • THE PROPRIUM • THE PROBLEM OF THE KNOWER • FEELINGS OF INFERIORITY • CONSCIENCE • CONCLUSION AND SUMMARY

T HE psychology of personality harbors an awesome enigma —the problem of the self. The self is something of which we are immediately aware. We think of it as the warm, central, private region of our life. As such it plays a crucial part in our consciousness (a concept broader than self), in our personality (a concept broader than consciousness), and in our organism (a concept broader than personality). Thus it is some kind of core in our being. And yet it is not a constant core. Sometimes the core expands and seems to take command of all our behavior and consciousness; sometimes it seems to go completely offstage, leaving us with no awareness whatsoever of self.

A complete theory of personality cannot shelve this difficult problem of the subjective (felt) nature of the self, but must face up to it. Let us ask first why the problem is so difficult and elusive. There

110

seem to be three principal reasons. (1) The term *self* is used in a great many ways by a great many theorists. Often the term *ego* is employed instead. And since no clear and consistent distinction has been made between *ego* and *self,* we shall need to treat them as equivalent. (2) Although each of us has an acute awareness of self, we cannot tell just what we are aware of. Some thoughts and acts *seem* to us more "self-relevant" than others, but there is no sharp dividing line. Therefore it is impossible to fix boundaries to assist our definition. (3) The subject opens up profound philosophical dilemmas concerning the nature of man, of "soul," of freedom and immortality. It is easy to see why many psychological discussions of personality avoid the problem altogether.

But evasion is not allowable. Again there are three reasons. (1) The one and only sure criterion of our personal existence and identity lies in our sense of self. To leave out this subjective pivot of personality is to keep the rim but discard the hub of our problem. (2) As we have already seen, our theories of learning, motivation, development cannot be complete or correct without distinguishing what is "self-relevant" in personality from what is not. (3) Although psychology cannot hope to solve the ultimate dilemmas of philosophy, it is obligated to provide a careful factual account of the evolving sense of self in order to assist philosophy in its task.

The present chapter, therefore, considers the factual aspects of the problem. The most helpful approach is to trace the developing sense of self from infancy onward.

Early Infancy

We do not know what an infant's conscious experience may be like. Years ago William James called it a "big, blooming, buzzing, confusion," and he may be right. One thing is quite certain: the young infant is not aware of himself as a *self.* He does not separate the "me" from the rest of the world. And it is precisely this separation that is the pivot of later life. Consciousness and self-consciousness are not the same, neither for the infant nor for the adult. The infant, though presumably conscious, lacks self-consciousness completely; the adult has both, but they are not identical.

Self-consciousness, as we shall see, is a gradual acquisition during the first five or six years of life, making most rapid strides with the coming of language in the second year. Although the process is gradual, it is no doubt the most important development that occurs during a person's entire life.

Sometimes we mistakenly say that a young infant is egocentric, wholly "self-centered." We point to his insistent demands, to his uncontrolled impulses, and to his unsocialized tyranny over his environment, including, of course, his mother. The young infant does not know that he is hungry, wet, or in pain. He just *is,* and howls until he no longer is. We might speak of him as "solo-centered" but not as "self-centered." And, we repeat, there is no single transformation during the course of life so momentous as the gradual passing from the stage of utter solo-centeredness to the stage where the child knows himself to be different from others, to be separated from the environment, and to be able to perceive events as significant for himself as an independent being.

The stage from birth to approximately a year and a half is sometimes called the *sensorimotor* stage. The child receives impressions and reacts, but there is no mediating self between. He feels and responds to pressures in his body or on the skin, as well as to soothing sounds; but these sensorimotor reactions are lost in a shapeless "all," in what Piaget calls an "undifferentiated absolute" of self and environment.[1]

In the fifth and sixth months the child studies his fingers and toes. He can grasp objects but cannot intentionally drop them. They get brushed off or else he shoves them into his mouth. The fingers and the object he holds are all one to him. When he stares at his feet he may grasp them and put the toes into his mouth. If he hurts his foot he cries but has no idea at all that *he* has hurt *him.*

At eight months his image in the mirror may cause him to stare. He recognizes his parents in the mirror long before he knows his own image. By ten months he will try to reach and play with the image, but he still does not know that it is his.

All the while there seems to be developing a vague distinction between "out there" and "in here." Gratifications do come from outside; the mother whom he usually "melts into" does not instantly gratify his needs. Loved objects can be frustrating. When the baby begins to creep and walk he has frequent collisions and receives many

[1] D. E. Berlyne, Recent developments in Piaget's work, *Brit. J. educ. Psychol.,* 1957, **27,** 1–12.

bumps. There is, he gradually learns, a hard outer reality. There is a dawning world of the "Not I" before the reciprocal sense of "I" fully evolves.

At eight months the child often cries when strangers appear. The familiar figures of mother and father, brother or sister, are now recognized, and this sense of the identity of another precedes the sense of self-identity. For this reason it is said, "The Thou is earlier than the I." One investigator who has worked extensively with babies would date the awareness of the "I" around fifteen months of age.[2]

Bodily Self

Probably the first aspect of selfhood to evolve is the sense of a bodily me. The infant receives a constant stream of organic sensations from the internal organs of the body, from muscles, joints, tendons. There is a continuous postural strain; especially the head region feels the strain because of its anatomical position. This fact, together with the importance of the eyes in every spatial adjustment, results in a tendency to "locate" the self in the region of the head, often in the middle of the brow, slightly behind the eyes, in a kind of "Cyclopean" eye.[3] At least this is the report given by most adults when asked where they feel the "self" to lie.

Of course sheer bodily sensation in the child would not give rise to a sense of self—it does not do so in the newborn—unless it is recognized as recurrent. Probably there is no recognition of recurrence until there is an appropriate maturation in the cortex that will retain "traces" of experience. It seems likely that the young infant has the nervous equipment to retain simple response habits before it is ready to retain "memories" such as are required for a sense of self-continuity.

The sense of the bodily me grows not only from recurrent organic sensation but from frustrations arising "out there." A child who cannot eat when he wants to, who bumps his head, soon learns the limitations of his too, too solid flesh.

Throughout life the sense of the bodily me is the basic attest of

2 R. A. Spitz, *No and yes: on the genesis of human communication* (New York: Int. Univ. Press, 1957), Chap. 12.
3 E. Claparède, Note sur la localisation du moi, *Arch. Psychol. Genève*, 1924, **19**, 172–182.

our existence. Our sensations and our movements feed us with constant awareness that I am I.

Recent work on sensory deprivation has shown how much we depend on our sensory stream for our sense of selfhood. Subjects who lie inactive on a bed for a day or so, receiving absolutely no outside stimulation, and a very minimum of internal stimulation, complain that they virtually lose all sense of self.[4]

The bodily sense remains a lifelong anchor for our self-awareness. It is true that in health the normal stream of sensations is often unnoticed, while in a state of ill-health or pain or deprivation, the bodily sense is keenly configurated. But at all times the underlying support of the bodily me is there. How very intimate it is can be seen if you imagine the following situation. Think first of swallowing the saliva in your mouth, or do so. Then imagine spitting it into a tumbler and drinking it. What seemed natural and "mine" suddenly becomes disgusting and alien. Or, to continue this unpleasant line of thought for a moment, picture yourself sucking the blood from a prick in your finger; then imagine sucking blood from a bandage around your finger. What you perceive as belonging intimately to your body is warm and welcome; what you perceive as separate becomes instantly cold and foreign.

Important as bodily sense is, it is not the whole of one's self. Those who have suffered extreme torture report that while feeling pain, they also feel a detachment. "This," they say, "is happening to my body, not to *me*." "I shall come through this somehow, and continue to be the same self I have always been." And so the sense of self depends on more than the bodily me.

Self-identity

Today I remember some of my thoughts of yesterday, and tomorrow I shall remember some of my thoughts of both yesterday and today; and I am certain that they are the thoughts of the same person—of myself. Even an oldster of eighty is sure that he is the same "I" as at the age of three, although everything about him—including the cells of his body and his environment—has changed many times over. This sense of self-identity is a striking phenomenon,

4 Cf. W. A. Bexton, W. Heron, and T. H. Scott, Effects of decreased variation in the sensory environment, *Canad. J. Psychol.*, 1954, **8**, 70–76.

since change is otherwise the invincible rule of growth. Every experience we have modifies our brain, so it is impossible for the identical experience to occur a second time. For this reason every thought, every act is altered with time. Yet the self-identity continues, even though we know that the rest of our personality has changed.

This particular property of the self is sometimes considered as the *whole* of the problem of selfhood. A dictionary of psychology, for example, offers the following definition:

> Self = an individual regarded as conscious of
> his own continuing identity and of his
> relation to the environment. *Syn.* = ego.[5]

Some philosophers are so impressed with this sense of personal identity that they argue that each personality contains an unchanging and imperishable soul-substance. This substance is what guarantees unity to a given life from birth to death—and probably thereafter. Others say no, that the mere overlap of successive states of consciousness and the interlocking and reviewing of memories are all we need to account for the sense of self-identity.

However that may be, we can point to one very important psychological factor in establishing the sense of identity in the second year of life, and to its continuation—the factor of language. When the child can speak and think in terms of toys, or his shoes or daddy, he has tools for relating the it to the I. By sometimes leaving and sometimes returning to the object and speaking its name, the inference grows that the I is the continuing factor in these intermittent relationships.

The most important linguistic aid of all is the child's own name. He hears constantly "Where is Johnny's nose?" "Where are Johnny's eyes?" "Good Johnny," "John naughty." By hearing his name repeatedly the child gradually sees himself as a distinct and recurrent point of reference. The name acquires significance for him in the second year of life. With it comes awareness of independent status in the social group.

Personal pronouns, however, are hard to cope with. The two-year-old often confuses the first, second, and third persons. He may be overheard to say to himself, "You be careful. William get hurt.

[5] H. C. Warren (Ed.), *Dictionary of psychology* (Boston: Houghton Mifflin, 1934).

No, I won't get hurt." The confusion (which is common at least until the age of two and a half) reflects the difficulty the child has with his own identity.[6]

There is plenty of additional evidence of incomplete selfhood. The toddler may not be aware that he is cold, that he feels feverish or fatigued, or that he needs to eliminate. He may wet or soil himself without being aware that he is doing so. He feels none of the disgust or fear that an adult would feel regarding alien or harmful objects. The boundaries between "out there" and "in here" are still vague. Emotions, for example, are not always his. He will yell, laugh, even cry, for no good reason except that someone near him is doing so. Nursery schools often report these waves of contagious but hollow emotion.

Even after self-identity is partially established, the child readily surrenders his identity in play. He may lose it so completely that he grows angry if other people fail to recognize him as a bear, an airplane, or whatever his fantasy has wrought. His night dreams are as real as his daytime experiences. He cannot yet fully separate what is "in here" from what is "out there." The tiger of his dream is terrifyingly real.

Various objects besides the child's name provide important anchorage for self-identity. Clothing, ornamentation, and special grooming play a part. Children of two or three are enhancing their sense of identity when they proudly display their new shoes, a hair ribbon, or a toy. Clothing helps mark the child off from the environment. Some child psychologists have noted that little children speak more freely and frankly when unclad. It is as if self-consciousness were a garment to be shed as readily as a shirt. Perhaps nudists hope that by abolishing clothing they can regain some of a child's freedom from oppressive self-consciousness.

We have been speaking, of course, of self-identity in Western cultures. Other cultures do not insist on so sharp a separation of the self from the nonself. The I of the Western man sticks out like a stubbed thumb. In other cultures it blends more readily with nature and with society. The primitive medicine man through his incantation feels that he "becomes" the rain; the father in couvade identifies himself with his wife suffering in childbirth. Parts of the

6 Cf. L. B. Ames, The sense of self in nursery school children as manifested by their verbal behavior, J. genet. Psychol., 1952, 81, 193–232.

bodily self, for example, the hair or fingernails, are sometimes treated as equivalent to the whole self, as in black magic and other witch-craft practices.[7]

Even the languages of other cultures show that the separation of the I from the it or from the thou is less sharp.

Among the Wintu Indians in California, for example, the boundaries of self are not the same as with us. If a Wintu mother tells you her child is hungry, her words are, "I am hungry—my child." If she wants to say that she has fed her child, "I ate—my child." A man may say, "I am ill—my horse." Whatever engages one's affection is included as part of one's self-concept. The Wintu may if he wishes also speak in a more closed-self fashion, as when he says, "I alone did this." But in European languages the I is always a narrow and closed identity.[8]

The most important anchorage to our self-identity throughout life remains our own name. Shakespeare assures us that one's good name is one's most precious possession:

> Who steals my purse steals trash . . .
> But he that filches from me my good name . . .
> . . . makes me poor indeed.[9]

Our name is warm and central, a symbol of our whole being. How quickly we overhear it spoken in a room filled with conversing people. We feel offended if someone forgets it.

How closely names and self-esteem are related is shown in a study by Strunk. People were asked to indicate whether they liked or disliked their own first names. They were also studied to determine the degree to which they accepted (liked) themselves as persons. Low self-acceptance is defined as "extremely dissatisfied to be the kind of person he is." It turns out that people who dislike their own first names generally do not like themselves.[10]

Here again we see that one's name, though only a symbol, is closely tied to one's self-esteem as it is to one's sense of self-identity.

[7] H. Werner, *Comparative psychology of mental development* (Rev. ed.; New York: Int. Univ. Press, 1957).

[8] D. Lee, Notes on the conception of the self among the Wintu Indians, *J. abnorm. soc. Psychol.*, 1950, 45, 538–543.

[9] *Othello*, Act III, Sc. 3.

[10] O. Strunk, Attitudes toward one's name and one's self, *J. indiv. Psychol.*, 1958, 14 64–67.

Self-esteem

Before the age of two a child wants to push his stroller, wants to control his world, wants to make things *do* things. He has a fierce passion to manipulate objects. What does ink do? paint? lipstick? a razor blade? What can one do with cupboards, bureau drawers, matches, electric switches, cats, dogs, grandma's wig? Within a few minutes the curious two-year-old can wreck the house.

This passion, the bane of every parent, is not a direct reflection of selfhood. It is simply the normal adient relation between child and environment—the "exploratory drive," if you wish. The sense of self enters when these activities are thwarted.

A two-year-old went to the bathroom with his father to have his face washed. Saying, "Let me," he struggled to turn on the faucet. He persisted without success. For a time the father waited patiently, but finally "helped" the child. Bursting into screams of protest the child ran from the bathroom and refused to be washed. His father had spoiled everything.

Such incidents are common at this age. When the exploratory bent is frustrated the child feels it a blow to his self-esteem. The ego is thwarted, resulting in humiliation and anger. The child becomes acutely aware of himself as a self. So conspicuous is this behavior that some psychologists say that the *need for autonomy* is the outstanding mark of selfhood in the second and third year of life.[11]

Negativism. Thus the growth of self-awareness reaches a critical stage around the age of two. One symptom is the burst of opposition to feeding, dressing, taking orders—to almost anything the parent desires. Levy has studied this type of "oppositional behavior" in nearly 1,000 children brought to the clinic for medical examination and testing. The first signs of negativism (usually the cry "No! No!") appear in half the cases by eighteen months of age, but the negative mode may continue to the age of four.[12] One boy, not yet three, made

11 For example, E. H. Erikson, Identity and the life cycle, *Psychol. Issues,* 1959, 1, No. 1. (New York: Int. Univ. Press.)
12 D. M. Levy, The early development of independent and oppositional behavior. In *Midcentury psychiatry* (Springfield, Ill.: Charles C Thomas, 1953), Chap. 5. See also D. P. Ausubel, Negativism as a phase of ego-development, *Amer. J. Orthopsychiatr.,* 1950, 20, 796–805.

a daily visit to his grandmother's house across the street to announce (apropos of nothing), "Grandma, I won't."

The child of this age regards almost any adult proposal as a potential threat to his integrity. And so he develops a generalized habit of saying "No," even though on second thought, he meant "Yes." To him it seems safer to resist any adult proposal in advance, as a protection to dawning self-esteem. Incidentally, we may point to the fact that some adults seem to have preserved the childish trait of negativism. They are chronically countersuggestible; the French would say *contredisant*. To every proposal they offer resistance, to every argument a counterargument. Like the preschool child, they seem to fear that if they do not do so they will somehow be "stepped on."

Although he is negativistic the child of two is not yet competitive. Only by the age of three can he be taught to "get ahead." Between three and four, about half acquire the sense of "I beat you." By the age of six or seven in our culture we can safely say that self-esteem acquires a competitive flavor. In other cultures it is not so. Anthropologists tell us that while in some cultures individual competition is keen, in others it is impossible to arouse rivalry within the group. The individual identifies his self-esteem with his esteem for the group.[13]

In Western cultures, however, individual self-esteem and self-love are such prominent parts of our nature that Western writers have declared that unabashed *egoism* is man's supreme trait. Whole philosophies have been built on this assumption (by Hobbes, Nietzsche, Stirner, Le Dantec, and many others). Some modern psychologists have likewise claimed that in all our actions our principal aim is to keep the "ego-level" (i.e., our self-esteem) as high as possible.[14] William James once said that what every person craves most is *praise*.[15]

Think how much of our social life centers around self-esteem. To put a man to *shame* is to shatter his self-esteem. Conversely, to employ *tact* is to avoid offense to the ego. If we do not employ tact the

13 See M. Mead, *Cooperation and competition among primitive peoples* (New York: McGraw-Hill, 1937).
14 Cf. F. Hoppe, Erfolg und Misserfolg, *Psychol. Forsch.*, 1930, 14, 1–62. Also A. W. Combs and D. Snygg, *Individual behavior* (2d ed.; New York: Harper, 1959).
15 H. James (Ed.), *The letters of William James* (Boston: Atlantic Monthly, 1920), II, 291.

result is *resentment,* which is the impulsive assertion of an aggrieved self-esteem. Closely related is the common experience of *embarrassment* (called self-consciousness), which means that our egos stand exposed. Stage fright is a conspicuous example. *Pride* is one common synonym for self-esteem, *self-love* another.

Pervasive as this aspect of selfhood is, it is not in all lives sovereign. And it is far from constituting the whole of the problem of self.

The Early Self: Summary

We have been saying that three aspects of self-awareness gradually evolve during the first three years of life:

> Aspect 1: Sense of bodily self
> Aspect 2: Sense of continuing self-identity
> Aspect 3: Self-esteem, pride

Contributing to the development are many influences: maturation (anatomical and physiological), recurrent bodily sensations, memory aided by verbal concepts, one's proper name as an anchorage point, frustrations during the process of exploring and manipulating the environment, a period of negativism where the child practices his emerging sense of self. At this stage the child begins to feel himself autonomous and separate from others. But even now he can easily "depersonalize" in play, and feel himself to be an object, an animal, or another person.

It is, of course, *people* who stimulate the child most of all. He learns that their acts and his response, as well as his acts and their response, always go together. The ego and the alter play a constant game of interaction—like adults at tennis. There is a continuous "conversation of gestures" between them.

G. H. Mead, the principal depicter of this process, believes that the original sense of the me is made up largely of the attitudes, words, gestures, of others which the child perceives, imitates, and responds to. His sense of self is thus a product of other people's behavior toward him. Some treat him as an offspring, some as a sibling, as a playmate, or as a stranger. These are, so to speak, his "looking-glass selves," or his roles in life, and while he develops a sense of continuity and identity, he never shakes himself free from seeing himself in terms of the roles he plays, i.e., in terms of the images other people have of him. The self, says Mead, in all its aspects, is predominantly a social product.[16] In general we agree with Mead, though he inclines to overstate his case.

Four to Six

The processes we have described continue through the preschool years and beyond. The evolution of the self is still far from complete. As we have said, the preschool child easily loses his self-identity. He is distressed if we do not recognize his transformations. Fantasy and reality merge. Fiction dominates the play life. Imaginary companions appear, usually a child or an animal. Fully 20 percent of children in the four-to-six age range have imaginary companions— probably more.[17]

And the child of this age may still have trouble with his pronouns. Stone and Church report a dialogue between a bright four-year-old and his teacher.[18]

STUART: *Me* is a name, you know. My name.
TEACHER: *Me* is my name, too.
STUART: No, it is mine. How can it be yours? I am *me*.
TEACHER: I am, too.
STUART: No, you are not *me*. I am *me*. You are you. (After a pause): I am *me* to me, but you are *me* to you!

This is a good example of learning by insight (page 103). The sudden shift in Stuart's point of view is likewise an instance of what Piaget calls "reciprocity." After a time the child is at last able to take the standpoint of "the other," and by so doing sharpens his own sense of separation from others.[19]

The sense of bodily self becomes keener in this period. A five-year-old boy facing a tonsillectomy said, "I do not like myself not

[16] G. H. Mead, *Mind, self and society* (Chicago: Univ. of Chicago Press, 1934).
[17] L. B. Ames and J. Learned, Imaginary companions and related phenomena, *J. genet. Psychol.*, 1943, **62**, 147–167.
[18] L. J. Stone and J. Church, *Childhood and Adolescence* (New York: Random House, 1957), p. 124.
[19] Full-scale "reciprocity" is not possible until about the age of twelve, when the child usually comes to realize that another person's point of view may be as good and as right as his own. A study shows that Swiss children before the age of twelve feel certain that Frenchmen at heart really wish they were Swiss. Only in puberty do they understand that another person's outlook on life seems as right and desirable to this person as the child's outlook seems to him. Full-scale reciprocity is a slow achievement. Even some adults fail to attain it. See J. Piaget and A. Weil, The development in children of the idea of the homeland and of relations with other countries, *Int. soc. Sci. Bull.*, 1951, **3**, 561–578.

to be myself, and that is what will happen if even my littlest tonsil is taken away from me."[20] Freudians would call this boy's fear a type of castration anxiety. All parts of the body, especially the genitals, come to seem private and important to the child. Unwise adults who threaten bodily harm to the child (perhaps to "cut it off" when the child indulges in sex play) plant deep-set fears and thus menace the growing desire for autonomy and integrity. Our bodies are our preferences. Even when we are old enough to know their limitations, and even though we suffer inferiority feelings because of them, we still agree with Touchstone: "An ill-favored thing, sir, but mine own."

In one sense the child of four to six is vastly egocentric. He regards the world as existing for his benefit. The sun, he thinks, follows him to see whether he is a good boy. To him God, or Santa Claus, is a Being whose primary duty is to serve him. The child is virtually unaware of any framework of thought other than his own (only meager beginnings of reciprocity exist). He takes his point of view as absolute, believes that others think as he thinks, and feels no need to explain his statements. But all this egocentricity is not, strictly speaking, self-centered; it comes merely from the subjective nature of the child's thought at this period. He does not know it is his alone.

During this period we may date the appearance of two aspects of selfhood in addition to the three we have previously discussed.

Aspect 4: The extension of self
Aspect 5: The self-image

We have said that the sense of competition starts only after the age of three. With it comes the sense of possession. This ball is *mine*. *I* own the tricycle. My daddy, my brother, my dog, my house are felt to be warm parts of one's self. The child cannot yet, of course, extend himself to embrace his country, his church, or his career. But the foundations are laid for this important extension of selfhood. At the adult level we sometimes say, "A man is what he loves." (See Chapter 12.) By this statement we mean that we know personality best by knowing what the extended-self embraces. But the young child has only the rudiments of such self-extension.

Rudimentary, too, is the *self-image*. The child begins to know

20 L. J. Stone and J. Church, *Childhood and adolescence* (New York: Random House, 1957), p. 161.

that his parents want him to be a "good" boy, and also that at times he is "naughty." By the interaction process he comes to know what his parents expect of him, and to compare this expectation with his own behavior. Of course, as yet, he has no clearly developed conscience, nor any image of himself as he would like to be in adulthood. He is, however, laying the foundations for the intentions, goals, sense of moral responsibility, and self-knowledge that will later play a prominent part in his personality. In childhood the capacity to think of oneself as one is, as one wants to be, and as one ought to be is merely germinal.

Six to Twelve

The child's sense of identity, his self-image, and his capacity for self-extension are greatly enhanced by his entrance into school. His classmates are frank and brutal regarding his weaknesses or idiosyncrasies. They call him "Four-eyes" or "Fatso." Such critical nicknames may hurt, but they also help establish an identity and render more acute the inner sense of selfhood.

The child soon learns that what is expected of him outside the home is very different from parental standards. Tribal (peer) standards of clothing and of speech are something new. A boy must soon learn to shift rapidly from the harsh and obscene talk of his peers to the politer world of his parents, and somehow to incorporate both worlds into his own being. When children enter their peer society they have a sharp lesson in "reality testing." They learn in effect to say, "Now I must do this. Now I must do that. Now I must be careful. Now I can do as I please." Such shifts intensify the sense of self.

It is well known that children of this age become moralistic and legalistic. Rules of the game must be followed rigidly. Parental rules are important, but the rules of the gang are utterly binding. The child does not yet trust himself to be an independent moral agent. His sense of self is comfortable only if he adapts to outer rules, extends himself into the gang, and develops a self-image of a safe conformer. The child fiercely believes that his family, his religion, and also his peer-group are right. While he may feel conflict between parent and peer standards, he is firmly loyal to these particular extensions of himself. In this period "identification" becomes an important principle of learning.

All the while the child's intellectual life is developing. Early in the school years he becomes addicted to riddles and puns, and a little later to codes, cryptograms, and foreign words. Objective knowledge fascinates him, and the question "Why?" is always on his lips. He begins to sense a new power, a new aspect of his selfhood:

Aspect 6: The self as rational coper

It is true that from early months the child has been able to solve simple problems, but only now does he fully realize that he has a rational capacity to bring to bear upon them. Previously he *thought,* but now he *thinks* about thinking.

The self as a "coper" coincides fairly well with Freud's definition of the ego. For Freud the ego is the conscious portion of personality whose duty it is to find a solution to the problems created by impulses (the id), by the outer environment, and by the prohibitions taken over from one's parents and from society (the superego). Like a horseback rider the rational self tries to pick his way to avoid the traps laid by these three "tyrants." The ego, of course, is not always fully rational. It is often merely "defensive." Its duty includes the inventing of excuses and "rationalizations" to prevent injury to self-esteem. It may deny that obstacles exist and invent escapes and strategies that are mere fake solutions to life's problems.

It is, we admit, somewhat arbitrary to date the evolution of this aspect of selfhood as late as the period six to twelve, but we do so because it is during this period that children begin to engage in reflective and formal thought. They now fully know that the self is a thinker, and this function becomes for them warm and central, like all other aspects of selfhood.

Adolescence

Erikson points out that the chief feature of adolescence is the renewed search for self-identity.[21] The two-year-old, we recall, has already gone through the preliminary stage. But later he has lost himself again, so to speak, in his family and gang loyalties. Now in adolescence the problem once more becomes acute. The central teen-age problem becomes, "Just who am I?"

The central question is, "Am I a child or an adult?" Parents are

21 See Note 11, above.

of no help. Sometimes they treat the youth like a child; sometimes they expect him to shoulder mature responsibilities. The parents' vacillation may be the cause of his own. While the youth holds on to many childhood attitudes, he is now physically and sexually mature enough to play adult roles. Eighteen-year-olds can be drafted, but in most states they cannot vote. Are they mature or are they not? Certain rites marking the transition from childhood to adulthood are set at the age of twelve or thirteen: confirmation, Bar Mitzvah, graduation from elementary school. Do these rites really mark entrance into the age of discretion? The adolescent may be permitted to drive a car at fourteen, sixteen, or eighteen, depending on his place of residence. Who can say where maturity starts? The adolescent doesn't know; but neither does society.

The adolescent's self-image is dependent on others. He seeks popularity and is fearful of ostracism. His hair, his tastes in music, even his jalopy conform to the standards of his group. Seldom does the adolescent defy teen-age mores. His self-image and sense of identity are not firm enough to stand the strain.

The youth who is late in physical maturing is miserable among his contemporaries. The youthful male may agonize over the slow growth of his beard or over his skinny frame and negligible biceps. His sister may wistfully linger over advertisements for bras. At the same time no adolescent likes to hear an adult say, "My, how you have grown!"

The well-known rebelliousness of the adolescent has an important relationship to his search for identity. It is his final bid for autonomy. Rejecting one's parents, in whole or in part, may be a necessary, if cruel, stage in the process. It is the adolescent counterpart of the toddler's negativism.

The search for identity is revealed in the way an adolescent tries on different masks. He first develops one line of chatter, then another, one style of hairdress and then another (always within the range permitted by the peer-group). He imitates one hero and then another. He is still searching for a garb that will fit. What he really wants is not yet fully present—his adult personality. Since parents are usually scornful of these experiments the youth tries them out with his peers, and chiefly with the opposite sex, and often over the telephone, to which he is greatly addicted. The adolescent is seeking assurance that he or she can attract and hold, and can play an acceptable role in the serious business of mating. Even falling in love is often a device for testing one's self-image. Partners in puppy love will converse endlessly, trying out this *persona* and then that to see the effect. They are hurt, make up, talk it over, probe the future, and embrace. On the whole they seem to prefer to converse than to embrace.

At the same time conflict over sexual needs becomes acute. The youth has already learned the stern prohibitions, and finds it difficult to harmonize carnality with convention. He hopes to find a road to identity that will enable him to blend his contradictory impulses. The solitude, suffering, and storm and stress of adolescence (in Western culture) are well known. Sometimes the conflicts lead to suicide, more often into religion, and in religion the youth may find solutions that will endure, or, on the contrary, intensify his anguish.

The core of the identity problem for the adolescent is the selecting of an occupation or other life-goal. The future, he knows, must follow a *plan,* and in this respect his sense of selfhood takes on a dimension entirely lacking in childhood. Often youth aims too high. Idealism is a frequent, and lovable, quality. Many adolescent ideals are so high that a bad tumble is in store. Perhaps during the late twenties the youth will discover that he has less talent than he thought, that he will make less of a mark on the world, and that his marriage is less perfect than he had hoped. Paring down the self-image and aspirations to life-size is a task for his adult years.

But the important point is that in adolescence long-range purposes and distant goals add a new dimension to the sense of selfhood. We shall speak therefore of

Aspect 7: Propriate striving

Various writers maintain that the cement holding a life together is its "directedness" or "intentionality." In order to be normal an adolescent, and especially an adult, needs a defining objective, a line of promise. It is not necessary that the goals be rigidly focused, but only that a central theme of striving be present.[22]

This important aspect of self is not present in earlier life. The young child, to be sure, "wants" to be a fireman or a pilot when he grows up, but at this time there is no integrated effort. Until youth

[22] W. McDougall, *The energies of men* (London: Methuen, 1932). Also, C. Bühler, *Der menschliche Lebenslauf als psychologisches Problem* (Leipzig: Hirzel, 1933; rev. ed., Bonn: Hogrefe, 1959).

begins to plan, the sense of self is not complete. Some adolescents, it is true, drift into adulthood without any appreciable sense of purpose. When this is so, we can say that their personalities are of an "opportunistic" and immature order. Their sense of selfhood is still rudimentary.

William James once defined the self as a "fighter for ends." He was here accenting the propriate (central striving) aspect of selfhood. James, however, was well aware of additional aspects we have described. With his rubrics of "bodily," "material," and "spiritual" selves, he anticipated our present more detailed analysis in terms of bodily sense, self-identity, self-esteem, self-image, self-extension, and propriate striving.[23]

The Proprium

Is there no way to unite these seven aspects of selfhood? They are all states of self-relevance that we *feel*. Each in its way is an intimate region of personality involved in matters of importance to the organized emotional life of the individual. Together they compose the me as felt and known.

So it seems reasonable to unite these aspects (even though they are phenomenologically different, i.e., differently experienced) under a single name. Let us choose the term *proprium*. Why not simply the term *self*? There are two reasons: (1) Most writers, as we have seen, use *self* or *ego* for only one or two of the limited aspects we have treated. We prefer a fresher and broader label. (2) There is one remaining philosophical problem pertaining to the self to which we now turn, the question of "the knower." Since this aspect of selfhood is also properly termed *self*, we suggest using *proprium* to cover the self "as object" of knowledge and feeling. We are directly aware of the proprium in a sense that we are never directly aware of the "knower."

Before proceeding with this issue let us explain why it is necessary in personality theory to give a place to the proprium in its various aspects. One reason, of course, is that the subjective (felt) side of personality is what everyone knows about; it would be foolish to overlook it as some psychologists prefer to do. Another reason, very

23 W. James, *Principles of psychology* (New York: Holt, Rinehart and Winston, 1890), Vol. I, Chap. 10.

important, is that people's *behavior* varies greatly according to whether they feel self-involved or merely task-involved in what they are doing. Thus in our discussion of learning in the previous chapter we saw that learning is far more efficient when it is felt to be self-relevant than when it is impersonal.[24] And many psychological experiments prove that not only learning but almost every performance is altered, depending upon the presence or absence of propriate-involvement. This difference turns up in measurements of attention, judgment, memory, motivation, aspiration level, productivity, and in the operation of personality traits.[25]

The concept of the proprium, therefore, we find to be not only justified, but entirely indispensable in psychological theory.

It is important to point out that the proprium is not at all moments conscious. True, we *derive* the concept from experiences of self of which we are fully aware. But the traces of these experiences are effective even when we are not observing them. In propriate striving, for example, we characteristically "lose ourselves," because we are deeply absorbed in what we are doing. But it is nonetheless true that ego-involved interest is still playing a persistent role. And as we earlier pointed out, we are not constantly aware of the bodily me, perhaps hardly at all until pain or sensory deprivation forces such awareness upon us. Yet all seven propriate functions play a part, an important part, in the "go" of personality, sometimes consciously, but often unconsciously.

The Problem of the Knower

This puzzling problem arises when we ask, "Who is the I who knows the bodily me, who has an image of myself and sense of identity over time, who knows that I have propriate strivings?" I know all these things and, what is more, I know that I know them. But who is it who has this perspectival grasp?

[24] The objection may be made that ego-overinvolvement is injurious to learning efficiency. This is true: too intense a propriate involvement may be disruptive (as when in stage fright we forget our carefully memorized lines). A balance is required so that the emotions attending involvement do not swamp the integrative neural mechanisms. Discussions of this matter are contained in R. M. French, Goal, mechanisms and integrative field. *Psychosom. Med.*, 1941, 3, 226–252. Also in M. Scheerer, Problems of performance analysis in the study of personality, *Ann. N.Y. Acad. Sci.*, 1946, 46, Art. 7, pp. 653–678.
[25] Cf. G. W. Allport, The ego in contemporary psychology, *Psychol. Rev.*, 1943, 50, 451–478.

Philosophers beyond count have racked their brains with this problem. It is beyond our present scope to enter into the argument. Let us be content with a brief statement of two contrary views.

The philosopher Emmanuel Kant argued that we never experience the knowing self in the same way we experience the object-self (proprium). The knowing self is just there, a transcendental or pure ego. The knower apprehends but is not itself apprehended. We catch bare glimpses of its shadow, but nothing more.

The opposite solution, offered by William James and John Dewey among others, holds that there is no substantive knower apart from the process of knowing. Each moment of consciousness overlaps with the previous moment, and the knower is somehow embedded in what is known. It is only when we stop the normal process of knowing, and grow reflective about the matter, that we imagine the problem to exist. The knower is nothing more than the organism itself.

We shall not here presume to choose between these two solutions, or others that have been offered.[26] There is, for example, the view that holds the self to be a central *agency* within personality. It knows, it wants, it strives, it wills. The self is the center of personal energy. This so-called self-psychology takes various forms, but the general position is the same.[27]

It has the merit of focusing, as we have done, on the unity and coherence that mark the propriate functions of personality, and of setting them off to some extent from the large balance of mere organismic and nonego-relevant functions.

It has, however, one serious danger from the scientific point of view. If we admit the self as a separate agent that knows, wills, wants, and so on, are we not in danger of creating a personality within a personality? We seem to be postulating "a little man within the breast." If we ask why Jim works hard, it explains nothing to say that "his self wills it." If we ask why this hospital patient is depressed, it is not helpful to say that "the self has a wrong self-image." To say that the self does this or that, wants this or that, wills this or that, is

26 For a fuller discussion of the problem see G. W. Allport, *Becoming: basic considerations for a psychology of personality* (New Haven, Conn.: Yale Univ. Press, 1955), pp. 36–62.
27 Cf. P. A. Bertocci, The psychological self, the ego, and personality, *Psychol. Rev.*, 1945, 52, 91–99; J. Macmurray, *The self as agent* (London: Faber & Faber, 1957); and M. B. Arnold and J. A. Gasson, *The human person: an approach to an integral theory of personality* (New York: Ronald, 1954).

to beg a series of difficult questions. The psychologist does not like to pass the buck to a self-agent.

It is my position that in the structure of *personality*, if rightly understood—including, of course, the propriate structure—we shall find the explanations we seek. It is unwise to assign our problems to an inner agent who pulls the strings.

For certain philosophical purposes it may be justified to regard the self as a continuing entity—perhaps endowed with immortality. But in psychology we do well to avoid the sharp separation of the self "as agent" from the functioning of the propriate systems within the personality.

Feelings of Inferiority

Many important problems in the psychology of personality can be approached only via the sense of self. The so-called inferiority complex is one; conscience, another.

All of us often experience failure. Our accomplishment falls short of our pretension. Our performance falls below our self-esteem and jars upon our self-image. When this occurs we normally stiffen our efforts or change our objective, and stop worrying.

Often, however, when failures are recurrent and have propriate significance, we cannot brush them aside. They remain as latent and haunting memories. And so a deep-seated sense of deficiency may develop and be steadily aggravated. This sense of deficiency may be due to different causes: physical weakness, unpleasant appearance, sexual impotence, social inadequacy (poverty, lack of education, awkwardness, poor vocabulary, slowness of wit). Or it may be due to feelings of unworthiness, of guilt and sin. As failures multiply, the "complex" deepens. If a definition is desired, we may say that an inferiority complex is a strong and persistent tension arising from a somewhat morbid emotional attitude toward one's felt deficiency in his personal equipment.

Most people know the type of discomfort. One study shows that less than 12 percent of a group of college students report that they do not know what it is to suffer from gnawing feelings of inferiority. As the table shows, there seem to be four main types. On the whole the college women seem to be somewhat worse off than the men. The higher ratio among women no doubt reflects the disadvantage they

Type of inferiority feeling	Men 243	Women 120
	Percentage reporting persistent inferiority feelings	
Physical	39	50
Social	52	57
Intellectual	29	61
Moral	16	15
None at all	12	10

feel in a "man's world." In this particular college sample the high incidence of intellectual inferiority feelings may be due to the fact that males greatly outnumbered females. In general, college students of both sexes say that the life of a male is more desirable than that of the female; and they tend to ascribe more favorable qualities to the male sex.[28] Thus it seems that even in the United States the emancipation of woman is not complete.

Needless to say, feelings of inferiority cannot be taken as an index of actual inferiority. The girls in this study were highly selected students; by no reasonable test could half or more be considered actually inferior in physical, social, or intellectual abilities. Yet the objective facts seem to make little difference. The second best prize fighter, or the second best chess player, or the second best actor might suffer from a deep-seated feeling of inferiority. It is purely a subjective phenomenon pertaining to the self, and is measured by the ratio that obtains between one's *success* and one's *aspirations* in a given direction.

It seems safe to say that many of these students, now in late adolescence, have already outgrown earlier feelings of inadequacy. Other studies show that during early adolescence most males report haunting fears of physical inferiority. Short stature, obesity, pimply faces are grim obstacles in the search for identity. And we may well ask whether young children, simply because they are small, do not harbor a nascent feeling of physical inferiority. It was the recognition of genuine and imaginary organic weakness that led to the first form-

28 J. P. McKee and A. C. Sherriffs, The differential evaluation of males and females, *J. Pers.*, 1957, **25,** 356–371.

ulation of the "inferiority complex" by Alfred Adler around 1912.[29]

For our purposes what is especially important is the way this chronic wound to self-esteem sometimes develops into a generalized trait of personality. A strong sense of failure in one department of life may leave a person with a general feeling of insecurity and lack of confidence.

In one study people were asked to tell how well satisfied they were with their bodily features—hair, complexion, nose, teeth, and the like; also with their intellectual and artistic ability; and with their own morals. Later the same people took tests of "social security" which measured their normal level of self-confidence. The correlation between feelings of inferiority and general insecurity was around .50.[30]

Other studies show that some people tend to be generally optimistic and self-confident, even after failure, whereas others take a characteristically downcast and pessimistic view of their ability.[31] Interestingly enough, people in the former category tend to believe that the average citizen can have much, or at least "some," influence on important governmental policies, through voting, writing letters, and so on, whereas people who feel inferior and insecure think that the average citizen can have little or no effect on the course of events in a democracy.[32] These examples illustrate what is meant by a generalized trait of personality (Chapters 14, 15). Inferiority feelings may saturate one's attitude toward life in general.

Compensation. What does one do with inferiority feelings beside suffer? One cannot escape them for long since they are rooted in the proprium. Some sustained form of combat is required, and to this form Adler gave the name *compensation.*

Several types may be distinguished. *Direct action* (compensation in kind) occurs when the sufferer persistently attacks the *source* of an actual inferiority and removes it. When the original weakness is not only removed but turned into a source of strength, we speak of

29 A. Adler, *Organminderwertigkeit und ihre psychische Kompensationen* (1912; transl. 1917), *Nerv. & Ment. Dis. Monogr. Series,* No. 24. See also H. L. Ansbacher and R. R. Ansbacher (Eds.), *The individual psychology of Alfred Adler* (New York: Basic Books, 1956).
30 S. M. Jourard and P. F. Secord, *Body-cathexis and personality, Brit. J. Psychol.,* 1955, **46**, 130–138.
31 J. Nuttin, *Tâche, réussite et échec* (Louvain: Éditions universitaires, 1953).
32 E. Douvan and W. M. Walker, *The sense of effectiveness in public affairs, Psychol. Monogr.,* 1956, **70**, No. 429.

overcompensation. Demosthenes, legend tells us, worked so hard to overcome his stammer that he became not merely a normal speaker but a great orator. Theodore Roosevelt, whose early frailty was a burden, worked to build up his physique and ended by overcompensating. He became a lion hunter and a Rough Rider (not merely a partridge hunter and a gentleman rider). The successful self-made man in America may have started as an immigrant bedeviled with feelings of social inferiority. Through hard labor he has compensated —and perhaps overcompensated—for his handicap.

We speak of *substitute compensation* when a person cannot remove his handicap but develops other satisfactions. The hunchback cannot correct his deformity, but may become the power behind a throne. A plain girl may develop compensatory charm and wit, and the nonathletic youth may excel in his studies.

Defense mechanisms are compensations designed to deceive others. The adolescent may hide his insecurity by developing an exaggerated handshake. The bluster of a bully may hide inner weakness. Beards, thick-soled shoes, ingratiating manners may mask physical or social inferiority feelings.

Rationalization is a form of compensation that fools others not so much as oneself. A pale, nonathletic chap said, "I am sick of hearing about red-blooded athletes. You know red blood is the blood that never flows through the brain." Such sour-grapes rationalizations are common, as is the sweet-lemon type. One man with a cadaverous face consoled himself with the thought that it made him look distinguished "like Savonarola or Dante." Rationalization is aided by the mass media. People with feelings of intellectual or social inferiority may find comfort in reading about, or in watching films depicting, the evil ways of high society, the uncouthness of college students, the foolishness of "eggheads," and the superiority of homely virtues and the common man.

Autistic thinking is a fantasy compensation. Through our daydreams we can succeed. A certain youth, persecuted by his tougher schoolmates, fled to his room every afternoon to play his two favorite games. In one he was schoolmaster and administered floggings to the tough boys. In the other he was a millionaire and wrote large checks for his favorites and entertained important guests. When autistic compensation goes far we find the personality strongly introverted, perhaps even "schizoid" (a condition bordering on abnormal schizophrenia where the individual lives almost entirely spun in a web of his own fantasies).

Few people are free from one or more of the forms of compensation we have described. But unless the process is habitual and ingrained we cannot speak of compensation as a *trait* of personality.

Conscience

Conscience, like feelings of inferiority, represents a patterning of several propriate states—especially self-esteem, self-image, and propriate striving. A "good" conscience seems not to have a sharp configuration. When our conscience is "quiet" or "at rest" we go on functioning in our normal way, enjoying a smooth psychic and moral equilibrium.[33] But a "bad" or "outraged" conscience nags us and tells us we have somehow violated our preferred style of being. We must then either "salve" it through rationalization or do penance and make amends. Often conscience is integrated with a religious sentiment, but sometimes it is not; nonreligious people often have acute consciences. Indeed, we may safely say that, except for a few "psychopathic personalities," conscience is a normal development within every human being. It is an indicator—something like a fever thermometer—that tells us some activity on our part is disrupting, or has disrupted, an important aspect of our self-image.

There are two central problems in the psychology of conscience: the first concerns its *development;* the second concerns its *adult structure.* Broadly speaking, we may consider the evolving conscience in childhood a *must* conscience, and the mature, adult form an *ought* conscience. Fromm calls the former an "authoritarian conscience" and the latter a "humanistic conscience."[34]

Without doubt the *must* conscience—the only form a child has—evolves out of parental restrictions and prohibitions. As early as eighteen months the child becomes fearful and frustrated when he hears the parental warning "No! No!" The sugar bowl is "No!" The TV is "No!" Dirt is "No! No!" Some form of punishment often accompanies these words. As language further develops, the child learns the word "must." He must wash his face, and he must not

33 C. I. Jenkins, The significance of conscience, *Ethics*, 1955, **65**, 261–270.
34 E. Fromm, *Man for himself* (New York: Holt, Rinehart and Winston, 1947). An instructive account of the stages of development in conscience is R. F. Peck *et al.*, *The psychology of character development* (New York: Wiley, 1960).

cross the street alone. These words are signals of parental power: they betoken rewards and punishments that will follow. The child does not know, of course, why he must or must not. (Indeed, the reasons for "must" and "must not" are highly complex: in some cases the "must" means, "You'll get hurt if you come too close to the stove," i.e., nature will punish you; in some cases, "I, your parent, will punish you because you annoy me"; sometimes, "People in society will punish you for such and such behavior"; and, finally, the sanction behind the *must* may rest with God, who will punish you if you steal or do not obey your parents.)

The child then—with great difficulty—learns obedience. He is most obedient, of course, when the parent is standing over him; but gradually he "interiorizes" the external voice of authority, and behaves himself (fairly well) even when he is alone. The forbidden cooky jar, however, is a temptation for years—unless the monitoring mother is on the scene.

From about the age of six, morality based on adult demands is firmly fixed. The child becomes a "moral realist" (Piaget). Acts are evaluated entirely in terms of their keeping to, or departure from, the rules laid down. The habit of expecting and obeying rules is by now so well generalized that even at play the child (6–12) is outraged if games aren't played according to rules.

There seems to be no doubt that this early stage of conscience is, as Freud argued, due to the internalization of tribal and parental rules. Violation causes anxiety and guilt even though immediate punishment does not threaten. It is not uncommon for a child to seek external punishment after he has done something wrong, for in this way he hopes to restore his psychic and moral equilibrium. And often he punishes himself by suffering pangs of conscience and making little indirect acts of retribution.

In adolescence the youth faces a new crisis. For one thing, he decides that most parental restrictions are foolish. He engages in many forbidden acts—though he may still feel some guilt. Around the age of fourteen there are disciplinary problems at home and at school because the youth will "get away" with antisocial acts if he can; he does not yet *want* to place his backbone on the inside; he prefers strong leaders and monitors to keep him in order, even though at the same time he is in revolt.

But gradually, as the self-image grows, and as the youth develops an ideal for himself, the negative aspects of the *must* conscience give way to a wholly different *ought* conscience. We say it is "wholly different" because it is no longer sustained by fear of punishment, but blends into the positive structure of propriate striving. The youth who has chosen a career knows that he should study for it, and if he fails to do so he violates his own chosen style of being. Conscience gradually shifts its center from specific habits of obedience to the proprium. The "feel" of conscience in maturity is rarely tied to the fear of punishment, whether external or self-administered. It is rather a feeling of obligation.

There remain many "musts" in adulthood, but they spring now from a rational recognition of consequences and are seldom felt any longer as matters of conscience: I *must* obey traffic regulations. I must have the electric wiring repaired. I must not show her my true feelings. But, on the other hand, I *ought* to vote. I ought to write that letter. I ought to study harder. I ought to pursue the good as I see it. These are propriate value-judgments. No one will punish me if I fail to live according to my own preferred style. To argue that I fear future pangs of conscience is to confuse a possible outcome with the wholly positive sense of obligation.[35]

Mature conscience, then, is a sense of duty to keep one's self-image in an acceptable shape, to continue one's chosen lines of propriate striving—in short, to build (and not tear down) one's style of being. Conscience becomes a kind of generic self-guidance. Emphasis has shifted from tribal and parental control to individual control.[36]

It is unfortunate that some psychological interpretations do not recognize the transformation that normally occurs from the *must* to the *ought*. Some writers claim that a person's "superego" is nothing more than a lifelong stencil of parental and tribal rules and admonitions. It is true that some adults suffer an arrest in moral development. They continue to suffer from infantile guilt, from unresolved conflicts with early authority figures. But this pathology

[35] Cf. P. A. Bertocci, A reinterpretation of moral obligation, *Phil. & phenomenol. Res.*, 1945, **6**, 270–283; and Allport; *Becoming: basic considerations for a psychology of personality*, pp. 68–74. Note 26, above.

[36] The analysis offered here is similar to the much fuller argument of H. Bergson in *The two sources of morality and religion* (First published in France in 1932; Garden City: Doubleday, Anchor, 1954).

of conscience—a not uncommon ailment—does not alter the rules governing its transformation in the normal course of growth.

Conclusion and Summary

This chapter has been devoted to the *sense* of selfhood, not to the *nature* of selfhood. Our discussion therefore is primarily psychological, not philosophical, in nature. As Moustakas has said, it is much easier to *feel* the self than to *define* the self.[37] Final definitions we leave to philosophy.

It is, however, a psychological fact that the human mind is able to regard itself as an object in much the same way that it regards objects in the outer world. Whenever personal states are viewed as "peculiarly mine" the sense of self is present. We have shown that at different stages of life various aspects of self-awareness emerge.[38] Although the seven aspects of the proprium do seem to evolve at successive stages of life, I do not mean to imply that they function separately. In our daily experience several, or even all, aspects co-exist.

Suppose that you are facing a difficult and critical examination. No doubt you are aware of your high pulse rate and of the butterflies in your stomach (bodily self); also of the significance of the exam in terms of your past and future (self-identity); of your prideful involvement (self-esteem); of what success or failure may mean to your family (self-extension); of your hopes and aspirations (self-image); of your role as the solver of problems on the examination (rational agent); and of the relevance of the whole situation to your long-range goals (propriate striving). In actual life, then, a fusion of propriate states is the rule. And behind these experienced states of selfhood you catch indirect glimpses of yourself as "knower."

The problem of the knower arises when we ask, "Who is the self that knows these self-functions?" We are not only aware of what is

---

[37] C. E. Moustakas (Ed.), *The self: explorations in personal growth* (New York: Harper, 1956), Chap. 1.
[38] A helpful diagrammatic representation of this emergence is offered by T. R. Sarbin, Preface to a psychological analysis of the self, *Psychol. Rev.*, 1952, **59**, 11–22. In part the stages he depicts overlap with mine, but in part they are different.

peculiarly ours, but we are also aware that we are aware. This puzzle has led to the postulation of a special self-agent (either as a pure knower—a transcendental ego—or else as a combined knower-wanter-striver-willer). This latter point of view seems to set up a master coordinating agent within the personality, a little man within the breast who pulls the strings.

It seems on the whole sounder to regard the propriate functions of wanting, striving, willing as interlocked with the total personality structure. They are felt as self-relevant, but are not caused by a separate agent within the personality. As for the knower, whether it is simply an inference we make at a high level of complexity, as James, Dewey, and others hold, or whether it is necessary to postulate a pure knower, a continuing transcendental self, as Kant holds, is a riddle we have not solved.

To return to the sense of self, there are two familiar patterns that have merited our special attention—feelings of inferiority and of conscience. These patterns involve, in various proportions, many, perhaps all, of the aspects of the proprium. They are important subjective conditions that affect the functioning and structuring of personality.

Finally, we turn back to our discussion of the principles of learning in the previous chapter. We have argued that the sense of self is gradually acquired. (It is not inconsistent to say, if one wishes, that every child has an innate latent capacity to develop a self.) Since the self is acquired, then the laws of learning must apply. Specifically, in the first year or two—as we have previously explained—quasi-mechanical principles account for the emergence of early selfhood. Conditioning, reinforcement, repetition are clearly necessary before the young child can connect his bodily sensations, experiences, and verbal tags (e.g., his name) into an emerging self-identity. This form of "opportunistic" learning precedes the forms of propriate learning that we described. In short, we argue for a certain discontinuity in the learning sequence. Quasi-mechanical principles account for the emergence of the proprium; but once established, the proprium becomes the principal source of subsequent learning.

CHAPTER 7

The Unconscious Stratum

THEORIES OF STRATA • FREUD'S VIEW OF THE UNCONSCIOUS •
THE NEUROTIC AND THE NORMAL • MECHANISMS OF DEFENSE
• SUMMARY

OF the whole of our natures we are never directly aware, nor of any large portion of the whole. At any given moment the range of consciousness is remarkably slight. It seems to be little more than a restless pencil point of light darting here and there within the large edifice of personality, focused now within, now without.

Yet for all its feebleness, consciousness provides each of us with the only sure test of our personal existence and identity. At one moment we think back to some event of childhood; the next moment we have an image of what will happen tomorrow; then immediately we are aware of some present event. Our sense of self, as well as our knowledge of the outside world, is wholly dependent on this criss-cross of conscious states.[1]

---

[1] The fugitive and undependable nature of consciousness has led some psychologists to deny it any place at all in psychological science. Behaviorism, positivism, stimulus-response psychology incline to do so. And yet the objective method preferred by these psychologists depends completely upon the testimony of their own conscious experience. Of what use are pointer readings unless they are consciously perceived and interpreted? We cannot escape the fact that consciousness plays some sort of integrative role in behavior.

But since the range of consciousness at any given moment is so slender, we have no alternative but to say that most of what goes on in our personalities belongs in some way to a nonconscious stratum.

The surface flow of our conscious lives takes its course largely from hidden contours and from rivulets intruding from below the surface. Impressions of which we are not aware may nonetheless leave their mark. This fact can be demonstrated by experiment.

Kolers asked his subjects to look at an apparently blank screen. On it was flashed at very low illumination a geometrical figure. It was so dim that the subjects were unaware that they were "looking" at anything. Following this "blank" experience the subjects were asked to solve a problem, the solution of which involved the use of this same unperceived figure. The subjects proceeded to solve the problem although totally unaware that they were making use of the unconscious (subliminal) impression they had previously received.[2]

This principle is applied in so-called subliminal advertising. A faint picture or printed message appearing on a movie or television screen is thought to have unconscious effects on the potential buyer even if he does not know he is being affected. Whether an urge to buy the product can actually be instigated in this way is a disputed question. But such unperceived cues may launch a train of thought, arouse a latent interest, or start a chain of worry—and we ourselves will never know the causal sequence.

Theories of Strata

How shall we think of the unconscious as it enters into the structure of personality? The metaphor of levels or layers or strata seems most natural. (In general, psychologists are partial to spatial figures of speech. They speak of *breadth* of emotion, *span* of attention, a *field* of force, of *barriers,* of a *split* personality; and the unconscious is said to be *submerged,* requiring *depth* analysis to reach it.)

One theory depicts *layers* running from outside to inside—like an onion. This particular theory (Lewin) is not concerned so much

2 P. A. Kolers, Subliminal stimulation in problem solving, *Amer. J. Psychol.,* 1957, **70,** 437–441.

with what is conscious and what is unconscious, but with the total structure of personality.

As Figure 14 shows, the person, for Lewin, is a differentiated region separated by a permeable boundary from his external environment. (See also Figure 11, page 97.) In direct contact with the environment are certain perceptual-motor systems engaged in sensing stimuli and acting directly upon them. For the most part these systems are fluid, for they require quick adaptability to demands of the environment and do not reflect the more permanent dispositions of personality, although they are affected by them.

Inward from this layer are the peripheral regions of the inner personality. They are more firmly structured than is the perceptual-motor region, but do not contain the central (propriate) systems. Among the peripheral systems we may include various cultural habits —such as our skill in speaking our native language. Ordinarily such a system proceeds without a sense of self-involvement—although of course on occasion (for example, if a conqueror should forbid us to speak our native language), the system may become central and ego-involved. In other words, peripheral systems may become motivational if they are placed under tension, but ordinarily they run their course with no conflict or strain. Most of our habits belong in this group.

Proceeding inward we find the more central regions representing

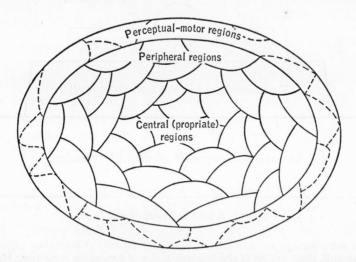

Figure 14. The "Onion Layer" Conception of Personality Structure (after Lewin)

deeper motives and interests, lasting sentiments, and prejudices. These central regions correspond to our concept of *proprium*. The heart of the inner-personal region is the most intimate zone, comprising our most cherished images and aspirations. Lewin calls this innermost region the *self*.

A valuable feature of this representation is the allowance it makes for uniqueness of pattern. No two structures are differentiated in precisely the same way. Furthermore, it allows for a change in the boundaries of regions over time, and even from moment to moment. A given pressure from the environment may place one or more regions (traits) under tension and thus produce a single dynamic force. In short, the representation allows for structure but also for flexibility—two of the essential attributes of personality.[3]

Other authors are more directly concerned with dividing the conscious from the unconscious stratum, and prefer a vertical to a concentric picture. A typical view might be that represented in Figure 15.

In this figure the familiar metaphor of the iceberg comes to mind. Most of the structure of personality is submerged under the surface; it is subliminal. The present moment of *awareness* is at the summit. The *coconscious* is a stratum that immediately supports the shifting

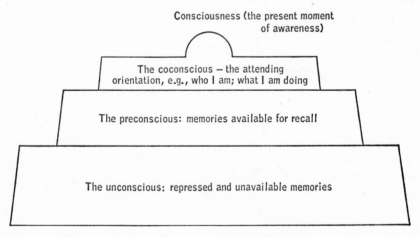

Figure 15. A Basic Representation of Strata

3 For a fuller account see K. Lewin, *Principles of topological psychology* (New York: McGraw-Hill, 1936), pp. 166 f.; also *Dynamic theory of personality* (New York: McGraw-Hill, 1935), Chap. 7.

summit. We always "know" who we are, what we are doing, our physical orientation. The *preconscious* is somewhat further from the surface, but contains all memories and associations that will arise to consciousness if called upon. The deepest layer, the *unconscious,* is not ordinarily accessible, but may under unusual conditions (in dreams, in therapy) become conscious.

There are many variations on this basic design. The oldest is Plato's. This ancient philosopher assured us that man has three parts to his nature, each anchored in a bodily region. The abdomen is the center of appetites and desire; the breast contains striving, courage, and volition; the head is the seat of intellect and reason. We have already said that some modern theories divide personality into the same three components: *affection, conation, cognition.* This particular trichotomy, however, does not deal directly with the problem of the unconscious.

Most strata theories point out that the unconscious layer has two functions. It is the storehouse of buried memories; and it is also a source of energy or motivation not fully understood by the individual. We might say that, like a dwelling, the basement contains both an accumulation of articles in storage and a heating system.

An appealing feature of some strata theories is their evolutionary flavor. Anatomists distinguish between the "old brain" and the "new brain." The old brain includes the thalamus and hypothalamus, which are, roughly speaking, the seat of the emotions. The new brain is the cerebral cortex, an agent of inhibition, control, intelligence. A decorticated animal will, at the slightest provocation, fly into a rage. And men, too, if suffering from cortical damage, often behave in primitive ways. It seems logical, then, to say that in each of us dwells a "cortical man" and a "depth man." Lersch calls the latter the "endothymic ground" of existence, and the former the "personal superstructure." The vital, vegetative, emotional functions of life are "endothymic," whereas the controlling power of reason, of planning, of decision resides in the less stable superstructure. The same basic distinction is the core of Klages's theory of the expression of personality (handwriting, gesture, voice, and the like), as we shall see in Chapter 19.[4]

---

[4] An instructive review of German stratification theories is A. R. Gilbert, Recent German theories of stratification of personality, *J. Psychol.,* 1951, **31,** 3–19. See also P. Lersch, *Der Aufbau des Charakters* (1st ed.; Leipzig: Barth, 1938).

Especially in postwar Germany numerous versions of strata-theory have been proposed. Thomae resembles Plato in distinguishing three strata: an *impulsive ego,* containing reflexes, instincts, and drives; a *propulsive ego* containing free energy and aspiring to self-actualization; a *prospective ego* which plans, foresees the future, and coordinates the two lower egos as best it can. The latter is an intermittent agent, and is able only partially to control impulse and propulsion.[5]

Another proposal—somewhat similar—calls for five layers: (1) a vital layer present in all life; (2) a vegetative and nutritional layer; (3) animal drives and instincts; (4) peculiarly human emotions and endowments; (5) the personal layer.[6]

Still another scheme enlarges the levels to seven: vitality, drive, sensation, feeling, fantasy, understanding, and will. But in this case there is no clear hierarchy. The role of each level is determined by its closeness to, or remoteness from, the "nuclear" structure of the developing personality.[7]

A point on which all stratification theories agree is that the cortical, or personal, or prospective layer—whatever one calls it—does not always succeed in dominating lower levels. There is conflict between them. In St. Paul's words, "The flesh lusteth against the spirit, and the spirit against the flesh." Especially in times of war and social crisis, the lower, emotional, impulsive, archaic layers erupt and seize control of personalities otherwise rationally and morally balanced—a phenomenon seen in Hitler's Germany.

Although all schools of thought agree that in some sense the unconscious layers make trouble for the conscious, and even on occasion may overwhelm it, there is one issue of sharp disagreement that we must keep in mind.

The issue is this: Does the conscious layer (Freud calls it the ego) have an autonomy and function of its own, or does it *always* serve the purposes and motives that are deeply embedded in the unconscious? Long ago Schopenhauer said that the intellect cannot act by itself if the will (the lower layers of passion and desire) is active. More recently Kempf made the same point in arguing that the cen-

---

[5] H. Thomae, *Persönlichkeit: eine dynamische Interpretation* (Bonn: Bouvier, 1951).
[6] E. Rothacker, *Die Schichten der Persönlichkeit* (Bonn: Bouvier, 1948).
[7] A. Wellek, *Die Polarität im Aufbau des Charakters* (Bern: A. Francke, 1950).

tral nervous system is essentially the servant of the autonomic (vegetative and emotional) system (see page 74 f.).

Such views as these (and Freud's among them) argue in effect for the primacy of the unconscious. The "psychic surface" of life, they say, is deceptive. It is due to a late evolution, and lacks the stability and dynamic power needed to transform the archaic contents of the unconscious into contemporary conscious motives of the sort the "prospective ego" would approve. The well-dressed man who lives in the penthouse is not likely to know about, nor be able to control, the subterranean boilers, pipes, and valves that maintain the edifice in which he lives.

The issue is central for our theory. The questions are simply these: Does the unconscious (with its primitive and archaic charac-ter) dominate the structure and functioning of personality, or does the conscious stratum do so? If both are effective, under what condi-tions and in what proportion does each take control?

Freud's View of the Unconscious

We commonly hear that Sigmund Freud "discovered the un-conscious." Also that for this reason his contribution to psychology is the greatest since Aristotle (who first formulated a psychology of conscious mental life). While the statements are too extreme, they are nonetheless basically just. Freud was more successful than any other writer in history in calling attention to the hidden formative processes that often shape our personalities without our knowing that they do so. Thanks to Freud, even the man in the street now knows that we often act for reasons we do not understand, and that we harbor unconscious sentiments that would surprise us if we knew we had them.

According to Freud the unconscious, as we have said, does double duty. On the one hand, it stores up forgotten or repressed memories that have dropped or been thrown—so to speak—into a deep pit. On the other hand, it contains a steam boiler of basic energies, a "seeth-ing cauldron" of instinctual drive (chiefly sex and aggression). The dynamic id is the original system of personality out of which other systems differentiate.

The id has no recognition of outer reality. It is self-seeking, oper-ating wholly for gratification of the instincts. It therefore operates on the "pleasure principle." To avoid pain and obtain pleasure it has only two items of equipment: *reflex action* and the *primary process*. The newborn infant, by virtue of its reflex equipment, can sneeze, blink, suck, eliminate, for the purpose of gratifying the id. Primary process refers to the wish-fulfilling tendency that we note in our dreams and in our fantasies. We picture gratification of the id directly. Our instincts make us think of (hallucinate) objects of gratification but can do nothing to bring about such gratification, except what reflex action will do.

The ego therefore comes into existence early in life for the purpose of serving the id. It operates by the "reality principle," with the aid of *secondary process*. The ego's job is to solve problems, think, plan, protect itself and the id. It is an executive agent, mediating between instincts and the outer world. Its task is a hard one, and frequently it cannot make the difficult adjustments required. Under frustration and conflict it often breaks out in anxiety. Anxiety, if prolonged and unresolved, results in some form of neurotic behavior. Anxiety, says Freud, is the "alpha and omega of neurosis." Neurosis (a term covering a vast variety of disorders of personality) is due to the simple fact that the ego, borrowing its energy from the id, and carrying out its impulsive orders, finds that the outer world is too resistant to handle. The strange quirks that result are "neurotic."

The poor ego is a slave not only to the two "tyrants" of id-impulse and outer reality, but likewise to a third: the superego. This tyrant, one's conscience and ego-ideal, is a set of habits learned from parents and from society that require the individual to carry out his task according to prescribed rules of the game. It is a "must" conscience (page 134).

The key conception in Freudian psychoanalytic theory is "primary process."[8] The id wants its way. It refuses to be socialized or civilized—and yet society (via parents) demands "correct" behavior. To satisfy the id and yet be reasonably "correct" is the task of our

8 E. Glover, The future of "dynamic" psychology, *Brit. J. med. Psychol.,* 1957, **30**, 219–229. Secondary expositions of Freud are numerous. Especially useful are C. S. Hall, *A primer of Freudian psychology* (Cleveland: World, 1954; and W. Healy, A. F. Bronner, and A. M. Bowers, *The structure and meaning of psychoanalysis* (New York: Knopf, 1930). To make a start in Freud's own writings, it is well to begin with *A general introduction to psychoanalysis* (Rev. ed.; New York: Liveright, 1935), and *New introductory lectures on psychoanalysis* (New York: Norton, 1933).

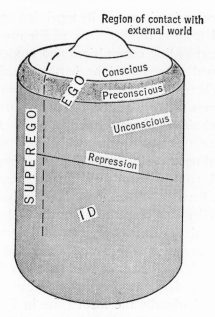

Figure 16. Structure of Personality According to the Freudian View

"secondary process." Intelligent problem solving helps, but could not succeed without the important aid of *repression*.

Repression forces a dangerous idea or memory out of consciousness and prevents it from returning—at least in an uncensored form. Some desires of the id (for example, sexual love for the parent) are so deeply taboo that they may never be allowed conscious recognition, even by the child. As socialization continues, the superego will see to it that more and more repressions occur. In Figure 16 an "escape hatch" is allowed for, whereby repressed content of the unconscious may slip through—if suitably disguised and displaced. Dreams, for example, often reveal the primary process in spite of repressions that operate during waking hours. Likewise, slips of the tongue and pen may betray wishes or hatreds that are buried but not dead. A tired and unwilling hostess said to her departing guests, "Good night, I'm so sorry you came." Her repressed thoughts and hostile feelings slipped through. Repression is like putting a flaming wastebasket into a closet and closing the door. Sometimes the flames may die out of their own accord, but often they cause serious damage.

The goal of psychoanalysis is to enable a patient to strengthen

the ego through enlarging its scope. By regaining and facing dangerous thoughts and feelings the problems of life can be met realistically without the crippling compulsions and anxieties that are the
product of repeated repression. The battle cry of psychoanalysis,
says Freud, is, "Where the id was, there shall the ego be."

Let us look more closely at the terms *primary* and *secondary*
process. Freud's choice of these terms betrays his whole theory of
the nature of man. What is instinctual, blindly self-centered, immediately demanding, largely unconscious is *primary*. What is rational, controlled, adult is *secondary*. To be sure, the terms have
also an innocent flavor of time: the infant's primary demand for
gratification is *earlier* than all secondary rational developments. But
Freud means more than this. Not even an adult escapes the *primacy*
of the primary process in his life. Freud insists that "the ego has no
energy of its own."[9] It does not exist until energy is diverted from the
id to sustain the secondary processes that constitute the ego.

Now this is undoubtedly the moot issue in Freudian doctrine.
Many followers regret that Freud held this view; others reinterpret
him; still others say he died before completing his "ego psychology."
Many psychoanalysts today depart radically on this issue, and have
established a neo-Freudian ego-psychology.[10]

The issue, as we have said, is of highest importance for personality theory. If we regard all the acquisitions of an adult (his
altruism, his ideals, his mature tastes, and his "ought" conscience)
as "secondary," or, as Freud has said, as "transparent sublimations"
of id processes, we have an animalistic view of the nature of normal
adult personality.

But Freud's picture of an id that "never changes" can be, and has
been, sharply challenged. Early in the history of psychoanalysis Jung
dissented vigorously from Freud. Simply because the roots of ill-
health are sometimes found in the unconscious, it is not necessary,
says Jung, to conclude that the deeper regions of human nature contain only what is evil, dirty, and dangerous. (Someone has quipped

[9] See Hall, *op. cit.*, p. 36.
[10] For example, D. Rapaport (Ed.), *Organization and pathology of thought* (New York:
Columbia Univ. Press, 1951), especially chapters by Rapaport and H. Hartmann; E.
Erikson. *Identity and the life cycle* (Monogr. No. 1 of *Psychological Issues;* New York:
Int. Univ. Press, 1959); and E. Kris, Ego psychology and interpretation in psychoanalytic
therapy, *Psychoanal. Quart.*, 1951, **20**, 15–30.

that in exploring the unconscious Freud goes down deeper, stays longer, and comes up dirtier than any other psychologist.)

For Jung the unconscious contains more than aggressive and sexual impulses embedded in tabooed and rejected memories. It harbors likewise "racial memories" (archetypes) which are thought-forms basic to human existence. Thus the concepts of mother, of orderly nature, of immortality are categories of a universal human order and seem to lie in a latent form in the unconscious. There are likewise creative urges and energies available in the unconscious to draw on. Furthermore, the unconscious contains the complement of our everyday personalities, for qualities reside there that are the reciprocals of our ordinary natures: a strongly extraverted person is likely to have an introverted unconscious.[11]

Thus one may challenge Freud's account of the furnishings of the unconscious. One may also challenge its primacy throughout life. Our instincts, Freud says, may form attachments to new objects (cathexes), but the same instinctual forces remain—overlaid, cathected —but not fundamentally changed. The picture still leaves the ego frail and relatively inconsequential. It ascribes to consciousness a passive and secondary role. It is this one-sidedness that modern ego-psychology tries to correct.

The point at issue, we repeat, is the relative importance of unconscious and conscious functions in forming and maintaining personality. Whatever else consciousness is, it is clearly associated with the highest level of metabolic activity in the cortex. It would not have evolved unless it had a part to play in the economy of human life. At the very least it provides a regulatory field wherein problems that cannot be solved by unconscious habit or instinct receive the interplay of forces (reflection, analysis, imaginative testing, and decision) that bring about a solution. We note that we are most acutely conscious when there are problematic situations that cannot be dealt with automatically.[12]

On a hundred occasions I have approached my door, taken my key from my pocket, and let myself in—all without being

11 For a good secondary account of Jung's theory of personality, including the unconscious, see C. S. Hall and G. Lindzey, *Theories of personality* (New York: Wiley, 1957), Chap. 3.
12 Cf. R. M. Collier, Outline of a theory of consciousness as a regulatory field: preliminary statement, *J. Psychol.*, 1955, **40**, 269–274.

conscious of the sequence. On the hundred and first occasion my hand does not encounter my key, and I find myself locked out. Instantly I am acutely conscious of the problem. Is the janitor around? Where is my roommate? Can a window be entered? All these trial solutions rush to mind, and from this conscious welter some decision emerges to solve the problem.

As William James put it, consciousness seems to have evolved in order to regulate a nervous system grown too top-heavy to regulate itself.

But is all this regulation merely in the service of an id whose "structure never changes"? It seems most unlikely. Our conscious choices leave traces; they build up a self-image, they form a generic conscience, they construct new systems of interest. The ego, formed in this fashion, becomes relatively autonomous of the id.

Like other writers I have been critical of Freud's depreciation of the role of consciousness, but there is residual truth in his formulation—especially in accounting for neurotic trends in personality that are often due to unconscious motives and unconscious conflicts.

The Neurotic and the Normal

There are some who argue that we are all neurotic, that no person is normal, that there are only degrees of acceptability to others. If I manage my relationships so that others do not avoid me or commit me to a hospital or prison, then I am said to be normal. According to this view everyone has neurotic, criminal, or even psychotic bents; everyone is a bit crazy, though some are less objectionable than others.

This view is consistent with the Freudian position, for Freud felt that psychoanalysis offered the "entire foundation" for the science of psychology. He felt that his formulations were not confined to "morbid processes," but characterized all human mental life.[13] It is precisely this position that we challenge. Freud was a clinician who worked year in and year out with disordered personalities. His insights are more applicable to these cases than to personalities marked by healthy functioning.

Unlike the normal person, the neurotic is not able to work out

13 See Hall, *op. cit.,* p. 12. Note 8.

the balanced give-and-take required for sound friendship, for smooth relations at work, and for domestic felicity. Instead of balance we find a compulsive imbalance. The neurotic is demanding and possessive, jealous and self-pitying, hysteric and accusatory; he (she) may develop physical ("conversion") symptoms: ulcers, eczema, functional deafness, lameness, even paralysis. Although disorders of love life are often, perhaps always, involved, there are also other fierce but unguided motives in the neurotic pattern: hate, fear, resentment. The truest and most general statement about the neuroses seems to be that they are a reflection of uncontrolled self-centeredness. Someone has said that the neurotic will do anything to be loved except to make himself (herself) lovable.

Without assistance no neurotic fully understands the roots of his unhappy behavior. It may be that he is suffering from a bad start in life. Harsh memories, unwelcome impulses are repressed and cut off from the integrative channels of growth. Although we cannot rule out the possibility that certain constitutions are inherently "weak" and thus tend to develop hysterical splits and to lack a capacity for firm integration, it is probably true that neurotic tendencies are due chiefly to poor mental hygiene—to wrong child training, to a failure to confront one's needs, impulses, and ideas with reality. Here we are agreeing with Freud.

Now all of us have had rough spots in our histories. Are we not all, therefore, to some degree neurotic? Perhaps, but there is still a great gulf between lives that are *on the whole* well integrated and balanced (in spite of minor neurotic threads) and lives that are dominated by possessive, compulsive, badly understood conflicts. Normal people may be selfish, anxious, and demanding. It is not the quality of an act that makes it neurotic. The distinction lies rather in the automatic, compulsive, dissociated character of neurotic conduct.

The distinction between normal and neurotic does not hinge on whether something is good or bad, clean or dirty, selfish or generous, courageous or fearful, guilty or virtuous, constructive or destructive, implying activity or indolence, arrogance or penuriousness, ambition or apathy, ruthlessness or gentleness, conformity or rebellion, success or failure. It is not the value which attaches to the act nor its frequency or rarity which determines whether the act is healthy or neurotic. Whether any act is healthy or neurotic depends only upon the nature of the constellation of forces which determines it. If those forces . . . are of such a nature that they *predetermine the automatic repetition of the act, irrespective of any considerations,* then that act is a neurotic act and the forces which determine it are neurotogenic. This is the essence of that which is psychopathological in human behavior.[14]

Thus a true neurosis is dominated largely by the unconscious. Inappropriate acts persist "irrespective of any considerations." The act is usually self-defeating, as in the case of an overly possessive mother who succeeds only in driving her children away from her. The normal person, by contrast, can usually balance his impulses and conform to all relevant considerations: suiting his act to appropriate time and place, using appropriate means, and relating the act to the standards of his own conscience and to the convenience of others.

This is a point of deep importance for our theory of motivation. A neurotic system of motivation is blind, largely unconscious, automatic, and disconnected from the remainder of the life. For these reasons it is usually self-defeating. Its origin probably lies in early life, and though its effects endure in later years, it has an infantile flavor. Normal motivation, by contrast, is flexible, largely conscious, and "at age." Normal motivation breaks its ties with early life. It is "functionally autonomous" (Chapter 10). The archaic id structure does not prevail.

A diagram adapted from Kubie (Figure 17) represents the wide difference that exists between lives ordered largely by conscious plans, purposes, and intentions (autonomous ego) and lives driven primarily by unconscious compulsions and neurotic formations.

The diagram calls attention to the presence of the preconscious in all lives. It suggests that this region of available memories is especially important in creativity. The creativeness of the normal person depends more on the cooperation of the preconscious and the conscious than is the case with neurotics, where the unconscious enters more compulsively and in larger proportions.

The diagram also recognizes a continuous series of personalities from those almost completely dominated by their conscious purposes and in continuous contact with reality, through personalities with less insight and less integration and somewhat more dominated by both preconscious and unconscious functions, to the clearly abnor-

---

[14] L. S. Kubie, The neurotic process as the focus of physiological and psychoanalytic research, *J. ment. Sci.,* 1958, **104,** 518–536.

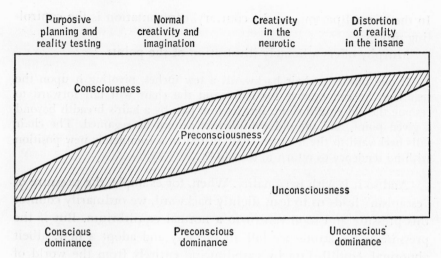

| Purposive planning and reality testing | Normal creativity and imagination | Creativity in the neurotic | Distortion of reality in the insane |

Consciousness

Preconsciousness

Unconsciousness

| Conscious dominance | Preconscious dominance | Unconscious dominance |

Figure 17. Varying Proportions of Conscious and Unconscious Dominance in Personalities (adapted from Kubie)

mal cases whose lives are more and more controlled by dissociated and unconscious systems.

Now in one sense this hypothesis of strict *continuity* between the normal and the abnormal is acceptable. A strong point in its favor is the existence of borderline cases. There are in our midst mild neurotics, semipsychotics, borderline paranoiacs (suspicious personalities), and the like. Descriptively, then, we can say that normality-abnormality is a matter of degree.

But this unbroken continuum is one of *symptoms,* not of *processes.* The processes making for normality and for abnormality are very different. Let us take an example. To *confront* the world and its problems is intrinsically a wholesome thing to do, since it brings about appropriate adjustment and mastery. To *escape* from the world is intrinsically a dangerous and diseased thing to do. Extreme escape is found in the most severe forms of mental disorder, the psychosis. But now, you ask, do we not all do some escaping? Yes— and what is more, we may obtain recreation from it and find our daydreams eventually constructive. But such harmless and even beneficial results can come about *only if the dominant process is confrontation.* Left to itself, escapism spells abnormality. In the psychotic (and in some neurotics) this process has the upper hand.

In the normal person, on the contrary, confrontation is the controlling process.

Murphy offers a homely illustration of the point:

If one pushes a chair backwards a few inches, pivoting it upon the rear legs, he can remove his hand and the chair will fall forward to resume the old equilibrium. But let him pass by a hair's breadth beyond a given point, and the old equilibrium cannot be regained. The chair falls backward to the floor, to come to rest in a completely new position with no tendency to return to the old.[15]

And so it is with personality. When, for example, the pressure of "escapism" leads us to lean slightly backward, we ordinarily counter this pressure and soon return to a normal equilibrium. But if the pressure is too strong we fall all the way and adopt a new, albeit abnormal, equilibrium by withdrawing entirely from the world of reality.

Let us list some of the processes which *intrinsically* make for abnormality and for normality:

Making for abnormality	*Making for normality*
escapism (fantasy)	confrontation (reality testing)
ineffective repression (with troublesome aftereffect)	effective repression (total exclusion of unwanted impulses and thoughts; see page 158)
self-deception	self-insight
disintegration (dissociation)	integration (progressive organization)
narrowing thinking to concrete adjustments	abstraction (ability to think *about* things)
uncontrolled impulsivity	frustration tolerance
fixation at juvenile level	autonomy appropriate to age and experience

Why do we label the second list as "normal" processes? The reason is simply that these modes of functioning, and others like them, produce continuous flexible development within the per-

15 G. Murphy, *Personality: a biosocial approach to origins and structure* (New York: Harper, 1947), p. 85.

sonality. The "abnormal" processes, taken by themselves, lead to a rigid and closed mode of existence, and to an arrest in the process of individuation and becoming. It is true that all judgments concerning normality, health, soundness, maturity involve a value-standard. Philosophers would caution us that it is not easy to prove, for example, that confrontation is "better" than escape from reality. But everyone seems to agree in general that it is. We return to the question of the criteria for the normal and mature personality in Chapter 12.

To sum up, Freud, for all his merits, has smudged the boundary line between neurotic and normal mental functioning. He has done so by postulating (in all people) an unconscious heavily laden with antisocial impulses and repressions. The counterforce, the ego, is regarded as essentially weak and secondary (in all people). My point of view is considerably different. People who are relatively sound and healthy have a far more active and autonomous ego than Freud allows (although many of his followers are now conceding the point). The normal processes of growth and becoming are, in the main, neglected in Freud's theories of personality. Although traces of neurotic traits and mechanisms may be found in many healthy people, these threads are minor as compared with the sturdier weave of wholesome growth.

Mechanisms of Defense

It is not necessary to accept Freud's theories of motivation and of the unconscious in order to appreciate his brilliant account of the protective strategies we all employ in order to guard our self-esteem. Self-love and pride are universal in human nature, even though in mature personalities they are not necessarily sovereign. Every day we experience grave threats to our self-esteem: we feel inferior, guilty, insecure, unloved. Not only big things but little things put us in the wrong: we trip up in an examination, we make a social boner, we dress inappropriately for an occasion. The ego sweats. We suffer discomfort, perhaps anxiety, and we hasten to repair the narcissistic wound.

The mechanisms of ego-defense (Freud's term) are sly devices by which we try to circumvent discomfort and anxiety. These self-protective strategies are common, but they do not by any means constitute the normal person's entire repertoire of adjustive actions. Often he faces up to his weaknesses and failings, and proceeds to cope with them realistically. He meets his guilt, his fears, his blunders head on, and works out a way of life that fully and consciously takes them into account and makes of them building blocks for a more integrated personal edifice. The opposite of *defense,* then, is *coping.* The neurotic shows much defense, less coping. In the healthy personality coping ordinarily predominates.

Many philosophers prior to Freud have dealt with our human tendency to sidestep or prettify our failings—among them Hobbes, Nietzsche, Bentham—but to Freud goes the credit for permanently inscribing this chapter in the science of psychology.

What is the nature of this pervasive self-protective motive? Older philosophers were wont to say, "Self-defense is nature's oldest law," or, "By whatever name we call the ruling tyrant, self is all in all." For Freud it is a matter of the ego defending itself against anxiety. Among psychologists Koffka speaks of "a force which propels the ego upward."[16] McDougall finds at the center of every personality a sentiment of self-regard which plays "the most powerful all-pervasive role in the higher life of man."[17] Psychoanalysts speak of "basic narcissism." In the previous chapter we gave an important role to "self-esteem," although we pointed out that it is only one of the propriate functions of personality.

What are some of the chief strategies of ego-defense? Freud rightly gives first place to repression.

Repression. The individual frequently denies conscious outlet to unwelcome wishes and thoughts. "Everything contradictory to the ruling tendencies of the conscious personality, to its wishes, longings and ideals, and everything which would disturb the good opinion one likes to have of oneself is apt to be repressed."[18]

Repression has first place on our list because all other mechanisms of defense seem to depend on it in one way or another. If all our wishes, memories, and conflicts were fully available to consciousness we would normally employ *coping* rather than defense. It is precisely because we find coping too difficult that we resort to re-

16 K. Koffka, *Principles of Gestalt psychology* (New York: Harcourt, Brace, 1935), pp. 670 ff.
17 W. McDougall, *Energies of men* (New York: Scribner, 1933), p. 233.
18 F. Alexander, *The medical value of psychoanalysis* (New York: Norton, 1932), p. 79.

pression. And when the true nature of the conflict is no longer clearly understood we are ripe for new strategies of self-deception.

To take an example, deans and departmental chairmen in colleges are often astonished by the number of academically deficient students who "forget" that they have received letters of warning about their college work. To them the threat of separation from college is unwelcome and the simplest thing to do is to repress the thought. Having conveniently "forgotten" the threat the student is then free to have a good time, and also to build up his self-esteem in a variety of minor ways. He can excuse his previous failures, blame his instructors, rationalize his laziness— until the tragic reality finally catches up with him. Even if he has not really forgotten the warning, he has at least dulled its significance and assured himself that it was for some reason not applicable to him.

Denial. Even if one does not actually forget a threat, one may still deny its existence.[19] A common example occurs after the sudden news of a catastrophe or a bereavement. We are likely to say and believe, at least for the time being, "It just can't be so."

A child of three was told that his mother was to have another baby. His jealousy aroused, the child said, "No baby," and kept repeating this formula for many weeks. When the infant arrived he persisted in overlooking its presence, and still kept up his chant, "No baby, no baby."

Let us return to the theory of repression. Sometimes the attempt to repress is ineffective, but sometimes it succeeds. In the neuroses it is ineffective for it causes compulsive and not-understood behavior. But there is another kind of repression which is wholly benign, serving well the normal function of coping. Every day we deliberately suppress much material, banishing what is not useful and what does not square with our chosen style of life—and we suffer no ill consequences.

[19] Anna Freud, *The ego and the mechanisms of defence* (New York: Int. Univ. Press, 1946), Chap. 7.

An experiment illustrates the point. McGranahan warned his subjects that they would receive an electric shock if they gave the name of any color in a word-association test. A person who could not inhibit the tendency to say "green" to the stimulus-word "grass" was given an uncomfortable shock. The experimenter, by the very nature of his negative instructions, was in effect inviting a mental set for color, but he was also asking the subjects to repress this set. Most of his subjects had no difficulty with the task. They suppressed the color set by adopting a non-color set. Thus, they might set themselves to give superordinate terms, or synonyms, or contrasting words. By adopting a safe mental set, they avoided the dangerous and unwanted set. They repressed it, and the repression was all to the good.[20] They escaped the shock. Others, however, could not effectively suppress the tabooed idea of color, even though repeatedly punished by receiving an unpleasant shock.

Repression, then, is the process of excluding from consciousness all or part of a conflict situation. (If the process is deliberate, as in this experiment, we speak of *suppression;* if not deliberate, of *repression.*) When the suppression or repression serves the interests of coping by banishing irrelevant and unwanted impulses and memories, it is benign. Sometimes, however, as we have seen, the banishment is unhealthy; suppressed impulses and memories continue to disturb the personality. The flaming wastebasket cannot safely be put into a closet and the door closed.[21]

Rationalization. The term *rationalization* applies broadly to any form of self-deception.[22] It is an absurdity of the English language

20 D. V. McGranahan, A critical and experimental study of repression, *J. abnorm. soc. Psychol.*, 1940, **35**, 212–225. See also L. Belmont and H. G. Birch, Re-individualizing the repression hypothesis, *J. abnorm. soc. Psychol.*, 1951, **46**, 226–235.

21 Although Freud himself was much more concerned with ineffective and unhealthy repression than with benign, he does not deny the possibility that unwelcome wishes may be "actually destroyed or annulled." Not every impulse lingers in the unconscious. See E. Jones, *The life and work of Sigmund Freud* (New York: Basic Books, 1957), III, 259.

22 The term was first used in 1908 by Ernest Jones, Rationalisation in every-day life, *J. abnorm. Psychol.*, 1908, **3**, 161–169. The process itself, however, has been recognized under many names: *fictions* and *fallacies* (Bentham), *ideology* (Mannheim), *derivations* (Pareto), *hypocrisy* (Le Dantec), *myth, folklore, thobbing,* and the like. See G. W. Allport, Historical background of modern social psychology. In G. Lindzey (Ed.), *Handbook of social psychology* (Cambridge, Mass.: Addison-Wesley, 1954), Vol. I, Chap. 1.

that the term signifies the *opposite* of "rational" or "reason." Reason
is the capacity to shape one's belief and conduct to accord with one's
knowledge of the world, and if one's knowledge is insufficient, the
capacity to acquire more knowledge pertinent to the issue in hand.
Reason fits one's impulses and beliefs to the world of reality; rationalization fits one's concept of reality to one's impulses and beliefs. As someone has said, reasoning discovers *real* reasons, rationalization *good* reasons for what we do.

In one experiment people were confronted with uncomplimentary
opinions about themselves. Sometimes they were told that a stranger gave
a harsh judgment of them, sometimes that a friend did so. A few people
took this information to heart and seriously considered whether they
ought not revise their own self-judgments in a downward direction. But
more frequently they saved face through rationalization. The stranger,
they said, "is a poor judge of people," or "he just doesn't know me." The
friend gave more trouble; but some people claimed, "He couldn't have
said that," or "He really meant something different." And after a time
many subjects distorted their memories of what the friend had said, and
reported that the judgment was more favorable than in fact it was.[23]

Rationalizations range from the trivial to the grandiose. On impulse we jump to justify our misdeeds. As Emerson said, "That
which we call sin in others is experiment for us." Our irritability or
laziness we readily blame on the heat or the humidity. When our
child breaks a neighbor's window we minimize the deed by calling
it "kid stuff." A dozen times a day we find ways of defending our
good opinion of ourselves and our families.

At a more complex level we build up elaborate fictions and
ideologies. According to Lotze, a man's philosophical creed is more
often than not an attempt to justify a fundamental view of things
adopted once for all early in life. Belief in the innate inferiority of
the Negro is a comfortable rationalization for white people whose
self-esteem and economic advantage depend on keeping Negroes "in
their place." One historian has gone so far as to say that nearly all of
the writing of the past in social sciences, politics, and ethics "may
be brushed aside by future generations as mainly rationalizing."[24]

But this line of thinking becomes dangerous. To reduce all
theory to rationalization cuts the ground from under us all. Is Dar-

[23] O. J. Harvey, H. H. Kelley, and M. M. Shapiro, Reactions to unfavorable evaluations
of self made by other persons, *J. Pers.*, 1957, **25**, 393–411.
[24] J. H. Robinson, *The mind in the making* (New York: Harper, 1921), p. 47.

win's theory of the survival of the fittest a mere rationalization of nineteenth-century cutthroat economic competition? Is Freudian psychology nothing more than a rationalization of his "decadent, sex-ridden" life? Was Kant's emphasis on the role of reason only a comforting escape from his lack of success in his emotional and active life? One may admit that thinking is often tendentious without concluding that it never has objective validity. Reason transcends rationalization; its function is to distinguish the false from the true; and unless we believe this fact we cannot hope to establish a science of psychology—or of anything else. Rationalization is certainly common in human thought, but its role should not be exaggerated.

Projection. The important defense mechanism of projection is a special type of rationalization. It is basically the form of self-deception wherein one ascribes one's own unwelcome thoughts, wishes, and shortcomings to another person.

If we can blame others we are saved from the pain of blaming ourselves. Somehow we feel especially righteous and free from sin when we comfortably talk about our own shortcomings in others. Do I tell lies? Well, look at Tony. He is an inveterate liar! This particular form of projection Ichheiser has called the "mote-beam mechanism." The other fellow has evil impulses, so too do I; but thanks to projection I behold only the mote in his eye and overlook the beam in my own.[25]

Sometimes, of course, the other fellow hasn't even a mote—he is wholly innocent. Yet I can "see" my failures in him. An extreme example would be the psychotic who thinks that everyone except himself is crazy. A more common example is groundless gossip which tells nothing true about the victim but a great deal about the inner conflicts of the gossiper.

In *complementary projection* we do not ascribe our own states of mind to others, but rather ascribe to them motives and behavior that would explain (or complement) our own distress.[26] The timid child thinks that the dog, or the boy next door, or the Chinese laundryman has aggressive designs against him. The paranoiac believes that others are plotting his destruction. Through complemen-

---

[25] G. Ichheiser, Projection and the mote-beam mechanism, *J. abnorm. soc. Psychol.,* 1947, **42**, 131–133.
[26] Cf. G. W. Allport, *The nature of prejudice* (Cambridge, Mass.: Addison-Wesley, 1954), Chap. 24.

tary projection our fears, guilt, or worries receive an "explanation." Do I feel depressed? Well, it is because other people don't treat me fairly.

Displacement is a special form of projection. A disgruntled workman is much irritated by his foreman, but he can neither retaliate nor directly cope with the issue; and so at night he vents his annoyance on his wife and children. Bottled-up humiliations for defeat in World War I, plus an array of social disorders and personal conflicts, led Nazi Germany to make scapegoats of the Jews. It is particularly interesting that Hitler's bill of particulars against the Jews contained the very items of which he himself was guilty (greed for power, warmongering, sexual perversion). Prejudice against minority groups often takes the form of blaming Jews, Negroes, politicians—almost any group—for frustrations in our own lives. It seems easier to blame them than to seek out and cope with true causes.[27]

Fixation and Regression. A not infrequent defense mechanism is to avoid being one's true age. No one expects much from a baby, a child, or a young person. And so the child may remain babyish, the young person childish, and the adult adolescent in behavior. This infantile drag betokens an attempt to avoid the responsibilities appropriate to one's age.

In times of crisis some people regress. The bride who finds married life too exacting may return to her mother. The husband, not fully mature, confronts his wife with a recital of his own mother's virtues as cook, homemaker, comforter. Temper tantrums in an adult are regressive in nature.

Neurasthenia (habitual invalidism), too, may be a regressive self-protection. If I am ill no one can expect me to cope with my problems at an adult level. Imaginary invalidism thus becomes a safe defense.

Reaction Formation. Reaction formation is an odd form of defense. To hide the source of conflict from others and even from himself, a person may vigorously pretend the exact opposite to what he feels. He does not hate his offspring, but loves them passionately; he is not fearful, but an adventurous daredevil. Extreme priggishness may be a reaction formation to hide lewd impulses. A mother who dislikes her child may actually smother it with devotion. "Usu-

27 *Ibid.*, Chap. 21.

ally a reaction formation is marked by extravagant showiness—the person protests too much—and by compulsiveness."[28]

Sublimation. In Freudian theory the process by which repressed instinctual impulses are expressed in socially and personally acceptable channels is called *sublimation.* Since sex and aggression cannot often be expressed directly they remain as "aim-inhibited wishes," and they seek substitute outlets. By becoming a nurse a woman may sublimate her desire for maternity; a boys' club leader may by this activity sublimate repressed homosexuality; a surgeon sublimates his repressed sadism by carving people in a socially approved way. The poet finds that he can "chew and suck beautiful lines" rather than his mother's breast. Psychoanalysis says that such adult interests as these are "transparent substitutions" for the true (but now unconscious) wishes that the individual harbors.

Although there may be occasional (neurotic) cases that fit such formulation, the doctrine of sublimation implies far too much. It implies that all our mature desires are nothing more than a "cover up" for repressed instinctual wishes. The primary process remains supreme, the structure of the id never changes, and what we regard as a mature socialized person is little more than a wolf in sheep's clothing. In Chapters 9 and 10 I shall argue further against this false picture of adult motivation.[29]

Compensation. The concept of compensation, which we discussed earlier, is Adlerian and not Freudian. It does, however, overlap the present discussion of defense mechanisms. Compensation is a counteractive measure taken against a person's feelings of inferiority. Some compensations, however, are clearly of the coping variety. Demosthenes the orator, Roosevelt the Rough Rider, the immigrant who became a tycoon are all instances of compensation by coping. The nonathletic youth who substitutes brains for brawn is also manifesting coping rather than defense. But many compensations are genuine instances of ego-defense. Daydreams, bluster and

[28] Hall and Lindzey, *op. cit.,* p. 50. Note 11, above.

[29] For a more detailed analysis of the concept of sublimation see G. W. Allport, *Personality: a psychological interpretation* (New York: Holt, Rinehart and Winston, 1937), p. 185. In replying to this critique Sappenfield argues that Freud's conception of sexuality can be broadly interpreted to cover all instances of positive cathexis (satisfaction of the person as a whole), and that in this sense all forms of adult motivation are genuine sublimations. B. R. Sappenfield, *Personality dynamics* (New York: Knopf, 1954), pp. 356–362. It is a serious question whether Freud's concept of sexuality can with propriety be so far extended.

bullying, sour-grapes and sweet-lemon rationalizations, neurasthenic invalidism can with perfect propriety be considered to be both compensations and instances of ego-defense.

Summary

There are various ways of viewing the structure of personality in terms of layers or strata. This approach has been particularly fashionable in postwar German theory. Most, but not all, strata theories postulate a less stable level of consciousness and conscious control, various intermediate levels (e.g., the co- or preconscious), and an unconscious layer viewed as the seat of instinctual life forces as well as of buried and nonavailable memories.

The most famous of the strata doctrines is Freud's. It includes not only a theory of the structure of human personality, but an immensely influential theory of motivation as well. It is offered as a basic system of psychology for all personality theorists to follow. It is even more audacious, for it argues a bold philosophical conception of the nature of man.

Criticisms of Freud are directed chiefly at his picture of a relatively passive ego. A person's conscious life, he holds, has no energy of its own; it is by nature merely a servant of the id. Many psychoanalysts have turned away from this one-sided emphasis and have introduced an "ego-psychology." There is also a serious question whether the unconscious is furnished as exclusively as Freud depicts with antisocial impulses and destructive thoughts.

In general the Freudian theory seems best to fit certain types of neurotic disorder, but falls short as a formula for the healthy personality. In order to establish this point we have found it necessary to argue that normality and abnormality are not governed by the same developmental processes. Although there is a continuity of symptoms between the normal and the abnormal, there is a discontinuity between balancing and unbalancing mechanisms. In normal people balancing mechanisms have the upper hand; in neurotics and psychotics they do not.

Freud has given us a helpful analysis of ego-defense mechanisms: repression, denial, rationalization, projection, displacement, fixation, regression, and reaction formation. These concepts are of value in understanding our strategies for guarding our own self-esteem.

To accept and employ these aids we need not subscribe to the full Freudian dogma concerning structure and motivation. Sublimation is a concept of doubtful value.

Ego-defense mechanisms are present in all personalities. When they have the upper hand we are dealing with a badly disordered life. Normal persons employ them more sparingly and often with a corrective measure of self-insight and humor.

CHAPTER 8

Culture, Situation, Role

"Real Culture" and the "Culture Construct" • Culture and Personality • Acculturation of the Child • Basic Personality • Situation • Role • Catastrophic Social Change • Individual Structure and Collective Structure • Summary

Everyone admits that culture is vastly important in shaping personality. No Australian aborigine could have a personality like that of an American businessman. A Viennese is unlike a Vietnamese, and both are unlike a Venetian. Could anyone confuse an African with an *Afrikaner?* Even differences in subcultures make for great differences in personality. A dirt farmer in the Bible belt has little resemblance to a beat denizen of the art colony. A Negro cotton picker is unlike a Negro professor. The personalities of a cinema star and of a schoolteacher are seldom alike.

The impact of culture is so indisputable that some writers regard it as the *all*-important factor. We read many assertions to this effect: "Apart from sociocultural life there are organisms or psychobiological egos but not persons." "The factor of acculturation makes a person out of a human organism." "Personality cannot be ripped out of its [cultural] setting except by a type of surgery that will kill the patient."[1] And on page 24 we saw that one type of definition sees personality as nothing more than "the subjective side of culture." These enthusiastic cultural statements have merit, though they seem to us overzealous.

"Real Culture" and the "Culture Construct"

It is vital to observe a distinction drawn by Linton.[2] *Real culture* is flexible. Although it prescribes limits for personal behavior and broad guidelines for the developing personality, it allows a wide range of freedom. Every native-born American, for example, speaks English, but a wide array of accents and degrees of expertness is allowed. In most societies every man and woman is clothed in public, although latitude for personal choice of garments is permitted. In some countries every child is required to attend school for a minimum period of time, although he may continue far beyond this minimum. There is, then, factually a wide range of acceptable conduct within the cultural mold. The result is, therefore, the creation of only broad and approximate resemblances among different members of the same culture.

The *culture construct* pays no attention to the range of acceptable conduct. It tells us only what is the usual, the common, i.e., the modal, practice. The German culture, we say, is technologically efficient (but in reality, many individual Germans are not). The Navaho culture, we say, has a belief in witchcraft (but the intensity of belief will vary from person to person, and some will be wholly devoid of such belief). America, we say, prizes democracy (but plenty of practices are undemocratic). In short, a "culture construct" is an oversimplification. It gives the essence of a pattern, but in truth not every personality is fitted to the stencil.

Now this distinction is of great importance. The historian, the anthropologist, the sociologist will justifiably emphasize the culture construct. Their interest does not lie in the fate of any single individual. It is the culture system as such that concerns them. While persons are born and die, a society or a culture goes on. For the

---

[1] These statements can be traced in S. S. Sargent and M. W. Smith (Eds.), *Culture and personality* (New York: Viking Fund, 1949), pp. 17, 41 f.
[2] R. Linton, *The cultural background of personality* (New York: Appleton-Century-Crofts, 1945), p. 46.

survival of a sociocultural system no particular individual is important. And yet for the psychologist the individual is all-important. The abstract culture concept seems remote, and even misleading, from the psychologist's point of view. No individual is a mirror-image of the modal or average culture pattern. We are molded by *real* culture and not by the anthropologist's distilled image of it. To apply this image directly to people is to falsify the diversity of personality found within any single culture.

Now it is true that for some societies the culture construct comes closer to matching the real culture than in other societies. So-called primitive societies, for example, stress tribal solidarity, uniformity of behavior, and strict obedience to cultural forms more than do societies of the Western tradition. In the Western pattern emphasis is actually placed on the separateness of the individual. We assign our children to separate seats in school (not to a communal bench); give them individual plates and cups at mealtime, distinctive clothing, separate sleeping arrangements. We *want* them to become different from others—but not *too* different. In this particular case a modal trait of the culture construct of the West (prizing individuality) relates closely to the real cultural latitude that exists. Also, in rigid primitive societies the culture construct and real culture are not far apart. Yet it is still true that "the culture" which ethnologists describe is almost invariably an oversimplification of the facts —justifiable for certain purposes, but misleading so far as the study of individual personality is concerned.

Culture and Personality

Culture shapes personality chiefly because it provides ready made, pretested solutions to many of life's problems. Out of his own life experience a child could hardly be expected to invent a language or a scheme of medical treatment; he could not evolve a science, an ethics, or an embracing religion. He must rely on the experience of his race. Culture offers him stored-up solutions—not always accurate but at least available. Culture has an answer (sometimes merely rough and ready) to every question that can be asked. It is a prearranged design for living.

For example, take episodes that occur too seldom for the individual to benefit from personal experience. He ordinarily marries

only once in a lifetime. The formula for marriage (and the prescription of monogamy) is laid down for him. His marriage license,
the authorities who may perform the ceremony, even the smallest
details of wedding etiquette are prescribed. True, in the real culture
he has some latitude of choice, but only within the permitted cultural framework. Another example: most people see a total eclipse
of the sun not more than once in a lifetime. Their culture determines how they shall view the phenomenon, whether with a superstitious or a scientific orientation.

Culture is in part a set of inventions that have arisen in various
parts of the world (or with subgroups of populations) to make life
efficient and intelligible for mortals who struggle with the same basic
problems of life: birth, growth, death, the pursuit of health, welfare,
and meaning. The solutions are passed on from one generation to
another.

It would not be quite accurate to say that a culture is nothing but
a set of devices for meeting individual needs. It does, of course,
fulfill this function, telling us, for example, how to satisfy (without
conflict with our fellows) the needs for food, for excretion, for mating, for affiliative relations with others. It tells us how to handle our
need for recreation and for self-esteem, and our sorrow after bereavement. But in time culture also becomes a "way of life." We
come to love the practices and the values and the interpretations we
have learned from our culture. We desire (and need) the Hopi way,
the Italian way, or the American way. At first culture is an instrument that trains us and satisfies our needs. Gradually it becomes a
value in its own right, and our love and loyalty to our culture are a
prime, autonomous motive whose force we feel most keenly when we
are deprived of our cultural anchorage.[3] We come to say to ourselves, "This is the only way I can live." Thus our culture, at least
those features that we "interiorize," may become motivational in
our lives.

Of course, we do not mean that every feature of every culture
comes to be loved by its members. Many cultural practices remain
peripheral habits for the person, residing not in the propriate but in
the outer layers of personality (page 141). Perhaps it is only our own

[3] Chapter 10 develops the theory of functional autonomy. See also Dorothy Lee, Are
basic needs ultimate? In C. Kluckhohn, H. A. Murray, and D. M. Schneider, *Personality: in nature, society, and culture* (New York: Knopf, 1953), Chap. 20.

private culture construct that we have in mind when we say that we love the Hopi, the Italian, or the American way.

In terms of real culture what seems to happen is that the individual, according to his temperament and evolving sense of self, selects from the "tolerable range" allowed by his culture the features that fit best his own style of life. He may, of course, find that almost every feature suits him; if so he becomes a full-blown conformist, a true stencil copy. Many people, on the other hand, deviate in practice and thought from cultural models and conform only within necessary limits. Some, of course, are total misfits and rebels. Most of us lie between the extremes.

It is interesting to recall that Mahatma Gandhi vigorously endorsed many Hindu cultural values and taught them faithfully. Among these were the dream of independence for India, traditional piety, self-discipline through yoga, home industry, and the like. But he forcibly opposed Indian culture in respect to its expensive pageantries and its caste system.

Acculturation of the Child

The human infant could not survive at all if he depended on his own instincts and abilities. More than any other type of organism he is dependent on the good will and help of others. A baby monkey can cling tenaciously to its neglectful mother while the latter swings from tree to tree. If the baby hangs on long enough it may receive the attention it needs. But the human infant can't even cling.

Since the young child has few native resources for survival, it is, unlike other organisms, a completely dependent prisoner of its culture. The mother carries out cultural practices in tending the baby's needs. The home situation, the language he learns, the school, the economic practices, and the prescriptions for eating, sleeping, excreting—all impose cultural demands. True, the child grows "from within" (there is no other way to grow), but his models for learning are all outside himself. Early he begins to learn the values of his culture. Many of them are taught repeatedly—at home, by the church and school, through newspapers, comics, on the radio and television. No child can escape the common heritage. A cultural value is a way of life deemed desirable by most members of a society.

It is important to note that the adoption of cultural models comes about chiefly in the earlier years of life. Individuation and rebellion come later. Revers proposes that we regard the process of acculturation as occurring in three stages: (1) adoption of the cultural model, (2) reaction against this model, (3) an incorporation of the revised model as a firsthand fitting of the mature personality.[4] We may illustrate these stages by referring to one familiar cultural pattern, handwriting:

A six-year-old will laboriously copy letters or numbers as precisely as he can from his copybook or from his teacher's blackboard model. His graphic production has virtually no individuality. The written papers on the classroom display board are almost all alike. The young children are, in respect to handwriting, prisoners of their culture. Toward puberty true individuality in handwriting begins to appear. By now the child has mastered the cultural forms; they are second nature to him. He begins to take liberties with them (always within limits). His formation of letters, slant, embellishments are his own. Occasionally his script becomes negativistic toward the culture, to the point of sheer illegibility. All this experimentation need not be conscious, but it clearly violates the original cultural model. Finally, the graphic style settles down, and hereafter displays what Revers calls a "revised cultural model"—adapted to the individuality of the person. Handwriting is simply one example of the compromise we all reach between cultural obedience and individual integrity.

The same stages are seen in virtually all departments of life. Everyone knows the rigid "moral realism" of the child between approximately five and ten years of age. Every story must be told in the same "right" way; every game must be played according to rule; the tribal ("must") conscience reigns supreme. Everyone knows, too, about the rebelliousness of adolescents in respect to parental and social mores. The adolescent begins to question, among other things, the culturally taught religion, although in his younger years he accepted it as final. To find one's individual identity is more important than to conform to tradition. Finally, in adulthood, there is

[4] W. J. Revers, Vorbilder persönlichen Werdens, Sinnbilder menschlichen Seins, *Jahrb. f. Psychol. u. Psychother.*, 1955, 1, 26–36.

ordinarily a successful blending of the traditional and the personal, of culture and self-image.[5]

We have been speaking as if culture were a uniform succession of influences acting alike on all members of a group. Such a picture is false, for even within close-knit communities the influence may vary. At school you will have one teacher, I another; you will read one book, I a different book. Even children in the same family are subjected to different expectations and treatments. For the son some aspects of culture are accented, for the daughter others are given weight. Oldest, middle, and younger children, because of their position in the family constellation, receive different social influences.[6] The impact of real culture is not monolithic; it is selective depending on the person whom it strikes and the conditions that prevail.

Nonetheless children *do* learn their culture (defined so as to allow for the "real" variability that occurs). And in a given society they learn approximately the same cultural ways (but never exactly). How they learn them is an infinitely subtle matter. Every one of the principles we examined in Chapter 5 is relevant to the process. Certain principles, however (for example, *identification*), have been specially pointed out as methods by which the relatively uniform acculturation of young children in a given society takes place.

Basic Personality

A traveler made the following observation. Leaving the United States on an American ship, he found that among the passengers were many children. The children roamed everywhere; they had the run of the ship, and no one seemed to mind. Sitting in his

[5] These stages are described for the religious sentiment in G. W. Allport, *The individual and his religion* (New York: Macmillan, 1950), Chaps. 2 and 3.
[6] Cf. R. Stagner, *Psychology of personality* (Rev. ed.; New York: McGraw-Hill, 1948), Chaps. 18 and 19; and W. Toman, Family constellation as a basic personality determinant, *J. indiv. Psychol.*, 1959, 15, 199–211.
We are not in this chapter distinguishing precisely between *cultural* and *social* influence, nor between cultural systems and social systems. A more detailed analysis should do so. The *cultural system* contains traditional practices and values that affect persons, whereas the person's interaction with others in carrying out these values creates *social systems*. Thus traditional religion is a fact of the cultural system, whereas the interaction of clergy and parishioners in a given parish comprises a social system. The third system, personality, is analytically distinct from both, although at countless points there is intersection of all three systems. Cf. T. Parsons and E. A. Shils (Eds.), *Toward a general theory of action* (Cambridge, Mass.: Harvard Univ. Press, 1951), pp. 22 f.

deck chair he'd find, as likely as not, a strange youngster climbing into his lap. At a foreign port he changed to a British steamship line. Arriving on deck of the new vessel he encountered a conspicuous sign: "Dogs and children not allowed in this salon." On this ship the children were supervised, controlled, and, from the American point of view, suppressed.

This small fragment of cultural practice, added to others of the kind, leads to the generalization that America has a "child-centered" culture whereas Britain has not. British people often say that Americans let their children run wild, neglect their manners, and spoil them. Americans may say that the British bring up their children to be too reticent, inhibited, and class-conscious.

Without taking sides in this argument we point out that steady pressure in the direction of culture pattern must inevitably affect the course of the developing personality, and lead to certain traits that are basic and common in most members of a culture. When the growing individual reaches adulthood he will probably (in some degree) have a personality that reflects the "national character."

The *basic personality type* is defined by Kardiner as "that personality configuration which is shared by the bulk of the society's members as a result of the early experiences which they have in common."[7] The conception assumes

    a. that cultural tradition determines the lessons the parent will teach the child, and the way in which the lessons are taught;
    b. that different cultures have different ways of training the child —and different lessons to teach;
    c. that the child's early experience exerts a lasting effect upon his personality; and
    d. that similar experiences will tend to produce similar personalities within the culture.

The conception implies a cycle which continues from generation to generation in endless circularity. The culture prescribes the goals and method of child training (in general); this early training fashions within the culture a basic personality type (in general), and adults reinforce and continue the cultural tradition which they find habitual and congenial (in general).

7 A. Kardiner, *The psychological frontiers of society* (New York: Columbia Univ. Press, 1945), pp. vi–viii.

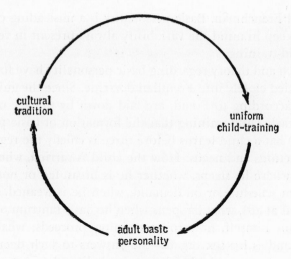

Figure 18. Culture-Personality Cycle

The logic is sound, and helps us to understand why the personalities of the bushman and the American businessman are different. It also helps us to understand why one bushman is similar to another. The scheme, however, fails to account for the differences between individual bushmen, or between individual businessmen. In other words, the formula is only broad and approximate.

Take, for example, the hypothetical case of a French child, Henri. If we know that he is born into a middle-class Parisian family we can predict (approximately) that he will undergo a certain type of training in cleanliness and discipline, in taboos and positive values, in the control of his aggression and in his development of humor, economic habits, and general outlook.

Now when Henri is grown we may think of him as a typical Frenchman—as animated, domestic, penny-wise, an ardent lover, as possessing, in short, all the traits of the French "national character."

The trouble here is that we confuse real culture with the cultural construct. We forget that Henri's training will not conform exactly to the model of the construct, and that the end-product of his personality will be affected by his innate temperament and selective experience so that he may end quite unlike the stereotype (construct) of a typical Frenchman. Basic personality is a misleading conception unless we keep in mind the variability always present in real culture and in child-training.

Research and theory regarding basic personality have for the most part been tied closely into Freudian doctrine. Since the guidelines to character, according to Freud, are laid down by the age of three, it is in very early child-training that the formation of basic personality must lie. What a child learns before three is chiefly the regulation of bodily functions and needs. How the child is carried, whether he is swaddled, where he sleeps, whether he is breast-fed or not, whether he is fed on schedule or on demand, when he is weaned, how he is punished (if at all), what happens when he has a tantrum or when he wets or soils himself, how toilet training proceeds, what happens when he fondles his sex organs—the answers to such detailed questions as these are sought by those who believe basic personality is fashioned in the earliest years. Critics of this approach incline to dismiss it as misguided "diaper anthropology."[8] Probably proponents claim too much for it, opponents too little.

Of course, the concept of basic personality—which leads in turn to the concept of national character—has merit whether or not we follow the psychoanalytic model. Any kind of uniform learning at any stage of life would lead to similarities.

There are a growing number of studies of national character from diverse points of view.[9] But culture does not follow national lines alone. There are cleavages in terms of races, occupations, social classes, none of which follows national boundaries. Class differences have been extensively studied. We know, for example, that children of lower social classes tend to want their gratifications here and now, while those of higher classes have learned to delay their pleasures and satisfactions. The sexual behavior of males with higher education is (on the average) less promiscuous than that of males with a lower degree of education. Negro boys, according to various tests, see the

8 The amount of research on basic personality, mostly from the psychoanalytic point of view, is extensive. Examples are G. Gorer, Themes in Japanese culture, *Trans. N.Y. Acad. Sci.*, 1943, Ser. II, Vol. V, pp. 106–124; G. Gorer and J. Rickman, *People of Great Russia* (London: Cresset, 1949); F. Goldman-Eisler, Breastfeeding and character formation. In Kluckhohn, Murray, Schneider, *op. cit.*, Chap. 11 (Note 3 above); J. Whiting, The cross-cultural method. In G. Lindzey (Ed.), *Handbook of Social Psychology* (Cambridge, Mass.: Addison-Wesley, 1954), Vol. I, Chap. 14.

9 See A. Inkeles and D. Levinson, National character: the study of modal personality and sociocultural systems. In Lindzey, *op. cit.*, Vol. II, Chap. 26.

world as less friendly and more hostile and threatening than do white boys. Other differences between racial and ethnic groups exist, though they turn out to be less than is commonly thought.[10]

One method of studying national or other group differences is to administer tests for attitudes or traits, and in this way determine the differences between the average group scores. Another method is to see how successful we are in predicting an individual's traits solely from our knowledge of his group membership. If we know only that a man is a professional army sergeant we already know a good deal about his personality (in all probability). If we know a woman is an unmarried, middle-aged nurse from a middle-class Protestant mid-western background we can (probably) predict other features of her personality. Experiments show that clinical psychologists do achieve fairly successful predictions merely from their knowledge of the group memberships of their clients.[11]

Enthusiasts for the conception of basic personality or of group (or national) character often use the term "shared." They speak of similarities as due to "shared traits," "shared attitudes," "shared habits," "shared values." They may even speak of "shared person-ality." This is a misleading use of terms. No two army sergeants, or two nurses, or two Englishmen "share" any of their habits, traits, or values. Each is unique in the organization of his personality. At most we can speak of *similarity* or *comparability* in aspects of their person-ality structure.

Situation

Suppose that we place a pound of butter in the refrigerator for a few hours. Then suppose that we take it out and put it in the sun for a few hours. It is the same butter chemically, but its shape and texture are vastly altered by the situation. And so it is with human personality. Any theory that regards personality as stable, fixed, invariable is wrong.

Whenever we act or speak we must decide (perhaps coconsciously) just where we are, what is expected of us, what to avoid, how much of ourselves to disclose, and what the rules of the game are. We do

---

10 For a discussion of the extent and nature of likeness within ethnic groups see G. W. Allport, *The nature of prejudice* (Cambridge, Mass.: Addison-Wesley, 1954), Chap. 6.
11 R. Dymond, Can clinicians predict individual behavior? *J. Pers.*, 1953, **22**, 151–161.

all this automatically and our personalities (at least as perceived by others) vary accordingly.

We never encounter personality apart from some situation. Even when a man breathes, the act involves outer air as well as inner lungs; digesting requires food as well as appetite. What is inner requires something outer in order to create a circuit of behavior. John Dewey has written:

> Honesty, chastity, malice, peevishness, courage, triviality, industry, irresponsibility are not private possessions of a person. They are working adaptations of personal capacities with environing forces.[12]

Dewey adds that it is an easy error to think of personality as a product of "unreal privacy of an unreal self." There is nothing personal that is not at the same time a reflection of the physical, social, and cultural environments.

> A student writes: I don't believe I have any stable traits. On Monday I am dominant, but on Tuesday I encounter a number of petty failures throughout the day. By Wednesday I feel inferior and have become humble and submissive. Likewise I am an autocrat under some sets of external conditions, but an anarchist under other sets. My personal traits are so unstable that I doubt they have any substantial existence.

We recall that William James recognized situational variability when he said that each of us has as many "selves" as there are groups of people whose opinion we prize (page 100 f.).

Sometimes our behavior varies because we choose to speak truly or falsely. If a prospective employer asks Jim, "Do you like to meet strangers?" Jim will probably give an affirmative answer in order to get the job. If his psychiatrist asks the same question Jim may say, "Strangers make me feel nervous and inferior." If a public opinion interviewer asks the same question he may say, "It all depends on the stranger."[13]

> In one polling study (intended to measure anti-Semitism as an attitude of personality) the question was asked, "Do you think

12 J. Dewey, *Human nature and conduct* (New York: Holt, Rinehart and Winston, 1922; Modern Library ed., 1950, p. 16).
13 J. W. Getzels, The question-answer process, *Publ. Opin. Quart.*, 1954, 18, 80–91.

the Jews have too much power in the United States?" Two groups of interviewers were employed: one Jewish-looking with Jewish names; the other not Jewish-looking and with non-Jewish names. The first group of interviewers discovered that only 6 percent of the people said "Yes" to this question; the latter group reported that 21 percent said "Yes." Apparently 15 percent in the first group covered up their true attitude because they did not wish to offend the Jewish interviewer.[14]

But situational variability is by no means due only to our capacity to tell lies and to mask our private natures. Very often people do in fact harbor contradictory attitudes. In studying institutional versus private attitudes, for example, Schanck found that many people were authentically inconsistent with themselves. The investigator asked questions concerning religious doctrine. At one time he framed the question, "As a member of your church how do you feel about (your Bishop), (drinking alcohol), (the proper form for baptism), (other like topics)." The replies tended to conform to the expected (official) position of the church. But when asked, "Now, how do you feel about the matter personally?" the same respondent might give a flatly contradictory reply. In short, the public and private attitudes often differed, but the individual in a sense really holds them both, depending upon the situation with which he identifies himself at the moment.[15]

It is not necessary to pile up examples of inconsistency. We all seem to be bundles of contradiction. The tendency is so marked that some theorists say that there is no *inner* consistency in personality. Everything depends on what the situation elicits. We are bundles of tendencies-in-a-situation, nothing more. It is not we who are integrated; it is only that the environments in which we move have some stability and therefore elicit characteristic behavior in given situations.[16]

14 D. Robinson and S. Rhode, Two experiments with an anti-Semitism poll, *J. appl. Psychol.*, 1946, **30**, 169–181.
15 R. L. Schanck, A study of a community and its groups and institutions conceived of as behavior of individuals, *Psychol. Monogr.*, 1932, **43**, No. 2.
16 For discussions of situational variability see W. Coutu, *Emergent human nature* (New York: Knopf, 1949), and Consistency and inconsistency in intergroup relations, *J. soc. Issues*, 1949, **5**, No. 3; also G. Murphy, *Personality: a biosocial approach to origins and structure* (New York: Harper, 1947), Chaps. 38 and 39.

From this point of view it is senseless to administer personality tests in the classroom or laboratory because you cannot tell what your subject will do when he gets out into the wider world. Above all, you cannot tell what he will do when he meets new and unexpected situations. The emergencies of life bring forth combinations that never existed in the person's experience. He himself does not know whether he will behave courageously or be panicked, whether he will assume or evade new responsibility when faced with sudden bereavement, illness, or financial disaster.

The situational theorist is right when he claims that psychological theory looks too much inside the skin. But it is likewise true that the situationist looks too much outside the skin. He errs when he says that personality tests taken in the classroom or clinic fail completely to predict behavior in other situations. (If they failed they would have been discarded long ago as having no validity.) Nor is it true that we are completely helpless in predicting how a person will act in new situations or in emergencies.

Three facts should be kept in mind. When confronted with a strange situation most people tend to become reserved, silent, withdrawn. They tend, if possible, to avoid any action. A person is much more active and expressive in a familiar situation. This fact would suggest that for adults situations do not determine what we will do so much as what we will *avoid* doing. We like to be ourselves and when we cannot be, we tend to withdraw.

The second fact is that young children are far more "situational" than adults. They throw themselves into the hilarity, fearfulness, or despair of the immediate situation, and seem to lack "inner personality" while they do so. We have said that children are prisoners of their culture (page 169); so, too, are they prisoners of the situation. Adults are so to a lesser degree.

A third fact of importance is that most people do a good deal to *create* the situation to which they respond. A party-minded person gives a party. A situationist might come along and say, "See, her gaiety is a function of the situation." But what is this situation itself a function of? A man who likes baseball will seek out a baseball game. In brief, the situations we find ourselves in are often the direct product of our previous (and continuing) personalities.

Now the question as to how much of our behavior is due to "inner personality" and how much to "outer situation" can, with some measure of success, be submitted to experimental study.

Suppose we throw together a small group of strangers and give them a common task to do. Who will become the leader of the group? Is it true that some people are "born leaders" and will come to the top under any circumstance, and that others are followers "by nature"? Another way to put the question, "Does the possession of certain measured personality traits dispose a person to assume leadership in a new group of people who are all strange to one another?"

In a careful survey of research on this problem Mann concludes that "inner personality" is indeed a condition of leadership. Thus, people with high intelligence, who are well adjusted personally and who tend toward extraversion, are more likely than others to become leaders; also, to be popular in the group, and to contribute positively to the group activity. Likewise favoring the assumption of leadership are such traits as dominance, masculinity, and liberalism. Now these trends are all genuine and statistically significant, but they are not by any means universal. Inner personality is one, but definitely not the only, factor determining leadership.[17] (And, of course, today's "inner personality" is in part a result of interaction with yesterday's situation.)

It turns out that the role of personal traits is greater in situations that are "unstructured"—where, for example, the task assigned to the group is discussion rather than skilled action. Personal traits are less important when the task is not of the discussion variety but concerns a mechanical or technical problem. We may safely venture a generalization: Situational determinants are most important where duties and roles, where tasks and functions, are heavily prescribed. Personality determinants are most important where the task is more free and open and unstructured.

Since personality (considered as a system of inner traits) is not the sole determinant of behavior in small groups, what else do we need to know in order to predict accurately how an individual will perform?

Setting himself this problem, Couch did extensive experimentation. First he found, as did Mann, that there are reliable

17 R. D. Mann, A review of the relationships between personality and performance in small groups, *Psychol. Bull.*, 1959, **56**, 241–270.

(but not large) relationships between a person's needs and traits and what he does in groups. The traits he measured include anxiety, extraverted expression of emotion, aggressiveness, authoritarian conformity, optimism, and wish-fulfilling fantasy.

It is helpful to know a person's standing on these traits. But in order to predict with greater certainty how he will behave in a group it is necessary to know also (a) to what degree he normally conceals his personality, i.e., what ego-defenses he employs; (b) how he perceives others in the group—does he like them? does he think they like him? does he think the group worth while? (c) what the actual pressure is upon him—is he expected to lead? what is the assignment of work? All these variables enter into the total situation and we need to know them in order to predict behavior correctly beyond what a knowledge of personal traits will do.[18]

In other words, we see from available evidence that what a person will actually do is the result of at least four conditions:

a. enduring personality characteristics;
b. defenses and concealments used by the person; his degree of self-disclosure;
c. how he perceives the present situation and its relevance to himself; and
d. what the situational assignment actually calls for and expects of him.

We may say that the first two conditions are products of the personality, and the last two products of the situation. To understand behavior we need to know both sets of determinants.

Let us probe a little more deeply into factors (c) and (d). No person can "perceive the present situation" nor execute "what the assignment actually calls for" except in terms of the capacities he already has. In other words, the personality is itself a factor in the so-called situation. Even in new and unexpected situations I can act only within a range of personal variability permitted by my abilities and traits.

We are forced, therefore, to the conclusion that while the situation may modify behavior greatly, it can do so only within the limits

18 A. S. Couch, "Psychological determinants of interpersonal behavior." Unpublished doctoral dissertation, Harvard College Library, 1960.

of the potential provided by the personality. At the same time, we are forced to concede that traits of personality must not be regarded as fixed and stable, operating mechanically to the same degree on all occasions. Rather we should think of traits as *ranges of possible behavior*, to be activated at varying points within this range according to the demands of the situation.

It is wrong to say that Jim has y-amount of anxiety, or of extraversion, or of aggressiveness. Rather we should say that he has *upper and lower limits* of these traits. This would mean that he never shows more than x-amount and never less than z-amount. His exact location within the range at any given time will depend on what the situational cues bring forth. To put the matter slightly differently, we may conceive of situation as "pulling" a person higher or lower on his scale of potentialities, but always within his particular limits.

To sum up: if there is no personality apart from situation, it is equally true that there is no situation apart from personality. The pull of the situation is, however, so powerful that we are forced to regard personality as never a fixed entity or pattern but a complex system of potential ranges of behavior that may be evoked (within the limits of possibility for the person) by the various physical, social, and cultural conditions that surround him at any given time.[19]

Role

A *role* is a structured mode of participation in social life. More simply, it is what society expects of an individual occupying a given position in a group.

Consider an average family in Western culture. As a general thing the father is expected to leave the house in the morning, go to work, provide for the family, discipline the children, play with them, and in various ways abet the mother. The role of motherhood comprises a multitude of prescribed duties and tasks, even appropriate thoughts and feelings, and also, perhaps, a few privileges. The child's "structured mode" is, broadly speaking, one of obedience, plus privileges of play and receiving nurture. The oldest child is expected to help care for the younger and assist in the housework. The male child soon occupies a special role appropriate to his masculinity; he is supposed to do boyish things, including fighting back if attacked by a school-

[19] The concept of the "range of personal variability" is employed by S. Rosenzweig, Idiodynamics in personality theory with special reference to projective methods, *Psychol. Rev.*, 1951, 58, 213–223.

mate. The daughter is expected to learn housekeeping, and to be more modest and reticent than her brother (again speaking broadly). The interaction of all these roles is exceedingly subtle, and constitutes what we call the *family social system*.[20]

While the child is fulfilling his own role he is also learning the roles of his father, mother, and siblings. Their roles are reciprocals of his own, but they are likewise models which he may imitate. A two-year-old after a misdeed will often call himself "naughty," just as his mother might do; a four-year-old will imitate his father's motions in driving the family car. These role-assumptions, added to the child's own role, play a large part in socializing and acculturating him for the requirements of adult life.[21]

Let us follow the father as he leaves home in the morning to carry out his duties, some of which are incident to his father-role. He soon finds himself at the hospital, where he is resident physician. Swiftly the physician's role takes control of his behavior (while the father-role persists latently). At noon he presides at a Rotarian luncheon where new role-expectations in a new social system confront him. Later he visits his aged mother and behaves in his customary filial role. For recreation he joins his bowling team and plays the role appropriate to his membership in this sporting organization. At dinner time he rejoins his family and the latent father-role again becomes regnant.

Thus his life, like all lives, can be viewed as a succession of roles, relating the individual to an intricate series of social systems. In our culture the number of possible "structured modes and codes" seems endless; there are prescribed roles for pupil, neighbor, voter, car-owner, church member, suitor, husband, wife, parent, lawyer, manager, secretary, and so on, in addition to the modes and codes assigned to different ages of life (childhood, adolescence, young adulthood, middle age, retirement) and for the two sexes. In virtually all cultures sex-typed roles for male and female are particularly strict.[22]

Our numerous roles frequently conflict. A busy professional woman who is also a mother of young children finds her roles difficult

20 See Parsons and Shils, *op. cit.,* Chap. 4. Note 6 above.
21 See E. E. Maccoby, Role-taking in childhood and its consequences for social learning, *Child Develpm.,* 1959, **30**, 239–252.
22 For a discussion of both age- and sex-typing, see T. Parsons, Age and sex in the social structure of the United States. In Kluckhohn, Murray, and Schneider, *op. cit.,* Chap. 22. Note 3 above.

to reconcile. A school superintendent discovers that in his job he is confronted with a network of often conflicting role-relations. Suppose an unruly boy has to be disciplined. The teachers (whose views he is supposed to represent) wish the boy expelled. The superintendent's own pastor pleads for a second chance for the lad. The school committee (his official boss) recommends suspension. The PTA (of which he is a member) blames the boy's teacher—and so the crisscross goes. The superintendent's numerous roles pull him this way and that.[23]

An imaginative experiment demonstrates the same phenomenon. Stouffer and Toby put various questions to a large number of college students. One question asked what they would do if they had taken a job to proctor an examination and discovered one of their good friends cheating on the test. Would they report the dishonesty to the dean as the rules required? Or would they not report it on the grounds that the role of friendship calls for the protection of a friend? From this and other questions involving similar role-conflict it was found that some students consistently choose the "universalistic" standard, i.e., they follow the official code of justice and make no exceptions even for their friends. Others, however, consistently resolve the role-conflict in favor of the "particularistic" code, favoring the role-relation of friendship.[24]

So much for the unquestioned importance of roles. How shall we now relate the role-concept to personality? As was the case with culture and with situation, we find some social scientists so enthusiastic about the concept that they would give role the pre-eminent place in personality theory. We give two examples:

The person is composed of the roles he enacts.[25]
An individual in the course of his life performs a number of different roles, successively or simultaneously; the synthesis of all the social roles he has ever performed from birth to death constitutes his social personality.[26]

23 N. Gross, W. S. Mason, and A. W. McEachern, *Explorations in role analysis: studies of the school superintendency role* (New York: Wiley, 1958).
24 S. A. Stouffer and J. Toby, Role conflict and personality, *Amer. J. Sociol.*, 1951, 56, 395–406.
25 H. Gerth and C. W. Mills, *Character and social structure* (New York: Harcourt, Brace, 1953), p. 80.
26 F. Znaniecki, *The social role of the man of knowledge* (New York: Columbia Univ. Press, 1940), p. 14.

Before we can answer our question we must distinguish carefully four meanings of role—all legitimate but too frequently confused.

1. *Role-Expectations.* Role-expectations are located in the social system. They are what the culture or subculture prescribes for the father, the mother, the pupil, the physician. They constitute the rules of the game and are what most people in a society come to expect of any member that occupies a certain position in any current social system.

2. *Role-Conception.* The picture a *given* father or *given* teacher has of his role may or may not correspond to the role-expectations. Of course, broadly speaking, a father or a teacher knows what others expect of him. But the question here is what does he expect of himself? He *defines* his role in his own way. One father believes that he should supervise his adolescent son closely, another that he should allow the lad latitude and freedom. One teacher conceives of good teaching as a matter of strict drill and severe punishment, another favors individual project work and permissive methods.

3. *Role-Acceptance.* People sometimes love their roles (whether defined in terms of the expectation of others or in terms of their own conception); some people are indifferent to them; others hate "the station in life to which they have been called." There are willing mothers and unwilling mothers. Some college presidents and some coal miners like their jobs; others hate them. And some like their own conception of their roles but resent the expectancies that others have of them. Until we know the answers we cannot decide whether the role is warm and central (propriate) to the personality or whether it is merely a peripheral and disagreeable cultural prescription.

4. *Role-Performance.* What the individual actually does with his role assignment depends on all these foregoing conditions. Is he vigorous or halfhearted? Is the schoolboy cooperative or reluctant and unruly? Role-expectations alone will not tell us. Schoolboys, mothers, executives, salesmen differ greatly among themselves in their role-performance. The expectations are uniform and prescribed, but the variation that occurs through differing conceptions, degrees of acceptance, and all attendant features and traits of personality, modifies greatly the eventual role-performance.

Figure 19 shows the position of these various role-concepts.[27] It

27 I am indebted to John P. Hill for suggesting this diagram.

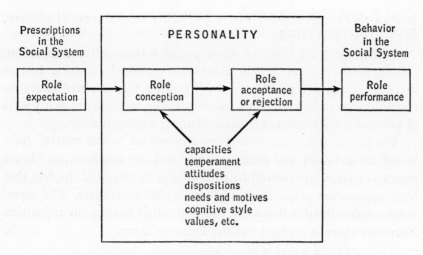

Figure 19. Four Meanings of "Role" in Relation to Personality

suggests that in two senses we may view roles as belonging to the social system (and not to personality). Role-expectation serves only as the external model and stimulus (which may be reinterpreted, accepted, or rejected by the person). Role-performance is again a point of intersection between the personality system and the social system. The performance is by a person, but it affects the social system and can be evaluated as part of this outer system. In two senses, however, the role-concept belongs within the personality. How the individual defines the role for himself and whether he accepts it and makes it propriate, or fulfills it in a perfunctory or inadequate fashion, is a subjective matter.

As a rule those who conceive their roles as society does, and who accept them gladly, are people who tend to support the current institutional structure of society. Those who redefine their roles drastically and dislike them—in either their societal or their personal definition—are rebels. We do not mean that every role-satisfied person is a conservative, nor every role-dissatisfied person is a radical; but there seems to be a tendency in this direction.

We cannot agree that personality is a mere colligation of roles—any more than we could agree that it is only the subjective side of culture, or a puppet at the mercy of changing situations. At the same time we concede that the "personal range of variability" is great.

Within this range activity varies according to the press of culture, of situation, and of role.

Fortunately, all three of these social forces—culture, situation, role-expectancy—allow much latitude in personal conduct. Just as there are many acceptable ways of speaking English, and many acceptable ways of behaving at a sporting event, so there are many ways of being a good mother, a good executive, a good teacher.

We can therefore reconcile the emphasis on "social system" (preferred by sociology and anthropology) and the emphasis on "inner personal system" (preferred by psychology) by virtue of the fact that both approaches allow for a wide range of variability. The social system makes flexible demands; the individual has flexible capacities. Normally there is no fatal conflict between them.

Catastrophic Social Change

One problem remains. We have said that culture, situation, and role heavily determine both personal behavior and the structure of personality. If this is true we should expect a change in social and cultural systems, and in situations, to bring about changes in personality. If personality were nothing more than "the subjective side of culture" or "a collection of roles" the parallel would be perfect.

The logic is clear: In order to maintain our personalities we need the nourishment provided by a stable environment in which we have lived a long time, and from which we derive continual support from the presence and memories of those who have known us for years on end. Unless our environment is stable and integrated, how can *we* be stable and integrated? In favor of this view we may cite the evidence that "sensory deprivation" is highly upsetting to a person's orientation and even to his sense of selfhood (page 114). An additional study shows that periods of medical illness in many lives coincide closely with upsets in their social environment which has suddenly become psychologically threatening and overdemanding. The study finds that not only are the so-called psychosomatic illnesses (ulcers, asthma, allergies, and so on) greater in times of personal stress, but all manner of medical ailments increase.[28]

28 L. E. Hinkle and H. G. Wolff, Ecological investigations of the relationship between illness, life experiences and the social environment, *Ann. intern. Med.*, 1958, **49**, 1373–1388.

Although it is certainly true that our conduct and our health vary from situation to situation, and with changes in our roles, still we usually maintain a kind of stubborn integrity, or at least try to.

Occasionally social scientists have the opportunity to study cases of catastrophic social change and its effects on individual personalities.

> One such study was conducted by the anthropologist Margaret Mead, who at one time investigated the culture of the Manus in Polynesia and became well acquainted with many individual members. Twenty-five years later she visited them again. Meanwhile the whole culture had changed drastically. From a primitive level the tribe had advanced to a complex Western type of civilization. Centuries of social change had been condensed into a single generation. Yet she noted the *stability* of individual personalities. One man, now a middle-aged judge, reflected the same pomposity that marked him as an adolescent. Another who was distrustful, reticent, and apathetic in early life had the same temperament and traits a generation later.[29]

Such observations, of course, do not prove that gross social change has *no* effect on personality. Of course it has, but we are warned against the easy generalization that personality is only a mirror-image of culture.

A second example is likewise instructive:

> During the Hitler era in Germany thousands of people completely lost their customary support in the social system. They were barred from their employment, persecuted, stripped of their property, arrested, tortured; families were broken up. Some escaped the ultimate fate in concentration camps and managed to flee the country and take up residence in foreign lands where they had no roots at all. What, then, happened to their personalities? A careful study of ninety such cases showed how persistent and vigorous were their efforts to retain their own propriate natures, both before leaving Germany and in their new home.

[29] Margaret Mead, Cultural discontinuities and personality transformation, *J. soc. Issues,* Suppl. Ser., No. 8, 1954.

The investigators report that a vivid impression gained from the case material is the extraordinary continuity and sameness of individual personalities. A suppressed, colorless teacher of mathematics loses his job, manages to emigrate and becomes a suppressed, colorless teacher of mathematics in the New World. An optimistic, extraverted, affable advertising man is ruined by the Nazis, but eventually turns up in South America as an optimistic, extraverted, affable advertising man. A highly competent Jewish woman, a writer with much sparkle of manner, leaves Austria under dangerous circumstances, but lands in Israel, where she writes a volume of memoirs with her usual verve.[30]

We are forced to conclude that for most individuals the changes within personality are, at the very least, not *proportional* to changes in the culture or in the situation. Even under conditions of social *anomie* (disintegration of values) the person manages to retain his personality system more or less intact. And yet beyond a certain point he cannot do so. In the present troubled era we have vivid proof that a person, however intense his efforts, cannot permanently withstand complete collapse of his social supports.

Brain Washing. In brain washing we have a case where strangers want desperately to alter the stubborn value-systems that one has build up through a lifetime of learning. The victim may be an American missionary or a newsman taken prisoner in North Korea or in China. Or he may have been a democratically minded German arrested for his political views and thrown into a Nazi or a Russian concentration camp. Grim experiments in "brain washing" or "soul surgery"—a more sedate label would be "ideological remolding" or "coercive persuasion"—enable us to trace the results.

As we reconstruct the story from now numerous reports, the process starts with a dramatic arrest, often at midnight or in the early hours of the morning, accompanied by the brandishing of pistols and other weapons. The prisoner may then be blindfolded, handcuffed, and led to a cell. Interrogation starts immediately, usually under a very bright light which induces eyestrain and fatigue. The inquisition starts by saying, "The Government knows all about your crimes, but

[30] G. W. Allport, J. S. Bruner, and E. M. Jandorf, Personality under social catastrophe: ninety life-histories of the Nazi revolution, *Charact. & Pers.*, 1941, **10**, 1–22.

it is now up to you to confess everything." The prisoner is astonished and confused, for he knows of no crimes—other than privately disagreeing with the regime. He protests innocence, but is told, "The Government does not arrest innocent people." Under questioning he must tell about his job, what he is doing in the country, who his associates are, and complete facts of his social life and economic status. He must try to recollect exhaustive details about conversations he has had. If he tries to cooperate he is told, "There is more. You are not telling us all frankly." As fatigue increases he is told to confess and he will soon be released from the ordeal.

From a physiological point of view we can say that his nervous system is being overloaded with products of fatigue and emotional frustration. Inhibitions of his customary habits and beliefs set in. He becomes preoccupied in seeking escape, and he is told the only way to escape is to confess. He has nothing to confess, but the idea takes root and becomes more attractive as the fatigue and the threat of physical torture loom larger. Often, as he grows more and more confused and unsure, he is taken to his cell and permitted to sleep— but only for an hour or two. This partial rest serves to disorient his customary habit systems still further. Interrogation—often torture— begin again. None of his customary habits help him to escape the intolerable situation. All protests or attempts at reason are met with, "Confess. Say the truth. Confession will save you." With the idea so firmly planted, after hours perhaps days of deprivation of food and sleep, time filled with pain and total frustration, the victim feels weak and wants to give in. He wants to "help" his tormenter who is so insistent, especially, of course, because in this way he can escape. But nothing he says satisfies the examiner. The ordeal is not over.

In his cell he is put with more "advanced" criminals, further along in brain washing, and these people violently turn on him, probably displacing onto him their own months of anguish. He is accused of being "an arch-criminal imperialist who refuses to recognize his crimes."

The physical suffering continues:

You are obliged to stand with chains on your ankles and holding your hands behind your back. They don't assist you because you are too reactionary. . . . You eat as a dog does, with your mouth and teeth. You arrange the cup and bowl with your nose and try to absorb some broth twice a day. If you have to make water they open your trousers. . . .

You are never out from the chains. . . . Nobody washes you. The lice grow and grow. . . . They continually tell you to confess all, and you will be treated better. . . . You start to think how to get rid of the chains. You must get rid of the chains.[31]

The story of such tortures has been told many times in recent years. The breaking point is postponed, confessions may be withheld for months. But what happens eventually—after months or years of such existence—is a genuine collapse of the edifice of personality as it existed prior to arrest. Oddly enough, sudden kindness from the judges helps break down resistance and causes the victim to regress to a childhood level. He craves comfort, kindness, and will do anything to merit it. The confession itself can be a superficial thing, but jailers know this and are intent, having obtained this wedge, on driving it deeper and deeper into the personal integrations until they split and shatter. One victim said, "They build up a spy mentality. What you invented becomes a reality. If you confess you gave forty spy messages, next time you say you gave fifty. And this fifty becomes a reality to you."

It becomes too painful to retain one's former standards of truth and falsehood, justice and injustice. It is easier to accept the standards offered; to say, "Yes, I am a spy, a criminal, an enemy of the people. I deserve what you are giving me. You are right and I am wrong. You are great and just judges. I am nothing." A missionary priest in China, after this sequence of experiences, reasoned that he was indeed a spy, trained in missionary schools to go to China in order to do espionage under the cloak of religion; his local mission is a spy organization; the Vatican is the main center for spies; his whole lifework has been against the interests of the Chinese people.

Such shattering of old habits and sentiments is extremely difficult to achieve, but it can be done—at least in many cases. It takes much time and catastrophic suffering to invert established beliefs and values. Bettelheim tells of his own struggle for many months in the concentration camp at Buchenwald to preserve his sense of self. He would say, "This torture is happening to my body but not to me." But even Bettelheim places an outside limit of about three years to the resistance. Older prisoners often became abject slaves of their

31 R. J. Lifton, "Thought reform" of Western civilians in Chinese communist prisons, *Psychiat.*, 1956, **19**, 173–195; by the same author, *Thought reform and the psychology of totalism* (New York: Norton, 1961).

Nazi jailers, agreeing with their preachments, even seeking bits of their clothing to carry about as a sacred fetish.[32]

Thus it comes about that under conditions of a totally controlled external environment, exerting maximum pressure upon the individual, the personality (or important regions of it) may be turned upside down. Whether those who finally escape from the coercive environment can ever fully recover their previous systems of belief and value is not yet known.

Some investigators have advanced the view that these extreme transformations are due to the operation of three forces: *debility, dependency,* and *dread.* This "DDD theory" holds that intense and simultaneous operation of these forces will sooner or later break down all resistance to the suggestions given by the persecutors.[33] Probably the theory should stress more than it does the loss of customary social supports and the total inversion of the social system, situation, and roles in which the victim finds himself.[34]

Figure 20 attempts to generalize the findings from various studies of social stress and pressure upon personality. What seems to happen

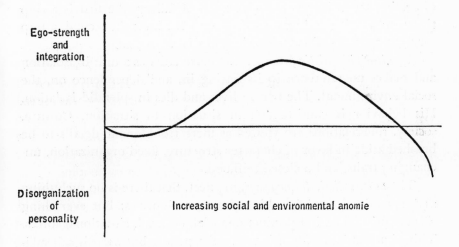

Figure 20. Generalized Relationship between Ego-Strength and Stressful Social Change

[32] B. Bettelheim, Individual and mass behavior in extreme situations, *J. abnorm. soc. Psychol.,* 1943, **38**, 417–452.

[33] I. E. Farber, H. F. Harlow, and L. J. West, Brainwashing, conditioning, and DDD, *Sociometry,* 1957, **20**, 271–285.

[34] For fuller discussion of the theory see Lifton, *op. cit.* Also W. Sargant. *Battle for the mind* (New York: Doubleday, 1957); and E. Schein *et al., Coercive persuasion* (New York: Norton, 1961).

is that normally a stressful change in the social situation at first induces a disorganized type of reaction, arousing some of the mechanisms listed on page 154 as "intrinsically abnormal." When sudden illness, loss of job, bereavement, or arrest occurs, the individual may well feel depressed and disoriented, become defensive, or deny the misfortune. When the pressure increases (as on the victims of the Nazis or in the early months of imprisonment) there is greater resistance. The person seeks rational solutions, vows to keep his integrity, works hard to carry on with his old beliefs and values. Finally, however, as in the brain-washed cases, the personality may be turned upside down and conform (without resistance) to the greatly altered conditions. There is presumably a breaking point for most personalities, some earlier, some later. Fortunately for most people the ultimate limit is never tested.

Individual Structure and Collective Structure

In this chapter we have undertaken the difficult task of relating the personality system to the social system. We have tried in our discussion to avoid two opposite types of fallacy—the first is a trap that psychologists and psychiatrists often fall into; the second, a trap for unwary sociologists and anthropologists.

The *individualistic fallacy* views personality as a unit in isolation and makes no reference to its setting in, and dependence on, the social environment. The person lives and dies in splendid isolation. His behavior is consistent from situation to situation. Culture, society, role-relations are viewed as mere troublesome details to be brushed aside in favor of character structure, fixed organization, unchanging traits, and a closed selfhood.

The *culturalistic fallacy* says, in effect, that there is no such thing as personality. There is a biological organism, yes; but everything this organism does is a product of social, cultural, situational forces. This view denies self-sufficiency to the person but awards self-sufficiency to cultural institutions, to social systems, and to role-relations. From this point of view the individual is a mere nuisance for social science.

Many writers place "the social" and "the individual" in dialectical opposition. They view them as in constant conflict. Jung tells us that we cannot escape the impress of archetypes and social tradition; at the same time each of us has a drive toward individuation, a negativism to tribal ways and a desire to be oneself. Angyal likewise postulates two opposing needs: one to fit ourselves in with other people (homonomy), the other to be independent in one's life (autonomy).[35] A man is both a mirror of his culture and a lamp unto himself.

But this dialectical way of handling the matter seems unsatisfactory for the simple reason that nothing in personality is purely "social" and nothing purely "individual." There is no such concrete separation. We do, of course, recognize the truth in what these authors say, but they scarcely provide us with a scientific framework for solving the problem of the duality.

The best approach, we believe, is to distinguish two frames of discourse. We can readily identify the personality system, existing within the skin. It confronts us with many problems of "individual structure." We can also identify the institutions we find in culture and the social systems involving role-relations of many people. Here we are dealing with "collective structure." Both approaches are valid. And for a *complete* account of human action (which no single science yet attempts) we need them both.

Let us take an example. A kindly lady takes a plant to a sick friend in the hospital. This simple act may, if we wish it to, lead us to the "inside structure" (the personality system). We ask, Is this a characteristic act? Yes, we find that she is almost always thoughtful and generous in her deeds. The act flows naturally from her system of beliefs and values, from her habit and trait structure. Having thus fitted the act to our assessment of her personality we rest content.

But the same act, if we wish it to, leads us also into the "outside" or collective structure (the social system). She could not have bought the plant unless she had played the role of a customer in the florist shop, and had thus been a cog in the mercantile system of her culture. She could not deliver the plant to the hospital unless she fitted the visiting hours and prescriptions of this "outside" social system. In many ways this good lady's personality system intersected the mercantile, transportation, and medical systems of her community.

Personality, in short, is "an aggregate within an aggregate, a

[35] A. Angyal, *Foundations for a science of personality* (New York: Commonwealth Fund, 1941).

structure within, and constituting a part of, a larger structure."[36] It is futile to ask which structure is more "real." It so happens that psychologists are interested particularly in the personality system; the sociologist and the anthropologist, in the outside structures. All are justified in their chosen focus. But all need to watch for, and freely recognize, the numerous points of intersection and the mutual interdependence of the two structures—as this chapter has attempted to do.

Summary

Personality is a system within a matrix of sociocultural systems. It is an "inside structure" embedded within and interacting with "outside structures." The outside (collective) structures could not exist at all if the constituent personality systems were destroyed. But neither could any given personality system be what it is, or endure for long, without the environing collective systems.

Some theories neglect the outer systems. Perhaps psychoanalysis, existentialism, and personalism could be so accused. It is also common to find neglect of the personality system. Role-theorists, culturalists, Marxists, and some sociologists would have to plead guilty. To strike a proper balance is difficult. And we may excuse one-sidedness to some extent by pleading that each specialist is entitled to his own preferred assignment.

In this chapter we have tried to preserve a reasonable balance—although the remainder of the volume deals primarily with the "inner system." Our specific purpose has been to examine the points of intersection.

Inevitably the child acquires (through the principles of learning) cultural ways; inevitably he grows to accept the roles appropriate to his status within the family. Later he finds himself playing many assigned roles within many social systems. His behavior is modified within limits by every social situation he encounters. Throughout life he reflects the "basic personality" appropriate to his culture and subcultures. He bends to some extent with the winds of social change. If the change is violent and extreme, as in brain washing, his whole personality may undergo alteration.

[36] The quotation and the example are drawn from F. H. Allport, *Theories of perception and the concept of structure* (New York: Wiley, 1955), p. 107.

At the same time we find that real culture permits a wide range of acceptable variation in personal behavior. Social situations are likewise, to a considerable extent, permissive, and there are more ways than one of carrying out role-expectations. The considerable play in the social system allows for great (though not limitless) personal variability.

Correspondingly the structure of personality allows a range of variability. Traits and attitudes are structured with upper and lower limits. Because of this latitude the person can more easily meet the requirements of his culture, of the momentary situation, and of his roles. By virtue of this flexibility within both the social and personality systems a mutual adaptation and successful intersection are normally achieved.

CHAPTER 9

The Development
of Motives

ADULT VERSUS INFANT • EMOTION • THEORIES OF UN-
CHANGING MOTIVES • CRITIQUE OF THEORIES OF UNCHANGING
MOTIVES • THEORIES OF CHANGING MOTIVES • SUMMARY

THE problem of motivation is central to the psychological
study of personality. Some writers insist that the two topics are
identical. Although we need not accept this extreme view it is nonetheless true that any theory of personality pivots upon its analysis of
the nature of motivation. By motive we mean any internal condition
in the person that induces action or thought.

Adult versus Infant

The course of life, broadly speaking, starts in infancy with
total *dependence,* progressing in youth to relative independence, and
achieving in adulthood a measure of *social responsibility.* Such a
thoroughgoing transformation of personality must involve major
changes in motivation.

Consider first the two-year-old. However much we may love him
we are forced to admit that he is an unsocialized horror. Excessively
demanding, he can brook no delay in gratifying his impulses. He is

196

pleasure-seeking, impatient, vastly destructive, devoid of conscience, and wholly dependent. His own hunger, his own fatigue, his own bodily urges, his need for activity, play, and comfort—these are his sole concerns. Never does he consider the convenience or welfare of others. He can tolerate no frustration, no rivalry. From his point of view his mother, his family, his world must devote themselves to the instant gratification of his whims. If an adult were half as self-centered as a two-year-old he would be considered a psychopathic criminal. The philosopher Hobbes once said, "The wicked man is but a child grown strong."

By contrast the mature adult possesses motives that are controlled, socially relevant, and fairly well integrated into a planned career. Chesterton's description of Tolstoy depicts such a person:

Tolstoy, besides being a magnificent novelist, is one of the very few men alive who have a real, solid, and serious view of life. . . . He is one of the two or three men in Europe, who have an attitude toward things so entirely their own, that we could supply their inevitable view in any-thing—a silk hat, a Home Rule Bill, an Indian poem, or a pound of tobacco. There are three men in existence who have such an attitude: Tolstoy, Mr. Bernard Shaw, and my friend Mr. Hilaire Belloc. They are all diametrically opposed to each other, but they all have this essential resemblance, that given their basis of thought, their soil of conviction, their opinions on every earthly subject grow there naturally, like flowers in a field. There are certain views of certain things that they must take; they do not form opinions, the opinions form themselves. Take, for in-stance, in the case of Tolstoy, the mere list of miscellaneous objects which I wrote down at random above, a silk hat, a Home Rule Bill, an Indian poem, and a pound of tobacco. Tolstoy would say: "I believe in the utmost possible simplification of life; therefore, this silk hat is a black abortion." He would say: "I believe in the utmost possible simplification of life; therefore this Home Rule Bill is a mere peddling compromise; it is no good to break up a centralized empire into nations, you must break the nation up into individuals." He would say: "I believe in the utmost possible simplification of life; therefore, I am interested in this Indian poem, for Eastern ethics, under all their apparent gorgeousness, are far simpler and more Tolstoyan than Western." He would say: "I believe in the utmost possible simplification of life; therefore, this pound of tobacco is a thing of evil; take it away." Everything in the world from the Bible to a bootjack, can be, and is, reduced by Tolstoy to this great funda- mental Tolstoyan principle, the simplification of life.[1]

[1] From G. K. Chesterton et al., Leo Tolstoy (London: Hodder & Stoughton, 1903), pp. 3 f.

We may dismiss as literary exaggeration Chesterton's claim that only "two or three men" are so well integrated that one can supply their inevitable view in anything. Among our acquaintances you or I could name several more. Nor need we believe that Tolstoy's motives are as perfectly single-pointed and integrated as the author claims. Yet the sketch serves our purpose by showing how far the motivational systems of adults have come from the impetuous, disconnected, self-centered motives of early childhood.

Emotion

Motive and *emotion* have the same Latin root (*movere*—to move). Emotions move us; so, to, do motives. What, then, is their connection?

Emotion is best defined as a "stirred up condition of the organism." Some emotions are specific to a present need: pain, hunger, fear, sexual desire; others are more pervasive and longer lasting: anxiety, depression, tenderness, reverence. Whatever their feeling tone or duration, emotions are valuable as a signal that things are not going right with us, or as an assurance that they are. They are often tonic in helping the individual secure what he needs for his physical survival and for the protection and further growth of his personality. But when they are violent they are disruptive and seem to serve no adaptive purpose.

The nature of emotion is still not fully understood, although it constitutes a major chapter in the field of general psychology. So far as personality is concerned we may say that emotion is the subjective coloring of motives, especially of motives that are blocked or thrown into conflict, or that make sudden and unexpected progress toward their goal. Since our task is to understand the lasting structure of motives we shall omit discussion of the "stirred up" emotional condition that often attends them.[2]

Theories of Unchanging Motives

In spite of the apparently vast difference between the motives of a two-year-old and an adult several important theories tell us that

[2] The relation between motive and emotion is considered at length by Magda Arnold, *Emotion and personality* (2 vols.; New York: Columbia Univ. Press, 1960).

the motives of mankind are essentially the same from birth until death. The same drives, needs, or instincts haunt us from the cradle to the grave. Let us examine some of the major statements of this point of view.

"Pleasure and pain are our sovereign masters." This famous statement by Jeremy Bentham has always had plenty of supporters from the time of the ancient Greeks to the present day. In olden times the Cyrenaics claimed that all human beings are motived to seek positive pleasure; the Epicureans felt that man's chief goal was the avoidance of pain. During the nineteenth century the utilitarian school of thought dominated much of the economic and social theory and policy of the West. It held with Mill that a man is physically unable to desire anything unless the idea of it is pleasurable. In current psychology emphasis is again placed, as with the Epicureans of old, on the avoidance of pain or discomfort. "Tension-reduction" is the alleged sovereign motive. All our conduct, it is said, is a striving toward equilibrium, detumescence, homeostasis, or escape from tension (cf. pages 86–89).

Psychological hedonism, as this type of theory is called, has a sirenlike attraction. It seems only sensible and obvious to say that men seek happiness and seek to avoid pain. Does not the formula hold from birth to death? The two-year-old seeks pleasure; Tolstoy seeks pleasure (by reducing the complexities of life); you and I seek pleasure (or happiness). It is all so simple. Or is it?

A group of young factory girls were discussing their life-motives. They came to the unanimous decision that "being happy" was their sole motive. A psychologist was present and asked them to look at two photographs, one representing a smiling girl, obviously of the working class; the other a depressed-looking girl, obviously wealthy. All the girls agreed that the former was happy and the latter unhappy. They were then asked, "Which of the two would you most like to be?" All chose to be the unhappy but wealthy girl. Some of them laughed at their choice. One said, "I know it is funny because I want to be happy; but that is how I feel." This revealing (if slightly tricky) experiment suggests that *social status* is for these girls a stronger and more concrete motive than happiness.

There are many difficulties with the concept of happiness as motive. Most serious of all is the simple fact that one cannot aim directly at the achievement of happiness. It is therefore not a concrete motive. Someone may *think* that if he obtains a college degree, marries Susan, earns a good living, he will be happy; but these *concrete* accomplishments are the tangible goals. Happiness is at best a by-product of otherwise-motivated activity. One who aims at happiness has no aim at all.

Let us examine our own consciousness. When absorbed in a task, in carrying through a motive, are we aware of a happiness incentive? We know that we aim to pass a test, to write a poem, or to win a game. We expect, in a vague way, that success will bring us satisfaction; but we aim to reach a specific goal; the anticipation of satisfaction is itself nothing more than a distant penumbra.

And this satisfaction is often of a grim order, not in any intelligible sense "happiness." Where is the happiness for a crash-dive bomber who loses his life for his country? Where is happiness for the dedicated but overworked and harassed statesman? for the devoted mother of a condemned criminal? Whenever we do something because we "ought" to do it we are violating the creed of hedonism. Many things we are motivated to do merely increase our tensions, diminish our chances for pleasure, and commit us to a strenuous and risky course of life. Bismarck once said, "We are not in this world for pleasure, but to do our damned duty."

But, in spite of these critical comments, there are certain positive relationships between pleasure and motive that may be pointed out. It is certainly true that a pleasurable feeling tone often accompanies the satisfaction of drives: food, sleep, activity, elimination, sexual activity, even the breathing of fresh air. It is also true that much of the behavior of a young child is impulsive (drive controlled), and so may be called "hedonistic" in this sense. Youth, too, is a "pleasure-seeking" age (in the sense that parties, athletics, dating are short-run objectives with a quick yield of pleasurable feeling). True also that many adults are hedonists in the sense that all through life they seek immediate sensuous gratifications. We concede these facts. Also we can concede that pleasure and pain are nature's signals to us that our motives are being facilitated or blocked. Even a person pursuing his duty experiences some flickers of pleasure or satisfaction. But as the evolutionary development of man has progressed it seems that nature's signals (and signals are not motives) become less and less reliable. A cave man's motives may have been well tuned to hedonistic signals. But in the modern day we find a poorer paralleling between the realizing of an ideal, a duty, a responsibility and the signal flag of pleasure. And much that is pleasurable is inconsistent with an adult's principal goals in life.

In sum, we cannot build a theory of motivation on hedonism, because it is a vague principle, insufficiently supported by evidence or by our own introspections, and because the paralleling of pleasure and goal-attainment is not close.[3]

Instincts. A second simple, but probably erroneous way to view motivation is to ascribe it wholly to instinct. We shall mention three types of instinct doctrine.

Ad hoc listings. It is easy to invent instincts according to one's need. An economist wishing to account for man's economic behavior may glibly postulate an instinct of *workmanship,* of *competition,* or of *acquisitiveness.* He may build a whole system on his assumptions— but the assumptions are gratuitous and unproved. An educator may "need" an instinct of *play,* of *curiosity,* of *thought*—and presto! he invents them for his purposes. A sociologist may, to help his theorizing, decide that man has four basic "wishes": for *novelty,* for *security,* for *recognition,* for *mastery.* And there they are.[4] Many years ago L. L. Bernard surveyed the literature of psychological and social science and discovered approximately 14,000 alleged (and arbitrarily invented) instincts.[5] Although inventions of this sort may have pragmatic utility, they do not rest on sound motivational theory.

Hormic theory. A more orderly theory is presented by William McDougall.[6] It argues that animals are clearly guided by instinct. If

[3] It seems to be a fact that younger students and younger scholars often argue vehemently for some version of the doctrine of hedonism, whereas older scholars tend to argue against it. E. L. Thorndike and S. Freud are among those who altered their own views as they grew older. It may be that older scholars lose their zest in living, or that they grow in wisdom. One's view of this matter will probably depend on how old one is.
[4] We should not disparage the usefulness of such *ad hoc* inventions. In their system of sociological thought, W. I. Thomas and F. Znaniecki make elegant and systematic use of these four wishes: *The Polish peasant in Europe and America* (2 vols.; New York: Knopf, 1927).
[5] L. L. Bernard, *Instinct: a study in social psychology* (New York: Holt, Rinehart and Winston, 1924).
[6] McDougall's highly influential statement of his views was first published in *Social psychology* (New York: Luce, 1908). A later statement, enlarging the number of basic "propensities" is *The energies of men* (London: Methuen, 1932).

we accept evolution, as of course we must, men, too, have basic propensities that are their prime movers. Not all propensities are evident at birth, but they ripen (through maturation) and provide the essential dynamos of all human conduct. Each instinct has a primary emotion attached to it. The blending of these instinctive energies with one another and with later learning, accounts for all the rich diversity of human motives. Examples are the parental instinct (with the emotion of tenderness), flight (with the emotion of fear), pugnacity (anger), gregariousness (loneliness). When habitual objects become attached to these instincts we develop *sentiments,* and it is out of sentiments that personality itself is compounded. This theory thus gives us simultaneously an account of the structure of motivation and of personality.

Although McDougall's system is closely reasoned we cannot accept it as an adequate account of motivation. It is wholly speculative, and requires a given number of mainsprings in human nature (the number varies between eight and eighteen in various editions of his writing) which, in fact, have never been established. The truth of motivation is certainly more complex, and individual differences far greater than the theory would allow.

Freudian instinct. Freud says, "The structure of the id never changes." The id is filled with "instinctual energies." What these energies may be is less clearly stated than in McDougall's system; but, as everyone knows, Freud postulated sex and aggression as two dominant instincts. Between them they can account for most of man's behavior and character.

If the instincts never change, how can we account for the difference between our obstreperous two-year-old and a Tolstoy? Freud offers two explanations. For one thing, the adult (Tolstoy, for example) acquires new *object cathexes.* To satisfy his aggression and his love-life he now wants different objects. But the basic instincts are the same. Second, he is capable of sublimation. Perhaps Tolstoy's longing for the simple life was merely an "aim inhibited wish." Instead of desiring directly the comfort of his mother's body (Oedipus complex) he masks this now-unconscious desire by playing peasant, where mother earth substitutes for his own mother.

As in the case of McDougall's theory there is no proof that Freud has achieved a basic list of man's root motives, nor that as the individual grows and develops, his root motives remain unchanged.

When we compare age two with maturity the assumption seems most improbable.

The three types of instinct theory we have mentioned contend that (1) all men have essentially the same dynamos of action, (2) these are inborn, (3) they are capable of being attached to various objects and therefore of being channeled (cathected, displaced, sublimated). In short, in all personalities we find the same root motives from birth to death; and adult personality is in effect a blend of channeled, unchanging motives. This logic seems to us inadequate to account for the qualitative differences between infant and adult (e.g., the emergent motives of social responsibility), and also for the extraordinary diversity of adult motives, unique in each particular personality.[7]

We may now mention two additional theories that may roughly be classed with doctrines of instinct.

Needs. Many psychologists would like to operate with a definite list of fundamental human urges, but they are cautious concerning inbornness. They say, in effect, we do not care whether the basic motives are strictly speaking *instinctive,* but they are so fundamental and widespread that they act *like* instincts. Let's call them *wishes, desires, wants, ergs,* or *needs.* The last term seems to be most widely favored. Among the needs often studied are *achievement, affiliation, acquisition, aggression, autonomy, deference, dominance, nurturance, sex.*[8]

The advantages of this type of theory are many. It sidesteps the nature-nurture controversy, allowing in a rather vague way for the role of learning. It encourages research on one motive at a time or on motives in combination.[9] Like McDougall's system it allows for the

---

[7] In current psychology the term *instinct* is used in a different sense. The modern school of "ethology" studies the perceptual configurations to which animals and infants respond without prior experience. Thus the social smile is elicited in the baby normally from 3 to 6 months of age when he sees a human face or reasonable facsimile thereof. The face may be a mask or even a scarecrow, but must have two eyes, be fully visible, and show movement. It need not be a smiling face (a fact that rules out imitation), nor need it belong to a familiar person. Cf. R. A. Spitz and K. M. Wolf, The smiling response: a contribution to the ontogenesis of social relations, *Genetic Psychol. Monogr.,* 1946, **34,** 57–125. This type of innate response exists, and is important for a full understanding of infant psychology. It does not, however, deal with motivation directly. The only instincts we are here concerned with are *instinctive motives.*

[8] A basic defense of this approach to motivation is H. A. Murray *et al., Explorations in personality* (New York: Oxford, 1938).

[9] Cf. D. C. McClelland, J. W. Atkinson, R. A. Clark, and E. L. Lowell, *The achievement motive* (New York: Appleton-Century-Crofts, 1953).

development of needs into sentiments, thus tying together motivation and the resulting structure of personality.[10] The needs can also be regarded from the Freudian point of view, as repressed, displaced, cathected, and sublimated. The system, however, employs far more basic motives than does Freud's, and allows more scope for conscious needs.

But like the preceding theories, the doctrine of needs says, in effect, that while desired objects may vary from person to person, the basic kinds of desire do not. Men may want different things, but there are only a few reasons why they want them. Two men, for instance, may have a strong need for abasement; one perhaps becomes a sexual masochist, the other a well-disciplined monk. The two directions taken by these two lives are so different that it seems highly artificial to give them identical scores on *n* Abasement. Need theory, like instinct theory, seems too abstract, too disembodied, and depersonalized to represent the ongoing motivation of actual individuals.[11] We prefer a theory that will depict the actual motivational systems of the sexual masochist and of the well-disciplined monk without the speculative derivation of two such different systems from one remote (and unproven) common source of "abasement."

"Dependable motives." None of the theories thus far considered rests on solid research. At best it is common-sense observation or clinical work with patients that is the undergirding for the postulated lists of instincts or needs. Klineberg, however, has made a praiseworthy attempt (by studying the records of cultures) to find out what every human being in every culture of the world without exception wants (or needs).[12] This anthropological search yields a list

10 Cf. H. A. Murray and C. Morgan, A clinical study of sentiments *Genet. Psychol. Monogr.*, 1945, **32**, 3–149.
11 This point seems to be admitted by Murray, who writes, "Every need is associated with traces (or images) representing movements, pathways, agencies, goal objects, which taken together, constitute a need-*integrate*." *J. Psychol.*, 1936, **3**, 37. This conception of a need-integrate is a great improvement over the skeleton need. It fulfills well our demand for a unit of analysis that is concrete, lifelike, and personal, provided only that the need-integrate is understood to be not merely a momentary organization but a mental structure that endures and is a constant characteristic of the person. It is no doubt true that *comparisons* between individuals cannot be made quite so readily on the basis of need-integrates as on the basis of common needs; but comparison is only a secondary goal of the psychology of personality. The primary goal is the representation of the single life with maximum fidelity.
12 O. Klineberg, *Social psychology* (Rev. ed.; New York: Holt, Rinehart and Winston, 1954).

of "absolutely dependable motives": hunger, thirst, rest and sleep, elimination, breathing, activity, sensory hunger. There are also "highly dependable motives," found in all cultures but exceptions would have to be made for individuals: sex, postmaternal behavior, self-protective behavior. Then with diminishing frequency Klineberg finds aggressiveness, flight, gregariousness, acquisitiveness, and other common patterns.

The most interesting aspect of this research is the character of the "absolutely dependable" motives discovered. They are, without exception, the *biological drives* whose satisfaction is necessary for biological survival.

Drives. The fact that drives are essential to survival has led many psychologists to argue that here at last is the simple and sovereign concept on which to found *all* motivational theory. Drives are with us from birth to death; they underlie all our early learning; and if we allow for the conditioning and extension of drives—so that "secondary drives" result—we can cover all the motives of men.

Although a drive theory invites (indeed, requires) a theory of learning, yet the basic energies are always regarded as being the drives themselves—and so we must class this type of thought (embraced by behavioristic, i.e., stimulus-response, psychology) in our category of "unchanging energies."

In Chapter 5 we dealt with this point of view. There we showed how the concepts of conditioning and reinforcement by "stretching" drives are intended to account for all the diversity of men's response-habits.

We shall soon point out the insufficiency of drive theory, but first two important points must be urged in its favor. In the first place, as Klineberg clearly shows, all human beings in all the world do have drives, and these are prepotent (when aroused they usually take precedence over all other motives). If somone is very hungry, very much in need of oxygen, water, or rest, all other motives fade away until the drive is satisfied. No theory of motivation can overlook this central fact.

In the second place, since most if not all infant behavior can be traced to drives—including, of course, the activity and esthetic drives—then drives are the original (but not necessarily permanent) foundation of our motivational life. It is clear that much that an infant learns has to do with modes of satisfying drives (to hold his bottle, to avoid hot radiators, to control his mother in order to obtain food and other comfort). We are saying that the drive theory seems adequate (or almost adequate) in accounting for motivation during the first two years of life (and to a limited extent, all through life); it seems adequate also in accounting for motivation in animals.

There is, as we shall now see, some question as to the listing of drives. We recall that among the "absolutely dependable motives" Klineberg included an *activity* and an *esthetic* drive. Are these, like hunger and thirst and fatigue, specific "tissue tensions" that require tension reduction? Or are they motivational endowments of a different order? We shall return to this problem later.

Critique of Theories of Unchanging Motives

I have implied that none of the theories thus far considered allows sufficient flexibility and change to account for the vast diversity of adult human motives. I shall now state in somewhat fuller detail my objections to the two most widespread doctrines: the Freudian and the stimulus-response (drive) theories.

First, I venture what I hope will be a helpful digression. Let us take note of the large number of crucial terms in contemporary psychology that start with the prefix *re: receptor, reaction, response, reflex, repression, repetition, reward, reinforcement, regression*—to name some but not all. The flavor of these terms suggests (1) a passivity of human nature (which receives and reacts to outside pressures), and (2) a retracing or reinstatement of past conditions. From this array we rightly conclude that most psychological theories dominant today are somehow *receptive, recapitulative, reverberative* in their emphasis. There is far less terminological assistance in pointing to what is to come, to activity that is future-oriented. The prefix *pro* is seldom found in the technical lexicon of psychology. We hear much of *reaction* but seldom if ever of *proaction*. We hear of *regression,* but not of *progression.* We conclude that while human beings are busy living their lives into the future, much psychological theory is busy tracing these lives backward into the past. And while it seems to each of us that we are spontaneously *active,* many psychologists are telling us that we are only *reactive.*

This state of affairs is reflected in the leading theories of motivation, and points to their weakness. Although the Freudian and the stimulus-response theories are unlike in many respects, both agree in their emphasis upon the *reactive* nature of motivation.[13]

According to the Freudian view the totality of organic tensions or drives comprises the id. These tensions or drives are our "instinctual energies" and they alone "cause" us to act. Sex and aggression are perhaps the most important of these id drives because they encounter the most opposition from the outside world and thus are repressed. Repression augments their flame. Our present personality, according to Freud, is pretty much a relic of the various ways in which we have attempted to gratify the id needs in the face of opposition from both the outside world and from our own conscience, which is an interiorization of the rules impressed on us by our parents.

Psychoanalysis attempts to trace all adult interests, aspirations, and strivings back to the instinctual roots of sex and aggression. The main device is to assert that adult interests (in music, medicine, art, agriculture, politics and religion, education or anything else) are matters of *sublimation*. Sublimation is redirecting an "aim inhibited wish." The poet turns to the mouthing of beautiful phrases because he was frustrated in his "oral gratification" as a child. The evidence for the doctrine of sublimation is slender and it cannot, of course, predict which of many possible ways of displacing an "aim inhibited wish" a person will adopt.

Freud also suggested that some of the energy to sustain adult motives may come from a fusion of the sexual and aggressive drives. These drives, when fused, become "neutral"; that is, they lose their specific aim, and become nondirective in aim; the free energy may be used to animate the individual to seek almost any goal that has happened to become "cathected" (associated with) this neutral drive.

One feature of the theory of sublimated or neutral energies should be noted. Sublimation can never discharge more than a certain portion of the id energy, nor can a fusion of aggression and sex drives ever be completely satisfied with substitute activities having nothing to do with sex or aggression. *Therefore acquired adult interests*

[13] R. S. Woodworth labels them both "need-primacy" theories, and opposes them to doctrines that allow for changing and expanding energies, which he calls "behavior primacy" theories. In certain respects the present critique parallels Woodworth's own argument. R. S. Woodworth, *Dynamics of behavior* (New York: Holt, Rinehart and Winston, 1958), Chap. 5.

persist. Poetry cannot satisfy the oral erotic needs, and so these needs keep pressing and sustaining this semifutile sublimation. Surgery does not really satisfy the sadistic fusion of sexual and aggressive needs, and so these fused needs continue to goad the surgeon. It is for this reason that his interest in his profession persists a lifetime.

This general picture of motivation makes personality almost a wholly reactive product of two archaic forces. It also puts chief emphasis on early life when the frustrations, repression, and cathexes were largely built. Freud taught that the guidelines of a person's character are established by the age of three.[14]

Of course we gladly grant that adult motives often reflect sex and aggression, and that some traces of infantile motivation may be found in some (especially neurotic) adult conduct; yet we cannot believe that Freud does justice to the diversity, uniqueness, and contemporaneity of most adult motivation.

Turning to the stimulus-response theories we find another "tension-reduction" view of motivation. Here drives are the sole motivators; they are less protean than Freud's instinctual energies. They are regarded as specifiable and separate tensions, hunger, thirst, sex, withdrawal from pain being prominent examples much used in experimental work with animals. Hull and other defenders of the S-R approach spend more effort than does Freud in attempting to explain how all adult motives and interests are in the last analysis derived from the primitive drives. *Learning* is the important ingredient in the theory. In outline it runs as follows. Here we are restating and extending the argument already presented in Chapter 5.

Whenever a primary drive is satisfied, e.g., hunger for food, the tension of the motive is reduced. (All motivation seeks "tension-reduction.") Now, whatever activity led to (or was closely associated with) this tension-reduction is easily learned, because it is affected by *primary reinforcement.* The law of "reinforcement" states that the means employed in reducing tensions will be retained through learning. Thus we learn to "like" (build favorable habits toward) our bed, our breakfast menu, our sex partner.

But sometimes the things we like are only remotely connected with tension-reduction. In such cases we speak of *secondary reinforcement.* Let us take a well-known example from animal research:

14 E. Jones, *The life and work of Sigmund Freud* (New York: Basic Books, 1953), I. 13.

A chimpanzee was trained to take a poker chip from the floor and insert it into a vending machine, which thereupon delivered a grape or a raisin. One may say that the use of the poker chip token was learned by primary reinforcement. But the chimp was then forced to learn an additional act in the sequence to food. He discovered that in order to obtain his poker chips he had to work another machine that delivered poker chips. He would spend each chip as he got it. But if he was prevented from doing so he would "hoard" his tokens. He liked to amass "wealth," so to speak. And this hoarding illustrates the principle of secondary reinforcement. It is an act associated with another act that leads to tension-reduction.[15]

The S-R theorists are quite certain that within this model somewhere we shall find the explanation for all complex adult motives. Even the most elaborate motives are somehow remote anticipations of primary drive satisfaction. We like the rug that was in the dining room during our childhood. We want to go fishing because we were taken fishing by our father (secondary reinforcement), who satisfied many of our childhood wants (primary reinforcement). We find we have an aversion to a certain town because it vaguely reminds us of (i.e., has partial cues corresponding to) a town where we suffered a long and painful siege with a childhood disease (secondary negative reinforcement). And so it goes.

There are three serious objections to this line of reasoning—any one of them serious enough to tell us it is on the wrong track:

1. According to the theory all motivation presses toward the reduction of primary drive tensions. If there is no such reduction, then in the long run the reinforcing value is lost, and the habit or instrumental activity disappears. In the chimpanzee experiment cited above, unless the chimp *sometimes* obtains the reward of grapes he loses all interest in the poker chips. The hoarding suffers "experimental extinction." But a human miser does not behave this way. Money may at first have been a means to buy drive satisfaction, but now it becomes an end in itself; he continues to amass his useless horde.

[15] J. B. Wolfe, Effectiveness of token-rewards for chimpanzees, *Comp. Psychol. Monogr.*, No. 60, 1936; J. T. Cowles, Food tokens as incentives for learning by chimpanzees, *Comp. Psychol. Monogr.*, No. 71, 1937.

Nearly all experimental studies that build secondary reinforcements show the loss of the instrumental habits and secondary interests unless they do in fact lead to primary drive gratification. The chief exception is what is known as "avoidance conditioning," where the use of electric shock or other intensely painful stimuli will lead an animal all its lifelong to avoid the situation that led to the shock. There is apparently no extinction of avoidance habits.

One experiment placed dogs in a two-compartment box with a separating wall low enough for the animals to jump over. A buzzer sounded and shortly thereafter the dogs received a severe electric shock. They jumped over the wall to escape. But the second compartment was likewise wired, so that the dogs received the same treatment there. Still by jumping as soon as the buzzer sounded from one compartment to the other the dogs managed to avoid the shock. The point of the experiment is that after the first few trials (which were sufficient to establish the habit) the compartments were unwired. There was no more shock. But the dogs kept on for 400 trials or more, manifesting the conditioned response with full force. The experimenters then gave up the attempt to "extinguish" the conditioning. It was too persistent. It looked like a lifelong inextinguishable habit.[16]

Avoidance, therefore, becomes a motive that loses its dependence on primary reinforcement. It exemplifies a kind of "functional autonomy" which we shall soon discuss more fully.

Hull felt that additional very intense conditionings may remain without primary reinforcement. He writes:

The present hypothesis does not imply that secondary reinforcement will necessarily suffer experimental extinction when the support of the primary need reduction is withdrawn. If the primary reinforcement has been sufficiently profound during the establishment of a secondary habit or interest, anticipation of the primary reward may be intense enough to take the place of the actual reward and so resist extinction indefinitely.[17]

16 R. L. Solomon, L. J. Kamin, and L. C. Wynne, Traumatic avoidance learning: the outcomes of several extinction procedures with dogs, *J. abnorm. soc. Psychol.*, 1953, **48**, 291–302.
17 C. L. Hull, *Principles of behavior* (New York: Appleton-Century-Crofts, 1943), p. 101. See also Woodworth's discussion, *op. cit.*, p. 113. Note 13 above.

Yet the whole logic of the "secondary reinforcement" position does insist, as Dollard and Miller say, that "learned drives should be weakened by nonreinforcement,"[18] and ultimately reinforcement can come only by reducing the tension of primary drives.

In animal experiments the evidence for experimental extinction (except in avoidance conditioning) is overwhelming, whereas the evidence for the loss of acquired human adult interests is not. We do not lose our liking for the dining room rug simply because for forty years we have not eaten in its presence. We do not lose our love of fishing simply because our father no longer satisfies our primary drives. We do not cease to save money because it is not converted into edible "grapes." We do not give up our interest in music because we no longer have a parent or a teacher to administer positive and negative reinforcements. An older woman does not lose her good taste in clothes when clothes are no longer a device for attracting a suitable husband. An ex-sailor still has a craving for the sea, though it is fifty years since he made his living at it.

2. The second objection is less technical, and more common-sense. Does it seem credible to suppose that the contemporary interests of personality are relics of past satisfactions? The theory says in effect that I now like fishing because once upon a time my father comforted me. As a *historical* fact the statement makes some sense, but as a *functional* fact it does not. The "go" of my passion for fishing is here and now, stretching into the future—I hope to go fishing next Wednesday—and not into the past. Adult motives are infinitely varied, self-sustaining, *contemporary* systems. They are not fossils.

3. Finally, and most fatally of all, much motivation has no ascertainable relation to primary drives. It is easy to recognize hunger, thirst, sex, fatigue, oxygen-hunger as motives stemming from tissue change in the body, from a deficit or excess stimulation of nerve endings. But many of the complex motives of adults have no demonstrated relation whatever to these drives, nor, for that matter, to Freud's "instinctual energies." The S-R psychologist or psychoanalyst may *claim* that adult interests can be traced to his chosen unchanging energies, but he cannot *prove* that they are. An adult may want to be a stamp collector, a scientist, a traveler, a philanthropist, a priest;

[18] J. Dollard and N. E. Miller, *Personality and psychotherapy* (New York: McGraw-Hill, 1950), p. 88.

he desires to support the United Nations, to provide opportunities for his children, to carry through his responsibilities. None of these interests can be directly traced to drives.

The neurologist Goldstein has said that it is only the sick man who is driven by drives. It is only the mentally ill who are obsessed by their need for food, comfort, elimination, sex gratification. Normal folk handle these drives in their place, but are more concerned with what Goldstein calls "self-actualization"—a term that covers the main interest systems of adulthood.[19]

Theories of Changing Motives

Contrasting with these reactivity theories we now examine what Woodworth calls "behavior primacy theories."[20] These insist that the major share of our day's activities does not contribute to gratifying basic drives. Our behavior for the most part has to do with outgoing, exploring, adjustive dealing with our environment. The child's "play"—an all-absorbing motive for him—is a good example. Even when his primary drives are fairly strong, the child keeps on with his play. A child must be very hungry to cease. When the drives reach a high degree of intensity, and he finds himself very thirsty or fatigued or needing to eliminate, the play is temporarily (but only temporarily) interrupted.

Unlike the primary drives, it seems impossible to satiate this type of motive. A given toy may begin to pall, but the child does not then become quiescent (as in "tension-reduction") but turns to new exploratory and play activities. The adult, too, is primarily motivated to keep in touch with his environment, through manipulating, watching, exploring, gossiping.

No one denies that organic drives are important factors in motivation. The question is whether they can possibly explain all that a man does with his equipment. A musician's combination of interest and skill is profoundly motivational; so too is the scholar's, the nurse's, the explorer's. Each becomes energized with his own style of dealing with his world. Drive theory, it is said, takes care of the

19 K. Goldstein, Organismic approach to the problem of motivation, *N.Y. Acad. Sci.*, 1947, **9**, 218–250.
20 See Note 13 above.

essentials in motivation; but fails to take care of the "priceless non-essentials."

Explorative Tendency. For many years animal psychologists overlooked the potential significance of the ceaseless investigatory behavior of animals. They were too busy studying the primary drives of hunger, thirst, sex, fatigue. In recent years, however, the essential difference between this explorative tendency and other drives has been noted.[21]

Exploration is a continuous activity, the basis of much learning, and is not satiated as are the "tension-reduction" drives. This fact leads us to conclude that the "esthetic" and "activity" drives are not properly drives at all but should be classed under an altogether different conception of motivation.

Competence. R. W. White proposes the concept of "competence" to cover all that the child is doing when he is not under the immediate influence of discomfort, strong drives, or danger.[22] Conflict-free activity includes exploring, manipulating, looking, listening, pulling-pushing-dropping objects, running, climbing, "making" things, imitating parents, interacting with playmates. None of this spontaneous activity "reduces tension" as do drive-instigated actions. As White says, "as soon as a child begins to play in his crib he knows that the tension-reduction hypothesis is wrong." This author adds that the Freudian doctrine that the ages of six to thirteen constitute a "latency period" is indeed a curious myth. The child's development in this period is far from "latent." He is acquiring competence by leaps and bounds. The "myth" arose on the assumption that the

---

[21] Important discussions are T. A. Ryan, Drives, tasks and the initiation of behavior, *Amer. J. Psychol.*, 1958, **71**, 74–93; also H. L. Ansbacher (Ed.), Symposium on expansion and exploration, *J. individ. Psychol.*, 1958, **14**, 103–127. For a survey of relevant experimental literature see D. E. Berlyne, *Conflict, arousal, and curiosity* (New York: McGraw-Hill, 1960).

[22] Other authors have suggested different labels: *superiority* (Adler); *function-pleasure* (Bühler); *mastery* (Woodworth, also W. I. Thomas); *activity-drive* (G. Murphy, O. Klineberg); *primary ego-autonomy* (H. Hartmann). White's argument that drive theory cannot adequately account for the healthy growth of the normal personality is in two articles: R. W. White, Adler and the future of ego psychology, *J. individ. Psychol.*, 1957, **13**, 112–124, and Motivation reconsidered: the concept of competence, *Psychol. Rev.*, 1959, **66**, 297–333.

The reader may ask, "If competence is a dominant and permanent need, why is it listed under theories of *changing* motives?" The answer is that under the concept of competence we must allow for a continuous change of *specific* motives and goals. To be competent in adulthood is to have a wholly different goal-orientation from the child's. Such is not the case in theories of fixed and classified motives.

chief motive in life is (broadly speaking) sexual, and that, according to Freud, no striking changes in the psychosexual development occur during this interval.

Much of the competence a child seeks is in the social realm. He desires attention, he wants love, and he enjoys playing with other children. In these cases he undoubtedly learns in part by the rewards or rejections he receives from others. But in most nonsocial matters the child (and the adult) is the best judge of his own success. He knows what enhances his self-esteem, what strikes him as a failure or as a worthy accomplishment, what fulfills his own image of himself. Hence if the theory of reinforcement has explanatory value it must be considered largely in terms of self-reward and self-punishment.

When we come to adulthood we need the concept of competence just as much as in childhood. Most of what an adult does springs from his store of personal skills and interests. Like the child he has plenty of biological needs (for food, shelter, sex) which may fuse with, or may distract from, his interests. But they cannot explain the enduring pull of esthetic, intellectual, religious, or economic activities.

Although we cannot derive normally healthy adult interests *entirely* from the individual's mode of handling his infantile instinctual problems (as Freud's theory of sublimation and ego defense would hold), yet we must not deny that many of the passionate interests of adulthood may contain some admixture of unconscious aggressive or symbolic sexual force. Indeed, the more "passionate" (obsessive) the interest the more we may suspect it to be infused with unconscious sexual or aggressive pressures. (See page 151.) But normally the central motives of adulthood have their foundation in a cooler kind of interest—the interest that implies competence.

It would be wrong to say that a "need for competence" is the simple and sovereign motive of life. It does, however, come as close as any need (closer than the sexual) to summing up the whole biological story of development. We survive through competence, we grow through competence, we become "self-actualizing" through competence.

Related to exploration and competence are other current concepts. These also shift emphasis from the treadmill of reactivity to proaction and future-pointing in man's motives.

Deficit Motives and Growth Motives. A. H. Maslow propounds a highly suggestive theory. He holds that in the course of childhood development it is important first of all that basic drives (deficit motives) be gratified so that the child may later be freed to adopt less self-centered (growth) motives. Thus a child who has a sufficiency of food, care, safety, and love need not as he grows older be obsessed by these basic needs. He will feel secure, and can therefore reach out to expanded goals. If he has known basic drive-gratification and security he can later in life tolerate a frustration of these same drives more readily than a person whose whole personality is permanently pivoted on needs that were never adequately gratified.[23] (Some animals, it is known, will develop stronger habits of hoarding if in early life they were deprived of earlier food satisfaction.)

In this theory Maslow recognizes, as we have done, that primary drives are central in infancy; he also indicates a way in which the turn from early to more mature motivation may take place. His theory helps to explain the "neurotic" person who fails to develop functionally autonomous systems of motives—who all his lifelong may be "acting out" infantile complexes. Freud, of course, first called attention to this type of personality, but unlike Freud, Maslow allows *normal* people to outgrow this dependence in their course of development.

Self-actualization. Growth motives, as Maslow calls them, lead to self-actualization. Goldstein, in fact, insists that all motivation (of whatever type) partakes of this character. Self-actualization is at bottom the only motive of men. The concept is not specific, but has the merit of pointing to the ultimate individuality of motivation; each personality is different from all others, and strives to maintain its integrity and fulfill its own destiny in its own way. The concept also has the advantage of seeing more in motivation than pressures, drives, conflicts. It implies that while these forces cause the person to react, there is over and above sheer reactivity a large scope for conflict-free growth and self-realization. The concept is definitely pointed toward the future, whereas theories of reactivity point toward the past or at best toward the immediate present.[24]

Ego-Psychology. Without doubt the chief error in orthodox

[23] A. H. Maslow, *Motivation and personality* (New York: Harper, 1954), Chap. 5.
[24] For a discussion of self-actualization see K. Goldstein, *Human nature in the light of psychopathology* (Cambridge, Mass.: Harvard Univ. Press, 1940).

Freudian psychology lies in its contention that "the ego has no energy of its own." Today many, perhaps most, followers of Freud admit the blunder and excuse it by saying that "Freud died before he had finished his theory of the ego." As we saw in Chapter 7 there has grown up a neo-Freudian school of thought that denies that the only source of energy is the id. Correspondingly it denies that adult interests and motives are sustained entirely by the sublimation of sexual and aggressive instincts or, at best, by a neutralized and de-sexualized energy that comes from inhibiting sexual and aggressive aims.

Ego (or neo-Freudian) -psychology speaks freely of "ego auton-omy," meaning thereby that the self-conscious region of personality is not wholly a slave to id impulses, nor to environmental pressures. There are such things as "conflict-free ego functions." We live our lives, at least in part, according to our conscious interests, values, plans, and intentions. Our motives are at least relatively autonomous of pressures from drives, instincts, and surrounding situations.[25] To acknowledge the existence of conflict-free ego functions is to turn traditional Freudian psychology on its head. The admission means that much of our life is lived on the basis of mature and reportable schemes of values and purposes, and not merely as a conflicted defense against primitive instinctual forces. To a person who has reached this stage of development Fromm gives the label "productive personality."[26]

How does it happen that the ego can develop a relative autonomy of instinctive id forces and of the environment? Seeking to answer this question Hartmann postulates first an *apparatus of primary autonomy.* This "apparatus" is nothing more than man's adaptive powers, as represented in the functioning of his perception, memory, motor capacity, of all that helps him to fit in with environment. To adapt means to solve problems, overcome obstacles, search out mean-ings, and, in general, use one's brains. The relation between this type of motivation and what other authors have called *exploration* and *competence* is close. Other writers have made the point in dif-ferent ways. Long ago Graham Wallas insisted that among man's

25 D. Rapaport traces the drift of psychoanalysis toward ego-psychology in two articles: The autonomy of the ego, *Bull. Menninger Clin.,* 1951, 15, 113–123, and The theory of ego autonomy: a generalization, *Bull. Menninger Clin.,* 1958, 22, 13–35.
26 E. Fromm, *Man for himself* (New York: Holt, Rinehart and Winston, 1947).

motives must be included an "instinct of thought." Bartlett has seen a basic dynamism in the "effort after meaning." Gestalt psychology has considered intellectual "closures" as an important dynamic tendency; Festinger speaks of "cognitive dissonance" as a motivating force. Cantril and such existentialists as Frankl regard man's search for meaning, for the "why" of his experience as an ultimate—perhaps *the* ultimate—motive in life.

To ascribe dynamic force to the intellectual functions, to the cognitive aspect of life, is an advance of great importance over the various "unchanging energy" theories we have previously discussed. It means that human purposes are not limited by a strict list of drives or instincts, but that they change in time, with varying conditions, and keep pace with one's course of becoming.

Hartmann speaks likewise of an *apparatus of secondary autonomy*, which is not primordial but derivative.[27] Granted that the ego does often serve instinctual drives (as Freud maintained), still in the course of growth its instrumental activities and interests may become "estranged" from their instinctual sources. What was once a service function of the ego, or an ego-defense may undergo a "change of function." The young man who once wanted to become a politician because of his early father fixation may become interested in politics for its own sake: as a means of carrying out his own style of being, as a way of actualizing his own potentialities.[28]

It would be misleading to say that all modern Freudians accept the autonomy of the ego. Some of them deny it altogether; others speak guardedly of *relative* autonomy. And they are, of course, correct in denying that ego-motives are always to be accepted at their face value. Much motivation, we repeat, is unconscious, infantile, and hidden from oneself. The important point, however, is that *some* motivation is functionally autonomous, especially in personalities that we consider normal, mature, sound.

[27] H. Hartmann, The development of the ego concept in Freud's work, *Int. J. Psychoanal.*, 1956, **37**, 425–438. See also H. Hartmann, Ego psychology and the problem of adaptation. In D. Rapaport (Ed.), *Organization and pathology of thought* (New York: Columbia Univ. Press, 1951), pp. 362–396.

[28] When thinking is on the right track, as it is here, the question of priority fades in importance. Yet the historically minded reader may care to note that my own conception of *functional autonomy* antedated the "apparatus of secondary autonomy" by several years. See G. W. Allport, *Personality: a psychological interpretation* (New York: Holt, Rinehart and Winston, 1937), Chap. 7.

Summary

Motivation is the "go" of personality, and is, therefore, our most central problem. Psychologists are not agreed in their accounts of what internal conditions induce action and thought. Some say that all conduct is instigated by unchanging instincts or by drives. Such theories stress the reactive side of man's behavior. Severe restrictions must be laid on theories of this order (whether of the psychoanalytic or stimulus-response order). They fail to allow for the extensive transformation in motives from infancy to maturity, or for the extreme diversity of motives that we find in adulthood. Current theories are tending to allow for an additional principle: they claim that competence, self-actualization, and ego autonomy are equally basic features of human motivation. A final theory of motivation will have to admit the truth that lies in all these views.

CHAPTER 10

The Transformation of Motives

REQUIREMENTS FOR AN ADEQUATE THEORY OF MOTIVATION •
FUNCTIONAL AUTONOMY • TWO LEVELS OF AUTONOMY •
WHAT PROCESSES ARE NOT FUNCTIONALLY AUTONOMOUS? •
HOW DOES FUNCTIONAL AUTONOMY COME ABOUT? • TRAU-
MAUTIC TRANSFORMATIONS • SUMMARY

Personality, like every other living thing, changes as it grows. And since motives are the dynamos of personality we must expect motives also to grow and to change. To account for the vast transformation that occurs between infancy and adulthood is not an easy task. The process is gradual and subtle. Nor can we say that all motives change in equal degree. Drives remain with us. And even in complex adult motives the past is sometimes, to some degree, still alive in the present. But our task is to discover how much of the past is fire and how much of it is ashes.

The previous chapter laid the groundwork for our analysis. The reader will recall that it distinguished theories that postulate *unchanging* energies from theories that postulate *changing* energies.

219

Requirements for an Adequate Theory of Motivation

We propose that an adequate theory of human motives will meet the following requirements:

1. *It will acknowledge the contemporaneity of motives.* Whatever moves us must move now. Hence motivational theory must look at the *present* state of the organism. The past is not important unless somehow it can be shown to be dynamically active in the present. Take, for example, the following case:

> George is a youthful criminal. He has pilfered, committed arson and armed robbery, and made vicious attacks on several policemen. The reason, it is clear to see, lies in his early, miserable home life. His mother whom he loved died when he was five. After that tragedy he lived only with his father, who was cruel and a drunkard and who alternately rejected and abused George.

Does this history "explain" George's conduct today? In a sense, yes, for it gives historical facts that are essential to an understanding of George's total course of life. But other boys with the same grim history may today not be delinquent. In fact, a certain dedicated Jesuit missionary of my acquaintance has a very similar family history. What, then, is the difference? The answer seems to be that George is still actively troubled by his conflict and is currently still acting out (and displacing) his hostility toward his father. The missionary, on the other hand, has somehow outgrown the conflict, and has supplanted earlier hostile motives with others of a more benign order. Hence we cannot say that past history automatically determines the contemporary "go" of motives. As we have said, past motives explain nothing unless they are also present motives.

For this reason the doctrine of "secondary drives" is beset by fatal illogicality. The doctrine, we recall, regards present motives as deriving their energies from past reinforcement. If you like fishing, is it because your father once upon a time took you fishing, and because when you were a child he satisfied many of your primary drives? Historically this may be the true sequence. But now, today, you have a passion for fishing; and the "go" of this passion is not the "go" of the primary drives of infancy (with which your father and later fishing were associated).

There are no "secondary" motives in the dynamic sense. Secondary in time, yes, for all present motives grow out of previous motives. Also, we may speak of motives that have secondary importance in the personality. But if we are speaking of the *energies* or *dynamics* of a motive we must concede that they are all "primary." None has its "go" in the past, but always and only in the present.[1]

2. *It will be a pluralistic theory—allowing for motives of many types.* In addition to the error of anachronism (defining present motivation in terms of past events), another shortcoming of much motivation theory is its oversimplification. Various writers have assured us that all motives are reducible to one type: to drives, or to pleasure-seeking, or to the unconscious, or to power-seeking, or to self-actualization. None of these formulations can be adequate, for there is some truth in all of them. To brush a mosquito from one's cheek is a motivated act, but so, too, is devoting one's life to the eradication of yellow fever or malaria; to seek a drink of water is no more and no less motivational than to seek the Olympic championship for swimming.

We recall Maslow's helpful distinction. He speaks of *deficit* motives and of *growth* motives.[2] The former include drives and elementary psychological needs—thirst, hunger, sleep, safety, comfort, basic security. The latter include the ambitions, interests, outthrusts of the normally developing adult. An adequate theory must encompass both.

Some motives are transient, some recurring; some are momentary, others persistent; some unconscious, others conscious; some opportunistic, others propriate; some tension-reducing, others tension-maintaining. Motives are so diverse in type that we find it difficult to discover the common denominator. About all we can say is that a person's motives include all that he is trying (consciously or unconsciously, reflexly or deliberately) to do.

If we admit this principle of pluralism we must be ready to face the fact that motives in animals will not be an adequate model for motives in men; neither will the motives of adulthood always con-

---

1 One author who insisted with special clarity on the contemporaneousness of all motivation was Kurt Lewin. See *A dynamic theory of personality* (New York: McGraw-Hill, 1935).
2 A. H. Maslow, *Motivation and personality* (New York: Harper, 1954). A similar position is taken by Charlotte Bühler, who on the basis of extensive work with life-histories, concludes that every human being seeks both equilibrium and expansion: Maturation and motivation, *Dialectica,* 1951, **5,** 312–361.

tinue the motives of childhood; and, finally, motivation in a neurotic personality will not necessarily define motivation in a normal individual. Many investigators, hoping to unravel the tangled skein of human motivation, have endeavored to reduce its strands to the simplified model of the machine, the animal, the child, or the pathological. None is adequate.[3]

3. *It will ascribe dynamic force to cognitive processes—e.g., to planning and intention.* We are emerging from an epoch of extreme irrationalism when human motivation has been equated with blind will (Schopenhauer), with the struggle for survival (Darwin), with instincts (McDougall and others), with the steam boiler of the id (Freud). Under the powerful influence of these doctrines the role of "the intellect" has been considered negligible. At best it was seen as an instrument for carrying out a motive. Cognitive functions are mere servants. In physiological terms the central nervous system is regarded as the agent of the autonomic nervous system.[4]

Gradually a current of protest has set in. Over forty years ago, after surveying McDougall's theory of instincts, Graham Wallas proposed that we add an "instinct of thought" to the list.[5] More recently the Gestalt psychologists have ascribed dynamic force to cognitive operations. We shape our perceptions, alter our memories, solve our problems because of dynamical "self-distributing" tendencies in the brain field which have no necessary connections with drives, instincts, or other urges. Bartlett sums up such forces under the phrase "effort after meaning"—a conception that plays a large part in the writings of many modern psychologists—experimentalists, cognitive theorists, and existentialists.[6]

Although there is no doubt that men greedily seek to know the meaning of their present experiences and of their existence as a whole, we should not sharply separate such cognitive motives from

3 Cf. G. W. Allport, Scientific models and human morals. In *Personality and social encounter* (Boston: Beacon, 1960), Chap. 4.
4 Cf. E. J. Kempf, The autonomic functions and the personality. *Nerv. & ment. Dis. Monogr. Ser.*, 1921, No. 28. We described this point of view in Chapter 4.
5 G. Wallas, *The great society* (New York: Macmillan, 1914).
6 In varying ways the following writers place considerable weight on the dynamic force of cognition: F. C. Bartlett, *Remembering* (Cambridge, England: Cambridge Univ. Press, 1932); S. E. Asch, *Social psychology* (Englewood Cliffs, N.J.: Prentice-Hall, 1952); H. Cantril, *The why of man's experience* (New York: Macmillan, 1950); L. Festinger, *A theory of cognitive dissonance* (Evanston, Ill.: Row, Peterson, 1957); R. May, E. Angel, and H. F. Ellenberger (Eds.), *Existence: a new dimension in psychiatry and psychology* (New York: Basic Books, 1958).

those that are traditionally called conative or affective. More typically we find that people are trying to do something in which their wants and their plans readily cooperate. Instead of being related as master and servant, the desire and the reason fuse into a single motive that we may call the "intention."

Intention is a much-neglected form of motivation, but one of central importance for the understanding of personality. It enables us to overcome the opposing of motive and thought.

Like all motives, intention refers to *what the individual is trying to do*. There are, to be sure, immediate and short-run intentions (getting a glass of water, brushing off a fly, satisfying any drive); but the term has particular value in pointing to the long-range dispositions in personality. We can *intend* to order our lives by some ethical code, to search out a meaning for our existence. A religious intention leads us to order our life in the hope of attaining at the end a beatific vision.

The concept of intention enables us to admit several important features of motivation:

1. The cognitive and emotive processes in personality become fused into an integral urge.

2. The intention, like all motivation, exists in the present, but has strong future orientation. Use of the concept helps us to trace the course of motivation as lives are actually lived—into the future and not, as most theories do, backward into the past. It tells us what sort of future a person is trying to bring about, and this is the most important question we can ask about any mortal.

3. The term has a flavor of "tension maintained" and thus reflects the true condition of all long-range motives.

4. When we identify major intentions in a life we have a device for holding subsidiary trends in perspective.

A young college student *intends* to become a surgeon. This is a basic motive. The intention inevitably selects certain of his abilities for sharpening and others for neglect. (Hence we cannot know him only by studying his present abilities.) The intention may well bring disappointment to his parents, who had planned a business career for the boy. (Hence we cannot understand his personality by observing its effect on others.) The intention also inhibits contradictory motives. Although he wishes to marry, his surgical intention may delay this goal; while he likes football he sacrifices it to his studies. (Hence we cannot know him simply by listing his drives and desires.)

Although it is useful to know what a person can do, what his effect is on other people, and what his impulses and desires may be, the picture is always incomplete unless we know also what he is intending, what future he is trying to bring about.[7]

Agreeing with the discoveries of psychoanalysis, we admit that an individual does not always know precisely what his own intentions are. Consciously he may misinterpret the line of his own endeavor. A neurotic frequently does so. A mother who unconsciously resents and hates her offspring may conceivably be full of conscious solicitude and overly protest her love ("reaction formation"). Her intentions need clarifying to herself through psychiatric aid. But in most mortals we find that impulse and planning, desire and intention, conflicts and discordant intentions are reflected fairly accurately in their conscious report.

Unfortunately the concept of intention is not prominent in current psychology. The reason is that it connotes purpose, the efficacy of conscious planning, and a "pull" that man's image of the future exerts on his present conduct. As pointed out in Chapter 5, the more favored "physicalistic" conception would say that he is *pushed* by his motives (not *pulled* by his intentions). Many psychologists would say that "drives" take entire care of what we here call intention. Yet drives as such are blind. They do not allow for organization and direction by cognitive attitudes, by foresight, by cortical control. And yet all these psychological functions are bound into the total course of motivation.

The point at issue is illustrated by two different psychologists' replies to the inquiry, "What is the most important question you can ask a person in order to understand his personality?" The first, a "depth" psychologist, replied, "I'd ask what types of fantasy the man has" (thus tapping unconscious pushes). The other, a consulting psychologist with long experience, said, "I'd ask

---

[7] Cf. F. Heider, *The psychology of interpersonal relations* (New York: Wiley, 1958), Chap. 4; also G. E. M. Anscombe, *Intention* (Oxford: Basil Blackwell, 1957).

where he wants to be, what he wants to be doing, five years from now" (thus tapping his long-range intentions).

Before we leave the concept of intention, let this be said: If the term seems unacceptable (perhaps because it dates back to Brentano and even to St. Thomas Aquinas, or because it has a "mentalistic" flavor), the point can be preserved satisfactorily by placing stress on the concept of *interest*. A person's intentions are, after all, his characteristic interests. Diamond defines interest as

the disposition to engage in some culturally elaborated activity without regard for any consequent gratification other than through the mere exercise of this disposition.[8]

The phrase "culturally elaborated" calls attention to the difference between the complexity of an interest and the relative simplicity of a drive. An interest may or may not include an element of primary drive, but it always includes more. Even when we say that an individual is interested in food or sex, we recognize that it is not the drives, but learned ways of satisfying the drives, that define the interest. And at the opposite extreme we speak of architecture, the United Nations, or religion as interests. In these cases there may be no detectable drive element at all.

4. *The theory will allow for the concrete uniqueness of motives.* What is the difference between a concrete and an abstract motive? In the left-hand column we list certain motives as we find them in studying actual lives; in the right-hand column we see how they may be fitted to various abstract theories.

Concrete	*Abstract*
Mary has a strong desire to become a professional nurse.	She is cathecting an aim-inhibited sexual wish (Freudian).
Jim is passionately fond of music.	His interest is a secondary drive developed from his musical mother, who satisfied his early primary drives (S-R theory).
William hopes to become a top-notch mechanic.	He is thus expressing his need-achievement (Need theory).
Irene has a terror of all open spaces (agoraphobia).	The instinct of flight is the root motive (Instinct theory).

[8] S. Diamond, *Personality and temperament* (New York: Harper, 1957), p. 294.

Concrete	*Abstract*
Thomas hopes to be elected president of his club.	The wish for mastery is the motive.
Sam seems always to be seeking praise.	He has a need-nurturance.
Patricia loves to entertain guests in her home.	The desire for competence is the root.

These examples are sufficient to show the difference between the concrete and the abstract view of motives. The latter are always fitted to some theoretical system, and derive from classifications of allegedly basic and common motives of men. They concern personality-in-general. Their fit to the concrete case is loose. Not four wishes, nor eighteen instincts, nor thirty needs, nor any combination or derivation of these, seem adequate to account for the endless variety of goals sought by an endless variety of mortals.

Take the final example in the series. It is true that Patricia is in a sense manifesting "competence" in her entertaining. But there are surely a million kinds of competence in life which do not interest Patricia at all. Her motive is highly concrete. Entertaining, not abstract competence, is the bread of life to her, and any abstract scheme misses that point completely, and therefore sheds little or no light on her personality as it actually functions. It is a caricature of a person to view his interests merely as changes rung on a common pattern.

This stress on the uniqueness of developed motives will cause consternation. "How," you ask, "are we ever to have a *science* of motives unless we generalize?" The answer to this objection is that general principles of motivation (such as this chapter and the preceding chapter deal with) may help us to understand how uniqueness comes about. It is an error to assume that a general principle of motivation can lead only to a uniform schedule of motives common to all men.

Functional Autonomy

We turn now to one general law of motivation that allows fully for the concrete uniqueness of personal motives, and observes all other criteria for an adequate theory of motivation. It is by no means the only valid principle pertinent to the development of human motives; nor does it explain *all* motivation. It is, however, our attempt to escape the limitations of uniform, rigid, abstract, backward-looking theories, and to recognize the spontaneous, changing, forward-looking, concrete character that much adult motivation surely has.

Functional autonomy regards adult motives as varied, and as self-sustaining, contemporary systems, growing out of antecedent systems, but functionally independent of them. Just as a child gradually outgrows dependence on his parents, becomes self-determining, and outlives his parents, so it is with many motives. The transition may be gradual but it is nonetheless drastic. As the individual (or the motive) matures, the bond with the past is broken. The tie is historical, not functional.

Such a theory is obviously opposed to all conceptions of "unchanging energies." It declines to view the energies of adults as infantile or archaic in nature. Motivation is always contemporary. The life of modern Athens is *continuous* with the life of the ancient city, but in no sense *depends* upon it for its present "go." The life of a tree is continuous with that of its seed, but the seed no longer sustains and nourishes the full-grown tree. Earlier purposes lead into later purposes, but are abandoned in the latter's favor.

Let us take a few commonplace examples. An ex-sailor has a craving for the sea, a musician longs to return to his instrument after an enforced absence, a miser continues to build up his useless pile. Now the sailor may have first acquired his love for the sea as an incident in his struggle to earn a living. The sea was "secondary reinforcement" for his hunger drive. But now the ex-sailor is perhaps a wealthy banker; the original motive is destroyed, and yet the hunger for the sea persists and even increases in intensity. The musician may first have been stung by a slur on his inferior performance into mastering his instrument; but now he is safely beyond these taunts, and finds that he loves his instrument more than anything else in the world. The miser perhaps learned his habit of thrift in dire necessity, but the miserliness persists and becomes stronger with the years even after the necessity has been relieved.

Workmanship is a good example. A good workman feels compelled to do a clean-cut job even though his income no longer depends on maintaining high standards. In fact, in a day of jerry-building his workmanlike standards may be to his economic disadvantage. Even so he cannot do a slipshod job. Workmanship is not an instinct, but so firm is the hold it may acquire on a man that it is no wonder Veblen mistook it for one.

A businessman, long since secure economically, works himself into ill-health, perhaps even back into poverty, for the sake of carrying on his plans. Hard work, once a means to an end, becomes an end in itself.

Neither necessity nor reason can make a person contented on an isolated country farm after he is adapted to active, energetic city life. Citified habits urge him to a frenzied existence, even though health may demand the simpler life.

The pursuit of literature, the development of good taste in clothes, the use of cosmetics, strolls in the public park, or a winter in Miami may first serve, let us say, the interests of sex. But every one of these "instrumental" activities may become an interest in itself, held for a lifetime, even after they no longer serve the erotic motive.

Some mothers bear their children unwillingly, dismayed at the thought of drudgery in the future. The "parental instinct" is wholly lacking. The mother may be held to her child-tending by fear of what her critical neighbors will say, or by fear of the law, or perhaps by a dim hope that the child will provide security for her in her old age. Gross as these motives may be, they hold her to her work until gradually, through the practice of devotion, her burden becomes a joy. As her love for the child develops, her earlier practical motives are lost. In later years not one of these original motives may operate. The tenacity of the maternal sentiment is proverbial, even when, as in this case, it can be shown to be not an original but an acquired motive.

Let us add one more example. Many boys choose occupations that follow in their fathers' footsteps. Also, most young boys go through a period of passionate "father identification." Joe, let us say, is the son of a famous politician. As a young lad he imitates everything his father does, even perhaps giving "speeches." Years pass and the father dies. Joe is now middle-aged and is deeply absorbed in politics. He runs for office, perhaps the self-same job his father held. What, then, motivates Joe today? Is it his earlier father fixation? Conceivably yes, for Joe may never have outgrown his Oedipal complex (trying to be like Daddy in order to win his mother's affection). If Joe's political activity today is of this neurotic variety we shall probably find him behaving in a compulsive, rigid, even maladaptive manner. The chances, however, are that his interest in politics has outgrown its roots in "father identification." There is historical continuity but no longer any functional continuity. Politics is now his dominant passion; it is his style of life; it is a large part of Joe's personality. The original seed has been discarded.

All our illustrations have one feature in common. The adult interest we describe began as something else. In all cases the activity that later became motivational was at first instrumental to some other end (i.e., to some earlier motive). What was once extrinsic and instrumental becomes intrinsic and impelling. The activity once served a drive or some simple need; it now serves itself, or in a larger sense, serves the self-image (self-ideal) of the person. Childhood is no longer in the saddle; maturity is.

Functional autonomy, then, refers to any acquired system of motivation in which the tensions involved are not of the same kind as the antecedent tensions from which the acquired system developed.[9]

[9] Functional autonomy (without the label) has been acknowledged by many writers. Many years ago F. Brentano called it a "well-known psychological law" that "what at first was desired merely as a means to something else, comes at last from habit to be desired for its own sake." *The origin of the knowledge of right and wrong* (Transl. by C. Hague; London: Constable, 1902), p. 16. E. C. Tolman speaks of "acquired adherences to specific types of means objects" as having the power to set up "in their own right," and acquire "a strangle hold." *Phil. Sci.*, 1935, 2, 370. Elsewhere Tolman acknowledges "independent tertiary motives" which for all practical purposes must be regarded as functionally autonomous. In T. Parsons and E. A. Shils, *Toward a general theory of action* (Cambridge, Mass.: Harvard Univ. Press, 1951), pp. 321 f.

A more familiar statement is R. S. Woodworth's phrase "mechanisms may become drives." "The fundamental drive towards a certain end may be hunger, sex, pugnacity, or what not, but once the activity is started, the means to the end becomes an object of interest on its own account." *Dynamic psychology* (New York: Columbia Univ. Press, 1918), p. 201. W. Stern makes the same point when he writes that "phenomotives" may turn into "genomotives." *General psychology from the personalistic standpoint* (Transl. by H. Spoerl; New York: Macmillan, 1938). H. Hartmann's concept of "secondary ego autonomy," as we saw in the previous chapter, supports our position.

In spite of this extensive endorsement, many critics have shown marked resistance to the concept. In general, they argue that if instinct theory or drive-reduction theory are extended far enough they will cover all cases of "functional autonomy." Illustrating this critical literature are the following references: P. A. Bertocci, Critique of Gordon W. Allport's theory of motivation, *Psychol. Rev.*, 1940, 47, 501–532; and O. Oppenheimer, The functional autonomy of motives, *J. soc. Psychol.*, 1947, 25, 171–179.

Among the critics who believe that stimulus-response psychology remains adequate are D. C. McClelland, Functional autonomy of motives as an extinction phenomenon, *Psychol. Rev.*, 1942, 49, 272–283; and Dorothy Rethlingshaefer, Experimental evidence for functional autonomy of motives, *Psychol. Rev.*, 1943, 50, 397–407.

Whether the present exposition of the case for functional autonomy will satisfy these critics is doubtful. And yet the argument has benefited from their criticisms and is, I hope, more convincing (when taken in conjunction with Chapters 5 and 9) than the original exposition published in *Personality: a psychological interpretation* (New York: Holt, Rinehart and Winston, 1937), Chap. 7.

Two Levels of Autonomy

Examples of functional autonomy could be multiplied end-lessly and aimlessly. Better, however to be more systematic about the matter. After giving some years of thought to the problem, I am now inclined to believe that the phenomenon should be inspected on two levels. We shall do well to speak of (1) *perseverative* functional au-tonomy, and (2) *propriate* functional autonomy. The former level skirts close to what are (or may be assumed to be) simple neurologi-cal principles. The latter level, however, frankly depends upon cer-tain philosophical assumptions regarding the nature of human per-sonality—not that these assumptions contradict in any way known neurological fact, but they reach beyond present knowledge of the way the nervous system operates.

Perseverative Functional Autonomy. Let us speak first of certain animal experiments. One scarcely knows how much weight to give them. On the one hand, animals possess the basic neural and emo-tional rudiments that are also found in man. On the other hand, the higher cortical centers are so poorly developed that the capacities for symbolization, delay, and self-reference are largely or wholly lacking.

1. *Animal evidence.* An experimenter feeds a rat at regular intervals. The rat is most active just prior to the time for feed-ing. After a while the experimenter starves the rat. But though it is now hungry all the time, the previous rhythm of maximum activity (just prior to the usual feeding time) persists.[10]

Even a mollusc, whose habits of burrowing in the sand and reappearing depend on the movements of the tide, will, when removed from the beach to the laboratory, continue the same rhythm without the tide.[11]

A rat who has learned a maze under the incentive of hunger will, even when fed to repletion, run the maze correctly, not for food, but apparently "for the fun of it."[12]

One investigator applied collodion to the ears of an animal, thus setting up removing and cleaning movements. A month after

[10] C. P. Richter, A behavioristic study of the activity of the rat, *Comp. Psychol. Monogr.*, 1922, 1, No. 2.

[11] S. C. Crawford, Characteristics of nocturnal animals, *Quart. Rev. Biol.*, 1934, 9, 201–214.

[12] J. D. Dodson, Relative value of reward and punishment in habit formation, *Psycho-biol.*, 1917, 1, 231–276.

the beginning of the experiment when the ears of the rats as studied by the microscope showed no further trace of irritation, the number of "cleaning" movements was still very great.[13]

As far as they go these experiments and many like them show what we mean by *perseveration*. A mechanism set in action because of one motive continues at least for a time to "feed" itself. Here we have the most elementary instance of functional autonomy.

As yet it is not possible to designate the underlying neurological basis for perseverative functional autonomy of this type. The phenomena just mentioned, as well as those listed below, indicate the presence of self-sustaining circuits or substructures, no longer geared exclusively to stimulus-control. Neurologists acknowledge the phenomena and speculate concerning the nervous mechanisms involved.[14]

2. *Addictions*. No one will deny that the craving for tobacco, alcohol, or opiates is an acquired appetite, or that the craving may be very intense. An alcoholic under treatment writes:

> Those craving paroxysms occur at regular intervals, three weeks apart, lasting for several days. They are not weak, namby pamby things for scoffers to laugh at. If not assuaged with liquor they become spells of physical and mental illness. My mouth drools saliva, my stomach and intestines seem cramped, and I become bilious, nauseated, and in a shaky nervous funk.[15]

13 W. C. Olson, *The Measurement of nervous habits in normal children* (Minneapolis: Univ. of Minnesota Press, 1929), pp. 62–65.
14 Thus D. O. Hebb believes that "open assemblies of cells in the brain" may allow for some enduring reverberative activity: *The organization of behavior* (New York: Wiley, 1949). Morgan speaks of "central motive states." C. T. Morgan, *Physiological psychology* (New York: McGraw-Hill, 1943), Chap. 22. J. C. Eccles holds that while old learning is never lost it may be reorganized in such a way that it no longer manifests itself in the behavior-pattern to which it initially "belonged." *The neurophysiological basis of mind* (Oxford: Clarendon, 1953). Olds introduces the concept of self-stimulation to account for "long-run continuities": J. Olds, *The growth and structure of motives* (Glencoe, Ill.: Free Press, 1956).
  A related line of speculation is offered by W. S. McCulloch, A hierarchy of values determined by the topology of nervous nets, *Bull. math. Biophysics*, 1945, 7, 89. This author holds that the nervous system is not organized on a linear basis, but that cortical neurones are ordered in a circle. An impulse does not fire a motor neurone until it has passed continuously around the circle, and his been modified accordingly. In all these speculations we note the recurrence of the concept of a reverberating cortical circuit. This principle may turn out to provide a neural base for perseverative functional autonomy.
15 Inmate Ward Eight, *Beyond the door of delusion* (New York: Macmillan, 1932), p. 281.

One may say that such physical hunger, artificially induced by drugs, is not a fair example. Yet recent work on addiction indicates that the dynamism involved is largely psychological. Thus, monkeys and medical patients who are injected with opiates become habituated and suffer greatly from "withdrawal"; but once cured they show no desire to use the drug again. True addicts, on the other hand, even after a cure, when all withdrawal symptoms have vanished, still, in a vast majority of cases, return to their addiction. It cannot be because of *physiological* hunger, but because a subsystem of personality has been formed which handles life's frustrations by taking to narcotics. Thus the person who is "hooked" is one who has developed an acquired and autonomous motivational structure.[16]

3. *Circular mechanisms.* Everyone has observed the almost endless repetition of acts by a child. The good-natured parent picks up a spoon repeatedly thrown down by a baby. The parent wearies of the game long before the infant does. The child's babbling, early manipulations, and play show the same self-perpetuation. Each activity seems to "feed back" into the sensory channels, thus maintaining a "circular reflex."[17] Admittedly this example illustrates only a temporary functional autonomy. It is, however, an important example in showing that there is some neural machinery for maintaining activity patterns without our needing to trace every act to a drive-motive.

4. *Task perseveration.* Many experiments show that incompleted tasks set up tensions that keep the individual at work until the task is completed—no matter how long it takes. Even a trivial task can become haunting for a considerable time. Ask a subject to spend an hour thinking of, and writing down, all the words he can beginning with the letter *c.* When he leaves the experimental room, even during his sleep, and perhaps into the next day, he will continue to perseverate, and without wishing to do so will recall many new

---

16 A. Wikler, *Opiate addiction: physiological and neurophysiological aspects in relation to clinical problems* (Springfield, Ill.: Charles C Thomas, 1953); A. R. Lindesmith, *Opiate addiction* (Bloomington, Ind.: Principia Press, 1947).

17 E. B. Holt, *Animal drive and the learning process* (New York: Holt, Rinehart and Winston, 1931), especially Chaps. 7 and 8. On a higher level of speculation, F. H. Allport raises the question whether all "event structures" at the physical, psychological, and social levels do not by their inherent nature have the property of self-maintenance: *Theories of perception and the concept of structure* (New York: Wiley, 1955), especially Chap. 21.

words beginning with c.[18] Here, too, the functional autonomy is of short duration, but the point is that no hypothesis of self-assertion, rivalry, or any other basic need is required to explain the self-maintaining dynamic system temporarily in force.

Gestalt psychologists speak of a "closure tendency" (*Gestaltdrang*) which persists until the completion of a task. It is known that the memory for incompleted tasks is better than for completed tasks.[19] There is pressure to continue work on any unfinished assignment.

Woodworth originally spoke of "habits becoming drives." This statement is only partially acceptable. When once learned, most habits seem to become merely instrumental skills. We use our typewriter, our automobile, or our language habits only in the service of active motives. Yet "habits on the make" are highly dynamic. The child who is just learning to talk or to walk seems driven to perfect these skills. The adolescent is haunted until he completes his skill in skating, dancing, or driving. Of course, some skills are never really perfected. The concert pianist feels driven every day to hours of practice. We may conclude the matter this way: It is not the perfected talent nor the automatic habit that has driving power, but rather the imperfect talent and the habit-in-the-making.

5. *Familiarity and routine.* John Dewey has written:

> It is the essence of routine to insist upon its own continuation. Breach of it is a violation of right. Deviation from it is transgression.[20]

Especially in childhood, as we have seen, does repetitiveness have a compelling quality. If you tell a story to a young child he will not let you vary it in the retelling. Familiar playthings, foods, family customs are preferred. Trips away from home, perhaps to a summer camp, often bring acute homesickness. Childhood morality, as Piaget points out, is largely a morality of custom, obedience, and routine.[21]

The reader may object that a familiar setting is only a conditioned assurance that our drives will be met. Thus, our customary bed is associated with refreshing sleep; we like it because it is a "secondary reinforcer" of rest. But this explanation is not satisfactory.

18 Isabel Kendig, Studies in perseveration, *J. Psychol.*, 1936, **3,** 223–264.
19 B. Zeigarnik, Über das Behalten von erledigten und unerledigten Handlungen, *Psychol. Forsch.*, 1927, **9,** 1–85.
20 J. Dewey, *Human nature and conduct* (New York: Holt, Rinehart and Winston, 1922), p. 78.
21 J. Piaget, *The moral judgment of the child* (New York: Harcourt, Brace), 1932.

The pleasure that comes from a familiar bed is not the pleasure of somnolence but of simple familiarity. A child finds no more gratification of hunger in a familiar food than in a novel one, but he wants the familiar. And what drive does the exact repetition of a story satisfy?

The dynamism of routine may be found where no drives are present—even when they are thwarted. It sometimes happens, for example, that we enter a new city and lose our sense of direction. We think east is north, or that north is south. This condition of being "turned around" is annoying and certainly satisfies no drives; but it persists. A frame of reference is quickly established that for us becomes routine and almost impossible to correct. We don't want it, but we can't shake it off.

In a series of experiments Maslow has shown that people rapidly develop preferences for works of art and even for foreign names that they have previously encountered. They think a Russian name they have heard once or twice previously more euphonious, and like it better, than a totally novel Russian name.[22]

Suppose that you attend a conference which has morning and afternoon sessions. Do you not find everyone making for the same seat in the afternoon that he occupied in the morning? And if the conference continues over several days the space habit is firmly set. This routinization satisfies no drives unless the desire for sameness (familiarity) is itself a drive.

Gardner Murphy has introduced a concept that partly, but only partly, overlaps functional autonomy. He names it *canalization*.[23] This author points out that the pull of familiarity is often closely tied to the satisfaction of drives.

We want our drives satisfied in a familiar way. Most of us eat three meals a day, not two or five. This mealtime rhythm is not independent of the hunger drive, but does define it and imposes upon it an acquired preference. Some people cannot sleep well

22 A. H. Maslow, The influence of familiarization on preference, *J. exp. Psychol.*, 1937, 21, 162–180.
23 G. Murphy, *Human potentialities* (New York: Basic Books, 1958).

unless they have one pillow, two pillows, or, sometimes, none at all. Everyone needs oxygen, but some people are fresh-air fiends, and like to have gales of air blowing into their bedrooms; others prefer only to let it filter through cracks. The times, places, and seasons that we select for our eating, drinking, elimination, and sex activity are highly individual, and are profoundly important ingredients in the total motivational pattern.

But, strictly speaking, such acquired attachments are not functionally autonomous, for a basic drive motive is always present. At the same time, the drives can sometimes scarcely operate at all unless the highly individual, acquired tastes are ful-filled. And so we conclude that while there is a surface resemblance, the concept of canalization belongs fundamentally among theories of "unchanging energies" and not with functional autonomy.

Propriate Functional Autonomy. Up to now we have fixed our attention on relatively "low-grade" processes that manifest a shift of earlier dynamisms into later dynamisms. The latter derive from the former although they no longer depend on them. In all our illustrations we have assumed that some kind of servo- or feedback mechanism is at work helping to sustain systems at their contemporary level even while these systems undergo internal change.

We shall not, however, succeed in accounting for all adult motives if we stop at this point. For one thing, if we did so, the resulting picture of personality would be like that of a jeweler's repair shop filled with unrelated self-winding watches. Although personality contains many such self-maintaining systems, its principal energies are master systems of motivation that confer more unity on personality than disparate perseverating systems can do. Our account, therefore, cannot be complete until we relate the concept of functional autonomy to the propriate functions of personality (pages 126–128). Let us consider a few examples from this level of functional autonomy.

1. *Ability often turns into interest.* It is an established fact that ordinarily people *like* to do what they can do well (the correlation between abilities and interests is high). Now the original reason for learning a skill may not be interest at all. For example, a student

who first undertakes a field of study in college because it is required, because it pleases his parents, or because it comes at a convenient hour may end by finding himself absorbed in the topic, perhaps for life. The original motives may be entirely lost. What was a means to an end becomes an end in itself.

It is true that rewards are often given to an able person for exercising his talents. But does he exercise them merely to get a reward? It seems unlikely. No such motivation accounts for the drive behind genius. For the genius, creative passion itself is the motive. How hollow to think of Pasteur's concern for reward, or for health, food, sleep, or family, as the root of his devotion to his work. For long periods of time he was oblivious of them all, losing himself in the white heat of research. And the same passion is seen in the histories of geniuses who in their lifetimes received little or no reward for their work: Galileo, Mendel, Schubert, van Gogh, and many others.

It is important to note that major life-interests are seldom clearly formed or even indicated in childhood (musical prodigies being an exception).

One study of children between the tenth and twelfth grades showed that the strength of their interests over a three-year period correlated only +.57, whereas the same test showed a stability of interests over a twenty-two-year period following graduation from college to a much higher extent (+.75).[24]

Clearly youthful interests are less stable than adult interests. Further, it seems safe to say that the interests of most children, even into the teens, are very much like those of other children, whereas adults grow in uniqueness (individuation). The ruling passions of adults are exceedingly diverse. One man is absorbed in business and golf; another, in religion and art. An old woman in a home for the aged pivots her life solely on the hope that "some people may remember me kindly."

Whether we shall call these propriate motives *interests, sentiments, values,* or something else, does not for the moment matter.

[24] L. Canning, *et al.,* Permanence of vocational interests of high school boys, *J. educ. Psychol.,* 1941, **32,** 481–494; E. Strong, Permanence of interest test scores over twenty-two years, *J. appl. Psychol.,* 1951, **51,** 89–91.

Whatever we call them, they are acquired pre-eminent motives. Since the tensions involved are not of the same kind as the tensions of the seed motives, they are, by our definition, functionally autonomous.

2. *Acquired interests and values have selective power.* In the following chapter we shall show that what a person perceives, remembers, and thinks is in large part determined by his own propriate formations. As an interest grows it creates a lasting tensional condition that leads to congruent conduct, and also acts as a silent agent for selecting and directing whatever is related to the interest. Thus people with a strong esthetic interest respond more quickly to words connected with this interest than to words relating to interests they lack.[25] Given a newspaper to scan, they will read more items pertaining to art than will nonesthetic people.[26] The same selective tendency is discovered in all forms of interest that have been tested.

3. *Self-image and life-style are organizing factors.* It would be an error to think of interests as single and separate mainsprings. Together they form a complex self-image or life-style which is also functionally autonomous. It evolves gradually in the course of life, and day by day guides and unifies all, or at least many, of a person's transactions with life.

I am speaking here of the highest levels of organization in personality. Most theories of personality (especially those postulating "unchanging energies") overlook the motivational power of higher-level formations. My position is that, although lower-level self-maintaining (perseverative) systems exist, the more important instance of functional autonomy is found in the complex propriate organization that determines the "total posture" of a mature life-system.

A prominent ingredient of this master dynamism is the sense of responsibility one takes for one's life. The way one defines one's role and duties in life determines much of one's daily conduct. (McDougall calls this level of organization the "self-regarding sentiment"; others call it the "ego-ideal.")

[25] H. Cantril, General and specific attitudes, *Psychol. Monogr.*, 1932, No. 192; N. Jenkin, Affective processes in perception, *Psychol. Bull.*, 1957, **54**, 100–127.

[26] H. Cantril and G. W. Allport, Recent applications of the *Study of Values*, *J. abnorm. soc. Psychol.*, 1933, **28**, 259–273; also W. C. Engstrom and Mary E. Power, A revision of the *Study of Values* for use in magazine readership research, *J. appl. Psychol.*, 1959, **43**, 74–78.

What Processes Are Not Functionally Autonomous?

I have argued that for the most part personality structure is postinstinctive: it is not wholly dominated by innate drives; nor is it dominated normally by early formations of juvenile complexes. Unlike Freud or Adler, I do not hold that the guidelines of personality are ordinarily laid down by the age of three or five.

Yet not all motives are functionally autonomous. Several types are not.

1. *Drives.* From birth to death a human being is subject to biological drives. He must eat, breathe, sleep, and eliminate, and his body must make countless homeostatic adjustments to maintain the delicate balance of life. To be sure, it has been pointed out above that most drives develop canalized styles of expression and seek satisfaction in some preferred manner. But canalization is not true functional autonomy. For our first generalization, then, let us say that if a motive is primarily traceable to drive-tensions it is not an instance of functional autonomy.

2. *Reflex action.* The eye blink, the knee jerk, the digestive process—although they, too, manifest individuality of functioning—are not to be considered functionally autonomous. They are automatic responses, capable of only slight modification, geared to specific stimulation, and doubtfully to be classed as motivational at all.

3. *Constitutional equipment.* Some capacities and formations are best regarded as relatively fixed and unchanged in the course of life. We refer primarily to the "raw materials" of *physique, intelligence, temperament* (Chapter 4). We may add here individual limitations of bodily strength and health. Of the same order are the given constitutional laws of development (such as the maturation of capacities with age, the occurrence of puberty, and so on). Although none of these items directly constitutes "motives," it is well to have in mind their limiting effects on the transformation of motives.

4. *Habits.* Although it was argued that "habits-on-the-make" nicely fit into our conception of perseverative functional autonomy, still it is not wise to hold that habits-in-general are examples of functionally autonomous motivation. Indeed, most habits are not motivational at all. They are instrumental systems brought into play in the service of motives.

5. *Primary reinforcement.* All patterns of conduct that require

primary reinforcement fall outside the conception of functional autonomy.

A little neighbor child comes to our door and receives a cooky. He returns again and again. Has he acquired a new (functionally autonomous) motive? To find the answer we shall have to abolish the cooky. If the child stops coming it shows that his motivation was tied wholly to his sweet tooth. He has not formed a new interest *in us*.

If a workman depends upon praise in order to maintain his standards we cannot say that workmanship is for him an acquired motive. Similarly, if he receives a legacy and stops working altogether, we can safely say that for him his occupation was only an extrinsic habit (serving his need to make a living) and not an intrinsic functionally autonomous motive.

I hope that my position on "reinforcement" is now clear. Whenever, as in the above instances, a form of behavior is "extinguished" unless it satisfies an original drive, we cannot speak at all of the transformation of motives. Functional autonomy is not involved. As for "secondary reinforcement" it was shown in Chapters 5 and 9 that this explanation of the transformation of motives is too vague and still too tied to "unchanging energies" to provide a satisfactory theory of the growth of mature interests.

6. *Infantilisms and fixations.* Whenever an older person is acting out an infantile or juvenile conflict, we cannot speak of functional autonomy. He is following an urge that is basically unaltered from early years.

A girl of twelve had a most disconcerting habit of smacking her lips several times a minute. Analysis finally revealed that eight years previously her mother had told her that when she inhaled air it was "good" air, but when she exhaled it the air was "bad." These moralistic terms distressed the four-year-old because she understood from them that she had been naughty in making the air "bad." Deeply perturbed, she tried not to breathe at all. Failing in this heroic effort she invented the ritual of kissing the air she exhaled to "make it well again." The habit persisted, but the whole affair was so distressing that she repressed the memory of the event; but the tic still persisted. It took a psychoanalysis to bring the buried conflict into consciousness and to cure the tic.

In this case conduct at the age of twelve is in reality acting out an unresolved conflict at the age of four.

The astute reader may ask, "Do we not have here a case of *perseverative* functional autonomy? The little girl seems to have suffered from a dissociated, self-maintaining motivational system." The observation is a good one. Compulsions of hand-washing, facial tics, nail-biting, scratching, thumb-sucking do certainly act like self-feeding systems. Scarcely is the compulsive act completed before it seems to set off a repetition of the same compulsive act. We may do well to allow the conception of perseverative functional autonomy a place in the theory of compulsive neuroses.

At the same time there is an essential difference. We note that the little girl was *cured* when her eight-year-old conflict was removed. Her neurotic behavior then was not *primarily* self-sustaining.

7. *Some neuroses.* The problem of neurotic behavior, as our example shows, is complicated from the point of view of functional autonomy. Basically we should like to maintain that neurotic motives are not functionally autonomous, for the present acts of a neurotic person are laden primarily with bygone considerations. Some echo of early life is haunting his conduct. The neurotic seems unable to focus adequately on the present or the future. Freud has taught us that the roots of a neurosis often lie in the first years of life.

But now there is another side to the picture. Any neurosis is a complicated interlocking system of maneuvers designed to maintain life under difficult conditions.[27] It is a learned style of survival, and may be viewed without reference to early unfulfilled needs. It seems possible for a neurotic style of life to be rigidly set, and no longer harbor in any clear sense past conflicts. Especially what is called a "character neurosis" reflects a self-image badly matched to reality, but nonetheless persistent and permanently stylistic. Is it not therefore functionally autonomous?

There is at least a theoretical distinction to help us decide. If under psychoanalysis the patient relives the past (as did our twelve-

27 Cf. A. Angyal, A theoretical model for personality studies. In D. Krech and G. S. Klein (Eds.), *Theoretical models and personality theory* (Durham, N.C.: Duke Univ. Press, 1952), p. 141.

year-old girl), and learns what repressed incidents have been troublesome, and *if this backward tracing effects a cure* (because the patient sees that the troublesome element has no place in his current motivational system), then the neurosis was *not* functionally autonomous. If, on the other hand, a "character neurosis" is so firmly structured that it now constitutes the life-pattern, and if nothing can dislodge it, then we have no choice but to admit that it is an acquired, functionally autonomous, motivational system.

There is a moral here for psychotherapy. It would seem wise for the therapist to determine whether the patient's symptoms are to be relieved by "going to the root of the problem" or whether the most that can be hoped for is to reconcile the patient to his own developed style of life. In the first instance he is assuming that the neurosis is not functionally autonomous. In the latter case it is, and can be handled better by re-education than by reliving.

Psychoses can be looked at from the same point of view. Some psychotic upsets are temporary, reflecting unbalance in the existing systems of motivation. The disturbance is not functionally autonomous. Some mental patients, however, are wholly unable to handle their existence and permanently "go over to another world." Such a patient adopts a delusional pattern and a shrunken range of behavior as his permanent life-style, and for him this new level of existence becomes functionally autonomous. He "gets used" to his malady, and builds his life around it.

Finally, let us glance back at the case of the politician who is following in his father's footsteps (page 228). There we raised the question whether his occupational interest as an adult is merely a neurotic "acting out" of his early father-identification. If it is so (as shown by his compulsiveness and rigidity), then this interest is not to be regarded as functionally autonomous. If, however, he has long since worked through his juvenile dependence, and now has an interest in politics for its own sake, the motivation is functionally autonomous. We mention this case here to emphasize the fact that it is necessary to examine each specific instance in order to determine to what extent, and in what way, functional autonomy may be involved.

8. *Sublimation*. Freud's familiar theory holds that all adult motives—even the most socially prized and idealistic—are "transparent sublimations" of the primitive motives of sex and aggression. The physician, the artist, the missionary are displacing their "aim inhibited wishes"; they are finding substitutes for the things they *really* want in life. Undoubtedly "transparent sublimations" do sometimes exist, but that they account for *all* adult motives we emphatically deny.

Critics of functional autonomy cite special cases to prove their point. One student writes:

My own bias is biological, mechanistic, and Freudian. Let me describe a case that fits my bias and seems to deny functional autonomy.

I have a friend who appears to be motivated by a strong esthetic value. Everything he does seems consistent with this well-integrated motivational system. He looks up from his perusal of photographs of armless Aphrodites and sighs, "Ah, if there were only people like these alive today." Every week end he dates a different girl, looking for the perfect one. Returning from one such foray he said, "She's all right but she hasn't any *bust.*" He loves poetry. When he reads it he drops the words out of his mouth like marbles. He quotes Noel Coward. And in many other ways he is an archesthete. Does his love of beauty and of what is charming constitute a functionally autonomous motive? I think not.

Lars is his name. His divorced mother and he are extremely devoted to each other. His "ideal girl" is, after all, his mother. His preoccupation with breasts, his "chewing and sucking" of the beautiful lines of poetry—all show his desire to possess (or return to) his mother. The estheticism of Lars is neurotic—a mere transparent sublimation of his true motives.

If the case is essentially as the student states it, there is no basis for assuming that Lars's esthetic style of life is functionally autonomous. It is not intrinsic to his nature but exists in the service of another stronger, and at best half-conscious, motive.

Here is another case, also written by a student skeptical of functional autonomy.

I am interested in the case of a priest whom I recently met. Many people had told me that he is a man with a single motive in life: to raise money for a convent he hopes to build. Until I met him I could not even imagine the overpowering dominance of this one motive in all his conduct.

For example, my errand with him was to see about renting his school's auditorium for a teen-age dance. He asked what percentage of the profits he would receive for his convent project. I tried to discuss the needs of adolescents for some recreational facility; he was not interested. I tried to discuss the interreligious tensions of the community; he tossed them off. To every conversational gambit he replied, "How much do I get for the convent?"

His relations with people in the town are poor, for he hounds them unmercifully for money. In his office is a large picture of the proposed convent, not hung on the wall, but displayed on a conspicuous easel. Even the Archbishop does not seem strongly to favor the priest's project because he is thought to have misappropriated some of his parish funds for this purpose.

Now how can we explain his singleness of purpose? Shall we accept the psychoanalytic interpretation that the celibate is sexually repressed and thus is eager to gather nuns about him? While conceivably valid, I doubt this explanation, for there seems to be no other evidence of sexual interest in his behavior—and he is a very old man. One can scarcely accept the hedonistic explanation, for not only is he unpopular because of his unpleasant persistence; he is actually not making much headway. His behavior is more punished than rewarded.

Perhaps to say that this ruling passion is functionally autonomous is the best statement we can make. But is it not a doctrine of despair? It does not even attempt to explain his central motive!

In this case, as in many others, we simply do not know enough about the life in question to reach a clear decision. On the one hand, the highly obsessive nature of the priest's behavior raises the question whether a compulsive neurosis is involved, displacing some aim-inhibited wish (sexual perhaps). On the other hand, many people, like Faust of old, have found their whole reason for living in some limited project of a similar scope. In this priest's life the project may be merely the concrete focus of a religious motive and style of life. We may have to accept it as the way in which all his complex life-influences, integrating with his evolving needs and interests, have converged into a unique pattern of propriate striving. From this point of view his convent-building motive is functionally autonomous. We cannot actually say in this case whether "sublimation" or functional autonomy is the best fit to this case—simply because we do not know enough about the life in question.

We must add a word concerning the writer's complaint that the doctrine of functional autonomy "does not even attempt to explain his central motive." If the writer means that he would like a historical explanation in terms of the steps in the priest's life that led him to his present ruling passion, there is no objection to his attempting to reconstruct the life-story. But historical explanation is *not* functional explanation. In a very real sense a functionally autonomous motive *is* the personality. We cannot ask for any further reduction. Life itself is the energy and the "explanation." We need not, and cannot, look "deeper"—not if the motive is functionally autonomous.

We may, however, tie any functionally autonomous motive to the total propriate system, and discover its relative importance in the life-style. Functional autonomy is not a "doctrine of despair." Rather, it is a straightforward labeling of one important, and widely neglected, aspect of human motivation.

To sum up: if we are dealing with sublimation, transparent or otherwise, then we do not have a case of functional autonomy. On the other hand, to declare without proof that all adult interests are masquerades for what man really wants (chiefly sex and aggression) is as improbable as gargoyles.

Degrees of Functional Autonomy. Our discussion has made clear that it is not always possible to determine whether a given motive is rooted in drives, in infantile fixation, in sublimations, or in wholly adult formulations of life. For that matter, a motive may reflect a combination of forces: infant and adult, instinctive and intentional, conscious and unconscious, extrinsic and intrinsic. Even drives, as we have seen, by virtue of canalization, acquire new and highly individual tastes. For these reasons we cannot declare that a motive is always *either/or*. We must allow for the possibility that life's motives may show many degrees of purity and impurity in respect to functional autonomy.

Hence, to the question "When is it not so?" there can be no categorical answer. The decision can come only after an intensive study of each individual life. Practically, the decision is often hard to make. In principle, however, we can say that *to the extent that a present motive seeks new goals (i.e., manifests a different kind of tension from the motives from which it developed) it is functionally autonomous.*

How Does Functional Autonomy Come About?

It would be scientifically satisfying if we could give a simple answer to this troublesome question of how functional autonomy comes about. Unfortunately we cannot do so—and for two reasons. In the first place, we lack knowledge of the *neurological processes* that may be involved in the transforming of old systems and the maintaining of new systems of motivation. In the second place, present-day psychology has no consistent theory of the *nature of man*. The phenomenon of functional autonomy will never be clearly understood until we know more about relevant neurological mechanisms and about the correct formulation of the purposive nature of motives.

At the present time, therefore, we shall attempt only to point our answer in what seems to us to be the right general direction. We shall label the first group of considerations "quasi-mechanical" and the second group "propriate."

Quasi-mechanical Considerations. We have called attention to various perseverative systems as representing a relatively low level of functional autonomy. Although these self-maintaining systems by no means exhaust the range of functionally autonomous motives, they already give difficulties to prevalent learning theory. Commenting on this matter, Miller writes:

. . . we say that a strong acquired drive might seem not to be extinguished for a considerable number of trials and still eventually extinguish. When generalization, higher-order reinforcement, and shifts from one reinforcing agent to another are added to this possibility, it can be seen how difficult it is in complex human situations to determine whether or not a habit actually is functionally autonomous.[28]

What this passage shows us is that Stimulus-Response theory would like *if possible* to deny functional autonomy by explaining the phenomenon in familiar S-R terms.[29] These terms, unfortunately, grow exceedingly vague when applied to what Miller calls "complex human situations."

Let us review a few quasi-mechanical considerations that are relevant, and may be helpful.

1. *Delayed extinction.* In the passage cited above Miller holds that some persistent acquired systems are really on the road to extinction. Thus the little boy who learns to like fishing because this activity has been associated with receiving love and attention from his father, may hold his interest in fishing for a time, but if it is not reinforced by attention from the father, he will eventually lose the

[28] N. E. Miller, Learnable drives and reward. In S. S. Stevens (Ed.), *Handbook of experimental psychology* (New York: Wiley, 1951), Chap. 13.
[29] Other attempts, in addition to Miller's, are cited in Note 9 above.

interest. If this happens, then, of course, the interest in fishing has not become functionally autonomous. We admit the point but must call attention to the numerous cases where acquired interests *never extinguish.*

In this connection we recall the well-established fact that avoidance motives, when once learned, seem to defy extinction. This fact is admitted by S-R theorists.[30] The explanation seems to be that the animal (or human being) "plays safe" by never allowing himself to be in a position of suffering the shock (or burn, or illness) where he was first injured. ("The burned child avoids the fire.") All of us have a vast repertory of such avoidance motives, and we do not need to return to the first painful experience in order to sustain these avoidances. They last a lifetime, and do not extinguish.

Let us therefore conclude that if with the passage of time an acquired interest disappears (extinguishes) we are not dealing with a case of functional autonomy; but many cases of "delayed extinction" are apparently *permanently* delayed, and in these cases we conclude that functional autonomy is therefore involved.

2. *Self-maintaining circuits.* A familiar term in modern neurological theory is *feedback.* It refers to the fact that the end-situation (a response) sends return neural impulses to the brain. These return-impulses discharge in the open pathways, and thus tend to maintain in a circular fashion (or slightly modified fashion) the system that is operating.[31] We have already mentioned as an elementary example of such reflex-circle the infant's babble and other repetitive sequences of acts.

What we do not know is how permanent such a system may be. All that we can say at present is that self-maintenance seems to be a basic neural property and offers some basis for the concept of functional autonomy.

3. *Partial reinforcement.* It has been discovered that activities that are rewarded only part of the time seem more resistant to extinction than are activities that always receive a reward. In the latter case when the reward is no longer given, the activity promptly dies out.

---

[30] R. L. Solomon and L. C. Wynn, Traumatic avoidance learning: the principles of anxiety conservation and partial irreversibility, *Psychol. Rev.,* 1954, **61**, 353–385.
[31] See Notes 14 and 17 above; also H. T. Chang, The repetitive discharge of corticothalamic reverberating circuits, *J. Neurophysiol.,* 1950, **13**, 235–257.

Let us take an animal example. Pigeons who are fed every time a light goes on will soon . . . change their habits of pecking if after a time they get no food. But if they are sometimes fed and sometimes not, the habit continues. With this irregular reinforcement, Ferster and Skinner find that even after receiving no food, the pigeons peck long and ardently—for thousands upon thousands of trials.[32]

At the human level gambling is a good example. The inveterate gambler needs to win only *occasionally*. The *hope* of winning seems to sustain his passion. Similarly, the unpredictable factor in angling may help sustain the fisherman's zeal.

In the case of the pigeons we see that although "aperiodic reinforcement" prevents extinction, drive satisfaction is still clearly involved. In the case of gambling and fishing, on the other hand, no known elementary drive is satisfied. What seems to be happening is that goals are more attractive if they are sometimes reached and sometimes not. This element of "risk" is, of course, evident in many interests of maturity. Thus our "gamble" on a course of conduct may be a factor in conferring autonomy.

4. *Blend of the novel and familiar.* Perhaps the dynamic effects of partial reinforcement may be a special case of a wider principle enunciated by Hebb. This author points to the fact that self-sustaining interests seem to reflect preoccupation with the novel when commingled with the familiar.[33] A scientist is fascinated by what is new in a combination with what is familiar; the musician is absorbed in tackling new and more difficult pieces within his total range of ability; a child likes a toy if it conforms to some of his expectations, but not to all of them. To master the art of walking is an absorbing motive for a child of fifteen months, for it stretches his present capacities. When skills are mastered they have no longer any motivational character. It is habits-on-the-make, or taming the novel into the familiar, that seem to endow the neurophysical system with autonomy.

This type of central motivating state—though we do not know its neural nature—corresponds well to the type of functional autonomy we have called "task perseveration" (page 232). Tasks are hauntingly

[32] C. B. Ferster and B. F. Skinner, *Schedules of reinforcement* (New York: Appleton-Century-Crofts, 1957).
[33] Hebb, *op. cit.*, pp. 224–231. Note 14 above.

coercive until they are accomplished—and, we note, some are never solved in our lifetime. Explorers, scientists, searchers for ultimate religious truth set themselves new tasks within familiar settings; and pursue their goals until death. We have previously referred to a kind of preference for the familiar (for routine) that marks much of our motivational life (page 233). Without denying this dynamism, it is perhaps well to accept Hebb's amendment: The motivational character of routine is much enhanced if it contains within itself the complicating stress of novelty.

5. *Primacy of high-level gating.* It is an accepted neurological principle that high-level organizations select, screen, and "gate" specific responses of all types. This principle in itself favors the development of functional autonomy.

We may illustrate in this manner: The hunger drive, we grant, is with us from birth to death. It is not functionally autonomous. In the course of development, however, we have developed many specific canalizations (we will eat this food but not that), and we have developed some very general attitudes toward the cleanliness, appearance, quality of our nourishment. Some eaters are thoroughgoing gourmands; others have a curiously finicky approach to eating. Now, whenever hunger is aroused and food is consumed these obviously acquired styles are activated and they definitely control and direct the manner of eating.

In his critique of functional autonomy mentioned above, Miller speaks of "generalization" and of "higher-order reinforcement." It seems to us pertinent to think of these factors as the "gating" by higher-order acquisitions of specific habits and responses, rather than as reinforcements of specific drives. The error of S-R theory lies in its old-fashioned image of neural organization in terms of a bundle of myriad specific drives and reinforced separate habits. Just as physics has ceased to think of nature as a composite of centimeter-gram-second units, so modern neurophysiology turns away from the specific reinforced habit to the dynamic neural field that has primacy over specific response habits.

In this connection we may refer to Piaget's genetic theory of intelligence. This author maintains that in the course of life new and higher-order "schemata" evolve—so that our thinking is controlled by new systems. He rightly states that older schemata remain dormant, and can often be re-used. We "regress" to them at times. But normally we work with our acquired systems in preference to their antecedents.[34]

6. *Multiple mechanisms.* It is a principle of mammalian behavior that survival is overdetermined; that is to say, a good mode of adaptation is sustained by many mechanisms. Should one mechanism fail, a dozen others remain that will sustain the same outcome. Nature does not put all eggs into one basket. Therefore, it is highly probable that functional autonomy may be due to, or aided by, any and all of the principles to which we have called attention—as well as to additional principles to which we now turn.

Philosophy of Growth: A Crucial Issue. Before continuing in our effort to tell "how functional autonomy comes about" the reader should pause and consider the most crucial issue in all psychological theory: the question concerning the *nature of man.*

The customary view tells us something like this: man is an equilibrium-seeking animal. He is made up of a great many discordant drives. Each by itself seeks reduction of tension. When some particular mode of successful adjustment is found (i.e., when an act is rewarded) it is learned. Hence man is a bundle of rewarded modes of responding.

In this portrait of man we note that separate segments of his being are treated as if they were self-sufficient. Thus we say that an *activity* is rewarded, not that the *person* is rewarded. We say a drive is satisfied, not that a person is satisfied. We treat each system as separate, and do not look at the functioning of the life as a whole.

This view of man we have called the *homeostatic* theory (pages 88–90).[35] The concept of homeostasis refers to the maintaining or restoring of "steady states" within the organism. The balancing feats among the glands, metabolic systems, and biological drives and needs are so intricate and remarkable that Cannon speaks of them as "the

[34] J. Piaget, *The psychology of intelligence* (Transl.; London: Routledge & Kegan Paul, 1950).

[35] Cf. R. Stagner, Homeostasis as a unifying concept in personality theory, *Psychol. Rev.,* 1951, 58, 5–17; Homeostasis: corruptions or misconceptions?—A reply, *Psychol. Rev.,* 1954, 61, 205–208; O. H. Mowrer, A cognitive theory of dynamics. Review of R. S. Woodworth, *Dynamics of behavior, Contemp. Psychol.,* 1959, 4, 129–133.

wisdom of the body."[36] But at best they result in the upkeep of an existing order.

Many psychologists see nothing in human personality beyond this basic law. Yet Cannon, who formulated it, did not regard it as accounting for all human conduct.

He writes:

With essential needs answered through homeostasis, the priceless unessentials could be freely sought.[37]

In other words, man wants a great deal in life beyond a healthy biological balance and satisfaction of his drives. Coming home from work a man finds himself tired and hungry, wanting food and rest. But when he has been replenished and restored, what then? If he is healthy, he wants new activity, turns to his hobby, reads a stimulating book, or goes out for the evening.

What Cannon calls the "priceless unessentials" of life are the most conspicuous feature of human personality—unless illness or utter destitution have reduced the individual to a purely drive, homeostatic, equilibrium-seeking level of existence. Without denying the truth of homeostasis we need a vital supplement to it if we are to account for human motivation.

Propriate Considerations. Returning to functional autonomy, we are therefore prepared to assert that in addition to the quasi-mechanical considerations offered above as partial explanation, we need at least three additional principles, all closely related to the propriate functions of personality. Taken together they amount to saying that functional autonomy comes about because it is the essence or core of the purposive nature of man.

1. *Principle of organizing the energy level.* Consider the man who, after a good dinner and rest, looks around for new worlds to conquer. He, like all healthy people, must do something with his energy. If his routine motives (for survival and drive-satisfaction) do not absorb his power he will have to "invent motives." A healthy woman who reaches middle age and no longer has children to care for will look eagerly "for something to do." Such a woman is unfortunate indeed unless she can develop new interests in politics, social service, art work, study, or some similar goals.

36 W. B. Cannon, *The wisdom of the body* (New York: Norton, 1932).
37 *Ibid.,* p. 323.

Although this line of thought does not explain how a particular motive arises, it provides us with an important ground plan for a theory of acquired motives. There must be motives to consume one's available energies; and if existing motives do not suffice, new ones will develop. If the idle adolescent does not have constructive interests to occupy his time he easily takes to rebellion, vandalism, or crime as an outlet for his energy.

We are saying that man's nature is such that new motives *must* grow up in healthy lives to supplement the inadequate minimum of homeostasis.

2. *Principles of mastery and competence.* Here we refer to the discussion of those motivational theories that allow for "changing energies" (pages 212–217). Some of them assume that mastery ("behavior primacy") is the basic urge in life, which at different ages takes new and different forms. The principle of "competence" or "adequacy" is similar; so, too, the postulation of "growth motives" and "self-actualization." In short, many theories of personality believe that the "go" of human life lies not so much in satisfying primary drives and their derivatives as in carrying through transactions beyond this level of bare existence.

In tracing the development of mature motives, Charlotte Bühler points to a commonly encountered sequence. First, new and strange objects cause anxiety (an infant may be startled by the click of an electric light button; or an adult may become disoriented and anxious in a new and strange city). Soon, however, there is a normal recuperation from the anxiety. Then comes "a need to know and control" the new and "dangerous" object or condition. Finally there is constructive use of it enabling the individual to expand his previous range of competence and control. "In other words, the individual progresses from adapting to the environment to adapting the environment to himself."[38]

Thus, it is clear that many authors reject the "reactive" view of man. Man has energies to use that reach way beyond the need to react. For one thing, he has an expanding image of himself (a conception of what he would like to be), and the pursuit of this goal directs much, if not most, of his conduct.

[38] See Note 2 above.

3. *Principle of propriate patterning.* The conception of functional autonomy does not mean that in the mature pattern each motive is autonomous of every other; it does not mean that motives fly off as so many independent mainsprings without dependence on propriate structure. Except for certain isolated perseverative systems, functionally autonomous motives are highly propriate, i.e., well anchored to the self. Indeed, to a large extent they constitute the self (Chapter 6).

Therefore an important part of our answer to the question of how functional autonomy comes about is that the self-structure of man demands it. A young person intends to become a physician, a man of the world, a politician, or a hermit. None of these ambitions is innate. They are all acquired interests. We contend that they do not exist *now* because of remote reinforcements. Rather, they exist because a self-image, gradually formed, demands this particular motivational focus.

Should we then say that it is the existence of the "self" that explains functional autonomy? This answer is dangerous, since it implies that a mysterious inner agent (a soul) ultimately shapes the dynamic forces of a life. We have already taken a strong stand against the question-begging procedure of seeking explanations in terms of a separate self.

We prefer to say that the essential nature of man is such that it presses toward a relative unification of life (never fully achieved). In this trend toward unification we can identify many central psychological characteristics. Among them are man's search for answers to the "tragic trio" of problems: suffering, guilt, death. We identify also his effort to relate himself to his fellow men and to the universe at large. We see that he is trying to discover his peculiar place in the world, to establish his "identity." As a consequence of this quest— which is the very essence of human nature—we note that man's conduct is to a large degree proactive, intentional, and unique to himself. In the total process the sense of selfhood, or the self-image, is involved. Yet it is not the self (as a separate agent) that brings it about. Selfhood is reflection of this fundamental human process of becoming.

From this point of view functional autonomy is merely a way of stating that men's motives change and grow in the course of life, because it is the nature of man that they should do so. Only theorists wedded to a reactive, homeostatic, quasi-closed model of man find difficulty in agreeing.

Traumatic Transformations

Changes in motives are often so gradual that we cannot tell where one leaves off and another begins. Love of music for its own sake may only gradually replace obedient practice; religious longing may slowly develop from religious routine; concern for others may displace step by step childhood self-centeredness. Changes may operate as gradually as the tide that lifts a grounded ship until suddenly it is afloat.

And yet some transformations are abrupt and far-reaching. A few lives seem pivoted upon one decisive event: the conversion of St. Paul or of Tolstoy, the Italian journey of Goethe, or Nietzsche's infection by a prostitute. Such traumatic transformations constitute a special instance of functional autonomy.

Traumatic changes may be either of the perseverative type of functional autonomy or of the propriate type. Let us consider each briefly.

Perseverative Traumata. We have noted that motives of avoidance seem never to extinguish. The burned child dreads the fire— forever. If the dread is unusually deep and compulsive we speak of a *phobia*. Many people have irrational but ineradicable fears of this order.

A child less than three years of age was so terrified by an onrushing locomotive, when he was temporarily separated from his mother, that his whole life was dominated by a dread of separation from security. As an adult he could scarcely travel more than a few blocks from his house. The situation grew worse as he grew older. At last the sufferer, who was a teacher, was compelled to hold his college classes in his own home.[39]

David Levy, a child psychiatrist, writes that an "anxiety-laden event occurs frequently, according to my records, within the first

---

[39] W. E. Leonard, *The locomotive God* (New York: Appleton-Century-Crofts, 1927). This autobiography is highly recommended for its literary merit and psychological fascination. Perseverative neuroses in animals are described by J. H. Masserman, *Behavior and neurosis* (Chicago: Univ. of Chicago Press, 1943).

two years of life."[40] Children who cannot yet comprehend or control their environments are at the mercy of frightening occasions. A surgical operation, becoming "lost" on a city street, electrical storms, thoughtless acts of rejection on the part of the parents, moving to a new neighborhood, death in the family—all these and other specific events may set up once and for all phobic tendencies, with perhaps curious preventive rituals on the part of the child. And these systems may continue for years, sometimes for a lifetime. Some psychiatrists (O. Rank, for example) have argued that the trauma of birth is a catastrophic event that is likely to leave a permanent scar on every mortal. One may, however, question whether the nervous system at birth is mature enough to bear a lasting impress of the birth-event.

Be that as it may, it seems reasonable to agree with Levy that before the child can verbalize his experiences he may be especially susceptible to shocks that he cannot comprehend or master or even discuss. The arrival of a new baby with consequent feelings of jealousy, an early experience of bereavement, or perhaps adoption into a foster family are all ripe occasions for traumatic experience.

When at about the age of six the child leaves the shelter of his home for the harder environment of the school and playground, new experiences of failure and ridicule await him. Especially a child who is lame or who carries some visible scar (or a child of a minority group) may suffer merciless taunting from other children. Such traumata leave long effects. A sensitive child may grow permanently morbid, or develop an inferiority feeling which lasts a lifetime— even though he achieves resounding success in later years. These are all examples of "perseverative functional autonomy" due to incisive "psychic wounds" inflicted on a definite, datable occasion.

A period of special importance in the life of the American boy is puberty, when he must establish himself on the ascending ladder of manhood. He must surmount the critical "sissy hurdle." Perhaps a fist fight, a foot race, or a grown-up haircut, or some act of daring may do the trick. If so, a "normal boy's" life lies ahead for him. If the hurdle is not successfully passed, the result may be a radical alteration in the life; new compensations, a new self-image may develop.

Soon come other demands from the peer group, including rela-

40 D. M. Levy, On evaluating the "specific event" as a source of anxiety. In P. H. Hock and J. Zubin (Eds.), *Anxiety* (New York: Grune & Stratton, 1950).

tions with the opposite sex. Religious interests develop. Experience of success and failure, of remorse and guilt, of conversion, of puppy love may be of supreme importance. There are new worlds to conquer, college examinations to be passed, a vocation to be selected, a living to be earned. At all these crucial stages traumatic experiences can occur.

In adult years shocks due to business failure, to illness, to bereavement may also effect swift and profound alterations. As a rule, however, personality after the age of thirty is much less subject to sudden upheavals than it is before that age. Critical and abrupt changes seem to be most numerous during adolescence.

We must not assume that all lives are marked by some traumatic changes. On the contrary, in most lives change is only gradual—even though all people can point to vivid and impressive emotional experiences. Actually it is not possible to draw a sharp line between traumatic and gradual transformation.

In one set of autobiographies from college students, it seems that not more than 10 percent report distinctly traumatic events that in some way seem to effect a sudden transformation in a major region of their personalities. When questioned directly, 48 percent claimed to have had unusually impressive emotional experiences, but in few cases did these result in a sudden reorientation of the life.

Propriate Traumata. The impressive single event may, as we have said, leave some perseverative system uppermost (a phobia, an aversion, a ritual). But such events may also start a recentering of the self-image, and thus affect the evolution of functionally autonomous propriate states. Some traumata merely freeze fears and limit growth; others change the direction of growth.

The late anthropologist Ruth Benedict tells of her serious shock at the death of her father when she was only two years of age. Somehow, in spite of the grief, the tragic scene at her father's coffin gave her the impression that the world of death was peaceful and beautiful. Later at the age of six, she regarded her hiding place in the haymow as her "grave." She writes, ". . . it came to me with a brilliant flash of illumination that I could always without fail have myself for company, and that if I didn't talk to anybody about the things that mattered to me no one could ever take them away. I think that was the fundamental knowledge that I lived on until I was thirty-five. . . ."[41]

Out of these episodes at the age of two and six Ruth Benedict forged a style of life that lasted many years. The following two episodes deal with traumatic experiences in school and college.

A woman now sixty years of age traces her lifelong devotion to poetry largely to an episode in her Virgil class in high school. She was performing a routine translation, difficult and dreary. The teacher, trying for the hundredth time to give significance to the task, asked how the passage would be expressed in the Bible. Happily she caught the allusion, and said, "Incline thine ear unto my supplication." Her artistic success on this occasion was a traumatic experience, a dawn of poetic beauty, to which she was ever after devoted.

A certain freshman in college, coming from an uncultured home, held a supercilious view of all intellectual activities. Badly adjusted to college, with poor habits of study, and as nearly illiterate as a college youth can be, he had special difficulties with his course in English composition. One day when his weary instructor was scolding him, the boy countered with his customary defense: "I don't like English, I never did, and never shall like it." The instructor, bored but persisting, said, "It isn't English I'm talking about at the moment, it's your life." The effect was wholly unpredictable. The thrust somehow struck home. The lad not only reformed his precarious ways, but became devoted to the subject, obtained a high grade, made Phi Beta Kappa, and eventually became a teacher of English.

Needless to say, there must always be preparation in a life to accept and utilize such traumatic experiences. What seems to happen is that the old materials in the personality are abruptly regrouped and endowed with a new significance. William James spoke of effective religious conversions as "recentering" a life. The term well

41 Margaret Mead (Ed.), *An anthropologist at work* (New York: Basic Books, 1959), p. 102.

describes what seems to happen in all cases of traumatic transformation.

Summary

This long chapter has had much to say. It has argued that a simple homeostatic theory of motivation is inadequate. It has argued also that we cannot understand the part that adult motives play merely by tracing them back to their origins in childhood. The differences between juvenile and adult motives are vast.

The phenomenon of transformation we call *functional autonomy*, a term that refers to any acquired system of motivation in which the tensions involved are not of the same kind as the antecedent tensions from which the acquired system developed.

Some functionally autonomous systems are perseverative, meaning that they are local, self-sustaining systems; others, however, are central to the major trends of the life and must be viewed in terms of propriate development, a characteristic of the very nature of man. Thus, there are quasi-mechanical functions involved in functional autonomy, but also propriate functions. Most transformations are gradual, though some are traumatic and abrupt.

CHAPTER 11

Cognition and Personality

MENTAL SET: KEY TO THE EDIFICE OF PERSONALITY • VERIDI-
CAL AND NONVERIDICAL COGNITION • CULTURAL PROCEPTION
• INDIVIDUAL PROCEPTION • COGNITIVE FIXEDNESS AND FLEXI-
BILITY • UNDERSTANDING THE PERSON IN HIS WORLD • SUM-
MARY

As our motives grow and change, so too do our habits of thinking. Every person—from childhood onward—is kept busy attaining some degree of order in his thought-life to correspond to his evolving motives. As a matter of fact, it is artificial to distinguish thinking from motivation. Both are "continuous, effortful, goal-directed, self-experienced activities."[1]

It would, of course, be more convenient if we could slice personality into its major faculties. From Plato onward, writers have tried to do so, and have even agreed that the major faculties are three in number: *thinking, doing* (willing), and *feeling;* sometimes

[1] Cf. F. Wyatt, Some remarks on the place of cognition in ego psychology, *J. proj. Tech.,* 1953, 17, 144–151. The same essential point is made by J. Nuttin, *Psychoanalysis and personality: a dynamic theory of normal personality* (Transl.; New York: Sheed & Ward, 1953).

these are called *cognition, conation, affection.* One contemporary theorist makes neat use of this ancient trio by asserting that personality is composed of three kinds of units: *schemata* (cognitions), *traits* (habits of doing), and *motives* (affective dynamisms).[2]

Such an analytical framework has its appeal, but it is at best artificial. It slices personality in a wholly fictitious way. People are not (like Gaul) divided into three parts. Although each life has its own systems and subsystems (see Chapters 14 and 15), these do not correspond to the ancient faculties of feeling, thinking, acting.

When we watch the intense play of children we see that it is all of a piece: it cannot be broken down into such and such feelings, such and such thoughts, and such and such acts.

And the same is true of adults. If Mr. X has a deep interest in corporation law, if Mrs. Y is concerned with welfare work with children, these systems are a blend of desiring-doing-willing-thinking-feeling. It is artificial to distinguish one aspect from another.

Some theorists—the "irrationalists," such as Schopenhauer, Kempf, Freud, and others—have held that cognition (our thought-life) is essentially the servant of our needs and drives. If this were always so we might reasonably be justified in separating cognition from motivation. But nowadays we cannot accept this easy judgment. When we say that we have "scientific curiosity," or that all men make an "effort after meaning," or that everyone tries to resolve "cognitive dissonance," we are saying that the desire to know is itself a motive, and that there are cognitive, as well as drive, motives to reckon with.[3]

Difficult as it may be, we shall have to find a way to talk about thinking and cognition as parts of a single personal style where thinking and knowing are blended with emotions, wishes, orientations.

Mental Set: Key to the Edifice of Personality

The human mind operates as it does principally because it is replete with "sets." And personality is structured as it is because it is

---

2 D. C. McClelland, *Personality* (New York: Sloane, 1951).

3 The trend toward a new emphasis on "cognitive motives" is seen in S. Asch, *Social psychology* (Englewood Cliffs, N.J.: Prentice-Hall, 1952); F. C. Bartlett, *Thinking: an experimental and social study* (London: Allen & Unwin, 1958); L. Festinger, *The concept of cognitive dissonance* (Evanston, Ill.: Row, Peterson, 1957).

made up of extended "sets" that can be called traits, predispositions, preferred patterns, attitudes, personal characteristics, trends, or something similar.

Let us start with simple examples. Suppose I ask you to solve the following problem in arithmetic.

$$\frac{\begin{array}{r}11\\7\end{array}}{}$$

You naturally ask, "Well, shall I add, subtract, or multiply?" You cannot proceed a single inch with this problem (nor with any of life's tasks) until you have some directional set.

Suppose I ask you to translate from the French: *Pas de lieu Rhône que nous.* You correctly retort that this mishmash of words makes no sense. Nor does it—in French. But shift your set to English and pronounce the words aloud. A well-known proverb results. Everything depends on whether your set is for French or for English.

Take a typical "brain teaser" (most of them have to do with set). A hungry boy was asked by a baker to deliver some dough-nuts to a customer. Not trusting the lad, the baker wrote in Roman numerals the number nine, thus notifying the customer how many to expect. The lad could not resist temptation and ate three. Wishing to cover up his misdeed he took a pencil (without an eraser) and doctored up the Roman numeral so that the number corresponded to the remaining contents of the box. How did he do so? The problem is easily solved if you have the right set.[4]

Our examples are trivial, but they demonstrate the crucial role that set plays even in transient mental operations. Any set like these, adopted for a particular purpose at a particular time, is sometimes called "task attitude," "problem set," or by the German name, *Aufgabe.*

But even in these examples we note the operation of long-stand-ing, enduring, sets. We could not add, subtract, or multiply; we could not think in French, in English, or in the Roman numeral

4 Most people visualize the IX as "Roman." But the delivery boy was set for plain English, and inserted the letter S in front of the "numeral."

system unless we had once learned these "permanent possibilities for action." We now carry them as latent abilities and find them ready for action under appropriate circumstances.

We may call the latent readiness the *tonic* aspect of set. When aroused, it guides, steers, and fashions the *phasic* contractions that lead to the solving of the problem or the performing of an act. Physiologically considered, sets are cortical and postural structures that have the capacity to "gate" or guide specific phasic reactions. It is only the phasic aspect that is overt and visible; the tonic is carried somewhere in the still-mysterious realm of neurodynamic process.

Tonic sets are of many kinds. They may be of short duration, as when we "get set" to run a race, or to expect a telephone call. They may be lasting skills or habits—as our ability to drive a car, to skate, or to speak a foreign language. They may be still more dynamic and represent pressing systems of interest, ambition, or aspiration. Personality is a constellation of sets—of all orders of specificity and generality, and of different degrees of availability and urgency.[5] In Chapters 14 and 15 we shall examine more closely those "sets" that comprise the major structural traits of personality.

Sets or dispositions, then, govern our mental life completely. It is our present purpose to show that mental life (or what is often called the "higher mental processes") can best be viewed as meshing closely with the rest of personality. And this is achieved via *sets*. We repeat, it is artificial to distinguish motivation from higher mental processes, since both are merely aspects of a single personal style of life.

Veridical and Nonveridical Cognition

The basic requirement laid upon all men is to handle the world competently enough to survive. Unless we keep reasonably close in tune with "reality," we die. Hence in the course of evolution our sensory and brain processes have become well developed to provide us with true ("veridical") cognitions and perceptions. Eyes perceive color, line, and shape with exquisite fineness; ears register a wide range of air vibrations with exactness. If the skin is imperfect in telling us size and shape it is very sensitive to gradations of tem-

[5] For a fuller discussion of set see F. H. Allport, *Theories of perception and the concept of structure* (New York: Wiley, 1955).

perature. Insofar as we have a pervasive motive to survive and master our world, our passion for veridical perceptions and cognitions is a part of this motive. For the most part our perceptions and our knowledge are true, trustworthy, and verifiable.

Yet by following the same line of reasoning we can say that perception and cognition must likewise depart from true mirroring in order to be of maximum use to us. Not every tree in the forest comes into perceptual focus, but only the one we are chopping. Not every man in the street is clearly perceived, but only our friends or our enemies. If you hear a babble of vague conversation how quickly *your* name stands out if it is mentioned. Selective perception is as much a functional necessity as is veridical perception.

And it would make no sense at all if we had to start every day building up a new and veridical cognition of the world we live in. It is far more efficient to take new experiences and dissolve them into our old experiences. We do not cognize them afresh, but *re-cognize* them in terms of our own past history, interests, and habitual sets. If the new were not soluble in the old we would have no continuing personality. Every day would start a new chaos.

The reason we perceive on the whole accurately is in order that we may cope realistically. But coping requires more than mirroring. Coping means to fulfill our needs, to find safety and love and self-respect, freedom from worry, opportunities for growth, and, ultimately, a satisfying meaning for our existence. Thus it comes about that our coping may be best served by disregarding some stimuli entirely, by modifying our interpretation of others, and by blending incoming meanings with our past habits, present desires, and future directions.

We can see, therefore, that the process of perception (which is the basis of cognition) is not only veridical but also personal. When we dissolve incoming information into familiar meanings we do so because of "perceptual readiness." When we are quick to perceive matters of importance to us (such as our own name) we speak of "perceptual vigilance." When we block off unwelcome information ("None so blind as he who will not see") we speak of "perceptual defense." Now all these processes have been experimentally established by what has been called "new look" perception theory. The term (borrowed from the label given to the fashion in women's dresses around 1950) refers to the fact that psychologists are no longer interested only in veridical perception but also in personal perception.[6]

The personal factor in perception and cognition is demonstrated in many experiments. A few samples will suffice.

College students who feel themselves to be "alienated" (pessimistic, distrustful) tend to hear and recall more gloomy-sounding words than do students who are happier and better adjusted.[7] Personality is the sensitizer; what is admitted and what is retained resonates with the personality structure. Much work has been done with hungry people. In general, it turns out, that hungry people perceive, imagine, think about food (or at least about implements and ways of obtaining food) more readily than do people whose stomachs are well filled. In a similar way, coins of monetary value are "seen" to be larger than are worthless cardboard disks. Again, people who are known to have high esthetic, religious, or other values are perceptually sensitized to words or objects having to do with these values. (For example, if the word "priest" is flashed briefly before a man whose dominant interest is in money and banking, he is much less likely to recognize the word than a man whose dominant interest is religious.)[8]

Although such experimental studies are numerous, they scarcely seem necessary to establish the presence of the personal factor in perception and cognition. It is fully evident, as William James long ago pointed out, that four men who go to Europe—a politician, an artist, a businessman, and a playboy—will see, hear, note, and remember entirely different scenes and events.

A great deal of our selectivity is related to our own self-esteem (egoism). A student will note and remember the teacher's words of praise addressed to him, but perhaps not at all if addressed to others. Indeed, we attach so much importance to ourselves that we readily

---

[6] Much of the "new look" literature has been reviewed by N. Jenkin, Affective processes in perception, *Psychol. Bull.*, 1957, **54**, 100–127. Within the space of a scant decade at least 300 researches focused upon the influence that personality (or motivational) factors exert upon "perception." Although many criticisms have been made of the experiments and theory (e.g., F. H. Allport, *op. cit.*) the trend of the evidence is consistently positive.
[7] A. Davids, Past experience and present personality dispositions as determinants of selective auditory memory, *J. Pers.*, 1956, **25**, 19–32.
[8] Literature on these and many comparable experiments can be traced through Jenkin, *op. cit.* Note 6 above.

imagine that other people's words and acts are for the purpose of bringing us good or ill—although they seldom are. Each one of us has more *egocentric perception* of this sort than is good for us.

Percept versus Procept. The reader will note that I have been using the term *perception* broadly. Many psychologists do so.

Strictly speaking a percept is *sensation plus meaning.* Some sensation (hearing or seeing or touching) should be involved when we speak of perceiving. Now in the illustration I have used it is not always possible to say that the subject *sees* coins to be larger than the same-sized discs, or whether he merely *judges* or *reports* them to be so.

H. A. Murray finds that after playing a scarey game of "murder," children claim that photographs of men shown to them are hostile, unfriendly, and threatening, more so than before playing the game. Do the children actually *see* a change in the lineaments of the faces, or does their scared mood merely lead them to *judge* and *report* differently?

When we say, "None so blind as those that will not see" do we mean that perceptual defense keeps him literally from seeing, or that he quickly passes over and forgets what is uncongenial?

The truth of the matter is that when a stimulus strikes a sense organ a vast array of higher mental operations is put rapidly into motion. The sensory core reaches the brain, where it is acted upon by expectancy, habit, lightning swift recognition, bewilderingly rapid associations. Judgments and thinking result, also sometimes distortions, repressions. By the time the person responds (or fails to respond) we can seldom be sure just what the *sensory* experience has been.

Nor for our purposes does it greatly matter. We are interested only in establishing the influence of all kinds of personality "sets" upon the broad functions of perceiving and cognizing.

But in order to avoid terminological squabbles we may, if we wish, borrow the label *proception* from the philosopher Justus Buchler.[9] The term recognizes the fact that each individual carries with him his past relations to the world, his emotional dispositions, and his own expectancies for the future. These "proceptive directions" provide his potentialities for seeing, hearing, doing,

9 J. Buchler, *Nature and judgment* (New York: Columbia Univ. Press, 1955).

thinking, making, and saying. Buchler adds, "Were there no proceptive direction, there could be no characterization of the course of an individual life, and hence no individual life except in a purely biological sense" (p. 114).

In the balance of the discussion I shall employ the term *proception* to cover any and all influences of set that intervene between sensory input and act. Whereas the term *perceive* should rightly refer to sensory appearance, the term *proceive* covers whatever influence set may have not only on sensory appearance, but also on imagery, remembering and forgetting, judgment, reasoning, and reporting.

Cultural Proception

Our proceptive dispositions are in part acquired from our culture. A culture we have defined (Chapter 8) as a set of ready-made answers to all the common problems of life. When society has firmly implanted these "answers" in us, we are ready to "proceive" the world accordingly. While we retain some idiosyncrasies, in the main our perceptions, cognitions, and conduct conform to cultural standards. Examples are endless.[10]

A chieftain from Swaziland "saw" all the London traffic officers as immensely friendly (because in Swaziland an upraised arm is a warm greeting).

A physician in a village in India will be proceived as a powerful and revered figure if only he pronounces the confident words, "The patient will recover." But in Chile the same confident prediction will make the physician seem arrogant and hence to be distrusted.

In Zululand it is possible with tact to persuade acute cases of tuberculosis to go to a sanitorium for treatment. But the patient will resist if he is told he is a "carrier" of the disease. Such a charge is proceived as an accusation of witchcraft. And no one will acknowledge that he is a witch.

All stories of ethnic character illustrate the point—such as the treatise on elephants. The Englishman titled his, "Elephants I

[10] Many relevant instances are offered by M. Sherif, *The psychology of social norms* (New York: Harper, 1936). See also G. W. Allport, Perception, proception, and public health. In *Personality and social encounter* (Boston: Beacon, 1960), Chap. 18.

Have Hunted"; the Frenchman, "Love Life of Elephants"; the German, "A General Prolegomenon to the Philosophy of Elephantine Quadrupeds."

American health workers state as their goal "the inculcation in each individual of a sense of responsibility for his own health." And this dictum is readily accepted by upper- and middle-class culture. But it is proceived differently by members of the lower classes. To them it is a slap at their cherished domestic values. What is important is to take care of the members of one's family in times of trouble and to be taken care of by them. Self-responsibility is proceived as isolationism; it is even disloyal.

It is unnecessary to multiply instances, for virtually all our proceiving follows—in part at least—cultural stencils. Some veridicality plus some cultural patterning prepare our higher mental processes to cope with the basic conditions of our existence. But for all this standardization, we find that every proceptive system, every individual, is still unique. The veridical and the cultural are fused into the personal.

Individual Proception

Thus to exist as a person means to go beyond the veridical and the cultural, and to evolve one's own outlook on the world. At every moment each of us is conducting his "ego-world" transaction in his own way. Over a period of time we build up our own characteristic "ego-world constellations."[11]

It would be impossible to list all the broad types of proceptive directions that serve to distinguish men from one another. Some, as Whitehead points out, have a dominant mentality of the past, some of the present, others of the future.[12] For some the world is a hostile place where men are evil and dangerous; for others it is a stage for fun and frolic. It may appear as a place to do one's duty grimly; or a pasture for cultivating friendship and love.

Psychologists find it difficult to study such "total" life-styles—

[11] J. Nuttin is one theorist who conceptualizes personality in this manner. See H. P. David and H. von Bracken (Eds.), Personality dynamics. In *Perspectives in personality theory* (New York: Basic Books, 1957), Chap. 10.
[12] A. N. Whitehead, *Symbolism: its meaning and effect* (New York: Macmillan, 1927), p. 63.

though many studies of "value orientations" do approach this level (pages 296–300). It is somewhat easier to study relatively limited proceptive dispositions in respect to which men can be compared. Sometimes these are called "perceptual response dispositions," or "personal constructs," or simply "cognitive styles."[13]

Nuttin set himself to discover whether people's "optimistic" and "pessimistic" dispositions would color their proceptions of a particular laboratory task. He confronted them with a series of short problems. By manipulating the method of scoring he could induce a feeling of success or of failure according to a pattern. All subjects went through the same procedure, and were asked afterward whether they "mostly succeeded" or "mostly failed." There were large differences: for some the memory of success was dominant; for others the memory of failure. For our purposes the important finding is that these same people were independently characterized as chronic optimists or chronic pessimists by their friends and associates. In the laboratory, as in life, they behave true to type (i.e., consistent with their proceptive sets).[14]

Rather than multiply examples, let us concentrate upon one proceptive dimension that has received especially intensive study.

Cognitive Fixedness and Flexibility

From different approaches several investigators have made a single central discovery. To state it in the simplest terms: *some people are chronically unable to change their sets when objective conditions demand it; others, by contrast, are flexible.*

Witkin and his co-workers call the first group *field-dependent*, the latter group *field-independent*. In one experiment the subject sat in a tilted chair. He was then asked to adjust a movable rod so that it would be vertical. The field-dependent subject tended to keep the rod parallel to his own body and line of sight. He

13 L. Postman, Perception, motivation, and behavior, *J. Pers.*, 1953, 22, 17–32; G. A. Kelley, *The psychology of personal constructs* (2 vols.; New York: Norton, 1955); G. Klein, Need and regulation. In M. R. Jones (Ed.), *Nebraska Symposium on Motivation: 1954* (Lincoln: Univ. of Nebraska Press, 1954).
14 J. Nuttin, *Tâche, Réussite et Échec: théorie de la conduite humaine* (Louvain: Éditions universitaires, 1953).

could not abstract the "true vertical" from his own situation in the field. By contrast, the field-independent person was able to correct for his own position and handle the pointer as the objective conditions required.

The important point is that the subjects behaved in a similar way in other tests involving space orientation. Indeed, they acted consistently on quite different tests. Thus, in a modified Gottschaldt design, using patterns similar to those in Figure 21, they were, if field-dependent, unable to pick out certain embedded elements.

Now let us look at the personalities of the field-dependent—those who cannot shake themselves free from the constraints of the situation in which they find themselves. After administering tests and employing interviews and other techniques, the investigators tell us that these subjects are people who in general are very dependent on environmental supports; they lack ability to initiate, are in many respects passive, and submit readily to the forces of authority; they are not insightful regarding their inner life, and fear their own aggressive and sexual impulses; they tend to have low self-esteem and low self-acceptance.

By contrast, the field-independent subjects do not demand environmental supports; they have initiative and organizing ability; they are active and want to achieve; they are aware of their own inner life and accept their impulses even while they have good control over them; they have high self-esteem and self-acceptance.[15]

This study marks a bold attempt to demonstrate that the person approaches his world with a broad proceptive disposition. In many (perhaps most) of his dealings he shows a consistent tendency to be passively rigid or actively and flexibly adaptive. It is also evident that what he sees in the outer world is related to what he feels about the inner world.

Although a single bold investigation of this type may run into

15 H. A. Witkin, H. B. Lewis, M. Hertzman, K. Machover, P. Bretnall Meissner, and W. Wapner, *Personality through perception* (New York: Harper, 1954). A principal limitation of this research is its use of only extreme cases. That such types exist seems established, but the in-betweens show no clear cognitive style of this order. For a more general criticism see A. Gruen, A critique and re-evaluation of Witkin's perception and perception-personality work, *J. gen. Psychol.*, 1957, 56, 73–93.

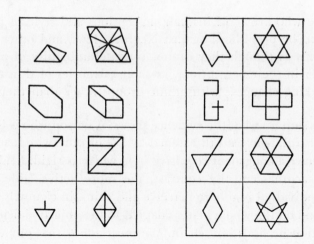

Figure 21. Embedded Designs (selected from K. Gottschaldt, Über den Einfluss der Erfahrung auf die Wahrnehmung von Figuren, *Psychol. Forsch.*, 1929, 12, 46).

pitfalls of method and interpretation, we have in this case a good deal of supporting evidence. Approaching the same problem from fresh angles, other investigators have come to similar conclusions.

Klein discovers what he calls *levelers* (individuals who characteristically hold tight to their categories of perception and judgment), and *sharpeners* (who seem, like the field-independent, to be more adventurous in coping with environmental data).[16]

Similar is Eriksen's distinction between *repressers* and *intellectualizers*. The former "play safe" by keeping strictly within the field—excluding adventuresome perceptions and judgments. The latter are able to detach themselves from the field and make bolder judgments suited to the objective demands of the situation.[17]

Goldstein and Scheerer distinguish between *concrete* thinkers, who keep close to literal-minded reality, and *abstract* thinkers who can be detached and flexible.[18]

Particularly interesting in this connection is the discovery that

16 G. S. Klein, Personal world through perception. In R. W. Blake and G. Ramsey (Eds.), *Perception: an approach to personality* (New York: Ronald, 1950).

17 C. W. Eriksen, The case for perceptual defense, *Psychol. Rev.*, 1954, 61, 175–182.

18 K. Goldstein and M. Scheerer, Abstract and concrete behavior: an experimental study with special tests, *Psychol. Monogr.*, 1941, 53, No. 239.

people who are rigid in their perceptions and style of thinking tend to be prejudiced against Negroes, Jews, and other groups. It seems as though they cannot tolerate ambiguity of any sort: neither in their perceptions, in their categories of thinking, nor in "taking chances" with ethnic groups other than their own.[19]

Let us sum up what the evidence shows. A person who is insecure, self-distrustful, who feels threatened by life or otherwise inadequate, tends to have a congruent cognitive style which is rigid, field-bound, concrete, acquiescent. By contrast, the more active, able, secure, relaxed individual is able to perceive and think in channels that are flexible and on the whole better adapted to the objective demands of the situation he finds himself in. We must admit that our evidence is from scattered sources, that we know little about the "in-between" cognitive styles, and that many other individual cognitive styles are overlooked. But the evidence is still good enough to make our point that personality and procepts go hand in hand.

How does it come about that children develop such differing cognitive styles?

Working with ten-year-olds, to whom perceptual tests similar to Witkin's had been given, it was found that the background and training of the field-dependent and field-independent children differed markedly. Parents of field-dependent children on the whole had punished them more severely, using both aggressive modes of punishment and the withdrawal of love. They had forbade them to show assertive or overly independent behavior, and in general imposed their own standards upon the children. By contrast, the parents of field-independent children encouraged them to make their own decisions and were more likely to give punishment for being too passive or babyish than for asserting independence. In short, these children were free to develop autonomy and were not punished for it.[20]

Thus the roots of these cognitive styles seem to lie partly at least in patterns of child training.

[19] See G. W. Allport, *The nature of prejudice* (Boston, Mass.: Addison-Wesley, 1954), Chap. 25. Also Else Frenkel-Brunswik, Intolerance of ambiguity as an emotional and perceptual personality variable, *J. Pers.*, 1949, 18, 108–143. Even by the age of seven there seems to be a correlation between rigidity of thinking and ethnic prejudice. See B. Kutner, Patterns of mental functioning associated with prejudice in children, *Psychol. Monogr.*, 1958, No. 460.
[20] J. Shaffer, S. Mednick, and Judith Seder, Some developmental factors related to field-independence in children, *Amer. Psychol.*, 1957, 12, 399.

Understanding the Person in His World

If we wish really to know a person it is not enough to be acquainted with his scores on personality tests, nor with his past history, nor with what he may say in an interview. Understanding requires that we take him whole as a unique being-in-his-world. This is the great truth that existentialism teaches. It is also the art of the dramatist, the novelist, and the biographer. By comparison with these artists the psychologist fumbles badly in trying to tell how a man views his world and in depicting his proceptive directions.

And yet all of us, the psychologist included, develop some skill in understanding the cognitive styles of others. We know how our friends think, and how their main values and orientations will color their judgments and conduct. Their cognitive styles are their distinctive ways of living in the world. Sometimes these styles are worm-eaten with ego-defense and prejudice. But on the whole we respect them, for human dignity, we feel, rests ultimately on the validity of human thought.

Mental disorder occurs when a person loses partial touch with reality. His perceptions and cognitions are defective in veridicality.[21] It seems as though tried and trusted (but still false) preconceptions provide him with the only sense of order and safety that he has. It may help us to understand the development of such perverse proceptive dispositions if we examine the case of Karl, an eleven-year-old boy who is in the process of evolving a crippled cognitive style.[22]

Karl: A Cognitive Cripple. We begin with his attitudes toward minority groups. Karl says of Negroes: "They make trouble and start wars. They should be kicked out of San Francisco because they get drunk and kill people. I would like to have a couple for good fighters. They are good fighters when they fight with a knife." The Japanese he wants "to put on an island and throw bombs on them." The Jews "think they are smart and dress up

21 There is experimental evidence that people who are badly adjusted or abnormal do in fact make more errors in ordinary perceptual tasks than do well-adjusted people: F. Barron, Personal soundness in university graduate students. *Publications in Personality Assessment and Research,* No. 1 (Berkeley: Univ. of California Press, 1954). A. H. Maslow, Two kinds of cognition and their integration, *Gen. Semantics Bull.,* 1957, Nos. 20 and 21, pp. 1–6.

22 Adapted from Else Frenkel-Brunswik, Patterns of social and cognitive outlook in children and parents, *Amer. J. Orthopsychiat.,* 1951, 21, 543–558.

in all kinds of jewelry. Some just kidnap girls and boys and use them for slaves."

Karl is a fat and passive boy with a history of many illnesses. Although he rejects minority groups, he often speaks of their strength as fighters. About Filipinos he says, "They are good fighters and definitely good to go through jungles with." Pre-occupation with jungles, where one can be lost, and with wild animals dominates Karl's fantasy in general.

Hitler, says Karl, "is a little bit O.K." though "sometimes he got a little bit too mean and did dirty stuff like putting lighted matches in the toenails of Americans." Although Karl had admira-tion for Hitler he had none for the German people. "We should put all the Germans and Japs on an island and put an atom bomb to it."

Like most prejudiced children, Karl thinks almost always in terms of violence. He thinks "there is always going to be a war," and believes people are marked by avarice, selfishness, and are "out to get you."

When asked, "How would you like to change America?" he replies, "I would like to have a filling station every couple of blocks or so" and "have all the back yards cleaned up." "Every store should have all kinds of candy and bubble gum." Preoccu-pation with food and with cleanliness is common among preju-diced children. Rigid order is demanded, harsh punishment for malefactors, strict conventionality—all of which sharply contrasts with their own turmoil and aggression. Feeling inwardly insecure, they demand outward order and control.

This ambivalence concerning authority is shown by Karl's statement that he likes his teachers—especially if they are strict. At the same time he complains at their injustice: "A lot of them make you go to the principal's office for something you didn't do. I had that happen lots of times."

The same ambivalence is shown toward his father. On the one hand he states "my father is good to me," but then criticizes him for giving him inadequate spending money. On the surface Karl shows submissive obedience, but is at the same time ridden by fears and rebellious thoughts which he tries to repress. He denies that he has any desire to change his parents in any way, but when looking at pictures of older people he shows great hostility toward father and mother figures.

Although Karl seems to idealize his parents when talking about them, he would not choose any member of his family as a companion on a desert island. He wants food and water, and "a girl." It is clear from his dreams and talks that he connects the idea of a girl with feeding her or being fed by her, and with being safe from the threats he feels in connection with boys or men. Karl is by no means sure of his own masculinity. The stories he tells are full of murder and gore; so, too, are his dreams. He seems to live in terror of "dangerous men." Girls are safe. Karl admits that "some boys want to be girls"—a possible projection of his own deep-seated but unwelcome wish.

Although Karl has trouble with his own sexual identity, he takes a rigid view of the position of women. Their place is in the home, and girls should not try to talk when a boy is talking. This conventionalism, like his insistence on cleanliness, order, obedience, is a way of handling an existence that he feels to be too threatening. No doubt his physical weakness is a factor, and so, too, is his home life.

Both parents had foreign-born mothers and fathers. They had to struggle to attain middle-class respectability. Probably as a result of their own insecurity they made strict rules for Karl. He has to be in bed "sharp at six without fail." Asked whether he ever had tantrums, the mother replied, "I should say not. He had better not." Punishment was severe and overpowering. The father says, "It seems like Karl is afraid of me." The mother believes in astrology and thinks Karl will go far and wide. "The stars show it." The father will not let Karl do work in the home, for that is "women's work." This sharp dichotomy of sex roles often goes with ethnic prejudice. Both parents are open about their hatred for Negroes and Jews.

These are a few hints of the kind of home Karl lives in. His own insecurity, his rigid style of "safety thinking," and lack of trust of people seem to follow naturally from the home's influence.

The case of Karl is more or less typical of what has been called the "authoritarian personality." It is condensed here to show that cognitive outlooks may become set in the fairly early years of life;

also, that such outlooks have clear functional significance for the life (providing a kind of safety and self-esteem in lives lacking basic trust). We offer it, too, because the pattern is probably the most common form of cognitive crippling in a society where men and women have not yet learned to accept the uncertainties of life, nor to be confident of their own identity and worth.

Summary

Personality, it is said, is an individual's unique way of perceiving his environment, including himself.[23]

This definition has the merit of raising cognitive operations to a level of primary importance. It counteracts the common misconception of higher mental processes as mere shadows (servants and rationalizations) of underlying motives. There is nothing secondary about cognition. The hunger to know, to comprehend our environment, is a basic motive in life.

It would be still more accurate to say that all motives are an inextricable blend of feeling and cognition. The root factor in both is a "set" or "tendency" (both cognitive and affective). The most important sets are personal traits which are basic modes of striving-and-thinking. These sets direct our perceptions, images, judgments (in short, our proceptions) of our personal world.

There results for each individual a "cognitive style." To some extent culture slants this style, thus accounting for much of the uniformity in people's thought and behavior. But, in the last analysis, each person is unique in the way he blends veridicality, culture, and his own personal existence.

Disordered lives inevitably show cognitive crippling. Their style is marked by a rigid, nonventuresome way of looking at life—an endeavor to find security and safety in a world of flux. There is evidence that the way a child is trained at home has much to do with the rigidity or flexibility of his proceptive sets.

One of the requirements of a mature and healthy personality, as we shall now see, is that its cognitive style be broad, confident, flexible.

[23] R. Stagner, *Psychology of personality* (Rev. ed.); New York: McGraw-Hill, 1961).

CHAPTER 12

The Mature Personality

PROPOSED CRITERIA OF MATURITY • EXTENSION OF THE SENSE OF SELF • WARM RELATING OF SELF TO OTHERS • EMOTIONAL SECURITY (SELF-ACCEPTANCE) • REALISTIC PERCEPTION, SKILLS, AND ASSIGNMENTS • SELF-OBJECTIFICATION: INSIGHT AND HUMOR • THE UNIFYING PHILOSOPHY OF LIFE • PSYCHO-THERAPY • A NOTE ON AGING • SUMMARY

Our long survey of the development of selfhood, of motivation, of cognitive styles brings us at last to the crucial question: What is the *mature personality* like?

We cannot answer this question solely in terms of pure psychology. In order to say that a person is *mentally healthy, sound, mature* we need to know what health, soundness, and maturity are. Psychology alone cannot tell us. To some degree ethical judgment is involved.

When Freud was asked, "What should a normal person be able to do?" he replied, "He should be able to *love* and *work*." While we may find ourselves in agreement with this statement, we also ask, "Is that all a normal person should be able to do?" Another physician, Richard Cabot, doubled the list: *work, love, play,* and *worship.* These are the activities a healthy person lives by[1] Whether we prefer the first list or the second, our choice is based on ethical grounds, and not on *scientific* fact. Science alone can never tell us what is sound, healthy, or good.

Different cultures have somewhat different conceptions of healthiness. In some regions the only "sound" person is one who loses himself completely in following the traditions and advancing the welfare of his tribe. In the Western world the standard places more emphasis on individuality, on realizing one's own personal potentialities.

Fortunately in Western culture there is considerable agreement on the norms for soundness, health, or maturity (we shall use these terms interchangeably). Our task in this chapter is to examine and clarify this common ground of agreement. Before we do so four preliminary remarks are in order:

1. Today we witness a great burst of interest in this problem. It is discussed up and down, before and behind, by psychologists, psychiatrists, and by others.[2] The burst of interest is due in part to the acute menace of mental disorder and emotional ill-health that alarms all nations today. In part also the interest springs from a desire to discover common values among sound mortals as a groundwork on which to build a more peaceable world society.

2. The distinctive richness and congruence of a fully mature personality are not easy to describe. There are as many ways of growing up as there are individuals who grow, and in each case the healthy end-product is unique. Although in this chapter we seek universal criteria of wholesome adult lives, we must never forget the wide play of individuality of pattern.

3. It is questionable whether we should ever expect to find in

---

[1] R. C. Cabot, *What men live by* (Boston: Houghton Mifflin, 1914).
[2] Among discussions of the problem I would call particular attention to Marie Jahoda, *Current concepts of positive mental health* (New York: Basic Books, 1958); L. B. Cole, *Human behavior: psychology as a bio-social science* (Yonkers, N.Y.: World Book, 1953); E. Fromm, *Man for himself* (New York: Holt, Rinehart and Winston, 1947); G. W. Allport, Personality: normal and abnormal, *Sociological Rev.*, 1958, **6**, 167–180. This last reference makes an important distinction between statistical norms (what most people are like) and ethical norms (what the healthy person should be like). M. B. Smith makes it clear that there is no single entity of mental health. The only way to handle the problem is by enumerating the many constituent values (which is the procedure followed in the present chapter): Research strategies toward a conception of positive mental health, *Amer. Psychologist*, 1959, **14**, 673–681.

the flesh a paragon of maturity. We shall be talking more about an *ideal* than about an actual person. It is significant that when we ask people to name some person who seems to them to have a "mature personality" they nearly always select someone outside their own family and of the opposite sex. Why? Perhaps because familiarity makes them all too aware of the weaknesses of their closest associates and of their own sex. Some people approach true maturity. But does anyone ever fully achieve it?

4. Maturity of personality does not have any *necessary* relation to chronological age. A well-balanced lad of eleven, "wise beyond his years," may have more signs of maturity than many self-centered and neurotic adults. A sound college student may have greater maturity than his own parent, or even grandparent. Often, of course, riper experience and the continual meeting and mastering of obstacles and of suffering, do confer greater maturity with advancing age. But the parallel is far from perfect.

Proposed Criteria of Maturity

One terse definition says that a healthy personality actively *masters his environment*, shows a certain *unity of personality*, and is *able to perceive the world and himself correctly*. Such a personality stands on his own two feet without making excessive demand on others.[3] So far as it goes, this definition is satisfactory.

A fuller set of criteria is offered by Erikson, who specifies the period of life at which each attribute is (or should be) normally achieved:

Infancy: a basic sense of trust
Early childhood: a sense of autonomy
Play age: a sense of initiative
School age: industry and competence
Adolescence: personal identity
Young adult: intimacy
Adulthood: generativity
Mature age: integrity and acceptance

Erikson's principal emphasis is upon the sense of *identity*, the formation of which is a particularly acute problem in adolescence. Without

[3] Marie Jahoda, Toward a social psychology of mental health. In M. J. E. Senn (Ed.), *Symposium on the healthy personality* (New York: Josiah Macy Jr. Foundation, 1950).

a firm sense of identity (who am I?) true maturity cannot be reached.[4]

Although it is true that an ethical or value-judgment enters into every definition of health, maturity, and soundness, still a good deal of corrective and guiding light may come from the use of clinical and laboratory investigations. We give an example.

Using the concept of "soundness," the Institute of Personality Assessment and Research at the University of California employed the following method. Members of the various university departments rated graduate students on a nine-point scale for "all round soundness as a person" defined as "the balance and degree of maturity which the individual shows in his relations with other people." Six ratings were obtained for each of the students, and the over-all reliability of the ratings (.68) is as good an agreement as ratings of personality ordinarily yield. Eighty of the rated students, randomly selected, came together in groups of ten for an intensive period of testing and living together for two full days. Several psychologists were on the study staff and *did not know* what rating for "soundness" the departments had given to the subjects. At the end of the study it turned out that the staff, which had given independent ratings on soundness, agreed with the department ratings to an extent represented by a correlation of .41, significantly high but by no means perfect.

What interests us especially in this study are the differences discovered between those whom the departments regarded as sound and not so sound.

First, there were appreciable average differences in their home environments. "In general, the more highly rated subjects had somewhat easier developmental histories, with a lower incidence of serious illness or trauma in childhood, more stable home environments, and more successful and highly respected parents to serve as models for their own development." This finding reinforces our earlier conclusion that security and stability in childhood augur well for a continued advance in personality development. The investigators, however, found some sharp exceptions to this rule—cases of high soundness with wretched family backgrounds. They warn that a bland and easy childhood is not the

[4] E. H. Erikson, Identity and the life cycle: selected papers, *Psychol. Issues,* Monogr. No. 1 (New York: Int. Univ. Press, 1959).

secret of maturity. The secret lies in the "way of responding to the problems set by life." A favorable childhood may *help* master later problems, but it is not the whole story.

The chief personality differences between sound and not so sound students (as ascertained by tests, interviews, controlled ratings) were four in number.

1. *Effective organization of work toward goals.* The departments' more highly rated subjects turned out to be steadier, more able to resist stress; to have more vitality, and to be more adaptable and resourceful. In laboratory tests of perception they showed less fluctuation and irrelevance in their visual performance.

2. *Correct perception of reality.* Not only in perception tests were the high subjects more accurate, but they turned out to have in general better judgment, to have more correct knowledge of themselves (self-insight), and to be more skeptical of miraculous-seeming events.

3. *Character and integrity in the ethical sense.* The high subjects gave evidence of being more dependable, serious, responsible, and tolerant. They had strong "internally determined principles."

4. *Interpersonal and intrapersonal adjustment.* The more highly rated subjects were less defensive, less egotistical, and less distrustful. They more often described themselves as "happy most of the time." They showed fewer traces of neurotic and other abnormal tendencies.[5]

The merit of this study is that it succeeds to some degree at least in reducing the everyday judgments we make of "soundness" or "maturity" to some concrete measurable aspects. If the method has loopholes, it nonetheless possesses the great advantage of confirming the *judgment* of soundness (by the departments) through the *analysis* of soundness carried out in a laboratory setting.

A further study by Maslow uses a method somewhat less objective but still allowable.[6] He made an intensive analysis of cases, of both living and historical personalities, who by a "folk definition"

[5] F. Barron, Personal soundness in university graduate students. *Publications in Personality Assessment and Research*, No. 1 (Berkeley: Univ. of California Press, 1954).
[6] A. H. Maslow, *Motivation and personality* (New York: Harper, 1954).

would be considered mature, or, as he prefers to say, "self-actualizing." He took pains to exclude people with strong neurotic tendencies, although he found that minor foibles and foolishness existed in even the most clearly self-actualizing lives.

The attributes he discovered can be briefly summarized:

1. *More efficient perception of reality and more comfortable relations with it.* The subjects, like the "sound" people in the California study, judge situations and people accurately. Perhaps for this reason they were "uniformly unthreatened and unfrightened by the unknown." They do not, like immature people, show a "catastrophic need for certainty, safety, definiteness, and order."

2. *Acceptance of self, others, nature.* They are at home with nature and with human nature. They accept bodily needs and natural processes without disgust or shame, but also appreciate the "higher" qualities that help make up human nature.

3. *Spontaneity.* Maslow makes much of the capacity to appreciate art, good times, and zestful living. The mature person is not weighed down by conventionality but can capture "peak experiences" of living easily.

4. *Problem centering.* Like the California cases, these people work effectively and with persistence at objective tasks. They can lose themselves in authentic problems without being preoccupied with themselves.

5. *Detachment.* Self-actualizing people have a need for privacy and for self-sufficiency. Their friendships and their attachments to family are not of the clinging, intrusive, and possessive variety.

6. *Independence of culture and environment.* Closely related is the ability to take or to leave idols of the market place. Neither flattery nor criticism disturbs their fundamental course of development.

7. *Continued freshness of appreciation.* Here again we encounter an aspect of spontaneity and responsiveness to new experience.

8. *Limitless horizons.* Most subjects express some concern with the ultimate nature of reality. Maslow characterizes this feature as "mystical" or "oceanic." It is the religious factor in maturity.

9. *Social feeling.* They have a basic feeling of "identification, sympathy, and affection" in spite of occasional anger or impatience. Compassion for one's fellow mortals seems to be an earmark of maturity.

10. *Deep but selective social relationships.* Complementing the attribute of "detachment" we find self-actualizing people capable of unusually close personal attachments, with their own egos more or less obliterated. The circle of close attachments may be small, but even surface relationships outside this orbit are handled smoothly and with little friction.

11. *Democratic character structure.* Maslow finds that his subjects generally feel respect for and show "respect to any human being just because he is a human individual." As other studies have shown, ethnic and religious tolerance is associated with other features of maturity.[7]

12. *Ethical certainty.* None of the subjects was unsure about the difference between right and wrong in daily living. Expressed differently, they did not confuse means with ends, and held firmly to the pursuing of ends felt by themselves to be right.

13. *Unhostile sense of humor.* Punning, joking, and hostile wit are found less often than "thoughtful philosophical humor which elicits a smile more usually than a laugh, which is intrinsic to the situation rather than added to it, which is spontaneous rather than planned, and which very often can never be repeated."

14. *Creativeness.* As a type of summary characteristic Maslow calls attention to an unfailing attribute of his subjects. Without exception, their style of living has a certain strength and individuality that puts an impress upon whatever they do, be it writing, composing, shoemaking, or housework.

Maslow does not claim that these criteria are independent of one another. Clearly they are not, but all seem to flow together in personalities that we variously call mature, healthy, sound, or self-actualizing.

A group of psychiatrists were chatting informally. Someone asked them what they understood by "mental health." One or another

---

[7] G. W. Allport, *The nature of prejudice* (Cambridge, Mass.: Addison-Wesley, 1954), Chap. 27.

of the members mentioned cheerfulness, optimistic serenity, ability to enjoy work, ability to enjoy play, capacity to love, ability to achieve goals, no extreme show of emotions, self-insight, appropriate reaction to situations, and social responsibility. Now these attributes are biased by the psychiatrist's need to treat sick people. But the list is suggestive for the very reason that it is based on much professional experience with cases of not-so-sound personalities.

Healthy persons are not always as happy and as free from conflict as the psychiatrists' list might seem to imply. To accept and handle suffering, guilt, and death is part of the human lot. Shoben attempts to derive the criteria of normality from the essential qualities of being human (such as the long period of youthful dependency and the ability to deal with symbols). This approach leads him to emphasize the serious side of maturity. For him normality means "self-control, personal responsibility, social responsibility, democratic social interest, and ideals."[8]

The criteria advanced by existentialists also stress the serious side of maturity, and include the achievement of meaning and responsibility, as well as acceptance and "the courage to be."[9]

The wars of the twentieth century with their attendant misery have focused attention on human suffering. Suffering cleaves two ways: sometimes it seems to break, and sometimes to make, personality. Injury, disease, imprisonment, "brain washing" often bring a permanent collapse and despair; but often, too, these same conditions bring firmness, richness, and strength. Although people never seek suffering, nor wish it for their children, it is a question whether an easy life ever paves the path to maturity.[10]

All the criteria we have reviewed point to an ideal seldom, if ever, achieved. The sturdiest of personalities have their foibles and

---

[8] E. J. Shoben, Jr., Toward a concept of the normal personality, *Amer. Psychologist*, 1957, **12**, 183–189. See also P. Halmos, *Towards a measure of man: the frontiers of normal adjustment* (London: Routledge & Kegan Paul, 1957).

[9] P. Tillich, *The courage to be* (New Haven, Conn.: Yale Univ. Press, 1952); and V. Frankl, *From death camp to existentialism* (Boston: Beacon, 1959). See also T. A. Kotchen, Existential mental health: an empirical approach, *J. indiv. Psychol.*, 1960, **16**, 174–181.

[10] A biography that brings out this point with extraordinary vividness is E. Barnes, *The man who lived twice* (New York: Scribner, 1956). It tells how Edward Sheldon, the playwright, afflicted by total arthritic paralysis and blindness, surmounted his handicap and became the wise and much sought-after counselor of innumerable friends and stage associates.

their regressive moments; and to a large extent they depend on environmental supports for their maturity. Yet it is perfectly clear that some people, in spite of circumstances, lead lives far closer to this ideal than do others.

We now turn to the task of summarizing in our own way the criteria of maturity we have reviewed. It is arbitrary to say they are *six* in number. Yet six seems to give a reasonable balance between distinctions too fine and too coarse for our purpose.

Extension of the Sense of Self

The sense of self built up gradually in infancy is not fully formed in the first three, or ten, years of life. It continues to expand with experience as one's circle of participation becomes larger. As Erikson points out, adolescence is an especially critical time. Battling against "identity-diffusion," the youth wants to know just who he is. Which facts and experiences and roles are for him propriate, which peripheral, or not suited at all to his life-style?

Puppy love illustrates the point. It focalizes powerful but discordant impulses: sexual tonicity, assertive and submissive tendencies, ambitions, esthetic interests, family sentiment, even religious emotion. But what is important is that this intimate surge attaches itself to another person. The boundaries of self are rapidly extended. The welfare of another is as important as one's own; better said, the welfare of another is *identical* with one's own.

It is not only adolescent love that enlarges the "oneliness": new ambitions, new memberships, new ideas, new friends, new recreations and hobbies, and, above all, one's vocation become incorporated into the sense of self. They are now factors in one's identity.

Here we clearly need the principle of functional autonomy (Chapter 10). To the mature person, life is more than food, drink, safety, mating; more than anything that can be directly, or even indirectly, related to "drive-reduction." Unless a person develops strong interests "outside himself" (and yet still part of himself) he lives closer to the animal level than to the human level of existence. We are, of course, speaking here of *propriate* (and not merely perseverative) functional autonomy.

Let us put the matter another way. The criterion of maturity we are now examining calls for authentic participation by the person in some significant spheres of human endeavor. To be *participant* is not the same as being merely *active*.

Take, for example, Citizen Sam, who moves and has his being in the great activity wheel of New York City. Let us say that he spends his hours of unconsciousness somewhere in the badlands of the Bronx. He wakens to grab the morning's milk left at the door by an agent of a vast Dairy and Distributing system whose corporate manoeuvers, so vital to his health, never consciously concern him. After paying hasty respects to his landlady, he dashes into the transportation system whose mechanical and civic mysteries he does not comprehend. At the factory he becomes a cog for the day in a set of systems far beyond his ken. To him (as to everybody else) the company he works for is an abstraction; he plays an unwitting part in the "creation of surpluses" (whatever they are), and though he doesn't know it his furious activity at his machine is regulated by the "law of supply and demand," and by "the availability of raw materials" and by "prevailing interest rates." Unknown to himself he is headed next week for the "surplus labor market." A union official collects his dues; just why he doesn't know. At noontime that corporate monstrosity, Horn and Hardart, swallows him up, much as he swallows one of its automatic pies. After more activity in the afternoon, he seeks out a standardized day-dream produced in Hollywood, to rest his tense but inefficient mind. At the end of his day he sinks into a tavern and unknowingly victimized by the advertising cycle, orders in rapid succession Four Roses, Three Feathers, and Vat 69.

Sam has been active all day, immensely active, playing a part in dozens of impersonal cycles of behavior. He has brushed scores of "corporate personalities," but has entered into intimate relations with no single human being. The people he has met are idler-gears like himself meshed into systems of transmission, far too distracted to examine any one of the cycles in which they are engaged. Throughout the day Sam is on the go, implicated in this task and that—but does he, in a psychological sense, *participate* in what he is doing? Although constantly *task-involved*, is he ever really *ego-involved?*[11]

What precisely is wrong with Sam? He has not extended his sense of self into any of the significant areas of his life. Like those of all other people, his existence touches upon many spheres of human concern: the economic, educational, recreational, political, domestic, and religious. Sam passes them all by, incorporating none into himself.

It is probably too much to expect even a mature person to be-

11 G. W. Allport, The psychology of participation. In *Personality and social encounter* (Boston: Beacon, 1960), Chap. 12.

come passionately interested in all these spheres of activity. But unless autonomous interests have developed in some of these areas— unless our work, our study, our families, hobbies, politics, or religious quest become significantly propriate—we cannot possibly qualify as mature personalities.

True participation gives direction to life. Maturity advances in proportion as lives are decentered from the clamorous immediacy of the body and of egocenteredness. Self-love is a prominent and inescapable factor in every life, but it need not dominate. Everyone has self-love, but only self-extension is the earmark of maturity.

Warm Relating of Self to Others

The social adjustment of the mature person is marked by two quite different kinds of warmth. On the one hand, by virtue of self-extension, such a person is capable of great intimacy in his capacity for love—whether the attachment is in family life or in deep friendship. On the other hand, he avoids gossipy, intrusive, and possessive involvements with people (even his own family). He has a certain detachment which makes him respectful and appreciative of the human condition of all men. This type of warmth may be called *compassion*.

Both intimacy and compassion require that one not be a burden or nuisance to others, nor impede their freedom in finding their own identity. Constant complaining and criticizing, jealousy and sarcasm are toxic in social relationships. A woman of marked maturity was asked what she considered the most important rule of life. She answered, "Do not poison the air that other people have to breathe."

This respect for persons as persons is achieved through an imaginative extension of one's own rougher experiences in life. One comes to know that all mortals are in the same human situation: they did not ask to come into the world; they are saddled with an urge to survive and are buffeted by drives and passions; they encounter failure, suffer, but somehow carry on. No one knows for sure the meaning of life; everyone is growing older as he sails to an unknown destination. All lives are pressed between two oblivions. No wonder the poet cries, "Praise the Lord for every globule of human compassion."

It is here that we encounter tolerance and the "democratic character structure" so often advanced as earmarks of maturity. By contrast the immature person feels, as it were, that only he himself has the distinctively human experiences of passion, fear, and preference. He and his kind matter; no one else. His church, his lodge, his family, and his nation make a safe unit, but all else is alien, dangerous, to be excluded from his petty formula for survival.

More should be said about the deeper personal attachments. It is safe to assert that no one, mature or immature, can ever love or be loved enough. But it seems that the less mature person wants to be loved rather more than he wants to give love. When he gives love it is usually on his own terms, which is to say that strings are attached: the other must pay for the privilege. A possessive, crippling love—such as some parents burden their children with—is common enough but unwholesome for both giver and receiver. It is a hard lesson for a parent to learn—or for a wife, husband, lover, or friend —that he should desire the other's company, wish him well, and accept him for what he is, without placing iron bonds of obligation upon him.

Genitality. Some psychoanalysts are wont to equate maturity with what they call "genitality." Sex is such a dominant theme in most lives that it is easy to see why some theorists hold that the attainment of complete orgastic genital gratification is a principal mark of maturity. They argue that the free play of the sexual function is the best measure of the individual's capacity to surmount the repressive forces of society as well as the press of infantile sexual fixations. Since, however, rapists and perverts may be capable of complete orgastic gratification, it becomes necessary immediately to modify the criterion by limiting sexual gratification to that experienced "with a loved partner of the opposite sex." Erikson states the argument as follows:

Psychoanalysis has emphasized *genitality* as one of the chief signs of a healthy personality. Genitality is the potential capacity to develop orgastic potency in relation to a loved partner of the opposite sex. Orgastic potency here means not the discharge of sex products in the sense of Kinsey's "outlets," but heterosexual mutuality, with full genital sensitivity and with an over-all discharge of tension from the whole body. . . . The idea clearly is that the experience of climactic mutuality of orgasm provides a supreme example of the mutual regulation of complicated patterns and in some way appeases the potential rages caused by the daily evidence of the oppositeness of male and female, of fact and fancy, of love and hate, of work and play. Satisfactory sex relations make sex less obsessive and sadistic control superfluous.[12]

Persuasive as the argument is, we are nonetheless aware of exceptions. It is not proved that every genitally mature individual is healthy in all regions of his life. Nor is it clear that the sex drive is so closely tied to all regions of the personality as the theory requires. Finally, there are the innumerable instances of celibates, both male and female, and even of sexual deviants, whose accomplishments and whose conduct are so outstanding that we cannot possibly consider them as "immature."

What, then, shall we conclude? It seems wise to admit that in many lives genital maturity does accompany general personal maturity. At the same time, we cannot possibly maintain that mature people experience no frustrations and no deviations in handling their drive impulses, including the ramified impulses of sex. The difficulty here seems to lie in identifying adult motivation almost exclusively with the sex-drive. One can readily concede that such an important drive, if handled in a mature way, may well harmonize with, and reinforce, general maturity, without at the same time reducing the entire problem of maturity to genitality.

Emotional Security (Self-acceptance)

We readily note the difference between the person who has emotional poise and one who is emotionally clamorous and who gives way to outbursts of anger and passion—including overindulgence in alcohol and obsessive outbursts of profanity and obscenity. The egotist, the roué, the infantile person have not passed successfully through the normal stages of development. They are still preoccupied with bits and pieces of emotional experience.

Many writers speak of *self-acceptance*. This feature of maturity includes the ability to avoid overreaction to matters pertaining to segmental drives. One accepts his sex drive and does the best he can to handle it with the minimum of conflict in himself and with society; he does not constantly seek the salacious and the scatolog-

12 E. H. Erikson, Growth and crises of the healthy personality. In Identity and the life cycle: selected papers, *Psychological Issues*, Monog. No. 1 (New York: International Universities Press, 1959, p. 96). Quoted by permission of the publishers.

ical, nor is he prudish and repressed. Everyone has fears, both of
immediate dangers and of ultimate death, but these can be handled
with acceptance. If not, there develops a neurotic preoccupation with
the danger of knives, of high places, with health foods and medicines,
with self-protective superstitions and rituals.

Especially important is the quality called "frustration tolerance."
Irritations and thwartings occur daily. The immature adult, like
the child, meets them with tantrums of temper, or with complaining,
blaming others, and self-pity. By contrast, the mature person puts
up with frustration, takes the blame on himself (by being "intro-
punitive") if it is appropriate to do so. He can bide his time, plan
to circumvent the obstacle, or, if necessary, resign himself to the
inevitable. It is definitely not true that the mature person is always
calm and serene, nor is he always cheerful. His moods come and go;
he may even be temperamentally pessimistic and depressed. But he
has learned to live with his emotional states in such a way that they
do not betray him into impulsive acts nor interfere with the well-
being of others.

He probably could not do so unless he had evolved a continuous
sense of security in his life. His early childhood experiences of
"basic trust" will have something to do with this development. And
at later stages he has somehow learned that not every pinprick to his
pride is a mortal wound, and not every fear portends disaster. The
sense of security is by no means absolute. No one has control of
time, tide, taxes, death, or disaster. As the sense of self expands, one
takes on new risks and new chances of failure. But these insecurities
are somehow held with a sense of proportion. One becomes cautious
without panic. Self-control is a reflection of a sense of proportion.
The mature person expresses his conviction and feelings with consideration for the convictions and feelings of others; and he does
not feel threatened by his own emotional expressions or by theirs.
Such a sense of proportion is not an isolated attribute in personality.
It comes about because one's outlook is generally of a realistic
order, and because one possesses integrative values that control and
gate the flow of emotional impulse.

Realistic Perception, Skills, and Assignments

Thought, as the preceding chapter showed, is an integral part
of personality. One might say that the life of feeling and emotion is

the warp and that higher mental processes are the woof of the fabric.

We have already seen that the everyday perceptions and cognitions of the sound personality are on the whole marked by efficiency and accuracy (pages 270, 279). One might say that the sound person has "sets" that lead to veridicality to a greater degree than do persons not so sound. Maturity does not bend reality to fit one's needs and fantasies.

Does this fact mean that no person can be healthy and mature unless he has a high IQ? There is truth, but also danger, in such a judgment. Manifestly a sturdy minimum is required of memory ability, verbal (symbolic) power, and general problem-solving capacity. To be mature means to have these basic intellectual abilities. Yet the equation is not reversible. Plenty of people with high intelligence lack the emotional balance and intellectual organization that constitute a wholesome personality.

The psychologist Terman studied a population of gifted children whose scores on intelligence tests were so high that each child was literally "one in a thousand." Not only was their intellectual endowment great but as a group they had every advantage in health, physical form, and socioeconomic support.

Yet in following up these cases twenty-five years later, it was found that the failures in personality organization were not less numerous than those in the general population of the same age. Alcoholism and psychosis were just as prevalent. Maladjustment was present, even very serious maladjustment, though it would be hard to compare the extent with an average population. To be sure, many were successful in fulfilling their earlier promise.[13] But on the whole we are forced to conclude that exceptional intelligence alone does not guarantee maturity.

Not only are the perceptions mostly veridical, and cognitive operations accurate and realistic, but appropriate skills are available for solving objective problems. An otherwise sound person who lacks the know-how of his trade—be it mechanics, statecraft, or housekeeping—will not have the security or the means for self-extension that maturity requires. Although we often find skillful people who

13 L. M. Terman and Milita H. Oden, Genetic studies of genius: IV. *The gifted child grows up* (Stanford, Calif.: Stanford Univ. Press, 1947).

are immature, we never find mature people without problem-pointed skills.

Along with veridicality and skill we must list the capacity to lose onself in ones' work. Freud, Maslow, the California study—all make this point. Mature people are problem-centered. Something objective is worth doing. What this means is that egoistic impulses of drive-satisfaction, pleasure, pride, defensiveness can all be forgotten for long stretches while a task takes over. This particular criterion can be related to the goal of "responsibility" which is stressed by existential thinkers. It was in the spirit of existentialism that Harvey Cushing, the brain surgeon, once said, "The only way to endure life is to have a task to complete."

In short, a mature person will be in close touch with what we call "the real world." He will see objects, people, and situations for what they are. And he will have important work to do.

Here we should add a word concerning "economic maturity." For most people the struggle to earn a living, to remain solvent, to meet fierce economic competition is a major demand of life. It causes strain and begets crises often more devastating than the crises of sex and self-identity. College students do not always estimate correctly the challenge they will face when they enter into competition for the dollar. Youthful personalities sometimes seem relaxed (even serene) prior to their ordeal of the market place. To be able to support oneself and one's family (in America with an ever-advancing standard of living) is a frightening demand. To meet it without panic, without self-pity, without giving way to defensive, hostile, self-deceiving behavior is one of the acid tests of maturity.

Self-objectification: Insight and Humor

To achieve the good life, said Socrates, there is one paramount rule: *know thyself*. This is not an easy assignment. Santayana wrote, "Nothing requires a rarer intellectual heroism than willingness to see one's equation written out." Lord Chesterfield was perhaps too self-satisfied when he wrote to his son, "I know myself (no common piece of knowledge, let me tell you). I know what I can, what I cannot, and consequently, what I ought to do."

Most people *think* they have good self-insight. In various courses in psychology 96 percent of the students claimed to have average or better than average insight, only 4 percent admitting possible deficiency. Since we think about ourselves so much of the time it is comforting to assume that our thinking is veridical—that we really know the score.

The term *insight* (often called *self-insight*) comes from psychiatric usage according to which a mental patient, who knows that he (and not everybody else) is suffering from disorientation, is credited with insight. Extending this usage to the normal population, we may say that accurate self-knowledge is a dimension where people occupy positions ranging from high self-insight to little or none.

Autobiographies make an interesting study in this connection. Some writers make a point, even a virtue, of admitting their defects, and write their confessions "objectively" for the world to read. The chances are that they guard some secret tabernacles against prying eyes, even their own. There are some incidents of meanness or shame that would be too humiliating to disclose, or even to face. And, of course, many autobiographies are little more than elaborate self-justifications.[14]

How is the psychologist to tell whether or not an individual has insight? According to an old adage, Everyman has three characters:

1. that which he has;
2. that which he thinks he has; and
3. that which others think he has.

Ideally, insight is to be measured by the ratio between the second item and the first, for what a man thinks he is in relation to what he really is provides a perfect definition and index of his insight. Practically, however, proof positive of what a man *is* in the biophysical sense is difficult to obtain. Ultimately, therefore, the most practicable index becomes the ratio between the second and third items—the relation of what a man thinks he is to what others (especially the psychologist who studies him) think he is. If the man objects that all the world, including the psychologist, is wrong about him, he cannot be disproved. In such a case the evaluation of his insight must be left to heaven.

[14] This problem is discussed more fully in G. W. Allport, *The use of personal documents in psychological science* (New York: Soc. Sci. Res. Council, Bull. No. 49, 1942).

Psychologists know that there are certain correlates of insight. For example, those who are aware of their own objectionable qualities are much less likely to attribute them to other people, that is to say, they are less given to "projection" than are those lacking insight.[15] Also, people with high insight are better judges of other people and are likely to be accepted by them.[16] There is likewise evidence that those with good insight are on the average relatively high in intelligence.[17] We recall also (page 279) that students rated high in "soundness" stood high on insight.

Humor. Perhaps the most striking correlate of insight is the sense of humor. In one unpublished study where subjects rated one another on a large number of traits, the correlation between ratings on insight and humor turned out to be .88. Such a high coefficient means either that personalities with marked insight are also high in humor, or else that the raters were not able to distinguish between the two qualities. In either case the result is important.

> The personality of Socrates shows the close association of the two traits. Legend tells how at a performance of Aristophanes' *Clouds* he stood up in order that the amused audience might better compare his face with the mask that was intended to ridicule him. Possessed of good insight, he was able to view the caricature in a detached way, and to aid the jest by laughing at himself.

What, then, is a sense of humor? The novelist Meredith says it is the ability to laugh at the things one loves (including, of course, oneself and all that pertains to oneself), and still to love them. The real humorist perceives behind some solemn event—himself, for instance—the contrast between pretension and performance.

The sense of humor must be distinguished sharply from the cruder sense of the comic. The latter is a common possession of almost all people, children as well as adults. What is ordinarily considered funny—on the stage, in comic strips, on TV—consists usu-

---

15 R. R. Sears, Experimental studies of projection: I. The attribution of traits, *J. soc. Psychol.*, 1936, **7**, 151–163.
16 R. D. Norman, The interrelationships among acceptance-rejection, self-other identity, insight into self, and realistic perception of others, *J. soc. Psychol.*, 1953, **37**, 205–235.
17 P. E. Vernon, Some characteristics of the good judge of personality, *J. soc. Psychol.*, 1933, **4**, 42–58.

ally of absurdities, horse play, or puns. For the most part it consists in the degredation of some imagined opponent. The aggressive impulse is only slightly disguised. Aristotle, Hobbes, and many others have seen in this "sudden glory" of one's own ego the secret of all laughter. Related to aggressive wit (which derides the other fellow) is laughter at the risqué which seems due to the release of suppressions. Aggression and sex are at the basis of much that we call comic.

A young child has a keen sense of the comic, but seldom if ever laughs at himself. Even during adolescence the youth is more likely to view his failings with acute suffering than with laughter. There is evidence that people who are less intelligent, who have low esthetic and theoretical values, prefer the comic and lack a sense of humor based on the real relationships in life.[18]

The reason why insight and humor march hand in hand is probably because at bottom they are a single phenomenon—the phenomenon of self-objectification. The man who has the most complete sense of proportion concerning his own qualities and cherished values is able to perceive their incongruities and absurdities in certain settings.

As with insight, almost everyone claims to have a rare sense of humor. The same students who evaluated their own insight in comparison with that of other people were asked to estimate their sense of humor. Ninety-four percent replied that it was as good as or better than the average.

Stephen Leacock has observed the same conceit. In *My Discovery of England,* he writes: "A peculiar interest always attaches to humor. There is no quality of the human mind about which its possessor is more sensitive than the sense of humor. A man will freely confess that he has no ear for music, or no taste for fiction, or even no interest in religion. But I have yet to see the man who announces that he has no sense of humor. In point of fact, every man is apt to think himself possessed of an exceptional gift in this direction. . . ."

It is only fair to state that up to now psychologists have had very little success in measuring either insight or the sense of humor. We

---

[18] C. Landis and J. W. H. Ross, Humor and its relation to other personality traits, *J. soc. Psychol.,* 1933, **4,** 156–175; also R. Grziwok and A. Scodel, Some psychological correlates of humor preferences, *J. consult. Psychol.,* 1956, **20,** 42.

are dealing here with the subtler reaches of personality—a territory which we hope psychologists will explore with more success in the future than in the past.

Affectation. The precise opposite of the criterion we are describing is the tendency of some people to appear outwardly to be something they cannot be. The affected person is not aware that his deception is transparent, or that his pose is unbecoming. We have spoken of the adolescent's bent for trying on all manner of "identities" for size. The mature person, by contrast, unless he is deliberately play-acting for fun, knows that he cannot counterfeit a personality.

It is true that most of us try to put our best foot forward, and even pretend to virtues and achievements that stretch the truth. But the mature person does not let this social effort collide too seriously with his true nature. Insight and humor keep such egotism in check.

The Unifying Philosophy of Life

Humor, we have said, is indispensable to a mature outlook on life. But it is never sufficient. An exclusively humorous philosophy of existence would lead to cynicism. Everything would be regarded as trivial, displaced, and incongruous. Reason would be distrusted, and all serious solutions rejected. Although the cynic may find amusement along the way, he is at bottom a lonely soul, for he lacks the companionship of a life-goal.

Maturity requires, in addition to humor, a clear comprehension of life's purpose in terms of an intelligible theory. Or, in brief, some form of a unifying philosophy of life.

Directedness. One psychological approach to the matter is Charlotte Bühler's research in the life histories of many individuals, famous and average.[19]

This investigator feels it necessary to introduce the conception of *Bestimmung*, a German term somewhat inadequately translated as "directedness." In analyzing some two hundred life histories it appeared that each life is ordered or steered toward some selected goal or goals. Each person has something quite

[19] Charlotte Bühler, *Der menschliche Lebenslauf als psychologisches Problem* (Leipzig: Verlag von Hirzel, 1933; rev. ed.; Bonn: Hogrefe, 1959).

special to live for, a major intention. The goals vary: some stake everything on a single great objective; others have a series of definite purposes. A parallel study of suicides shows that life becomes intolerable only to those who find nothing to aim at, no goal to seek.

In childhood, objectives are at first lacking; in adolescence they are vaguely defined; early maturity brings definiteness in the pursuit. Everyone encounters obstacles. Lives plagued by bad luck may take a more modest goal (lowering the "level of aspiration"). Often there is grim persevering with little hope of success. Some defeated personalities remain bound to life by "sheer indignation," but even this focus serves as a goal for combat.

Using this concept we may say that in mature personalities the *Bestimmung* is more marked, more outwardly focused, than in lives less mature. A problem arises among youths who have no directedness in sight. One study of college students estimates that approximately one fifth are in a stage of "not knowing why they live." They seem devoid of any but simple momentary motivations, and are neither mature nor happy.[20] Some may develop directedness later, but the outlook is not favorable, for ordinarily in adolescence we expect to encounter high ambitions and idealism.

A common postadolescence crisis is often overlooked. Bühler points out that in the late twenties, after the ideals of adolescence have been given a trial, disappointment sets in. It is in the late twenties that a person may learn that his abilities and circumstances require a trimming down. We have already spoken of the difficulty of attaining "economic maturity." Salaries may not be as high as hoped for; marriage may not be as rosy; he may not outgrow all his personal handicaps. But in spite of this stage of disillusionment it seems a better prognosis for youth to have high aspirations and later scale them down, than for youth to have no firm direction at all.

The problem arises in a different way in old age. Although old people spend much time in evaluating their total effort, they still wish to maintain their direction even though their activity must be greatly curtailed. The goal may now be very modest. (We recall the old woman, inmate of an almshouse, who expressed as her sole

20 C. W. Heath, *What people are: a study of normal young men* (Cambridge, Mass.: Harvard Univ. Press, 1945).

desire that "some will remember me kindly after I am gone.") In general there is great social waste in cutting older people off, through retirement or isolation, from their directions of growth. When at last they are no longer capable of secular achievement they may profitably spend their time in piecing together what they know of life and continue to seek its pattern in philosophical or religious study and thought.

Value-Orientations. A closely related way of approaching this criterion of maturity is to seek for the unifying philosophy in terms of some standard classification of values. One might say that a given person is a Communist, a Christian, a pacifist, or a "beatnik." One would thereby imply that much or most of the unity in the life came from following the value-orientation of one of these standards. Two sustained psychological investigations of this order merit report.

Morris formulated a long paragraph describing each of thirteen "ways to live." These were composed principally from leading world ideologies. One, for example, would stress "sympathetic concern for others"; a second, "stoical self-control"; a third, "group activity and enjoyment"; a fourth, "dynamic integration of diversity." Youth in many lands were asked to read all thirteen "ways" and select their own first choice. American youth, it turns out, subscribed more frequently than other youth to "dynamic integration of diversity," showing that they wished a rich, full life and abhorred both routine and boredom in their existence.[21]

Such a study has the merit of remaining close to existing cultural ideologies and invites a comparison of youth in many lands. The approach is basically one of cultural anthropology. Both Morris's study and the one described below differ from Bühler's *Bestimmung*, which allows an infinite diversity of directions for human lives to take. She does not predetermine the number of "ways to live."

Spranger, somewhat in the manner of Morris, defines six major value-types. This author contends that every actual person can be regarded as approaching (but not fitting perfectly within) one or more of these value-directions. Human life, it seems to Spranger, harbors six main types of value, and these appeal in varying degrees to individuals who build the unity of their lives about them.

[21] C. W. Morris, *Varieties of human value* (Chicago: Univ. of Chicago Press, 1956).

It should be clearly understood that Spranger does not argue that there are six main types of *people*. The typology is one of pure *values*, not of actual persons. The term *ideal type* is used in this connection. The label does not mean that the types are necessarily good, or that they are ever found in their pure form. An ideal type is rather a "schema of comprehensibility"—a gauge by which we can tell how far a given person has gone in organizing his life by one, or more, of these basic schemes.[22]

1. *The theoretical.* The dominant interest of the "ideal" theoretical man is the discovery of *truth*. In the pursuit of this goal he characteristically takes a "cognitive" attitude, one that looks for identities and differences, one that divests itself of judgments regarding the beauty or utility of objects, and seeks only to observe and to reason. Since the interests of the theoretical man are empirical, critical, and rational, he is necessarily an intellectualist, frequently a scientist or a philosopher. His chief aim in life is to order and to systematize his knowledge.

2. *The economic.* The "ideal" economic man is characteristically interested in what is *useful*. Based originally upon the satisfaction of bodily needs (self-preservation), the interest in utilities develops to embrace the practical affairs of the business world—the production, marketing, and consumption of goods; the elaboration of credit; and the accumulation of tangible wealth. This type is thoroughly "practical" and conforms well to the prevailing conception of the average American businessman.

The economic attitude frequently comes into conflict with other values. The economic man wants education to be practical, and regards unapplied knowledge as waste. Great feats of engineering, scientific management, and "applied psychology" result from the demands that economic men make upon learning. The value of utility likewise conflicts with the esthetic value, except when art serves commercial ends. Without feeling inappropriateness in his act, the economic man may denude a beautiful hillside or befoul a river with industrial refuse. In his personal

22 E. Spranger, *Lebensformen* (3d ed.; Halle: Niemeyer, 1923; transl. by P. Pigors, *Types of men;* New York: Stechert, 1928).

life he is likely to confuse luxury with beauty. In his relations
with people he is more likely to be interested in surpassing them
in wealth than in dominating them (political value) or in serving
them (social value). In some cases the economic man may be said
to make his religion the worship of Mammon. In other instances,
however, he may have regard for the traditional God, but inclines to consider Him as the Giver of good gifts, of wealth,
prosperity, and other tangible blessings.

3. *The esthetic.* The esthetic man sees his highest value in
form and *harmony.* Each single experience is judged from the
standpoint of grace, symmetry, or fitness. He regards life as a
manifold of events; each single impression is enjoyed for its own
sake. He need not be a creative artist; nor need he be effete; he
is esthetic if he but finds his chief interest in the artistic episodes
of life.

The esthetic value is in a sense diametrically opposed to the
theoretical; the former is concerned with the diversity, and the
latter with the identities of experience. The esthetic man chooses
with Keats to consider truth as equivalent to beauty, or else to
agree with Mencken, that "to make a thing charming is a million
times more important than to make it true." In the economic
sphere the esthete sees in the process of manufacturing, advertising, and trade a wholesale destruction of the values most important to him. In social affairs he may be said to be interested in
persons but not in the welfare of persons; he tends toward indi-
vidualism and self-sufficiency. Esthetic people often like the beautiful insignia of pomp and power, but oppose political activity
when it makes for a repression of individuality. In the field of
religion they are likely to confuse beauty with purer religious
experience.

4. *The social.* The highest value for this ideal type is *love*
of people, whether of one or many, whether conjugal, filial,
friendly, or philanthropic. The social man prizes other persons
as ends, and is therefore himself kind, sympathetic, and unselfish.
He is likely to find the theoretical, economic, and esthetic attitudes cold and inhuman. In contrast to the political type, the
social man regards love as itself the only suitable form of power,
or else repudiates the entire conception of power as endangering
the integrity of personality. In its purest form the social interest

is selfless and tends to approach very closely to the religious attitude.

5. *The political.* The political man is interested primarily in *power.* His activities are not necessarily within the narrow field of politics; but whatever his vocation, he betrays himself as a *Machtmensch.* Leaders in any field generally have high power value. Since competition and struggle play a large part in all life, many philosophers have seen power as the most universal and most fundamental of motives. There are, however, certain personalities in whom the desire for a *direct* expression of this motive is uppermost, who wish above all else for personal power, influence, and renown.

6. *The religious.* The highest value for the religious man may be called *unity.* He is mystical, and seeks to comprehend the cosmos as a whole, to relate himself to its embracing totality. Spranger defines the religious man as one "whose mental structure is permanently directed to the creation of the highest and absolutely satisfying value experience." Some men of this type are "immanent mystics," that is, they find their religious experience in the affirmation of life and in active participation therein. A Faust with his zest and enthusiasm sees something divine in every event. The "transcendental mystic," on the other hand, seeks to unite himself with a higher reality by withdrawing from life; he is the ascetic and, like the holy men of India, finds the experience of unity through self-denial and meditation.

One advantage of such portraits, even though they are too perfect in consistency to exist in real life, is that they lend themselves to measurement. A personality test entitled *A Study of Values* (described in Chapter 18) makes it possible to discover to what degree an actual individual does subscribe to each of these value-directions.[23] It turns out that although these values as measured are of equal popularity in the population as a whole, they have very different strengths of attraction for individuals. One person, we find, is interested in *theory* and in the *beautiful,* but not in *power* or *religion.* In another the emphasis is perhaps reversed.

We may ask whether these value-directions exhaust the possibil-

[23] G. W. Allport, P. E. Vernon, and G. Lindzey, *A study of values* (3d ed.; Boston: Houghton Mifflin, 1960).

ities. They do not. We may also object that they tend to flatter human nature, since many people have no values beyond the hedonistic, the sensual, the vital, and temporary needs for adjustment. We may also complain that the values are defined too broadly. Although John may be interested in philosophical theory, let us say, theories of physics may leave him cold. Henry may relish power in his community but not in politics. But the scheme is not intended to fit all individual cases. It offers, nonetheless, an important contribution to the study of value-orientations as an integrating factor in mature personality.

The Religious Sentiment. When we speak of a person's "unifying philosophy of life" we are likely to think first of his religion. (Spranger, we saw, regarded it as the most comprehensive and integrative of all value-orientations.)

But here an immediate distinction must be drawn. The religious sentiments of many people—perhaps of most people—are decidedly immature. Often they are holdovers from childhood. They are self-centered constructions in which a deity is adopted who favors the immediate interests of the individual, like a Santa Claus or an overindulgent father. Or the sentiment may be of a tribal sort: "My church is better than your church. God prefers my people to your people." In cases of this sort religion merely serves self-esteem. It is utilitarian and incidental in the life. It is a defense mechanism (often an escape mechanism) and does not embrace and guide the life as a whole. It is an "extrinsic" value in the sense that the person finds it "useful" in serving his immediate ends.

> Studies show that ethnic prejudice is more common among churchgoers than among nonchurchgoers.[24] This fact alone shows that religion is often divisive rather than unifying. Extrinsic religion lends support to exclusions, prejudices, hatreds that negate all our criteria of maturity. The self is not extended; there is no warm relating of self to others, no emotional security, no realistic perception, no self-insight or humor.

In short, we certainly cannot say that the religious sentiment is always a unifying philosophy of life.

24 Cf. G. W. Allport, *The nature of prejudice* (Cambridge, Mass.: Addison-Wesley, 1954); also Religion and prejudice. In *Personality and social encounter*, Chap. 16. Note 11 above.

At the same time the religious sentiment may be of such an order that it does provide an inclusive solution to life's puzzles in the light of an intelligible theory. It can do so if the religious quest is regarded as an end-in-itself, as the value underlying all things and desirable for its own sake. By surrendering himself to this purpose (not by "using" it), religion becomes an "intrinsic" value for the individual, and as such is comprehensive and integrative and motivational.[25]

It may help to understand the religious sentiment thus defined if we compare it with humor. In one respect only are they alike. Both set a worrisome event in a new frame of reference, smashing, as it were, the context of literal-mindedness. Both humor and religion shed new light on life's troubles by taking them out of the routine frame. To view our problems humorously is to see them as of little consequence; to view them religiously is to see them in a serious scheme of changed meaning. In either case a new perspective results.

In all other respects they are different. Humor depends on seeing incongruity in events; religion sees an ultimate congruity. Since experiences cannot possibly be regarded at any one time as of great moment and as trivial, it follows that we cannot be simultaneously both reverent and jesting. We may joke and pray about the same disturbing events in life, but never at the same time.

What keeps the religious person from becoming a cynic—as thoroughgoing humorists must be—is the conviction that at bottom something is more important than laughter, namely, the fact that he the laugher, as well as the laughter itself, have a place in the scheme of things. When this important issue is decided there is still plenty of room for jesting. In fact, a case might be made for the superior sense of humor of the religious person who has settled once and for all what things are sacred and of ultimate value, for nothing else in the world then needs to be taken seriously. He can see that hosts of happenings are ludicrous, that men and women, including himself, are given to amusing vanities, actors upon a stage. To him nothing in their coming and going is of consequence unless it happens to touch the matter of their ultimate value in the scheme of things.

It is only the core and aim of a religious outlook that are beyond

---

[25] The criteria of intrinsic (mature) religion are described more fully in G. W. Allport, *The individual and his religion* (New York: Macmillan, 1950).

the reach of humor. Human foibles related to the religious intention are possible sources of amusement, examples being incongruous episodes that occur in church. But such incongruity does not affect the priority of the "ultimate concern."

Religion always involves more than a man's cognitive processes; nevertheless, being a response of the total self, rational thought is not excluded. All faith—whether religious or not—is an affirmation where knowledge, though made use of, is not the decisive factor. It is a truism that all men live by faith, for no one has knowledge that his values are worth while; he only has faith that they are. Religious faith differs from other faith chiefly in its comprehensive character. It holds that, if knowledge were present, one would find that the universe as a whole, the facts of existence, the puzzling clash of good and evil, all make coherent sense. As for the content of one's religious faith, one takes what to him is the best and most rational "fit." Mature (intrinsic) religion is a completely embracing theory of life but it is not a theory that can be proved in all detail.

Here we must reject the view that all religious impulses in a life are infantile, regressive, or escapist. That such "extrinsic" religion exists there is no doubt. Nor can we accept the view that institutional and orthodox religion is always a childish submission to authority and therefore immature. Plenty of thoughtful people find historic and traditional forms of religion the "best fit" to their own groping in terms of meaning and comprehensiveness. And so even orthodox religion may reflect more than childish awe and habit; it may reflect a carefully chosen, mature, and productive philosophy of life.

But we must not make the reciprocal error and assume that religion is the only unifying sentiment. Logically perhaps, since it aims to encompass all that lies within experience and all that lies beyond, it is ideally designed to confer unity. But the fact remains that many people find a high degree of unification in other directions.

W. H. Clark obtained judgments from approximately three hundred well-educated persons, nearly half of whom were listed in *Who's Who*. When they were asked to rate the constructive factors leading to creativity in their lives, the chief factor turned out to be "interest and satisfaction in work for its own sake," followed by a "desire to know and understand." Third came the desire to aid society. On the average, "religious motivation" came lower on the list, about equal to the "desire to create beauty." But an important fact is that people differ greatly in their ratings of the importance of religion. They tend to give it a high place or a very low place. The fairly low average ranking is due to the fact that the majority of cases studied did not consider it as their chief source of motivation.[26]

Thus we cannot say for certain how common is the comprehensive religious sentiment as a unifying philosophy of life. There is evidence, however, that college alumni, when they are a decade or two out of college, are more religious than they were in college.[27] The search for religious meaning seems to grow with advancing years.

Generic Conscience. Conscience, as John Dewey has said, is that which is taken to have rightful authority in the direction of conduct. If a person's conscience lays down comprehensive guidelines for all (or nearly all) of his conduct it is obviously a unifying force. To take *responsibility* is an existentialist ideal for maturity, but duty and responsibility are the cementing factor in many lives that do not have an articulate philosophy.

In Chapter 6 we traced the evolution of conscience. It passes through many stages. And human beings are so constructed that they not only have certain likes and dislikes but also like or dislike themselves for liking or disliking certain things and for performing certain acts. Thus conscience is a universal possession of man, except for a few individuals who, because of moral obtuseness, are called *psychopathic*. But there is a wide difference between the tribal or the child's erratic conscience and the generic conscience of maturity.

A mature person has a relatively clear self-image by virtue of which he can imagine what he would like to be and what he ought to do as a unique individual, and not merely as a member of his tribe or as the child of his parents. He says to himself in effect, "I ought to do the best I can to become the sort of person I partly am, and wholly hope to be." This type of conscience is not the obedient

[26] W. H. Clark, A study of some of the factors leading to achievement and creativity, with special reference to religious skepticism and belief, *J. soc. Psychol.*, 1955, **41**, 57–69.
[27] Cf. E. N. P. Nelson, Patterns of religious attitude shifts from college to fourteen years later, *Psychol. Monogr.*, No. 424, 1956; E. L. Kelley, Consistency of the adult personality, *Amer. Psychologist*, 1955, **10**, 659–681; I. E. Bender, Changing patterns of religious interest, *The Humanist*, 1958, **18**, 139–144.

"must" of childhood; it is less troubled by the specific and unrelated commandments that the young child learns. It is not overwhelmed by minor slips and sins; nor does it confuse cultural custom with basic personal morality, even though, of course, the person accepts selected standards from his culture that seem relevant to his self-ideal.

Now conscience may or may not be religiously toned. It certainly will be if its possessor is in any sense a religious person. A utilitarian extrinsic religion will be accompanied by a spotty and inconsistent conscience readily soothed by self-justification, or perhaps neurotically obsessed by specific fragments of guilt. By contrast, the intrinsic and mature religious sentiment is accompanied by a generic conscience whose quality is one of total directedness.

It is of considerable interest to note that many people (as in Clark's study, page 302) feel that their desire to serve society is a more important generic incentive for them than the fulfillment of some religious destiny. We conclude, therefore, that an integrated sense of moral obligation provides a unifying philosophy of life whether or not it is tied to an equally developed religious sentiment.[28]

Psychotherapy

When people are dissatisfied with their personalities they may undertake counseling, psychotherapy, or psychoanalysis. What are the goals sought by these remedies? To some extent each therapist selects his own goal. Horney, it seems, emphasizes security and escape from anxiety; Fromm, the overcoming of alienation from the world and increase in productiveness; Frankl seeks to enhance meaning and responsibility in the patient's life; Erikson, to rebuild the foundations of the patient's identity.

Without discussing each individual point of emphasis we can hazard the statement that *most* therapists seek three goals: (1) to remove unwanted symptoms; (2) to adjust the person to the society in which he lives; (3) to enhance his experience of wellness.

The first goal is obviously insufficient, though desirable. When symptoms are removed, the person is not fundamentally different; and it is doubtful whether symptoms can be removed unless the second two goals are also met.

---

[28] For a fuller discussion of the "must" conscience of childhood and the "ought" conscience of maturity, see G. W. Allport, *Becoming: basic considerations for a psychology of personality* (New Haven, Conn.: Yale Univ. Press, 1955).

As to the second goal, it seems a doubtful benefit. Society itself is sick. Why, then, make a patient content with its injustices, hypocrisies, and wars? And to what society shall we adjust the patient? To his social class, thus making him provincial and depriving him of aspiration? To his nation, thus giving him no vision of mankind as a whole? It is doubtful that we can accept society (any society) as a standard for a healthy personality. A head-hunter society demands well-adjusted head-hunters as citizens, but is the deviant in this group who questions the value of decapitation necessarily an immature human being?

Also, the sense of well-being is an elusive criterion. No one would claim that a sense of ill-being should be sought, and yet euphoria, happiness, or even "peak experiences" give only an elusive feeling of maturity. Moreover, oddly enough, well-being can only be experienced in contrast to suffering. Hence maturity must have a quota of suffering, if only that it may be surmounted.

Critical though we are of these common therapeutic goals, there is merit in all of them, provided they are supplemented by a somewhat fuller conception of human destiny. According to the psychoethics of this chapter we maintain that some kind of continual growth and development into the stage of maturity is what fully fashioned human beings seek. We suggest that the goals of psychotherapy should be framed in these terms, and that specifically the six criteria of maturity we have described be accepted as the objectives of all counselors, parents, and therapists who would help others along life's road.

An important postscript to this brief discussion should be added. Is maturity the only ultimate "good" value for personality? Do we not all know immature people who are highly creative, heroic in special ways, and possessed of other desirable attributes? It seems that especially the value of *creativity* is present in many lives that are otherwise warped, retarded, even neurotic and psychotic. And the world needs creativity. We must concede this point, and admit that there are many good things in life besides soundness and maturity of personality. We can yield on this matter, but still maintain as a generally desirable goal the development of personalities toward the highest attainable level of maturity. We shall always fall short of this goal, but when we do so, fortunately many sound values remain.

A Note on Aging

We have insisted that the process of aging is not necessarily the same as "maturing" in personality. Yet growing old is a normal stage in life and merits special study in the field of personality theory. The great increase in interest in the subject in recent years is due to the fact that since 1900 the average life has lengthened from about forty years of age to seventy. In the future more and more "personalities" will be in the advanced stage of life than ever before. The problem of what to do with them is particularly acute because the "extended family" is a thing of the past. Parents and grandparents now seldom live with their married children and grandchildren. Their health, their economic well-being, their loneliness, and the question whether they can still be of use to society are all burning issues.

Recent researches indicate that most older people are far from being feeble or incapacitated. Though retired and forced into virtual isolation many still have high abilities and strong *directedness*. It is true that biological vigor declines after the twenties and thirties; so, too, do sensory acuity and the knack of passing "intelligence tests." Yet the capacity for comprehension, reasoning, and judgment do not measurably decline. On the contrary, they may improve because of the greater available store of experience.

Investigations show that the record of older people in industry is surprisingly good. They have fewer industrial accidents, have lower labor turnover, and have equal output when compared with young workers. They also tend to be more stable and loyal when not held under close supervision. At the same time, they are less efficient in work requiring continuous, rapid action.[29]

It is illuminating to consider the records of automobile accidents. Although youth below twenty-five years of age score consistently higher on tests of motor coordination and skill, yet their rate of driver accidents is far higher than among drivers over sixty. Insurance companies recognize this fact in the steeper rates they charge youthful drivers. It is apparent that aging people, by

29 R. A. McFarland, The psychological aspects of aging, *Bull. N.Y. Acad. Med.*, 1956, 2d ser., Vol. XXXII, No. 1, pp. 14–32.

using caution and judgment, may compensate for what they have
lost in motor skill.[30]

But it seems relatively superficial to discuss aging only in terms
of average competence, average attitudes, average problems. Having
developed throughout life a unique personality, no aging person can
be considered to fit merely an average type. Uniqueness persists to
the grave. The most important lesson we learn from the many psychological studies of aging is that old people are not much different
after retirement from what they were before. Their life-quest is not
yet complete. The tragedy lies in cutting off their opportunities to
seek further growth. Who can estimate the amount of wisdom society
may lose by dampening development during the last decades of life?

Summary

Psychologists cannot tell us what *normality, health,* or *maturity* of personality mean. Yet every practical-minded person, including psychologists and psychotherapists, would like to know. Surveying some of the vast literature on the subject, we find considerable
agreement, at least so far as the value-conceptions of Western culture
are concerned. In particular we find six criteria that sum up the area
of agreement. The mature personality will (1) have a widely extended sense of self; (2) be able to relate himself warmly to others
in both intimate and nonintimate contacts; (3) possess a fundamental
emotional security and accept himself; (4) perceive, think, and act
with zest in accordance with outer reality; (5) be capable of self-
objectification, of insight and humor; (6) live in harmony with a
unifying philosophy of life.

The goals of psychotherapy and counseling are sometimes stated
in a manner that fails to recognize all these criteria of maturity. The
same failure marks our policies in dealing with aging people. It
would be sounder ethics and sounder psychology to encourage the
development of human potentialities in all six directions from childhood to the end of life.

[30] H. R. DeSilva, Age and highway accidents, *Scientific Monthly,* 1938, 47, 536–545.
Also R. A. McFarland, R. C. Moore, and A. B. Warren, *Human variables in motor
vehicle accidents* (Boston: Harvard School of Public Health, 1955).

PART III STRUCTURE OF Personality

CHAPTER 13

Search for Elements

PSYCHOLOGY'S PECULIAR PROBLEM • THE SEARCH FOR UNITS IN THE PAST • STIMULUS-RESPONSE UNITS • IDENTICAL ELEMENTS • FACTORIAL UNITS • SUMMARY

MAN'S nature, like all of nature, is composed of relatively stable structures. The success of psychological science, therefore, as of any science, depends in large part upon its ability to identify the significant units of which its assigned portion of the cosmos is composed. Without its table of elements chemistry could not exist. Where would physics be without its quanta, or biology without the cell? All science is analytic, and *analysis* means "to loosen or unbind."

Psychology's Peculiar Problem

It is often said that psychology is "far behind" other sciences because psychology cannot discover its fundamental units. Within the past century many have been proposed (among them, *faculties, ideas, instincts, reflex arcs, sensations, images, feelings, drives, habits, factors, attitudes, sentiments, event-structures*). No fundamental agreement has been reached.

The lack of agreement comes from the fact that psychologists have different purposes in view. Wundt and Titchener, whose interest lay only in conscious mental life, thought *sensations, images, feelings* were the ultimate units. Experimenters with animals favor stimulus-

Terms for units

Different ideas of units

311

response units (*drive, habit*); physiological psychologists speak of *cell assemblies;* statistical workers of *clusters* or *factors;* clinical psychologists lean toward *need;* others concerned with personality favor *traits, attitudes,* or *sentiments.*

Units vary in grades of complexity. They may be major structures, substructures, or microstructures, depending on our level of concern. The truest statement that can be made about the human nervous system is that it is hierarchically arranged: structures as simple as a reflex pathway or as complex as a guiding philosophy of life—all are equally real. Let us take an example: a physiological psychologist interested in the alternate flexion and extension of the leg might decide that the *chained reflex* is the basic unit concerned; but an investigator concerned with classifying motor activities will elect *walking* as a more acceptable unit. If we are studying interpersonal behavior we might prefer the *habit of walking away from people.* If our concern is with more generalized dispositions of personality we may fix upon a *trait of withdrawal.* Fine-grained or coarse-grained units of all orders have their place.

But this variability of units is at best confusing for science. At least one school of psychology (field theory) condemns all "atomism" in psychology and places its emphasis only on configurations, patterns, and fields. This conception tries to keep close to the fluidity that marks all mental life and behavior.

Yet something must account for the *recurrences* and *stabilities* in personal behavior. Although we admit that units cannot exist in a "pure state" (for our daily conduct is determined by a confluence of many activated units), still we do find that personality is relatively stable over time and in different situational fields. How can we account for this fact unless we search for some sort of structures?

The Search for Units in the Past[1]

What we need in the study of personality are units of a relatively high order of complexity, for our job is to account for the broader (molar) orders of conduct, not for muscle-twitches.

[1] To a certain extent this discussion follows my chapter entitled, What units shall we employ? In G. Lindzey (Ed.), *Assessment of motivation* (New York: Holt, Rinehart and Winston, 1958).

An embracing theory of "structure" is contained in F. H. Allport, *The nature of perception and the concept of structure* (New York: Wiley, 1955). This theory helps to account for the stability of personal structures and at the same time for their modifiability in their contact with "outside" (natural or social) structures.

From the fourth century B.C. to the seventeenth century A.D., personality theory, such as it was, was written largely in terms of the four temperaments. It is an interesting fact that these temperaments were regarded as corresponding to the four Empedoclean elements of nature, and to the four parallel humoral elements (black bile-melancholic, yellow bile-choleric, blood-sanguine, phlegm-phlegmatic). As we saw in Chapter 3, the scheme is neat though untenable. It says in effect that physics, biochemistry, and psychology all rest on the same four cosmic elements. If the "unity of science" is ever achieved it will not be achieved in this oversimplified manner.

When the humoral units finally lost favor, the doctrine of *faculties* arose to dominate the scene. For the space of two centuries (roughly 1650 to 1850) man's nature was viewed as a mélange of faculties—the "powers" of memory, attention, reasoning, and so on. Toward the end of this period, Gall, the phrenologist, sought faculties that came closer to *personal* qualities: vanity, love of offspring, friendliness, and the like.

Under the influence of Darwin, personality theorists traded faculties for *instincts*. The ensuing era, lasting approximately sixty years, brought McDougall's elegant defense of instincts and their derivatives, the sentiments. McDougall thought these units could serve as a list of uniform motivational elements in respect to which all persons could be compared. Freud reinforced the search, though, unlike McDougall, he offered no clear classification of instincts. By 1924, Bernard reported that over 14,000 different instincts had been proposed, and that no agreement was yet in sight.[2]

The instinct doctrine shifted its form. Behaviorists postulated *drives* as the unlearned units on which personality is based. The drives were for the most part simple physiological appetites and aversions. Other psychologists transformed instincts into the doctrine of needs (pages 203–205). Unlike instincts, needs are not necessarily inherited; they are simply basic directions of motive. Among the needs are abasement, achievement, aggression, dominance, seclusion, sentience, sex. More recently Murray has adopted the concept of value-vector, which escapes the abstractness of needs. Typical values are *health, money, ideology, sex*. Each may be linked with a vector; e.g., *to acquire, to maintain, to avoid*. Murray lists fourteen basic values and twelve vectors. The resulting number of motivational

---

[2] L. L. Bernard, *Instinct: a study in social psychology* (New York: Holt, Rinehart and Winston, 1924), p. 220.

units is large but not unmanageable. The scheme is strictly nomothetic but has the advantage of integrating the object of desire with the desire itself—an improvement over more abstract classifications.[3]

These fragments of history serve to give some perspective to a search that began two thousand years ago, and has not yet reached a conclusion. Current proposals exist in a bewildering array. Besides *instincts, drives, needs, value-vectors,* and *sentiments,* we encounter *habits, attitudes, syndromes, regions, ergs, personal constructs, preferred patterns, dimensions, factors, schemata, traits,* and *trends.* One or more authors favor each of these types of unit and proceed to offer their definitions and subclassifications. But even if authors agree on favoring a certain type of unit (factors, for example) they often disagree as to what specific units should be recognized under the type.

We shall not attempt to define or explain all these proposals. Several of them, however, will be examined in this chapter and in succeeding chapters.

Stimulus-Response Units

At this point we must tackle a fundamental issue in personality theory. Let us call it the issue of *specificity.* This point of view, though less common than it was two decades ago, is still widespread in America. It holds that "personality is made up of thousands of independent and specific habits." In other words, there is no organization at higher levels, such as is suggested in the ordinary usage of the term *trait.* The essential element is the specific habit. The only unit is a "specific behavior tendency which must be defined in terms of a particular stimulus and a particular response."[4]

The evidence for this view is crisply stated by Lehmann and Witty:

Over and over, a battery of tests designed to measure traits such as persistence, or aggressiveness, or honesty, yields results so unreliable and un-

---

[3] H. A. Murray, Toward a classification of interactions. In T. Parsons and E. A. Shils (Eds.), *Toward a general theory of action* (Cambridge, Mass.: Harvard Univ. Press, 1951), pp. 463 f.

[4] Statements of this point of view may be found in H. Hartshorne, M. A. May, and F. K. Shuttleworth, *Studies in the organization of character* (New York: Macmillan, 1930); P. M. Symonds, *Diagnosing personality and conduct* (New York: Appleton-Century-Crofts, 1931), Chap. 9; W. Coutu, *Emergent human nature* (New York: Knopf, 1949).

dependable . . . that one is led to question the actual existence of the general traits.[5]

To some extent common experience confirms this view. We all know men who are neat in dress but slovenly at their desks, saintly on the Sabbath and diabolical on weekdays, timid at the office, tyrannical at home. But at the same time do we not also know people who are almost always neat, shy, cynical, or officious? We can predict their behavior correctly in new situations. Their traits seem to be generalized.

Specificists sometimes rest their case on the older *Character Education Inquiry*.[6] This research was ingenious and painstaking. The investigators set concrete tasks before hundreds of children. From their responses it was possible to study the evidence for and against the existence of such alleged traits as deception, helpfulness, cooperativeness, persistence, and self-control. The final conclusion was that such qualities as these are "groups of specific habits rather than general traits."

Here is an example of the results. Children were given opportunities to steal pennies (and it turned out that children had fairly consistent habits of stealing or not stealing). They were also given a chance to cheat on their school papers, and to lie about the cheating, also to cheat on games. Now the correlations between these forms of behavior were low. Thus, stealing pennies and lying about cheating correlated only $+.132$. A dishonest habit in one situation was independent of the dishonest habit in another.

The study, impressive though it is, is not fully convincing. Several important objections must be made:

1. In the example given, the results do not prove that the children lack traits, but only that dishonesty as measured is not itself a trait. A child who has the habit of stealing pennies may do so because he is saving up to buy a tool kit; or because he is revengeful in an anti-

[5] H. C. Lehmann and P. A. Witty, Faculty psychology and personality traits, *Amer. J. Psychol.,* 1934, 44, 490.
[6] H. Hartshorne and M. A. May, Vol. I, *Studies in deceit,* 1928; Vol. II, *Studies in service and self-control,* 1929; Vol. III (with F. K. Shuttleworth), *Studies in the organization of character,* 1930 (New York: Macmillan).

social way; or because he feels socially inferior and wishes to buy candy to curry favor from his playmates. A child who lies may do so because he is fearful of punishment; because he does not wish to hurt the teacher's feelings. Child F (Figure 22) may lie because he has a chronic hunger for praise and approval.

What the inquiry discovers is that the abstract conception of "honesty" is not as strong a trait in the children as are other personal dispositions. The research does not prove that "stealing pennies" is an isolated habit unrelated to any higher structures of personality organization in the child who steals.

2. The investigators set out to study ethical qualities, much complicated by social approval and disapproval. These rubrics of character are not basic personality rubrics, especially in childhood. A child's conscience, as we have seen, is not firm or well socialized in early years. The following case illustrates the point.

A boy of ten, accustomed to the respect of his own playmates at home, found himself for the summer among older boys who looked down upon him as an outsider and as a punk. He felt frustrated and chagrined. One day a member of the gang proposed "swiping" a few bars of candy from the corner store. At first the

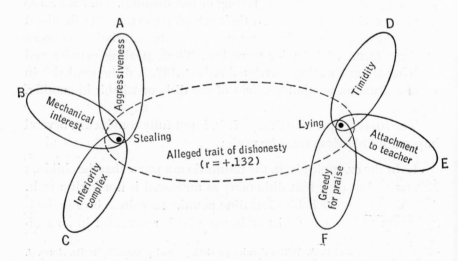

Figure 22. Critique of One Nomothetic Conception of Trait [Dotted ellipse represents the trait as conceived by investigators; solid ellipses, possible personal dispositions overlooked by them.]

lad's habits of honesty prompted him to resist the suggestion, but when the gang ridiculed him, his *major* desire for admiration and social standing became aroused. Alone he undertook the larceny, and in a few moments emerged from the store with a plentiful supply of chocolate bars. The less stable habits of honesty were destroyed by a stronger and more organized *trait*. The boy was consistent enough with himself, but his consistency did not happen to correspond to the social ideal.

3. Evidence is strong that older people become more consistent in their socialized behavior. They tend to be "honest all over," or perhaps "generally deceitful." We do not mean to say that every person is perfectly consistent, but only that adults are more consistent than children.

4. The C.E.I. investigators report that in securing a "total character score" for children, the average intercorrelation of the twenty-three tests used was $+.30$ (higher than for the stealing-lying comparison above). Whether the persistent positive relations should be regarded as evidence for specificity or for generality is a question. One author analyzing the C.E.I. data concludes that there is evidence for a general c factor of character. This conclusion, drawn from identical data, is directly opposed to the original investigators' conclusion.[7]

The doctrine of specificity has had somewhat mischievous results. Following the research reported, an important directive from the central New York office was sent nationally to leaders in a youth organization. It read in part: "Psychology no longer recognizes honesty as a general trait. . . . Character traits are not general traits, but rather a specific thing in each situation." That is to say, in training a child we can expect nothing more than a disarray of habits; we must train him not to take pennies from mother's purse, not to steal cookies, not to pick the lock of the grocery store. The child is considered incapable of generalizing standards of decency, of learning

[7] J. B. Maller. General and specific factors in character, *J. soc. Psychol.*, 1934, **5**, 97–102. The factor c is defined as the readiness to forego immediate gain for the sake of remote but greater gain. Recent studies by W. Mischel and R. G. H. Metzner indicate that this trait is relatively consistent in the child's personality. Some children develop a generalized ability to delay their gratifications; others of the same age demand immediate satisfactions.

wide respect for the interest of others. Something seems seriously wrong with this picture.

In spite of its manifest weaknesses, the doctrine of specificity has considerable appeal to American theories (not at all to the European). It fits the tradition of William James and E. L. Thorndike, who placed heavy emphasis upon the habit unit of conduct. It is congenial to stimulus-response doctrines that look for one measurable response to follow one measurable stimulus (a situation sometimes approximated in animal research). It is congenial to some sociologists who place heavy emphasis upon the situation. They like to think of recurrent situations (culture patterns) as causing whatever stability there is in man's conduct, rather than think of man as having stable traits that determine his behavior without marked dependence on the situation. Stated more broadly, the analytic tradition is strong in American thought; we like to reduce behavior to the smallest possible components.

But in spite of its congeniality to the American ethos, we cannot be content with specificity. The doctrine that all behavior (and therefore personality) is composed of countless specific habits is, for several reasons, unacceptable.

In the first place, the evidence is not convincing. When we fail to find consistency we may be looking in the wrong place for it. Suppose we ask whether people using the public library have traits causing them to take out only books with red or green covers. Of course they haven't. If only bindings were studied, no consistency should be expected. But if the subject matter of the chosen books is investigated, well-organized traits of interest would appear. Unless consistency is sought in the right direction, consistency will not be found.[8]

In the second place, we can never expect all people to be consistent by a method that relies only on *mass investigation*. We saw in Figure 22 that children may be consistent with themselves, but not with a nomothetically conceived rubric. A person may be entirely consistent with himself without being consistent in traits that are tested in a general population.

Third, evidence derived from common traits, though never indicating perfect reliability, does usually show considerable consistency.

---

[8] The illustration is from G. B. Watson, Next steps in personality measurement, *Charact. & Pers.*, 1933, **2**, 69.

Whenever a "personality test" has high reliability (internal consistency) it means that people who are aggressive, persistent, sociable (or what not) on one item are so, by and large, on all other items. Or if they stand low on one measure, they tend to stand low on others. Thus specificity is belied by whatever internal reliability exists in personality tests, and this reliability is usually much higher than the statement on page 314 implies.

Finally, everything that is known concerning the integrative action of the nervous system is incompatible with specificity. Belief in the "neural groove," where a specific habit was once supposed to reside, has been abandoned. Higher levels of integration exist, and these guarantee structures that are broader than mere specific habits.

Identical Elements

If one views personality as composed of "countless specific habits," one must answer the question, How do you account for the considerable consistency people show in their conduct? A traditional answer has been in terms of *identical elements*.

Let us see how the theory works. We may say of a certain boy that he is *courteous*. The theory of specificity (identical elements) says, "No, he has no general trait of courtesy." Rather, he "learns to take off a specific cap when coming in a specific door and in the presence of his mother. But in time he may take off his cap or hat or whatever he has on his head when entering any door, in any house whatsoever, whether or not in the presence of a person."[9] Courtesy, then, is nothing more than the repetition of the same habits over and over again when provoked by stimuli previously associated with these habits, or when the habits themselves have some threadlike connection. A diagram will make the theory clear.

The boy in the illustration has learned, by dint of drill, that when he enters an outside door (a) in his own home (Stimulus Field I), he should take off his cap (Habit 1), wipe his shoes (Habit 2), greet the occupants (Habit 3). Now, entrance doors have something in common (identical elements in different stimulus fields): they all provoke the boy to perform the same three habits (as, for example, when he enters a neighbor's door, a', Stimulus Field II). A misinformed observer might remark that here is a *courteous* lad. Not at all; he has

9 P M. Symonds, *The nature of conduct* (New York: Macmillan, 1928), p. 294.

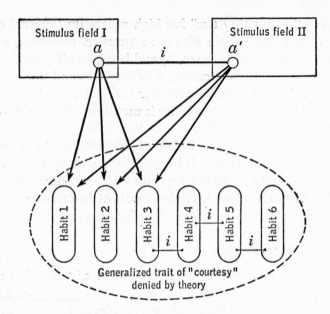

Figure 23. The Theory of Identical Elements. Identity may reside either in the stimulus fields, or else in parts of habits. [Solid connecting lines (*i*) indicate such identities. Arrows show lines of stimulation, and the ellipse with broken lines represents the hypothetical trait of *courtesy* denied by the theory.]

no general trait; his three habits are automatically set into motion whenever he encounters identical elements in different fields.

Now, the habits themselves are also capable of having identical features, so that the arousal of one may arouse another (by virtue of reintegrative action, page 93). Thus, greeting the occupants of the house (Habit 3) might through some commonly associated verbal components—for example, "Hello, how are you?"—set in motion a further inquiry concerning their health (Habit 4), which in turn by virtue perhaps of some commonly associated facial expression, might suggest a friendly smile (Habit 5). Finally, a friendly smile through further specific association leads to some additional act of "courtesy," such as asking his friend out to play (Habit 6).

Thus it is that identical elements in the stimulus fields, or in the neuropsychic structure, are responsible for the quasi-consistency of the boy's conduct. What is denied is that any generalized disposition exists to which the name "courtesy" might be properly attached. The boy is basically a creature of specific habits. Whatever relation there may be between the six habits here enumerated is due entirely to some still more minute and specific components of these habits, in short, to some identical elements.

This, then, is the picture of the structure of personality according to the theory of identical elements.

The reader should note that this point of view is often encountered in general psychology as well as in the psychology of personality. For example, it is often asked whether it is good to study Latin because it "trains the mind." The point of view of specificity would say, "No, except as identical elements may exist between Latin and other activities." For example, if one learns the word *amor* in Latin, this root is an identical element in the English *amorous*, in the French *amour* and *amour-propre*. The student, therefore, gains something of value in spelling or in vocabulary by the recurrence of specific elements. Or if in studying Latin a student develops the habit of sitting down with the grammar every evening, perhaps this habit will help him when he tackles the study of chemistry or any other subject.

The opposite point of view, traditionally called "formal discipline," says that studying Latin has far wider gains. It would stimulate the imagination (as a whole); it would develop a sense of precision in language (in general); it would, so to speak, exercise the intellectual muscles. To dispose of this issue: it seems likely that too little "transfer of training" is allowed for by the identical element theory, and too much by the old-fashioned "formal discipline" theory.

The tradition of specificity and identical elements has prevailed in Anglo-American psychology from the time of the British empiricists in the eighteenth century (e.g., Locke, Hume) down to modern stimulus-response theories. To summarize this view we may say that it first posits very small units (Locke's *simple idea,* Hume's *sensation,* the behaviorists' *reflex arc* or *habit*). It then seeks to account for higher-level structures by positing connections or associations between these small elements.

The whole matter comes to focus when we ask the question, What is *similarity?* In Goethe's line, "Green is life's golden tree," we do somehow feel the poet's meaning but where is there an identical element uniting life with golden tree and simultaneously with green? Similarity, yes; identical elements, no. In a metaphor once used to describe a popular but sentimentally trashy poet—"a purple-plushed exuder of poetic cheese pies"—where is the common element to unite the unfortunate poet with this withering image? This metaphor and others may strike us as apt expressions of similarity—and yet the tracing of a specific common element (whether sensation, habit, nerve tract, or any other identical bond) is impossible.

Now to bring the issue back to personality. A certain superpatriot (shall we call him McCarley?) has, let us say, a phobia against communism. This seems to be his leading trait. To him Russians, most college professors, all liberals, all peace organizations, the United Nations itself, antisegregationists, and Jews—all are "communist" and he hates them. It seems unreasonable to suppose that such diverse stimuli have elements in common. But to him they compose an organized concept (a similarity). Anything new or strange or foreign is likely to be included in this very general attitude (or trait).

Look for a moment at his behavior. Sometimes McCarley will give vent to his hatred by writing a letter to the local newspaper, sometimes by growing red in the face and blustering, or again by joining rioters and stoning the house of some Negro or other "communist." The behavior from situation to situation is similar, yes, but in no intelligible sense does it involve identical elements (in each case wholly different muscle groups may be involved).

What we are saying is that our personal traits (like our thought-life) are organized on the basis of similarities and that similarities cannot be reduced to identical elements. The term *similarity*, of course, has a subjective flavor. We *perceive* similarities. But we may, if we prefer, employ a more objective concept, and speak of *equivalence of stimuli* and *equivalence of response*. Many situations may

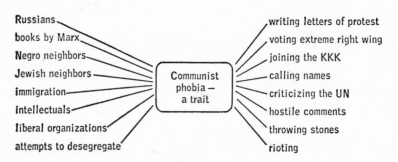

Figure 24. Generality of a Trait. The range of a trait is determined by the equivalence of stimuli that arouse it and by the equivalence of responses that it provokes.

arouse a generalized trait (or concept) and many forms of behavior may be equivalent in giving expression to the trait (or concept). The lad who takes off his hat and wipes his shoes on entering a house is not doing so just because elements in the two acts are mechanically tied, but because to him they have the same essential social meaning. He is generally "housebroken," and, as more equivalent acts are included in the system, we say he has a trait of courtesy, which means that many situations evoke the disposition of thoughtfulness-of-others, and lead to many varied forms of behavior, all having equivalent meaning.

There are several difficulties with the doctrine of identical elements. One is that the theory is unable to specify just what an element is, or just how identical an identity must be. But chiefly the theory runs afoul of much negative experimental evidence.[10] In the educational process we do not find that children learn new material in proportion to the number of identical elements in it and in old material; but they learn in proportion to their understanding of *principles* (i.e., seeing the wide sweep of similarity in cases).[11]

Evidence favors a theory of the opposite order, one in which integration and generalization play the leading part. Here transfer effects depend chiefly upon the equivalence of meaning to the individual of the fields that confront him. If they are similar, transfer takes place. Equivalence and similarity are not uniform for all; they are a personal matter, and hence it is impossible to predict for people en masse the transfer value of a single experience, or to arrange a program of school studies that will secure uniform transfer effects for *all* children.

So swiftly and so subtly do we group our experiences and form our own concepts and attitudes and traits that the process is admittedly baffling. The whys and wherefores of similarity and equivalence are beyond our present comprehension. We may borrow a phrase from William James and say that all human beings have "an electric aptitude for analogies." At present we cannot predict with exactness what stimuli and what responses will be equivalent for a person—

[10] The whole problem of identical elements and relevant evidence is reviewed at greater length in G. W. Allport, *Personality: a psychological interpretation* (New York: Holt, Rinehart and Winston, 1937), Chap. 10.

[11] See, for example, R. C. Craig, *The transfer value of guided learning* (New York: Columbia Univ., Teachers College, Bureau of Publications, 1953).

though we can often do so with some success. We can be fairly safe in saying that our Mr. McCarley will react negatively to anything "foreign." Or that our courteous boy will be thoughtful in almost any situation. But we may make mistakes.

It helps us to understand the formation of general concepts and traits if we recall the discussion in Chapter 11 of cognitive sets. A person who is timid may have from the start a disposition to develop fears of the strange; this insecurity is a kind of set that might, for example, account for the harsh cluster of qualities comprising McCarley's dominant trend. Or a child in school who learns a guiding principle (which is, of course, a form of mental set) will make rapid progress in organizing all relevant examples of this principle into a general concept. Or a person who has a definite self-image (seeing himself as a "friend of man") will cluster his experiences more readily because of this organizing set. What we have called "proceptive dispositions" help us understand the "electric analogies" that people make, and the firm patterns of personality that they develop.

In the following chapters I shall state may own view of the nature of the true units of personality. This view denies that specific stimulus-response units or identical elements are the foundation stones of personality structure.

Factorial Units

We shift our attention to a wholly different line of search. Factorial units do not rest on neural or behavioral assumptions, as does the doctrine of specificity, but rather on *statistical* assumptions. The theory of factors is a widely favored point of view.

Factors are popular because they attempt to answer the question that science persistently asks: What is the least number of concepts that can order and describe a multiplicity of phenomena? This question reflects the "law of parsimony," which admonishes science to avoid needless multiplication of concepts.

Factor-analysis applies the law of parsimony to the search for basic units of personality. Specifically it asks the question, What is the minimum number of separate clusters that can be considered to underlie a matrix of correlation coefficients? Although the mathematical computations required are complex, the essential nature of the factorial unit is not difficult to understand.

Let us take a simple hypothetical illustration. Suppose that an investigator measured several hundred or a thousand people on seven "traits." Perhaps he uses tests of these qualities, or perhaps he uses ratings gathered from their friends and acquaintances. Let us say the "traits" are these:

> D —Dominance
> F —Friendliness
> L —Leadership
> T —Talkativeness
> M—Moodiness
> S —Secretiveness
> P —Passivity

Now he quickly discovers that these are not "independent" traits. Some of them overlap heavily. Most people, for example, who stand high on dominance will stand high on friendliness, leadership, and even talkativeness; at the same time these same people tend to be low on moodiness, secretiveness, and passivity. An imaginary table of correlations indicates the situation.

The law of parsimony warns us, "You do not need seven separate units; you have only two basic clusters." Just what to name Cluster I is a problem. It seems heavily loaded with dominance and leadership, but also to some extent with friendliness and talkativeness. Naming Cluster II is no easier. Shall we call it withdrawingness? emotional introversion? recessiveness? or what?

Factor-analysis is a more precise way of discovering and purifying the overlap in a table of correlations, and establishing factors that will account for the clusters. Ordinarily, of course, many more inter-

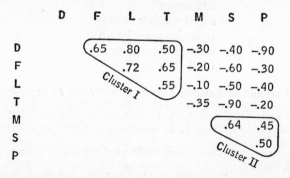

Figure 25. Hypothetical Matrix from which Factors May Be Extracted

correlations are included in a matrix, and the number of resulting factors is larger than in our simple illustration.[12]

Hundreds of factoring studies have been made of personality variables. Since the number of potential variables is vast, it is common to find investigators factoring some one area within the total field of personality. Thus, starting with 70 variables in the area of what they call "temperament" Guilford and Zimmerman assert that 13 factors cover the whole area. Every person could be tested or rated on these 13 basic factors:[13]

> general activity
> ascendance
> masculinity versus femininity
> confidence versus inferiority feelings
> calmness, composure versus nervousness
> sociability
> reflectiveness
> depression
> emotionality
> restraint
> objectivity
> agreeableness
> cooperativeness, tolerance

Or, to take an example from the area of human interests, a team of investigators used a scale made up of 1,000 items, all designed to measure many kinds of interests. After the table of intercorrelations is factored, the following 18 factors emerge:[14]

> mechanical interest
> scientific interest
> adventure
> social welfare
> esthetic appreciation
> esthetic expression
> need for diversion

[12] For a brief account of factoring procedures, see Anne Anastasi, *Differential psychology* (3d ed.; New York: Macmillan, 1958). For fuller accounts, R. B. Cattell, *Factor analysis* (New York: Harper, 1952); J. P. Guilford, *Psychometric methods* (Rev. ed.; New York: McGraw-Hill, 1954); L. L. Thurstone, *Multiple-factor analysis* (Chicago: Univ. of Chicago Press, 1947).

[13] J. P. Guilford and W. S. Zimmerman, Fourteen dimensions of temperament, *Psychol. Monogr.*, 1956, No. 417.

[14] J. P. Guilford, R. R. Christensen, N. A. Bond, Jr., and M. A. Sutton, A factor analysis study of human interests, *Psychol. Monogr.*, 1954, No. 375.

need for attention
business interest
outdoor work interest
physical drive
precision
thinking
orderliness
cultural conformity
clerical interest
aggression
sociability

This list illustrates an important limitation of factor-analysis. It does not include all possible interests, e.g., a religious interest. Why not? Because the original questionnaire contained *no* items dealing with religion. Factors are, as we see, a kind of second-order derivation from original data, and as such are wholly limited by what the original tests covered.

A more ambitious attempt to cover almost the whole field of personality is illustrated in the work of R. B. Cattell. On the basis of many studies he attempts to summarize the factors that he and others have discovered.[15] Besides intellectual factors there are the following:

competent assertiveness
restraint-timidity
hypomanic overcompensation
critical exactness
sociable willingness
energetic decisiveness
nervous, alert reactivity
neural reserves versus neuroticism
anxiety to achieve versus assuredness
accurate realism versus psychotic tendency
cultured introspective self-control
apathetic temperament

The question whether different factoring studies agree with one another is undecided. They use different kinds of tests, different initial dimensions, sometimes different statistical procedures. Diamond believes there is partial agreement. Over and over again certain

15 R. B. Cattell, The principal replicated factors discovered in objective personality tests, *J. abnorm. soc. Psychol.*, 1955, **50**, 291–314.

factors turn up which, though variously named, indicate that an *affiliative* (friendly, sociable) dimension exists, likewise an aggressive (dominant or ascendant) dimension; and two in addition: a *timid* (depressed) dimension and one having to do with *soundness or maturity* (opposite of neuroticism).[16] On the other hand we find critics who say that there is little agreement among factorists.[17]

A sweeping application of factor-analysis to the whole sphere of meaning has been made by Osgood and Suci.[18] The procedure in this case was to apply 50 rating scales of 7 steps each to 20 common nouns. Thus, if you are a rater, you would be asked to tell (in 7 steps or degrees) how *strong* or *weak*, how *good* or *bad*, how *wet* or *dry*, a "tornado" seems to you to be; also a "feather," even a "lady." The assignment may seem nonsensical, yet the upshot is mildly revealing. In general, all these ratings boil down to three major factors. They are in a sense "superconcepts" since they embrace roughly all the 50 concepts used in rating. They turn out to be the factors (or superconcepts) of *value*, of *power*, of *activity*. If this kind of analysis is extended or confirmed, it might bear helpfully on the basic ways in which personality is perceived and judged. Thus from the limited indication of this experiment we might hazard the guess that while we use thousands of adjectives to describe people we tend basically to see them in terms of their *value* (a character judgment), in terms of their *potency*, and in terms of their *activity*.

These various examples set forth sufficiently the intent and the merits of factorial units. They are statistical composites—as few in number as can account for a matrix of correlations.

The best use of factor-analysis in the field of personality, it seems, comes from its use in some well-defined, limited area—more limited in scope than is customarily the case. To give an example, Harsh undertook to study "annoyability." One person reports that he can't stand people who sniffle, and that he can't endure dandruff, crooked teeth, smutty stories, and aggressive salesmen. Others indicate different patterns of aversions. Studying hundreds of items checked by hundreds of people, Harsh finds that these annoyances cluster around four main pivots of irritation: (1) irregularities in personal appear-

16 S. Diamond, *Personality and temperament* (New York: Harper, 1957), p. 171.
17 P. E. Vernon, *Personality tests and assessments* (London: Methuen, 1953), p. 12.
18 C. E. Osgood and G. J. Suci, Factor analysis of meaning, *J. exp. Psychol.*, 1955, **50,** 325–338.

ance, (2) violations of customs and morals, (3) offenses against one's own ego, and (4) irritation at minor mishaps.[19]

Advocates of factor-analysis believe that this method may eventually lead us to a set of truly fundamental (or "source") qualities in human nature, corresponding, so to say, to the periodic table in chemistry. If basic elements of this order are discovered, then we can invent tests to measure each person's standing on each essential factor.

But there are serious complaints to be made of the whole conception of "factor." Its assumptions seem remote from reality.

1. In the first place, is it reasonable to assume that all people do in fact possess the same basic constitution of personality? Must the units of organization in all lives be the same? Must the factors, except for their differential weighting, be identical? At best a factor is a composite photograph, resembling no single individual in particular.

2. The statistical units discovered are remote from the individual organism. Scores on many tests from a large population of people are put into a statistical grinder, and the mixing is so thorough that what comes out is a link of factors in which every organic individual has lost his identity. His dispositions are mixed with everyone else's. The factors derived in this way seldom resemble the dispositions discovered by clinical methods when an individual is intensively studied. There is no proof whatsoever that the factorial units correspond to "source traits," i.e., to the genetic composition of human nature—as claimed by some enthusiasts.

3. A profound difficulty arises in the naming of factors. When they are finally named we discover that the name is largely arbitrary. Many investigators prefer to label the factors with letters, such as w, p, c, m, and so on, as though not quite daring to pronounce the names of the factors out loud. It seems safer to defend an abstract symbol than to argue boldly for such substantial units as *will, perseveration, cooperativeness, masculinity.* Sometimes the resulting factor simply cannot be named. One factorial cluster contained the following hodgepodge: spatial acuities, pulchritude, combined with drive, but having some negative relation to empathy and to spatial facility. Can any conceivable psychological sense be made of it? When

---

[19] C. M. Harsh, An inventory study of categories of annoyance (Berkeley: Univ. of California Library [unpublished], 1936).

we look at the ingredients of almost any factor that is isolated we fail
to find any name in plain English that can be applied accurately to
the product.

Let the reader ask himself whether the following responses indicate the presence of one underlying trait causing these responses:

Do you find that you have to avoid exciting situations because
   they fatigue you too much?   Yes

Do you think that much so-called progressive education is less
   sound than the old adage, "Spare the rod and spoil the child"? Yes

On the whole, do you enjoy more the company of books or
   people?   People

Are you uncontrollably afraid of some particular animal?   Yes

These are, in fact, sample ingredients of one alleged factor,
called "Guilt-proneness vs. Confidence."[20] Neither the coherence
of these responses with one another nor the relevance of any one
of them to the label given the factor is apparent. Statistically composed units often contain such obscurity.

4. We have spoken of the fact that nothing can come out of
factor-analysis that was not first put into it. To broaden the point
we may say that the method falls heir to all the errors of the preceding
measures and correlations upon which it rests, to inadequate sampling of people, to the unreliability and invalidity of the tests used, to
the narrowness of the battery of measurements, to experimental
errors and biases.

Various changes in factoring procedures have been introduced,
some of them attempting to surmount these criticisms, especially
aiming to weaken the force of the second criticism above, by taking
into account the recurrent behavior of the individual rather than
mere averages of everybody's behavior. The traditional factoring
procedure is called the r-technique. Recently inventors have introduced q, p, o, and other variant techniques.[21] To only a slight degree,
if at all, do these variants escape the basic criticisms here offered.

20 R. B. Cattell, *Personality and motivation structure and measurement* (Yonkers, N.Y.:
World Book, 1957). See Factor *O*.
21 For a brief definition of these techniques see Anastasi, *op. cit.*, pp. 336–339. Note 12
above.

Summary

Every science seeks the elements of which its subject matter is comprised. Psychologists have searched diligently for the elements composing mental life, but have never reached agreement concerning their number or nature. One reason is that some psychologists are interested in detailed (molecular) behavior, others (especially students of personality) are interested in broader (molar) behavioral trends. Units of many types have been proposed—as diverse as conditioned reflexes and needs, humoral elements and sentiments, faculties and factors.

Two current approaches are particularly prominent in Anglo-American psychology. These favor the stimulus-response and statistical points of view respectively. The unit endorsed by the stimulus-response approach is the specific *habit*. The favored statistical unit is the *factor*. Both proposals suffer serious limitations, the most apparent of which is their remoteness from the structure of human life as we ordinarily observe it.

The stimulus-response view has difficulty accounting for the more complex structures that the hierarchical organization of the nervous system clearly provides. The theory of connection via "identical elements" is unconvincing. Factorial analysis has difficulty representing the concrete individual life: its units are derived from a mélange of the responses of a great many people on a great variety of measurements. For certain limited purposes (such as discovering whether a hypothesized common trait—say "annoyability" or introversion—is really "unitary" or composed of separate factors) the method has its uses.

Thus far our search for basic components of personality has not seemed very rewarding. We have, however, proposed on the constructive side that the conception of equivalence of stimuli and equivalence of response prepares the way for understanding the organization of personality. To the individual a great many situations in which he finds himself are functionally equivalent ("similar" to him); and a great many separate kinds of acts are functionally equivalent in their intent and result (i.e., in their "meaning" to him).

It is this conception of equivalence that underlies the theory of traits presented in the next two chapters.

CHAPTER 14

The Theory of
Common Traits

THE CASE AGAINST TRAITS • ARE TRAITS VERIDICAL OR FIC-
TIONAL? • THE NATURE OF COMMON TRAITS • HOW ESTAB-
LISHED? • NORMAL DISTRIBUTION • TRAITS AND OTHER DETER-
MINING TENDENCIES • TYPES • NAMING COMMON TRAITS •
SUMMARY

SCARCELY anyone questions the existence of traits as the
fundamental units of personality. Common speech presupposes them.
This man, we say, is *gruff* and *shy,* but a *hard worker;* that woman is
fastidious, talkative, and *stingy.* Psychologists, too, talk in these terms.
One psychologist recently wrote a letter of recommendation for a
former student characterizing him as *ambitious, friendly,* an *enthusiastic teacher,* but having a *quick temper.* Even in their technical
research in personality most investigators have some kind of trait-
doctrine (as the preceding chapter has shown). At the same time
psychologists know that common sense is sometimes a faulty guide,
and the issue of traits is one of the areas where common sense, even
if fundamentally correct, needs to be critically examined and refined.

The Case against Traits

For one thing, trait-names, such as those in the preceding paragraph, imply too much. The young teacher is not always "friendly"; he is not uniformly "ambitious" in every direction; his "enthusiasm" surely depends on what and whom he is teaching.

During World War II the Office of Strategic Services established an Assessment Center where candidates for foreign secret-service work were examined. After testing and studying a man for several days, several psychologists would try to discover his traits and predict whether they would fit him or unfit him for such sensitive assignment. The research staff found their task enormously difficult, and the reason they give may be taken as a classic statement of the limitation of any trait-doctrine:

> It is easy to predict precisely the outcome of the meeting of one known chemical with another known chemical in an immaculate test tube. But where is the chemist who can predict what will happen to a known chemical if it meets an unknown chemical in an unknown vessel? . . . How, then, can a psychologist foretell with any degree of accuracy the outcome of future meetings of one barely known personality with hundreds of other undesignated personalities in distant, undesignated cities, villages, fields and jungles that are seething with one knows not what potential harms and benefits?[1]

This criticism is so true and so telling that we must admit at the outset that *no trait theory can be sound unless it allows for, and accounts for, the variability of a person's conduct.* Pressures from the surrounding environment, the companions he is with, and the countercurrents in the person himself may delay, augment, distort, or inhibit completely the conduct that we would normally expect to issue from a person's traits. (We have already discussed the case for "situationism" in Chapter 8.)

All this is true; yet in a person's stream of activity there is, besides a variable portion, likewise a constant portion; and it is this constant portion we seek to designate with the concept of trait.

The basic principle of behavior is its continuous flow, each successive act representing a mobilizing of much energy for a particular purpose in hand. Only one integrated activity takes place at any one

[1] OSS Assessment Staff, *Assessment of men* (New York: Holt, Rinehart and Winston, 1948), p. 8.

time, and this activity is the result of a final convergence of relevant energies and pressures. In other words, a given act is the product of the interaction of many determining forces, of which traits are only one.

The only thing we can observe is the *act,* and no act is the product of only one trait. When you write a letter, there may enter into this bit of behavior all sorts of determining factors: a sense of duty, a certain homesickness for your friend, a request you wish to make of him, the fact that you now have leisure to write, the availability of pen and paper, as well as the presence of memories, emotions, associations relevant to the activity. Such elaborate convergence of determining tendencies prevents us from saying that any single activity is the exclusive product of one or more traits. Traits are one of the factors that determine a present act, and they make that act seem "characteristic" of the person; but they are never the sole determinant.

Traits, unlike the "faculties" or "powers" of earlier psychology, are not "little men within the breast" who pull the strings of behavior. Traits are looser tendencies, each expression of a trait being slightly different because it confronts other determining conditions. Furthermore, after an act takes place, there is "feedback" to the nervous system, and in the future a trait will never be precisely the same as it was previously. Thus *continuous flow* is the primary fact. Yet we know that traits exist because, in spite of the continuous flow and change, there is considerable constancy in a person's mode of behavior. We can say that certain acts are characteristic of him. Traits underlie what is "characteristic" in conduct.

Are Traits Veridical or Fictional?

A metaphysical question arises at the outset of any discussion of traits, and if allowed to do so bedevils the whole problem. The sooner we can dispose of it the better. The question in brief is this: Are traits genuine, veridical dispositions? (The term *veridical* in philosophy means that the object under discussion is really *there.*) Thus a trait, if veridical, corresponds to some neurophysiological system. Or, on the other hand, are traits nothing more than nominal fictions, mere words, convenient groupings, of a plurality of unrelated acts?

As examples of the veridical view of traits we cite two definitions:

A trait is a constant directing psychic force which determines the active and reactive behavior of the individual.[2]

A trait is a dimension or aspect of personality, consisting of a group of consistent and related reactions that characterize a person's typical adjustments.[3]

The nominalistic view was expressed more than a century ago by Jeremy Bentham, who was ever on his guard against substituting fictitious entities for real ones:

Now disposition [trait] is a kind of fictitious entity, feigned for the convenience of discourse, in order to express what there is supposed to be permanent in a man's frame of mind.[4]

A more recent statement of the same point of view is the following:

Traits are only convenient names given to types or qualities of behavior which have elements in common. They are not psychological entities but rather categories for the classification of habits.[5]

This last quotation is in line with the "doctrine of specificity." Habits themselves are real, but traits reside not in the person himself but only in the eye of the beholder. Actually this is a curious position to hold. It says, in effect, that small units of behavior (habits) are veridical, but that broader dispositions (trait) are fictional.

The dispute here echoes Chapter 2, where we discussed veridical and nominal definitions of personality. Is personality really "out there," or is it something constructed in the eyes and mind of the beholder? Now we are asking if are traits really "out there," or if they are mere categories for the orderly description of behavior (i.e., orderly to the beholder).

Briefly stated, the arguments for the nominalistic position are as follows: (1) No one ever *saw* a trait of any person; nor can we prove

[2] F. Baumgarten, Character qualities. *Brit. J. Psychol.*, 1936, **26**, 290.

[3] L. F. Shaffer and E. J. Shoben, *The psychology of adjustment* (Rev. ed.; Boston: Houghton Mifflin, 1956), p. 317.

[4] J. Bentham, *Principles of morals and legislation* (Oxford: Clarendon, 1879), Chap. 9, p. 131.

[5] M. May, Problems of measuring character and personality, *J. soc. Psychol.*, 1932, **3**, 133. In the previous chapter the specificist argument was examined and reasons for rejecting it were given.

that a trait corresponds to neurophysiological structure. (2) All language, including the names we give to traits, is nominal. Words designate *social* and not *natural* categories. As we shall see later in the chapter, there are about 18,000 terms in the English language descriptive of alleged human traits, but these terms are classificatory tags; they have social utility but cannot be proved to derive from the cleavages in nature. (3) Everyone likes to oversimplify his perceptions and judgments of people. One may hold, for example, that Negroes (all Negroes) are *lazy, ignorant,* and *superstitious.* In this case the overgeneralization is obviously nonsensical.[6] Ascribing traits in such a coarse fashion always lands us in trouble. And yet we do tend to pigeonhole people (individuals as well as groups) with the aid of a few linguistic tags. No one is as simple and firmly structured as our labels imply.

Now all these arguments are sound, but they do not prove that persons are devoid of traits. They prove only that we should guard against our tendency to oversimplify the structure of *alter's* (the other fellow's) personality. We are warned not to assume that the words we use correspond precisely to the psychological unit we are attempting to name. Finally, the argument tells us that we need sound methods for establishing the existence of *alter's* traits since we can never observe them directly.

Although it is true that no one ever *saw* a trait, it is equally true that no one ever saw any of the structures and processes with which psychology inevitably must deal (drives, habits, expectancies, attitudes, categories). It has been proposed that when we feel the need to assume the existence of some veridical disposition to account for observed activity, we would do well to speak of a "hypothetical construct."[7] There is no objection to so doing, provided we do not confuse "hypothetical construct" with mere "fiction." As a hypothetical construct, *trait* is at present an inescapable inference and may some day be demonstrated directly. At one time the planet Pluto—or the lowly atom—was a "hypothetical construct." Given time, science was able to point directly

6 Cf. G. W. Allport, *The nature of prejudice* (Cambridge, Mass.: Addison-Wesley, 1954), Chaps. 10 and 11.
7 K. Mac Corquodale and P. E. Meehl, On a distinction between hypothetical constructs and intervening variables, *Psychol. Rev.,* 1948, **55**, 95–107.

to them. The case with traits we believe to be similar. Some day, we hope, neurophysiology will show us directly the processes of integration, gating, and phase sequence that correspond to our present hypothetical constructs.[8]

At present our evidence for the existence of traits comes from consistencies among separate observable acts of behavior. Separate acts, in Stagner's terms, are "indicators" of traits. As indicators of the trait of *seclusiveness* in John, for example, he lists such acts as his declining an invitation to a party, crossing a street to avoid meeting a recent acquaintance, planning his day so that social contacts will be unlikely to occur.[9]

Three indicators, of course, are not enough. Although all might point to a trait of *seclusiveness,* they might also be accounted for in terms of John's *busyness* or a temporary *mood.* But when we have not three, but scores, hundreds, or even thousands of acts that show a dependable regularity and consistency, we feel on firmer ground in saying that John *must* be a seclusive sort of chap. (And here we pause to remind ourselves that perfect consistency is never to be expected.)

The Nature of Common Traits

We have voted in favor of the veridical view of traits. We believe that a trait is a broad system of similar action tendencies existing in the person we are studying. "Similar action tendencies" are those that an observer, looking at them from the actor's point of view, can categorize together under one rubric of meaning.

But we take this veridical view with certain qualifications. First, we know that the verbal or mathematical tags we give are derived from our own perceptions of another's behavior, and that the act of categorizing our perceptions is bedeviled by the evil of simplification. We know, too, that we are forcing what we observe into the social or mathematical rubrics available to us (rubrics such as *aggressive* or *ardent,* or Factors A, B, or C).

We must add one further important qualification. We take a step away from the veridical conception when we try to force John into

[8] Possible neurophysiological patterns underlying traits are described by D. O. Hebb, *The organization of behavior* (New York: Wiley, 1949).
[9] R. Stagner, *Psychology of personality* (New York: McGraw-Hill, 1948), p. 151. (Rev. ed., 1961.)

a uniform schedule of traits that we try to apply to all people, including John. Every personality test, every rating scale does precisely this, as I shall now show.

Suppose we are interested in a trait that we may call *ascendance-submission* (or we might call it *dominance,* or *leadership*). We wish to test the strength of this trait in John. We can do so only by comparing him with other people on the same dimension. We therefore develop a scale, perhaps asking such questions as the following:[10]

Someone tries to push ahead of you in line. You have been waiting for some time, and can't wait much longer. Suppose the intruder is the same sex as yourself, do you usually

    remonstrate with the intruder   . . . .

    "look daggers" at the intruder or make clearly audible
        comments to your neighbor   . . . .

    decide not to wait, and go away   . . . .

    do nothing   . . . .

Do you feel self-conscious in the presence of superiors in the academic or business world?

    markedly   . . . .

    somewhat   . . . .

    not at all   . . . .

Some possession of yours is being worked upon at a repair shop. You call for it at the time appointed, but the repair man informs you that he has "only just begun to work on it." Is your customary reaction

    to upbraid him   . . . .

    to express dissatisfaction mildly   . . . .

    to smother your feelings entirely   . . . .

Now we ask a great many people in our "standardization group" to take the test, and we determine the average score for the group. Then we compare John with this norm, and we conclude that relative to other people he is the sort of fellow who yields and gives way. He is, we discover, in the lowest 10 percent of the population, and thus, we conclude, he has a strong trait of "submission."

Now there is good logic for assuming the existence of *common*

[10] G. W. Allport and F. H. Allport, *The A-S Reaction Study* (Boston: Houghton Mifflin, 1928). Described in *J. abnorm. soc. Psychol.,* 1928, **23,** 118–136.

traits and for measuring a given personality on a common dimensional scale along with other people. The logic is this: *Normal people in a given culture-area necessarily tend to develop somewhat roughly comparable modes of adjustment.* For example, people who live in English-speaking countries all develop more or less proficiency in the use of English, and it is entirely reasonable to give uniform tests of language achievement to see whether a person's mastery of English is at, above, or below average.

Or take the common trait *ascendance-submission.* In a competitive society, such as ours, every individual tends to find a level of assertiveness or ascendance that is congenial to his own way of life. One person may live quite comfortably (and charmingly) by being a "yielder." Another (by temperament or training) finds that dominance is a more congenial style of adjusting to, and mastering, his environment. Some people evolve a style of extreme aggressiveness; others, of extreme passivity. The point is that in our society people can be compared (roughly) in the way they have solved this problem of relating to the environment and to other people.

Years ago Herbert Spencer pointed out that the whole evolutionary struggle forces an animal as well as a human being to find his level of dominance. When the first two beasts met in the forest, said Spencer, one asserted himself as the *diner;* the other had to resign himself to becoming the *dinner.* Recent work has shown that there is a constant "pecking order" among hens and other animals, so that Animal A regularly dominates Animal B, B dominates C, and so on. For human beings there is the saying that everyone *must* be either a boot or a door mat.

Logical as it may be to evolve a uniform scale for ascendance-submission, the procedure is at best *approximate.* After all, there are endless varieties of dominators, leaders, aggressors, followers, yielders, and timid souls. The scale does not and cannot recognize the subtle shadings of traits in individuals. In the following chapter we shall examine more closely the problem of individual or personal traits.

Meanwhile let us restate the case for common traits. There are many aspects of personality in respect to which all people in a given culture may reasonably be compared. Besides ascendance-submission we may mention talkativeness, radicalism, money-mindedness, seclusion, anxiety, need for achievement, race prejudice, and hundreds of additional dimensions. *Common traits are, then, those aspects of personality in respect to which most people within a given culture can be profitably compared.*

As for veridicality, it should now be clear that we do rather more violence to the structure of John's personality if we *force* him into uniform trait categories than if we look at him as an individual in his own right and try to discover the actual internal systems of his own personal life.

To conclude the matter, common traits do not depart entirely from the natural cleavages of personality, because similarly constructed mortals in similar environments *would* develop similar goals and similar methods of obtaining them. At the same time, common traits are to some extent artifacts of our method of *forcing* categories upon individual persons. Common traits are therefore more nominal and less veridical than personal traits (Chapter 15). We might say, then, that they are only semiveridical, but are nonetheless indispensable whenever we undertake to study personality by scales, tests, ratings, or any other comparative method.

How Established?

Suppose you say that a certain friend of yours is *generous, punctual,* a *lover of art,* and a *humorist.* And suppose I ask, "How do you know he is?" Your reply would surely be, "Well, I've known him quite a long time and in situations where other people's interest and welfare are concerned he usually does the big-hearted thing. Whenever we've had a date, he is seldom late. He frequently goes to art exhibitions, paints a bit himself, and his bookshelves have many works on art; and in confronting the tangles of his life and of the world around him he frequently (but of course not always) manages the light touch, and gives the situation a humorous twist." In other words, the *frequency* with which a person adopts a certain type of adjustment is one criterion of trait. A second criterion is the *range of situations* in which he adopts this same mode of acting. A third criterion is the *intensity* of his reactions in keeping with this "preferred pattern" of behavior.

A psychologist uses precisely the same criteria. Look at the three test items on page 338. The first and third ask you what your "preferred pattern" is: whether ascendant or submissive. These items also ask you to judge what is usual or customary in your case (frequency). The second item asks how *intense* your response is. All three together (and many more in the same scale) ask over how wide a range of situations do you adopt an ascendant or submissive "preferred pattern." All three measures (frequency, range, and intensity) are quantifiable and permit statistical handling.

A psychologist need not, of course, use self-report as in this particular "pencil-and-paper" test. He may distrust self-report and choose to use direct observation. He could, for example, use "time sampling"—perhaps watching a given child in a playground for ten minutes a day. How frequently, how intensely, and over how wide a range of situations is this child dominant or yielding? He could observe adults in a group committee meeting (perhaps through a one-way screen) and count the "interacts" that are dominant or yielding. Or he might use a rating scale, and ask other people to judge how much or how little of a given trait John, Mary, and Tom may have. (If he uses a rating scale, and even if he makes the observations himself, the psychologist will want the judgments confirmed by other reporters—to establish what is called *observer reliability*.)

The statistical proof for the existence of a trait lies in various measures of *reliability*. If various observers or raters are employed, it is essential that they agree with each other. If a test is used, it is essential that approximately the same scores for all the different subjects turn up if the test is readministered after an interval of time (*repeat reliability*). It is likewise essential that if a person shows himself to be ascendant in one situation, he also shows himself (usually) to be ascendant in other situations. Since, as we have seen, this is a great deal to ask of an individual, the statistical measure used (*internal reliability*) merely determines whether in the long run, for a whole population of people, items do correlate with one another, and with the total score. This means that for all the people who take the test there is in general a tendency for high scorers on one item to be high scorers on other items. If so, the test is measuring a common trait with fair consistency.

We are saying that if it can be proved that one kind of activity is usually associated statistically with another kind of activity, there is evidence that something underlies the two activities, viz., a trait. It is a "common trait" if the evidence is derived from a whole population of people. Now the test for ascendance-submission, mentioned above, has a repeat reliability of .78 (1.00 would be perfect) and an internal reliability of about .85. We conclude, therefore, that people by and large do tend consistently to occupy a given spot on the continuum from high ascendance to low submission; and therefore may be profitably compared in respect to this common (generalized) attribute of personality.

Many (probably thousands) common traits have been established in this way. To name a few: *neuroticism, social extraversion-introversion, authoritarianism, manifest anxiety, need for achievement, masculinity* or *femininity* of interests, *conformity*.

The astute reader may detect a pitfall in this procedure. Suppose an investigator sets out to discover whether *generosity,* say, is a common and scalable trait. He first has to invent his scale. In so doing he manufactures a large number of imaginary situations. After pretesting his scale he finds that some situations do not hang together with others (the item reliability is low), so he discards these and changes the wording of others until he has a reliable scale. Thus what he *puts into* the scale determines what common trait he *pulls out.* This arbitrariness does some violence to pure naturalism (i.e., finding out what the comparable cleavages in human nature "really are"). This is one of the reasons why we cannot claim too much veridicality for common traits.

Failures to establish a common trait are enlightening. We would probably fail to find enough cases of *quixoticism, treasonableness,* or *kleptomania* to justify scaling individuals with respect to these variables. In certain individuals these may be important personal dispositions, but they are *not* common traits.

Attempting to discover whether *punctuality-tardiness* was a common trait, Dudycha discovered that for about 40 percent of the population there was indeed a reliable tendency for them to be consistently on time, or early or late in arriving at college gatherings (as diversified as basketball games, eight o'clock classes, meals, private conferences). But for about 60 percent there was too much variability to assume that they had any one "preferred pattern" of adjustment.[11]

The scientific evidence for the existence of a trait always comes from demonstrating by some acceptable method the *consistency* in a person's behavior. In the case of common traits it is also necessary to demonstrate that a whole population of people are reasonably consistent with themselves over time and in a range of situations. But what degree of consistency shall we demand? There is no strict answer. Statistically speaking, the higher the reliability measures, the better the evidence for a trait. If we use the traditional correlational measures (for repeat reliability, or for internal consistency), most psychologists would scarcely trust correlations of less than .80. When we consider the inherent variability of behavior, the effects of the immediate situation, and errors of measurement, it is small wonder that to achieve this minimum measure a scale often has to be revised several times (which, as we have said, makes the whole procedure somewhat artificial).

Normal Distribution

One usual (but not invariable) property of common traits is their so-called normal distribution. (The reader should note that this statement pertains only to common traits, for by their very nature individual traits, to be discussed in the following chapter, cannot be scaled in a population.)

Now the investigator *wants* to think of a common trait as "continuous," with scores arranged in a "bell-shaped" distribution. The bulk of the cases should have average scores, and the rest taper off toward the high and low extremes. Only if a trait has this normal distribution can we apply the ordinary statistical methods of measurement.

Figure 26 illustrates the situation with one common trait, namely, ascendance-submission. The figure shows a wide range of scores, actually 119 points, indicating that the scale is sensitive. It shows that extreme scores are not often encountered. Most people have moderate scores, clustering around the "dead average" (mean). An

[11] G. J. Dudycha, An objective study of punctuality in relation to personality and achievement, *Arch. Psychol.*, 1936, No. 204.

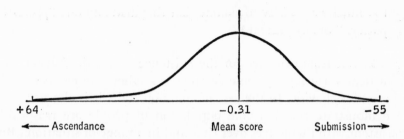

Figure 26. Distribution of Scores from a Test Measuring Ascendance–Submission. Constructed from the decile distribution of scores of the *A-S Reaction Study:* Form for Men. See page 426.

average score may result from endorsing "moderate" answers, indicating a disposition to avoid extreme modes of adjustment; or it may, and occasionally does, result from a cancellation of highly ascendant and highly submissive responses. (In the latter case, the average score is misleading, because the subject has two strong but contradictory dispositions.)

When the tester achieves such a normal distribution of scores he is well satisfied. He now can compare personalities in respect to a common trait. He knows that high and low scores are important deviations from the universal (or group) norm. He can use the results for many varieties of statistical purposes.

Although the normal curve is the tester's dream of delight, it is not easy to say just what it signifies. Actually it is usually a product of mixed circumstances. For one thing, it may in part reflect nature's preference for average (nondistinctive) levels; but in addition it reflects social pressure toward conformity with some accepted "average" level of conduct. The normal distribution often results from an arbitrary juxtaposition of opposite modes of adjustment into one linear scale. Finally, the distribution is to a certain extent affected by the inventor of the test, who sees to it that successive revisions of his scale yield a more and more symmetrical scatter of scores. There is no serious objection to this last procedure, nor to the normal curve thus obtained, since in any case the scaling of common traits is but a rough way of approaching personality. In the interests of sound theory, however, it is well to realize the extent of the complications introduced into one "simple" variable for purposes of convenient measurement. Only by so doing can we avoid the fallacy of presuming, as more than one writer has done, that "everything in personality is normally distributed."

Traits and Other Determining Tendencies

As we saw in Chapter 11, psychology cannot dispense with the conception of "set," implying a readiness for responses. Without such a conception it would be impossible to account for the stability and consistency of conduct.[12]

Since psychologists have always assumed that habits, drives, needs, memory traces, unconscious complexes, sentiments, mental sets, and many of the same sort of dispositions or systems exist in the neuro-psychic structure, it requires no new argument to add "traits" to this series.

What concerns us here is only a terminological matter. When shall the term *trait* be used and when some other term in this series?

Trait and Habit. Ordinarily the term *habit* applies to a narrow and limited type of determining tendency. The young child learns (with difficulty) to brush his teeth night and morning. For some years this habit stands alone, aroused only by appropriate commands from the parent as an item in the chain of acts he performs night and morning. With the passing of years, however, brushing the teeth becomes not only automatic (as is the way of habits) but it is woven into a wider system of habits, viz., a trait of *personal cleanliness.* Many adults have a generalized habit of removing all manner of dirt from their persons. If someone omits to brush his teeth, he is uncomfortable, not only because a habit is frustrated, but because the omission violates a more general trait of cleanliness.

---

[12] The weakness of the S-R formula is that it fails to allow for the enormously intricate internal organization that occurs when the stimulus is perceived, thought about, channeled into one rather than another pathway, receiving the imprint of personality along the way, before finally issuing into action. More acceptable is the S–O–R formula (*pattern of stimulation–internal organization–response to the products of organization*). The O in this formula is an acknowledgment of the existence of "determining tendencies" in the sense we are using the term. Strict methodologists say that we cannot know precisely what O is and so would do well to call it merely "an intervening variable." But by "intervening variable" even the strictest methodologist will, if pressed, admit he has in mind such possible "constructs" as drives, habits, attitudes, traits. The few extremists who try to approach psychological problems on the strict S-R basis ("empty organism") generally work with pigeons or rats, and do not contribute to personality research. If asked how they would approach problems of personality, the reply is vaguely to the effect "if we knew enough about the stimulus, we'd not need the concept personality." Not very convincing.

This example implies, quite correctly, that a trait arises, in part at least, through the integration of numerous specific habits that have the same general adaptive significance to the person. Habits do not integrate automatically, but they do so when the person has some general concept, or some self-image, that leads to their fusion under a higher system of organization. A child is never "generally polite." He learns at first to say "thank you," not to interrupt others while they are speaking, to hold open the door for his mother to enter the house. All these are specific bits of learning. When he becomes an adult, however, it may be said that he has a trait of politeness. The habits are now integrated into a conception of what one's own style of life should be. In the process of learning traits we must not forget that influences of temperament, intelligence, and constitution play their part. It is probably easier for persons with a certain innate make-up to develop the trait of politeness than for others.

A trait is, then, more generalized than a habit. It is likewise more variable in its expression. And this is a point of great importance. *Politeness* is more than a mere congeries of habits. A truly polite person will vary his behavior even to the extent of breaking his polite *habits* in order to maintain his *trait* of politeness. Ordinarily at dinner table it is not polite to drink out of one's finger bowl; but the story is told of the Washington hostess who did so in order to reassure her Oriental guest, who had already drunk from his. She violated her habit but maintained her trait.

A polite American while traveling will quickly learn to belch in satisfaction over his meal in some countries; in others, to avoid this hearty act. If he has a habit of taking the most uncomfortable seat in a room, he will quickly break his habit when in Germany he learns that the most uncomfortable seat is often the sofa which, however, is the seat of honor. In one country he will (in order to be polite) learn to ask his host how much he paid for his various possessions; in another country (in order to be polite) he will not ask such personal questions.

Here we refer again to the concept of *equivalence*. In all countries our polite traveler finds that most of his social relationships arouse in him his disposition to be polite. Many social stimuli are therefore *equivalent* in arousing the trait. On the response side, his activities, although exceedingly varied in type, are also equivalent in that they all *mean* politeness. Figure 24, page 322, has illustrated the point.

(The concept of equivalence is somewhat similar to the S-R conception of "stimulus generalization," discussed on page 94. The latter, however, seems to imply that generalization results automatically from frequent conditioning. "Equivalence" requires that the individual perceive common meaning in the range of stimuli to which he responds.)

A trait is, then, a *neuropsychic structure having the capacity to render many stimuli functionally equivalent, and to initiate and guide equivalent (meaningfully consistent) forms of adaptive and expressive behavior.*

Trait and Attitude. It is not always possible to distinguish between what should properly be called a *trait,* and what an *attitude.* Is *patriotism* a trait or an attitude toward one's native land? Is *extraversion* a trait or an attitude toward life? Does one have an *authoritarian* trait or attitude? In these and similar cases it is a matter of indifference which term we employ. Either designation is acceptable.

But *ordinarily* there are two distinctions between the two concepts: (1) An attitude always has an object of reference. One has an attitude *toward* parsnips, communism, or arctic exploration. A trait is aroused by so many objects that we do not attempt to specify them. Therefore, a trait is ordinarily considered to be more general (a higher level of integration) than an attitude. A person is conforming, expansive, shy, ascendant in so many situations that we do not, as in the case of an attitude, name them. (2) Attitudes are usually pro or con, favorable or unfavorable, well disposed or ill disposed; they lead one to approach or withdraw from their object. Andrew has a favorable attitude toward his church, a negative attitude toward his next-door neighbor, and an ambivalent (both favorable and unfavorable) attitude toward television.

This attribute of approach or avoidance gives a definitely motor cast to the concept of *attitude.* One is "set" for action. In most languages we find comparable terms that blend motor "stance" with inner state of mind. In an analysis of 12 languages Johnstone shows this to be the case, and also that the term for *attitude* is generally more tilted toward the motor than toward the inner state. Some languages make finer distinctions than does English. Thus in speaking of a political attitude (e.g., regarding

England's position in the Middle East) the Greek language uses the term *stasis;* whereas in speaking of a way of thinking and comportment (as in race relations) the same language uses *symperiphora.*[13]

But, as we have said, an attitude may be so broad in its range that it may be identical with a trait. If a man is fond of his dog but not of other creatures, he has an attitude; if he has a thoughtful and sympathetic attitude toward men and beasts, he has at the same time a trait of *kindliness.*

Both *attitude* and *trait* are indispensable concepts in psychology. Between them they cover the principal types of disposition with which the psychology of personality deals. In passing, however, we should point out that since *attitude* has to do with people's orientations to definite facets of the environment (including people, culture, and society), it is the favored concept in *social psychology.*[14] In the field of personality, however, we are interested in the structure of the person, and hence *trait* becomes the favored concept.

Traits and Other Forms of Readiness. Previously we have discussed such "intervening variables" as *drive, instinct, need.* Insofar as these prove to be useful units in comparing individuals and are thought to designate actually functioning dispositions, they may be subsumed under our conception of *common trait. Factor,* as we have shown, is a somewhat artificial construction, but it is nonetheless a cousin-concept to *trait.* There are additional current concepts that seem even closer. Let us mention them briefly. *Sentiment* stands between *attitude* and *trait.* We can generally designate the object of a sentiment as we can for an attitude; yet the objects are quite general.[15] Patriotism might be called a *sentiment* or an *attitude* or a *trait.*

Goldstein has introduced the concept *preferred patterns* of behavior. Although this term may cover more than traits, it is apt.[16]

13 J. Johnstone, "Attitude" in psychology and psychosomatic medicine, *J. nerv. ment. Dis.,* 1953, **117,** 287–299.

14 Almost every textbook in social psychology features *attitude* as its central concept. The history of the term and its systematic use in social psychology are described by G. W. Allport, Attitudes. In C. C. Murchison (Ed.), *A handbook of social psychology* (Worcester, Mass.: Clark Univ. Press, 1935), Chap. 17.

15 Sentiment is the unit of personality favored by W. McDougall, *Energies of men* (New York: Scribner, 1933); and by H. A. Murray and Christina D. Morgan, A clinical study of sentiments, I, *Genet. Psychol. Monogr.,* 1945, **33,** 3–149.

16 K. Goldstein, *The organism* (New York: American Book, 1939), Chap. 7.

Lewin speaks of a *region* (either "inner-personal" or "perceptual-motor").[17] Although this spatial metaphor implies a field-theoretical model, it is highly suggestive and has been described in Chapter 7. Other terms refer to certain kinds of traits, and will be merely listed here: *interest, value, complex, ego-system* (Koffka), *generalized habit* (Dewey), *style of life* (Adler), *syndrome* (Maslow).

Having drawn these various distinctions, let us now attempt a summary statement. The statement is, in effect, a condensation of our discussion thus far in the present chapter:

> *A common trait is a category for classifying functionally equivalent forms of behavior in a general population of people. Though influenced by nominal and artifactual considerations, a common trait to some extent reflects veridical and comparable dispositions in many personalities who, because of a common human nature and common culture, develop similar modes of adjusting to their environments, though to varying degrees.*

If this statement seems too technical, the reader may prefer the simple though less precise statement that a common trait is any *generalized disposition in respect to which people can be profitably compared.*

Types

Common speech tells us that a person *has* a trait but *fits* a type. This bit of usage suggests that types exist not in people or in nature, but rather in the eye of the observer. In other words, traits are to be regarded at least in part as *veridical,* but types as only *nominal.* Traits reside in the person; types in some *outside* point of view.

The truth of the matter depends largely on what sort of typology we are talking about. Let us consider first some typologies of a nominalistic cast. These seem to be devices for exalting the special interest of an author at the expense of the individual. One author says that mankind can be divided into two groups, *Philistine* or *Bohemian;* another prefers a different dichotomy, *Apollonian-Dionysian;* another, *inner-directed* and *other-directed.* Psychologists interested in imagery suggest *visual-kinesthetic-auditory* types. William

---

[17] K. Lewin, *Principles of topological psychology* (New York: McGraw-Hill, 1936), Chap. 17.

James spoke of *tender-minded* and *tough-minded;* Sheldon, of *viscero-tonic, cerebrotonic, somatotonic;* Spranger prefers *theoretical, esthetic, economic, social, political,* and *religious.* The list could be lengthened greatly.

What strikes us first about this heterogeneous series is that the author is imposing his own interests on human nature. *In his eye* mankind seems to be divisible according to *his* scheme. He is not interested in intact individuals at all but only in those portions of individuals that can be ordered to his scaffolding. Figure 3 (page 18) illustrates the dismemberment process.

Thus far our discussion defines types as abstractions created by taking bits of people and forcing them into a category of special delight to some investigator.

Empirical Types. There is, however, a sense in which type may be regarded as a *superordinate common trait.* This possibility arises when the investigator claims to cover a large area of the personalities of many people. In this case the evidence for a type is of the same kind as the evidence for a trait. If by empirical investigation it can be shown that many habits, traits, and attitudes are manifestations of a more embracing organization (and if many people are found to have this embracing organization), then these people constitute a type. (We may even violate customary usage and say they *have* a type.) Figure 27 illustrates the situation.

From this point of view an empirical type doctrine stands between the level of traits and the level of the total personality. It claims to cover much of the whole personality organization, if not quite all of it. It is from this point of view that one might argue that *introversion* or *somatotonia* (page 61) is an empirical type.

But even empirical types (established on good evidence that activities, attitudes, and traits tend to cluster) run into difficulty. The difficulty is that the very conception of type implies discontinuity. It implies that some people fit one type; others fit another type; and still others fall out entirely. The trouble is that clear-cut divisions of this sort are not found in the human population. We can only say that some people have some of the attributes of some of the types.

To preserve the doctrine of empirical types at all it is necessary to say that most people are a "mixed type." They are, for example, both introvert and extravert, both cerebrotonic and somatotonic.

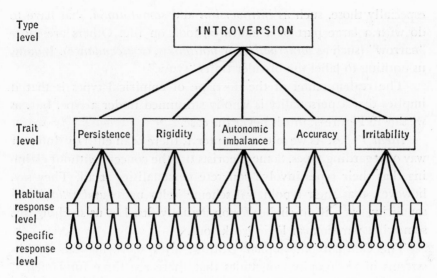

Figure 27. Type as a Higher-Level Trait (adapted from H. J. Eysenck, The organization of personality, *J. Pers.,* 1951, 20, 103).

This device retains the flavor of discontinuity while allowing for factual continuity. As Figure 28 shows, this solution means, in effect, that the term *type* applies properly only to the extremes of a continuum.

We conclude, then, that the empirical type doctrine is not really helpful in representing the structure of human personality. It implies a clean-cut discontinuity among "types" of human beings that is not actually found to exist. The truth that lies in empirical types is already fully recognized in our concept of *common traits.* That is to say, we fully grant that some measurable common traits are broad,

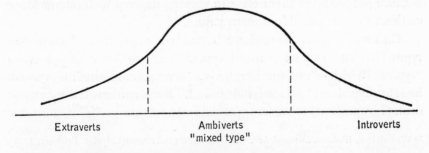

Figure 28. Empirical Types as Extremes of a Continuum

especially those, such as *introversion* and *somatotonia,* that have to do with a large part of a man's outlook on life. Others are more "narrow" (such as *punctuality,* or *politeness,* or *ascendance*). It gains us nothing to label the broader traits "types."

The real mischief of the doctrine of empirical types is that it implies that a personality is wholly subsumed under a type, but, as we saw in Figure 3, this is never the case.

Ideal Types. As we saw in Chapter 1, there is an entirely different way of regarding types. Some theorists use the concept without claiming that their types involve concrete personalities at all. They say, however, that their typological scheme helps us to *understand* personalities, even if no single person actually fits. Let us see how this somewhat paradoxical logic works out.

The German philosopher Dilthey, after surveying the world's systems of philosophy, concludes that there are three fundamental forms of philosophy. He labels them *idealism of freedom, objective idealism, naturalism.*[18] Now what has this to do with personality?

Well, if all fundamental views of life are three in number (three types), then individual men may be looked at to see whether they fit into (or at least approximate) one of these "ideal" types. We have seen that in a similar but more sophisticated way, Dilthey's pupil, Edward Spranger, makes an a priori analysis of fundamental human values. According to him they are the *theoretical,* the *economic,* the *esthetic, social, political,* and *religious* (see page 297). He does not claim that any given person fits without remainder into any single type; but he does say that to some degree we may understand a person by examining his values with the aid of these rubrics. They are "schemata of comprehensibility." They help us understand people because people align themselves to varying degrees with one or more of these various possible human values.[19]

Cultural Types. Somewhere between ideal types and empirical types falls an array of cultural types. We say of one man he is a "typical Britisher"; of another, he is a "true cosmopolite"; of a third, he is an ingrained "professional soldier." Such epithets tell us a great deal. Occupational types seem particularly revealing. A rich syndrome

18 W. Dilthey, *Weltanschuungslehre.* In *Gesammelte Schriften* (Leipzig: Teubner, 1931), VIII, 75–118.
19 E. Spranger, *Types of men* (Transl. by P. Pigors; Halle: Niemeyer, 1928).

of traits comes to mind if I say that John is a "typical" lawyer, merchant, unskilled laborer, farmer, barber, clergyman, or politician.

As we saw in Chapter 8, some writers hold that by knowing a man's occupation, or his status, roles, and position in society, we know more about his personality than if we study his traits. This statement is misleading. In the first place, the soldier in question may not be typical of his group but may be a marked deviant. In the second place, the statement overlooks the fact that even for the typical soldier, these traits are now *his*. They reside inside his skin (and not in his profession).

This point is important. It is never safe to characterize human personality in terms of roles, occupation, social status, or any other cultural or sociological rubrics. When we say that Max is a farmer, a suburbanite, a Catholic, an Italian physician, a business executive, or a member of the "upper middle" class, we are *not* describing his personality. He may be a deviant; and even if he is "typical," it is his own traits that now regulate his personality. Although his traits may be influenced by his membership, we should not confuse these memberships (social type) with his own functioning personality.

Types as Propaedeutic. In spite of our somewhat negative opinion of typology, we may admit that to start with a "hunch" about types (of any kind) is often a productive device. In recent years research has been stimulated by the postulation of constitutional types (Chapter 4), perceptual and cognitive types (Chapter 11), types of maturity and immaturity (Chapter 12), to name a few instances. Type doctrines, in short, may be a good springboard for psychological theory, but they make a poor point of arrival. To put the point more concretely, one might say that having started with *types,* investigators often end up with useful information concerning complex *traits,* but with nothing else of consequence.

Naming Common Traits

There are approximately 18,000 words (chiefly adjectives) in the English language designating distinctive forms of personal behavior.[20] At first sight this array seems like a semantic nightmare. Yet it is obvious that trait-names bear some relation to the underlying

[20] G. W. Allport and H. S. Odbert, *Trait-names: a psycho-lexical study, Psychol. Monogr.,* 1936, No. 211. The present section quotes freely from this source.

structural units of personality, and it is our duty to discover, if we can, what this relation is.

These thousands of terms have originated from two separate kinds of interest. First of all, we can be sure that men experience a desire to label what is truly present in human nature. If our fellow mortals did not *have* capacities and dispositions, we would be unlikely to name them. What is more, names are to some extent self-correcting, for there is no gain in preserving through names an erroneous belief in fabulous entities; there is everything to gain by using terms that designate true psychic structures. This is one reason we have trait names; if it were the only reason, the correspondence between our dictionary and psychological truth would be close, much closer than it is.

A second influence upon our lexicon of trait-names is wholly different; it comes via fads and fashions in cultural interest. Very early, thanks to the persistence of Galenian medicine, English used such trait-names as *sanguine, choleric, melancholic, phlegmatic, good-humored, bad-humored,* as well as *cold-blooded, hearty, heartless,* and *cordial* (derived from the belief that the heart is the seat of intellect and feeling). The Protestant Reformation, with its emphasis on inwardness and introspection, brought many useful trait-adjectives, among them *sincere, pious, bigoted, precise, fanatic,* also many of the compounds of *self: self-regard, self-assurance, self-love, self-confidence, self-esteem. Selfish* is a term coined by the Presbyterians about 1640. The growing subjectivity of literature in the eighteenth century brought *apathy, chagrin, depression, daydream.* Courtly circles added *demure, gawky, interesting, boresome.* To recent years belong many expressions, some still regarded as slang: *booster, climber, beatnik, hoodlum, yes-man, four-flusher, sad-sack, jitter-bug, chiseler, gigolo, ex-urbanite.* To this ever-increasing vocabulary of human characteristics psychology has contributed *introverted, neurotic, regressive, psychopathic, somatotonic, schizoid,* and many more. Although some symbols become extinct, the tendency is for trait-names to multiply—a reflection no doubt of ever-rising interest in human nature.

We conclude, therefore, that in part our available trait-names point to common characteristics in respect to which people may be compared. In other words, many terms strive to designate truly veridical endowments of men. About 25 percent of the terms are of this order.

But language is tricky. It also serves an evaluative purpose. When we say a woman is *attractive,* we are talking not about a disposition "inside the skin," but about her effect on other people. About 30 percent of our trait-names have this predominantly evaluative flavor: among them, *adorable, angelic, boresome, disgusting, enviable, evil, magnificent, trying, winning.*

The line between veridical and evaluative terms is often hard to draw. For one thing, a term of praise or blame, such as *honest, law-abiding,* or *unselfish,* may come to represent a desired self-image, and a person may strive (that is, develop a trait) to correspond to the social ideal.

There are two additional classes of terms. We designate temporary states of mind, mood, emotion, or present activity; for example, *abashed, gibbering, rejoicing, frantic.* Although such terms describe conduct, they do not refer to permanent "preferred patterns." About 25 percent of the 18,000 words are of this sort. Finally, we have to admit a large array (20 percent of the total) that seems metaphorical or questionable, such terms as *alive, amorphous, roly-poly, prolific.*

When we say that the list of humanly descriptive single terms totals about 18,000, we are omitting the vast number of hyphenated and compound expressions: *nature-lover, a hater of affectation, the sort of person who never bothers with detail,* and so on. One wonders whether the number of possible descriptions of human beings in the English language (or in other highly developed languages) is not almost infinite.

To sum up, our theory of trait-names holds that the labels offered by the lexicon are symbols socially devised from a mixture of psychological, cultural, and ethical concerns. Terms that are evaluative and censorious have little relevance to the study of the structure of personality, however useful they may be in studying the social impact of one individual upon others. Perhaps the number of single, nonjudgmental terms pointed clearly to the designation of permanent (nontemporary) traits is between 4,000 and 5,000. Yet so many combinations of words are possible that the number of accessible trait-designations is far, far greater.

At best trait-names are *range-names.* That is to say, when we designate Tom and Ted both as *aggressive,* we do not mean that their aggressiveness is identical in kind. Common speech is a poor guide to psychological subtleties. But words are nothing more than ragbag categories. We put into them a vast array of meanings that are roughly, but only roughly, comparable with one another.

But dissatisfied as we may be, verbal tags are about all we have to work with. Perhaps some day psychological science will have other symbols to designate traits (factorial or mathematical), but progress in this direction to date is too slight to tempt us to abandon primary allegiance to our mother tongue. Our fate is to analyze traits in words, doing the best we can along the way to *define* our terms.

Summary

Personality can be analyzed—to a certain extent and with partial success—in terms of common traits. These are dispositions—more general than habits or attitudes—in respect to which people in a population can be profitably compared. Common sense leads us to make such comparisons constantly. One man, we say, is more *dominant* than another. Psychologists do the same thing, though they may sometimes prefer to speak of "dimensions," "factors," or "variables," instead of traits.

Common traits are empirically established whenever personality tests (or other indicators) prove to be reliable, showing that people respond consistently over a period of time and with characteristic intensity. Hundreds of common traits have been established in this way, most of them showing a normal distribution in the population at large.

A common trait of unusual breadth and inclusiveness is sometimes called an empirical type, but it is questionable whether the concept of type is of any scientific advantage. Whether types are empirical, ideal, or cultural, they do considerable violence to the concrete individual who is forced into them. Common traits offer a better method and theory for the comparative study of personalities. Personal dispositions, as the next chapter will show, offer the best method and theory for the morphogenic study of personality.

Although common trait-names create many ambiguities and difficulties, we are compelled to use them in the analysis of personality.

CHAPTER 15

Personal Dispositions

The Uniqueness of Personal Dispositions • The Inter-dependence of Dispositions • The Consistency of Dispo-sitions • Genotypical, Phenotypical, and Pseudo Disposi-tions • Cardinal, Central, and Secondary Dispositions • How Many Dispositions Has a Person? • How Study Per-sonal Dispositions? • Personal Dispositions and Motives • Definition • Résumé

For a moment we shall continue our discussion of trait-names. Some of these, we find, are derived from individual historical or fictional characters: *quixotic, narcistic* (originally Narcissusistic, then narcissistic, now narcistic), *chauvinistic, sadistic, puckish,* a *quisling.* Some are spelled with capital letters, *Boswellian, Lesbian, Chesterfieldian, Rabelaisian, Pickwickian, Emersonian, Falstaffian, Homeric, Faustian.* We say a person is *Christlike,* a *Don Juan,* a *Beau Brummell,* a *Xantippe.* In all these cases, and many more like them, we note that some particular outstanding characteristic of a single person gave us a new label to apply occasionally (not often) to other people.

In such instances we are not dealing with a common trait. It would be absurd to try to compare all people—or any large number of them—on a scale designed to measure the peculiar *fastidious exhi-*

bitionism of a Beau Brummell or the *sexual cruelty* of a Marquis de Sade. Yet the very fact that we now name the characteristic shows that we have abstracted it from the individual life with the intention of applying it to other lives to which it may fit. Words are general. Even if we say "this boy," we are using two abstract words to point to a particular. Only a proper name, such as Franklin Roosevelt, comes near to designating one unique personal event in nature.

The Uniqueness of Personal Dispositions

We come again to the proposition that seems so shocking to science. Franklin Roosevelt was a unique historical event in nature, and the fabulously complex organization of his mental processes and nervous system was likewise unique. It could not be otherwise considering the individuality of his inheritance, the individuality of his life experience—all as explained in Chapter 1. Even the subsystems of his personality were ultimately unique. When confronted with this unassailable logic, one outraged psychologist exclaimed, "I think it is nonsense to say that no two men ever have the same trait. I mean, of course it is true, but it is one of those truths that can't be accepted." We reply: Unfortunately, this is one truth that the study of personality *must* accept, however great the difficulties it creates.

In order to keep the problem distinct from that of common traits, we shall adopt a different terminology. We could with propriety speak of *individual* (or of *personal*) traits as distinct from *common* traits, for there is similarity between the two conceptions (both, for example, refer to a complex level of organization). Yet for purposes of clarity we shall designate the individual unit not as a trait, but as a *personal disposition* (and shall occasionally use the abbreviation *p.d.*).[1]

Much that we have said concerning common traits applies also to

---

[1] Another possible label for the unit I have in mind is *morphogenic trait*. This term properly suggests a unit that carries the "form" of the personality structure, and helps to maintain this form over considerable periods of time.

Morphogenesis is a branch of biology that tries to account for the patterned properties of a whole organism. It is a relatively neglected area of biology, where major effort is expended on finding the ultimate elements that are common to all life. Molecular biology has demonstrated that these ultimate units, in terms of nucleic acids, proteins, genetic principles, are remarkably alike in all organisms whatever their form. This discovery, of course, makes it more imperative (not less imperative) that the forces accounting for the patterned integrity of individual organisms be sought. The parallel with psychology is almost perfect. With analytical zeal we have sought uniform units of all personalities (common traits, needs, factors, and so on), but have lost sight of internal morphogenic patterning along the way.

personal dispositions. Both are broad (generalized) determining tendencies; both differ in the same way from habits, attitudes, and types;
both refer to the level of analysis most suitable to the study of personality; the existence of both is inferred by the occurrence of activities having "functional equivalence."

Similarities of p.d. & c.t.

But there are differences. It makes no sense to speak of the "normal distribution" of p.d.'s, since each is unique to one person. Trait-
names fit common traits better than they fit p.d.'s. (Generally several
words are needed to designate a disposition, as when we say, "Little
Susan has a peculiar anxious helpfulness all her own"; or, "He will
do anything for you if it doesn't cost him any effort.")

dissimilar

Our contention is that, if correctly diagnosed, p.d.'s reflect the
personality structure accurately, whereas common traits are categories into which the individual is forced.

For example, by common trait methods, we find that Peter
stands high in *esthetic interest* and *anxiety,* but low in *leadership*
and *need-achievement.* The truth is that all these common traits
have a special coloring in his life, and—still more important—they
interact with one another. Thus it might be more accurate to say
that his personal disposition is a kind of *artistic and self-sufficient
solitude.* His separate scores on common traits do not fully reflect
this pattern.

But, one asks, is it not "more scientific" to work with common
traits? We shall answer this question gradually. For the moment we
merely insist that common traits are at best approximations. Often
they fail to reflect the structure of a given personality.

An illustration of the point comes from Conrad's study of
ratings. Three teachers rated a number of children of preschool
age upon 231 common traits, thus being forced to make the assumption that all the children did possess exactly these self-same

---

Still another helpful suggestion comes from F. H. Allport's conception of *trend.* This
unit is a highly energized system or meaning-cycle characteristic of the individual
personality. "It represents, in familiar terms, what the individual is 'characteristically
trying to do,' that is, what meaning he is always trying to achieve. . . ." Trend structures are "interstructured into larger systems (unity of personality)." F. H. Allport,
Theories of perception and the concept of structure (New York: Wiley, 1955), p. 656.
Although these suggestions reinforce the argument of the present chapter, it seems
best for our present purposes to employ the simpler descriptive label, *personal disposition.*

qualities in some degree. Proceeding on this precarious assumption there was only a low agreement among the teachers, with a median correlation of $+.48$. Many of the children, it seems, were rated by guesswork, simply because the investigation *required* that each child receive a rating on every quality. But in the course of the same study, the teachers were asked to *star* their ratings on such qualities as they considered to be of "central or dominating importance in the child's personality." On this part of their task the teachers agreed almost perfectly, their ratings correlating approximately $+.95$. This result shows that low reliability of rating may often be due to the fact that the subjects are forced into a common trait comparison where they do not belong. In a few cases (the starred qualities) the common trait concept seemed to correspond fairly well to some striking individual p.d., but in most cases the common dimensions fell wide of the mark.[2]

Let the reader bear in mind that we are not condemning the common trait-approach. Far from it. When we wish to compare people with one another, it is the only approach possible. Furthermore, the resulting scores, and profiles, are up to a point illuminating. We are simply saying that there is a second, more accurate way, of viewing personality: namely, the internal patterning (the morphogenesis) of the life considered as a unique product of nature and society.

We view personality—in the only way it can be intelligibly viewed—as a network of organization, composed of systems within systems, some systems of small magnitude and somewhat peripheral to the central or propriate structure, other systems of wider scope at the core of the total edifice; some easy to set into action, others more dormant; some so culturally conforming that they can readily be viewed as "common"; others definitely idiosyncratic. But in the last analysis this network—employing billions and billions of nerve cells, fashioned by a one-time heredity and by environmental experiences never duplicated—is ultimately unique.

The diehard nomothetic scientist replies, "Well, everything in the world is unique—every stone in the meadow, every old shoe, every mouse; but they are all composed of the same elements.

[2] H. S. Conrad, The validity of personality ratings of preschool children, *J. educ. Psychol.*, 1932, **23**, 671–680.

Uniqueness appears when common elements appear in different proportions. Organic chemistry is chiefly concerned with the various combinations of six or seven elements, and it has been estimated that about three million combinations of these few elements are possible. Allowing for still more elements (including common traits) we can ultimately account for the final uniqueness of every person."

My answer is this: Personality exists only at a postelementary state; it exists only when the common features of human nature have already interacted with one another and produced unique, self-continuing, and evolving systems. This is not to say that the search for common elements or common human functions is undesirable. For the most part the science of psychology does this and nothing else. I insist only that if we are interested in *personality*, we must go beyond the elementaristic and reach into the morphogenic realm.[3]

The Interdependence of Dispositions

With this picture before us let us ask whether it is reasonable to think of an individual personality as composed of separate dispositions. Is not the organization so interlocked that we cannot dismember the individual into p.d. components?

It is certainly true that we can never see one p.d. at a time. The continuous flow of behavior employs simultaneously all manner of determining tendencies. Consider the act of writing a letter: it requires the convergence of mental sets, motives of the moment, skills, stylistic habits, as well as deep personal convictions and values. Behavior always demands the effective convergence of many determining influences. Generalizing the illustration, we can say that no single performance is ever a univocal product of any one single trait or p.d.

At the same time, since adaptive acts distributed over a period of time show repeatedly the same purposes and the same expressive quality, it becomes necessary to assume some stable and continuous influences at work. A *talkative* person, who starts his stream of speech at the slightest provocation, must have some neuropsychic tendency that channels his conduct in this direction. His loquacity, provoked so easily (by an equivalence of stimuli), leads to fluent speech wherein

---

[3] A morphogenic point of view in biology is reflected in E. W. Sinnott, *The biology of the spirit* (New York: Viking, 1955). This author holds that the configuration of human personality is maintained chiefly by goal-directed motives (not by drives).

all manner of ideas and words may be employed (equivalence of response). Though it is not easy to conceive in neurological terms, there must be some neural system with a low threshold of arousal capable of engendering this consistent behavior. At any one time, to be sure, the form the loquacity takes is determined also by other operative factors—by his ideas and attitudes toward the topic of the discourse and toward the interlocutor, by the availability of a listener, as well as by other p.d.'s in his nature.

The expression *foci of organization* represents what we mean by personal dispositions. The average individual will have certain sets of interests and values, certain modes and manners of expression, and perhaps a magnificent obsession or two. These focalized dispositions can be aroused by a wide range of stimuli and lead to a wide range of equivalent responses. (See Figure 24, page 322.) But the boundaries between these systems are not rigid. Even so-called "logic-tight compartments" are not entirely separate; their boundaries are at least semipermeable.

A p.d., then, is identifiable not by sharp contours or boundaries, but by a nuclear quality. The nuclear quality will be some important goal or meaning, or sometimes a style of expression. All these betray the individual's effort at survival and mastery, and give shape or form to his personality.

The Consistency of Dispositions

Since the primary principle of behavior is its convergent flow, we cannot expect dispositions to be totally consistent and predictable. Yet our test for a p.d. (as for a common trait) lies in the demonstrable recurrence of "functionally equivalent" behavior. A New York executive, almost always decisive, orderly, and prompt, may be reduced to virtual paralysis when confronted in a restaurant with a tray of French pastry. Why? Perhaps it is just fatigue at the end of the day; perhaps it is a buried complex traceable to punishment in boyhood for stealing tarts. Dispositions are never wholly consistent. What a bore it would be if they were—and what chaos if they were not at all consistent.

We have already discussed inconsistency due to situation. Some authors, as we saw, go so far as to declare that personality has no inner consistency at all, but owes its uniformity to the likeness of situations recurrently faced. We have argued against this position. Even a person who is at one time ascendant and another time yielding, at one time gruff and another time sugary, must have these contrary tendencies *within himself*. Sometimes a person may harbor p.d.'s that are exactly opposite. Conquering and yielding, extraverted and introverted, saintly and sinful, dispositions may reside within one breast. Goethe creates Faust from such paradoxical trends. Jung's system of psychology rests heavily on the concept of contraries. A masculine person, for example, will have in his nature an unconscious *femina*.

One situation calls forth one p.d.; another calls forth another. We cannot deny this fact. But we should point out that what appears to be contradictory behavior is often not contradictory at all. The apparent contradiction comes from the fact that we have made a superficial diagnosis.

Take the case of Dr. D, always neat about his person and desk, punctilious about lecture notes, outlines, and files; his personal possessions are not only in order but carefully kept under lock and key. Dr. D is also in charge of the departmental library. In this duty he is careless; he leaves the library door unlocked, and books are lost; it does not bother him that dust accumulates. Does this contradiction in behavior mean that D lacks personal dispositions? Not at all. He has two opposed stylistic dispositions, one of orderliness and one of disorderliness. Different situations arouse different dispositions. Pursuing the case further, the duality is at least partly explained by the fact that D has *one* cardinal (motivational) disposition from which these contrasting styles proceed. The outstanding fact about his personality is that he is a self-centered egotist who never acts for other people's interests, but always for his own. This cardinal self-centeredness (for which there is abundant evidence) demands orderliness for himself, but not for others.

We conclude, then, that the consistency of a disposition is a matter of degree. There must be some demonstrable relationship between separate acts before its existence can be inferred. Yet the occurrence of dissociated, specific, and even contradictory acts is not necessarily fatal to the inference. And we usually find that contradiction diminishes if we spot correctly the deepest (most propriate) disposition that is operating.

Genotypical, Phenotypical, and Pseudo Dispositions

This last point brings us to a helpful distinction proposed by Lewin. Descriptions in terms of "here and now" are *phenotypical*. Explanatory accounts, seeking deeper dispositions, are *genotypical*. In the case of D, he has both orderly and negligent ways of behaving (phenotypical), but these opposed readinesses (each covering a range of equivalent situations and responses) are anchored in a more fundamental (genotypical) p.d. that we identified as *self-centeredness*.

It would not be correct to say that phenotypical dispositions are not true dispositions. They are "true" in much the same sense that common traits are true. In other words, although they may not reflect the core-dynamics and central structure of the individual personality, they at least show some consistency in a person's behavior.

Psychoanalytic theory holds that the quality of *miserliness,* for example, is a reflection of an anal-erotic character syndrome. *If* this be the case, then miserliness is a phenotypical disposition. Only the anal-erotic character would be properly considered genotypical. But some misers may not have this particular underlying genotype. Perhaps their hoarding started out of dire necessity and became functionally autonomous. They simply like the feel of gold (or its equivalent). In this case the miserliness is conceivably a true genotype (that is to say, it is as fundamental a p.d. as one is likely to find in their personalities). This example shows that *only by studying exhaustively the single life can we hope to distinguish genotype from phenotype with reasonable success.*

Sometimes our inference can be wholly erroneous. We may, for example, think that a person who gives gifts is a *generous* person. But perhaps he is merely trying to buy favor. In this case we are not dealing even with a phenotypical disposition, for the person has no bent at all for generosity. The phenotypical disposition is bribery (not generosity), and the underlying genotype, for all we know, may be a kind of core feeling of insecurity in life. *Pseudo traits,* then, are errors of inference, misjudgments that come from fixing attention solely upon appearances. Here again we see that only the soundest methods and the utmost of critical skill will lead to a proper diagnosis. It is chiefly by its ability to separate true dispositions from pseudo dispositions that psychology makes an advance over common sense.

Cardinal, Central, and Secondary Dispositions

In every personality there are p.d.'s of major significance and p.d.'s of minor significance. Occasionally some p.d. is so pervasive and so outstanding in a life that it deserves to be called a *cardinal* disposition. Almost every act seems traceable to its influence. The list of terms on page 357 derived from the proper names of historical and fictional characters (even allowing for exaggeration and over-simplification) suggests what is meant by cardinal dispositions. No such disposition can remain hidden, an individual is known by it, and may become famous for it. Such a master quality has sometimes been called the *eminent trait,* the *ruling passion,* the *master-sentiment,* the *unity-thema,* or the *radix* of a life.

It is an unusual personality that possesses one and only one cardinal disposition. Ordinarily the foci of a life seem to lie in a handful of distinguishable central p.d.'s. How many is the question we shall ask presently. Central dispositions are likely to be those that we mention in writing a careful letter of recommendation. Conrad's study cited on page 359 also deals with the central (starred) dispositions in the personalities of preschool children (where, of course, we should not expect to find structures as firm as later in life).

On a still less important level we may speak of secondary p.d.'s—less conspicuous, less generalized, less consistent, and less often called into play than central dispositions. Secondary p.d.'s are likely to be more peripheral and less propriate than central p.d.'s.

It goes without saying that these three gradations are arbitrary and are phrased mainly for convenience of discourse. In reality there are all possible degrees of organization, from the most circumscribed and unstable to the most pervasive and firmly structured. It is helpful, however, to have these distinctions at hand when we wish to speak roughly of the relative prominence and intensity of various dispositions in a given personality.[4]

---

[4] A word should be said about "intensity." In one sense if a p.d. is regarded as unique, it cannot exist in "degree" because there is no outside standard to compare it with. Yet if we take the individual as our reference point we may—as we have here—estimate the intensity of one p.d. in relation to others, and thus arrive at our rough scale: *cardinal-central-secondary.* If, however, we try to compare some p.d. with similar p.d.'s in other people, then, of course, we have transformed p.d. into *common trait.*

How Many Dispositions Has a Person?

How many dispositions has a person is a most audacious question, and can be answered in only a preliminary and speculative way. For many reasons the question is audacious: Behavior is in continuous flow; dispositions never express themselves singly; people manifest contradictory dispositions in contradictory situations; furthermore, diagnostic methods are too ill developed to enable us to discover the answer.

Still, a few guesses can be made on the basis of partial evidence, provided we confine ourselves to the level of cardinal or central p.d.'s. We shall not even venture a guess concerning secondary dispositions.

We turn first to the realm of biography. In his definitive life of William James, Ralph Barton Perry writes that in order to understand this fascinating figure it is necessary to deal with eight leading "traits" or "ingredients." He first lists four "morbid" dispositions—tendencies which, taken by themselves, would prove to be severe handicaps: (1) hypochondria, (2) preoccupation with exceptional mental states, (3) marked oscillations of mood, and (4) repugnance to the processes of exact thought. Blended with these morbid p.d.'s, and redeeming them, are four "benign" dispositions: (5) sensibility, (6) vivacity, (7) humanity, (8) sociability. The labels Perry uses are, of course, common trait names; but he defines them in such a way that the peculiar Jamesian flavor of each is brought out. What is important for our purposes is the fact that, even after a most exhaustive study of a complex personality, Perry feels that a limited number of major dispositions (in this case eight) adequately covers the major structure of the life.

Let us consider a bit of experimental evidence. We asked 93 students "to think of some one individual of your own sex whom you know well"; and then "to describe him or her by writing words, phrases, or sentences that express fairly well what seem to you to be the essential characteristics of this person." The phrase *essential characteristic* was defined as "any trait, quality, tendency, interest, etc., that you regard as of major importance to a description of the person you select."

The average number listed by the students was 7.2. Only 10

percent of the writers felt that they needed more than 10 items to describe their friend's "essential characteristics."[5]

These are only suggestive bits of evidence, but they open a momentous possibility. *When psychology develops adequate diagnostic methods for discovering the major lines along which a particular personality is organized (personal dispositions), it may turn out that the number of such foci will normally vary between five and ten.* We state this proposition as a hypothesis subject to eventual scientific testing.

How To Study Personal Dispositions

Since psychology has so rarely fixed its attention on individuality, we have fewer methods for determining personal dispositions in single individuals than we should like. In most quarters the cliché prevails: "Psychology, as a science, deals with universals, not with particulars." For every study of individual traits we find a hundred, perhaps a thousand, studies of common traits. Yet methods—or suggestions of methods—are available, and we shall tell enough about them to show that our challenge to science is justified—namely, that it *can* do more than it does in exploring morphogenic organization.

Particularizing Common Traits. A first and fairly obvious method is to scrutinize the standing of individuals on universal testing instruments or rating scales. Significantly high or low scores on common variables may draw our attention to areas where, if we look more carefully, important personal dispositions will be found. For example, we refer again to Conrad's rating study (page 359), where the method of "starred" ratings among over 200 common traits showed which variables seemed to point to important dispositions in individual children. It will be recalled that teachers agreed particularly well on these starred items. Having thus identified probable p.d.'s, we could then proceed to discover the coloring of each as it exists in a given life.

Case Studies. The most obvious of all methods is the study of biography, life-history, or single cases. Offhand this would seem to

---

[5] See G. W. Allport, What units shall we employ? In G. Lindzey (Ed.), *Assessment of human motives* (New York: Holt, Rinehart and Winston, 1958), Chap. 9. The biographical evidence is found in R. B. Perry, *The thought and character of William James* (2 vols.; Boston: Little, Brown, 1936), Vol. II, Chaps. 90–91.

be the method of literature and common sense, but, as we shall show in Chapter 17, it can, through the use of safeguards and analytic tools, become an important scientific method.

Testing for Hypothesized p.d.'s. Suppose, like any sensible scientist, we first take a common-sense look at the object we are studying. We then hypothesize that the object—in this case a particular personality—will be found to consist of certain major dispositions. We then, like any scientist, try empirically to verify our hypothesis and, if need be, correct it. This method has been proposed by F. H. Allport in the following case.[6]

A certain boy at school showed exemplary conduct; he was orderly, industrious, and attentive. But at home he was noisy, unruly, and a bully toward the younger children. Phenotypically he showed contrary dispositions.

Now the psychologist might make the hypothesis: This boy's central disposition is a craving for attention. He finds that he gains his end best at school by conforming to the rules; at home, by disobeying them.

Having made this hypothesis, the psychologist could then actually count the boy's acts during the day (being checked by some independent observer) to see how many of them were "functionally equivalent," i.e., manifested a clear bid for attention. If the proportion is high, we can regard the hypothesis as confirmed, and the p.d. as established.

A wider use of this hypothesis method would lead us to a wholesome focusing on individual lives.

Empirical Analysis of One Person's Acts. If we have a large array of acts of a single person available for study, we can in various ways make a revealing "content analysis" of them. For example, the letters or the diary of a person contains recurrent groupings of thoughts. How to make scientific use of such data is shown by the work of Baldwin, who calls his method "personal structure analysis."[7]

This investigator analyzed over one hundred letters written by Jenny between her fifty-ninth and seventieth year. He asked

[6] F. H. Allport, Teleonomic description in the study of personality, *Charact. & Pers.*, 1937, **6,** 202–214.
[7] A. L. Baldwin, Personal structure analysis: a statistical method for investigating the single personality, *J. abnorm. soc. Psychol.*, 1942, **37,** 163–183.

the question, If Jenny mentions one subject, what else does she mention at the same time (in the same thought sequence)? By this method he determined that Jenny displayed only a few unmistakable central dispositions in her life. She was highly jealous of her son; she was paranoid concerning her relations with women; she had a strong esthetic interest; and she was scrupulous in matters of money.

Although these letters, of course, may not have revealed the whole structure of Jenny's personality, the method nonetheless shows that careful quantitative work can be conducted in the area of unique personal dispositions. Psychology *can* be concerned with the single case.

The Clinical Approach. Since counselors, consultants, or therapists deal with individuals, they unavoidably make judgments concerning personal dispositions. For the duration of the consultation they are absorbed by the client's own structure. They will, of course, think of general laws that may apply to the person's conduct or problem, but their attention is riveted upon the present personal pattern.

Unfortunately, up to now clinical psychologists, psychoanalysts, and other counselors have let their interest in general laws and actuarial (average) predictions take precedence in their theorizing. Sometimes they even disparage the value of studying the morphogenic formations in the individual life.[8]

It is, however, clear that the clinical approach in principle offers an enviable opportunity for investigating morphogenic dispositions. In the future we may hope for enlightening research from this source.

Enough has been said to establish our point: Science can and should deal with individual personality directly, and not merely compare persons in the customary common-trait manner.

Personal Dispositions and Motives

We come now to our most difficult question. What is the relationship between p.d.'s as we have described them, and our discussion of motives (Chapters 9 and 10)?

[8] Cf. P. E. Meehl, *Clinical vs. statistical prediction* (Minneapolis: Univ. of Minnesota Press, 1954). Also T. R. Sarbin, R. Taft, and D. E. Bailey, *Clinical inference and cognitive theory* (New York: Holt, Rinehart and Winston, 1960).

First, let us remind the reader that most theorists make a sharp distinction between motives and the other ingredients of personality. For example, Murray divides needs (the basic motives and most important ingredients of personality) from the ways of fulfilling needs (actones).[9] Similarly, Freudians believe that instincts are the motivational units, whereas cathexes represent the objects attached to them. Others sharply separate motives (why one acts) from attitudes (how one acts). We recall that McClelland assumes that personality is composed of three types of units: *motives, traits, schemata* (page 259). For McClelland a trait is merely "the learned tendency of an individual to react as he has reacted more or less successfully in the past in similar situations when similarly motivated."[10]

Our view is different. We cannot believe that the personality is neatly divided into motives on the one hand and manners (modes of achieving motives) on the other. All determining tendencies are dynamic (i.e., they cause behavior), and so in a sense all personal dispositions have some motivational power. We hasten to add, however, that many degrees of dynamism exist. Some personal dispositions, for example, are far more motivational than others.

Let us take an example. Mr. X has a consuming passion to give his children a better education than he had. Mr. X has also a consistent disposition of behaving politely. Now we can easily picture him leaving the house in the morning for the purpose of accomplishing his goal for his children. But he certainly never leaves the house merely in order to be polite to someone. Politeness is more of a *stylistic disposition* in his nature; serving his children, more of a *motivational disposition*. Yet neither is devoid of some degree of dynamic force.

[9] H. A. Murray, *et al., Explorations in personality* (New York: Oxford, 1938). In one connection Murray speaks of *need-integrate.* As we have said, this term in itself suggests precisely what we are seeking: a single system in which need and object and mode of behaving are all integrated into a single disposition. But Murray unfortunately uses the term not for lasting systems within personality but only for the momentary integration of need and response modes. More recently the same author speaks of *value-vector* as a unit of personality analysis. Although the term gives somewhat more object content to the need, it still implies an unfortunate separation of motivation from its goal. See T. Parsons and E. Shils (Eds.), *Toward a general theory of action* (Cambridge, Mass.: Harvard Univ. Press, 1951), P. IV, Chap. 3.

[10] D. C. McClelland, *Personality* (New York: Sloane, 1951), p. 216.

At this point we wish we could call upon neurophysiology. But we do not yet know what sort of complex network or cell-assembly corresponds to a disposition; nor do we know exactly how these networks exert pressure on behavior. We do know, however, that our nervous machinery is arranged in levels so that the more complex higher levels stand in the dual role of driver and restrainer to the lower simpler levels.[11] This fact may help to explain how a complex disposition selects equivalent stimuli from the environment and instigates or "gates" equivalent responses (all being consonant with the higher-level disposition).

At the same time, we have no evidence at all that a drive (or impulse or motive) ever acts separately and alone. On the contrary, Hebb insists, a drive impulse flows into a higher-level organization and creates a diffuse general motivational state where integrated pressure then "flows down" from the cortex to the brain stem and eventually into action.[12]

Although our knowledge of this machinery leaves much to be desired, the indications are that complex dispositions are more truly motivational than are drives, for the simple reason that the latter do not function without involving higher integrations.

Let us look at the so-called *sex drive,* which is so often talked about as a uniform need, central and demanding in personality. Our question is whether the sex need ever exists apart from some dispositional system. When we look at concrete lives, we see that sex is intricately fused with all manner of acquired beliefs, tastes, habits, and inhibitions. The nervous system does not conveniently keep the sex impulse in a separate compartment from these factors with which it fuses. The "cathexes" are part of the "motive."

To say, for example, that a certain man or woman is *homosexual* is by no means to characterize his or her motivation. There are myriad forms of homosexuality: overt, covert, active, passive, compulsive, sublimated, diffuse, specific, altruistic, gentle, sadistic, protective, adulatory, superficial, repressed, peripheral, central, temporary, lasting, esthetic, intellectual—ultimately, as many forms as there are individuals whose *need Sex* has been "ca-

[11] C. S. Sherrington, *The integrative action of the nervous system* (London: Constable, 1906).
[12] D. O. Hebb, *A textbook of psychology* (Philadelphia: Saunders, 1958), p. 160.

thected" toward their own sex—and think of the many other ways this abstract need can be cathected. Concretely, then, it seems artificial to a high degree to say that sex takes the same form or has the same significance in any two personalities. Each lives with his own particular pattern. Although we may learn something of the nature of these patterns by studying the common biological foundation, it would be a mistake to assume that the abstracted sex capacity is itself a separable unit of motivation.

But having thus argued that we cannot sharply distinguish motives from personal dispositions, we hasten once again to admit that some dispositions have more motivational force than others. Those involving sex are, for example, likely to be more compelling than a stylistic p.d. of politeness, forcefulness, or negativism. Although all dispositions are to a degree dynamic, some are so only in an instrumental sense. They direct activity that is motivated by other p.d.'s possessing greater stress-power. We may, for example, expect a polite person to act out his sex-involved dispositions with a special degree of considerateness for his partner.[13]

Whether a p.d. is motivational or instrumental is, then, a matter of degree. Dispositions range from absorbing passions, through mild predilections, to mere manners. Even in the stylistic disposition, however, we can discover some dynamic force, especially when frustrated. If a polite person is forced to behave impolitely, the resulting discomfort calls attention to the normal press that exists in even a stylistic p.d. Our styles of behaving, we find, are not wholly a matter of servicing stronger motives; they, too, have a certain directive force.

Is a disposition dynamic in the sense that it is self-active (spontaneously setting itself in motion)? In a sense, of course, there is always a sensory cue, outside or inside the body, that *instigates* the tension. Strictly speaking, therefore, any disposition has to be aroused before it is dynamically active.

But in another sense motivational dispositions are self-active. It is certainly not a ring on the telephone that causes an egotist to talk for half an hour unchecked about his latest exploits, or a gossip to recount at great length the doings of her neighbors. In these cases

13 W. Stern makes the distinction between motivational and stylistic dispositions using the German terms, *Richtungsdisposition* (directional) and *Rüstungsdisposition* (equipmental). *Die menschliche Persönlichkeit* (Leipzig: Barth, 1923), p. 83. This account owes much to Stern.

the response springs from deep-seated trends, not from the telephone ring. Indeed, the egotist and the gossip may be under such tension that they *seek* an excuse to talk. They call on a friend in order to release their flood. An author, a housekeeper, a craftsman, if deprived of their favorite occupation, may "itch" to return to their work. In these cases the dispositions are, for all practicable purposes, spontaneously self-active. Interests, ambitions, compulsions, phobias, general attitudes, inclinations, hobbies, values, tastes, predilections—all are p.d.'s, (some only secondary) and are at the same time motives.

To conclude, it is impossible to consider personal dispositions as units of personality wholly apart from motivation. In some cases they are the leading motives in life, especially if they are mature, functionally autonomous systems of purpose. They are not merely ways of *reacting* to the environment but ways of *meeting* it.

As we said in Chapter 10, some drives—such as pain and oxygen hunger—may operate in a reflex manner to bring about tension-reduction with little integration into higher-level systems. Other drives—such as sex and food hunger—seem to be highly integrated with cortical functions, and remain no longer as purely biological in nature. They become ingredients of personal dispositions.

It seems necessary to postulate a wide range of motivational force for personal dispositions. Some are compelling, self-active, the very steam boilers of life. Others are stylistic and instrumental in nature—but still dynamic in a lesser degree.

Definition

From this long discussion we are prepared to offer a definition of a personal disposition. It is closely similar to our definition of *trait* (page 347). The careful reader will note that every part of the definition has been explained:

A personal disposition is a generalized neuropsychic structure (peculiar to the individual), with the capacity to render many stimuli functionally equivalent, and to initiate and guide consistent (equivalent) forms of adaptive and stylistic behavior.

Résumé

In the last two chapters we have sought to establish the level of analysis that is most useful for the study of human personality. It may be called the "trait" level, and is, in fact, the level most commonly recognized both by psychologists and by our habits of ordinary speech. In considering this level, however, we find it necessary to distinguish between two ways of viewing trait-organization.

Common traits designate organized complexities regarded as common (or comparable) in a population of persons. Because of people's membership in a common species and in a common culture, we can with good reason look for categories of behavior that are fairly uniform. All comparative studies of personalities, all differential psychology, most attempts at measurement, proceed on the basis of such "common traits."

Personal dispositions are units of the same order of complexity, but are regarded as "nature's own cleavages." That is to say, they are the neuropsychic units that we actually find in individual persons. Occasionally, but only very occasionally, a person is so typical of his culture and his kind that he can be adequately characterized in terms of common traits. More likely his cardinal, central, and secondary dispositions are highly colored with individuality. The way his life is organized may not correspond at all well to any analytic scheme of common traits. The term *personal disposition* (which might be rendered as *individual trait* or *morphogenic trait*) calls attention to whatever generalized sets do factually reside in the neuropsychic system of the single person.

Both conceptions have their uses. For comparative purposes—and most studies of personality are comparative—common traits suffice. For the detailed study of the individual, personal dispositions should be identified.

It is impossible to observe traits or dispositions directly. We can only infer their existence. A specific act is always the product of many determinants, not only of lasting sets, but of momentary pressures in the person and in the situation. It is only the repeated occurrence of acts having the same significance (equivalence of response) following upon a definable range of stimuli having the same personal significance (equivalence of stimuli) that makes necessary the inference of traits and personal dispositions. These tendencies are not at all times active, but are persistent even when latent, and have relatively low thresholds of arousal.

It is one thing to admit traits and dispositions as the most acceptable units for study but another to determine their precise character in a given life. In order to avoid projection of his own nature and many other sources of error, the investigator must use all relevant empirical tools of his science to make his inferences valid. Traits and dispositions cannot be conjured into existence: they must be discovered.

In naming these organized complexities there are many pitfalls, one being the confusion of purely social judgments with objective fact. If we avoid eulogistic and dyslogistic terms, it is possible to achieve a psychological vocabulary of noncensorious trait names. Regrettable though it may be, the attributes of human personality can be depicted only with the aid of common speech, for it alone possesses reasonable subtlety and established intelligibility.

Some traits and dispositions are clearly motivational, especially those ordinarily known as interests, ambitions, sentiments, complexes, values. Others are less dynamic, having an ability to steer (to stylize) behavior rather than to initiate it. Sometimes units that are at first directive acquire later driving power, and those that are at first driving may become merely directive. An aging athlete may lose his zeal, but still retain an interest in athletics.

Even while traits and dispositions stabilize conduct they are never wholly consistent, nor are they independent of one another. Effective adjustment to the world requires flexibility, and the calling forth of varying determining tendencies in differing situations. A given personality may show contradiction and conflict—as novelists and clinicians never tire of telling.

Our view of personal dispositions does not deny the importance of social interaction in the shaping of human conduct. In Chapter 8 we recognized the effects exerted by situation, role, culture. We argue only that a given person has a wide range of habits and dispositions that may be activated to different degrees and in different combinations, depending upon the environmental and social demands of the moment.

Traits and dispositions are *modi vivendi*. They derive their significance from the part they play in advancing adjustment to, and mastery of, the personal world.

CHAPTER 16

The Unity of Personality

Retrospect • Philosophical Views • Unity as Striving • Unity and the Self-image • Propriate Functions and Unity • Correspondence versus Congruence • Empirical Approaches to Congruence • Summary

Personality is many things in one—a *unitas multiplex*. In the preceding chapters we have considered the multiplex in terms of traits and dispositions. We come now to the problem of unity. For two reasons it is a perplexing problem: first, because there are many senses in which the term *unity* may be applied to personality; and second, because it is questionable whether unity is ever achieved. Such unification as exists seems to be only a matter of degree. The German writer Von Herder said, "Man is never complete; his existence lies in becoming."

Retrospect

In preceding chapters we have already encountered various important aspects of the problem of unity. It will be helpful to recall them to mind.

In early infancy there is a high degree of "dynamical unity." In the first months of life the baby responds as a whole whenever he reaches, retracts, or expresses emotion. Indeed, for the first year or more he reacts in an "all or none" fashion, particularly when emotion is involved. He is incapable of delay, of discrimination, of gradation. As he grows older, and as differentiation increases, this primitive unity is lessened.

But as primitive unity lessens, a learned unity enters by virtue of the process of *integration*. Integration offsets the segmenting process of differentiation. To integrate means to form more embracing units. Though total integration seems never to be achieved, there is constant progress in this direction, even while the contrary process of differentiation continues. This dialectic of dividing and uniting we discussed in Chapter 5.

In this connection we should also recall the organic balancing that results from *homeostasis* (page 88). To maintain a "steady state" is to preserve unity of a fundamental though static kind.

In an entirely different sense, unity (of the moment) is seen in the principle of *convergence*. At any one time available energies are mobilized in one maximally integrated course of conduct. Although this course of conduct may be largely determined by present demands (such as changing a tire, waiting on a customer, or playing the piano) it is likely to focalize many deep-lying sets. Both motivational and stylistic dispositions are involved. We may say, "That little gesture of his spoke volumes," and we mean by this statement that many complex levels of his personality were unified with (converged with) the momentary act.

I hear someone coming up the wooden stairs near my open door. The footsteps are heavy but slow, a bit faltering and insecure. I think to myself the climber is perhaps not young and not vigorous, and that he is a person with conflicts, somewhat depressed, basically insecure and dependent. Let us say my diagnosis is correct (and we do often find that our judgments based on expressive activities such as gait are confirmed). The point is that much of this man's personality is converging in an ordinary daily activity. Much, but not all. Many important features of his life are not revealed in his gait. From it I cannot tell whether he is esthetic, sentimental, intellectually gifted, or an agnostic.

Although our discussion of traits and dispositions dealt primarily with the *multiplex* of personality organization, it also allowed for some unification. A *cardinal disposition,* for example, is, by definition, a mark of unity. Tolstoy's passion for the "simplification of life," or Schweitzer's guiding ideal of "reverence for life," like all cardinal traits, are unifying to a high degree.

Further, in our theory of traits and dispositions we allow for their *interdependence.* They interlace like a tapestry. When a person acts, several dispositions are called into play. One may extract twenty-eight kinds of ice cream from twenty-eight labeled containers; but the nervous system has no separate containers: it has only networks of organization.

Finally, and most importantly, our discussion of the evolving sense of *self* (Chapter 6) forms a prelude to our present discussion of unity. The very term *self* implies unity. After discarding the concept for some decades psychologists have returned to it, for they now recognize that without it there is no adequate way to speak of some of the morphogenic aspects of personality.

Philosophical Views

Many philosophers tell us that everything we do, say, or are presupposes unity. Even a simple and common experience, such as *disappointment,* does so. One cannot feel disappointed unless there are a series of previous stages: desire, expectation, lack of fulfillment, all being stages belonging to one continuing actor. The fact that we have conflicts and clashes of purpose within our breasts is proof of unity. A present conflict could not be known except in terms of prior unity, or a hoped-for unity in the future. Hence conflict, dissociation, even the disintegration of personality have no meaning apart from the supposition that the person—first, last, and all the time—is a fundamental and continuing unit.[1]

This issue has worried many, perhaps most, philosophers, but not all of them reach the same conclusion. The philosopher Hume, for example, concluded reluctantly and with no strong sense of conviction, that a continuing agent (a self) was more of an illusion than a fundamental fact. He decided that men are made up of discrete bits

[1] Cf. W. Stern, *General psychology from the personalistic standpoint* (Transl. by H. D. Spoerl; New York: Macmillan, 1938), p. 449. See also E. S. Brightman, *Person and reality* (New York: Ronald, 1958), Chap. 14.

of experience. William James—wrestling with the same problem—concluded that there is no single-cementing principle but that unity lies in the overlap of successive states and acts, much as the unity of a shingled roof consists of the overlay of shingles.

The opposite conclusion, as we saw in Chapter 6, is reached by Kant, who argues that since we know our separate acts to be *ours,* there must be a "pure ego" continuing to guarantee personal unity throughout life. Philosophers who follow Kant may take one of two views. Either they hold that the self is a passive guarantor of unity—a "continuing ground" without active participation and "intervention"; or else they hold that the self is an *agent* that wills, directs, steers, selects conduct, and thus actively forges unity.

Extending this latter point of view, Thomistic psychologists say that the unifying self has one objective and inevitable goal. It is the nature of self to strive (not always successfully) for a higher degree of perfection than now exists. Even the feeblest life manifests a basic tendency for enrichment, for progress beyond its present limits. The direction of the goal is the ideal of a perfect person as the individual conceives him to be. Since man is made in the image of God, there is then a norm of perfection (of man as he ought to be) that guides, however imperfectly, the unifying activity of the self. Man glimpses the road toward ultimate unity, and insofar as he follows it, by reason and by choice, he will achieve a factual unification of his personality.[2] This line of thought calls attention to the conviction of some writers that the question of unity cannot be considered at all without at the same time considering the problem of the ultimate nature and destiny of man.

Other philosophers avoid the assumption that the self is a unifying agent. They see unity in the essential "systemic" nature of personality. They postulate a "tendency to stability" (Fechner), a "systematic relevance" (Whitehead), or a "conatus" (Spinoza). In human beings, according to Spinoza, the conatus takes the form of a tendency to grow into one's own perfected form. These philosophers admit that lower forms of life achieve unity more easily than do human beings, who have so many more diversified potentialities claiming fulfillment. As Keyserling points out, a kingfisher alertly

[2] Cf. Magda B. Arnold and J. A. Casson (Eds.), *The human person: an approach to an integral theory of personality* (New York: Ronald, 1954).

catching food on the shores of a pond, is a more perfect, if less intricate, unity than is a human being in quest of his daily bread.

If these various philosophical solutions seem confusing, the reason is that they require far deeper study than we can here offer. Our purpose in calling attention to them is to show that philosophical sophistication is needed in order to reach a completely satisfactory theory of the nature of unification in the personal life.

Unity as Striving

One line of philosophical thinking is especially close to the psychologist's stock in trade. The so-called romantic philosophers of the nineteenth century were fond of saying, "A man is what he loves." We never fully attain what we love; we simply keep on loving it and wanting more and more of it. Love of learning, to take an example, is a unifying force; but possession of learning is not.

What integrates our energies is the pursuit of some goal. When the goal is attained, the energy is dispersed. A person centered on becoming what he wants to become is far more integrated than one who has reached his goal—and has no place to go. To reach a goal we have to overcome distractions, discords, and obstacles. The effort involved welds unity.

Goethe saw that it was Faust's relentless search for objectives, particularly for the life-goal he set himself ("a free people on a free soil"), that was his salvation. Mephisto made a wager with Faust that he could so beguile him that Faust would no longer struggle for completeness but would surrender to some tempting state of self-satisfaction along the way. Had Faust yielded to the illusion that he had found his objective, he would have been damned. In the end he was saved because he ceaselessly strove for the goal he never attained.

Like all great epics, Goethe's Faust gives us a profound insight into human nature; in this case into the conditions under which unification of personality is achieved. The psychologist Jung recognizes the same situation in his definition of *self*. According to Jung the *self* is not something we have, but something we are throughout our life span endeavoring to achieve. It is in this special sense that "self" confers unity.

The doctrine of unity-through-striving demands single-mindedness. The Bible makes this point. The Epistle of St. James warns that "a double-minded man is unstable in all his ways." The Gospel

of St. Luke says, "No servant can serve two masters." The existentialist Kierkegaard insisted that to be spiritually whole one should "will
one thing." Diffuse striving can destroy unity. One major goal is the
true unifier. The true joy of life, wrote George Bernard Shaw, is to
find that you are "being used for a purpose recognized by yourself as
a mighty one."

Unity and the Self-image

Implied in the doctrine of striving is the presence of a cognitive factor—a self-image (page 122). One psychologist, Lecky, defines personality as "an organization of ideas which are felt to be
consistent with one another." He adds that the one overpowering
motivation in life is to maintain the unity of this system:

> Behavior expresses the effort to maintain integrity and unity of the
> organization. . . . In order to be immediately assimilated, the idea formed
> as the result of a new experience must be felt to be consistent with the
> ideas already present in the system. On the other hand, ideas whose in-
> consistency is recognized as the personality develops must be expelled from
> the system. There is thus a constant assimilation of new ideas and the
> expulsion of old ideas throughout life.[3]

An important application of Lecky's theory is in the field of
learning. We learn only what fits into our image of the self-system.
(Another way to state the point is to say that we learn only, or best,
material in which we are *ego-involved*.) This point we discussed in
Chapter 5.

Another author, Carl Rogers, is concerned with the importance of
helping people attain a self-image that is accurate and complete.
Many people fail to achieve healthy unity in their personalities because of self-deception.

> It would appear that when all of the ways in which the individual
> perceives himself—all perceptions of the qualities, abilities, impulses, and
> attitudes of the person, all perceptions of himself in relation to others—
> are accepted into the organized conscious concept of the self, then this
> achievement is accompanied by feelings of comfort and freedom from
> tension. . . .[4]

[3] P. Lecky, *Self-consistency: a theory of personality* (New York: Island, 1945), p. 135.
[4] C. R. Rogers, Some observations on the organization of personality, *Amer. Psychologist*,
1947, 2, 358–368.

This line of thought identifies health in personality with a complete and unified self-image. The self-image includes not only a view of "what I am," but also "what I want to be" and "what I ought to be." By bringing these aspects of the self-image together one approaches unification.

A somewhat related approach is found in the neo-Freudian concept of *identity*. Erikson makes it the core of a modern version of psychoanalysis. It is especially during adolescence that one attempts to bring the sense of one's own identity in close accord with one's social relationships. Erikson writes:

> The sense of ego identity is the accrued confidence that one's ability to maintain inner sameness and continuity . . . is matched by the sameness and continuity of one's meaning for others.[5]

From this point of view, the task of Everyman is to discover "Who am I?" When this question is satisfactorily answered, a new unity and maturity of personality have been achieved.

An extension of this quest into the realm of mysticism is found in Zen Buddhism. Zen is aimed at total knowledge of one's own nature. The goal of Zen discipline is the experience of *satori* or enlightenment. Zen insists that the true self cannot be known by analytical concepts, or by believing—as Westerners are wont to do—that one's own identity stands apart from the underlying ground of one's existence. *Satori* is an experience of unity: self and not-self merge. It is difficult for a Western mind to achieve such a fully mystical experience, or even to comprehend its nature. Our habits of intellectual analysis prevent us from attaining such perfect subjective unity. Suzuki, the teacher of Zen, writes:

> The intellect obtrudes itself and breaks up the experience in order to make it amenable to intellectual treatment, which means a discrimination or bifurcation. The original feeling of identity is then lost and intellect is allowed to have its characteristic way of breaking up reality into pieces.[6]

Although this line of thinking is alien to the Western conceptions of personality, it finds reflections in the writings of Fromm[7] and

5 E. H. Erikson, *Identity and the life cycle: selected papers* (New York: Int. Univ. Press, 1959), p. 89.
6 D. T. Suzuki, *Mysticism, Christian and Buddhist* (New York: Harper, 1957), p. 105.
7 E. Fromm, Psychoanalysis and Zen Buddhism, *Psychologia* (Kyoto Univ.), 1959, 2, 79–99.

Maslow,[8] who believe that man can greatly enhance his own unity by learning to avoid affective-intellectual dichotomies and by cultivating the experience of creative immediacy which children possess but adults have lost.

Propriate Functions and Unity

Both striving and the self-image are *propriate* aspects of personality (Chapter 6). We may then venture a generalization: *unity in personality is to be sought primarily in propriate (and not in opportunistic or peripheral) functions.*

We recall the story of G. B. Shaw's *Pygmalion,* where the heroine, an ignorant flower girl, is taken up by Professor Higgins for speech training. He teaches her to speak in an educated way, and finds that she readily obeys his order. If he tells her to act like a servant, she does so; like a lady, and she does. Outwardly it would seem that Eliza Doolittle has no consistency at all in her personality. But underneath there is one unifying explanation of her conduct: she is in love with her teacher. Her love is a propriate factor. And it is propriate factors that explain such unity as is found in personality.

Let us refer to an experimental study.

Klein and Schoenfeld wished to study *confidence* as an attribute of personality. They gave a group of subjects a series of intelligence tests under two experimental conditions. In the first, the atmosphere was neutral, dull, not ego-involved. The subjects were merely laboratory guinea pigs going through routine motions. After each of the six tests they were asked to state the degree of confidence they felt in the accuracy of their performances. Among the six tests there was little consistency in these ratings of confidence. After an interval of time, a second equivalent set of tests was given and the atmosphere markedly changed. The subjects were placed under greater strain, were told to try hard since the results of these intelligence tests would be entered on their college records. The shift was effective. The confidence ratings became sharply consistent. A student who felt assured that he had done well (or poorly) on one test felt assured he had done well (or poorly) on the other five. The authors conclude that

[8] A. H. Maslow, *Motivation and personality* (New York: Harper, 1954), pp. 214–217.

confidence is a consistent personality trait *when the ego is involved,* but that it is variable and inconsistent when the subject has no propriate interest at stake.[9]

Ego-involvement in any situation seems to bring greater consistency. Public-opinion polls show that people who feel strongly about an issue will be quite consistent (unified) in endorsing all the propositions that are related to this issue. If they feel less strongly (less ego-involved) they are variable and inconsistent.[10]

To generalize our point: thoughts and behavior have greater consistency when they relate to what we consider to be warm, central, and important in our lives than they have when they are not so related. Or, to put the matter more briefly: propriate functions tend to unify personality.

Correspondence versus Congruence

A corollary follows. We must expect greater unification to be evident in personal dispositions than in common traits. Common traits are merely variables on which we compare a large population of people, whether or not these variables have a central importance in their lives.

Now it is true that statistical studies of common traits can give us *some* evidence of the consistency or unity of personality. When we say, for example, that a certain trait test (e.g., ascendance-submission) has a coefficient of reliability of .85, we are saying that most people respond in the same meaningful way from item to item and from time to time. And so most people, we conclude, hold to a fairly constant level of dominant, submissive, or average adjustment.[11]

Evidence for unity that comes from the correlation of measures in a general population we shall call evidence of *correspondence*. By this term we mean that subjects' scores on a common trait scale are fairly constant.

9 G. S. Klein and W. Schoenfeld, The influence of ego-involvement on confidence, *J. abnorm. soc. Psychol.*, 1941, **36**, 249–258.

10 H. Cantril, *Gauging public opinion* (Princeton, N.J.: Princeton Univ. Press, 1943), Chap. 5.

11 One may go further and study the amount of "integratedness" shown by single individuals in many traits. Do they answer questions day after day in the same way, or are they variable? Such a device for measuring the common trait of over-all "integratedness" is proposed by R. B. Cattell, Fluctuation of sentiments and attitudes as a measure of character integration and of temperament, *Amer. J. Psychol.*, 1943, **56**, 195–216.

But there are many instances where for *propriate* reasons a person's measures do not correspond. And yet we cannot say that his personality structure therefore lacks unity. In addition to the concept of correspondence (evidence of common trait unity) we need the concept of *congruence* (evidence of dispositional unity).

Eliza Doolittle, as we have seen, was absurdly unintegrated in her manners of speech and behavior; but she was well integrated in her love for Professor Higgins. When we know this fact, we see that even her inconsistent speech and behavior, though lacking correspondence, are entirely congruent. We are tapping a deep, genotypical disposition (page 364).

On page 363 we noted the case of Professor D, whose untidiness about the library, which was under his charge, contrasted (failed to correspond) with his meticulousness about his person and desk. A deep-lying genotype of self-centeredness explained both sets of contradictory acts. Again, there was low correspondence but high congruence in his personality.

There is the case of a thirteen-year-old girl who was referred for counseling because she used excessive make-up on her face. This habit seemed sadly at variance with her scholarly nature. Her teacher felt something must be "wrong." The apparent split in the girl's personality was readily explained. She had a heavy crush on her teacher, who was herself scholarly and enjoyed a high natural complexion. The little girl was entirely congruent in her striving to be like her beloved teacher.

It is easier to be "objective" in studying the correspondence of measures than in studying congruence. Standard operations are prescribed for statistical studies of correspondence, but to detect congruence we often have to make a clinical interpretation—the rightness of which is harder to prove. It is probably for this reason that the investigators in the field of personality tend to overlook the genotypical dispositions in the individual life that help to resolve the apparent contradictions in personal behavior. We admit, however, that it is not easy to establish with certainty our insightful diagnoses of congruence. Often we can be in error. Nor should we say that, if only we knew the root congruences, everything in personality would prove to be consistent with everything else. The following statement presses the point too far:

> The unity of a person can be traced in each instant of his life. There is nothing in character that contradicts itself. If a person who is known to us seems to be incongruous with himself, that is only an indication of the inadequacy and superficiality of our previous observations.[12]

After all, unity in personality is only a matter of *degree*, and we should avoid exaggerating it.

It is difficult to keep a balanced footing. On the one hand, there is no doubt that experimental and statistical studies tend to underestimate the unity of personality simply because their techniques fail to focus upon the propriate regions of the individual life. On the other hand, it is easy to read into discordant behavior some mythical unity, thereby substituting arbitrary interpretation for fact.

> In biographies, even full length, an inevitable exaggeration of consistency occurs. "Irrelevant" activities and traits are discarded. The discarding results in a picture of greater unity than is justified. Such exaggeration is especially clear in necrologies. The writer wishes to extract the "essence" or meaning of the life as a whole. A remarkable degree of unity emerges—more than was ever present in the living person.

Empirical Approaches to Congruence

The day of a truly morphogenic psychology has not arrived. We have made some progress in manufacturing building blocks (traits) and in labeling them, but little progress in architecture. What determines the total form of personality we do not know. As this chapter has shown, we have some ideas on the subject, but as yet we have few methods to help us establish these ideas on a scientific basis. Concepts such as congruence, life-style, total pattern remain for the most part mere concepts.

The task is made more difficult by the fact that complete unity is not to be expected. Integration is never perfect, and so at best we can

12 R. Franke, Gang und Charakter (Ed. by H. Bogen and O. Lipmann), Z. f. angew. Psychol., 1931, No. 58, p. 45.

hope to discover nothing more than roughness of design and partialness of pattern.

It is not strictly true that no progress has been made. The preceding chapter mentioned various methods for discovering personal dispositions. If the dispositions we discover are highly general and intense (cardinal or central) we are close to finding the unifying theme or themes of a life. (Yet, even if we firmly establish, say, four or five central dispositions in a life, we still wonder how they are related to one another.)

The following chapters deal with methods for assessing personality. Although most of these methods focus on one trait, or at most a few, other methods lead us further into the problem of interrelations. Before plunging into methods, we shall mention two techniques that have special relevance to our present problem.

Matching. The method of matching is an excellent way of demonstrating congruence, although it sheds no light on the reasons for the congruence. The method requires a judge to place together different records of *one* personality from an assortment of records taken from *many* personalities. The records may be of any type: lifehistories, photographs, specimens of handwriting, scores on various tests, artistic productions, or anything else. Or one may match these productions with the author's name.

The principle of matching is illustrated in Figure 29. The three musical manuscripts there depicted were written by three well-known composers: Bach, Beethoven, and Mozart. From your knowledge of these men you are asked to match their names with the proper musical script.

The method of matching has the advantage of permitting complex productions to be ordered with other complex productions, without first undergoing any process of analysis. It is easy to determine how many matchings would occur by chance, and then to determine how superior to chance a given judge may be. The method permits the quantitative study of qualitative patterns, though, as we have said, it does not tell us *why* a judge perceives congruence between them.[13]

---

[13] Directions for using the method, as well as a summary of earlier research using the method, are given by P. E. Vernon, The matching method applied to investigations of personality, *Psychol. Bull.*, 1936, **33**, 149–177. See also F. Mosteller and R. R. Bush, Selected quantitative methods. In G. Lindzey (Ed.), *Handbook of social psychology.* (Cambridge, Mass.: Addison-Wesley, 1954), I, 307–311.

I.

II.

III.

Figure 29. Musical Manuscripts of Bach, Beethoven, and Mozart (from W. Wolff, *The Expression of Personality*. New York: Harper, 1943, pp. 20f.)

Prediction. One of the principal aims of science is to make accurate predictions. If we know the deeper congruences of a life, we should be able to predict successfully much of its future course. (We could not, of course, predict the exact response but only a range of responses. Rarely can we foretell the precise words our friends will use in expressing pleasure at the gift we bring him, but that he will like it we are sure.) Insofar as we predict correctly on the basis of our knowledge of congruences we have fulfilled the scientific requirement for an objective proof of consistency in personality.

Now there are two kinds of prediction (see page 20 f.). *Actuarial prediction*—the sort used by insurance agencies—can be amazingly accurate en masse. By knowing average tendencies we can predict how many people will be born or will die in the next twelve months; we can predict fairly well how many auto accident deaths there will be on a holiday week end; we can even say that among couples having certain home backgrounds and personal qualities 70 percent are headed for divorce. Actuarial prediction always deals with mass statistics. It never foretells what will happen to a *given* person.

In fact, there is a serious logical error made in discussing actuarial prediction. If six in ten Americans attend the movies every week, you may be tempted to say that I have a 6 in 10 chance of going to the films this week. The statement is really nonsensical. I shall either go or not go, and only a knowledge of my attitudes, interests, and environmental situation will tell you whether or not I will attend.

Morphogenic prediction, as we shall call it here, is based on a thorough understanding of one person and his dispositions (i.e., on the idiodynamics of his life). If we know a person from the ground up, we should be able to tell much more successfully whether he will go to the movies, whether he will seek a divorce, whether he will meet with an accident, than by applying actuarial averages to his case. In fact, we may say that the whole position presented in this chapter and in previous ones argues for the superiority of morphogenic prediction over the actuarial as applied to the future of any single individual.

Correct matching in Figure 29: I = Beethoven; II = Mozart; III = Bach. Most people quickly perceive the unities: the spritely fastidiousness of Mozart, the ordered and steady flow of Bach, the tempestuousness of Beethoven—qualities reflected not only in their music and handwriting but in their personal lives as well.

But a lively controversy rages on this matter. We have already cited the opinion that the most successful predictions come from knowing a person's class membership. Thus in Chapter 8 we pointed to the view that to know a man is a "professional soldier" is to give us basis for prediction better than if we know only his "vague" traits. Although it is true that most professional soldiers may have certain styles of behaving, it is also true that a person's future behavior depends in the last analysis upon what he *is*—and not upon what groups he belongs to.

As we saw in Chapter 1, the psychologist Meehl, intrigued with the problem, examined the evidence from such prediction studies as have been made. He concluded that those made on the basis of simple test scores and other actuarial criteria were as good as, if not superior to, those made on the basis of sheer clinical insight. Unfortunately the studies he cites are so partial in nature, and so little comparable with one another, that we cannot regard the problem as yet solved. The root of the difficulty, I believe, is that psychologists have not yet learned how to discover personal dispositions upon which to base their predictions.

Summary

The problem of the unity of personality is many-sided. Neurophysiologists tell us that the outstanding mark of the nervous system is its integrative capacity. Morphogenic biologists point to the formal properties in every living creature that make it a self-maintaining unity. Philosophers, poets, theologians—all have something to say.

From the strictly empirical point of view, psychology has as yet hardly entered this field of inquiry. Perhaps its most certain conviction is that no personality is wholly unified. A pattern is never complete. The most we can hope to find are degrees of congruence and more or less consistent directions of development.

Empirical methods for the establishment of personal dispositions would seem most promising in helping us to find the major unity-themes in a life. The specific techniques of matching and prediction aid in testing the accuracy of our perceptions of congruence. We may hope that, in the future, statistical methods will increasingly be applied to the integratedness of the single life.

Although empirical methods lag, a number of psychological concepts are proposed to account for such unity as exists—among them, self-image, self-identity, propriate (as opposed to peripheral) functions, and other representations of selfhood; likewise, life-style, and various related existential concepts (to be discussed in Chapter 22).

Perhaps the most useful concept of all is one that psychologists share with many philosophers—unification comes via striving. It is the pursuit (not the attainment) of major goals that configurates a life. The more unattainable the goal the more formative it can be. A poet has said that man achieves greatest unity when he reaches consistently for "the high that proves too high, the heroic for earth too hard."

PART IV ASSESSMENT OF Personality

CHAPTER 17

A Survey of Methods

How Shall We Classify Methods? • 1. Constitutional
and Physiological Diagnosis • 2. Studies of Sociocultural
Membership, Status, Role • 3. Personal Documents and
Case Studies • 4. Self-appraisal • 5. Conduct Sampling •
6. Ratings

Having now paid tribute to the *unitas* of personality
(insofar as it is a *unitas*), we turn back to the problem of the *multi-plex*. Most of the methods so far devised for the study of personality
do not deal with the whole. (One skeptic remarked that there is
nothing to be done with a "total personality" except to send it
flowers.) Most of our present methods of assessment deal with sub-structures within the whole. Some of them focus on small detail;
others, more comprehensive and synoptic, move in the direction of
the elusive whole.

Personality is so complex a thing that every legitimate method
must be employed in its study. We exclude, of course, the sloppy and
illegitimate ways that science has long since learned to avoid: gossip,
prejudiced inference, the exaggerated single instance, unverified
anecdote. Also, we exclude some avenues of popular "character read-

ing," since at the present time they seem unpromising—among them, astrology, numerology, palmistry, phrenology. But there remain a great many legitimate and promising methods, each with a proper place.

The basic method of psychology as of all science (as well as of common sense) is *observation* of a datum and *interpretation* of its significance. Like other sciences psychology has evolved a number of special techniques to make observation systematic and to safeguard interpretation. The goal of psychological study is to improve our ability to assess personality *beyond the level of accuracy we can reach by unaided common sense*. In this chapter we are concerned with devices that are intended to lead toward this goal.

Personality is not a datum exclusively for psychological science. In Chapters 3 and 4 we recognized the contributions of biological science, and in Chapter 8, of sociocultural science. Figure 30 helps us to place in perspective the wide range of disciplines involved in the complete study of personality. The figure does not include the contribution of the literary and philosophical methods whose importance we also recognize.

How Shall We Classify Methods?

There are many logical principles by which we might order the methods of assessment that are actually in use. For example, we might classify methods in accordance with

1. the theories underlying the invention of the instrument (whether derived from psychoanalysis, factor analysis, behaviorism, and so on);
2. the regions of personality explored (e.g., traits, opinions, fantasies, abilities, cognitive or motor functions);
3. the type of stimulus presented to the subject (e.g., pencil-and-paper, apparatus, definite versus indefinite instructions, structured or unstructured objects);
4. the type of response required (e.g., forced choice between two alternatives, multiple-choice, entirely unguided reactions as in writing an autobiography);
5. the conditions of administration (whether in the laboratory, in the classroom, or in a natural everyday situation);
6. the principles of construction (whether the instrument is

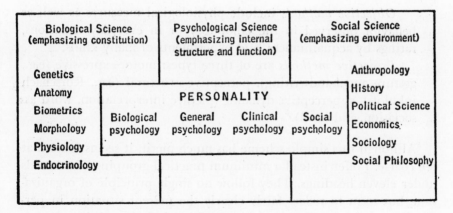

Figure 30. The Position of Personality among Various Sciences

standardized or unstandardized, whether rationally designed or empirically derived, whether nomothetic or idiographic);

7. the manner of interpretation (whether detailed and prescribed, or open and free; whether quantitative or nonquantitative; whether limited to one trait or holistic).

Other principles as well could serve as a framework of classification. The difficulty is that if we distinguish instruments according to one principle only we necessarily blind ourselves to all other equally valid principles.[1]

It is desirable, of course, to adopt as simple a scheme for classification as possible. Rosenzweig suggests ordering methods under three rubrics: the *subjective, objective,* and *projective* techniques.[2]

Under *subjective methods* he would include any form of self-report, whether in autobiography, in self-rating, in an interview, or via a pencil-and-paper personality test.

[1] Cf. G. Lindzey, On the classification of projective techniques, *Psychol. Bull.,* 1959, **56,** 158–168. Also D. T. Campbell, A typology of tests, projective and otherwise, *J. consult. Psychol.,* 1957, **21,** 207–210.

[2] S. Rosenzweig, Investigating and appraising personality. In T. G. Andrews (Ed.), *Methods of psychology* (New York: Wiley, 1948). An additional threefold scheme is advanced by Super, who chooses, as main categories for classification, *observational* methods, *projective* methods, *self-description* methods. D. E. Super, Theories and assumptions underlying approaches to personality assessment. In B. M. Bass and I. A. Berg (Eds.), *Objective approaches to personality assessment* (Princeton, N.J.: Van Nostrand, 1959), Chap. 2.

Objective methods include physiological measures as well as behavior observed in the laboratory or in everyday situations, ratings by acquaintances, and experiments of many kinds.

Projective methods are of three types: motor-expressive (e.g., gesture and handwriting), perceptive-structural (e.g., Rorschach inkblots), apperceptive-dynamic (picture interpretation, word association, and so on).

Although this simple scheme has much merit, it seems somewhat too coarse. I offer instead a minimum practical grouping of methods under eleven headings. They follow no single principle of organization, but seem to reflect fairly clearly the present situation in personality assessment. Figure 31 is a graphic tabulation of these broad, major types of method.

The number and sophistication of present-day techniques make those of a generation ago seem naïve and primitive. And the techniques in use today will seem naïve a generation hence. Yet this broad grouping of methods was valid a generation ago and may perhaps continue to serve as a *general* framework into which future inventions and improvements can be fitted.

1. Constitutional and Physiological Diagnosis

The biological correlates of personality are important. Constant research is needed in genetics, biochemistry, endocrinology, anthropometry to give us knowledge of the foundations of personality (Chapter 4). Studies of body build, of glandular and autonomic functions, of the psychogalvanic skin reflex, of electrical brain waves, of identical twins—all are in their infancy. Delicate measures of physiological functions can now be made with the aid of electronic polygraphs, and progress in the correlation of these measures with attributes of temperament is assured.[3]

Studies in heredity can be made from the family record charts employed by eugenic associations, as well as by the study of identical twins (page 70 f.). Somatotyping (pages 59–63) is a method holding promise. Electroencephalography is well advanced; it seems to be established that abnormal brain waves are frequently found in certain forms of disordered personality (especially among epileptics).

[3] A survey of physical, chemical, and physiological methods is given by R. M. Allen, *Personality assessment procedures* (New York: Harper, 1958).

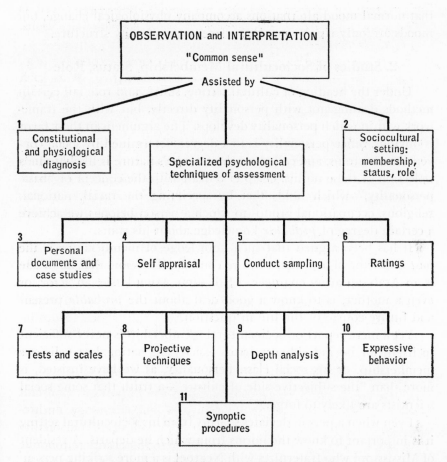

Figure 31. A Classification of Assessment Methods

Chapter 1 pointed to the vast range of biochemical individuality. If we interpret correctly the research that has been done we would say that there seems to be no known specific correlates between the activity of glands or metabolic functions and traits of *normal* personality, but that when excessive malfunctioning occurs, the personality is likely to suffer corresponding disorder. If this impression is correct we would conclude that normal personality is not regulated in detail by specific glandular or physiological functions, but that molar patterns (e.g., the somatotype) and especially gross abnormalities are reflected in personality formation. It seems also quite likely that normal mood alternations accompany physiological change, but moods are only ripples on the surface of personality structure.

2. Studies of Sociocultural Membership, Status, Role

Under the heading of cultural setting, status, and role fall certain methods dealing not with personality directly, but with the framework within which personality develops. The argument in their favor is obvious. Since personality is to a degree determined by social conventions, customs, and codes, much of a man's nature is likely to be a reflection of these norms. Chapter 8 dealt with the concept of "basic personality," which holds that by specifying the racial, national, religious, occupational groups to which a person belongs we achieve a certain degree of *probable* knowledge about his traits.

It has been argued that such knowledge of memberships is the *best* predictor of a person's future conduct. To know that he or she is an Arab, an army engineer, a Salvation Army lassie, an actor, or even a mother, is to know a good deal about the *probable* present and future course of the life in question.[4]

Yet a mere report on sociocultural membership is never sufficient in itself, for no individual mirrors exactly his national or religious membership, or his social class. Personality, as we have insisted, is more than "the subjective side of culture"—a truth that some social scientists are likely to forget.

Even when a person deviates sharply from his sociocultural setting it is important to know the norms from which he departs. A resident of Mississippi who fraternizes with Negroes is a more striking personality than is the northern white man who does the same thing. A rich man's son who becomes a socialist presents a different psychological problem from the son of a revolutionary leader who becomes a socialist. No personality is an exact replica of prevailing norms, but to understand the deviating as well as the relatively typical case, knowledge of norms and roles is needed.

[4] E. R. Guthrie asserts that knowledge of a person's memberships enables us to make a better prediction of his future conduct than measures of traits will do: Personality in terms of associative learning. In J. McV. Hunt (Ed.), *Personality and the behavior disorders* (New York: Ronald, 1944), pp. 170–213. P. F. Secord and S. M. Jourard have pointed out that male judges ascribe almost uniformly the same traits to their respective mothers—a fact that suggests there is a "basic personality" type corresponding to the mother's role: Mother concepts and judgments of young women's faces, *J. abnorm. soc. Psychol.*, 1956, **52**, 246–250.

And so a proper assessment of personality will without fail include statements regarding

    sex
    age
    occupation
    social class
    racial, national, regional memberships
    other relevant norms
    roles in the principal groups to which the person belongs

Since these studies of sociocultural setting are not the province of psychology we need not enter into a detailed discussion of methods for gathering the relevant information. For some purposes census data are employed; for other purposes, ethnological field methods, participant observation, cross-cultural files, linguistics, cultural history, interviews, and the like. All valid methods of determining the social setting of the life are admissible.

3. Personal Documents and Case Studies

We come now to methods developed within the framework of psychological (rather than biological or sociocultural) science. The first one we deal with, however, is still to some extent interdisciplinary. What we call "personal documents" are of interest not only to the psychologist but to the historian, biographer, and novelist.

We may define a *personal document* as any freely written or spoken record that intentionally or unintentionally yields information regarding the structure and dynamics of the author's life.[5] Among these we would surely include (1) autobiographies, whether comprehensive or topical; (2) diaries, whether intimate or daily log-inventories; (3) letters; (4) open-ended questionnaires (but not standardized tests); (5) verbatim recordings, including interviews, confessions, narrative; (6) certain literary compositions.

It is important to note that these are all first-person documents. In addition to these we have varieties of third-person records: case studies, life-histories, biographies.

Perhaps the first thing to determine about any first-person docu-

[5] A fuller discussion of this method will be found in G. W. Allport, *The use of personal documents in psychological science* (New York: Soc. Sci. Res. Council, Bull. No. 49, 1942).

ment is the motivation for writing it. There would seem to be at least a dozen distinguishable motives.

1. *Special pleading.* A writer may outdo himself to prove that he is more sinned against than sinning. Perhaps no autobiography is entirely free from self-justification, but the intensity of this motive varies greatly from document to document.

2. *Exhibitionism.* Closely related is the document in which egotism runs riot. The author seeks to display himself—both sins and virtues—in as vivid a light as possible. Rousseau opens his *Confessions* with the following bit of self-display: "I have entered upon a performance which is without example, whose accomplishment will have no imitator. I mean to present my fellow-mortals with a man in all the integrity of nature; and this man shall be myself. . . ."

3. *Desire for order.* Just as there are people who continually tidy their rooms and order their possessions, so there are diary keepers who cannot sleep at night until certain experiences of the day are entered in writing. This motive seems compulsive but the product may be valuable simply because it is circumstantial, as in the case of Pepys' famous diary.

4. *Literary appeal.* Many personal documents are written in an artistic form to give the author and reader a sense of symmetry and perfection. The result may be as idyllic as Selma Lagerlöf's *Mårbacka* or as vigorous as Richard Wright's *Black Boy*.

5. *Securing personal perspective.* Many sincere documents are attempts to take stock at a crossroads in life, often in middle age. H. G. Wells gives this as his prime motivation for writing *Experiment in Autobiography*.

6. *Catharsis.* Many documents are written to secure relief from tension. Documents of this type are both action-substitutes and action-silencers. The writer who cannot gain relief in action may express himself in a rush of writing.

7. *Monetary gain.* Sometimes students, the unemployed, refugees are attracted by the psychologist's offer of payment in return for autobiographical documents. Judging from productions under this incentive the quality is not necessarily compromised. But whenever cash fetches forth good documents it is

probable that the authors were attracted to the task for other reasons as well.

8. *Assignment*. In college courses students can be invited to write autobiographies. (It is bad taste to *require* such an assignment, though experience shows that given their choice of writing a case study of another person or an autobiography, about 80 percent of students chose to write about themselves.)

9. *Assisting in therapy*. A patient who produces an autobiography or other personal document for his therapist does so in order to assist in his own cure. Although documents of this type are likely to be trustworthy, they are tipped toward the side of disorder rather than to normal functioning.

10. *Redemption and social reincorporation*. The confessions of the ex-criminal, the spy, the alcoholic, the dope addict contain implicit pleas for forgiveness and social reacceptance. They are generally motivated also by a true conversion and desire to help others.

11. *Public service*. Similar are documents motivated to achieve a social or political reform. Clifford Beers in *A Mind That Found Itself* wished to improve the lot of the insane. Autobiographies of some Negroes, settlement house workers, political crusaders fall into this category.

12. *Desire for immortality*. Personal documents often reflect a man's "battle against oblivion." To be forgotten is to die a second and more complete death. This motive, though not rare, is seldom openly expressed.

13. *Scientific interest*. Cultivated individuals, including students, sometimes offer their diaries or other documents to psychologists for scientific study. While the documents were not prepared for this reason, they are released with this laudable intention.

We list this wide variety of motives simply in order to illustrate our first methodological problem. Unless we know how and why the document came into being we cannot decide how much trust to place in it, nor can we evaluate its completeness of coverage.

Even the fullest and most candid of documents suffer inherent disadvantages. The problem of early life is a serious stumbling block. No one has accurate reminiscence back to infancy, nor to the early years when, according to some theories, the guidelines of personality are fixed (pages 75–82). A person's account of his own heredity is likely to have little value. And it is also true that memory distortion occurs for later years as well as for younger. Finally it is probable that some bitter or shameful but important episodes will be kept secret even in documents that make a big show of candor and confession.

An interesting phenomenon arises in the writer's loss of perspective regarding recent events. As the recorded story approaches the present it seems to lose perspective. The account fans out, delta-wise, into many shallow channels. The writer can show the course of the past, but is confused regarding the significance of present events and experiences. It is well to stop an autobiographical composition at some definite point in the past, perhaps two or three years previous to the time of writing.

The autobiographies of children have little value. Until the age of thirteen or after, the child records events in external terms. He does not say, "I felt this . . . I thought that," but rather, "I did this . . . I did that." Subjective life grows important only as adulthood approaches.

Autobiographies, as we have said, may be comprehensive, "telling all," or may be topical, dealing with only one aspect of life. William James has made brilliant use of personal documents emphasizing only the religious experiences of "great souled persons wrestling with the crises of their fate."[6] Other authors have specialized in life-histories written with a focus on political events.[7] An interesting variation is the analysis of autobiographies of the future, written under the assigned title "My Life from Now Until the Year 2000."[8]

Thus the psychologist can elicit self-written biographical documents by varying the instructions and focusing upon matters of special interest to him. It is not uncommon to give the writer a general outline to follow so that he will not forget to include data that the investigator thinks will be of value.[9] Some psychologists, on

---

[6] W. James, *The varieties of religious experience* (New York: Longmans, Green, 1902).
[7] For example, G. W. Allport, J. S. Bruner, and E. M. Jandorf, Personality under social catastrophe: an analysis of 90 German refugee life histories, *Charact. & Pers.,* 1941, **10**, 1–22.
[8] J. M. Gillespie and G. W. Allport, *Youth's outlook on the future* (New York: Random House, 1955).
[9] Some guides of this order are listed by Allen, *op. cit.,* Chap. 16. Note 3 above.

the other hand, make systematic use of freely written autobiographies that were not intended for scientific analysis.[10]

The most personal of personal documents is the *diary*, provided the writer sets down events, thoughts, and feelings having propriate significance for himself. The diary (unless it is a mere log) is normally less constrained than the autobiography, letters, or interviews. Long-term diaries provide an excellent source for the study of continuities and shifts in personal development. Diaries usually escape the fallacy of attributing to earlier years thoughts, feelings, and interpretations appropriate only to the moment of writing. There are fewer errors of memory. There is less deliberate structuring of the record. A mere log of the weather, sports events, school grades, travel is, of course, of slight value. But the *journal intime* is perhaps the best of all subjective reporting. It is important, however, to note that diaries deal chiefly with conflicts. That which does not pose a problem receives little mention. In health a person does not write about his body; if happy with his family he takes the felicity for granted and seldom refers to it. For this reason a diary needs supplementary materials to place the entries in true perspective.

Adolescents are especially prone to keep diaries, probably more girls do so than boys. It is true that there are interruptions in the continuity; entries may be missing for months. Also, some diaries strike a pose for the benefit of possible future readers. Finally, the intimate journal takes much for granted, and may fail to describe persons or situations, knowledge of which the diarist merely assumes.

In spite of its limitations the idiographic study of a single diary, or the comparative (nomothetic) study of several, provides an important channel into lives as actually lived.[11]

Diaries, someone has said, have only one parent, whereas *letters* have two: the writer and the recipient. But like diaries, personal letters—provided they have not been written with an eye to publication—are always interesting. Perhaps their fascination lies in the fact

[10] E.g., G. W. Allport, The study of personality by the intuitive method: an experiment in teaching from *The Locomotive God, J. abnorm. soc. Psychol.*, 1929, **24**, 14–27.

[11] In a review of 120 English diaries Ponsonby reports that women writers seem more cautious than men, but that women have a tendency to write voluminously if they write at all. He also notes the frequency with which religion is a topic of concern, no doubt because diaries deal with the "inside half" of a life. A. Ponsonby, *English diaries* (London: Methuen, 1923). Examples of the use psychologists make of diaries are contained in G. W. Allport, *The use of personal documents in psychological science*, Chap. 8. Note 5 above.

that when we were children we were punished for reading other people's letters—an offense like putting one's eye to a keyhole. The existence of this taboo betrays the fact that letters, like diaries, are intimate. Unlike diaries, however, personal letters raise the problem of the dyadic relationship, the tie between two personalities.

Up to now psychologists have made less use of correspondence than of diaries, probably because of the various social complications that enter into letter writing. It is not easy to come by a series of letters in which self-revelation is spontaneous and continued, and not varied for the benefit of different recipients.

On page 368 we referred to one particularly successful analysis of this type. A. I. Baldwin worked with a large and revealing collection of letters from a widow written during the last eleven years of her life. The letters set forth her abnormal attachment to her son, the story of his death and of her loneliness. The investigator employed a method of determining how frequently any two classes of ideas were related in the writer's mind (i.e., mentioned in the same context). A portrait resulted of a dramatic personality, esthetically sensitive, scrupulous in financial matters, possessive of her son's affection, suspicious and paranoid regarding women.

This study is of importance, representing as it does, a contribution to the exact (quantitative) analysis of the structure of the unique single personality on the basis of personal documents. It sets forth a new conception of "population" for statistics: a population of events and traits within the boundaries of one person.[12]

In using personal documents (including the types we have not described—open questionnaires, verbatim recordings, literary productions) the psychologist, as we have said, strives to go *beyond common sense*. Anyone, of course, can read these documents and form interpretations in the common-sense way. The psychologist, however, uses special devices. The investigation just described does

12 A. L. Baldwin, Personal structure analysis: a statistical method for investigating the single personality, *J. abnorm. soc. Psychol.*, 1942, **37**, 163–183. Essentially the same method has been applied to the analysis of a diary by T. G. Andrews and G. Muhlhan, Analysis of congruent idea patterns as a study in personality, *Charact. & Pers.*, 1943, **12**, 101–110.

so, the technique being called "personal structure analysis." Other forms of content analysis may be used to determine the exact frequency with which certain ideas or themes occur. The psychologist will also try to determine whether the documents he uses are trustworthy and typical of the person; he will want to know whether other analysts will make the same interpretations that he himself makes. In short, the basic tests of reliability and validity will be employed so far as practicable. He will also spend considerable effort to find the central traits (ideational systems, constructs) that are revealed in the material before him.

G. A. Kelly believes that one can control to advantage the production and analysis of personal documents by asking the subject to write about himself but in the third person. The instructions are: "I want you to write a character sketch of (subject's own name is inserted here), just as if he were the principal character in a play. Write it as it might be written by a friend who knew him very *intimately* and very *sympathetically*, perhaps better than anyone ever really could know him. Be sure to write it in the third person. For example, start out by saying, '(Subject's own name) is . . .' "

Having obtained documents in this way Kelly proceeds to give rules for analyzing the product in terms of areas of interest, themes, views (constructs) of the world.[13]

Turning from first-person documents to third, we enter the large field of *case studies* and *life-histories*. Psychiatrists, clinical psychologists, social workers, employment managers, college deans, magazine writers, and members of other professions—all try their hands at writing up cases or life-histories. Properly done, the product is very revealing. Badly done, it becomes a meaningless chronology, a confusion of fact and fiction, of guesswork and misinterpretation.

The content of any case is limited by the purpose of the writer. The social worker's case may be overbalanced by facts pertaining to family budgets and to health; a probation officer is interested chiefly in whereabouts and misconduct; the employment manager stresses ability; the clinician tells more about illness than about health;

13 G. A. Kelly, *Psychology of personal constructs* (2 vols.; New York: Norton, 1955), Vol. I, Chap. 7.

biographers for popular magazines sometimes produce exciting distortions. Yet taken in its purest form, the case study is part of the art of biography.[14]

There are many suggestions for the writing of a good case study.[15] The difficulty with these suggestions is that since individuality is never repeated, the form of a study must vary. It is not possible to prescribe in detail the information that it shall include or the exact manner in which it shall be presented.

A case study, of course, is a comprehensive framework into which all relevant and significant data pertaining to a single life are compiled and arranged. It is a device for avoiding an embarrassing mass of test scores, items of past history, and unrelated fragments of information. It has the advantage also of keeping attention riveted upon a single concrete life—where the psychologist's attention should be riveted more often than it is. When many cases are in hand various comparisons may be made (e.g., concerning the differences in personality among members of social classes or among people with contrasting national, racial, or developmental backgrounds).

If two investigators each write a case study of a single person they are likely to agree on *what* has happened in the life far better than on *why* it happened. To interpret the causal relationships is difficult, and constitutes the problem of *conceptualization*. A writer wishes to make "theoretical sense" of the life he is describing. He implicitly conceptualizes whenever he selects material for inclusion, and he does so by classifying or grouping his statements. He then explicitly conceptualizes by stating relationships among acts ("So and so has such interests, habits, attitudes, traits"). He does so also when he infers causal relations among environmental forces, among the person's motives, defenses, early experiences, and the like. Or he may conceptualize deliberately in terms of his favorite psychological theory (psychoanalysis, need theory, learning theory).

When is a conceptualization correct? This is the most difficult question we could ask. If we could answer it successfully we would

14 On the history of biography and its overlapping relation with psychology see J. A. Garraty, *The nature of biography* (New York: Knopf, 1957). Also H. Thomae, Die biographische Methode in den anthropologischen Wissenschaften. *Stud. gen.*, 1952, **5**, 163–177. For an example of psychological analysis of literary biography see R. K. White, *Black Boy: a value analysis, J. abnorm. soc. Psychol.*, 1947, **42**, 440–461.

15 E.g., J. Dollard, *Criteria for the life-history* (New Haven, Conn.: Yale Univ. Press, 1935); G. W. Allport, *Personality: a psychological interpretation* (New York: Holt, Rinehart and Winston, 1937), pp. 390–398; D. C. McClelland, *Personality* (New York: Sloane, 1951), especially Part 5.

have our hands on the secret of validation. The truth of the matter is that we have no sure way of telling whether our interpretation (conceptualization) is wholly accurate. (As remarked in Chapter 1, literary interpreters do not worry about this matter, but psychologists must.)

Let us list briefly the principal tests by which the psychologist can attempt to assess the validity of his interpretation:

1. *Feelings of subjective certainty.* The illuminative power of an interpretation for the investigator who propounds (or accepts) it is by no means an adequate proof of its validity. Yet subjective certainty of this sort is perhaps the test we most commonly employ, and it is not altogether worthless.

2. *Conformity with known facts.* Obviously the interpretation we offer must be relevant to the facts of the case, and no important facts should remain unaccounted for in our theorizing about the life.

3. *Mental experimentation.* We try to imagine the life without the presence of some crucial factor, or without the formative process that we think is important. If the "experiment" succeeds, then the factor or our hypothesis is wrong. A conceptualization can be right only if we cannot even imagine the life being what it is without this crucial interpretation.

4. *Predictive power.* If an interpretation enables us to make successful predictions about the life, then it is presumably valid; but we must beware lest we assume that our theory was essential for the correct prediction. (The ancient Greeks predicted that the sun would rise tomorrow because Apollo never failed to drive his chariot.)

5. *Social agreement.* If many people, especially experts, accept an explanation, there is presumption of its validity. Yet, here are pitfalls, since there are fashions in concepts, and prestige-suggestion may play a part. The criterion is better if investigators have come *independently* to the same conclusion.

An extension of this test is to submit the conceptualization to the subject himself. If he (who knows the "inside half") accepts it, the chance of its being a correct explanation is enhanced.

6. *Internal consistency.* Parts of an interpretation can be made to confront one another. Logical contradictions raise the suspicion of invalidity. Granted that lives are not wholly consistent, yet

interpretations should certainly not be more complex than the life itself. The closer one comes to the "radix" of a life (page 365) the more valid the interpretation will be.

From this list we have omitted the purely authoritarian test of correctness. Simply because an interpretation is orthodox Freudian or Marxist or behaviorist does not automatically make it right.

The difficulty of interpreting personal documents and case histories has been emphasized in order to show fairly why many psychologists will have no truck with such "loose" methods. To some they seem subscientific. Certain it is that we have far to go in learning how to use them as tools in personality assessment. As yet we cannot honestly say that psychologists have learned to analyze documents or to write histories in a way that surely leads them beyond the level of accuracy achieved by unaided common sense.[16]

And yet who can deny that a life-history is precisely what we are talking about when we speak of human personality? To leave out the total ground is unthinkable. Terman, who devoted his life to testing, correctly said, "A true picture of personality cannot be pieced together from any number of test scores. A total is an organismic, not an additive, total."[17] More recently Dailey has expressed dissatisfaction with fragmented methods of research because they cannot be interpreted correctly apart from the "mainstream of personal life" as revealed in the life-history.[18] The life-history is, after all, the basic criterion against which all other methods should be tested.

4. Self-appraisal

Under this heading we include all methods that invite the individual to report explicitly and deliberately concerning selected aspects of his own personality.[19]

Self-rating. If you ask a friend whether he is above average, about

16 Cf. P. E. Meehl, *Clinical vs. statistical prediction* (Minneapolis: Univ. of Minnesota Press, 1954).
17 L. M. Terman, The measurement of personality, *Science*, 1934, **80**, 605–608.
18 C. A. Dailey, The life history as a criterion of assessment, *J. consult. Psychol.*, 1960, **7**, 20–23.
19 Immediately we discover that our scheme of classification—like all schemes—is faulty. On page 407 Kelly's method of eliciting a personal document was described. This procedure is clearly a self-appraisal, but because of its "wide-open" character it is included under autobiography. Also when we come to *tests* (Chapter 18) we shall be dealing likewise with a type of self-appraisal, although not as explicit and deliberate as the methods we are now considering.

average, or below average on some common trait (perhaps aggression, humor, or sociability) he will have no trouble telling you—perhaps correctly or perhaps incorrectly. You can also complicate the procedure by asking him to employ highly elaborate types of rating scales (pages 418–420). In either case self-rating is the most direct method of obtaining quantitative self-appraisal.

The method has one persistent source of error. Most people are self-flattering; they overestimate those qualities they consider desirable and underestimate those they consider undesirable. At least this tendency is marked for most self-ratings in the American culture where self-confidence is encouraged. In some foreign countries, perhaps especially in the Orient, a "set" of modesty or self-effacement leads to the opposite type of error. Among German subjects Becker finds that a self-rating is usually a compromise between what a person's conduct is and what he wishes it to be; i.e., self-rating falls somewhere between the real state of affairs and the self-conceived ideal.[20]

Although self-ratings tend to be weighted with self-flattery, or occasionally with self-abnegation, we cannot assume they are worthless. Some people have good insight and objectify themselves very well. Even if the results cannot be fully relied upon it is important to know what the self-image is, if for no other reason than to discover how blind the subject is when his self-rating is compared with the results of other diagnostic methods.

Sometimes a simple self-appraisal turns out to be the best of all methods of assessment. During World War II an experienced psychiatrist discovered in working with draftees that the best diagnostic device was the simple question, "Do you think you are emotionally ready to take Army service?" Most of those who said "No" were, in fact, very bad risks. This direct report seems to have screened inductees better than did tests or scales.

W-A-Y Technique. A very different and specialized method of self-appraisal asks subjects to write three short answers to the direct question, "Who are you?"[21] This simple task elicits a wide variety of

[20] Cf. Allport, *Personality: a psychological interpretation*, pp. 444 f; Note 15, above. See also H. Becker, Selbsterkenntnis und Fremderkenntnis, *Psychol. Forsch.*, 1954, **24**, 399–459.

[21] J. F. T. Bugental and S. L. Zelen, Investigations into the self-concept: I. The W-A-Y technique, *J. Pers.*, 1950, **18**, 483–498.

responses. Some people give humdrum answers, perhaps writing their name, occupation, and nationality. Others may write more revealing statements: "I am a person with a destiny to fulfill but who is uncertain of his strength for the task." "I am the girl Jim loves." Just what to make of these varied answers is not clear, but in some cases important information concerning identifications and images of oneself come to light.

Q-Sort. Another method of eliciting the self-image is to present the subject with many (perhaps 100) statements written on cards, and ask him to sort them into piles according to their "fit." The statements may be of any type desired by the investigator. For example,

> Feels insecure
> Is religious
> Communicates easily with others
> Is rigid: inflexible in thought and action

The inventor of the method, W. Stephenson, recommends the use of eleven piles, requiring the subject to place a prescribed number of statements in each pile (in order to force him to make fine distinctions in his self-appraisal). If 100 statements are employed the prescribed distribution might be:

	MOST DESCRIPTIVE OF SELF									LEAST DESCRIPTIVE OF SELF	
Pile	1	2	3	4	5	6	7	8	9	10	11
Number of cards	2	4	8	11	16	18	16	11	8	4	2

The device has the advantage of wide coverage (many qualities and traits) and of forcing the subject to decide which are central, which secondary, and which nonexistent in his personality. The method does not prevent subjects from claiming the most flattering attributes as their own; but it is particularly valuable in studying the change of self-image over time, especially if used before and after a period of counseling or psychotherapy.[22]

22 W. Stephenson, *The study of behavior* (Chicago: Univ. of Chicago Press, 1953). See also C. R. Rogers and R. F. Dymond (Eds.), *Psychotherapy and personality change* (Chicago: Univ. of Chicago Press, 1954).

Self-anchoring Scale. The self-anchoring scale offers a unique measure of a person's satisfaction with his situation in life. The authors, Kilpatrick and Cantril, employ a wholly idiographic procedure.[23] They seek first to elicit from the subject a statement regarding his own "very best or ideal way of life." The subject may indicate, for example, that for his ideal situation he would want good health, more material possessions, satisfaction in his job, and domestic felicity. The subject is then asked to describe what he would consider the very worst way of life for himself. He might reply by mentioning poverty, dependency, illness, moral degradation. Having thus anchored the extreme ends of his own "reality world" he is asked to imagine himself on a ladder, standing somewhere between the worst and the ideal extremes. He is shown the diagram in Figure 32 and asked, "Where on this ladder would you say you are now?"

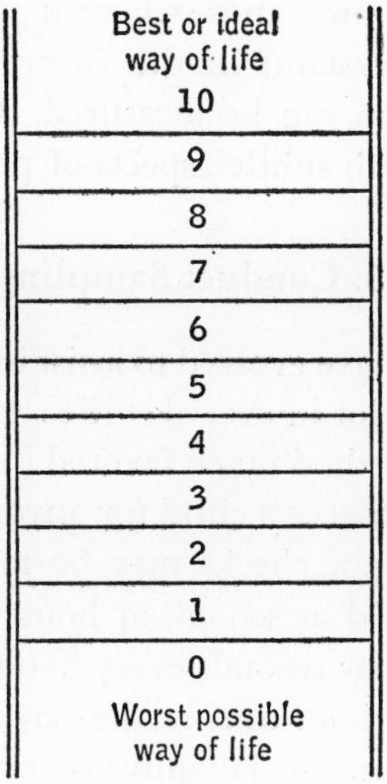

Best or ideal way of life
10
9
8
7
6
5
4
3
2
1
0
Worst possible way of life

Figure 32. The Ladder Scale

[23] F. P. Kilpatrick and H. Cantril, Self-anchoring scaling: a measure of individual's unique reality worlds, *J. indiv. Psychol.*, 1960, **16**, 158–170. An earlier approach to the "reality world" technique is the *philo-phobe*, a questionnaire that asks, among other matters, "What would you rather have than anything else in all the world?" "What would be your second choice?" "What are you most afraid of?" "What is the most unpleasant feeling you have ever had?" J. N. Buck, Personality appraisement by use of the philo-phobe, *Amer. J. ment. Deficiency*, 1943, **47**, 437–444.

He can also be asked, "Where on this scale were you two years ago?" "five years ago?" "Where do you think you will be five years hence?"

The method has the advantage of anchoring the scale at top and bottom in terms of the person's own values, goals, and fears. It thus employs a self-defined continuum. In using it a picture is obtained of the distress or depression, of the happiness and hope in a given life. Important, too, is the trend that is noted: does the person feel he is gaining or losing ground?

Used in this fashion the method is, as we have said, wholly idiographic. It does, however, yield important nomothetic data. The authors find, for example, that there are ethnic, occupational, and national differences in the depressed or hopeful outlooks of members of such groups. The method may also be shifted to nonpersonal judgments. Thus, the subject may be asked to describe the best and worst conditions possible for his nation; and then to judge where on the ladder the nation now stands, where it stood five years ago, and where it will probably stand in the future. In this way national optimism and pessimism can be measured. The method is versatile and deals effectively with subtle aspects of personal value.

5. Conduct Sampling

Several techniques have evolved to assist in the systematic observation of a person's behavior in everyday life situations.

Time-sample is a method much favored in the study of children.[24] Since it is difficult to observe a child (or anyone) continuously over a long period of time, spot checks may be made of his behavior at chosen intervals. A child at school, at home, or on the playground can be observed for a few seconds every five minutes, or perhaps for five minutes at stated times during the day. Whether he is idle or active, leading or following, laughing or crying, playing with materials or with children can easily be determined. In the long run a convincing picture of his preferred patterns can be developed. Since an adult's behavior is less spontaneous than a child's—restricted as it is by prescribed duties—the method is less applicable. A variation,

24 R. G. Barker, J. Kounin, and H. F. Wright (Eds.), *Child behavior and development* (New York: McGraw-Hill, 1943). See also R. G. Barker and H. F. Wright, *One boy's day*. (New York: Harper, 1951).

however, has been invented for adults: the *time-budget* whereby an
adult keeps a record for later analysis of the amount of time each day
he spends in various forms of activity, including recreation.[25]

Miniature Situations. With a bit of ingenuity we can compress
the sprawly situations of everyday life into a smaller scope. The
would-be pilot of an airplane need not be tried out in a real flight;
he can be screened for his fitness in the laboratory with the aid of
tests of equilibrium, visual acuity, and coordination. Psychotechnics
has developed countless "vocational miniatures" that help to assess
fitness for many types of occupation by presenting the subject with a
cameo edition of the full vocational pattern.[26] An employment officer
had a custom of placing a magazine on the floor of the waiting room
and noting whether the prospective applicant would replace it on the
table. Perhaps this is an unsafe test for neatness and orderliness, but
it illustrates what is meant by a "miniature."

An elaborate use of the method was made by the *Character Education Inquiry,* which presented to children miniature life-situations
in which they were tempted to steal pennies or to cheat on a problem,
and in other ways to betray vices or virtues. In Chapter 13 we discussed the findings and limitations of this particular study.

During World War II an intensive miniature situation was developed. Applicants for secret-service work spent a three-day session
at an isolated estate. During this "house party" they encountered
many assignments, tests, and interviews—and were constantly observed—to determine their personal fitness for the exacting work.
They were tested for their leadership ability, for their ability to resist
frustration and acute stress, even for their tolerance for alcohol. One
might say that all the future demands on their personality were tested
with the aid of an intensive miniature situation.[27] The house party
method has been adapted to cover the selection of military personnel,

25 P. A. Sorokin and C. Q. Berger, *Time-budgets of human behavior* (Cambridge, Mass.:
Harvard Univ. Press, 1939). A method that combines the time-budget and an interpretive
daily diary is described by B. Pauleikhoff, Die Tageslaufanalyse als Methode zur
Untersuchung der Persönlichkeit in ihrer Situation, *Z. f. Psychother. u. med. Psychol.,*
1960, **10,** 140–157.

26 The use of situational tests is described by Anne Anastasi, *Psychological testing* (New
York: Macmillan, 1954), Chap. 23.

27 OSS Assessment Staff, *Assessment of men: selection of personnel for the Office of
Strategic Services* (New York: Holt, Rinehart and Winston, 1948).

and also of members of the clergy. It is useful for other purposes where intensive assessment is desired.[28]

Whenever multiple examiners are involved, as is necessarily the case in prolonged sessions such as those just described, it is customary for them to confer in a *diagnostic council*.[29] Here they are allowed to pool their judgments (and also check for their agreement). The resulting assessment has the advantage of being a consensus of experts, and not merely a fragmentary judgment of one examiner.

Laboratory Experiments. I do not mean to imply that subjects are brought to an assessment center or to a psychological laboratory only for the purpose of an intensive and comprehensive diagnosis. They may be brought in for a single experiment. Any experiment dealing with personality is intended to be a miniature and controlled life-situation. To the layman the experiment may seem artificial, but to the psychologist it is an attempt to capture typical behavior under strictly controlled conditions. The range of possible experiments relevant to personality is enormous. In Chapter 11 we mentioned many examples dealing with proceptive tendencies—whether, for example, an individual tends to be *field-dependent* or *field-independent* in handling his visual perceptions. This important cognitive disposition could scarcely be determined except under controlled laboratory conditions. Experiments range widely and profitably over many regions besides the cognitive. Physiological functions require laboratory conditions. Dominance, leadership, sympathy, repression, frustration tolerance, conformity, special skills are among the legion of functions that can be assessed in contrived laboratory situations.

The Interview. In a sense interviewing is a miniature situation which seeks to secure verbally as much information of a personal nature as is relevant to the purposes of the interviewer. Verbal conduct is elicited in as brief and efficient a manner as possible. It is true, of course, that some form of interviewing may be auxiliary to all major methods of studying personality. But it can be, and often is, used as the primary technique. In psychological counseling, in

28 The work of the Personality Assessment Center at the University of California is of this order. A typical publication is F. Barron, *Personal soundness in university graduate students* (Berkeley: Univ. of California Press, 1954).
29 On the use of the diagnostic council see H. A. Murray, *et al., Explorations in personality* (New York: Oxford, 1938). Also M. B. Smith, J. S. Bruner, and R. W. White, *Opinions and personality* (New York: Wiley, 1956).

psychotherapy, and in some forms of guidance, it is the only method employed. It is used for both diagnosis and for therapy.

Most writers agree that interviewing is an art. It is clear, however, that the skills involved are to some extent teachable.[30] At the very least the interviewer can be warned against certain pitfalls. He must be a good listener, for if he does the talking he will not learn about the motivations, aspirations, conflicts, and defenses that are important aspects of the other's personality. His own biases and stereotypes are obstacles to be guarded against. Skill in framing questions can be learned.[31]

Interviews may be totally unstructured and random, they may be "focused" upon one aspect of the subject's life, or they may follow a strict question-answer form. For the purpose of learning as much as possible concerning the interviewee it is well to have at least a rough schedule to follow, though the order in which questions are asked is not ordinarily important. The interviewer may, for example, wish to follow some such general guide as the following:

1. age
2. nationality and cultural background
3. degree and type of education
4. sickness and accidents
5. occupational history and plans
6. hobbies and recreation
7. cultural interests
8. ambitions (e.g., what he hopes to accomplish within the next few years)
9. personal attachments (who influences him most)
10. daydreams
11. fears and worries
12. humiliations and disappointments
13. marked aversions
14. sex experience
15. neurotic difficulties
16. religious experience
17. philosophy of life

[30] W. V. Bingham and B. V. Moore, *How to interview* (3d ed.; New York: Harper, 1941); H. H. Hyman, *et al.*, *Interviewing in social research* (Chicago: Univ. of Chicago Press, 1954).
[31] S. L. Payne, *The art of asking questions* (Princeton, N.J.: Princeton Univ. Press, 1951).

Such a guide guarantees that important information concerning biological and sociocultural factors will come to light. It also includes items that permit one to understand the dynamics and future trend of the life. The interviewer may, of course, discover that the subject is reticent or evasive. If his evasiveness is extreme, the interviewer may have to abandon the method—or seek improvement in his own skill.

6. Ratings

Rating is a formal estimate of the strength of one or more qualities in a personality made upon the basis of direct acquaintance with that personality. Teachers, army officers, personnel directors, supervisors are among those who use ratings extensively for practical purposes. Even psychologists, in spite of their distrust of subjective judgments, are forced to rely time and again upon ratings as basic criteria in their investigations.

Ratings yield quantitative comparisons of people in respect to one variable at a time. It is a tool for the study of common traits—a device of differential psychology. There are basically two types of rating scales: the *scoring* and the *ranking*.

Scoring Scales. In a scoring scale the rater assigns a score without directly comparing the subject with other people in a defined group. To be sure, in order to make a quantitative judgment the rater requires some frame of comparison, but generally it is the "general population" he has in mind. To put his judgments upon a scale the rater uses whatever units are prescribed. It may be a percentage scale with 100 intervals. (If so, the rater usually finds that he cannot use so fine a scale and tends to employ round numbers, e.g., 60%, 70%, 80%. If a 10-point scale is used there is a curious tendency to favor odd numbers; 5, 7, 9, being popular.) Some evidence exists for saying that the *seven*-point scale is optimum for ratings of the scoring type. Scales with more than seven intervals demand a high degree of discrimination that lowers the reliability among raters. Fewer intervals are too coarse.[32]

[32] See Allport, *Personality: a psychological interpretation*, p. 438; Note 15 above. For a general survey of rating methods see P. E. Vernon, *Personality tests and assessments* (London: Methuen, 1953), Chap. 7. Also L. W. Ferguson, *Personality measurement* (New York: McGraw-Hill, 1952), Chaps. 10 and 11.

A *graphic rating* scale is a variant of the scoring scale. The judge makes as fine a discrimination as he chooses, placing a mark upon a straight line anywhere he wishes between the extreme of low and high. Figure 33 gives an example. In practice, however, since the graphic scale is more finely graduated than is warranted by its accuracy, it is always reconverted by the investigator into a small number of arithmetical units.

Still another variant of the scoring scale that has achieved recent popularity is the *adjective check-list*. The rater is asked merely to check in a list of qualities those which are characteristic of the subject. Such a list might begin with *absent-minded* and continue through *zany*.[33] Here we have, in effect, a two-interval scoring scale: a term checked signifying the presence of the trait; not checked, its absence. This simple check-list technique can, of course, be used in self-appraisal as well as in rating others.[34]

Ranking. The second major form of rating is used when a group of associated individuals are to be rated in relation to one another. We can take a class of students (if not too large) and place them in order according to their grades for the course. We can also, if we wish, place them in rank-order according to such variables as extraversion, self-insight, cooperativeness, sociability, and the like. In such a scale there are no true arithmetical units, since it is impossible to

Motivation					
	apathetic	vacillating	usually purposeful	effectively motivated	highly motivated
Influence on others					
	negative	cooperative	sometimes influential	effective in important affairs	always a leader
Disposition					
	usually unpleasant	up and down	even-tempered	cheerful	euphoric

Figure 33. Excerpts from a Graphic Rating Scale

33 H. G. Gough, *The adjective check list* (Berkeley: Univ. of California Press, 1952). Also by the same author, The adjective check list as a personality assessment research technique, *Psychol. Rep.* 1960, **6**, 107–122.
34 Cf. T. R. Sarbin and B. G. Rosenberg, Contributions to role-taking theory: IV. A method for obtaining a qualitative estimate of the self, *J. soc. Psychol.*, 1955, **42**, 71–81.

demonstrate that the intervals between successive individuals in the rank-order are equal. The usefulness of the ranking method is limited to such studies as employ a single group of individuals and require no units other than the serial positions of these subjects. The method is not applicable to large groups of subjects because concrete person-to-person comparisons cannot then be made. Persons who stand extremely high or low in a group on some common trait are likely to be reliably ranked, but those in between receive their ranks almost by guesswork.

Precautions. The use of rating scales, though very common in the world of business, education, and psychological research, is beset with pitfalls. All manner of errors and subjective bias can destroy their value. Perhaps the chief weakness is the tendency to give over-generous ratings (a trap for scoring scales but not for ranking, since even a choir of angels will have its least favored member).

The fallacy of generosity is found especially in the rating of friends, but also in the ratings of one's associates, of members of one's own sex, of one's own students. Compliments are paid to those belonging to in-groups more readily than to those belonging to out-groups. Yet many raters are softhearted even about strangers.

Akin to the complimentary fallacy is the "halo effect." We tend to have a general attitude toward a person; we like him or we dislike him in general. When we are asked to rate specific qualities we are influenced by this general set.[35] Thus a college teacher who believes that George is a generally good student is likely to fill out a rating blank (perhaps for medical school admission) ascribing to George high ratings in integrity, bedside manner, and leadership, although the teacher has in fact no knowledge about these particular qualities.

Although it is not possible to eradicate completely these sources of error, they can be minimized (1) by warning against them, (2) by employing clearly defined variables, (3) by using a scale that requires a wide spread of ratings, (4) by avoiding censorious terms, (5) by

---

35 The term *halo effect* suggests the luminous disc found in religious paintings. It is not the best term, therefore, to describe the failure of judges to make discriminating ratings. Sometimes, for example, antagonism to a person will lead uniformly (and erroneously) to low ratings on all desirable qualities. A better label for the rater's tendency to make a constant level of judgment regardless of the trait considered would be *perseveration error.* See G. J. Dudycha, A note on the "halo effect" in ratings, *J. soc. Psychol.,* 1942, **15,** 331–333.

so varying the presentation of the traits that a fresh consideration of each is demanded, (6) by avoiding haste and perfunctoriness in making the ratings, and (7) by averaging together the ratings of several judges so that individual prejudices may cancel out.

At best, ratings are secondhand. They endeavor to discover what a person is by asking friends or associates. Ratings rest, therefore, on reputation, and reputation is at one remove from personality. But often—especially in industry, in the armed services, and sometimes even in the psychological laboratory—ratings afford the only evidence we can obtain. In speaking of "reputation" John Locke said, "Though it be not the true principle and measure of virtue . . . yet it is that which comes nearest to it."[36] Though second-best, ratings have their uses.

[36] Some thoughts concerning education. In C. W. Eliot (Ed.), *Harvard Classics* (New York: Collier, 1910), XXXVII, 44.

CHAPTER 18

A Survey of Methods (Continued)

7. TESTS AND SCALES • 8. PROJECTIVE TECHNIQUES • 9. DEPTH ANALYSIS • 10. EXPRESSIVE BEHAVIOR • 11. SYNOPTIC PROCEDURES • SAFEGUARDS IN ASSESSMENT • ARE SO MANY METHODS NEEDED? • A MEASURE OF VALUES • CONCLUSION TO CHAPTERS 17 AND 18.

WE are now considering various analytic aids employed in the psychological study of personality. *Analysis,* as was pointed out in Chapter 13, means to loosen or unbind. The task of every science is to look at its assigned subject matter *in detail.*

So far as personality is concerned, all methods of analysis raise this haunting problem: Are the dimensions or elements we take such pains to analyze out of the total fabric of personality really *parts* of the life as actually lived, or are they artificial constructs? My own view is that in studying common traits (and most methods lead to common traits as defined in Chapter 14) we must rest content with mere *approximations* to the structure of the individual personality. A few methods, to be sure, focus directly on personal dispositions and on the internal consistency of a single life. But most methods yield only scores by which one individual can be compared with others. Such a procedure is perfectly legitimate, for common traits are useful constructs in comparing people, but they are not necessarily real *parts* of persons. That is to say, they cannot be readily synthesized into the prior living pattern.

Having pointed to this limitation, we now continue our survey of methods, starting with the most popular of all—the pencil-and-paper test for common traits.

7. Tests and Scales

The number of common traits that psychologists have identified and attempted to measure is very large—just how large we cannot say.[1]

One investigator, R. D. Mann, set himself the task of finding how many personality traits had been studied in connection with small-group research. He found five hundred. More than half of these had to do with seven major trait-areas: *intelligence, personal adjustment, extraversion, dominance, masculinity, conservatism, interpersonal sensitivity*.[2]

But small groups are only one of many settings where traits are studied. If we should review all investigations of social attitudes, values, abnormal dispositions, and traits relevant to industry, business, education, religion—we should extend the list enormously.

In Chapter 14 we reported that the English language contains approximately eighteen thousand trait-names. Psychologists have not yet presumed to measure *all* of these (and we hope they never will); but they have invented for measurement many additional dimensions not in the English lexicon (Factors S T D C R, mollity-durity, *n* defendance, and the like).

However one accounts for this tumult of testing, it is surely a tribute to the inventiveness of the psychologist and to the patience of the public. Both parties seem to like personality tests as much as they like parlor games.

[1] Extensive, but not complete, lists are contained in O. K. Buros, *The fifth mental measurements yearbook* (Highland Park, N.J.: Gryphon, 1959). Also, E. B. Greene, *Measurement of human behavior* (Rev. ed.; New York: Odyssey, 1952).
[2] R. D. Mann, Personality and performance in small groups, *Psychol. Bull.*, 1959, **56**, 241–270.

Personality testing grew out of intelligence testing. The success of Binet and other pioneers in measuring intelligence (the IQ) early in the twentieth century gave impetus to the measurement of non-intellectual dispositions. Within a generation after Binet, several such scales were in existence, some of which endure today. A personality test is an abbreviated standard experiment designed to measure some basic feature or features of a subject's personality in comparison with a normative population.

Here we will consider only standardized questionnaires (pencil-and-paper tests). Behavioral (as opposed to verbal) tests are more commonly encountered in connection with conduct sampling (pages 414–418), projective techniques (pages 437–445), and expressive movement (Chapter 19).

Since it is impossible to describe the hundreds (more likely, thousands) of scales in existence, we shall arbitrarily select a few samples —first to illustrate *single-trait* scales and then *multidimensional* scales.

Psychoneurotic Inventory. One of the earliest tests had an entirely practical purpose. During World War I the United States Army wanted a screening device (to supplement the Army intelligence test) that would identify draftees or recruits who might suffer breakdown under stress. R. S. Woodworth designed a "Personal Data Sheet" that asked many direct questions requiring only a simple "Yes" or "No" answer.[3] One hundred sixteen of these items were found to be of some value, and served as a model for many subsequent questionnaires of the type. Sample questions were:

> Do you feel tired most of the time?
> Do you make friends easily?
> Do you feel like jumping off when you are on high places?

We note first that such items have "face validity," that is to say, one has an immediate hunch that they may distinguish between neurotic and normal people. To validate the test more soundly it is necessary to see whether genuine neurotic cases give a larger number of un-favorable answers than do normal people. In this case it turned out that on the average neurotics gave thirty-six unfavorable answers, whereas the average score for normal men was only ten. Thus we see that there is some *probability* (though no certainty) that a high score

3 R. S. Woodworth, *Personal data sheet* (Chicago: C. H. Stoelting, 1919).

on the scale may indicate nervous instability, and therefore a poor military risk.

Later developments (especially in World War II) improved the screening power of the test. The Cornell Index, used mainly at induction stations, was able to predict that 50 percent of all men with a score of more than twenty-three unfavorable answers would be subsequently rejected for service on psychiatric grounds.[4]

Another variation seeks to mask the real purpose of the test by using a forced-choice form.[5] The examinee must choose between two alternatives, both of which seem to him "bad." One item, however, is known to be symptomatic of maladjustment, the other not. For example:

> I often have a feeling that things are not real.
> I often have trouble making up my mind.

When the diagnostic items are masked in this way it is thought that the examinee is less able to "fake" the test.

Surveying the diagnostic value of these and like instruments in eighty-four different investigations, Ellis concludes that in fifty-eight studies the inventory was successful in discriminating psychoneurotic from normal populations, but unsuccessful in twenty-six investigations.[6] This type of finding is typical of results with personality tests —broadly speaking. In *general* there is demonstrable validity in the scale, but in *some* cases the test falls wide of the mark. When it is applied to a single individual we therefore conclude that a test may sometimes measure what it purports to measure, but sometimes not. For this reason marked caution is needed before scores are accepted at their face value. We should always look for additional sources of supporting evidence and never rely on a single measuring instrument.

Ascendance-Submission. Another early single-trait test deals with the habitual role a person takes in his social relationships. Does he tend to dominate and lead, or to yield and follow? In other words, is he characteristically in the "active voice" or the "passive voice," or is he somewhere in between? (See page 338.)

---

[4] A. Weider, *et al., Cornell index* and *Manual* (New York: Psychological Corp., 1948).
[5] W. C. Shipley, F. E. Gray, and N. Newbert, The personal inventory—its derivation and validation, *J. clin. Psychol.,* 1946, **2,** 318–322.
[6] A. Ellis, Recent research with personality inventories, *J. consult. Psychol.,* 1953, **17,** 45–49. The practical utility of such screening procedures in the military services is reported likewise by C. W. Bray, *Psychology and military proficiency* (Princeton, N.J.: Princeton Univ. Press, 1948).

The full logic of the scale is presented elsewhere.[7] Sample items from the *A-S Reaction Study* appear on page 338. Additional illustrative items with score values are given below. Each seeks to assess the individual's tendency to dominate his associates or be dominated by them in face-to-face contacts of everyday life.

Someone tries to push ahead of you in line. You have been waiting for some time, and can't wait much longer. Suppose the intruder is of the same sex as yourself, do you usually

remonstrate with the intruder	(+2)
"look daggers" at the intruder or make clearly audible comments to your neighbor	(−2)
decide not to wait and go away	(−3)
do nothing	(−2)

Do you feel self-conscious in the presence of superiors in the academic or business world?

markedly	(−4)
somewhat	(0)
not at all	(+2)

Have you haggled over prices with tradesmen or junk men?

frequently	(+2)
occasionally	(0)
never	(−1)

Most of the items draw on recollections of actual behavior rather than on feelings, and for this reason are less subjective and more reliable. Note that the scale tries to sample behavior in a wide variety of daily situations.

The question arises how shall such items be scored? A mere guess would be of little value. Actually, an empirical scoring procedure was devised. In a large group of men and women (the test has separate forms for each), seven friends were asked to rate the subjects on the trait in question. The group was then divided into quarters, depending on whether their average ratings were high, low, or moderate on ascendance and submission. Then their

[7] G. W. Allport, A test for ascendance-submission, *J. abnorm. soc. Psychol.*, 1928, **23,** 118–136; G. W. Allport and R. Ruggles, Recent applications of the A-S Reaction Study, *J. abnorm. soc. Psychol.*, 1939, **34,** 518–528; G. W. Allport, *Personality: a psychological interpretation* (New York: Holt, Rinehart and Winston, 1937), pp. 410–414.

replies to the questions were examined. If a given answer were approximately four times as common among those rated as highly ascendant, this answer was given the score of plus 4; if an answer were nearly twice as common among submissive people, it was scored minus 1; and so on. The diagnostic power of each reply was thus determined empirically. In some cases there was no differential frequency between subjects rated ascendant and those rated submissive. In such cases the scoring value is 0.

Although the test can be faked (if the subject wishes to do so) it has considerable practical value in helping the cooperative subject to gain insight into his own level of adjustment (scores for men range from +64 to −64). It also has obvious value in vocational counseling. A highly ascendant woman, for example, would probably be badly placed as a dressmaker, servant, private secretary, or assistant librarian; she would do well, if she has the other requisite qualifications, as professional hostess, manager, or a teacher in a reform school.

Since dominance is a visible, overt, and important common trait it is not surprising that several additional types of measures have been invented.[8]

Extraversion-Introversion. A third "old stand-by" for testers is the dimension made famous by Carl Jung. Even before Jung coined the terms, William James had called attention to the difference between "tough-minded" and "tender-minded" people—between those who turn outward and those who turn inward. The extravert, says Jung, is dominated by external and social reality; the introvert approaches the world subjectively—in terms of its relevance to himself. Jung elaborates the typology to include the following characteristics.[9]

Extravert	Introvert
Directly oriented to objective reality	Subjective world is decisive
Governed by practicality and necessity	Governed by absolute principles

[8] For example, A. H. Maslow, A test for dominance-feeling (self-esteem) in college women, *J. soc. Psychol.*, 1940, **12**, 255–270; H. G. Gough, H. McClosky, and P. E. Meehl, A personality scale for dominance, *J. abnorm. soc. Psychol.*, 1951, **46**, 360–366. See also the discussion of variants on dominance scales in L. J. Cronbach, *Essentials of psychological testing* (2d ed; New York: Harper, 1960), p. 468.

[9] C. G. Jung, *Psychological types* (Transl.; New York: Harcourt, Brace, 1923).

Extravert	Introvert
Adjusts readily to new situations	Is rigid and inflexible
Affective life not finely shaded	General delicacy of feelings
Weak in self-criticism	Given to self-analysis and criticism
Direct action and compensation in kind	Compensations in escape and fantasy
Typical psychoneurosis is hysteric	Typical psychoneurosis is anxious or obsessive

Jung felt that both types should be subdivided according to the prominence of four subsidiary functions: *thinking, feeling, sensation, intuition.*

The first single-trait test (Freyd-Heidbreder) tried to lump together in one scale many of the diverse expressions of extraversion-introversion.[10] Subjects merely scored themselves as + or — on items such as the following:

> Prefers to read a thing rather than experience it
> Is reticent and retiring; does not talk spontaneously
> Keeps in the background on social occasions
> Blushes frequently; is self-conscious
> Keeps a diary
> Limits acquaintances to a select few

The final score is the algebraic sum of plusses and minuses, the higher the ratio of plusses, the more introverted. (We note at once the danger of "response set." A subject gets a "general feel" of the scale and slips into a habit of giving "Yes" or "No" answers, instead of making a fresh judgment on each item. This error can to some extent be guarded against if items are phrased in a varied direction, so that plus sometimes indicates extraversion and sometimes introversion.)

It was inevitable that several improved tests should be developed, for this dimension is of great interest to psychologists.[11] But it soon became evident that the dimension is too broad and coarse. A person

10 E. Heidbreder, Measuring introversion and extroversion, *J. abnorm. soc. Psychol.,* 1926, 21, 120–134.
11 Some of these variant scales are reported in R. M. Allen, *Personality assessment procedures* (New York: Harper, 1958), pp. 60–66.

may be introverted in one respect, but extraverted in another. One of the newer scales restores Jung's original suggestion that the types be subdivided according to the prominence of *thinking, feeling, sensation, intuition* in the life.[12]

Another method of refining the concept is to use factor-analysis. In the omnibus scales employed it was found that some items cluster together closer than others. With the aid of factor-analysis Guilford finds that in his scale of 175 items (many drawn from the original Freyd-Heidbreder test), five different factors occur; that is to say, there are five kinds of extraversion; therefore, instead of giving a person a single score, it is more discriminating to give him a separate score on five common traits.[13] Guilford describes his factors as follows:

S — social introversion, as exhibited in shyness and tendencies to withdraw from social contacts

T — thinking introversion, an inclination to meditative thinking, philosophizing, and analyzing one's self and others

D — depression, including feelings of unworthiness and guilt

C — cycloid tendencies, as shown in strong emotional reactions, fluctuations in mood, and tendency toward flightiness or instability

R — rhathymia, a happy-go-lucky or carefree disposition; liveliness and impulsiveness

Although there is some tendency for intercorrelations to occur (the largest—as might be expected—being a −.54 between S and R), it seems well to accept this finer method of measuring five forms of extraversion and introversion instead of accepting a single common trait.

R. B. Cattell, likewise using factor-analysis, finds no value in the traditional dimension, for to his mind it conceals several common traits which are analytically distinct.[14] In his list of "Primary Traits" of personality we find several (starred) that are reminiscent of extraversion-introversion:

---

[12] I. B. Myers and K. C. Briggs, *Myers-Briggs Type Indicator* (Research ed.); Princeton, N.J.: Educational Testing Service, 1961).

[13] J. P. Guilford, *An inventory of factors STDCR* (Beverly Hills, Calif.: Sheridan Supply Co., 1940). The same author has greatly extended his factorial analysis into other regions of personality beyond extraversion-introversion.

[14] R. B. Cattell, *Description and measurement of personality* (Yonkers, N.Y.: World Book, 1946). Also by the same author, *Personality and motivation: structure and measurement* (Yonkers, N.Y.: World Book, 1957).

*Cyclothymia
Intelligence
*Emotional maturity
Dominance
*Surgency
*Sensitivity
Socialized
Positive integration
*Charitable, adventurous
*Neurasthenia
*Hypersensitiveness
*Surgent cyclothymia

What shall we conclude? The history of extraversion-introversion is typical of much that has happened. At the start some psychologist formulates a "rational" conception of a dimension or type according to which people may be profitably compared. Enthusiastic measurement gets under way. A host of empiricists and statisticians use refined techniques to explore and modify the original conception. In principle one cannot object to the refinements of analysis. But often they go to such lengths that the original conception is lost in confusion, and its original merits vanish. My own view is that statistical refinement is desirable *so long as* a clear, rational conception remains. We are in danger of passing beyond this limit.[15]

Conformity (Suggestibility, Persuasibility). Are some people conformists and some nonconformists? Interest in this common trait has grown in our era of wars, dictators, and mass behavior. David Riesman tells us that Americans as a whole are more conformist (more "other-directed") than they used to be when our pioneer tradition encouraged people to be individualistic ("inner-directed").[16]

Traditionally the phenomenon of "social yielding" has been called *suggestibility*. For decades it (and the related concepts of hypnosis, imitation, persuasibility) have played a leading part in psychological theory. We might say that we have here a rational concept well worth reworking into a common trait in order to see

---

15 Such seems to be the conclusion we reach from a comprehensive review of the field by P. M. Carrigan, Extraversion-introversion as a dimension of personality: a reappraisal, *Psychol. Bull.*, 1960, 57, 329–360.
16 D. Riesman, *The lonely crowd* (New Haven, Conn.: Yale Univ. Press, 1950).

whether it is truly general and normally distributed in the population.

More than half a century ago Binet (also a pioneer in intelligence testing) invented tests of suggestibility. He found that children differed among themselves in the readiness with which they accepted suggestions. Child leaders he found to be more resistant than their followers.

The question immediately arises whether it is reasonable to expect anyone, child or adult, to be equally suggestible toward all topics. (Technically this is the question whether a scale has internal consistency.) A child who has lived on a farm is not likely to accept false accounts of country life as readily as will a city child. A layman may be susceptible to health advertisements, whereas his physician is resistant. A woman may be suggestible about machinery and finance but not about cooking or homemaking. The question, therefore, is whether we should expect suggestibility to be a good example of a common trait. Is it not rather an instance of behavior that is situationally determined (Chapter 8)?

The problem is an empirical one. Tests of suggestibility (persuasibility, conformity) can be administered, and the degree of generality experimentally determined.

One such study used a laboratory technique.[17] The investigators asked ninety individual judges to give their answers to three types of problems: (1) judging the number of clicks made by a metronome, (2) expressing an opinion regarding such propositions as, "There is no progress without war," and (3) solving problems in mental arithmetic. But before giving an answer each subject listened through earphones to what purported to be the answers of four subjects preceding him in the series. Actually these answers were "doctored" on tape, and were sometimes correct (for the factual problems) and sometimes erroneous. The question was how much did the ninety subjects yield to the suggestion of the four "predecessors."

The results show that people who yield in one situation tend to do so in other situations (a general correlation of .87 being

17 R. R. Blake, H. Helson, J. S. Mouton, The generality of conformity behavior as a function of factual anchorage, difficulty of task, and amount of social pressure, *J. Pers.*, 1947, 25, 294–316.

obtained). The nature of the situation, of course, had some effect; thus wrong solutions to difficult arithmetic problems were more readily accepted than erroneous solutions to easy problems. But on the whole the experiment demonstrates well that conformity tendencies are to a considerable extent "personality based."

Another study, conducted at Yale University and using a very different method, likewise demonstrates considerable generality in the trait of persuasibility which the authors define as "a predispositional factor reflecting an individual's susceptibility to influence from many different sources, on a wide variety of topics."[18] In this particular investigation high school students were used, and the test consisted of persuasive arguments on several controversial social issues, for example:

> The United States Civil Defense organization should be greatly expanded to include twenty-five million men and women;
> An effective cure for cancer can be achieved within one or two years, provided half of all medical research specialists concentrate on the task;
> General von Hindenburg was in reality a democratic leader and great statesman.

With this technique, it turned out that students did indeed have a general disposition to yield to persuasion (even accepting two contradictory positions on the same proposition when strong suggestions were made), or else to resist attempts to sway them, or to take a moderate place on the persuasibility scale.

While this study proves that persuasibility is a scalable common trait (at least among adolescents) it also establishes the fact that the trait is not isolated in the child's life. Those who were highly persuasible were found to be likewise low in self-esteem, given to inferiority feelings, and to be social isolates. In general they were insecure youth. By yielding they seem to be seeking approval and acceptance. Boys who were known to be in rebellion against their parents were generally more resistant to persuasion than boys who were not. In this particular study girls were more persuasible than boys (perhaps because the opinions tested had to do with public affairs with which they were less concerned). In short, the study tells us not only that the trait is general enough to be measured, but that

18 C. I. Hovland and I. L. Janis (Eds.), *Personality and persuasibility.* Vol. II of *Yale Studies in Attitude and Communication* (New Haven, Conn.: Yale Univ. Press, 1959).

it is embedded in a syndrome of personal qualities and needs. In an entirely separate investigation Eysenck finds that people who yield to suggestion are more likely than others to stand high in measures of neuroticism.[19]

The Yale study turned up a small group of obsessively hypercritical children. They were adolescent "negativists" (cf. page 125) who constantly refuted the ideas expressed by parents, teachers, and peers. They aggressively tore other people's arguments to shreds. We occasionally meet such *contredisant* individuals as adults. They illustrate the fact that some people cannot be fitted to a single common trait continuum; their pattern is too unusual. And we must likewise not forget that, although conformity seems to be a measurable common trait, we must expect situational factors, personal knowledge, and private motives to affect an individual's response in this area of social behavior.[20]

Authoritarianism. During the past decade a widely used test is the so-called *F-scale*. Its rational basis is the assumption that a complex syndrome of personality (not a simple trait) underlies the allegiance of many people to fascistic, authoritarian ideas and forms of government. The prod to the intensive study of authoritarianism has been the political and social unrest of our day. Literally hundreds of researches have employed the F-scale, and methodological discussions of its properties have been numerous.[21]

The test is composed of propositions with which the subject may agree or not agree as he chooses. The items are selected to reflect various aspects of the syndrome. For example, the following proposition is intended to measure conventionalism: "A person who has bad manners, habits, and breeding can hardly expect to get along with decent people." Another item aims to tap authoritarian aggression: "Sex crimes, such as rape and attacks on children, deserve more than mere imprisonment; such criminals ought to be publicly whipped,

---

19 H. J. Eysenck, *Dimensions of personality* (London: Routledge & Kegan Paul, 1947).
20 A vigorous warning against considering conformity as exclusively personality-based is given by E. P. Hollander, Reconsidering conformity in personality. In H. P. David and J. C. Brengelmann, *Perspective in personality research* (New York: Springer, 1960). Ingenious experimental studies in this area are reported by S. E. Asch, *Independence and conformity*. To be published.
21 The original publication was in T. W. Adorno, E. Frenkel-Brunswik, D. J. Levinson, and R. N. Sanford, *The authoritarian personality* (New York: Harper, 1950). A useful later exposition is by R. N. Sanford, The approach of the authoritarian personality. In J. L. McCary (Ed.), *Psychology of personality* (New York: Logos, 1956), pp. 253–319. For a general critical examination see R. Christie and M. Jahoda (Eds.), *Studies in the scope and method of the authoritarian personality* (Glencoe, Ill.: Free Press, 1954).

or worse." Other aspects of the syndrome (having appropriate propositions) have to do with authoritarian submission, anti-intraception (opposition to the subjective or imaginative way of life), superstition and stereotypy, power and toughness, destructiveness and cynicism, projectivity, exaggerated concern with sex. The general theory from which this syndrome is derived is psychoanalytic. It holds that rigid and punitive ways of rearing a child will result in an apprehensive, fearful, prejudiced, authoritarian type of personality.

Many studies have demonstrated that high scores on the F-scale are associated to a marked degree with racial and ethnic prejudice, and with other forms of hostile and autocratic social conduct.[22]

The findings have been so timely and so impressive that psychologists have devoted much zeal to analyzing, checking, criticizing, and modifying both the original scale and the theory involved.

An unfortunate error was made in composing the original scale. The same "response set" bias mentioned in connection with the Freyd-Heidbreder test (page 428) turns up again. The items are unidirectional: an agreement is always scored as authoritarian. This fact has led some critics to claim that there is no elaborate authoritarian syndrome involved, but merely a tendency to acquiesce, to say "Yes" to any and all propositions—a simple form of suggestibility.[23] The response set does not affect the positive results (the scale still correlates with ethnic prejudice), but the original elaborate theory of an authoritarian "character structure" is placed under strain. One author believes that a common trait of *dogmatism* is a better explanatory concept than the complex syndrome proposed by the original authors.[24]

The controversies aroused by this ingenious test have not yet been resolved. Their vigor testifies to the importance of this region of personality exploration.

Summary of Single-Trait Scales. Our sampling from among the

22 Cf. G. W. Allport, *The nature of prejudice* (Cambridge, Mass.: Addison-Wesley, 1954), Chap. 25.

23 More than a score of studies deal with this problem. To cite three examples, B. M. Bass, Authoritarianism or acquiescence? *J. abnorm. soc. Psychol.*, 1955, **51**, 616–623; R. Christie, J. Havel, and B. Seidenberg, Is the F scale irreversible? *J. abnorm. soc. Psychol.*, 1958, **56**, 143–159; and A. Couch and K. Keniston, Yeasayers and naysayers: agreeing response set as a personality variable, *J. abnorm. soc. Psychol.*, 1960, **60**, 151–174.

24 M. Rokeach, Political and religious dogmatism: an alternative to the authoritarian personality, *Psychol. Monogr.*, 1956, No. 425.

hundreds of available devices for measuring single traits has been selective. The examples deal both with long-established common traits and with instances of recent scaling techniques. Some traits have a simple definition (e.g., ascendance-submission), some rest on an elaborate definition (e.g., the authoritarian syndrome). The reader will note that sometimes a simple rational conception of a trait will grow complicated and confused when complex measurement techniques are applied and empiricism is pressed to its limit.

Multidimensional Scales. Empiricism and statistics have led some investigators away from the single-trait conception. They prefer an omnibus instrument that will fetch hundreds of replies from the subject, and thus permit the simultaneous measurement of *many* common traits. We have already referred to Guilford's Factors S T D C R, which in effect is a method of measuring five forms of introversion-extraversion with the aid of 175 questions, and therefore illustrates a relatively homogeneous, multidimensional scale.

Much more elaborate, however, is the Minnesota Multiphasic Inventory (MMPI), at present the most widely used of personality tests.[25] The scale has an initial rational foundation in its attempt to measure any person's tendency to fit into psychiatric categories. Among the common traits measured are hypochondriasis, depression, hysteria, psychopathic deviate, paranoia, psychasthenia, schizophrenia, hypomania. It is of interest to note that this most widely used test has a slanting toward abnormal psychology—a fact that shows widespread faith in the continuity of the normal and abnormal (cf. pages 150–155). From the same pool of items (over 500) the authors also derive additional scales to measure more "normal" dimensions: social introversion-extraversion, masculinity-feminity, and so on.

Let us consider just two of the 500 or more items. The subject responds by marking True, False, or ?:

I believe I am being plotted against
It takes a lot of argument to convince some people of the truth

Quite obviously *True* to the first statement suggests a paranoid trend in a personality (and it is in fact often so answered by actual paranoid patients in mental hospitals—hence the item is included as diagnostic).

[25] S. R. Hathaway and P. E. Meehl, *An atlas for the clinical use of the MMPI* (Minneapolis: Univ. of Minnesota Press, 1951). See also G. S. Welsh and G. W. Dahlstrom, *Basic readings on the MMPI in psychology and medicine* (Minneapolis: Univ. of Minnesota Press, 1956).

But what does the second item signify? On the face of it we might also expect the item to indicate a paranoid insistence upon the rightness of one's own ideas, but actually the paranoid criterion group did not validate this item. At the same time it turned out that hysteric patients usually answered *False* to this item, and so any taker of the test who gives that answer gets a positive score on hysteria. Just why is hard to see, but empiricism follows a logic of its own. Correlation is king. The whole aim is to discover what correlates with what.

Let us look a little more closely at the consequences of empiricism. An early test was the Bernreuter *Personality Inventory*, an omnibus of 125 questions, drawn largely from three preexisting "logical" scales (one being the A-S Reaction Study described on page 425 f.). Each of these original scales is intended to measure one and only one common trait. With the aid of the 125 questions, Bernreuter attempted to measure four common traits: *dominance, self-sufficiency, introversion,* and *neuroticism.* All answers to all the items receive four scores (some of them being zeros) according to their statistically derived relationship to other items in the same scale. Thus, one question reads, "Do you often feel just miserable?" If your answer is "?" (meaning either that you don't know how you feel or don't know what the tester means) you are scored -3 on introversion, -1 on dominance, and 0 for both neuroticism and self-sufficiency. Yet a response of "?" to such a question seems to bear no rational relation to any of the four traits.

Pursuing this same case further, Flanagan then applied factor-analysis to the Bernreuter scale and found that by regrouping the items, by separating them into independent dimensions, two main factors resulted, which he christened *self-confidence* and *sociability* (quite different conceptions from the original scheme). After this ceremony, it turns out that if you "feel just miserable" you score $+4$ on self-confidence, and 0 on sociability. As the statistics grow better and better, the intelligibility grows less and less. (From another empirical scale comes an extreme instance: children who give the response word "green" to the stimulus word "grass" receive a score of $+6$ for "loyalty to the gang"—surely an example of empiricism gone wild.)[26]

26 Cf. Allport, *Personality: a psychological interpretation,* pp. 328 f. Note 7 above.

Multidimensional scales cover more territory and give a broader picture of the individual, but they depart from the clear logic of the one-trait scale. As Cronbach says, "The theoretically oriented instrument often is confined to one single trait. To validate a test as a measure of even one construct requires extensive and painstaking research, and it is a brave investigator who tries to advance on more than one theoretical front at a time."[27]

We have said that the MMPI measures chiefly common traits that have a pathological flavor. A different omnibus test (but using many of the same items) is the California Psychological Inventory (CPI), focused on more positive (normal) variables. This scale of 480 items yields scores on 18 common traits: dominance, capacity for status, sociability, social presence, self-acceptance, sense of well-being, responsibility, socialization, self-control, tolerance, good impression, communality, achievement via conformance, achievement via independence, intellectual efficiency, psychological-mindedness, flexibility, femininity. One virtue of the CPI is that it attempts to help the tester interpret the complex individual profiles that result when so many separate scores are plotted.[28] In other words, there is an attempt to overcome the fragmentation inherent in differential psychology discussed on page 16.

8. Projective Techniques

A large array of instruments were christened "projective" by L. K. Frank in 1939.[29] Their theoretical origin lies in Freud's discovery of the importance of the unconscious stratum in personality. Several projective techniques were well developed before Frank invented the label. Their common principle is the use of vague or ambiguous stimuli to invite the subject to reveal submerged levels of personality. The response he gives presumably comes from deep (unconscious) psychodynamic processes.

It is convenient to classify projective techniques under three headings: the *perceptive*, the *apperceptive*, and the *productive*.[30] A few examples of each follow.

---

27 Cronbach, *op. cit.,* p. 469. Note 8 above.
28 H. G. Gough, *Manual for the California Psychological Inventory* (Palo Alto: Consulting Psychologists Press, 1957).
29 L. K. Frank, Projective methods for the study of personality, *J. Psychol.,* 1939, **8,** 389–413.
30 A more detailed scheme is offered by G. Lindzey, On the classification of projective techniques, *Psychol. Bull.,* 1959, **56,** 158–168.

Perceptive Techniques. Chapter 11 described certain simple perceptual tasks that are diagnostic of deep personal qualities of cognitive style. Some people, for example, are *field-dependent* in their perceptions, unable to sort out significant features from context. This quality seems characteristic of people who are insecure or not insightful.

Another purely perceptual task is illustrated by the flicker-fusion experiment. When a person looks at a light through spaces in a rotating shutter, at low speeds he sees "flicker," at high speeds only light. As the speed of rotation changes from low to high the subject can report the point where the flicker just disappears. For any given person the "fusion threshold" is stable, but there are marked individual differences. What does it signify if a person requires a high rate before he reports fusion? Some evidence exists that such people are more normal, more discriminating, and have higher "ego strength." It is the weaker psychic constitution that soon "gives up" and perceives an early fusion.[31]

In such tests as these we are not dealing with true "projection" in the psychoanalytic sense. It is not the unconscious stratum that we explore, but rather the basic cognitive style and constitutional structure. These methods do, however, offer insight into the logic of projective tests.

In most perceptive techniques the subject sees or hears ambiguous stimuli and tells what they "mean" to him. The most widely used instrument of this kind is the Rorschach Inkblot Test, dating from 1921 (although inkblots were used to test "imagination" as early as 1898.[32] Even Hamlet noted that a cloud could appear like a camel, a weasel, or a whale, depending on one's set[33]).

What objects one sees in the ten inkblot pictures used in the Rorschach method of diagnosis is not the primary consideration. The responses are scored chiefly according to formal characteristics: does the subject see moving or stationary objects? does he look at parts of

---

[31] On the flicker-fusion technique see W. C. Halstead, Biological intelligence, *J. Pers.*, 1951, **20**, 118–130; H. von Bracken, Komponenten der Ermüdung, *Zbl. f. ArbWiss. u. soz. Betriebspraxis*, 1952, **6**, 161–166. H. Schmidtke, Über die Messung der psychologischen Ermüdung mit Hilfe des Flimmertests, *Psychol. Forsch.*, 1951, **23**, 409–463.

[32] For the English edition of this test see H. Rorschach, *Psychodiagnostics* (New York: Grune & Stratton, 1942). A brief history of projective methods is given by Allen, *op. cit.*, pp. 153–156. Note 11 above.

[33] Act 3, Sc. 2. The use of nebulous visual materials for psychological testing was proposed by W. Stern, Cloud pictures, *Charact. & Pers.*, 1937, **6**, 132–146.

the blot or the whole? does he report objects in color? The common traits looked for (and presumably revealed by such reports) have to do with intellectual creativity, extraversion, practical-mindedness, and the like. The problem of scoring such a test makes difficulty. One school of thought wishes to employ uniform nomothetic signs (thus, associations involving color *mean* high emotionality). Another school insists that the total protocol be interpreted clinically on the basis of the examiner's experience with the instrument and the client. Yet a third school would effect a compromise between these views. Here we encounter one deficiency common to projective tests: they are far harder to score and interpret than most pencil-and-paper tests.

The tautophone, an "auditory Rorschach," presents the subject with speech sounds of low intensity, not intelligible. When asked what he "hears," the subject is very likely to report statements that disclose his own proceptive biases.[34]

Apperceptive Techniques. Here the subject goes beyond what he "perceives," and offers, instead of a simple report, a much more elaborate interpretation of meaning. (One must grant, however, that no sharp line exists between perception and apperception.)

A typical and widely used method is the Thematic Apperception Test (TAT).[35] Pictures such as those shown in Figure 34 are presented to the subject, who is asked to "tell a story" around each. Since a picture deals only with a momentary scene, the imagination is forced to play on events leading up to the scene, on the feelings involved, and on the probable outcome of the situation. In telling such a story the subject is likely to project into the picture his own preoccupations, his own needs, fantasies, fears, or hopes. The resulting story tells more about the subject than about the picture itself. For this procedure, as for all projective tests, scoring and interpretation present serious difficulties. Careful directions, however, have been worked out for diagnosing certain "needs" from the stories told—e.g., the need for achievement.[36] But here again it is a question whether

---

[34] B. F. Skinner, The verbal summator and a method for the study of latent speech, *J. Psychol.*, 1936, **2**, 71–107; D. Shakow and S. Rosenzweig, The use of the tautophone ("verbal summator") as an auditory apperceptive test for the study of personality, *Charact. & Pers.*, 1940, **8**, 216–226.

[35] H. A. Murray, *Thematic Apperception Test* (Cambridge, Mass.: Harvard Univ. Press, 1943; G. Lindzey and P. S. Herman, Thematic apperception test: a note on reliability and situational validity, *J. proj. Tech.*, 1955, **19**, 36–42.

[36] D. C. McClelland, *et al., The achievement motive* (New York: Appleton-Century-Crofts, 1953).

Figure 34. Japanese Thematic Apperception Test (copyright by and with permission of Professor Yukio Togawa)

the total protocol is not more revealing than specific scores that may be derived for specific needs.

Instead of visual material one or more words may be the stimulus. The word-association test was originally developed by Jung, but has been elaborated in recent years.[37] The subject is merely asked to reply to a word with the first word that comes to mind. Typical stimulus words are *table, dark, sickness, girl, afraid, whiskey*. Although common replies (such as *chair, light, health*) are not very revealing, a deep conflict may often be betrayed if the subject gives strange or senseless replies, or if he takes an unusually long or short time to react, or if he is so badly thrown off by a word that he repeats the same response over and over. Such "complex indicators" are numerous.

More elaborate is the sentence-completion method, which asks the subject to finish statements that start with only two or three words, for example:

> My mother . . . . . .
> My ambition is . . . . . .

Since the first-person pronoun may put the subject on guard, the technique is thought to be more successfully projective if third-person wording is used:

> A mother . . . .
> Frank's ambition is . . .

The device can be extended by asking the subject to complete not a single sentence but a short story. For example:

> It is a holiday. This boy goes for an auto
> ride with his parents. Returning home,
> he notes that his mother is sad. Why?

Still more free are "thematic compositions," i.e., imaginative literary productions. Here the focus of interest is on what the production reveals concerning its author—much as one might try to reconstruct Shakespeare's personality from his plays.[38] But at this level of analysis

---

[37] C. G. Jung, *Studies in word association* (New York: Dodd, Mead, 1918). J. B. Rotter, Word association and sentence completion. In H. H. Anderson and G. L. Anderson (Eds.), *An introduction to projective techniques* (Englewood Cliffs, N.J.: Prentice-Hall, 1951), pp. 279–311.

[38] A useful survey of "association methods" ranging from single-word response to story writing is offered by Allen, *op. cit.*, Chap. 13; Note 11 above.

psychology merges into literary criticism, for its methods would necessarily be similar.

Productive Techniques. Unlike perceptive and apperceptive methods, the productive techniques do not rely primarily on verbal response but on performance. The use of *drawing* and *painting* has a long history. This approach seems especially useful with children, who, for example, can be asked to "draw a person." What sex does the child choose to draw? Is hostility expressed in the drawing? Do certain exaggerated features call attention to his preoccupation with his own bodily features or inferiorities? The procedure can be varied almost indefinitely: "Draw the inside of your body," "Draw a tree."[39]

Some authors feel that scoring such spontaneous and uncontrolled productions is too difficult. They propose, therefore, to restrict the assignment, asking the subject merely to complete a drawing started in a uniform way (as in sentence-completion tests). Figure 35 shows the stimuli used in one drawing test.[40]

Among productive techniques we should list *psychodrama.* The rationale is simple. The individual is asked to act a role, being given only a skeleton plot. The instruction might be: "Your friend's mother has died, and you are trying to console your friend." Or, "You want a job very much and are trying to persuade the employer to hire you." Variations are endless.[41] For children psychodrama is less useful than the *doll-play* technique. With the aid of puppets, a doll house, and effigies representing parents, children, or playmates, the child's behavior is observed to note signs of conflict, hostility, special affections, or other states of mind which he may customarily repress but release freely in a "play" situation.[42]

Theoretical Note on Projective Techniques. We have barely

---

39 K. Machover, *Personality projection in the drawing of the human figure* (Springfield, Ill.: Charles C Thomas, 1948); A. B. Berman, A. A. Klein, and A. Lippman, Human figure drawings as a projective technique, *J. genet. Psychol.,* 1951, **45,** 57–70; K. Koch, *Der Baumtest* (Bern and Stuttgart: Huber, 1949); E. F. Hammer (Ed.) *The clinical application of projective drawings* (Springfield, Ill.: Charles C Thomas, 1958).

40 E. Wartegg, *Schichtdiagnostik: der Zeichentest* (WZT) (Göttingen: Hogrefe, 1954). Similar is the Horn-Hellersberg drawing test. See E. F. Hellersberg, *The individual's relation to reality in our culture* (Springfield, Ill.: Charles C Thomas, 1950). For a review of drawing tests, including finger painting, see Allen, *op. cit.,* Chap. 12. Note 11 above.

41 J. L. Moreno, *Psychodrama* (New York: Beacon House, 1946).

42 E. S. Shneidman, Manual of MAPS test, *Genet. Psychol. Monogr.,* 1948, **38,** 145–223. A review of play techniques is given by Anne Anastasi, *Psychological testing* (New York: Macmillan, 1954), pp. 618–621.

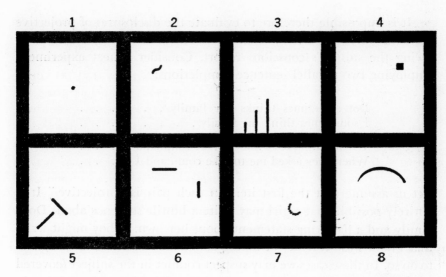

Figure 35. Wartegg Drawing Test (copyright by Verlag für Psychologie. Göttingen: C. J. Hogrefe, used with permission)

sampled the large array of imaginative inventions that aim to elicit unconscious processes in personality.[43] The creed of projective testing holds that the place to look for deep motivation, for conflicts, for basic character structure is in a person's fantasies; and these are best revealed not through direct questions (as in tests and scales) but by sly, slantwise, projective probes. The theory seems sound. Many authors claim that they are the *best* methods of assessing personality.

Let us, however, raise one important question. Will projective methods, if used *alone,* tell us what kind of personality we are dealing with? Suppose, for example, that a subject shows great anxiety in several projective methods. But suppose that by direct methods (tests, scales, questionnaires, self-appraisal) he denies feeling anxiety. Is he not a very different kind of person from one who *by both direct and projective methods* displays anxiety? The former case is clearly badly integrated and defensive, and perhaps neurotic. The latter case has excellent insight; he knows he is a nervous and an apprehensive person. For him projective methods yield nothing that conscious report does not yield.

[43] Fuller accounts are given by J. E. Bell, *Projective techniques* (New York: Longmans, Green, 1948); Anderson and Anderson, *op. cit.,* (Note 37 above); P. E. Vernon, *Personality tests and assessments* (London: Methuen, 1953); Allen, *op. cit.,* (Note 11 above); Cronbach, *op. cit.* (Note 8 above.)

It is impossible therefore to evaluate the disclosures of projective methods unless we also have an assessment based on direct methods giving the subject's conscious report. Consider a neat experiment employing two parallel sentence completions:

> Dot sometimes thinks her family . . . . . .
> I sometimes think my family . . . .
>
> When they asked Frank to take command he . . .
> When they asked me to take command I . . . .

Let us assume that the first item in each pair is "projective." It is entirely possible that a girl may write a hostile sentence about Dot's family and a flattering statement about her own. A boy might write that Frank was "fearful" of taking command; but that "I was glad" to do so. In these cases we may suspect conflict in the subject (covered up by his conventional defenses when describing himself). Other subjects (better integrated) give essentially the same meaningful replies to the direct and projective wordings.[44]

Of course we would not presume to base a diagnosis of neuroticism or normality, defense or integration, upon one fragment of evidence. But the example makes the point: unless *both* direct and projective techniques are employed we shall not be able to interpret the significance of the latter.[45]

9. Depth Analysis

We have said that projective techniques are for the most part sly handmaidens of depth psychology, which puts emphasis upon unconscious processes. But psychiatry and psychoanalysis have methods designed to attack this stratum more directly. *Psychiatric interviews* are of this order. The psychiatrist reaches his diagnosis by questioning and listening for evidence of hidden motives and obscure sequences of behavior. If the psychiatrist is a psychoanalyst he is likely to

44 J. W. Getzels and J. J. Walsh, The method of paired direct and projective questionnaires in the study of attitude structure and socialization, *Psychol. Monogr.*, 1958, No. 454. Evidence that neurotics do in fact give discrepant replies, and normal people congruent replies, is offered by A. Davids and H. Pildner, Comparison of direct and projective methods of personality assessment under different conditions of motivation, *Psychol. Monogr.*, 1958, No. 464.
45 A fuller statement of this argument is given by G. W. Allport, The trend in motivational theory. In *Personality and social encounter* (Boston: Beacon, 1960), Chap. 6.

employ *free association,* the patient lying on a couch and saying "anything that comes to mind." The psychiatrist may employ *analysis of dreams.* Some use *hypnotism* or *narcosynthesis* (drugs) to bring out buried but important memories. Even some questionnaires, firmly anchored in psychoanalytic theory, are used to discover whether the patient is, for example, of the oral, anal, or genital type.[46]

Since these methods are designed primarily for use with abnormal cases we shall leave them at this point. They should be included in any survey of assessment techniques, even though specialized for psychiatric use.

10. Expressive Behavior

Although they are often classified erroneously among the projective techniques I regard expressive-behavior methods as separate and deserving a fuller treatment in their own right. The following chapter is devoted to them.

Here it need only be said that projective performance is *elicited* by the investigator. Expressive behavior is freely *emitted* by the subject (in his spontaneous manner of walking, talking, gesturing, writing, shaking hands). What a subject says or writes in taking a Rorschach test is *projective,* whereas his tone of voice or style of handwriting is *expressive.* Both are revealing, but the former lies closer to the level of cognitive content, the latter is more primitive and motor. In taking a test a subject is always *coping* with an assigned problem; his *manner* of coping with it is *expressive movement.* In Chapter 19 we shall return to this issue.

11. Synoptic Procedures

The term *synoptic* means to have a general view of the whole or the principal parts of a thing. It is used here to cover a final group of methods which have to do with combining or relating information so as to strengthen our assessment of a given personality. We shall consider briefly four procedures of this general type: *psychography, identification, matching, prediction.*

The *psychograph* was defined in Chapter 1 (see Figure 2) as a method for plotting several scores for a single individual. From it we

[46] E.g., M. H. Krout and J. K. Tabin, Measuring personality in developmental terms: the personal preference scale, *Genet. Psychol. Monogr.,* 1954, **50,** 289–335.

can see at a glance what capacities and traits are high, medium, or low in magnitude in comparison with some normative group. Practically all multidimensional scales use this method of profiling the scores of individual subjects.

The limitation of the psychograph (or profile) is that it fails to tell us about the *interaction* of qualities. If a person stands low on intelligence and high on aggression we cannot tell whether he is an overbearing boor or an effective second-in-command. Personal behavior is a convergence of traits and not a mere summation of what appears on a psychograph. Nevertheless, psychography is a useful synoptic procedure so far as it goes.

Identification is the procedure we employ whenever we ask, "Can you guess who produced this record of behavior?" The common practice of spotting the author of a literary passage or a musical composition on the basis of previous knowledge of his creative style is an everyday instance of the method. In psychological research identification may be an aid in validating an assessment. Thus some person who knows the subjects personally may be given an assortment of scores, drawings, Rorschach protocols, or what not. He is then asked to identify the authors of these records. This is one version of a "blind analysis": from partial material a judge is asked to give fuller material (in this case the author's identity). Correct identification of authorship tells us that an assessment has been valid. It does not, however, tell us by what subtle psychological process the correct identification has been made.

A variant is the *Guess Who* technique, originally employed by Harthshorne and May.[47] Here an "ideal portrait" is offered, and the judge is asked to name someone who fits it. Thus children in a classroom may be asked to "guess who" is the most cowardly in the class, the biggest joker, the teacher's pet. Or, "These three people are always happy and enjoying themselves. It is impossible to annoy them. They never change. Who are they?" The device is simply a scheme to obtain children's judgments concerning outstanding qualities of certain classmates.

Matching. In discussing empirical approaches to the unity of personality (Chapter 16) we illustrated the method of matching,

---

[47] H. Hartshorne and M. A. May, *Studies in the organization of character* (New York: Macmillan, 1930), pp. 221–223. See also J. B. Maller, *Personality sketches* (New York: Columbia Univ., Teachers College, 1936).

using the musical scripts and the names of three well-known composers. The method consists simply of sorting out diverse productions and telling which of these were made by one and the same individual. Any kinds of material may be employed: specimens of handwriting, recordings of voice, photographs, themes, artistic creations. In one typical experiment the investigator wrote personality sketches based on an interpretation of drawings made by adults. These, it turned out, could be matched with considerable success against independent protocols prepared on the basis of Rorschach diagnosis of the same adults.[48]

Matching is perhaps the best method for demonstrating that the same essential patterning is revealed in two or more assessment methods. But the procedure has limitations. It can be used effectively with only a small amount of material at a time. Sometimes correct matching can be made on the basis of illegitimate cues (such as the subject's use of an unusual word in different sets of material). And the method fails to tell us *how* the correct matching was achieved.[49]

Prediction. Three statements concerning prediction seem incontestable: (1) To be able to predict with greater success than is achieved by unaided common sense is an important goal of science. (2) When successful predictions of human behavior are based on detailed assessment methods, such success is a sign of the validity of methods used. (3) Common sense, no less than science, employs prediction. Constantly we forecast the behavior of our associates. We predict, for example, that So-and-So will be a congenial roommate; that mother will like this particular birthday present; that X will be a satisfactory president of one's club, firm, or nation. All our decisions regarding human beings involve personality predictions.

When we have used a given test to predict outcomes, and have collected enough data to measure our successful and unsuccessful forecasts, we obtain for the test in question a "validity coefficient." We can say, for instance, that scores on one particular instrument for a group of subjects correlate, for example, $+.70$ with later demonstrated executive ability, grades in college, ratings as

---

[48] T. S. Waehner, Interpretation of spontaneous drawings and paintings, *Genet. Psychol. Monogr.*, 1946, **33**, 3–70.
[49] Cf. Vernon, *op. cit.*, p. 49. Note 43 above.

medical intern, successful salesmanship, or with some other measurable (or ratable) criterion.

Although prediction is certainly the most important synoptic method—for both common sense and for science—we are still uncertain regarding the answer to certain key questions: (1) How much better are our technical assessment methods than unaided common sense? In a few cases we have some evidence that they are better (thus tests of aptitudes in children are on the average better predictors of future academic success than raw ratings by teachers). But most of the assessment methods we have considered have not *proved* their superiority over common-sense prognoses. (2) Among the technical methods we have reviewed are some superior to others in making successful predictions? Specifically, are the more global, clinical methods superior to a mechanical ("cookbook") following of statistical scores? For example, is the psychiatric interview better than a mechanically scored Rorschach? Is a multidimensional test better than an autobiography? We do not yet know the answers. I do, however, venture one prediction of my own: When psychologists have learned to handle the interrelationships of traits in the single life, and to perceive their intrinsic congruences, predictions will be better than those from an averaging of weighted test scores on a computing machine. The latter procedure can at best give actuarial probabilities for masses of people, never certainties for the single person.

Safeguards in Assessment

How far the science of assessment has progressed beyond unaided common sense we cannot say for sure. At the very least, science has learned of various pitfalls that trap the unwary diagnostician. It knows the minimum rules for sound assessment.

A method should be reliable. A thermometer, a clock, or a speedometer is reliable only when it yields consistent measures—from day to day and in respect to the subunits of which it is composed. A reliable assessment method demands a reasonable degree of temporal *stability* (repeat-reliability). If a person takes a test today, and tomorrow takes it again with wholly different results, the test lacks reliability. And yet the person himself may have changed—in which case the test is not at fault. Most people, however, change little from day to day or from month to month, and so we have a right to expect that two administrations of the same test (preferably with equivalent forms) will on the average correlate highly (at least .80).

A second type of reliability required of any measuring instrument is *item homogeneity* (internal reliability). Unless the subunits of a method are all pointed to the same trait the instrument has no consistency. In other words, the subitems of a method should correlate with one another. Measures of internal reliability can be obtained for a test by correlating the scores obtained from even-numbered items with odd-numbered items (split-half reliability) or by correlating the score on each item with the total score obtained from all remaining items (item analysis). (An item that does not show a satisfactory correlation by this latter method should be discarded.)

Not all methods lend themselves to the determination of these two forms of reliability. Interviews do not, nor do personal documents. In these cases an important safeguard is *observer reliability*. Will two or more competent analysts make similar interpretations from interviews, personal documents, projective drawings, and the like? If not, we cannot place much faith in the method.[50]

A method should be valid. It is not enough for a method to have *face validity,* i.e., a mere appearance of measuring some trait. When the employment manager places a magazine on the floor and assesses the "orderliness" of applicants by their picking it up, he is relying on face validity. The technician must *prove* that his instrument measures what it is supposed to measure. There are various methods of establishing validity, and a combination of these should be employed whenever possible.[51]

We have spoken of *predictive validity,* resulting whenever we can correctly forecast significant and relevant behavior from the use of a method. *Construct validity* occurs when on the basis of some theory we can establish the fact that the scale behaves in the expected way. Thus, a successful test for dominance should correlate with other tests purporting to measure the same trait. Or, hospitalized neurotics should show greater anxiety on a projective instrument than non-neurotics. If they do not do so we question the validity of the instrument.

---

[50] For a fuller discussion of reliability see Anastasi, *op. cit.,* Chap. 5. Note 42 above.
[51] *Ibid.,* Chap. 6.

Whereas a reliable method does no more than agree with itself, a valid method has the power of predicting behavior beyond the immediate range of items contained in the instrument. It is far easier to prove the reliability of a technique than to prove its validity. But at the same time validity is the most important attribute of a method—without it the method is completely pointless.

A method should avoid unwanted response set. In a sense, of course, every method aims toward eliciting significant response sets, i.e., enduring dispositions to act in accordance with the trait-structure of the personality. But *unwanted* response sets may badly cloud the findings. One subject may be merely "acquiescent" and thus incline to agree with all sorts of scale items (if they are set before him in an "agree-disagree" manner). Another may wish above all else to make a good impression; another may have a dim view of himself and express only the worst side of his nature. Again, a subject may be one who likes to make extreme statements about himself and about his opinions. Conversely, he may be a cautious soul who endorses only moderate ("sometimes," "occasionally," "don't know") alternatives. Some people tend to give full and inclusive statements; others are reticent and meager in their replies. All these attitudinal biases are examples of unwanted response sets.[52] (Of course the fact that a person takes a certain response set tells *something* about him, but it does not tell what the tester wishes to measure by his instrument.)

Edwards has studied the troublesome set to give responses that are conventionally desirable.[53] He finds that the correlation between the *social desirability* of items and the tendency to endorse them is high, often over $+.80$. In one inventory, for example, appears the statement, "I like to be loyal to my friends." It has an extremely high social desirability rating, and is endorsed as applicable to themselves by 98 percent of the people taking this test. "I like to avoid responsibilities and obligations" is endorsed by only 6 percent.

No doubt there are more people who like to be loyal to their friends than who like to avoid responsibilities—among socialized

52 See L. J. Cronbach, Response sets and test validity, *Educ. psychol. Measmt,* 1946, **6,** 475–494.
53 A. L. Edwards, *The social desirability variable in personality assessment and research* (New York: Holt, Rinehart and Winston, 1957).

adults we would expect this result. Yet at the same time there is no doubt that many people give a less than honest account of themselves because they subscribe to the socially desirable: they deny irritability, hostility, self-pity, and claim for themselves conventional virtues such as loyalty, tolerance, unaffectedness. The tendency is especially strong in high school students.

Most personality tests are susceptible of faking if the subject wishes to fake them. The more clearly he perceives the purpose of the test, the easier it is for him to dissimulate. If a job depends on the results the temptation is almost too strong to resist.

In one study, Davids gave three measures of *anxiety* to two groups of subjects. One group consisted of "research volunteers," motivated only to tell the truth, the whole truth, and nothing but the truth about themselves; the other group consisted of "job seekers" who knew that the experimenter was seeking to hire "mature, well-adjusted" people. The former group, by all three measures, revealed higher degrees of anxiety than the latter. The tests were all of a type of self-report that permitted the subject to "see through" their intent.[54]

A battle of wits is on. Investigators try various methods of eliminating the faked answer or the undesirable response set. One method is to make sure that the answers to all questions have equal social desirability.[55] Another method is to shuffle the "direction of items" so that the subject cannot take a simple acquiescent set of saying "Yes." (If he does so the results are manifestly inconsistent.) Still another method is to include "jokers" in the battery to trap the unwary faker. For example, the MMPI includes a "lie" scale. A person scores high if he agrees with a large number of improbable statements, such as, "I never put off until tomorrow what I ought to do today."

But the best safeguard is to employ assessment procedures (of

---

[54] A. Davids, Relations among several objective measures of anxiety under different conditions of motivation, *J. consult. Psychol.*, 1955, **19**, 275–279.

[55] *The Study of Values* (see pages 453–457) is so constructed that all items used are known to have equal desirability in the population at large. In expressing his preference, therefore, the subject is revealing only his personal choice. Few scales are constructed on this principle.

any type) only with subjects who wish to study themselves objectively. A person who is interested primarily in finding out something about himself has no motive to fake, and is likely to avoid unwanted response sets. When assessment procedures are used for selecting people for jobs or for promotion, self-interest may lead to defensiveness and dishonesty. Tests of intelligence and achievement are much less open to willful distortion than are most tests of personality.

Interpretations of results should avoid glittering generalities. People, by and large, seem to be suggestible toward the results of assessment procedures. The prestige of the examiner is so strong that his statements are likely to be accepted even if he deliberately practices deception. In one experiment totally false scores on a personality test were reported to subjects, and when presented in a persuasive manner, all subjects accepted the results and agreed with the fanciful assessment.[56]

Popular character reading, even more than psychological assessment, is given to the use of "universal characteristics"—statements that apply to mortals across the board. When the analyst says, "You have a need for other people to like and admire you," the subject is likely to say, "How true! How acute you are!" He should, of course, say, "Who hasn't?" Similarly glittering and worthless are such diagnoses as, "You like change and variety and become dissatisfied when hemmed in by restrictions"; "Security is one of your major goals in life." Not only do such statements catch all mortals; they are likely to be interpreted in an individual way by each subject to fit his unique pattern of life, and he therefore credits the diagnostician with an acumen he does not have. Meehl has called this abuse of generalities "the Barnum effect." It is a trap to be avoided both by subjects and by ethical practitioners.

Are So Many Methods Needed?

Our survey of methods, extensive though it is, barely samples the profusion of inventions available for use today. It is obvious that investigators like to create assessment techniques and to try them out. It is too early to say for certain what the "best" methods are. But

---

56 J. F. Donceel, B. S. Alimena, and C. M. Birch, Influence of prestige suggestion on answers of a personality inventory, *J. appl. Psychol.*, 1949, **33**, 352–355. See also R. Stagner, The gullibility of personnel managers, *Personnel Psychol.*, 1958, **11**, 347–352. N. Sundberg, The acceptability of "fake" vs. "bona fide" personality test interpretations, *J. abnorm. soc. Psychol.*, 1955, **50**, 145–147.

in due time we may expect to reduce the present embarrassment of riches. We may answer our question by saying, "No, we do not need all the devices available, but at present we are in a period of free competition, hoping that fewer but improved methods will gradually emerge."

Our question, however, has deeper theoretical significance. If a personality is fairly well integrated, if there is consistency among its regions, then in principle very few diagnostic techniques need to be used. One and the same personality should shine through any and all methods. Theoretically we can say that if a method is valid and comprehensive (tapping all the main traits of a life) and if the life is well integrated, then this one method alone should suffice. Other tests would be simply redundant and confirmatory (if they too are valid).

But this ideal situation does not exist. For one thing, few tests are comprehensive. If they tap self-appraisal, they overlook the unconscious stratum; if they measure unconscious conflicts they almost certainly overlook conscious values. And so confidence cannot yet be placed in single instruments. We need well-conceived comprehensive batteries.[57]

Again, personalities are seldom as fully integrated as a "one-test diagnosis" would require. We have already argued (page 443) that for integrated normal subjects projective tests should reveal the same trends as direct methods reveal. For noninsightful neurotics the results would be different. But in order to know whether we are dealing with a normal or a neurotic structure, and with an insightful or a defensive neurotic, it is necessary to employ both direct and projective assessment methods. No single method yet discovered taps all the levels relevant to personality assessment.

We conclude, therefore, that experimentation with many techniques is still needed. In the long run, poorer methods will be eliminated, and we shall be left with fewer, but better, instruments.

A Measure of Values

Let us take a single method (a somewhat complex test of six common traits) for closer inspection. We shall ask about its rational

---

[57] R. W. White, What is tested by psychological tests? In P. Hoch and J. Zubin (Eds.), *Relation of psychological tests to psychiatry* (New York: Grune & Stratton, 1950), Chap. 1.

origin, how it developed into an empirical scale, and what its safeguards are.

We choose for our illustration the pencil-and-paper test, *A Study of Values*. One reason for this choice is our emphasis upon value-orientations as a particularly revealing level of human traits. We know a person best if we know what kind of future he is bringing about—and his molding of the future rests primarily on his personal values. A value is a belief upon which a man acts by preference. It is thus a cognitive, a motor, and, above all, a deeply propriate disposition.

In Chapter 12 we described at length the sixfold classification of ideal values propounded by the German philosopher Eduard Spranger.[58] These value-directions, we recall, are the *theoretical* (truth), the *economic* (usefulness), *esthetic* (harmony), *social* (altruistic love), *political* (power), *religious* (unity). Spranger, we recall, does not imply that a given man belongs exclusively to one or another of these ideal types. The types are conceptually pure (schemata of comprehensibility), but actual lives reflect various mixtures.

In selecting his six types, Spranger may be said to hold a somewhat flattering view of human nature. He does not allow for formless or valueless personalities; nor for those who follow an expedient or hedonistic philosophy of life. The neglect of sheerly sensuous values is a weakness in his scheme. Furthermore, the conception applies best to people who have a fairly high level of education and experience.

Our problem is to translate Spranger's "ideal types" into measurable dimensions. No person is purely theoretical, social, or religious in his interests. But he may have a preponderance of choices for one value-direction over others. The scale tests for preferences by a "forced choice" method. Given two or more alternatives, which does the person prefer?

A Study of Values offers 30 such choices in Part I, and 15 such choices in Part II. Each of the six values is paired an equal number of times with each of the remaining five. Figure 36 gives examples. In Part I the subject may score the two alternatives either 3–0 or 2–1,

58 E. Spranger, *Types of men* (Transl. from 5th German ed. of *Lebensformen* by P. J. W. Pigors; Halle: Niemeyer, 1928). American agent: Stechert-Hafner, 31 E. 10th St., New York 3, N.Y. *A Study of Values,* by G. W. Allport, P. E. Vernon, G. Lindzey, is published by Houghton Mifflin, Boston, Mass. (3rd ed., 1960).

Part I

6. Which of the following branches of study do you expect ultimately will prove more important for mankind? (a) mathematics; (b) theology.

7. Which would you consider the more important function of modern leaders? (a) to bring about the accomplishment of practical goals; (b) to encourage followers to take a greater interest in the rights of others.

8. When witnessing a gorgeous ceremony (ecclesiastical or academic, induction into office, etc.), are you more impressed: (a) by the color and pageantry of the occasion itself; (b) by the influence and strength of the group?

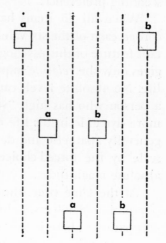

Part II

10. Which of the following would you prefer to do during part of your next summer vacation (if your ability and other conditions would permit) —
   a. write and publish an original biological essay or article
   b. stay in some secluded part of the country where you can appreciate fine scenery
   c. enter a local tennis or other athletic tournament
   d. get experience in some new line of business

11. Do great exploits and adventures of discovery, such as Columbus's, Magellan's, Byrd's, and Amundsen's, seem to you significant because —
   a. they represent conquests by man over the difficult forces of nature
   b. they add to our knowledge of geography, meteorology, oceanography, etc.
   c. they weld human interests and international feelings throughout the world
   d. they contribute each in a small way to an ultimate understanding of the universe

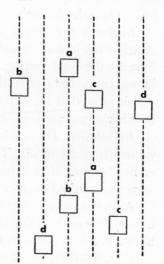

Figure 36. Sample Items from *A Study of Values* (G. W. Allport, P. E. Vernon, G. Lindzey. Boston: Houghton Mifflin Company, 1960).

depending on the degree to which he favors them. In Part II he ranks his first choice 4, and the remaining choices 3, 2, 1, in order of descending preference.

When all 45 items have been scored, the total preference accorded each of the six values is plotted on a psychograph. An important feature of this psychograph is its idiographic nature. The profile gives only the *relative* importance of the six values within the single life. No absolute levels can be inferred. In fact, the lowest value of a person who has high "value energy" might in absolute terms be more dynamic in his life than the highest value of a person who is generally apathetic and devoid of interests. The construction of the scale by the forced-choice method precludes the measurement of absolute magnitudes.

At the same time, the test yields norms for the standardization population (8,369 cases), broken down by sex, by college attended, by occupation. There is thus some guidance in terms of general norms for a comparison of the ranges and relative scores in individual profiles. In this way the test combines advantages of both an idiographic and a nomothetic method.

Response Set. The test is not transparent: the subject cannot see clearly what its aim is, nor what diagnostic significance his reply may have in the final scoring. Thus the scale is not easily faked. More important is the fact that the items have been selected through various revisions so that in a large population they have equal popularity, in this way precluding the response set of social desirability.

Reliability. The stability (test-retest reliability) ranges for the six values from .84 to .93. The item-reliability is very high: the preference for each item agrees on the average with the total preference score to a marked degree.

Although several attempts have been made to factor-analyze the battery, the authors feel that the intercorrelation of the values is not high enough to warrant their reduction to a smaller, "more basic" number. Further, factor-analysis cannot but destroy the initial logic upon which the scale is based, and which seems to be supported by the relative independence of the six scores.

Validation. The "construct validation" of the scale comes from the fact that selected occupations are clearly differentiated by the test. Engineers, for example, have relatively high theoretical and economic values, as might be expected considering their role in the social structure. Clergymen have relatively high religious and social values; students of business administration, relatively high economic and political values; artists, relatively high esthetic values; and so on. The test also predicts successfully the subjects' behavior on various proceptual and cognitive tests, thus showing that it taps a basic style of proceptive functioning.[59]

Uses and Limitations. This test has been found useful in teaching since it shows to the college student the hierarchy of his own values— a matter that he may not have previously thought about. It is helpful in counseling, and sometimes in vocational guidance. Prospective marriage partners gain from knowing in advance of marriage each other's profiles. In short, the test is primarily an aid to self-insight.

As we have said, it does not measure the absolute strength of values, but only their relative prominence in a given life. For this reason conventional comparisons of "trait strength," as made in differential psychology, are not possible. The test is also limited to the six value-areas postulated by Spranger, all of them, as we have said, somewhat flattering in type since they overlook the "baser" values of sensuality and opportunism.

This test has had the benefit of revision over a period of nearly thirty years. For this reason its merits and limitations are more clearly evident than is true of newer scales. Perhaps the main judgment to give is that since it stands the test of time its merit is established, but its limitations help us see why numerous methods are still required in assessment. Even this fairly comprehensive instrument taps only a selected region of personality.

Conclusion to Chapters 17 and 18

It was Aristotle who said, "It is the mark of an educated man to look for precision in each class of things just so far as the nature of the subject admits." At the present stage of scientific advance, personality does not seem to be a "precise" subject; it should be, however, a "careful" subject. Within recent decades marked advance has been made in approaching the topic with care and with a hope of eventual precision. Many humanists, no doubt, would say that the advances are vain show and that the topic should be left in the traditional way to art and literature. I disagree. Although the

[59] See the discussion of research uses of the scale in the *Manual* accompanying the test.

methods reviewed here are still vulnerable, I believe that they kindle some light. And, to quote another sage (Confucius), "It is better to kindle a little light than to chide the darkness."

Psychologists are remarkably inventive in creating new techniques for the analysis and assessment of personality. The task of classifying these techniques is difficult because many principles of categorization could be used. Below is a practical method of ordering them under eleven rubrics:

   1. constitutional and physiological diagnosis
   2. cultural setting, membership, role
   3. personal documents and case study
   4. self-appraisal
   5. conduct analysis
   6. ratings
   7. tests and scales
   8. projective techniques
   9. depth analysis
  10. expressive behavior
  11. synoptic procedures

Each of these major methods breaks down into specialized subdivisions. From our total panorama one principal conclusion emerges: There is no "one and only" method for diagnosing personality. Each method has its enthusiastic supporters; yet it is absurd to claim adequacy for any one procedure, be it word-association, endocrine analysis, the Rorschach test, the MMPI, the case study, or any other single device. The truth is that for some problems one method of attack is best; for others, different methods. A wise investigator will not place his faith in any one exclusively.

Some procedures, we note, are idiographic in their emphasis: for example, the life-history, the cluster-analysis method of dealing with personal documents, the self-anchoring scale in self-appraisal, various synoptic procedures, and (in part) A Study of Values. But it is not possible to classify procedures as exclusively idiographic or nomothetic in type, since the same device can often be used in either way. Most techniques, we may safely say, are extensions of the tradition of differential psychology and lead to a comparison of persons with one another rather than to the configuration (patterning) of traits within the single individual. The latter path still needs pioneering.

Most procedures lead to some form of quantification—the idiographic no less than the nomothetic. Basic methods of quantification are indispensable for determining the reliability and validity of methods. And in all forms of scaling and content analysis one must count *units*. Our only criticism of quantification comes when it is made the primary objective in research and theory rather than a tool and an incident in the total sequence of logic. Our criticism of excessively empirical scales, and of factor-analysis, is based on this consideration. We have argued that confusion is likely to result unless methods keep fairly close to their theoretical point of origin; that is to say, unless they start and end with a rational conception of the structure of personality. Quantification helps to clarify and correct hypotheses but is not a substitute for them. Statistics is a useful adjunct, but the field of personality should not be made a mere playground for the mathematically gifted.

Those who wish psychology to be a purely objective, repeatable, and positive science will, no doubt, criticize some methods reviewed here as being "unscientific," as making assessment into a subjective, impressionistic game. The defender of these "soft methods" would reply, "Your hard-headed methods yield mostly trivial and obvious information. Personality is too complex a thing for your machinelike methods. Above all else, personality is a problem of configuration, and the looser methods deal best with molar units and patterning." It is indeed a struggle to strike a balance between rigid and perfectionist standards that risk sterilizing research by yielding artificial fragments of behavior having no essential bearing upon personality, and loose standards that permit wanton assertions to go without check or proof. It is this balance that Aristotle advocates in advising us to demand the highest degree of exactness compatible with adequacy of conception and clear perspective upon the problem in hand.

These chapters have opened up the complex task of analyzing, measuring, understanding personality. Chapters 20 and 21 continue the discussion. But first we shall examine an important, and relatively neglected, avenue of assessment, *expressive behavior*.

CHAPTER **19**

•

Expressive Behavior

EXPRESSION DEFINED • EXPRESSIVE VERSUS COPING BEHAVIOR • THEORY OF EXPRESSION • ADDITIONAL DETERMINANTS • GENESIS OF EXPRESSIVE BEHAVIOR • ARE EXPRESSIVE MOVEMENTS CONSISTENT? • PSYCHODIAGNOSIS • EXPRESSIVE FEATURES • STYLE • SUMMARY

SUPPOSE that you go to a lecture delivered by a stranger. The lecture may be on any topic at all—let us say it is on "expressive behavior." You go primarily to hear *what* the lecturer will say, only secondarily, if at all, to note *how* he will say it. You are concerned with the content of his views, with the way he will cope with the topic. He, too, will be intent on the subject matter. Both of you are focused on this high-level process of communication.

But while the lecturer is speaking, a lower level process of communication is under way. Even if you are not particularly interested, you note—especially at the start of the lecture—many things about the speaker. He is tall, fairly young, neatly dressed, slender, incessantly active; he speaks rapidly but in a voice that is high and raspy. He repeats his phrases, smiles frequently, mops his brow though it is not hot, and scrawls illegibly on the blackboard.

Almost immediately—whether you wish to do so or not—you make some inferences about him as a person. The inferences are fleeting,

460

fringelike, usually unimportant. You think to yourself, "He is insecure, on the make, self-centered, but learned, humorous though slightly cynical; on the whole I don't like him and I pity his wife." Your judgments are shadowy and perhaps all wrong. But you cannot help making them and he by his *expressive movement* cannot help prompting them.

Before the lecture is ended, and especially if you hear many lectures by the same man, you become so accustomed to him that you pay no more attention to his manner. You tend to discount his style of expression and pay attention almost exclusively to his high-level communication, to what he is saying, how competent he is, and what it all means to you.

Sometimes, of course, we do become directly interested in manner, in style, in the expressive aspect of behavior. We put aside our usual preoccupation with content, with the intellectual, purposive, coping aspects of life. We ask ourselves what do this person's voice, speech, facial expression, style of clothing, handwriting, posture, gait, and pattern of gestures signify. We sometimes think—and rightly— that the *how* of behavior can be more revealing than the *what*. The *adverbial* manner of an act tells us much about the person we are dealing with.

Expression Defined

The term *expression* is used in psychology with at least three different meanings. First is the common-sense use. We say that a man expresses an opinion, or a preference, or a point of view. That is, he tells us directly and deliberately something about his ideas or himself. We also say that an artist, a musician, or a dancer is expressing his feelings as well as some symbolized meaning in his production. Whether intellectual or artistic, this type of expression is deliberate and conscious. It normally is our chief channel for understanding other personalities.

The term has a more limited meaning when it refers to such bodily changes as blushing, laughing, dilation of the pupil, quaking of the knees. Darwin's *The Expression of Emotions in Men and Animals,* first published in 1872, established this meaning firmly. In this sense expression signifies involuntary response to emotional stimuli.

The third use of the term is subtler, but most appropriate to the present chapter. It refers to one's manner or style of behaving. Unlike the first meaning, it has nothing to do with the *what* of an act, but only with the *how*. Unlike the second meaning, it has nothing to do with the release of emotional tension; instead, it deals with the oblique mirroring of personal traits. Of course, all three types of expression tell us something about a person, but for analytic clarity it is important to make the distinction.[1]

We can define expressive movement simply as *one's manner of performing adaptive acts*.[2] From our point of view, every single act a person performs has both its expressive and its adaptive (coping) aspects, sometimes more of one, sometimes more of the other. Let us examine this proposition more closely.

Expressive versus Coping Behavior

Every act that we perform copes with our environment. Even rest and sleep and play are no exceptions. There is a *task* in hand (the *what* of behavior). We must repair a lock, seek relaxation, summon a doctor, answer a question, or blink a speck of dust from our eyes. To cope with the task we employ our reflexes and habits or call upon our skills, our judgment and knowledge. But into this stream of activity there enter deeper trends in our nature. There are *styles* of repairing locks, calling a doctor, relaxing, answering a question, or blinking the eye. Every action betrays *both* a coping and an expressive aspect. One may think of coping as the *predicate* of action (what we are doing); expression as the *adverb* of action (how we are doing it).

Take the simple case of blinking the eye. The blink is provoked by irritation of the cornea. We cope with the irritation by closing the eyelid momentarily. But even this simple reflex activity shows the influence of other integrated neural centers. Some people blink with regularity, others in uneven rhythm, some close their eyes com-

---

1 Few writers distinguish between these three meanings of the term *expression*. Even those who have elaborate theories of expression lump them together, with the result that the theories become broad and muddy. A survey of such theories is given by P. Kirchhoff, *Allgemeine Ausdruckslehre: Prinzipien und Probleme der allgemeinen Ausdruckstheorie* (Göttingen: Hofgrefe, 1957).

2 An existential variation of this definition is given by Straus: "Expressive motions are variations of fundamental functions in which a person performs his being-in-the-world in a mode peculiar to him." E. W. Straus, The sigh: an introduction to a theory of expressions, *Tijdschrift voor Philosophie*, 1952, **14**, 1–22.

pletely, others do not.[3] Those who have seen cinema films of Mussolini may have noticed that his eyeblinks were infrequent but also astonishingly deliberate in appearance, as though his self-styled "indomitable will" exerted itself in even this remote corner of his coping conduct. Similarly, sighs, coughs, sneezes, knee jerks are marked by individual differences.

Some of the differences between coping and expressive behavior may be summarized as follows:[4]

a. Coping is purposive and specifically motivated; expressive behavior is not.

b. Coping is determined by the needs of the moment and by the situation; expressive movement reflects deeper personal structure.

c. Coping is formally elicited; expressive behavior spontaneously "emitted."

d. Coping can be more readily controlled (inhibited, modified, conventionalized); expressive behavior is harder to alter and often uncontrollable. (Changing our style of handwriting, e.g., can be kept up for only a short time.)

e. Coping usually aims to change the environment; expressive behavior aims at nothing, though it may incidentally have effects (as when our manner of answering questions in an interview creates a good impression and lands us the job).

f. Typically coping is conscious, even though it may employ automatic skills; expressive behavior generally lies below the threshold of our awareness.

Figure 37 represents the essential situation schematically. (We shall soon discuss the factor of cultural and situational determinants.)

Although both coping and expression are present in every act (even the eyeblink), their proportion varies widely. The man on the assembly line is held rigidly to his task. He must turn the wrench precisely so many millimeters, so many times a minute. Such behavior is frustrating to him, for it suppresses and holds in check all impulses arising from temperament and personality. It is no wonder

[3] E. Ponder and W. P. Kennedy, On the act of blinking, *Quart. J. exper. Physiol.*, 1927, **18**, 89–110.
[4] A similar but not identical list is given by A. H. Maslow, The expressive component of behavior, *Psychol. Rev.*, 1949, **56**, 261–272.

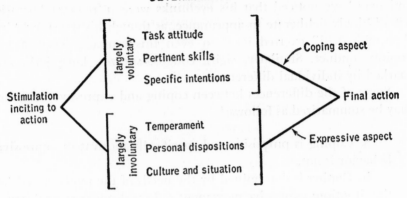

Figure 37. Behavior as Convergence of Coping and Expression

that job dissatisfaction is greatest when the mechanical prescription of movement is highest. In a technological society more and more occupations require precision in coping and a suppression of individual styles. In former days there was more pride of authorship among artisans, cabinetmakers, illuminators of manuscripts, and makers of doughnuts.

Effort to do a task in a prescribed manner destroys the impulse to do it stylistically. There is less individuality in the handwriting of a bookkeeper or librarian than in most people's scripts. A radio announcer must use his voice as an instrument of coping; the result is less expressive individuality. An actor who plays many roles must squeeze out so far as he can all his personal mannerisms.

Figure 38 represents the different proportions of coping and expression in various activities.

Theory of Expression

In Chapter 7 we spoke of "stratification theories." These are metaphorical ways of viewing the organization of personality in terms of layers. The method is favored by many German psychologists. A relatively early example comes from the work of Ludwig Klages, who made a sharp distinction between the upper overlaid layer, *Geist* (mind, intellect, adaptive performance) and *Seele* (soul, the diffuse elemental surge of life). Coping activity is a product of *Geist;* expressive activity, of *Seele.* The former acts as a restrainer, sometimes even as a destroyer of the basic rhythms that are carriers of vital expression. If we are to perceive the individuality of expressive behavior we must look beyond the specific intent of an act, beyond the con-

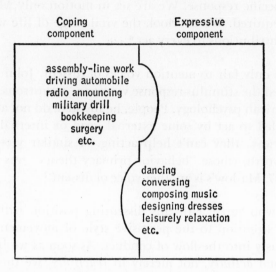

Figure 38. Varying Proportions of Coping and Expressive Component in Certain Activities

scious control, and beyond the conventions and skills employed in coping.[5]

Take handwriting, a special interest of Klages. It is clearly a product of both coping (*Geist*) and expression (*Seele*). On the one hand, the person is deliberately conveying his thoughts; he is employing conventions of writing taught him in school; he is adapting to the paper and pen he must use. All these reflect coping. At the same time his whole nature is, as it were, rebelling against prescribed convention. He departs from the school copy in ways that are individual to him; he betrays his energy, aggressiveness, hostility, fear, ambition or rigidity in his manner of departure. His own vital style of life (his temperament and his personal characteristics) surges into his performance. It takes little skill to understand the coping aspect of the performance; it takes much skill to read the underlying surge of expression.

[5] L. Klages, *Der Geist als Widersacher der Seele* (3 vols.; Leipzig: Barth, 1929–1932.) Klages was not himself an academic psychologist, but his deep influence on German psychological thought is shown in a volume of essays honoring him. H. Prinzhorn (Ed.), *Die Wissenschaft am Scheidewege von Leben und Geist* (Leipzig: Barth, 1932).

American psychology has developed no such comprehensive theory of expression. The reason is interesting. American psychology is, by and large, a psychology of "reaction." A specific stimulus demands a specific response. We are set in motion only when a coping action is required. We overlook the vital surge of life with its spontaneous contributions to every act.[6]

It is only fair to mention voices of dissent. John Dewey often criticized the stimulus-response view as a "monstrous assumption" of American psychology. People, he insisted, do not act only when compelled to act by some external goad or internal need. They act anyway; they can't help acting. A similar view is held by Woodworth, whose "behavior primacy theory" was discussed on page 207. Maslow's is another voice of dissent.[7]

Those who agree with this dissenting position will more easily turn their attention to the pervasive style of movement that enters spontaneously into the flow of conduct. As soon as we become interested in total *activity*, not merely in *reactivity*, we then appreciate the importance of expression as a complement to coping.

It is well, however, not to go to the opposite extreme. Every activity, even if loaded heavily with expressivity, has an origin somewhere. That is to say, some stimulus lies behind the scenes. Even a "spontaneous" act follows some sequence of instigation. The play of a child, the painting of a picture, dancing, laughing are heavily laden with expressivity, but something somewhere started off the playing, painting, dancing, laughing. As Figure 37 shows, coping and expression are both present in every act, however unequal their ratios may be. We are not making the "monstrous assumption" that the stimulus pulls the trigger and the act is a specific response. We are saying that spontaneity exists, though it should be defined simply as the contribution that the total organism makes to a coping performance. There seems to be no act that we can call purely and solely expressive, just as there is no act that is purely and solely coping.

At this point we need neurological theory to help us, but as yet

6 Even the vocabulary of American psychology reflects this bias. See G. W. Allport, The open system in personality theory. In *Personality and social encounter* (Boston: Beacon, 1960), Chap. 3.
7 A. H. Maslow, *Motivation and personality* (New York: Harper, 1954).

it is lacking. It is, however, consistent with what is known to view any act as a "final common path" representing the integration of many layers and levels of traces and impulses with the intention of the moment. Thus if I start to paint a picture there will necessarily be dominant coping movements (handling canvas and paints), but into the final product will flow concurrent impulses, traces, styles of expression—all that Klages would call my *Seele*.

Finally, the problem of expression raises questions of social value. It is said that the tragedy of our culture is that coping is in the ascendancy, and that creative expression is suppressed. A technological civilization necessarily brings this imbalance. Workmen are rigidly held to the precision of coping; their efforts to repress individuality of expression cause frustration and dissatisfaction on the job. True, they have more leisure, but the leisure is for many a matter of consuming prefabricated TV sports, TV shows, TV dinners. An age of mechanical conformity threatens us. When expression is starved, our personalities shrivel, falling far below our human potentiality.[8]

Additional Determinants

Our two-part analysis of the determinants of behavior is sound so far as it goes, but it is oversimplified. What shall we say about the following additional convergent factors that often help to shape the quality of an act?

    a. cultural tradition
    b. regional convention
    c. passing emotional moods
    d. conditions of strain and fatigue
    e. age
    f. sex
    g. native muscular structure and bodily build
    h. conditions of health and disease
    i. accidental deformations of the body
    j. special training (e.g., dramatics, military drill)
    k. conditions of physical environment (e.g., pen, ink, paper in writing; the ground and climatic factors in walking)

[8] Many critics of our modern age have made this point, and have written specifications and remedies. For example, E. Fromm, *The sane society* (New York: Holt, Rinehart and Winston, 1955); and D. McGregor, *The human side of enterprise* (New York: McGraw-Hill, 1960).

All these determinants are important, and although they complicate our two-part analysis they do not destroy it.

The first two factors, cultural tradition and regional convention, provide a kind of basic ground for the expressive component. A young child takes into himself the prevailing cultural habits of gesticulation, the general norm for handwriting, or the common intonations of voice. Insofar as he is socialized (or acculturated), these ground norms become a part of his own nature. (Hence these factors are included in Figure 37 as truly expressive factors.) He will, of course, vary his individual style around these traditional norms, but underlying them he will, if he is Chinese, display the Chinese mode. Schopenhauer wrote: "The English have a peculiar scorn of gesticulation and hold it to be something unworthy and common." By contrast, most Jews from Eastern Europe gesticulate dramatically, and even their gait has a cultural distinctiveness.[9]

Factors c and d, dealing with the temporary conditions of mood and fatigue, are often decisive. They, too, must be classed as expressive determinants, though in this case the expression is of transitory personal states, and not of enduring dispositions. How important mood is we shall see on pages 473–475.

Factors e to i represent certain structural influences. A woman, light in weight, cannot have as heavy a tread, as strong a grip, as the average male. A hand crippled by arthritis will affect gesture and script. A heavy physique cannot poise itself lightly on the edge of a chair. Infirm age does tremulously what youth does with vigor. It is difficult to classify such influences as applying only to the coping or expressive determinants. In part they affect movement via skill; in part they are related to change in personality and therefore are expressive.

The final factors, j and k, are properly regarded as special cases of coping determinants. Especially is this true of conditions in the physical environment. On a hot day or on uneven ground anyone is likely to slacken pace or shorten stride; with a scratchy pen anyone is likely to write with uneven pressure. As for special habits of skill (the trained voice, the military manner), to some

9 Cf. W. La Barre, The cultural basis of emotion and gestures, *J. Person.*, 1947, **16**, 49–68. See also D. Efron, *Gesture and environment* (New York: Kings Crown, 1941).

extent such training directly fashions personality, and therefore becomes incorporated into the expressive phase. Often, however, such conventions of movement are masklike and tend to conceal personal qualities.

Genesis of Expressive Behavior

If a young child is irritable he shows it openly in almost every movement he makes: he cries, fusses, whines, slaps. His expressiveness is diffuse and massive (cf. Chapter 5). An adult, by contrast, may show his irritable nature only by his restless fingers or shifting eyes. The growing differentiation and localizing of movement as a person matures is true not only of skilled coping but also of expression.

The fact that expression tends with growing maturity to become confined to limited regions of the body has important consequences for personality assessment. For one thing, it means that various features of expression are of unequal significance in different people. Some faces are open books; some are "poker faces." For some people gestures are merely conventional; for others, highly individual. Sometimes the style of clothing or the handwriting seems "just like" the person; in other cases, entirely nonexpressive. One person reveals himself primarily in his speech; another, in his posture and gait; a third, in his style of clothing or ornamentation. As a promising hypothesis we suggest that every person has one or two leading expressive features which reveal his true nature. If this is so, it is somewhat futile to study all people by the same cues, e.g., voice, eyes, or handwriting.[10] The cue that is revealing for one person is not necessarily revealing for another.

Every child is exposed to standard forms of expression which tend to limit his individual impulses in movement. He learns to write from a standard model, to play the piano or to dance according to rules. As Klages says, he tends to break away in part (but only in part), from the models. His handwriting acquires "graphic maturity," his musical interpretation and his dancing steps are his own. Even the stenographer in time modifies her system of shorthand, and

---

[10] It was this consideration that led W. Stern to repudiate what he calls "monosymtomatic" methods of psychodiagnosis. Graphology, for example, should never be employed alone, for it may in a given case draw a blank. It is safer to study many channels of expression before we draw inferences regarding personality. See W. Stern, Ausdruck und Leistung. In Prinzhorn, *op. cit.*, pp. 219–223. Note 5 above.

the physician, when no longer an intern, comes to practice his art in his own manner. But all people remain conventional to some degree. What is important is the extent to which they break through the prescriptions of training and convention, and develop their own stamp of individuality. And, as we have said, the stamp may be more apparent in some expressive features than in others.

The child, and especially the adolescent, is likely to adopt expressive styles by imitation. The small boy who envies the worldliness of the street-corner gang imitates their carefree manner of tilting the cap and spitting. The adolescent girl wears her hair as her favorite actress does. The college student apes the mannerisms of some coach or professor. Such superficial imitation is of psychological interest. At heart the youth wants the basic skills or attributes of his model. He is too young to attain them, and so he settles for the external expression of these attributes—for the kind of necktie or the haircut worn by the boss, for the swagger or stance of the athletic hero.

With maturity many of these imitative mannerisms are dropped. The office boy grown up to worldly wisdom can wear whatever necktie he likes; he no longer needs to ape the boss. And yet occasionally mannerisms in adulthood may be vestigial, indicating more the past history of one's development than its present state. Perhaps an expressive habit has become fixed by a kind of perseverative functional autonomy (pages 230–235). In such a case we are dealing with a residue of earlier life, and should evaluate it as such. Thus if an adult has a habit of averting his eyes, biting his nails, or picking his nose, he *may* be evincing present conflict and present trends, or he *may* be carrying out a dissociated perseverative mannerism from childhood. Only close study will tell.

Autistic Gestures. Let us look more closely at the part played by internal conflict in the creation of certain expressive mannerisms.

A fastidious house painter, who feels that his occupation is far beneath him, betrays his conflict through scrupulous care of his fingernails, which during work he polishes and inspects at frequent intervals.

A young man has a peculiar habit of jerking his arms whenever he thinks of embarrassing things. This habit goes back to a time when he had unpleasant compulsive thoughts of striking people on the street. At such times he would jerk his arms to throw off the impulse. But now he uses the mannerism whenever freedom from unpleasant thoughts is desired.

To such movements Krout gives the name *autistic gestures.* They have only unconscious meaning for the subject, and no meaning at all (unless carefully studied) for the observer. The theory holds that if a direct response is inhibited or tabooed it will be reduced to a mere vestigial state—to an autistic gesture.

Krout has ingeniously submitted the theory to experimental testing.[11] In the subject he arouses a conflict. For example, he secures the subject's agreement to the proposition that people keep their crushes secret; but then asks the subject to think silently for half a minute and admit to the experimenter his (her) own crushes. Or again, the experimenter says, "Now, no really normal person ever wishes his friends, especially his relatives, dead. Does he?" After the subject agrees, the experimenter says, "I want you to think now. Did *you* ever wish that one of your relatives was dead? I want you to think." During the interval of conflict thus induced—before the subject gives his answer—a record is taken of the movements of his hands. After the experiment the subject is asked what attitudinal state of mind he felt during the conflict.

By this procedure Krout reaches the conclusion that there are statistically significant equivalences between certain gestures and certain attitudes. The open hand dangling between the legs, he says, characteristically accompanies frustration; fingers folded at tips, suspicion or resignation; hand to nose, fear; finger to lips, shame; fist gestures, aggression; one finger enveloped by other hand, ego-inflation or encouragement.

These expressive signs Krout finds to be fairly general. The experiment is ingenious and may lead us eventually toward a general language of gesture. On the other hand, individuals also evolve their own personal patterns, and we cannot always read these from a

11 M. H. Krout, Autistic gestures: an experimental study in symbolic movement, *Psychol. Monogr.,* 1935, No. 208. Also, An experimental attempt to produce unconscious manual symbolic movements, *J. gen. Psychol.,* 1954, **51,** 93–152.

standard lexicon of gestures. Cultural norms, too, may differ, and the two sexes, as Krout shows, seem to favor different gestural patterns. We may suspect that some high-strung temperaments make many movements lacking deeper significance, and that some who suffer from conflict may remain outwardly placid. If we keep such cautions in mind we can still learn much from this pioneer research.

We do not imply that all expressive movements have their origin in conflict, though undoubtedly some do. From our point of view expression reveals the conflict-free as well as the conflicted aspects of personality.

Are Expressive Movements Consistent?

Let us try a short and easy experiment.

On a sheet of letter paper label four lines *a, b, c, d*. Write on lines *a, b, c* your own name just as you usually sign it. But on line *d* make deliberately an exact copy of what you wrote on line *c*.

Now compare lines *a* and *b;* also *c* and *d*. You will undoubtedly find that the first two are much more similar than the last two.

Figure 39 shows a typical result from this little experiment.

Why are lines *a* and *b* so similar? The reason is that the instruc-

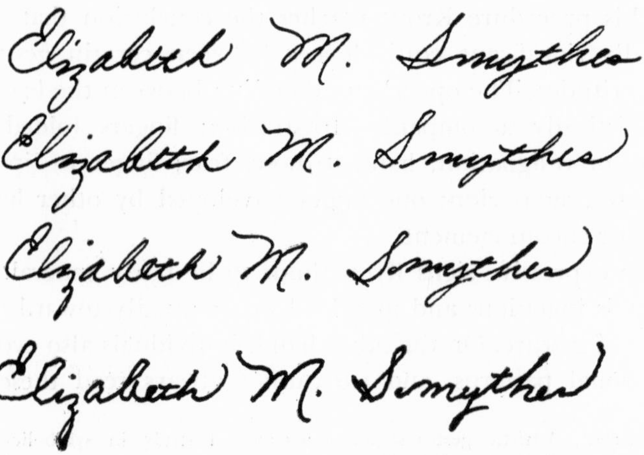

Figure 39. Signatures: Three "Expressive," One "Coping"

tions for coping ("write your name") were identical, and maximum freedom was allowed for expressive consistency. Line *d*, on the other hand, was written under very different conditions. The coping aspect was heavily loaded. It became a conscious task to "make an exact copy." Every movement was deliberate. Expressive consistency was suppressed. In the terms of Klages, the *Geist* took command and stifled the harmonious flow of the individual *Seele*.

This is a demonstration of expressive consistency. People develop highly characteristic styles of writing, talking, walking, sitting, gesturing, laughing, and shaking hands. At a distance we recognize a friend from his gait. Over the phone we know who greets us, not so much from what he says as from his voice and manner of speaking. Expression is perhaps the most stubborn part of our natures. Our coping is variable, depending on *what* we have to do. But *how* we do it carries an almost infallible signature.

For a given person patterns of expression are highly consistent over time. Mood does, of course, make some difference. If a person feels depressed his movements are relatively constricted; if he feels elated they are more expansive. His flow of speech is freer in elation than in depression.[12] But differences in mood seem to change chiefly the energy that goes into an expression. The pattern (e.g., handwriting) remains about the same in form.

To what extent do various expressive features of the body agree with one another? Is it true, as Lavater asserted of old, "one and the same spirit is manifest in all"? If Mr. X has an emphatic voice, are his gestures emphatic, is his stride, his handshake, his pressure in writing?

To some extent laboratory measurements help us to answer this question. In one study subjects were asked to perform many tasks: writing on paper, on the blackboard, with the foot (in sand); reading aloud, walking, drawing, making check marks, estimating distances, and so on. It turned out that the subjects were notably consistent. For example, they showed throughout the experiment a characteristic level of emphaticness, also of ex-

[12] Winifred B. Johnson, Euphoric and depressed moods in normal subjects, *Charact. & Pers.*, 1937–1938, **6**, 79–98 and 188–202. See also A. E. Wessman, D. F. Ricks, and M. McI. Tyl, Characteristics and concommitants of mood fluctuations in college women, *J. abnorm. soc. Psychol.*, 1960, **60**, 117–126.

pansive or constricted movement, also of outgoing (centrifugal) or inward (centripetal) movement.[13]

Besides laboratory measurement there is another way of demonstrating consistency: the method of *matching* (pages 387, 446). I might show you the photograph of a stranger, and with it three samples of handwriting. I then ask you to tell which sample of handwriting was written by the stranger in the photograph. Of course by chance you would be right one time in three. But if your success is consistently greater we have evidence that there is some perceptible consistency between facial and graphic expression. The method can be elaborated in many ways. Thus records of voice can be matched with occupations; written themes, with drawings; or all these, with all the others.[14]

Figure 29 in Chapter 16 invites you to match three musical notations with the names of three composers. From this experiment we find that correct matching occurs in 80 percent of the cases. The 20 percent of mistakes are made chiefly with the examples of Mozart and Bach. Mozart's balance and ease are sometimes confused with Bach's architectonic quality. Few people miss the explosive character of Beethoven's script.[15]

The method of matching helps us demonstrate to what extent we can *perceive* the same expressive quality in different expressive records. It does not, however, tell us on what basis we reach our decision. The cues are often so subtle that they elude us and we do not know why we make the matching we do. Matching demonstrates that congruence exists but tells us nothing more.

The evidence we have reviewed justifies three conclusions:

1. Expressive features of the body are not independently activated. Any one of them may be affected in much the same way as any other.

2. The congruence, however, is never perfect. One feature is not an exact replica of another. If it were we would be justified

---

13 These experiments are described more fully by G. W. Allport and P. E. Vernon, *Studies in expressive movement* (New York: Macmillan, 1933).

14 A discussion of the matching method is offered by P. E. Vernon, The matching method applied to investigations of personality, *Psychol. Bull.*, 1936, 33, 149–177. By the same author, *Personality tests and assessments* (London: Methuen, 1953), *passim*.

15 W. Wolff, *The expression of personality* (New York: Harper, 1943), pp. 21–22.

in diagnosing the personality from any one feature—from handwriting or from the eyes, hands, or limbs. As matters stand, however, we cannot safely do so.

3. The unity of expression turns out, as we would expect, to be a question of degree, just as the unity of personality is a matter of degree (Chapter 16).

Psychodiagnosis

Everyone "reads character" from expressive movement. We cannot help doing so. Literary authors use it as a major device, as a few examples show:

Hands in repose reflect breeding, sensibility, and regard for others.

Democritus knew Protagoras to be a scholar from seeing him bind up a faggot, and thrusting, as he did, the small twigs inward.

A man does not lay down his hat in coming into a room, or take it up in going out, but something escapes that reveals his nature.

Statements of this order are often charming and plausible but they leave us wondering as to their trustworthiness.

In a nutshell, expressive behavior is without doubt a potential guide to the assessment of personality; but unfortunately psychologists have given it very little study. Krout's painstaking experiment (mentioned on page 471) may eventually lead to a correct reading of significance of certain gestures. Soon we shall turn to a few other facts that have come to light in studying other expressive features. But on the whole the realm of expression has not been deeply studied as an aid to diagnosis.

Up to now psychologists have given attention almost exclusively to the "coping" aspect of personality. Most personality tests (including the so-called projective test) are coping tests. They instruct the subject to perform a task. The experimenter then measures the *what* of the product, not the *how*. The subject fills out a questionnaire, invents a "projective" story, or tells what he sees on a Rorschach card. What is measured is the content of the response. The content is, of course, revealing, but so, too, are the expressive movements that go to waste. Emphasizing the *Geist*, psychologists are blind to the *Seele* as reflected in postures, handwriting, eye movements, voice, and even doodles.

It will not be easy to bring the area of expression under scientific control to the point where we can be certain what the expressive aspect of an act signifies. As we have seen, many are the determinants that converge upon the "final common path." There are few simple one-to-one correspondences. We may say, for example, that a "social introvert" would "logically" make small and tight scribbles or doodles. Let us see what an experiment tells us:

> The investigators asked subjects to draw doodles, and measured their area (constrictedness versus expansiveness). It is true that on the average the socially introverted subjects did tend to draw small and tight doodles, but there were marked exceptions. Some drew exaggeratedly large ones. Similarly, social extraverts did tend to draw large doodles, but again some of them scribbled in a markedly tiny and tight manner. What accounts for this confusing result? It turns out that the deviants were, by other measurements, highly *anxious* people. The anxious social introvert *compensated* for his anxiety by expansive drawing; the anxious social extravert *compensated* in the opposite way.[16] Figure 40 gives illustrations.

This finding should not surprise us. We all know of cases where an insecure adolescent develops a powerful and exaggerated handshake, or other hearty mannerisms with which he hopes to conceal his feelings of inferiority. His act of deception may be deliberate, or it may have become habitual. In any case, we conclude that to read aright any expressive act we need to know whether it contains in itself some compensatory deception. In other words, it is not enough to rely on the obvious interpretation (the face-validity) of an expressive movement. Ego-defensiveness and other countercurrents may be affecting the production.

Judging One's Own Expressions. Perhaps you have had the following experience. You once wrote a theme, drew a picture, or gave a gift to a friend, but have forgotten the fact. Now, years later, you encounter this object but still do not recognize it as your own production. Yet you *feel* very favorable toward it; it seems *good* to you. You think it is smart, intelligent, in good taste.

This somewhat rare but significant experience has been pro-

16 M. A. Wallach and Ruthellen C. Gahm, Personality functions of graphic constriction and expansiveness, *J. Person.,* 1960, **28,** 73–88.

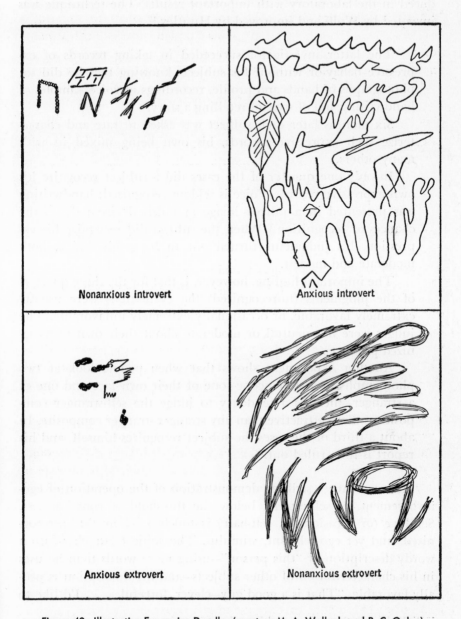

Nonanxious introvert	Anxious introvert
Anxious extrovert	Nonanxious extrovert

Figure 40. Illustrative Expressive Doodles (courtesy M. A. Wallach and R. C. Gahm)

duced in the laboratory with important results. The technique was invented by Wolff and improved by Huntley.[17]

The latter investigator succeeded in taking records of expressive behavior without his subjects knowing that he did so: photographs of hands and profile, recordings of voice, samples of handwriting and of style of retelling a story.

Six months later each subject was asked to rate and characterize such expressive records, his own being mixed in with many others.

In only one quarter of the cases did a subject recognize his own expressive record. (Voice is seldom recognized; handwriting was presented in a mirror image and this device reduces the chances of recognition.) When the subject did recognize his expression, his judgments turned out to be guarded, i.e., both moderate and modest.

The important finding, however, is that for the three quarters of the judgments (unrecognized) the evaluations were usually extremely favorable, or occasionally extremely unfavorable. The judges were not neutral or moderate about their own unrecognized products.

Another experiment shows that when people look at two photographs in a stereoscope—one of their own face and one of a stranger—there is a tendency to judge the self-stranger composite as more attractive than any stranger-stranger composite. In about a third of the cases the subject recognizes himself, and his report is then ruled out.[18]

Here we have a striking demonstration of the operation of ego-involvement, of self-esteem, below the threshold of consciousness. Self-love (or occasionally, self-hate) is touched off by the unrecognized, and yet ego-relevant, stimulus. The subject launches into a wordy description of "this person"—using more words than he uses in his characterization of other subjects—and the description is usually favorable. "That is a good guy—clever, forceful. . . . I'd like to

17 W. Wolff, Selbstbeurteilung und Fremdbeurteilung im wissentlichen und unwissent-lichen Versuch, *Psychol. Forsch.*, 1932, **16**, 251–329; C. W. Huntley, Judgments of self based upon records of expressive behavior, *J. abnorm. soc. Psychol.*, 1940, **35**, 398–427. 18 H. Beloff and J. Beloff, Unconscious self-evaluation using a stereoscope, *J. abnorm. soc. Psychol.*, 1959, **59**, 275–278.

know him, . . ." In the cases of unfavorable self-judgments the same type of explanation applies. When the normal controlling barriers are down, one's discontent and feeling of personal insufficiency may come to the surface as readily as does one's self-esteem.

Huntley's experiment offers ingenious confirmation of the argument of Chapters 6 and 7. A continuing high regard (or occasionally, low regard) for oneself may be carried at unconscious levels, ready to break through whenever the socialized guard (of modesty) is removed. To put the matter technically, we may say that this experiment shows the threshold of the proprium to be lower than the threshold of recognition. Or in other words, self-involvement comes into play before it can be controlled by recognition and therefore by the habits of socialization.

Expressive Features

Any mobile region of the body in rest or in motion is expressive—eyes, mouth, head, trunk, shoulders, hands, fingers, legs. And any of their motions may be analyzed for their expressive significance: jumping, standing, walking, running, strolling, dancing, sitting, lying down, positions in sleeping, gesticulating, talking, laughing, weeping, shaking hands, smoking, handwriting, painting, musical performance, scientific work, play, dress, ornamentation. All these activities and more besides can be studied, separately or in combination.

To consider all these channels of expression, or even to consider any one completely, would be impossible. A few, however, will be singled out to show how constructive research can be done.

The Face. By far the most expressive region of the body is the face. Nature has provided it most lavishly with nerves and subtle muscles; it is unclothed and therefore the most visible region; the seat of the distance receptors, it is the region where the person meets the world head-on. As we have seen, most people locate the "self" in close relation to the face. Our voice emanates from the face. And so, all in all, it is the region to which we give chief attention when we are observing others.

Psychologists have given much study to the facial expression of *emotion,* but this subject is not our present interest. In Chapter 3 we saw that from antiquity the art of physiognomy has persisted, but the insights of Aristotle, Lavater, and all other historical figures have never been scientifically proved.

Most modern research has been devoted not to what the face reveals, but to what people *think* it reveals. It is wise to start with this more modest problem. Some of the generalizations coming from experimental studies follow.[19] In general (at least among American judges) there is a tendency

1. to ascribe to dark-skinned people attributes of unfriendliness, hostility, lack of humor.
2. to ascribe to blonds various favorable qualities. One study shows that fiction tends to make its heroes blond, its villains swarthy and dark.[20]
3. to see faces with wrinkles at eye corners as friendly, humorous, easygoing.
4. to see older males as more distinguished, responsible, and refined than younger males.
5. to see older women as motherly.
6. to perceive people wearing eyeglasses or with high foreheads as more intelligent, dependable, industrious.
7. to perceive smiling faces as more intelligent. (The moral here is that if you are applying for a job submit a smiling photograph; if you are an employer pay no attention to it!)
8. to perceive women with thicker than average lips as sexy, and those with thin lips as asexual.
9. to consider bowed lips as indicating conceit, demandingness, even immorality.
10. to attribute to any Negro face the stereotypes of superstition, religiosity, easygoingness.
11. to see faces that are average in size of nose, hair grooming, set of jaw, and so on, as having more favorable traits than faces that deviate, e.g., by having prominent or receding features. Apparently we feel safer with someone who does not depart far from the cultural norm.

Although such judgmental tendencies seem to be fairly uniform, are they accurate? Probably only to a slight degree, if at all. They seem for the most part to be a product of an easy association of ideas.

[19] Some of these findings are drawn from P. F. Secord, Facial features and inference processes in interpersonal perception. In R. Tagiuri and L. Petrullo (Eds.), *Person perception and interpersonal behavior* (Stanford, Calif: Stanford Univ. Press, 1958), Chap. 20. See also F. Lange, *Die Sprache des menschlichen Antlitzes* (Munich: Lehmann, 1952).

[20] B. Berelson and P. J. Salter, Majority and minority Americans: an analysis of magazine fiction, *Publ. Opin. Quart.*, 1946, **10**, 168–190.

Most older women are mothers; a person wearing eyeglasses may have strained his eyes through study; people with high brows may have more room for brains—and so it goes. It seems that our experimental methods up to now succeed chiefly in uncovering what is stereotyped in our judgments of faces, not what is true.

A closer look at the relation between individual facial features and the impressions they create is achieved by a method invented by Brunswik and Reiter.[21] The six schematic faces in Figure 41 are selected from a larger series of similar drawings. There are quantitative differences in respect to (1) the distance between the eyes, (2) height of the brow above the eyes, (3) position of the nose, (4) length of the nose, (5) position of the mouth. The judges are asked to rate each face according to such characteristics as intelligence, mood, age, occupation, energy. Figure 41 indicates the modal judgments for the six faces.

This method permits us to come closer to a precise analysis of elemental facial patterns in their relation to judgments of personality, but whether the findings from schematized faces carry over to real faces seems doubtful.[22]

One finding from this experiment, and from others, is that in general the mouth is the most decisive facial feature in shaping our judgments.[23] The mouth is the most mobile region. And yet most people vote for the eyes as the most expressive feature. Eyes seem to us to be the visible center of another man's personality. But actually the eye is relatively inexpressive; it can't "do" as much as the mouth. Could it be that we *think* we learn most from another's eyes because we gain our impression through our *own* eyes? If so, there is a curious kind of projection under way.

It often happens that faces are asymmetrical. The right half does not exactly match the left. There are indications that when the asymmetry is marked we are more likely to be dealing with a neu-

---

21 E. Brunswik and Lotte Reiter, Eindruckscharaktere schematisierter Gesichter, *Z. f. Psychol.*, 1937, **142**, 67–134.

22 Cf. Myra R. Samuels, Judgment of faces, *Charact. & Pers.*, 1939, **8**, 18–27.

23 See also K. Dunlap, The role of eye-muscles and mouth-muscles in the expression of emotions, *Genet. Psychol. Monogr.*, 1927, **2**, No. 3; H. Rohracher's report of Winkler's research in The Psychological Institute of the University of Vienna, *Acta psychologica*, 1951–1952, **8**, 201–223. N. G. Hanawalt, however, suggests that the mouth region is superior only for happy emotions and not for surprise and fear. *J. gen. Psychol.*, 1955, **31**, 23–36.

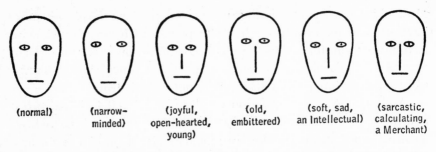

(normal)   (narrow-   (joyful,   (old,   (soft, sad,   (sarcastic,
             minded)   open-hearted,   embittered)   an Intellectual) calculating,
                           young)   a Merchant)

Figure 41. Brunswik-Reiter Schematic Faces. Employed for the quantitative determination of the influence of various features, separately and in combination, upon physiognomic judgments (courtesy Franz Deuticke, Vienna)

rotic personality.[24] And one investigator suggests that the right half of the face ordinarily indicates the more public and conscious side of personality, while the left betrays the unconscious life.[25] These are suggestive leads but require confirmation.

Another study of asymmetry is likewise challenging. The Lynns[26] find that a person who is right-handed and right-faced (as indicated by drawing up the corners of the mouth in smiling) is a better integrated and more outgoing individual than one where the dominance is crossed. Similarly, a left-left dominance (of hand and face) betokens an integrated personality. The neurological theory here is interesting. Homolateral dominance, where either the left or the right hemisphere of the brain is consistently in control, leads to a conflict-free, and therefore assertive, personality. By contrast, contralateral dominance throws the individual into slight motor conflict and retards activity, making him hesitant and unsure.

These are only samples of researches dealing with the face as an expressive agent. We are still far from reaching valid generalizations and laws, but the various lines of investigation hold promise.

Voice and Speech. Voice is only in part a coping instrument. To be sure, a person's enunciation must have a minimum of clarity; and for a professional singer, speaker, or radio or TV announcer, the proper adaptive use of the voice is of high importance. But untrained voices vary widely in pitch, timbre, and mannerism. Voice, therefore,

24 G. Lindzey, Blanche Prince, and H. K. Wright, A study of facial asymmetry, *J. Person.*, 1952–1953, **21**, 68–84.

25 Wolff, *The expression of personality*. Note 15 above.

26 J. G. Lynn and D. R. Lynn, Face-hand laterality in relation to personality, *J. abnorm. soc. Psychol.*, 1938, **33**, 291–322.

especially if it is untrained, is a highly expressive instrument. *Speech*, by contrast, is concerned largely with coping (though, as we shall see, it, too, has marked expressive components). Our speech is composed of conventional words, put together according to rules of syntax, and directed toward purposive communication.

Although voice is highly expressive, psychologists have tended to neglect it in favor of speech. Vocal features are fugitive and hard to analyze. They include the dynamics of intonation, rhythm, brokenness or continuity, accent, pitch, richness, roughness, musical handling. Individual peculiarities of pronunciation should be included.

By the matching method, where the unanalyzed voice is compared with other products of expression or with facts concerning the speaker, we discover the following tendencies:[27]

1. Untrained voices are more expressive (more often correctly matched than trained voices).
2. Age can usually be told within ten years.
3. Other physical features, such as height or complexion or physical appearance, are matched hardly above chance.
4. Deeper traits—whether the speaker is dominant, extraverted, esthetic, or religious in his interests, and so on, are judged with fair success.
5. *Complete* sketches of personality are matched with voice with still greater success. (This finding is important. It means that voice-as-a-pattern is highly congruent with personality-as-a-whole, and therefore suggests that too fine an analysis may lose the diagnostic revelation of expressive features.)

Research on voice requires that all the subjects read aloud the same written passage. Otherwise the individuality of speech styles would enter to confuse judgments based on voice alone.

Speech may be oral or written. In either case we can count individual peculiarities in a large number of dimensions. Sanford lists over a hundred such dimensions.[28] These include speed of speaking or writing; the characteristic length of an utterance or a sentence;

[27] From H. Cantril and G. W. Allport, *The psychology of radio* (New York: Harper, 1935).
[28] F. H. Sanford, Speech and personality: a comparative case study, *Charact. & Pers.*, 1942, **10**, 169–198. A still more extended analysis of the elements of speech-style is offered by R. Fährmann, *Die Deutung des Sprechausdrucks* (Bonn: Bouvier, 1960).

repetitiveness; tendencies to rephrase or rewrite; clause construction; use of adverbs; the tense, voice, mood of verbs; conjunctions; slang; metaphors; grammatical errors. Furthermore, complex indexes can be constructed. What is the verb-adjective ratio for the speaker, his demonstrative-descriptive ratio for adjectives, his definite-indefinite ratio for articles, and so on? One useful index is called the *type-token ratio,* which in effect measures a person's vocabulary. If a person uses 100 words in a speech sample, and if 50 of them are different words, the TTR is .50. The ratio can be determined for the total sample of speech or for any given part of speech (e.g., nouns or verbs).[29]

Perhaps the most striking finding from analytic research of this sort is the marked *consistency* of a person's speech. It is safe to say that every reported investigation proves that the speech style of a person is remarkably consistent from one occasion to another.

Relying on this fact, Yule applied the principle to determining the authorship of the famous book *Of the Imitation of Christ.*[30] Was it written by the German theologian Thomas à Kempis, as commonly believed, or by a contemporary fifteenth-century French theologian, Jean de Gerson, who also wrote in Latin?

> Yule counted the frequency with which certain nouns appeared in the *Imitations* and in *other writings* of each author. Correlating the frequency of the use of these nouns in both sets of writings, he finds that the *r* for Thomas à Kempis is .91; for Gerson, .81. On this basis Yule concludes that à Kempis is the true author. The high correlation for both authors is due, of course, to the fact that both were writing on the same religious subject. Both must have used *Deus* an enormous number of times!

There is a special reason for citing this study. The fact that Yule finds a characteristic difference in the use of *nouns* is surprising, for of all the dimensions of speech, nouns would seem to be least promising. Why is this? Because nouns are rigidly prescribed by our coping (by what we are doing). We have little expressive choice in the matter. Sanford's work, previously cited, suggests that the most

---

29 J. W. Chotlos, A statistical and comparative analysis of individual written language samples, *Psychol. Monogr.,* 1944, **56,** No. 2.
30 G. U. Yule, *The statistical study of literary vocabulary* (Cambridge, England: Cambridge Univ. Press, 1944).

individual and, therefore, the most expressive speech forms are verbs, adjectival and adverbial modifiers, and clause constructions. A person who uses active verbs, few modifiers, and simple declarative sentences is surely different from one who employs passive verbs, many modifiers, and many involved dependent clauses.

As for adjectival and adverbial modifiers, Doob discovers that people who use many of them also use active verbs. Furthermore, they give "field-independent" judgments (page 268); for example, they are able to pick out hidden figures in a complex visual field.[31] This little study shows well the whole logic of expression. People who are active, analytic, and discriminating in handling their environment show this same tendency in their stream of speech. They are not passive in accepting the outer environment—neither in their perception nor in their use of language.

We shall gradually learn just what aspects of speech are most useful for expressive diagnosis. Chapple has invented an apparatus, the "interaction chronograph," to tap important dimensions concerned with the length of speech samples and with the subject's tendency to interrupt or monopolize the conversation.[32] Thorndike tells us that in written speech punctuation is a consistent and revealing feature.[33] All these and other leads merit further exploration.

Posture, Gesture, Gait. The position and movements of the limbs reflect the influence of *coping, cultural convention,* and *personality.* The traffic policeman stops the flow of vehicles with his left arm and motions to pedestrians with his right. In this case the nature of the task and cultural convention are largely responsible for the pattern of motion. But even in this highly prescribed sequence we may detect subtle individuality of expression, sometimes suggesting friendliness, boredom, or arrogance.

Take posture. Man differs from the apes by his standing posture, a fact that has enormous consequences for his mobility and intelligence.[34] An anthropological investigation indicates that the human

---

31 L. W. Doob, Behavior and grammatical style, *J. abnorm. soc. Psychol.,* 1958, **56,** 398–401.

32 E. D. Chapple, The measurement of interpersonal behavior, *Trans. N.Y. Acad. Sci.,* 1942, **4,** 222–233. Also J. D. Matarazzo, G. Saslow, and Ruth G. Matarazzo, The interaction chronograph as the instrument for objective measurement of interaction patterns during interviews, *J. Psychol.,* 1956, **41,** 347–367.

33 E. L. Thorndike, Psychology of punctuation, *Amer. J. Psychol.,* 1948, **61,** 222–228.

34 E. W. Straus, The upright posture, *Psychiatric Quart.,* 1952, **26,** 529–561.

body is capable of assuming about one thousand different steady postures. "Steady" means a static position that one can maintain comfortably for some time.[35] To some extent these preferred positions depend on cultural habits (e.g., whether or not chairs are used), but still to a large extent the posture one finds congenial is a matter of his own choosing. Posture during sleep is also a highly stable personal characteristic.[36] Adler boldly suggests that "pessimists" curl themselves into the smallest possible space and draw the covers over their heads.[37] Psychodiagnosis has not yet tested this claim. Psychoanalysts tell us that the postures of patients upon the couch are revealing and merit study.[38]

Limbs in action are still more revealing, although here too we must read through the coping and cultural components. Culture, we know, has a marked influence on hand gesticulation.[39] Some movements, on the other hand, are more culture-free, and therefore potentially more revealing of personality; a good example is jumping.[40]

Psychologists, of course, would like to bring the problem under experimental control for closer study. Two attempts are described below.

Giese gave his subjects batons and asked them to beat time to various musical recordings. The room was dark and a bulb at the end of the baton permitted photographing the movements on a cinema film. From these records it was possible to identify the effects of sheer convention (beating time in the usual style of orchestra leaders), also a style of motion to accord with the composition (Beethoven versus jazz), and finally a definite individuality in movement (expressive only of the subject himself).[41]

Mira has developed a major method called *myokinetic diag-*

---

35 G. W. Hewes, World distribution of certain postural habits, *Amer. Anthrop.*, 1955, **57**, 231–244.

36 H. M. Johnson, T. H. Swan, and G. E. Wiegard, In what positions do healthy people sleep? *J. Amer. med. Assn.*, 1930, **94**, 2058–2062.

37 A. Adler, *Understanding human nature* (New York: Greenberg, 1927), p. 176.

38 F. Deutsch, Analysis of postural behavior, *Psychoanal. Quart.*, 1947, **16**, 195–213. For a fuller discussion of the significance of expressive behavior for the practice of psychiatry, see W. Malamud, *Outlines of general psychopathology* (New York: Norton, 1935).

39 Cf. Efron, *op. cit.* Note 9 above.

40 P. Halsman, *Jump book* (New York: Simon & Schuster, 1959).

41 F. Giese, Individuum und Epoche in Taktierbewegung bei verschiedenen Komponisten, *Arch. f. d. Ges. Psychol.*, 1934, **90**, 380–426.

nosis. The subject starts to copy a simple design, e.g., a staircase. As soon as he gets under way a shield is placed in front of his eyes so that he can no longer see what he is doing, but he continues the drawing. In this way the cues for coping are reduced and the expressive component becomes prominent. Does the subject continue accurately, does he wobble, does his hand start making exaggerated outward or inward errors? Does he become more expansive or more constricted? Mira claims that from these styles of deviation one can validly infer certain personal traits.[42]

Such methods are admittedly artificial, a long way from the fleeting gestures of daily life, but they may be the best way to bring the problem under control.

Gait is a topic of special fascination. In the Apocrypha we read: "The attire of the body, and the laughter of the teeth, and the gait of the man, shew what he is."[43] But here again controlled analysis is just beginning. Wilsmann suggests that there are seven measurable attributes in gait: regularity, speed, pressure, length of stride, elasticity, definiteness of direction, and variability.[44] To this list he adds an attribute pertaining to the total swing which he calls rhythm.

Over and over again in all the channels of expression the problem of rhythm recurs. It is a poorly defined concept. Sometimes it refers to the periodicity of some aspect of the movement pattern. But usually the term points to an unanalyzed (and perhaps unanalyzable) effect created by the whole pattern of movement. "Rhythm," like "style," is as yet a vague and nonoperational concept.

Since gait is an important topic for medical practice, considerable progress has been made in inventing instruments for the precise study of leg motions in walking, and in establishing norms for cadence, stride length, and speed.[45] Such basic research will serve as a

[42] E. Mira, *M.K.P.-Myokinetic diagnosis* (New York: Logos, 1958). One study, using an adapted M.K.P. technique, finds positive though low correlations between this test and the Thurstone measure of temperament: M. Talmadge, Expressive graphic movements and their relationship to temperament factors, *Psychol. Monogr.*, 1958, No. 469.

[43] *Ecclesiasticus* 19:27.

[44] A. C. Wilsmann, Charakterologische Bedeutung von Einzelmerkmalen. In H. Bogen and O. Lipmann (Eds.), Gang und Charakter, *Beihefte zur Z. f. angew. Psychol.*, 1931, No. 6.

[45] R. Drillis, Objective recording and biomechanics of pathological gait, *Ann. N.Y. Acad. Sci.*, 1958, 74, 86–109. See also G. Kreezer and A. D. Glanville, A method for the quantitative analysis of human gait, *J. genet. Psychol.*, 1937, 50, 109–136.

springboard for psychologists who, we hope, will soon concern themselves with the characterological significance of gait.

A particularly interesting discovery is made by Wolff, who finds
that subjects always recognize their own gait, far better in fact than
they recognize that of their friends.

> The experiment is conducted by dressing subjects in loose
> fitting garments to conceal the head and all additional cues of
> identification. Cinema records are made, and subjects asked to
> identify the walker.[46]

We recall from our earlier discussion (page 478) that self-recogni-
tion from expressive features is not accurate. A person rarely recognizes his own voice, hands, or mirrored handwriting. But gait is
another matter. It would seem that we identify the movement of our
trunk and limbs unerringly by a kind of *empathy* (Chapter 21). The
perception of the total swing immediately arouses like muscular
impulses which we promptly recognize as our own.

As with all other channels of expressive movement, the preliminary work in analyzing gait has gone further than the study of its
diagnostic significance. There is one study, however, that suggests
that the trait of dominance in personality can be read from gait "a
little better than chance."[47]

Handwriting is, of all the forms of expression, by far the most
popular. Graphologists may make a living by "reading character
from handwriting." Psychologists increasingly, if somewhat reluctantly, are turning their attention to this field of investigation. For
one thing, they have invented clever instruments for measuring the
three dimensions of script—its vertical length, its width, and its
pressure.[48]

There is a strong case to be made for handwriting analysis. It is,
as proponents argue, not merely handwriting, but also "brain writ-

46 W. Wolff, Zuordnung individueller Gangmerkmale zur Individual-charakteristik. In
Bogen and O. Lipmann, *op. cit.* Note 44 above.
47 P. Eisenberg and P. B. Reichline, Judging expressive movement: II. Judgments of
dominance-feeling from motion pictures of gait, *J. soc. Psychol.*, 1939, **10**, 345–357.
48 See, for example, W. Luthe, An apparatus for the analytical study of handwriting
movements, *Canadian J. Psychol.*, 1953, **7**, 133–139. Also C. A. Tripp, F. A. Fluckiger,
and G. H. Weinberg, Measurement of handwriting variables, *Percept. & Motor Skills*,
1957, **7**, 279–294; and K. U. Smith and R. Bloom, The electronic handwriting analyzer
and motion study of writing, *J. appl. Psychol.*, 1956, **40**, 302–306.

ing," influenced by all manner of expressive neural impulses giving individual flavor to the coping movements of the hand. As "crystallized gesture," it is by all odds the most accessible of expressive movements for study; all other movements are fugitive and more difficult to measure. Part, but not all, of the popularity of studying handwriting is due to its easy availability.

Critics who say flatly that there is "nothing in graphology" are simply wrong. Many studies show that graphologists are in fact able to diagnose some characteristics above chance.[49] And it is not only professionals who have skill; probably all of us have to some extent. For example, it is commonly found that a random sample of people can tell the sex of writers correctly from script alone in about 70 percent of the cases. Though far from perfect, this degree of success is above chance.[50]

If some critics claim too little for graphology, enthusiasts certainly claim too much. Sometimes charlatanry is involved, as when a graphologist gives us a "reading" of a well-known political figure or actress. The characteristics reported are probably not discovered from the script at all but merely repeat common knowledge about the personage in question.

Charlatans aside, many workers in the field make serious attempts to discover the most appropriate dimensions of handwriting for use.[51] Broadly speaking, there is a quarrel between those who favor specific graphic signs and those who look only at molar features of script. The former group might claim, e.g., that a forward slant indicates "sympathy," or that writing uphill signifies "optimism," or that a person who writes "o" open at the top is "open" and "generous." This is the graphic-sign approach, and probably is less valid.

[49] Studies on this point are numerous. Examples are H. J. Eysenck, Graphological analysis and psychiatry: an experimental study, *Brit. J. Psychol.*, 1945, **35**, 70–81; H. Cantril, G. W. Allport, and H. A. Rand, The determination of personal interests by psychological and graphological methods, *Charact. & Pers.*, 1933, **2**, 134–151; G. R. Pascal, The analysis of handwriting: a test of significance, *Charact. & Pers.*, 1943, **12**, 123–144.

[50] Cf. P. Eisenberg, Judging expressive movement: I. Judgments of sex and dominance-feeling from handwriting samples of dominant and non-dominant men and women, *J. appl. Psychol.*, 1938, **22**, 480–486.

[51] Cf. Thea Stein-Lewinson, Graphische Darstellung der handschriftlichen Dynamik, *Ausdruckskunde*, 1956, **3**, 145–180; H. de Gobineau and R. Perron, *Génétique de l'Écriture et étude de la personalité* (Neuchâtel: Delachaux & Niestlé, 1954); J. Kašpárek, A factor analysis of some quantitative and qualitative signs in handwriting, *Československá Psychologie*, 1957, **1**, 338–352.

Others prefer to study global features. We have seen that Klages's theory (page 465) requires that one start one's analysis by estimating the departure of a script from school copy, in order to determine the general level of expressivity that a person shows. Klages would also study such broad syndromes as "bonds and release," i.e., the constriction or expansion of writing. A person overwhelmed by the external world tends to write in a constricted fashion, as shown by such graphic bonds as smallness of script, heavy pressure, verticality, regularity, narrowness, long lower and short upper strokes, decreasing left margins, and so on. A person who masters his world would show the opposite graphic syndrome.[52]

Some investigators claim that handwriting has not only expressive but also "projective" (cf. page 442) significance. Like autistic gestures, it may tell much about specific unconscious conflicts in the personality.[53]

One problem that urgently needs exploration is this: What aspects of personality can be validly determined from script and what aspects cannot be? One study shows, for example, that a person's outstanding values can be fairly well identified (e.g., whether he is a markedly religious person), but we certainly cannot decide from handwriting alone whether the writer is a Catholic, Baptist, or Jew.[54] And also, in line with our argument on page 465, we must expect some people to reveal more of their personal traits in handwriting than others. A librarian, for example, might have an inexpressive script, but a revealing voice or gait.

These limitations lead us to our main conclusion: All avenues of expression deserve study. We dare not rest our practice of psychodiagnosis on any one "monosymptomatic" feature. To study expression adequately we should explore all channels.

Style

Originally *style* meant a pen or inscribing tool (stylus). It came later to mean handwriting, and then the whole flavor of a

---

[52] A good account in English of Klages's system is Thea Stein-Lewinson, An introduction to the graphology of Ludwig Klages, *Charact. & Pers.*, 1938, **6**, 163–176. See also J. E. Bell, *Projective techniques* (New York: Longmans, Green, 1948).

[53] W. Wolff, *Diagrams of the unconscious* (New York: Grune & Stratton, 1948). Also E. B. McNeil and G. S. Blum, Handwriting and psychosexual dimensions of personality, *J. proj. Techniques*, 1952, **16**, 476–484.

[54] See Cantril, Allport, and Rand, *op. cit.*, Note 49 above.

written, or any other, work in its entirety. Since man is, in a sense, a fusion of all his works, the French are wont to say, *Le style est l'homme même.*

For the psychologist the term means the complex and complete pattern of expressive behavior. It concerns the whole of activity, not merely special skills or single regions, unless, of course, we specifically limit the term by speaking of a *style of handwriting* or a *style of speaking.*

Each painter has a style of his own; so, too, each composer, musician, ball player, novelist, housewife, and mechanic. From style alone we recognize compositions by Chopin, paintings by Dali, and pastry by Aunt Sally. In all these cases we are speaking of the close tie between expressive layers of personality and highly integrated forms of coping. Style applies to the *personal idiom* that marks coping activity.

Style is of interest to esthetics as well as to psychology. In literature, we are told, style seems to be a product of peculiarities of sentence structure, vocabulary, favorite imagery, the use of metaphor, and other devices. We have already called attention to the large array of dimensions on which habits of speech and writing can be compared.

But is style only a summation of separate ingredients? Or is it unanalyzable? A little experiment will make the issue clear. In Figure 42 you are asked which drawing is properly named *quidikaka* and which *waleula?*

The drawings are essentially meaningless, but they leave you with a distinct "feel." You *know* which one should be called quidikaka and which waleula. If asked for your reasons you may say that there is something rounded and soft about the word waleula and also about A, something square and sharp about quidikaka and about B.

A   B

Figure 42. Waleula and Quidikaka

Yet the visual roundedness of A is not the same as the auditory roundedness of waleula. There is no "identical element" that binds them. Yes, there is similarity somewhere, but the similarity is highly elusive. All we can say is that the total auditory style of waleula corresponds to the total visual style of A. It is a case of "physiognomic," or unanalyzed, correspondence.[55]

And so it seems to be with all style. In Figure 29 we showed that it is easy to match complex musical scripts with complex personal qualities of composers. It is only our general impressions that correspond. The judgment is a high-level process; it is somehow the total pattern of traits that seems to be carried in the total pattern of style.

The fact that we make inferences not only from detailed expressive features but also from style as a whole is shown in an experiment.

Nine themes were gathered from each of seventy students, three in October, three in January, and three in May. The topics for the themes were uniform for all students.

After the themes were typed with the names removed, judges were asked to group the themes written by different students. On the whole this sorting was successful. Why? In some cases individual expressive features were the guide. Excessive use of semicolons might mark the writing of one student, or some other oddity of punctuation or spelling. But most identifications were made on the total "form quality" (style) of the theme.

The judges found themselves looking for features that corresponded to personal traits in the author. Thus one student's themes seemed always to reflect "a well-balanced sense of humor, a quiet, amused tolerance of social relations and situations." Another showed in all themes "a positive self-assurance but neither prejudiced nor opinionated." A third was "constantly bored. Looks at life as a monotonous experience in which one follows the least course of action." And so on.[56]

There is, then, an esthetics of being oneself. A person himself is the fundamental and unique unit of all activity. An artist, it is said, is not a special type of man; but every man is a special type of artist.

55 Cf. M. Scheerer and J. Lyons, Line drawings and matching responses to words, *J. Pers.*, 1957, **25**, 251–273.
56 F. H. Allport, L. Walker, and E. Lathers, Written composition and characteristics of personality, *Arch. Psychol.*, 1934, No. 173.

Perhaps in a limited way we can set up a typology of styles. Gough and Woodworth show, for example, that there are perhaps eight different styles reflected in the work of professional research scientists. Certain syndromes of work habits and personal qualities seem to go together. One man is primarily a "zealot," another an "initiator," a third a "methodologist," and so on.[57]

My own view, however, is that just as personality is unique, so too is the signature of style. As in all research in personality we may, if we wish, look for commonalities, types, and categories. But in the last analysis all such clusters will be rough and approximate. The situation is the same as with the structure of personality. We may seek out common traits or we may seek out personal dispositions. Just so we may seek general laws of expression or individual styles. There is justification for both scientific roads.

Summary

In Chapter 17 it was stated that the study of expressive movement was only one of the eleven basic methods for assessing personality. And yet it was necessary to devote a full chapter to this topic. I have done so because I feel the subject is important and too often neglected.[58] Most theories of personality lack a clear definition of expression, and often confuse it with projection. I have tried to make clear that projective techniques are special devices for tapping unconscious *content* in a life, whereas expressive behavior is the constant flow of *manner* and *style* which marks each and every act of adaptive behavior.

We may properly assert that every act a person performs invariably has two aspects: the coping and the expressive. Both are vitally important to an understanding of personality. What a person is trying to do is highly revealing, but so too is his manner or mode of doing it. We encountered this distinction in Chapter 11, where we referred to the content of cognition (what a person thinks) and to cognitive style (his way of thinking).

In ordinary life we pay more attention to coping behavior than to expressive. Coping is the foreground, expression merely the back-

[57] H. G. Gough and D. G. Woodworth, Stylistic variations among professional research scientists, *J. Psychol.,* 1960, **49,** 87–98.
[58] One recent text clearly recognizes the importance of the topic: H. Bonner, *Psychology of personality* (New York: Ronald, 1961), Chap. 13.

ground, of personality. We rapidly become accustomed to a person's manner and pay attention only to what he is doing. Psychologists, too, are prone to take manner for granted, and to concentrate their study upon the *what,* rather than the *how,* of performance.

This chapter has dealt with several theoretical problems—with the origin, consistency, and variability of expressive behavior. Likewise it has reported representative research on separate expressive features (the face, voice and speech, posture and gesture, gait and handwriting). Although much solid preliminary work has been done, we have not yet reached a point where we have a guide to psychodiagnosis. It is unsafe to claim that a given facial expression, a given gesture, or a certain handwriting always signifies such and such a trait. Probably we shall never reach this guidebook stage, for expressive behavior reflects the convergence of many determining tendencies, and we shall have to learn to trace the underlying network with more subtlety than we now command.

Yet for all its elusiveness, the expressive manner and style of the other is an important (perhaps the most important) factor in our understanding of personality—in what has come to be called "person perception." And to this topic we now turn our attention.

PART V UNDERSTANDING Personality

CHAPTER 20

Person Perception

OPENNESS OF THE OTHER • FIRST IMPRESSIONS • THE ABILITY
TO JUDGE • QUALIFICATIONS OF A GOOD JUDGE • SEX DIF-
FERENCES • SOME PROCESSES IN PERSON PERCEPTION • WHOM
DOES ONE KNOW BEST? • COMMON SOURCES OF ERROR • THE
FOCUS OF UNDERSTANDING • SUMMARY

No person can understand any other person completely
because no human being shares directly the motives, thoughts, and
feelings of another. The only self to which we have immediate access
is our own. Knowledge of other people comes to us indirectly and in
fragments. At best we catch glimpses of one another.

Yet we try ardently to bridge the chasm between mind and mind,
for our happiness and survival depend on correct judgments of persons. Many times a day we find ourselves smiling, nodding, saying,
"Yes, yes"—to assure our companion and ourselves that we understand what he is saying and what he is. Although our understanding
is at best partial, such as it is we put it on display.

> We seldom smile when we are alone. Almost always a smile is
> the special product of social encounter—a gesture to signify that
> we understand our companion, that we "belong together," that
> we have an agreed-upon basis for coexistence.

The infant smile has no such significance. In the baby a smile is an instinctive response, evoked after the first weeks of life by a full face (or mask) in motion. For this perceptual response to occur the child must be in a state of well-being and basically secure. It is only later, after the sense of self-and-other has evolved, that the smile takes on the meaning of "understanding."[1]

In this chapter and the next we shall see that psychologists (and philosophers) have puzzled deeply over the indirect and mysterious process by which we gain our *connaisance d'autrui*. At best our image of another person is only a *phenomenon*—a picture in our own mind —a rough and ready replica of the objective reality. As we saw in Chapter 11, perceiving is not a photographic camera, let alone an x-ray. It is a device that *orders* the external cues that come to our senses. Although we never know external reality directly, we do know that what we perceive corresponds to some extent to what is "out there."

This dilemma haunts all sciences. Even the physicist can know only phenomena (what he perceives), and not absolute truth. His effort, like the psychologist's, is to make his phenomenal world correspond as closely as possible to the unknowable *Ding an Sich* (thing-in-itself).[2] But, as we shall see, this Kantian dilemma is particularly pointed when applied to the problem of understanding people. In person perception there are many sources of error that do not trouble the natural scientist. For one thing, personal feelings are readily aroused in all our social dealings, even when we try to be objective. A person in love is certainly not the best judge of the personality of his beloved. The climate of the situation strongly affects our judgments of people. Research shows, for example, that when we are in a threatening or humiliating situation we rate people as far "less attractive" than in situations which flatter our self-esteem.[3]

But emotional bias is only one factor that complicates "person perception." (I employ this somewhat awkward phrase because it is

---

[1] R. Spitz, The smiling response, *Genet. Psychol. Monogr.*, 1946, **34**, 57–125; and K. Goldstein, The smiling of the infant and the problem of understanding the "other," *J. Psychol.*, 1957, **44**, 175–191.

[2] A helpful discussion of this issue is contained in B. B. Wolman, *Contemporary theories and systems in psychology* (New York: Harper, 1960), Chap. 10.

[3] R. J. Keliner, The effects of threat reduction upon interpersonal attractiveness, *J. Pers.*, 1960, **28**, 145–155.

becoming current in psychology. The reader will realize that we do not literally *perceive* others. As we saw in Chapter 11, it would be more accurate to say that we *proceive* them. In common speech we say that we "judge" them. For convenience we shall speak of the whole problem area we are dealing with as *person perception*. The "perceiver" we shall call the *judge,* and the person "perceived" the *other.*)

We shall give our attention to eight aspects of the complex problem that confronts us:

> Openness of the other
> First impressions
> The ability to judge
> Qualifications of a good judge
> Sex differences
> Some processes in person perception
> Whom does one know best?
> Some common sources of error

Openness of the Other

Mark Twain wrote, "Everyone is a moon, and has a dark side which he never shows to anybody." Granted that we all try to keep certain recesses of our natures secret from prying eyes, still we differ greatly in the extent to which we do so. In some lives the dark side of the moon covers a small area; in other lives, a large one.

Self-disclosure. Recent research proves this fact. People vary widely in the amount of information about themselves they willingly disclose, and in the range of persons in whom they will confide.[4]

The procedure for such a study is simple. Subjects can be asked whether they have recently talked over with their mothers, fathers, spouses, strangers, same-sex friends, opposite-sex friends, (or other "target persons") a variety of subjects, e.g., their political opinions, financial matters, personal dress, health, feelings of social inferiority, impersonal sexual topics, personal sexual topics, and so on.

[4] S. M. Jourard, Healthy personality and self-disclosure, *Ment. Hyg.,* 1959, **43**, 499–507; S. M. Jourard and P. Lasakow, Some factors in self-disclosure, *J. abnorm. soc. Psychol.,* 1958, **56**, 91–98; and M. A. Rickers-Ovsiankina and A. A. Kusmin, Individual differences in social accessibility, *Psychol. Rep.,* 1958, **4**, 391–406.

Some people, it turns out, let themselves be wholly known to a wide variety of fellow mortals; others "clam up" on most subjects with most people. Some we may say are voluntarily "open" and others deliberately "enigmatic." In general it seems that women (whose role in society is on the whole "expressive" and personal) disclose more than men (whose role is "instrumental" and impersonal). White college students disclose more than do Negro students. Mothers are confided in more than fathers. And, as might be expected, liking for the target person, similarity in values, degree of mutuality, and length of acquaintanceship are important factors. There are, of course, cultural differences. Lewin claims that Americans as a group disclose far more to acquaintances and to strangers than do Germans.[5] Mead points out that in Samoa all of a person's *activities* are known to the group, but that there is marked privacy concerning *motives*.[6]

Obviously the will to self-disclosure is a major factor in assisting person perception. And yet openness is not merely a matter of deliberate confiding. Some people, in their spontaneous daily activities, seem relatively transparent, whereas others by comparison are opaque. One study finds that people who are extraverted, adaptable, ascendant are people who can be reliably rated on these and on all other traits.[7] It also seems to be a rule that individuals who are most typical of their culture are more open (more correctly judged).

First Impressions

It seems self-evident (though it is not always true) that the more we see and hear of a person's behavior the more accurate is our judgment of him. What is surprising, however, is the extensive nature of our judgments based even on the slenderest of cues.

The astonishing rapidity with which first judgments are made can be easily demonstrated. While riding in a public conveyance close your eyes and turn your head toward some fellow passenger not previously observed, perhaps someone sitting obliquely opposite. Open your eyes for a brief glimpse lasting two or three seconds, and then with the eyes closed ponder the impressions as they arise. Here

5 K. Lewin, Some social-psychological differences between the United States and Germany, *Charact. & Pers.*, 1935–1936, **4**, 265–293.
6 Margaret Mead, *Coming of age in Samoa* (New York: Morrow, 1928), Chap. 9.
7 Cf. G. W. Allport, *Personality: a psychological interpretation* (New York: Holt, Rinehart and Winston, 1937), pp. 443, 508 f.

is a person, never before seen and completely unknown. With but the briefest visual glimpse a complex mental process is aroused, resulting within a short time, thirty seconds perhaps, in judgments of the sex, age, size, nationality, social class, and occupation of the stranger, together with some vaguer estimates of his temperament, his past suffering, his "hardness," his ascendance, friendliness, neatness, and even his trustworthiness. With further acquaintance many of these impressions would no doubt prove to be mistaken, but the exercise serves to call attention to the swiftly structured nature of our judgments. The fact that one perceives a personality at first contact, not by fragments pieced together with painful slowness, but as a unitary structure (in which a complex pattern of interrelated cues are instantly organized) is, as the following chapter will show, a matter of considerable theoretical importance.

In an unpublished classroom experiment an instructor invited a friend of his (a total stranger to the class) to come into the room and join him on the platform. He asked the stranger, "What do you think of the weather?" The latter made some neutral comments and after a minute left the room.

The students then wrote for three minutes in response to the instruction, "Will you please write down your impression of Mr. X? Anything that has come to your mind about him. Just list your first impressions."

On the average the students reported 5.6 separate impressions in the three minutes allowed. In all, 259 items were listed, distributed as follows:

	PERCENTAGE OF TOTAL REPLIES
Personal traits: quiet, humorous, cultivated, modest, and so on	56
Physical characteristics: dark, angular, well-dressed	14
Situational judgments: trying to please, unaccustomed to group, enjoys occasion	12
Ethnic characteristics: foreign-born, Jewish, European	7
Status and role: teaches science, may be photographer, belongs to wealthy class	7
Effect on judge's feelings: congenial, disconcerting, nice guy	4

Experiments of this sort are, of course, affected by the instructions given and by momentary conditions that prevail. Yet two results are probably typical of experiments on first impressions. (1) While personal traits are looked for and perceived, the judge often tries in addition to categorize the other; he classifies him physically, ethnically, and by occupation; also, he judges him in terms of his adjustment to the present situation. To a less extent the judge reacts subjectively (in terms of liking or disliking the other). (2) A considerable agreement exists among judges. (Whether the judgments are accurate is not here the question.) In this experiment virtually all judges agreed that Mr. X was intelligent, friendly, warm but shy, sensitive, well-mannered, and not opinionated. But occasionally there were marked disagreements, X being judged as both ill at ease and composed, as both a shallow and a deep thinker. In general it seems that a stranger's voice and manner arouse fairly uniform impressions in others. This means that in a given culture all judges tend to "type" cues in the same way, even though the typing may prove to be erroneous. Often we hear it said, "I know he gives everyone that impression at first, but once you get to know him . . ."

With modern experimental devices it is possible to study how added bits of information change judgments. For example, one can run a film showing a person's behavior for one minute and take the resulting judgment, and later add three, five, or ten minutes to the running time. Or one can introduce a subject only through his voice, then add his manual gestures, his face, and finally a personal meeting and discussion.

What happens when such increments of information are added? For one thing, judges generally become more complimentary and favorable. Also, they feel greater confidence in their judgments. And yet added information does not necessarily result in better judgments. In fact, some judges may be more correct if they make merely stereotyped judgments about people (according to their social, national, class memberships) than if they are forced to individualize and employ subtle cues beyond their capacity to interpret. Even clinical psychologists, it seems, may become confused and less efficient as judges if they try to absorb too much information about the other.[8]

[8] E. G. Beier and J. Stumpf, Cues influencing judgment of personality characteristics, *J. consult. Psychol.*, 1959, **23**, 219–225; W. J. Crow, The effect of training upon accuracy and variability in interpersonal perception, *J. abnorm. soc. Psychol.*, 1957, **55**, 355–359; and E. L. Kelly and D. W. Fiske, *The prediction of performance in clinical psychology* (Ann Arbor: Univ. of Michigan Press, 1951).

But judges differ. It seems that if their first impressions are numerous and rich and varied, they are flexible judges who with added information readily correct and enlarge their original judgment; whereas those who see little at first are likely to keep an impoverished and stereotyped impression even when more information is given.[9]

The Ability to Judge

Most mental abilities are neither entirely general nor entirely specific. For example, a person with artistic ability is not as a rule equally expert at drawing, painting, dancing, and composing music. Abilities run in somewhat narrower channels. On the other hand, artistic ability is not entirely specific. It is unheard of for a man to be able to sketch a good boat but an unrecognizable lighthouse, or to be able to compose one melody and not others. We should not expect a judge of people to be uniformly successful in estimating every quality of every person, but at the same time we should not expect him to succeed only in judging *one* quality in all people, or perhaps all qualities in only *one* person. The truth will lie somewhere between these extremes.

Experiments have been devised to explore this issue.

For example, Bronfenbrenner, Harding, and Gallwey studied two kinds of ability in their judges:[10] (1) a *sensitivity to the generalized other* (i.e., knowledge as to how people in general behave). The method required the judges to predict such phenomena as the results of public-opinion polls, average attitudes in a community, or the "typical response" of college students to items in a personailty test. (2) *Interpersonal sensitivity* refers to the ability to sense how a *given* person in a group feels about an issue or about the leader of the group, quite apart from any average opinion. This ability, of course, is what we usually have in mind when we speak of "a good judge of people."

The investigators point out that the two abilities are largely independent. Those who are good judges of "the public" are not necessarily good judges of "the person." A sales manager in a

[9] Elise S. Bartholomew, Changing impressions of personality: a study in cognitive restructuring. Unpublished doctoral dissertation, Radcliffe College Library, 1958.
[10] U. Bronfenbrenner, J. Harding, and M. O. Gallwey, The measurement of skill in social perception. In A. L. Baldwin, *et al.* (Eds.), *Talent and society* (Princeton, N.J.: Van Nostrand, 1958).

department store, for example, may predict what "the public will buy" but not be able to estimate the readiness of a given customer to make a purchase.

Further, so far as interpersonal sensitivity is concerned, it turns out that some judges are more accurate in understanding (predicting) men than women; others do better with women than with men. Likewise there is some evidence that people are best in judging others who are similar to themselves and whom they like.

Yet in spite of the discovery of factors that narrow the excellence of judgment, there is also strong evidence that interpersonal sensitivity is (in many people at least) a general ability.

On page 13 it was pointed out that three sets of norms are useful in the study of personality: (1) universal norms telling us how human beings in general behave; (2) group norms, telling us what practices are common in a given nation, culture, occupational group, or social class; (3) individual norms, dealing with the forms of behavior characteristic of a given person. From the study just cited we learn that skill in handling universal and group norms is not necessarily associated with skill in handling individual norms. (As many investigations show, psychologists who may be expert in universal or group trends, are often poor in assessing individual personalities.) The first form of skill, *sensitivity to the generalized other* (or sometimes called *stereotyped judgment*), is of course, extremely useful. It is useful not only in dealing with people en masse, but in dealing with the individualized other. The latter skill (*interpersonal sensitivity*) goes beyond the first in that it is based on a sense of personal patterning, an esthetic or structured feeling for the particular. We hazard the opinion that the very best judges have both types of skill.[11]

How does one discover whether the ability to judge people is

11 Although the discovery of two types of ability (sensitivity to the generalized other and interpersonal sensitivity) is helpful, we must not assume that no other "primary abilities" are involved. For example, P. E. Vernon suggests three ranges of skill: Some people understand *themselves* well; some are especially good at understanding their *friends;* others excel in judging *strangers.* Vernon finds some evidence to support this threefold distinction. Good judges of self are characterized by high intelligence and humor. Good judges of friends and associates are less socially inclined and less intelligent than good judges of self, but more artistic. Good judges of strangers are high in intelligence and in artistic gifts, but tend to be unsocial in many respects: Some characteristics of a good judge of personality, *J. soc. Psychol.,* 1933, 4, 42–58.

general or specific? The following experiment gives one illustrative procedure.[12]

Cline and Richards selected at random ten shoppers at a suburban supermarket. After filming these strangers during an interview they obtained their further cooperation in taking various personality tests. Then from the friends and acquaintances of these strangers they gathered additional data about them.

Fifty judges then viewed the films and afterward filled out the personality tests as they thought each shopper had done. They also attempted to rate the shoppers as they thought friends had rated them.

It turns out that if the judge does a good job on one of the instruments he tends to do a good job on the others and if he does a good job on one of the strangers, he tends to do a good job on all. If he is poor on one he tends to be poor on all.

Although this method is ingenious we must point out that the task of validating judgments of personality is not easy. What criterion have we for what the other "really is"? For us to fill out a personality test just as we imagine the other has filled it out is a quantifiable, but not entirely appropriate, method. For one thing, personality tests (and ratings by friends) are seldom high in validity. They do not necessarily represent what the other "really is." Furthermore, to predict the precise words a person will use on a test goes far beyond what we mean by successful judgment of people. Will he say "Yes" or only "Sometimes" to a question whether he is troubled by insomnia? The measure is too fine. Does he prefer tub baths or shower baths? Who cares? Many items on a personality test are trivial and irrelevant when it comes to ascertaining who is a good judge of people. They invite the judge to give a cautious and stereotyped answer, or to reply by assuming the other must be like himself, or to take some equally artificial way out of the assigned task.[13]

---

12 V. B. Cline and J. M. Richards, Accuracy of interpersonal perception—a general trait? *J. abnorm. soc. Psychol.*, 1960, **60**, 1–7.

13 Certain authors argue that these artifices cast doubt on the existence of any generalized ability. Thus Cronbach points out that a certain mental set might be responsible for the superiority of one person over another. For example, if a teacher adopts a narrow range of prediction—estimating that the IQ's in a class of students will fall between 90 and 110, she has less chance of error than if she uses a wide range, say from 70 to 130. Her success is merely an artifact of the range she chooses. L. J. Cron-

For all its shortcomings, the method of predicting responses to a personality test, or what acquaintances will say about the other, represents one of the few methods of controlling our validation of successful judgment. In some cases long-range validation is used. Has the judge successfully predicted that X will become delinquent, that Y will be a good leader of his group, that Z will suffer a mental breakdown? Such long-range predictions are difficult to check, and yet they would seem closer to what we ordinarily conceive as ability to judge personality.

To sum up, although we do not know just what subtypes may be involved in the ability to judge others, and although we have considerable difficulty in proving that judgments are good or poor, still the preponderance of evidence favors the view that the ability is to a considerable extent generalized.[14] It is certainly more of an error to say that the ability is entirely specific than to say that it is entirely general. Broadly speaking, therefore, we conclude that common sense is not too far off when it speaks of one man as "an excellent judge of character," and another as "continually taken in by people."

Qualifications of a Good Judge

Granted, then, that there is such a thing as a good judge of personality (while admitting that the ability is not completely "across the board"), we may ask what research shows concerning the good judge's attributes.[15]

bach, Processes affecting scores on "understanding of others" and "assumed similarity," *Psychol. Bull.*, 1955, **52**, 177–193. See also N. L. Gage and L. J. Cronbach, Conceptual and methodological problems in interpersonal perception, *Psychol. Rev.*, 1955, **62**, 411–422. Others argue that a person who gives stereotyped predictions (based on common human tendencies) will often do better than a person who tries hard to individualize his predictions. See W. J. Crow and K. R. Hammond, The generality of accuracy and response sets in interpersonal perception, *J. abnorm. soc. Psychol.*, 1957, **54**, 384–390.

Such methodological objections, although important for the refinement of procedure and for an understanding of the process of prediction, do not affect our basic conclusion that some people are better judges than others.

14 In addition to the studies cited, two reviews of evidence support this conclusion: J. S. Bruner and R. Tagiuri, The perception of people. In G. Lindzey (Ed.), *Handbook of social psychology* (Cambridge, Mass.: Addison-Wesley, 1954) II, 634–654; R. Taft, The ability to judge people, *Psychol. Bull.*, 1955, **52**, 1–21.

15 The following paragraphs represent a digest of evidence from various sources: Allport, *op. cit.*, pp. 513–516 (Note 7 above); R. Taft, *op. cit.*, pp. 6–19 (Note 14 above); V. B. Cline, Ability to judge personality assessed with a stress interview and sound-film technique, *J. abnorm. soc. Psychol.*, 1955, **50**, 183–187; J. E. Chance and W. Meaders, Needs and interpersonal perception, *J. Pers.*, 1960, **28**, 200–209; N. L. Gage, Judging interests from expressive behavior, *Psychol. Monogr.*, 1952, No. 350; J. S. Bruner and R. Tagiuri, *op. cit.* (Note 14 above); J. Bieri, Cognitive complexity—simplicity and predictive behavior, *J. abnorm. soc. Psychol.*, 1955, **51**, 263–268.

Experience. A good judge requires first of all maturity, which means not only the attainment of adult age but also a rich store of experience with human nature. An adolescent, as a rule, sees people in the narrow perspective of his limited experience, and often resorts to callow clichés in judging people. This acquaintance is a "square," that one "a good guy." What can the youth know of the conflicts peculiar to middle age and later? In spite of the protest by the younger generation that the elder fails to understand it, the chances are vastly in favor of youth misunderstanding its elders.

As we shall see in the following chapter, inference is an important factor in understanding personality. Each judgment partakes of previous judgments and is corrected by them. Without a broad and long-continued acquaintance with all manner of people, the elementary basis for logical inference is lacking.

Similarity. A special case of "experience" is similarity. The more the other resembles me, the more experience, so to speak, I have had with *him*. It is for this reason that members of the same sex, same race, same age, same culture are ordinarily the best judges of one another. Students are as a rule better judges of other students than of professors—and vice versa. Our perceptual discriminations are finer within the area of our own customary contacts. Western people are wont to complain that Orientals are all alike, even look alike; and Orientals return the compliment. Within our own racial group we are able to make finer and more accurate judgments.

It is important to distinguish between "real similarity" and "assumed similarity." Whereas real similarity is a definite aid to judgment, assumed similarity may be a bad handicap. Very often we predict that the other will behave as we ourselves would. Studies show that this is a common source of error (unless real similarity is also present).[16]

Intelligence. Most studies discover that some relationship exists between superior intelligence and the ability to judge others. The positive correlation holds even within the narrow range of high intelligence that characterizes the selected judges used in most experiments. The correlation need not surprise us, for the process of judging people is, like intelligence itself, a matter of discerning the relevance of cues, the relations between past and present activities,

---

[16] Cf. L. J. Cronbach, *op. cit.* (Note 13 above); I. E. Bender and A. H. Hastorf, On measuring generalized empathic ability (social sensitivity), *J. abnorm. soc. Psychol.*, 1953, **48**, 503–506.

between cause and effect. Perhaps, as Vernon suggests, intelligence is less important as a factor in judging friends than in judging self and strangers. (See Note 11.)

Cognitive Complexity. As a rule people cannot comprehend others who are more complex and subtle than they. The single-track mind has little feeling for the conflicts of a versatile mind. People who prefer simplicity of design and have no taste for the complex in their esthetic judgments are not as good judges as those with a more complex cognitive style and tastes.

Would it not follow, therefore, that the psychiatrist, since he deals with intricate mental tangles, should benefit by the possession of a complex personality? If he has neurotic difficulties of his own and manages them well, might they not add to his qualifications? Yes, it would seem advantageous for the psychiatrist to have a complex nature as well as a complex cognitive style. But this is not to say there is no place for the buoyant, uncomplicated psychiatrist whose role is not so much the understanding as the encouraging of patients caught in the snares of depression. Therapeutically it is often more valuable to radiate health and good spirits than to enter sympathetically into the tangles of the patient's life. Perhaps there are two types of successful psychiatrists: those who cure by tortuous reconstruction, and those who cure by radiant suggestion.

Self-insight. Although the evidence is not all in, it appears fairly certain that people who have accurate self-knowledge tend to rate another accurately—especially in relation to traits that are common to both of them. Here, obviously, the factors of experience and similarity are again playing their part.

We may hazard the guess that self-insight prevents a person from giving merely conventional or stereotyped judgments of others. In terms we have employed, he is not likely to confuse the norm for the individual with the universal or cultural norms. It seems reasonable to suppose that if we know our own complex motives, our inconsistencies, the uniqueness of our own pattern of life, we are more likely to allow for complexity in others. By a kind of "reciprocity" (page 121) we realize that others can be as individual and as well patterned as ourselves, and at the same time be very different in their structure.

Social Skill and Adjustment. Most studies show that good judges are socially skillful and emotionally stable. On the whole they are free from neurotic disorders. They are rated high in leadership and in popularity. They are outgoing and like to influence, supervise, or take care of others. The poor judge, by contrast, seems maladroit in social dealings; he is likely to score high on tests of aggression, is likely to report that he frequently disagrees with people, tells them off, makes fun of them, or takes revenge. Yet at the same time he often shows an excessive dependence on others.

Detachment. Although the good judge is successful in social relationships, and reasonably warm and friendly, he is also to a considerable extent detached. Very often he proves to be an introverted person who is himself enigmatic and hard to judge, even though he adjusts successfully to others. What is involved here is a certain distance from others that permits an impartial view and perspective. Poor judges are often overly social, excessively affiliative, dependent, or nurturant. We all know the warmhearted soul who feels so much sympathy, pity, love, admiration for others that he (or she) cannot take an impartial view of their failings. And we also know good judges—some novelists are in this category—who participate heartily enough at times, but also withdraw, and consider events and people with an almost grim objectivity.

Esthetic Attitude. Related to the capacity for detachment is the esthetic attitude. As a qualification it may stand above all others, especially in the case of the most gifted judges. The esthetic attitude seeks always to comprehend the intrinsic harmony of any object that is the center of attention (cf. page 298). The object may be as trivial as an ornament or as substantial as a human being. In either case the singleness and symmetry of the structure are what interests the esthetic person. This attitude is, of course, indispensable to the novelist and biographer. Even among the rank and file of people investigations show that ability to judge others is higher in persons who have dramatic and artistic interests. It seems probable that, when developed highly enough, this attitude may to some extent offset limitations of experience, of intelligence, of insight, of similarity and complexity.

Intraceptiveness. To our long list of attributes it seems well to add an extra qualification, although it overlaps to some extent with the others. Intraceptiveness is a trait (or syndrome of traits) that points to a certain kind of "psychological-mindedness."[17] Some people seem by nature to be concerned with the significance of subjective states—with inner feelings, fantasies, wishes, meanings. They are particularly sensitive to the shadings of motivation, conflict, suffering in others. Like primitive animists, they even tend to view nature in "human" terms. Almost by definition it would seem that such a person would be a good judge of personality. There is a "passion for the subjective" in his nature; he is a "born psychologist" in the sense in which we apply this term to Shakespeare or Dostoevski. Intraceptiveness is more than an attitude; it is a motivating value.

Lack of intraceptiveness is seen in the authoritarian character structure (page 433). An experiment reveals this fact.[18]

> Scodel and Mussen tested college students on a scale designed to measure authoritarianism. They then paired each high authoritarian with another student of the same age and sex who stood low on the same scale.
>
> For twenty minutes these students conversed informally about radio, television, or the movies. Through this casual conversation each formed an impression of the other. None knew the real purpose of the experiment.
>
> After conversing, each student was taken to a separate room and given a questionnaire to fill out as he thought his partner would fill it out.
>
> The results show that the high authoritarians "projected" their own attitudes; that is, they thought their interlocutor would answer the questions in an authoritarian manner (although, of course, their partners were all low on this scale). By contrast, the nonauthoritarian students estimated the attitudes of their partners more correctly. They not only perceived them as authoritarians, which they were, but also estimated more correctly other traits in their natures.

From this study we see that the nonauthoritarian is more flexible and less "projective" in judging others. The authoritarian, by con-

---

17 Cf. H. A. Murray, et al., Explorations in personality (New York: Oxford, 1938). Murray writes, "The intraceptive mode of apperception seems to be basic to an intuitive understanding of other people" (p. 213).

18 A. Scodel and P. Mussen, Social perceptions of authoritarians and nonauthoritarians, J. abnorm. soc. Psychol., 1953, 48, 181–184.

trast, believes that his own mental type is universal. He assumes that others are similar to himself, and rigidly projects his convictions upon them.

In postulating intraceptiveness as a qualification for a good judge of people I may seem to be begging the question. Am I not saying merely that a good judge of people is such because he has a flair for being a sensitive judge? Perhaps my logic is circular, but I prefer to frame the matter this way: our search is for the deepest reason why some people by and large are better judges than others. I have listed many differentiating conditions, experimentally discovered, including experience, similarity, intelligence, cognitive complexity, self-insight, social skill and adjustment, detachment, esthetic attitude. Do these attributes separately or in combination go to the heart of the matter? The concept of intraceptiveness overlaps with some of these conditions, but it points in addition to a basic trait that may lie at the heart of social sensitivity. More research is needed to clarify this point.

Sex Differences

The proverbial "intuition" of women is supposed to manifest itself especially in her judgments of people. Returning home from a dinner party a husband is likely to report, as the extent of his observation, that the hostess looked rather pretty in her new green dress. Whereupon his wife may add that the dress was not new, but formerly white; that it had been altered to bring it in style; further that the hostess is worried about money matters and about her husband's drinking, that she is having trouble with her children, and is something of a flirt—and all things considered it would not be surprising if there were a divorce in the family within the year.

Yet the case for woman's superiority can be easily exaggerated. Experimental studies establish only a slight (but persistent) margin in favor of women.[19]

A simple explanation for such superiority as exists may lie in the signal importance of personal relationships in women's lives. Her role in society requires that even a young girl learn to be sensitive to

[19] A few studies fail to find any sex differences, but the majority seem to discover a slight superiority among women. See, e.g., Taft, *op. cit.* (Note 14 above); Cline, *op. cit.* (Note 15 above); W. Toman, Das Lernen in der Ausdrucksdeutung. *Wiener Z. f. prakt. Physchol.*, 1950, **2**, 2–6; D. A. Trumbo and H. C. Smith, A test of the ability to predict behavior and its correlates, *Amer. Psychologist*, 1957, **12**, 412.

the needs and attitudes of others. A woman entering upon a business or professional career, for example, must know whether her male associates have a prejudiced, jocular, patronizing, or fair-minded attitude toward her presence. Her success depends upon reading such cues aright. Further, in a society where double standards of morality still exist, it is wise for a woman to be observant and circumspect about the qualities of her friends. Finally, in accordance with the principle of autonomy, she may develop a genuine interest in understanding people which becomes an incentive to study them and a source of satisfaction. Such an interest easily becomes integrated with the esthetic value which is known in our culture to be higher among women than among men, and which, as we have seen, is an important factor in making accurate judgments of others.

All in all there are plenty of reasons to account for women's superior judgment of personality. The wonder is that their superiority over men is not more marked than it is.

Some Processes in Person Perception

Some psychologists argue that our discussion of the accuracy of judging others, as well as of the qualifications of a good judge, is premature. They say that the process of judging is so complex that it should be carefully analyzed before we concern ourselves with accuracy.[20] Some add that since we can never know what a person "really is," the study of accuracy is bound to be futile and we do well therefore to confine our scientific curiosity to the conditions under which some people make one type of judgment, and other people a different type.

---

[20] This theme prevails throughout the symposium edited by R. Tagiuri and L. Petrullo, *Person perception and interpersonal behavior* (Stanford, Calif.: Stanford Univ. Press, 1958).

It is surely a good thing to analyze the process of person perception carefully. But it is quite another thing to make nihilistic assertions. Some authors deny that there is any such thing as a personality "out there." They even deny, in effect, that there is a judge "here" who perceives and interprets this object. In short, they tend to define personality as a relationship between two people (cf. page 23). To them a judgment cannot be either true or false; it is only a process. What the judge sees is a result of his assumed similarity to the other, of his degree of liking for the other, or of his stereotype concerning the social class, race, or role of the other. Granted that such relationships play a part in the process of judging, I prefer to consider them as complicating factors that have a helpful or hindering effect on the accuracy of judgment. At bottom the problem of I-knowing-you-as-a-person or you-knowing-me-as-a-person remains. Complex though the process is, this is the basic problem. *I* am a person; *you* are a person. How do we come to understand one another as well as we do?

I cannot agree with this line of thinking. Although it is certainly true that the judging process is complex, and that it is hard to find criteria for measuring the success of judgments, the fact remains that accuracy of judgment is a major goal in our social relationships, and that some people make more correct judgments than others. There is no reason why psychology should not study both *accuracy* and *process*.

In some ways the process of perceiving a person is much like that of perceiving any object. A person, like an object, can be touched, seen, heard, and sometimes smelled; he can be recognized as familiar or as something new; he can be regarded as attractive, interesting, dangerous. But at the same time much that is new and complex is added in our perception of persons. The other, I know, is more or less "like me"; he is a "self"; he has purposes (far more intricate than the simple type of causation I ascribe to objects). He is ordinarily far less predictable than objects; and he has a subtle and evolving relation to me that goes far beyond my tie with inanimate things. In short, we never perceive a person without at the same time perceiving that he *is* a person. We never concern ourselves with the intentions of objects, but are constantly concerned with the intentions of persons.

Following are some of the processes that come conspicuously to light in the perceiving of persons.

Common Judgmental Sets. When we "size up" a person we almost always have a special reason in view. Our reason will limit what we see in the other. Sometimes we are interested in fitting the other to a job (in matching him to a situation). Will he, we ask, have requisite skills? Will he get on well with the office staff? Will he be a good pastor for my church? On other occasions our interest is in personal congeniality. Will he be on *my* side? Will he be a good roommate? Can I trust him with my money? Again, our mental set may be "scientific"; we can judge from a "causal-genetic" point of view. What are his true motives? Is he displaying defensive behavior? How did he come to be the way he is? Thus according to our particular purposes we are likely to perceive a person in a special, and not truly comprehensive, way.[21]

Categorization Tendency. One of the first things we do in per-

[21] E. E. Jones and J. W. Thibaut, Interaction goals as bases of inference in interpersonal perception. In Tagiuri and Petrullo, *op. cit.*, Chap. 11. Note 20 above.

ceiving any object is to place it in a familiar category. People are no exception. Suppose we meet a stranger and are told only that he is a Frenchman. Forthwith we ascribe to him all the attributes of our own stereotype of the French. We do the same when we meet for the first time a professor, a janitor, a businessman. In other words, our first tendency is to place a person in the category of the *generalized other*. From this base line we start to individualize. If we have considerable experience with the category (thus, if we know many Frenchmen), we can all the sooner divest the person of stereotyped attributes and start the individualizing process. But the fact remains that our first judgments tend to be stereotyped.[22]

Now a stereotype, as we have seen, is not necessarily a source of error. Knowledge of the generalized other is often helpful. To know universal or group norms is a good starting point—and especially so if the other is typical of his culture or class, that is to say, if his pattern of qualities approaches the "basic personality" of his group (page 171). Studies show that judges who are familiar with a particular subculture (for example, with students in a given college) often do an excellent job in predicting the behavior of its members without individualizing at all.[23]

And yet such categorizing certainly falls short of expertness in judgment. All people, even the most "typical," deviate in some respects from stereotyped norms. Although it helps to know a person's memberships and status and the roles he plays, to stop with this information is to miss the individuality of pattern. Sarbin reports that in judging others, women tend to mention fewer status or role attributes (e.g., "doctor," "leader") than do men. They are more likely to look for "inner" traits ("aggressiveness," "modesty").[24] Perhaps it is by avoiding outer and stereotyped variables that, as noted above, women achieve a somewhat higher degree of accuracy than do men.

Combining Cues. In judging people we ordinarily have many bits of information to put together. In meeting Mr. X, for example, I perceive his courteous greeting, but note his frown, and hear a report that he is "a witty conversationalist." In making use of these

22 J. S. Bruner and H. V. Perlmutter, Compatriot and foreigner: a study of impression formation in three countries, *J. abnorm. soc. Psychol.*, 1957, **55**, 253–260.
23 Gage, *op. cit.* Note 15 above.
24 T. Sarbin, Role theory. In Lindzey, *op. cit.*, Vol. I, Chap. 6. Note 14 above.

and many other cues I do not merely add them together, but form a blend of all this information, and also leap beyond the information given and reach a highly general judgment of Mr. X. How is such a judgment made?

Bruner, Shapiro, and Tagiuri show that given one bit of information, e.g., that Sam is *intelligent,* most people infer (if asked) that Sam is also *active, clever, deliberate, efficient, energetic, imaginative, independent,* and that he is probably also *modest, considerate, cheerful, even-tempered, warm, neat, witty,* and so on. Clearly we go far beyond the information given. The experiment shows that people have a powerful generalizing tendency to make all the use they can of such cues as they obtain.[25]

Now suppose that we have two "contradictory" bits of information about Bruce. We learn that he is both *intelligent* and *inconsiderate.* By and large the associational value of *inconsiderate* is opposite to the associations listed above for *intelligent.* For example, although most people predict that an intelligent person will be *modest,* they predict also that an inconsiderate person will be *immodest.* What, then, do they predict for Bruce who is both intelligent and inconsiderate? The answer seems to be that they take the association with the heavier weight. It so happens that the associational pair *inconsiderate-immodest* is stronger in most people's minds than the pair *intelligent-modest.* Hence the attribute of *immodesty* is assigned to Bruce.

This particular experiment seems to suggest that rapid and unconscious weighting goes on when we combine multiple cues in our perception of people. We make inferences according to the strength of our habitual associations. With lightning rapidity we observe, weigh, and average out the cues, and come up with a judgment of others that fuses innumerable past experiences and meanings.

But we must not assume that the process is altogether mechanical and mathematical. Very often the outer configuration of the other person is so demanding that we "forget" to use this averaging of inferences, and proceed directly to construct a unique image of him.

[25] J. S. Bruner, D. Shapiro, and R. Tagiuri. The meaning of traits in isolation and in combination. In Tagiuri and Petrullo, *op. cit.,* Chap. 18, Note 20 above.

Ordinarily, as we shall see in the following chapter, the process of understanding is based both on common inference ("probabilism") and on uniqueness of pattern.

Asch has pointed out that not all items of information have equal weights.[26] Thus to say of a person that he has a "warm" nature is to color our picture of most of his traits. To say that he is "cold" will have the same effect. Thus to say of a person that he is "warm" will convey the impression that he is also wise, happy, imaginative, humorous. To say that he is cold implies that he is serious, reliable, but also humorless and unhappy. These two trait names, therefore, seem to have unusual *centrality* in depicting personality. They are pivots upon which almost all other traits seem to rest.

There are other "monopolistic concepts" of this type. To say of X that he is a *blind man,* a *foreigner,* a *laborer,* a *Negro* will tip (too greatly) the resultant image.

Whom Does One Know Best?

It was pointed out earlier that similarity between the personality of the judge and of the other is one of the conditions for accurate perception. It was also pointed out that knowledge of a subculture helps in judging members of that culture.

To specify, it seems to be true, broadly speaking, that men understand the personalities of men better than they do those of women; correspondingly, women are best understood by women. If one reads case studies and novels one finds that this generalization is supported. The women in Dickens are mostly fainting caricatures, the women in Trollope idealizations; Jane Austen and Charlotte Brontë created not men but puppets. A few exceptions come to mind, perhaps Tolstoy and Flaubert; but their success is often limited to portraits of one type of the opposite sex. Opinions may differ on these illustrations, but the reader is not likely to dissent from the rule.

The average male may be unable to free himself from self-consciousness in relation to the opposite sex; he may have idealistic or cynical biases that prevent objective perception; he may be unable to escape his "mother-image"; he may have preconceived ideas of the

26 S. E. Asch, *Social psychology* (Englewood Cliffs, N.J.: Prentice-Hall, 1952), Chap. 8.

proper role of women in society. Conversely, a woman may take a one-sided view of men because she dislikes her own role in a society where males are favored for most careers and enjoy more freedom; she may find male sexual aggressiveness so unpleasing (or so pleasing) that she judges men on this trait alone. And yet, of course, there are exceptions. One thinks of the female teacher who, on the basis of long experience, understands successfully the adolescent boys in her class; or of the male psychiatrist who specializes in the nervous disorders of women.

The most general rule seems to be that one understands best those personalities that are like one's own; similarity in race, sex, age, as well as in personal traits and values, is of great assistance.

Yet the situation is not so simple. For instance, we often seem to be able to understand with success natures directly opposite to our own. We understand the cheat by virtue of our own honesty. If we know our own impulses we are able to know the inhibition that causes others to restrain those impulses. To have a train of ideas in our own mind implies an understanding of an antithetical train of ideas. Opposites imply similars. Dostoevski believed that each man possesses a "double" that represents unconsciously the qualities directly opposite to those that he discloses. Jung's theory of the role of the unconscious is similar. An introvert, for all his incessant self-reference and brooding, can understand well enough the reckless extravert frame of mind he cannot attain. It is often said that "opposites attract." Insofar as this is so, it must be because of our unconscious sympathy for what is suppressed and therefore latent in ourselves.

For accurate understanding, similarity is important, and oppositeness is a shadowy kind of similarity. Yet we must also admit that long-continued practice, special experience, and giftedness may aid a judge to understand personalities quite unlike his own.

Common Sources of Error

Almost every conceivable way of committing an error in thinking is at the same time a way of misjudging people. Superficial observation, faulty memory, erroneous premises, mistaken inferences, superstitions, prejudice, rationalization, projection—the number of possible missteps is too great to classify. There are, however, certain special errors that are so common in person perception that they should be constantly borne in mind.

Oversimplification. Neither the longest novel nor the most elaborate case history can give a complete portrait and explanation of a character. Shorter accounts—including a psychograph—are almost inevitably caricatures. Usually we are well satisfied to give crisp characterizations of other people, but we object strenuously to having ourselves disposed of with a brief analysis. We have great resistance to being rubricized, and regard almost any brief account of ourselves as "a cheap form of cognizing."[27] We know we are more complex than others think, and we suspect that even an epic biography in three volumes would not do us justice.

Oversimplification is an inherent limitation of the human intellect. It is impossible to hold as many variables in mind as there are aspects of any single personality. Our cognitive processes are simply unequal to the task. But this failing is not peculiar to our perception of persons; it haunts us in our dealings with knowledge of any kind.

We seem, however, to have a special tendency to overestimate the unity of personality, to see form, to impose structure when unstructure prevails.[28] We discount inconsistencies as "exceptions that prove the rule." We are led to do so partly by our prevailing attitude of favor or disfavor toward the person. The "halo" (perseverative judgment) spreads over the whole scene (cf. page 420). Think how simplified and legendary are our images of historical personages: of Lincoln, Napoleon, Casanova, Hitler. Our dead friends and relatives become simpler and more worthy as our memory traces fade. And the same ascription of unity and consistency marks our judgments of our living associates.

Assisting oversimplification is our frequent use of some "monopolistic" concept. We have noted that to say that a person is "warm" is to tip almost all other judgments to fit this salient thought. Haire and Grunes have shown that to know a given person is a "workingman" makes it almost impossible to obtain a stereotype-free judgment of his personality.[29] When we see that the other is a Negro or French-

27 A. H. Maslow, Resistance to being rubricized. In B. Kaplan and S. Wapner (Eds.), *Perspectives in psychological theory: essays in honor of Heinz Werner* (New York: Int. Univ. Press, 1960).
28 G. Ichheiser, Misinterpretation of personality in everyday life and the psychologist's frame of reference, *Charact. & Pers.*, 1943, 12, 145–160.
29 M. Haire and W. F. Grunes, Perceptual defenses: processes protecting an organized perception of another personality, *Human Relations*, 1950, 3, 403–412.

man we often get no further than our own stereotype. Our image of a person as "successful" or "unsuccessful" spreads like a grease spot over our judgments of his traits.[30] And studies show that people often have a few favored categories in terms of which they judge others. One person looks for signs of charm, manners, cultivation; a second, for intelligence and competence; a third, for neurotic or pathological trends. What they see is thus relevant to their own interests rather than to the structure of the other's personality.[31]

The temptation to oversimplify seems to be especially acute when there are wide differences in age—a tendency to which we have already alluded. To a child most adults are merely "old people." And even in middle age we tend to see citizens of eighty as geriatric types rather than as individuals. A college student may look at his classmates and younger instructors as distinct persons, but regard senior faculty members as "old profs," devoid of individuality. Conversely, to older teachers all college students may look alike—and be so treated. Few adults note the striking individual differences among children (unless their own). If we consult a physician of our own age we are likely to mark the kind of person he is, but if the doctor is much older, he is seen merely as an impersonal oracle. To generalize the point, when there are marked differences the judge tends to perceive the other in terms of his status or role rather than as a unique personality.

Another specific source of error is *projection* (page 160).[32] The judge sees in the other person traits that reside only in himself, or else he exaggerates a quality in another person simply because he himself possesses it in high degree (mote-beam mechanism). This kind of error springs from "assumed similarity," although the assumption may be entirely unconscious. Much of our misunderstanding is colored by such egocentricism; we assume that the other fellow must feel and think as we do, and that he is merely perverse in not showing it more clearly.

In discussing the rating of personality we pointed to certain injurious response sets. A judge may try to be *complimentary* and so avoid giving offense. He may be *cautious*, and so avoid giving ex-

[30] G. Ichheiser, *op. cit.* Note 28 above.
[31] A. H. Hastorf, S. A. Richardson, and S. M. Dornbusch, The problem of relevance in the study of person perception. In Tagiuri and Petrullo, *op. cit.*, Chap. 5. Note 20 above.
[32] A. H. Hastorf and I. E. Bender, A caution respecting the measurement of empathic ability, *J. abnorm. soc. Psychol.*, 1952, 47, 574–576.

treme judgments, even when these might be more accurate. He may have a tendency to ascribe special meanings to terms and thus fail to communicate his judgments to others. All types of response biases are potential sources of error in judging people.

And yet I repeat our main conclusion: However complex the process of knowing others may be, and however many sources of error contaminate our judgment, still a major effort in your life and in mine is to bridge with understanding the gulf that separates us.

The Focus of Understanding

This major effort pivots on our attempt to comprehend each other's *intentions*. As Heider points out, the unique feature of person perception is its preoccupation with "personal causality," and personal causality springs from intention. The intention of a person "brings order into the wide variety of possible action sequences by coordinating them to a final outcome."[33] In short, the key to person perception lies in our attention to what the other is *trying to do*. His goals, his values—together with his abilities and available energy— are what fascinate us.

Thus to know another person well is to know his intentions, i.e., what kind of future he is trying to bring about. It is true that we also perceive all manner of incidental features about him, but our main effort is directed toward grasping the directions of his striving, for these (above all other things) cement his personality (just as they cement our own).

To put the matter in another way: Our own personalities center subjectively around our own concept of self. The dynamic ingredient in this concept is our own propriate striving (our own intentions). It is natural then, indeed inevitable, that when we concern ourselves with others, we look primarily for this same unifying theme.

Summary

Much of our lives is spent in trying to understand others (and in wishing others understood us better than they do). Our chief effort is to grasp correctly the motives and intentions of the other, for we would then know the guidelines of his life. But the task is

[33] F. Heider, *The psychology of interpersonal relations* (New York: Wiley, 1958), p. 112. See also A. R. Gilbert, The other person: how we "intend" it, *J. Psychol.*, 1961, **51**, 247–262.

not easy. A large number of factors influence our success or our failure.

People differ greatly in their accessibility: some are given to self-disclosure, others to secretiveness, and they differ in the "target" confidants they choose. And quite apart from deliberate self-revelation we find that some personalities are in their inherent structure relatively open, others enigmatic.

The complexity of the process is evident even in the study of first impressions. Just a glimpse of a person will start a swift and elaborate chain of inference and structuring which yields judgments reaching far beyond the information given. Our first impulse seems to be to fit people into familiar categories of age, sex, nationality, role, and thus to endow them with the stereotypes we hold for these classes; but we also swiftly form judgments concerning their personal dispositions. When more information is added to our first impressions we grow more confident in our judgment though not necessarily more accurate. It depends upon how good a judge we are, and how flexible.

The ability to judge others is not wholly general, nor is it altogether narrow and specific. It seems that some are gifted in "sensitivity to the generalized other," in knowing universal and group norms; they can predict well how typical members of a subculture will behave. Others are gifted in "interpersonal sensitivity"—in recognizing the individuality of pattern.

The gift of interpersonal sensitivity seems to be correlated with experience and maturity, with intelligence, with cognitive complexity, and with self-insight. Furthermore, a good judge is likely to be well adjusted and effective in groups, but also to be detached, high in esthetic values, and gifted with a special kind of psychological-mindedness called "intraceptiveness." Authoritarians, lacking this trait, are poor judges of people. On the whole, women are slightly better judges than are men, probably not because of an inborn capacity for intuition, but because their role in society requires the cultivation of the gift.

The process of perceiving persons is both like and unlike all other perceptual processes. The chief difference is that human objects, unlike other objects, impress us with their purposes, their animation, their intentions toward us, and their relative unpredictability. A peculiar excitement attaches to person perception.

Even more than in ordinary perception we find common judgmental sets playing a part: halo effects, stereotyping, assumptions of similarity, and all manner of emotional involvements. We combine in an intricate way the bits of information we receive; one characteristic of that intricate combination is rapid inference in terms of our experience with the cues we obtain. Another characteristic is the selection of central attributes, such as *warm* or *cold,* for emphasis. Frequently a monopolistic stereotype (such as race, occupation, social class) prevents us from making accurate and discriminating judgments. Seldom do we endeavor to assess a person as a whole; we are interested only in some one channel of relationship: Will he fit into my office staff? Will she be a congenial companion?

Broadly speaking, we know best people who are similar to ourselves—members of our own sex, culture, age-range, and like us in traits and in tastes. But people opposite to us in various traits may also be fairly understood since oppositeness is a type of similarity. Also, long experience with special groups may compensate for the lack of similarity, as may broad giftedness in interpersonal sensitivity.

The chief obstacle to accurate judgment lies in our tendency to oversimplify, to rubricize, our person perceptions. No life has all the unity and firmness of structure we customarily ascribe to it. And, of course, we are subject to other common sources of error: stereotyping, projection, leniency, halo judgments, and undue caution.

In spite of the complexity of the process we maintain that psychologists are not entitled to sidestep the problem of *accurate* knowledge as some are wont to do. My personality lies "in here," yours "out there." Although it is important to know the process by which I attempt to bridge this chasm, it is no less vital to know how well I succeed. *A major task in life is to achieve increasing success in our perception of one another.*

CHAPTER 21

The Nature of Understanding

INFERENCE IS IMPORTANT • INFERENCE IS NOT SUFFICIENT •
EMPATHY • THE DEMAND CHARACTER OF THE HUMAN BEING
• THEORIES OF CONFIGURAL COMPREHENSION • SUMMARY
THEORY: PATTERNED PERCEPTION

WE come now to a topic of lively dispute. It concerns the
various theories of cognition that are implicit in all discussions of
person perception. In the previous chapter we considered many of
the *conditions* that affect our perception of persons. But now the
question arises, *How is it possible to know the personality of others
at all?* Since we have no direct access to their experience how does it
come about that our understanding is as good as it is? That it can
never be perfect all theories would agree.

The spectrum of available theories is wide, ranging from *inference* at one extreme to *immediacy* at the other. A correct theory, we
shall hold, falls between these extremes, combining the convincing
features of both.

It is a curious fact that not only philosophers who are concerned with the theory of knowledge (epistemology), but also

psychologists concerned with the theory of cognition, argue with considerable heat about the issues involved. The reason for their emotion probably has something to do with cultural loyalty. Broadly speaking, the whole of the Anglo-American tradition in cognitive (epistemological) theory is derived from the British empiricists and associationists (Hume, Locke, Hamilton, Mill, and others). Similarly, the tradition on the Continent (especially in German-speaking countries) derives from phenomenology and from the doctrine of the "active intellect" (held, in various forms, by Leibnitz, Kant, Dilthey, Köhler, Bergson, to name a few). This latter group of thinkers argues that Anglo-American associationism and doctrines of inference fall short of accounting for our knowledge of others. Each of these Continental writers offers some additional postulates concerning the process of knowing.[1]

To illustrate the dispute we may take Locke and Leibnitz, late seventeenth-century contemporaries. The former can be considered the father of Anglo-American empiricism. His doctrine that our minds in the beginning are like a blank sheet of paper (*tabula rasa*) leads to the doctrine that sensations (impressions we receive from other people) are the sole basis of knowing; these sensations leave traces in our memories—a store of experience that is organized according to the laws of association. By calling on this store we are able to give meaning to the sensory cues that come from a new personality. Locke summarized his view by saying, "There is nothing in the intellect that was not first in the senses."

To this statement Leibnitz made a pointed addition. "Yes," said he, "there is nothing in the intellect that was not first in the senses—*except the intellect itself.*" Like Leibnitz, the great majority of cognitive theorists on the European Continent hold that Locke's scaffolding is too frail, that "something more" is involved in knowing than the simple formula

$$\text{Sensory cue} + \text{association}_1 + \text{association}_2 + \text{association}_n = \text{Understanding}$$

---

[1] A convenient discussion of these traditions will be found in B. B. Wolman, *Contemporary theories and systems in psychology* (New York: Harper, 1960), especially Chap. 10.

As we shall see, the Lockean-Leibnitzian dispute is still active today.[2]

Inference Is Important

When we say that our dog is "jealous," how do we know that it is jealous—or more accurately, why do we *think* it is? The only possible answer seems to be that in some remote way the dog's behavior is like the behavior of a jealous child with which we have had some experience. We judge by analogy. And how do we know that a child is jealous? Again we judge by analogy: his behavior is like our own, or like our memory of our own childhood jealousy. The words he uses (or his expressive bids for attention) reintegrate all sorts of past experiences we have had with jealousy (cf. pages 92–95). One author states the matter as follows:

Any experience or mental process in another organism can be inferred from structure, situation, history, and behavior only when a similar experience or mental process is or has been associated with similar structure, situation, history and behavior in oneself; and the probability of the inference will be proportional to the degree of similarity.[3]

No one denies the existence of this process of reasoning by analogy or inference. It has been accepted ever since Aristotle first stated the conditions of the syllogism. If a new event is an instance of a class of experience, it will be understood as having the same significance. For example, if it is our experience that all men are mortal, and if Socrates belongs to the class "men," then he, too, must be mortal. Or, if it is my experience that tall and thin men mostly have a cerebrotonic temperament, it follows in my reasoning that this new acquaintance, who is also tall and thin, will have the same temperament.

Inference, then, may be defined as a "cognitive process in which characteristics of a general class are attributed to an individual taken as an instance of that class."[4]

2 For a fuller discussion of Anglo-American versus Continental theories see G. W. Allport, *Becoming: basic considerations for a psychology of personality* (New Haven, Conn.: Yale Univ. Press, 1955), pp. 7–17. Also, European and American theories of personality. In H. P. David and H. von Bracken (Eds.), *Perspectives in personality theory* (New York: Basic Books, 1957), Chap. 1.

3 D. K. Adams, The inference of mind, *Psychol. Rev.*, 1928, **35**, 235–252.

4 T. R. Sarbin, R. Taft, and D. E. Bailey, *Clinical inference and cognitive theory* (New York: Holt, Rinehart and Winston, 1960), p. 5.

It is true that we are seldom aware of cognizing in this manner. The logic of the syllogism is rarely conscious. Most of the inferences we make in everyday life are amazingly swift, subtle, and largely unconscious. The following experiment shows neatly that we may be completely unaware of the factors going to make up our judgment.

> Subjects looked at the photograph of a face 20 times in one-minute exposures. The word *happy* or *angry* was superimposed on the face below threshold intensity (that is to say, the subjects did not know consciously that a word was present). In most cases the face presented with the label *happy* came gradually to be seen as "more pleasant." Likewise the face paired with *angry* grew "more unpleasant." Actually the photographs employed were chosen for their neutrality—having neither a pleasant nor an unpleasant expression.[5]

Although this experiment seems artificial from the point of view of everyday life, it nevertheless proves the case: inferences may be affected by cues, and these cues may be fitted to classes of experience (in this case with the aid of linguistic tag), without entering our awareness at all.

Many inferences, therefore, are unconscious. They are also exceedingly swift. In an earlier chapter, in a discussion of first impressions (page 500), it was suggested that the reader look for only an instant at a strange face in a public conveyance. This exercise is astonishing because of the flow of judgments that immediately occur. A brief glimpse arouses a large number of classes of experience (concerning sex, occupation, suffering, and the like) and delivers in a split second a large number of judgments.

The speed of the inferential process becomes still more baffling when we consider that we must also weight cues to determine their *probabilistic* validity. Some of our judgments seem certain, others uncertain. That our fellow passenger is a woman we are absolutely positive, for the visual cues we receive are always associated with the class (category) "female." But whether she is a young housewife or an office worker we are less certain; "on the whole" we judge she is

---

5 S. Bach and G. S. Klein, Conscious effects of prolonged subliminal exposures of words, *Amer. Psychologist*, 1957, **12**, 397.

a housewife because the cues we pick up seem to fit with greater probability into this experience-class.

Like a great sorting machine the perceiving mind seems to punch a card (with the visual cues), send it to the brain, where all other cards with similar punches are instantly assembled, and the attributes associated with the punches (in our example, the attributes of a housewife) are delivered with proper frequency weights in the form of a probabilistic judgment. The perceiver is like an infinitely complex coding machine.[6]

Thus inference can be viewed as a mechanical process along the lines of the models offered by modern "information theory." As we have already said, it can also be viewed in terms of unconscious syllogistic reasoning. Further, its tie with associationism, with the doctrine of reintegration, is likewise clear. It should be added that the theory of inference likewise can easily be fitted to the stimulus-response model.

A child, for example, who suffered from having a cruel and overbearing father, may, in later life, respond with fear and hatred to anyone whose physical features resemble his father's, or even to anyone who is in a position of authority over him. That is to say, the physical features and the role of authority are "conditioned stimuli" that reactivate the original fear response.

The point made here is that many schools of contemporary thought subscribe in one way or another to the theory of inference.[7]

The virtues of the theory of inference are undeniable. It accounts admirably for many of the conclusions reached in the preceding chapter. It explains why people know best those who are like themselves, why a wide experience in life is essential to a good judge of personality, why personalities that are subtle in structure are not well understood by judges who are themselves uncomplicated. It accounts for the chasms of misunderstanding that lie between the two sexes, between races, and between types of persons having incom-

6 The subtleties of the process of inference are too complex for analysis here. Valuable accounts are offered by Sarbin, Taft, and Bailey, op. cit. (Note 4 above). Also by J. S. Bruner, J. J. Goodnow, and G. A. Austin, A study of thinking (New York: Wiley, 1956).
7 Inference is the pivot of traditional logic, associationism, stimulus-response psychology, information theory, cybernetics, probabilistic functionalism, and the epistemological assumptions made by what today is called "cognitive theory."

patible values. It can handle well the common errors in judgment
that come from holding rigid stereotypes, from assuming similarity
between the other and ourselves when similarity does not in fact
exist. No theory of knowing others can deny the importance of
inference.

Inference Is Not Sufficient

For all its unquestioned merits, the theory of inference falls
seriously short of adequacy. Among its limitations are the following:

1. *Although there is some support, there is also much contrary
evidence from introspection.* Only rarely do we say to ourselves,
"Now what does that facial pattern mean? Well, it reminds me of X,
who often looked like that. Now X was a person I liked and trusted.
And so—although I am only 'probably' sure, I shall on the whole trust
this man." Such conscious inferences do, of course, occasionally take
place and so far as they go they support the inference theory. When
the inference is not conscious we must still allow generously for unconscious inference, for rapid, subtle, probabilistic coding. We
cannot expect introspection to follow the lighting process step by step.

Introspection does, however, raise a fatally embarrassing question.
Why do I always perceive the other person as a pattern that exists
"out there" and never "in here" (where all the inferring is taking
place)? Introspection is unable to factor out the lines in the other's
face + my own experience. In my perception his face and his suffering are parts of a single system. I do not perceive a face there and
add a meaning here (as the inference theory claims). The process
has an exclusively objective reference.

Köhler has pointed out that when we say that a man is *melancholy, embarrassed,* or *big-hearted,* it is clearly *he* and not we
ourselves who have these qualities.[8] A Dutch investigator, studying
judgments of facial expression, finds that in spite of the analytical
(inferential) frame of mind induced by the experiment, the most
impressive finding is that judges are wholly convinced that what they
see is "out there" and not "in here." The investigator concludes that
"no theory explaining understanding by means of experience alone
or of reasoning by analogy, could be correct; the impression received

[8] W. Köhler, *Gestalt psychology* (New York: Liveright, 1929), pp. 234–268.

being clearly located in the perceived face."[9] All understanding is pointed outward; it is the wind, the dog, the person who seems angry or gentle, not we ourselves.

2. *Inference requires external control.* When an acquaintance makes a certain gesture, what is it that holds our potential inferences to the significance of this gesture in *his* life? Why should not our associational train run perhaps as follows: *gesture*-ballet–Ballet Russe–Moscow–H-bomb–annihilation, and so on?

The associationist might answer: We have a *mental set* to confine our inferences to the task in hand, viz., judging the other. True, but what gives us this limiting mental set? Inference does not do so. There must be an additional factor—at the very least a "demand character" in the other that holds us to our task. The stimulus-person is the continuing and controlling factor in our chain of inferences.

The lightning speed of coding and weighting and the enormous complexity of the whole process make it essential that we seek out the organizing factors that are able to prevent chaos among inferences. To some extent the study of neurological mechanisms may aid us. There seems to be, for example, a natural tendency for the brain to function with general blocks of information (cell-assemblies, categories, high-level generalizations, modules—call them what you will). The cue that arrives from the appearance of an object or from the speech of another will activate this whole block. This "instantiation" of the cue into the category provides its "meaning."[10] But whatever the neural mechanics may be—and they are not yet understood—we still require a powerful orientation to the other in order to keep our chain of inferences anchored to *him*.

3. *Understanding is not proportional to the amount of available relevant experience.* Strictly speaking, the inference theory would say that we comprehend nothing unless we have previous experience with it; and further, that the excellence of an inference (and the probability of making it) will be proportional to the amount of

---

[9] N. H. Frijda, The understanding of facial expression of emotion, *Acta psychologica*, 1953, **9**, 354.

[10] The preferred categories of meaning into which we code sensory cues are called "modules" by Sarbin, Taft, and Bailey, *op. cit.*, Chap. 5 (Note 4 above). These authors likewise propose the term "instantiation" for the coding process. Speculative discussion of possible neural groundwork for inference is offered by D. O. Hebb, *The organization of behavior* (New York: Wiley, 1949). Also, by J. S. Bruner, Neural mechanisms in perception, *Psychol. Rev.,* 1957, **64**, 340–358.

relevant experience we have. The quotation from a thoroughgoing inference theorist (page 525) makes these assertions. But are they strictly true?

A boy, say ten years old, sees a movie in which a plumed knight swings his medieval lady up to his saddle and gallops across a drawbridge with a defiant flourish of his lance at a furious and frustrated dragon. The boy has never ridden a horse or carried a lance, and, to say the least, has limited acquaintance with medieval ladies and frustrated dragons. But is his "understanding" any less than that for a cinema based on a familiar playground or domestic scene? Perhaps, a little less—but not much.

Still more to the point, take infants. At the age of one year or less they often show appropriate response to expressions with which they have had no conceivable experience. The child who has suffered no actual punishment may respond with astonishing pertinency to a scolding or scowling face. We have already discussed the origins of the smiling response (page 498), which is clearly not based on previous experience. Ethologists tell us that, contrary to Locke, there are many such innate perceptions. Although it is certainly true (as pointed out in the last chapter) that children are less good judges of others than are adults, still we cannot say that their judgments are directly proportional to their experience.

Suppose that a friend tells us that he is feeling well, that he has no worries, and that he is happy, and suppose that his behavior gives circumstantial support for his statement. By all the laws of association and inference, we should accept his statements, and make a corresponding judgment that he enjoys well-being. The theory of probabilism should give us at least 99 percent certainty. But now suppose that some trivial cue, perhaps the absence of a familiar tone in his voice, or a tense line in his brow, belies the obvious. What he tells us and most of what we see, together with all our habits of inference, are now discounted. It is the *unfamiliar* (not the familiar) evidence that conveys meaning and forms our judgment. Something about the man himself—unfamiliar though it is—leads to a reversal of the expected judgment. Why does it do so? Probabilistic inference cannot explain.

Understanding another is often like understanding an unfamiliar metaphor. In Walt Whitman's phrase, *"the wide unconscious scenery of my land,"* for every single word, of course, we have past associations—but not for this new combination. Never have we heard the phrase "unconscious scenery." But suddenly it conveys a feeling for the unplanned variety of the American landscape. We do not add together the familiar words in this quotation and give to each its customary meaning. To do so would be probabilism. No, the novelty obtained by the juxtaposition of *unconscious* and *scenery* creates an understanding in spite of a lifelong *unfamiliarity* with this particular combination of words.

Each person is much like a novel metaphor. Separate past experiences do indeed enter into our comprehension, but their impact is in no sense additive. It is not exclusively our habits that determine our comprehension; the outside pattern is also determinative.

4. *The understanding of emotional behavior does not normally, as the inference theory would require, arouse similar feelings in the observer.* According to the doctrine of inference, the cue should normally tend to reinstate the full original experience with which it was associated. Our perception of an angry face should arouse an angry frame of mind in us; sensual gestures should arouse concupiscent feelings. But instead of their doing so, we find that such expressions usually provoke no feelings at all, or else quite contradictory feelings, perhaps amusement or disgust.

The associationist may, of course, reply that any part of an inferential train may be inhibited by concurrent cross-states in the perceiver. But this is an extravagant assumption. Would it not be simpler to say that the stimulus-object (the other) determines what we shall see? The task in hand is to understand *him*, and not to relive our own entire emotional history, and then discount part of it. Inference explains too much.

5. *Inference stresses what the other has in common with all men, not the pattern that belongs to him alone.* Inference theorists tell us that "the conditions for knowing any 'particular' are fulfilled only when its 'universal' or class membership is recognized."[11] This is an extreme statement. It means in effect that we cannot know Peter or Paul unless we fit him into stock-sized clothes. It means that we can know Peter only insofar as we can code him. He is, let us say, a white Protestant, a college male, mesomorphic in build, who has a hundred

[11] Sarbin, Taft, and Bailey, *op. cit.*, p. 255; Note 4 above. In the quotation given, the word "recognized" is, of course, unfortunate since the authors themselves emphasize the unconscious nature of the inferential process.

scores on a hundred personality tests, and can be tagged with general conceptual labels, such as *cordial, ardent, intense, extraverted.* All these classes, so the inference theories tell us, constitute Peter. But do they? The unity that is Peter has disintegrated into a mere powder of concepts. The continuity of Peter has been broken into discontinuous and static categories. His life "out there" is reduced to my conceptual furniture "in here." There is no way of reconstructing the true mobility and pattern of Peter from this debris of concepts.

The reader will recall that in Chapters 14 and 15, where the convenient assumption of "common traits" was discussed, we insisted that in nature only "personal dispositions" will be found. At the same time common traits were defended as useful in comparing people—and inference is now defended as a mode of comparison. But just as we argued earlier that common traits will not give us the patterned structure of an individual life, so, too, we now argue that inference puts too much weight on commonalities and not enough weight on the unity of the particular other.

The very process of inference begins by neglecting the special coloring of the individual, and by substituting for it an array of common categories applicable to all sorts of mortals, to which in turn the individual is fitted. Such a process deflects attention from the manner in which the traits of the other function together in the general interests of *his* organism.

The doctrine of inference, like the doctrine of common traits, puts emphasis on what is common, on what is average. Nearly all investigations of personality, we have noted, are made in terms of groups of people. It is inevitable, therefore, that the *average* is the anchor in research. But an average is something intermediate between people. It is not concerned with individuals at all. Indeed, the whole purpose of an average in statistics is to keep together a group as a whole.[12]

It is true that by knowing the average we can infer that Peter deviates from his group—but we can do so only for the class of qualities under investigation. True, we can also make smaller subclasses and tell how he deviates from the average in many narrower, measurable qualities. Yes, but we still do not deal with Peter primarily, but only with classes. If Peter deviates so many points in

---

[12] Cf. A. L. Bowley, The average and the individual (*Barnett House Papers*, No. 22; London: Oxford, 1939). See also A. Wellek, Der Stand der psychologischen Diagnostik im Überblick, *Stud. gen.*, 1954, **8**, 464–472.

extraversion from other college males, we are making a useful comparison. But the core problem is *how does Peter's extraversion relate to his intelligence, ascendance, values, and health?* What does it *mean* in his life? No juggling of subclasses will tell us.

We must, of course, admit that for some purposes a knowledge of the average leads to good predictions in the round. The actuary can tell almost exactly how many males in a given age or occupational group will die next year. And that is all he wants to know. He cannot tell whether Peter will die (and that is what Peter wants to know). Similarly, it is said that psychologists can make their best predictions by taking group (actuarial) statistics (i.e., by coding Peter according to his class-memberships).[13] And so, no doubt, they can for some purposes. But when, in the future, psychology develops its morphogenic methods and makes proper use of them, the predictions (which at best are now weak) should improve.[14]

Empathy

Shortcomings in the inference theory have led many writers (especially in Europe) to devise broader, and to them more adequate, accounts of the process of understanding.

The concept of *Einfühlung* (feeling oneself into) was introduced by Lipps at the turn of the century; the translation of the term as *empathy* was proposed by Titchener. Lipps applied it to the field of esthetics and especially to the understanding of persons.[15]

[13] P. E. Meehl, *Clinical versus statistical prediction* (Minneapolis: Univ. of Minnesota Press, 1954).

[14] I have been speaking of inference as if it were always a matter of calling upon our knowledge of people in general, or of classes of people. It is, of course, true that even in idiographic prediction we form a general concept of a given person, and infer the significance of his acts from this concept. But since no writer, to my knowledge, has this type of idiographic inference in mind it seems fair to direct our criticism to the actuarial inference intended by the authors we cite. It is, for example, the argument of Sarbin, Taft, Bailey, *op. cit.* (Note 4 above), that the uniqueness of a personality always reduces to variations within classes of the universal, and so inferences are always inferences from classes.

[15] For the historical background of this concept and critique, the following references are helpful: T. Lipps, Das Wissen von fremden Ichen, *Psychol. Untersuch.*, 1907, **1**, 694–722; G. Murphy, *Historical introduction to modern psychology* (Rev. ed.; New York: Harcourt, Brace, 1949), p. 167; G. W. Allport, *Personality: a psychological interpretation* (New York: Holt, Rinehart and Winston, 1937), pp. 530–533; G. W. Allport, Historical background of modern social psychology. In G. Lindzey (Ed.), *Handbook of social psychology* (Cambridge, Mass.: Addison-Wesley, 1954), Chap. 1; M. Scheler, *The nature of sympathy* (German original, 1913; Transl. by P. Heath; New Haven, Conn.: Yale Univ. Press, 1954).

As originally used, the concept referred primarily to the process of motor mimicry. Contemplation of a work of art, for example, involves many slight movements of the brows, eyes, trunk, and limbs which are in some way imitative of the stimulus-object. When one says that a Gothic spire *soars,* that the arch of the nave *is exalted,* that a waterfall *leaps,* or that a storm cloud *weighs heavily,* it is in reality one's own muscular responses that are being reported. In art we give judgments of pleasingness if our empathic movements are graceful, uninterrupted, but not too simple. Ugliness or boredom is our judgment if our imitative movements are jerky, unbalanced, or oversimple.

In person perception slight motor mimicry is likewise important. Watch the facial expressions of a sympathetic audience—the chances are that they show strains, smiles, and changes like those of the speaker. Actors and mimics are often good judges of personality. People who actively imitate a facial expression seem to be better judges of its meaning than those who do not.[16] Graphologists, when confronted with a new and strange formation of script, sometimes trace the formation with a dry pen in order to obtain the kinesthesis that will enable them to reconstruct in some degree the affective and motor impulses of the writer.

Ordinarily we are unaware of the extent to which this motor mimicry enters into the process of understanding. Figure 43 offers an illustration of this fact. Had not the camera recorded the strains and stresses in the spectators it would be hard to believe that the watchers are close physical mimics of the bowler.

Goethe once claimed that he could imitate a man for an hour after watching him for fifteen minutes. This remark calls attention to the deep anchorage of the empathic process. Once started, it enables us to "swing with" the mental life of the other.

The psychiatrist Sullivan felt that empathy is an important basis for mother-infant relationships. When the mother feels anxiety her expressions of this state induce similar tension in the child.[17]

It is important to note that in the main (though not in the case of the infant) empathic response fits well under the theory of infer-

16 F. H. Allport, *Social psychology* (Boston: Houghton Mifflin, 1924), p. 229.
17 Sullivan did not know how such postural transfer comes about. With characteristic humor he remarks, "So although empathy may sound mysterious, remember that there is much that sounds mysterious in this universe, only you have got used to it; and perhaps you will get used to empathy." H. S. Sullivan, *The interpersonal theory of psychiatry* (New York: Norton, 1953), pp. 41 f.

Figure 43. Empathy. All-Ireland road bowls championship (Derek Bayes for *Sports Illustrated*)

ence. By imitating the other we come to know how he feels and thinks simply because we know how we ourselves thought and felt when we made similar movements or held similar postures in the past. Empathy would seem to be simply a case of "kinesthetic inference."[18]

But Lipps avoided this trap. He insisted that although we employ our own past experience in empathy, the process itself has exclusively objective reference. We do not perceive our own body in action but the body of the other. There is no break between the strain, pride, sorrow, or playfulness which I feel empathically and the personality of the one I am seeking to understand. "A unitary object demands a unitary perception." The unity of the other is not a gluing together of fragments from my inferences but is something demanded by the unity of the object itself. "Otherness" is an inherent attribute in empathy, marking it off from the ordinary process of inference.[19]

In spite of Lipps's desire to remove empathy from the simple realm of inference, the fact remains that empathy is a "half-way" theory. It is loaded with kinesthetic inference, but it tries also to establish the *Thou* as having precedence in the process of perception. From the point of view of inference theory, Lipps is guilty of adding an intuitive element; from the point of view of many phenomenologists, he remains too close to the psychology of association.

It is regrettable that with passing years the original meaning of empathy as "objective motor mimicry" became hopelessly confused and lost to view. The term has broadened out to mean any process of successful understanding. A typical current definition is "the imaginative transposing of oneself into the thinking, feeling and acting of another."[20] Such a definition lacks theoretical value since "imaginative transposing" can occur through inference, empathy, or any

---

18 Freud felt that empathy is the process by which we try to perceive what is essentially foreign to our own ego. It is an intellectualistic endeavor to understand by mimicry and inference those activities which are not immediately intelligible. True understanding comes via *identification* and requires no forced mimicry. Empathy is at best a "trial identification"; it gives us hypotheses concerning the nature of the other which must be verified. S. Freud, *Group psychology and the analysis of the ego* (transl., 1921; New York: Liveright, 1949).

19 Mead's theory of role-assumption (see Chapter 8) emphasizes the subtle part played by muscular imitation in our understanding of others. Like Lipps, Mead agrees that the empathic act *presupposes* the consciousness of another self, and that this other self as *given* becomes intentionally the object of knowledge.

20 R. F. Dymond, A scale for the measurement of empathic ability, *J. consult. Psychol.*, 1949, 13, 127–133. See also F. Massarik and I. R. Weschler, Empathy revisited: the process of understanding people, *Calif. Mgmt. Rev.*, 1959, 1, 36–46.

of the configural processes soon to be considered. Today we hear much concerning "the measurement of empathy," but what is measured is successful judgment, not the particular process of judgment that Lipps had in mind. The theoretical coin has depreciated, probably beyond redemption.

The Demand Character of the Human Being

Before additional theories of understanding are described it is well to consider further the insistent mental set that dominates our perception of others.

Let us start with a not uncommon experience. You think you are alone in a room, but suddenly discover that someone else is present. You are startled—not because there is physical danger, but because you have to readjust from a nonpersonal orientation to one that is personal. What happens is that a cognitive "whirl" starts to form around the other person. Who is he, what is he doing here, what is his relation to me? My world is no longer my own. I cannot go about my business until I have located the other in my setting.

Suppose that a family is sitting in the living room of an evening. Through the years the members have "located" one another and live on a level of routine peace. The doorbell rings and an acquaintance enters. Immediately a new level of conduct appears. Bare legs are covered, hair is slicked into place, company manners are assumed, the so-glad-to-see-you look comes over all faces.

Is it not obvious that persons normally have the highest "demand" character of anything in our environment? They are very different from objects. If I see a man sitting on a chair, it is the man and not the chair that interests me. A person is seen as an intelligent, causal, moving, significant entity. A material object, such as a chair, will wait in place until I wish to move it. A person, on the other hand, is mobile, spontaneous, fraught with consequences for me. I must locate him in my world, must know his intentions, must adjust to him. Above all he has *purposes* which inanimate objects lack. As Buber would say, between me and the chair there is an I-it relation, between me and a person an I-thou relation. Every I-thou relation is more than an experience, more than a perception; it is a *meeting*, an *encounter*.[21]

21 M. Buber, *I and thou* (Transl. by R. G. Smith; Edinburgh: Clark, 1937).

Heider points out that so great is the priority of the human being in our perception that we tend even to humanize nonhuman objects. Like animists we view much of our environment with a humanizing mental set. Kittens are like babies; a stanch oak is like a sturdy man; pansies have "little faces"; willow trees sigh. Heider shows that even a two-minute film composed entirely of circles, squares, and lines in motion can scarcely be seen as such. The audience almost invariably sees these lines in motion as human beings undergoing a series of appropriate feelings and actions. Of course a person *knows* that the objects are mere lines, but he cannot help sensing human meanings in their movements.[22]

When we meet a human being we feel under great compulsion to see him as a pattern. We do not look at him as a congeries of acts typical of humanity at large, but as a unique self-system. Only by reference to this system as a whole do his acts make sense. Unless the *system* were prior in our interest we would perceive only fragments of activities whose personal relevance could not be understood. A gesture, for example, is never perceived by itself. Nor is it related exclusively to our stock of available inferences. We say, rather, that this gesture as performed by this man in this situation has such and such significance. His acts are not referred to universal laws but to the ongoing system of his nature that has compelling priority for us.

If we did not have this overpowering intention to perceive persons as individual systems we could not sensibly use the stores of information that are potentially available to the inferential process.

And so we see more clearly why the theory of inference must be modified to include the priority of the personalizing mental set which alone guarantees that the needed selection and channeling of inference will take place.

Theories of Configural Comprehension

Several theories hold that the objective pattern "out there" has a more direct impact upon our cognition than can be accounted for by inference, empathy, or even by a humanizing mental set.

22 F. Heider, *The psychology of interpersonal relations* (New York: Wiley, 1958), Chap. 2. Our tendency to anthropomorphize objects in motion is brought out by A. Michotte, *La perception de la causalité* (Louvain: Institut supérier de Philosophie, 1946). Also by R. Tagiuri, Movement as a cue in person perception. In H. P. David and J. C. Brengelmann (Eds.), *Perspectives in personality research* (New York: Springer, 1960), Chap. 9.

1. *Isomorphism*. The term *isomorphism* may be illustrated by the method used by a typical Japanese artist. When he wishes to represent an object suggesting strength—a cliff, the beak of a bird, the tiger's claw—he invokes in himself a sentiment of strength which he feels throughout his system at the moment of applying the brush. The theory of isomorphism holds that the inner feeling of strength will be conveyed through his stroke, through the excursions of his brush, through the painted product, to the retina, and thence to the brain of the beholder, so that the final esthetic experience of the perceiver will have the "same shape" as the original experience of the artist.[23]

Isomorphism holds that a perceiver does not merely create meanings from fragments of inference, but rather (and more important) he *receives* meanings. A person who is embarrassed, melancholy, anxious, or condescending does not emit unstructured light and sound waves of evidence which the perceiver assembles and fits to his own store of experience. Rather, the evidence is patterned throughout the series of events. Even when the evidence shifts from the "mental" to the "physical" level, it retains an essential pattern. Several stages are involved, but the same pattern persists through each. A simple table summarizes the stages.[24]

ISOMORPHIC LEVELS

A. The perceived person

Stage 1	His state of mind	psychological
Stage 2	Nervous system correlate of Stage 1	electrochemical
Stage 3	Movement of his body (in speech and gesture)	neuromuscular

B. Communicating media

Stage 4	Light waves, sound waves, touch	mechanical

C. The perceiver

Stage 5	Patterned excitation of sense organs	physicochemical
Stage 6	Projections to cortex	electrochemical
Stage 7	Perceptual judgment of other's state of mind	psychological

[23] The example is cited by R. Arnheim in his authoritative account of isomorphism: The Gestalt theory of expression, *Psychol. Rev.*, 1949, **56**, 156–171.
[24] Adapted from Arnheim, *op. cit.*, p. 161.

The important point is that from first to last there is a configurated character to the communication. Pattern persists—barring some unusual breakage. Interruption of the pattern may occur, for example, when the other decides not to betray his state of mind, and contrives to introduce a deceptive pattern at Stage 3. Or the perceiver may not see or hear the communication because of dim light or inaudible sound (Stage 4). Or again, strong stereotypes may prevent a correct registering of the pattern (Stage 7).

This theory, strongly advocated by Gestalt psychologists, does not deny altogether the contribution made by association and inference.[25] It gives us, however, a picture of what the restraining limits may be that help to keep inference within relevant bounds. It also has the merit of explaining the fact (noted above) that young children seem to have some direct comprehension of meaning that exceeds by far their own inadequate store of life experience.

One limitation of the theory may be mentioned. Our illustrations, it will be noted, have to do with transitory emotional moods or states of mind, and not with the realm of deep-lying and permanent traits. Isomorphic perception may tell us that the artist experiences a mood of strength, but not what sort of man he is. We may perceive isomorphically that Peter now feels embarrassed, but whether Peter is by nature a shy introvert we can tell only through prolonged acquaintance.

Related to isomorphism is the concept of "physiognomic perception." Figure 42 on page 491 presented two diagrams. The reader feels that one fits the name "waleula" and the other "quidikaka." Why? Simply because one name corresponds to (has the "same shape" as) one of the diagrams. A child may go further; he may say that quidikaka is *cruel,* that a walking stick is *proud,* that masks are *fearful,* and that hard candy is *angry.* It is not that the child has specific associations to account for these judgments, but to him stimuli are saturated with emotional and human attributes, depending on the form they take. Physiognomic perception recedes normally with age in our Western society. Analytical inference then becomes relatively more dominant.[26]

---

25 See K. Koffka, *Principles of Gestalt psychology* (New York: Harcourt, Brace, 1933), especially pp. 655–661; Köhler, *op. cit.,* Chap. 8 (Note 8 above); S. Asch, *Social Psychology* (Englewood Cliffs, N.J.: Prentice-Hall, 1952). Chaps. 7 and 8.
26 For a discussion of physiognomic perception see H. Werner, *Comparative psychology of mental development* (Rev. ed.; Chicago: Follett, 1948).

2. *Identification and sympathy.* Some writers feel that it is possible to enter more closely into the lives of others than any of the theories so far discussed allow. There is, says Bergson, a sympathetic attitude toward reality outside us that makes us seem to enter into it, to be one with it, and to live it.[27] This direct participation is the opposite of intellectual analysis and inference. Bergson holds that it is foreign to our normal course of understanding to judge in terms of universal concepts, categories, and inference. Our normal effort is to grasp the unity of a pattern which we know to be original and fresh. I can see the color of an orange, feel its shape, taste it, know its history and its class, but it is not possible to see, feel, touch or reason its *unity*. Its unity as an orange is something my consciousness seems directly to take possession of. Concepts are formed through associations and these do not yield unity. "The dilemma," says Croce, "is inexorable: either keep associationism and give up unity, or keep unity and give up associationism. No third way out of the difficulty arises."[28]

So far as person perception is concerned, the unity of the particular is even more demanding. We never perceive a person without perceiving that he *is* a person—a system of purposes, values, conscience, and even of contradictions. It is his unique system of intentions that we enter into and comprehend.

Whether close emotional ties improve our understanding is an empirical question we cannot yet answer. Perhaps overinvolvement (being in love, for example) makes for a certain blindness. But a minimum degree of sympathy seems necessary for comprehension. We recall that Freud argued that *identification* is the basic process of understanding. We resort to empathy, he said, only when we cannot fully identify with the other.

Even writers who seem satisfied with the inference theory sometimes add that a primary assumption must be made—that "after all, we are all pretty much alike."[29] At least this degree of sympathy with our common lot would seem to be required. It is not a matter of intellectual commonalities, but of compassion.

3. *Innate knowledge and identity.* Here we come to a more ex-

27 H. Bergson, *An introduction to metaphysics* (Transl. by T. E. Hulme; New York: Putnam, 1912).
28 B. Croce, *Aesthetic* (Transl. by D. Ainslie; New York: Macmillan, 1909), p. 171.
29 Cf. D. Bakan, Clinical psychology and logic, *Amer. Psychologist*, 1956, 11, 655–662.

treme view which argues that each person is but a single incarnation of a common mental life. Each of us must, therefore, share the essential structure and attributes of the minds of all our fellow mortals. Mutual understanding rests ultimately upon men's participation in a common objective mind. For Hegel and for others, "It is mind itself that understands itself in its separate individuations."

Islands are connected by way of the sea bed, and who knows, when we reach out below the level of our own island of consciousness, what intuitions we may have of the mental life of others? The point of view is found in Jung's conception of the racial unconscious and of archetypes, also in William James's account of religious experience. Theories of this type are out of fashion among Western psychologists today, for by assuming innate ideas and the existence of overindividual minds, they seem to deny the basic tenets of empiricism.

4. *Acquaintance with* versus *knowledge about.* Two Maine fishermen were chatting. They were discussing a college professor who was a summer resident. One said to the other, "He *knows* everything." The other drawled his reply, "Yup, but he don't *realize* nothing." The second fisherman was saying, in effect, that the professor had plenty of knowledge about the world, but he had somehow failed to digest it.

William James, like the fisherman, has called attention to the distinction between two kinds of cognition: *knowledge about* and *acquaintance with.*[30] One may know a great deal about Peter and yet not "realize" the pattern of his life.

To be truly acquainted with a person means to be able to take his point of view, to think within his frame of reference, to reason from his premises. Acquaintance leads us to realize that the existence of the other is rationally consistent from his standpoint, however disjointed it may appear to be from ours.

We do not imply that "acquaintance with" is a theory of cognition apart from other doctrines of configural understanding. It is simply an additional way of calling attention to the fact that the theory of inference is insufficient to cover completely the process of knowing others.

It is here that we must mention an embarrassing state of affairs.

[30] W. James, *Principles of psychology* (2 vols.; New York: Holt, Rinehart and Winston, 1890), I, 221.

Psychologists, as a professional group, are not particularly successful as judges of other people. After reviewing available evidence Taft concludes that "physical scientists, and possibly other non-psychologists, e.g., personnel workers, appear to be more capable of judging others accurately than are either psychology students or clinical psychologists."[31] How can we explain this professional ineptness? Our answer is that the present training of psychologists leads them to a *knowledge about,* rather than to an *acquaintance with,* human nature in its concrete manifestations.

5. *Verstehen.* In Chapter 1 we mentioned a German school of thought that makes a sharp contrast between the sciences of mind (*Geisteswissenschaften*) and the sciences of nature (*Naturwissenschaften*). It says in effect that while certain sequences in a man's life may be *explained* in terms of natural science, his life as a whole can be *understood* only by the method of mental and cultural science. It is only when the life and actions of another are intelligibly bound together as a unit that I understand him. To observe fragments of his behavior, and then to reason by analogy (which is to bind these fragments to the lives of other people) will never yield an understanding of individuality. *Verstehen,* then, is a mental process guided by consciousness of *structure.* Spranger defines it as the mental activity that *"grasps events as fraught with meaning in relation to a totality."*[32]

Now it is impossible to apprehend events "in relation to a totality" unless there is some focus in personality to provide a point of anchorage for the observer's attention. What should the observer grasp first in order to anchor the pattern that he perceives? The answer is, Identify the other's intention (page 520), i.e., his constellation of values. Personal values are the dominating force in life, and all of a person's activity is directed toward the realization of his values. And so the focus for understanding is the other's value-orientation—or, we might say, his philosophy of life.

What are the central value-patterns that we may look for? One answer is Spranger's typology of six major patterns to which we may

31 R. Taft, The ability to judge people, *Psychol. Bull.*, 1955, **52**, 12.
32 E. Spranger, *Proc. 8th int. Congr. Psychol.* (Groningen), 1927, p. 148. The literature on *Verstehen* and related processes is extensive. Earlier literature may be traced through Allport, *Personality: a psychological interpretation,* Chap. 19. Newer developments through E. Meyer, Zur Neuorientierung im Bereich der verstehenden Psychologie, *Psychol. Beitr.,* 1954, **1**, 426–434.

order the other's acts (the *theoretical, economic, esthetic, social, political,* and *religious* values, described on pages 297–299). In order to understand a life that fits into one or more of these "schemata of comprehensibility" we must understand the pure (ideal) type itself. We must know what the essential "theoretical man" is like in order to understand concrete men who may fit approximately into this value-direction. Hence, *Verstehen* requires cultural sophistication and much knowledge of history and society. To understand a given person requires that we comprehend also his context of thought and development. Some authors go so far as to say that such understanding is a wholly different process from that used in inference. The latter requires analysis into elements and association by classes. Understanding, by contrast, is descriptive, global, complete, contextual. We cannot grasp a historical event, such as Hannibal's crossing the Alps, simply through our knowledge about Roman legions, elephants, and Alps, but only through our feeling for the specific context of the event.

Critics point out that if defined in this way there can be no check on the accuracy of understanding. One judge's interpretation is as good as another's. Uncontrolled understanding yields mere dogmatic conviction, and may suffer from the common errors of projection and prejudice.

It can also be objected that the sharp opposition offered between analytic (inferential) knowledge and understanding cannot be defended. Although there is unquestioned truth in the claim that outer pattern is important, there is no denying that detailed associations and inference are ingredients in the total process. Stern states the objection clearly:

It is erroneous to place *verstehende* psychology as an independent discipline in opposition to psychology as a natural science. There is only one unitary psychology which seeks to know its objects in their elementary nature and in terms of the conceptual laws under which they may be subsumed, as well as in their totality as concrete value-structures possessed of unique significance.[33]

In short, our theory of knowing others must allow for both nomothetic and for idiographic knowledge, for both inferential and for configural comprehension.

[33] W. Stern, *Wertphilosophie* (Leipzig: Barth, 1924), p. 380.

Summary Theory: Patterned Perception

So much for the clash of theories.[34] There are those who believe to the bitter end in the sufficiency of analogy and inference; there are those who are convinced that associative processes are virtually irrelevant to the understanding of persons, and that our understanding is immediate and direct; finally, there are conciliators who believe that what is said by the proponents and opponents of each theory sounds sensible enough, and that a combined view is needed. We join the conciliators.

It does no good to assert that the whole dispute is an epistemological snowball fight, and that psychologists should forget it and return to their tests and measurements to collect *facts*. The sad truth is that facts alone tell little. Every fact concerning a human person requires interpretation, and interpretation may be analogical or structured, or both. The proportion of each is a matter of considerable methodological importance. The devotee of inference is likely to place his confidence almost entirely in those methods which tell him more about *populations* of people than about concrete personalities. The devotee of structure may be in danger of placing too much faith in unverified and incommunicable impression.

We seek a balance, a method that will season our knowledge *about* people with an understanding *of* them.

Modern theories of perception are in fact moving in the desired direction. We no longer think that sensations plus associations tell the whole story. The theory of inference taken by itself says that light waves reflected from your face and clothes, sound waves from your larynx, force upon my brain an array of elementary sensations. These touch off categories or classes of earlier associated experience which indirectly provide "meaning" for your personality. The result is that I assemble you, as it were, with lightning rapidity from light, sound, touch, smell vibrations. You are not *you*. You are merely a source of physical energy. I assemble you; I construct you; I unify you. Such are the assumptions of a pure inference theory.

---

[34] The reader may have marked, perhaps with surprise, that I have made no reference to *intuition* as a way of knowing others. The avoidance of this term is intentional. Long experience shows that the word is a red flag to the psychological bull. My aim is to invite a dispassionate consideration of the problem of understanding. For this reason it seems well to avoid terminology carrying excess emotional freight. Previous pages, however, have described the essential position of various "intuitionist" schools of thought.

What we need is a trenchant modification of this view that will allow for three unquestionable truths: (1) Personality is a structure "out there," capable of being understood with greater or less accuracy. It is *you*, not I, who are shy, sensitive, boisterous, or domineering. It is your qualities, not mine, that I perceive—except when I make the error of projection. (2) The sources of physical energy through which your qualities are communicated to me act in a patterned manner, not atomistically. Whether we can assume literal isomorphism is doubtful, but that structured and not chaotic transmission occurs seems certain. (3) My sensitivity to the pattern perceived is immensely sharpened by my humanizing attitude, that is to say, by the powerful demand character that persons as persons exert upon my attention and perceptual preference. If we wish to do so, we may negate this normally patterned attitude in favor of conceptual analysis (as when we look only at a person's scores on tests), but in proportion as we do so we lose grasp of the individuality of structure.

Briefly stated, the patterned perception of personality is *the comprehension of organization, with the aid of inference, but under a sustained interest in the structure of the other personality itself.*

Patterning exists at the very outset of our effort to understand another. Our first glimpse is of a complete individual. We do not yet know detail, but we cannot even start a train of inference unless we are guided by a sense of the whole. Thus a psychiatrist, a counselor, or an interviewer has no idea how to frame questions that will probe, until he comprehends, however dimly, the type of structure with which he is dealing. This point is important, for much effort is wasted in studying personality through using irrelevant variables and conceptualizations that are beside the point. The Procrustean bed is a poor setting for the study of a person. Too often an assortment of percentile ranks or Rorschach scores is solemnly offered as a psychological portrait of a person. The blunder would not occur if the psychologist sensed in the beginning the nature of the personal structure he is attempting to analyze.

The role of inference is especially apparent when there is a hitch in the course of comprehension. When Peter puzzles me by his behavior, I am likely to ask, "Now what made him do that?" It was an act incompatible with my previous perception of pattern. I desire to repair the structure. I seek parallel conduct from the stores of my previous experience. But even while I try one analogy after another, and draw tentatively this inference and that, my interest is always channeled toward a patterned understanding of Peter as a single individual.

The experience of knowing another seems to be most like an esthetic experience (though not necessarily tinged with pleasure as is the apprehension of beauty). An esthetic experience is immediate and unique. It never occurred before. It is not a repetition or summation of previous perceptions or feelings. To be sure, if we talk about it, we are forced to use the conventions of language—to use words we have used before. "What an exquisite color," we may say; or "The setting sun is like a Japanese lantern." Also, fragments of association play their part: unconscious memories of a similar sunset or other moments of beauty from our past. Even bits of scientific knowledge may enter—items of information concerning refraction, the Purkinje effect, or what not. But the pattern of the moment is whole, unique, never repeated. And most important, what we perceive follows closely the pattern that is objectively presented to our senses. The delight may be "in here," but the pattern is "out there."

Can patterned perception be taught? The child does not learn curiosity for objects in the outer world, nor does he learn to perceive configurations; his native perceptual capacity is already appropriately tuned. No one learns to *hear* the tonal pattern of a symphony, but one can be taught to *listen* to it, and to look for significant features. Most instruction in life is devoted to analysis, to giving knowledge about, and to building up a store of, available inferences. We cannot teach another to perceive the unity of an object (it is simply there), but we can teach so that his associational equipment is enriched. And so it is with personality: we cannot teach understanding of pattern, but we can call attention to detail, as well as to laws, principles, generalizations which can sharpen comprehension through comparison and inference. The danger, as we have pointed out, lies in overweighting the general so that the student loses his prior touch with the particular.

From all that has been said it should now be agreed that the process of understanding personality rests on both inference and on configural immediacy. There are indeed sensory cues, empathic responses, coding instantiation—all as asserted by the inference theory. But these activities are normally subservient to the structuring proc-

ess of the mind that takes place under the guidance of external
pattern, sustained by the demand character of the human being.
Thus, our understanding comes partly from within, but also partly
from without. In any given instance of understanding it is not possible to separate the contribution of inference from the contribution
of objective configural perception. Both are present.

Personality is, verily, a work of art. Unless we view it in detail
and in comparison with others, our impression remains naïve. But
unless we keep the objective pattern uppermost we start with analysis
and end with irrelevancy. Along the way we sacrifice our chance to
understand the living person. *Only by keeping objective pattern as
the center of our interest and attention can we employ analytical or
inferential knowledge appropriately.*

CHAPTER 22

The Person
in Psychology

POSITIVIST FORMULATIONS • PSYCHOANALYTIC FORMULATIONS
• PERSONALISTIC FORMULATIONS • EXISTENTIALIST FORMULA-
TIONS • A HINDU FORMULATION • STYLE OF LIFE • LINKS TO
PHILOSOPHY • PERSONALITY AS SYSTEM • PERSPECTIVE

TODAY people are asking more urgently than ever before, *What sort of creature is man?* Has he the potential for continued evolution and growth so that he may yet master the calamitous problems that face him—ideological schism, overpopulation, atomic disaster, and widespread disrespect of nation for nation and race for race?

Although the question is often addressed to philosophers and theologians, to historians and poets, the inquirer turns with special hope to the biological, psychological, and social sciences. For in an age of science he wants to hear what these relevant studies have to say.

So far as psychology is concerned, there is less agreement than we could wish for. Like other scientists and like philosophers, psychologists offer different sorts of answers—often only bare hints of answers, half-hidden in a network of unexpressed assumptions. Our task is to make some of the leading psychological answers explicit.

Positivist Formulations

We use the term *positivist* to stand for the traditional main stream of psychological science as it has existed in Western lands since the time of Locke and Comte. It is the empirical, experimental, chiefly associationist, and increasingly quantitative tradition known to all.

Perhaps the simplest way to characterize the positivist view of man is to say that he is regarded as a *reactive* being. What he does is determined by outer forces or by inner drives. Like traditional natural science, positive psychology sees movement as caused and determined by pressures. Man is like inanimate objects (including machines) and like elementary organisms.

The positivist view of man is seldom explicitly stated. Psychologists are too busy studying this reaction or that, in men or rats, to draw final implications from their work. They merely assume, in line with their procedures, that the human person is a purely reactive being. As pointed out in Chapter 9, even a cursory view of the psychologist's vocabulary shows that terms such as *reflex, reaction, response, retention* are far more common—perhaps a hundred times more common—than terms with *pro* prefixes, such as *proactive, programing, propriate, proceeding, promise.* Terms commencing with *re* connote againstness, passivity, being pushed or maneuvered. Terms with *pro* suggest futurity, intention, forward thrust. Psychology for the most part looks at man not in terms of *pro*action but of *re*action.[1]

Positivism does not pretend to be synoptic in its view of man. Its assignment is to find small facts under controlled conditions. The "fact" is bound to be small, since reliability can, as a rule, be obtained only when one deals with a limited fragment of behavior. Totalities of behavior are so inexact that the positivist turns away from them. Fragmentation yields firmer results. Therefore attention is devoted to the partial, the physical, the quasi-mechanical, the regular, the logical, because these aspects can be controlled. Attention is correspondingly withdrawn from the symbolic, the illogical, the uncoded, the configural because they cannot be reliably controlled.

Thus positivism teaches us how to be cautious and conservative,

---

[1] See also G. W. Allport, The open system in personality theory. In *Personality and social encounter: selected essays* (Boston: Beacon, 1960), Chap. 3.

how to check and validate, how to be accurate and precise. Much of the detailed general information that goes into the psychology of personality, as we have seen throughout this volume, is gathered by following the canons of experimental research. This procedure appeals to us because it offers the best means for verifying our discoveries. The price we pay is limiting our curiosity to only a portion of a human being. We suppress interest in the total pattern.

Since positivism seeks nomothetic generalizations about behavior it is likely to regard curiosity about the internal order of mind-in-particular as subjective and "unscientific." It somehow seems more scientific to send a platoon of white rats through a maze than to occupy oneself with the complex organization of a concrete personality. It is more respectable to pursue averages and probabilities for populations than to study the life-style of one person. Such preference is not hard to explain in a culture that is technological and machine-centered.

> It is interesting to recall that the founders of modern experimental psychology—Wundt, James, and Titchener—acknowledged the individual person as central in their definitions of psychology. The first wrote: *It [psychology] investigates the total content of experience in its relations to the subject.* The second: *Psychology is the science of finite individual minds.* The third: *Psychology is the study of experience considered as dependent on some person.* Yet none of these eminent authors developed his account of mental life to accord with his definition. All were preoccupied with the uniform aspects of mind. The tradition in which they worked prevented them from following their own definitions consistently to the end. Like their successors, they stripped the person of all his troublesome particularity, and for the most part sought a science of averages.

The only real difficulty with the positivist formulation is that it does not know (or rarely knows) that it is a prisoner of a specific philosophical outlook, also of a specific period of culture, and of a narrow definition of "science." Positivism seldom defends its deterministic, quasi-mechanical view of the human person; it merely takes it for granted. Its metaphysics is unexamined, and, as the philosopher

Whitehead once said, "No science can be more secure than the unconscious metaphysics which it tacitly presupposes."

It is certainly unfair to blame the positivist outlook in psychological and social science for the present plight of mankind, although
many critics do so. Positivism is more a reflection than a cause of the
fragmentation of personality in the modern world. The worst that
can be said is that by keeping itself "method-centered" rather than
"problem-centered" positivism has brought forth an array of "itty
bitty" facts at the expense of a coherent view of the human person
as a whole.[2] In fairness, however, we should thank positivism for the
wholesome safeguards it places on undisciplined speculation, and for
many useful, if disconnected findings.

Psychoanalytic Formulations

Much has been written concerning the psychoanalytic image
of man. Indeed, the image is so well known that only the briefest
comment is needed here to supplement our discussion in Chapters
7 and 9.

In some respects the picture is like that of positivism. Man is a
quasi-mechanical reactor, goaded by three tyrannical forces: the
environment, the id, and the superego. Man adjusts as well as he can
within this triangle of forces. His vaunted rationality is of little
account. Since he is full of defenses and prone to rationalize, his
search for final truth is doomed to failure. If perchance he claims to
find truth in religion, this discovery is dubbed an illusion and
charged up to his neurosis.

There is a deep pessimism in orthodox psychoanalytic doctrine
(Freudian style). Man is so heavily dominated by unconscious id
forces that he never fully escapes the ferocity and passion in his
nature. Sublimation is the best we can hope for. There is no genuine
transformation of motives. (See Chapter 10.)

Grim as the picture is, no theory of modern man can safely overlook its elements of truth. How can we hope to see man whole unless
we include the dark side of his nature? Many present-day psychoanalysts, however, feel that the image overweights the role of unconscious and libidinal forces in personality. Neo-Freudian "ego-

2 Cf. A. H. Maslow, *Motivation and personality* (New York: Harper, 1954), Chap. 2.

psychology" has broadened the perspective, and would agree in many respects with the schools of thought we shall next consider.

Personalistic Formulations

There are several versions of personalistic thought.[3] They all agree that the individual person as a patterned entity must serve as the center of gravity for psychology. The intention of personalism is to rewrite the science of mental life entirely around this focus.

Why should such thoroughgoing reconstruction be demanded by the personalists? The reasons they advance are too numerous to be given in full. A brief hint of some of the arguments must suffice.

Without the coordinating concept of *person* (or some equivalent, such as *self* or *ego*), it is impossible to account for the interaction of psychological processes. Memory affects perception, desire influences meaning, meaning determines action, and action shapes memory; and so on indefinitely. This constant interpenetration takes place within some *boundary*, and the boundary is the person. The flow occurs for some purpose, and the purpose can be stated only in terms of service to the person.

The organization of thought or behavior can have no significance unless viewed as taking place within a definite framework. Psychological states do not organize themselves or lead independent existences. Their arrangement merely constitutes part of a larger arrangement—the personal life.

Such concepts as *function, adaptation, use* have no significance without reference to the person. If an adjustment takes place it must be an adjustment *of* something, *to* something, *for* something. Again, the person is central.

All the evidence—introspective and otherwise—that forces

[3] The most detailed system is found in the writings of the German psychologist William Stern. See *General psychology from the personalistic standpoint* (Transl. by H. D. Spoerl; New York: Macmillan, 1938); also G. W. Allport, The personalistic psychology of William Stern, *Charact. & Pers.*, 1937, **5**, 231–246. The American philosophical school of personalism is exemplified in E. S. Brightman, *Introduction to philosophy* (New York: Holt, Rinehart and Winston, 1925); also in P. A. Bertocci, Psychological self, ego, and personality, *Psychol. Rev.*, 1945, **52**, 91–99. For a critical discussion see G. W. Allport, The psychological nature of personality. In *Personality and social encounter*, Chap. 2. A Thomistic version of personalism is M. B. Arnold and J. A. Gasson (Eds.), *The human person* (New York: Ronald, 1954). An eclectic textbook approach is that of G. Murphy, *Introduction to psychology* (New York: Harper, 1951).

psychology to take account of the *self* (Chapter 6) is here relevant. The very elusiveness of the self—James says that to grasp it fully in consciousness is like trying to step on one's own shadow—proves that it is the ground of all experience. Although seldom salient itself, it provides the platform for all other experience.

We cannot talk about strata of personality (Chapter 7) or of propriate, as distinguished from peripheral, states without implying that a superior totality includes both.

A creative person is presupposed in the creeds he creates. Even a scientist of the positivist persuasion intentionally limits his interest, designs his experiments, interprets the results. No sense could be made of this sequence without the assumption that the scientist himself is a prior creative unity.

Such are some of the philosophical arguments whereby personalistic psychologists (and self-psychologists) state their case for the reconstruction of psychology. They gladly consign to impersonal (natural and biological) sciences the task of exploring a certain range of problems. But they insist that psychology, whose task it is to treat the whole of behavior, cannot discharge its duty without relating the states and processes it studies to the person who is their originator, carrier, and regulator. There can be no adjustment without someone to adjust, no organization without an organizer, no perception without a perceiver, no memory without self-continuity, no learning without a change in the person, no valuing without someone possessed of desires and capacity to evaluate. Psychology must take seriously James's dictum that every mental operation occurs in a "personal form," and must take it more seriously than James himself did.

It is not uncommon in textbooks on general psychology to find wedged into the last chapter a separate and rather abrupt treatment of personality, as if to reward the reader who has waded through piles of abstractions concerning the generalized human mind. Personalistic psychology would reverse the procedure. The person would form the *point of departure*.

Stern's handling of space perception illustrates the point. Traditional psychology speaks of "visual space" or "auditory space" and treats these as wholly separate. Such a procedure, Stern argues, is misleading, a mere laboratory abstraction. There is only one space: *my* space. Tones and objects and touches are all related to *me*.

An impersonal psychology could not possibly account for the fact that my seatmate in a plane is distant from me while the friend toward whom I am riding (although still a thousand miles away) is already near to me. The essence of space, psychologically considered, is its personal relevance. Events are distant when they lack such relevance; near, when they possess it.

Time, too, is a personal, not chronological matter. A segment of life that is ten years behind me may be far nearer to me subjectively than a period two years ago; or some act I performed yesterday may today appear incomprehensible to me, a totally foreign element in my past.

Subjectively, space and time blend. We anchor experiences as here-and-now or as far-and-then. This personal blend is very unlike the psychologist's normal abstractions in classifying separately space perception (for separate modalities) and time perception.

To sum up, the personalistic point of view is based partly on philosophical argument and partly on appeal to immediate experience (phenomenology). It is in essence a rebellion against positivist science that tends to regard the individual as a bothersome incident. Different lines of personalism would answer somewhat differently the question, What sort of a creature is man? But they all agree that the final answer will disclose a creative unity, a purposive, growing individual—and not a dismembered reactor as pictured by positivism. The secret of man will not be found in a reductive analysis of his *being*, but only by tracing coherently the course of his *becoming*.

Existentialist Formulations

Existentialism, like personalism, has no single answer to our question concerning the nature of the human person. Indeed, in this movement we can find answers that in some respects are diametrically opposed to one another. One existentialist tells us that "man is a useless passion"; another, that "man is a being who exists in relation

to God." Existentialism is theistic and atheistic, despairing and hopeful, empirical and mystical—all depending on the devotee.

Yet certain features are common. One is the conviction that
positive science alone cannot discover the nature of man as a being-
in-the-world. Each special science is too narrow. None is synoptic.
And the methods of positive science tend to rule out the most
appropriate tool for research: phenomenology. It is not enough to
know how man reacts: we must know how he feels, how he sees his
world, what time and space are to *him* (not to the physicist), why he
lives, what he fears, for what he would willingly die. Such questions
of *existence* must be put to man directly, and not to an outside
observer.

Common also is a passion not to be fooled about man's nature.
If the Victorian image of man was perhaps too pretty, the Freudian
image may be too grim. But grim or pretty, *all* knowledge about man
must be faced. The findings of biology, psychology, anthropology are
important, but so, too, are the findings of history, art, philosophy.
We seek to know man in his entirety. Life demands that we know
the worst and make the best of it.

It is probably true to say that all forms of existentialism hope to
establish a new kind of psychology—a psychology of mankind. The
pivot of such a psychology will lie in the perennial themes and crises
of human life. Mere stimulus-response sequences, drives, habits,
repetitions tend to miss the catastrophic coloring of life. Psychology
should be more urgently human than it is.

What are some of the perennial themes and crises? A person is
born in a condition of dependency; he is ordinarily nurtured in love
and develops a measure of basic trust (pages 77–79). Gradually
there comes the poignant sense of selfhood and solitariness which he
never can lose; he relates himself to life through his interests, and
seeks always to enhance the value-experiences he has along the way;
he falls in love, mates, nurtures his offspring; he suffers basic anxieties
(fear of death, feelings of guilt, and a horror of meaninglessness); he
seeks always the "why" of existence; he dies alone. Since psychology
as a science has not oriented itself to these central themes it has not
yet dealt fully with man's existence.

There are too many varieties of existentialism to be considered
author by author. Many writers—Kierkegaard, Heidegger, Jasper,
Sartre, Berdyaev, Marcel, Binswanger, Frankl, Tillich, and others—

have made important contributions.[4] But we shall confine our attention to certain questions that pertain to the movement as a whole.

Is Existentialism Idiographic or Nomothetic? Each person is busy building his own peculiar constellation of ego-world relationships. His motives are his own, taking always the form of "personal projects."[5] His inheritance in unique; his experienced environment is unique; all his ego-world relationships are unique. Existence ultimately resides nowhere except in the individual's point of view. Certainly no counselor or therapist can succeed unless he can understand the patient's dilemma from the patient's standpoint. A million mortals will experience their ego-world quandaries in a million ways.

Thus, at bottom the existentialist approach to man is urgently idiographic. As yet, however, it offers no special methods for representing the unique structure of persons. Phenomenology, of course, is the approved method, but it is difficult to specify just how it can be used for a proper configural comprehension. Fiction and drama (Camus, Sartre) and case studies (Minkowski, Binswanger) are employed. But the movement has not yet evolved genuinely novel methods for the representation of individuality.[6]

What Is Man's Principal Goal? All existentialist writers agree that existence is essentially a *restlessness*. But is it a blind, disconnected, and useless restlessness? Only a few "beatnik" existentialists say that it is. Most writers find a more stable project at the core of life. Formulations differ, but all agree that there is an anxious out-

---

[4] Valuable historical surveys will be found in F. H. Heinemann, *Existentialism and the modern predicament* (Torchbook ed.; New York: Harper, 1958); also in R. May, E. Angel, and H. F. Ellenberger (Eds.), *Existence* (New York: Basic Books, 1958), Chaps. 1 and 2. The student will find special fascination in the brief volumes by V. Frankl, *From death camp to existentialism* (Boston: Beacon, 1959); and by P. Tillich, *The courage to be* (New Haven, Conn.: Yale Univ. Press, 1953).

[5] J. Nuttin, Personality dynamics. In H. P. David and H. von Bracken (Eds.), *Perspectives in personality theory* (New York: Basic Books, 1957), Chap. 10.

[6] Existentialist writers may dispute this implied criticism. They may say that it is not the purpose of existential analysis to become objective and scientific. To force existence into a theoretical system is to destroy it: "I am a moment of individuality, but I refuse to be a paragraph in a system." J. Wahl, *A short history of existentialism* (New York: Philosophical Lib., 1949), p. 32. If one wishes to study a rushing stream of water, one cannot dip down with a scoop and take out a sample, at least not without losing the restless rush—which is life. Another's existence cannot be pinned down or communicated by devices; an extrascientific grasp is the best we can hope for. The psychoanalyst Otto Rank gives an extreme statement of this point of view: "Therefore there can be neither a natural scientific nor an intellectual scientific psychology, but only a will and feeling psychology. . . ." *Will therapy and truth and reality* (New York: Knopf, 1950), p. 92.

reach, a compelling hunger in existence that goes beyond animal drives and sheer reactivity. The neurologist Goldstein, we recall, insists that only sick people in mental hospitals are reduced totally to the biological pressures of sex, thirst, hunger for food, oxygen, sleep, and so on. The rest of mankind, he observes, engage in activities beyond these basic drives. These activities amount to a striving for *self-actualization*.[7] Other authors formulate the core motive differently, but all agree that the quasi-mechanical view of motivation (Chapters 5 and 9) is insufficient to the dynamics of human life.

Perhaps the commonest terms employed by existentialists are *anxiety, dread, alienation*. Man finds himself "thrown" into an incomprehensible world. He can scarcely avoid an undercurrent of fear with eddies of sharp panic. He lives in a whirlpool of instability, aloneness, suffering, and is haunted by the ultimate specter of death and nothingness. He would like to escape from the burden of anxiety, but he would also like to know its meaning. Meaninglessness is more of a torture than is anxiety, for if there is a clear purpose in life, then anxiety and dread can be borne. It was Nietzsche who said that he who has a Why to live surmounts almost any How.

Man, then, is not a homeostatic creature. He does not seek equilibrium within himself and with the environment. His restlessness is systemic, and too deep-rooted to be drugged by temporary satisfactions. He seeks a more solid formula for living, something that will enable him to surmount alienation and suffering. There is something bloodless about homeostasis; it favors laziness and belies our specifically human capacity to outstrip ourselves.

Fortunately we have the capacity to make commitments and to take risks. We can, if we wish, gamble our life on the value of some "personal project," even though we cannot prove its worth or be assured of its success. Our faith in a project may be only half sure, but that does not mean that we need to be halfhearted. To be able to make a life-wager is man's crowning ability. Members of the French or the Norwegian underground resistance movement in Hitler's Europe felt that they had little chance of success. But the goal was something worth living for, and worth dying for. Suffering and dread are surmounted if we have an ideal of this magnitude.

[7] K. Goldstein, *Human nature in the light of psychopathology* (Cambridge, Mass.: Harvard Univ. Press, 1940). See also the sharp distinction between "deficit motives" and "growth motives" in Maslow, *op. cit.* Note 2 above.

When people are asked if they have projects for which they would willingly die, most of them reply in the affirmative. They may specify the welfare of their children, or their commitment to the cause of peace, or their religious faith. The whys may differ, but they are present in most lives.

Even people who are discouraged and depressed can often be led to a freshening of their purposes by asking them the blunt question, "Why don't you commit suicide?" In answering this question the patient reveals his half-forgotten values and commitments. In them lies a firm foundation for therapy and recovery.

And so one answer to our question concerning the nature of the human person is that he is a creature bent on enhancing the value-attributes of his experience.[8] Every day each of us is building many self-world relationships. Some of these become more and more meaningful, more propriate, more urgent. They are what make life worth while.

Some writers, Freud among them, feel that man's restlessness leads him to desire ultimate peace through annihilation. Religions of the Orient incline to this view, as expressed by the anonymous Japanese poet:

> Loathing both seas of life and death
> How deeply I long
> For the upland of Nirvana
> Untouched by the tides of change.

In theistic terms, Western religions echo the thought. St. Augustine wrote, "My heart is restless until it finds its rest in Thee, O God."

Short of this ultimate goal, and centering on the present course of life, many writers emphasize the indelible creativity of man, as does Buber:

Every person born into this world represents something new, something that never existed before, something original and unique. It is the duty of every person to know . . . that there has never been anyone like him in the world, for if there had been someone like him, there would have been no need for him to be in the world. Every single man is a new thing in the world and is called upon to fulfill his particularity in this world.[9]

[8] H. Cantril, *The "why" of man's experience* (New York: Macmillan, 1950).
[9] M. Buber, *Hasidism and modern man* (Transl. and ed. by M. Friedman; New York: Horizon Press, 1958), p. 139.

Here the emphasis turns to man's responsibility. It is not enough for man to question life concerning its meaning and purpose. More important are the questions life puts to each man: What creative acts will you perform? What responsibility will you assume for your existence now that you have it? Which of the world's needs (not your needs) will you fulfill?

This aspect of existentialist thinking goes beyond the goal of "self-actualization." For it asks in effect which of your many potentialities will you choose to actualize? To actualize all of them would be trivial self-indulgence. One must transcend himself, take an outside look at his abilities and desires within a context of meaning that is objective, even cosmic. From this point of view the capacity for self-transcendence and responsibility becomes the truly significant core of human nature.[10]

To sum up, there is a tendency among existentialist writers to seek for one basic intentional theme in human life. A fairly wide range of proposals is the result—and yet the varied proposals seem for the most part to be complementary and concordant, not in actual opposition. Man is inherently restless and anxious, desiring both security and freedom. He strives to counter his condition of alienation by seeking a meaning for existence which will cover the tragic trio of suffering, guilt, death. By making commitments he finds that life can become worth living. Along the way he enhances his own value experiences. If necessary he will sacrifice his life in order that some primary value can continue to be served. He is capable of taking responsibility, of answering by his deeds the questions life puts to him. In this way he rises above his own organic and spiritual urgencies, and achieves true self-transcendence. Although different writers place emphasis on different parts of this formula, the picture is consistent.

Is Man Free? All existentialists tell us that man is free. And in

10 V. Frankl writes: ". . . those theories of man which are circumscribed by the individual himself, whether based upon the reduction of his tension as in homeostasis theory, or [upon] the fulfillment of the greatest number of imminent possibilities as in self-actualization, when weighed, are found wanting. It is the contention of the author that an adequate view of man can only be properly formulated when it goes beyond homeostasis, beyond self-actualization—even beyond man himself!—to that transcendent sphere of human existence in which man chooses what he will do and what he will be in the midst of an objective world of meanings and values." Beyond self-actualization and self-expression, *J. existential Psychiat.*, 1960, **1**, 17.

giving this answer existentialism collides sharply with the traditional viewpoint of psychology.

The collision is due to a radical difference in the "altitude" at which the question is asked. Existentialism always takes the acting person's point of view. The person himself knows that all day long he makes decisions. Shall he do an errand now, or wait until later? Shall he study or watch TV? If he has pain, shall he go to the doctor or grin and bear it? If his nose runs—to borrow an example from Epictetus—shall he complain or shall he be glad he has a sleeve to wipe it on? None of us can prevent misfortunes from striking, but we can determine our attitudes toward the unkind shafts of fate. This is what existentialism says. Perhaps an all-wise God would know our decisions beforehand, but the person, from his own point of view, is free. He feels that his deeds and attitudes are a matter of choice, not of destiny. He cannot take the point of view of an all-wise God, nor even of the less-wise gods of science.

Psychology approaches the matter at the level of the demigod. It does not pretend to predict every act or thought of the person as might an all-wise God, but it knows so many limitations upon freedom that it inclines to assume that in the last analysis all conduct is determined and no act is free. It knows that personality is dependent on many "givens," on the inherent capacities and limitations of the human species, on native constitution (physique, temperament, intelligence), on the social environment in which personality is fashioned and from which it draws nutriment; it is dependent also upon the immediate situation which calls forth one or another of the potential modes of conduct available in the nervous apparatus. Such dependencies weave a net of determinism whose strength is greater than the person knows.

Strict determinism would have to say that no one ever *does* anything. The person does not live his life; it is lived for him. He is no freer than a billiard ball responding within a triangle of forces. The two major forces are internal drives and environmental pressure. To these two Freud added a third, namely, man's superego. This force, however, is only a derivative of parental and social teaching (environmental forces). The ego, having no energy of its own, is a victim of these tyrants.

Determinism of this order sees the person as an essentially passive, coerced, reactive, and determined product. There is evidence to support the view. During the past two generations we have learned a great deal regarding the coercive effects of constitution, drives, unconscious complexes, early learning, and situational pressure. Determinism may seem outrageous to the person who "knows" that he is free and who assumes that all other men are free; but psychology prefers to believe that in principle human nature is as predictable as the orbit of a satellite in space.

So much for thoroughgoing determinism. Its logical appeal is evident, and is needed to counteract the lavish and sometimes sentimental ascriptions of freedom that mark certain types of existentialist and theological writing. But there are difficulties. The case for rigid determinism is no stronger than the case for the positivist view of man's nature, which, as we have seen, is vulnerable.

First arises the problem of consciousness. We are conscious chiefly when we are in conflict, i.e., when there are problems to be solved. Now if consciousness plays no part, if it does not enter somewhere into the sequence of cause and effect, why has it evolved? If consciousness is merely the "squeak that the machinery makes," why do we have this worthless friction in our natures? It seems more sensible to assume that consciousness exists for a purpose; at the very least it can tip the scales at the moment of choice. We say, "Let it be this way rather than that."

But consciousness seems to do more than select the button to be pressed. It has the capacity for reflection. When we have an important decision to make we call upon our stores of past experience so far as they are relevant to the issue in hand. We ruminate and weigh, and "on the whole" decide that this is the best course of conduct to pursue. And here we encounter a neat paradox. A person whose stores of experience and knowledge contain many "determining tendencies" is freer than a person who has only a meager store. If I have only one relevant skill, or if I know only one solution, I have only one degree of freedom. I act in the only way I can. But if I have much relevant knowledge, a broad education, and have wide experience with the kind of problem I face, then I can select "on the whole" the most appropriate solution, or create a new one. A many-channeled mind is freer than a one-track mind.

Every school of therapy, even those based on positivism, assumes that the goal of treatment is to lead the patient to a relatively greater freedom of decision than his disorder originally allowed. A patient with a compulsion, a phobia, an obsessive thought has no freedom at all. His is ridden by his neurosis. After therapy he should have freedom *from* such domination, and also freedom *for* a life that will accord more closely with his self-ideal. The healthy person, with rich experience and maturity of outlook, is able to program his own identity. He surveys the possibilities and declares, "This builds my style of being," or "That tears it down." He can say, "This course is a good fit to my life-style," or "That course is a misfit, and for me a sin."

In this line of thought lies a possible reconciliation between the freedom claimed by existentialism and the determinism claimed by positivism. There are, we repeat, *degrees*. Precisely what do we mean when we say that the normal personality is relatively free to program his own identity? Not that he is liberated from all his drives (he still must sleep, eat, obtain oxygen, and he is strongly goaded by sex needs, by angry impulses, by ego-defenses). Not that he is entirely free from his early learning—many dispositions and attitudes acquired in childhood will be with him to the end. Not that he is independent of the continuous stream of "nutriment" that the environment gives him to reward and sustain his cultural attitudes and to insure his conformity to the roles he must play in family, in occupation, and in society.

All these pressures exist. But *becoming* is the process by which all these forces are employed by the creative urge to program a style of life for oneself. The basic existentialist urge to grow, pursue meaning, seek unity is also a "given." It is a major fact—even more prominent in man's nature than his propensity to yield to surrounding pressures. It is this desire for autonomy, for individuation, for selfhood, for existential uniqueness that enters into the shaping of the product. Growth toward this end is a law to which most personalities seem to conform. The *promise* I see for myself is the essence of my freedom. When a critical situation challenges me I call forth this promise—and it becomes a major factor in the solution of the problem in hand.

From this point of view freedom lies in our general posture toward life, in living out our hope of continuous becoming. In terms used by William James, freedom lies in "the ability to keep the selected idea uppermost." Through reflection and deliberation one keeps the image of what one wants to become uppermost, and from this superordinate system will flow deeds and decisions. The weakness of the habit theory lies in assuming that all acts, if equally often repeated and rewarded, will be equally strong. But in fact we know that habits appear and disappear not only in conformity with the laws of reward and frequency, but also in relation to the central control of propriate structure. Thus the "go" of normal life reaches far beyond its specific dependence on habit or circumstance.

It is true that in the process of becoming we often put forth a good deal of *effort*—to inhibit an impulse, or to keep the selected idea uppermost. But it is unfortunate that discussions of freedom have so often been confined to the topic of "will power." By cracking our knuckles and gritting our teeth we run the risk of reversing the desired effect. We sometimes do precisely the thing we are fighting against. Centering attention upon an impulse often brings with it an irresistible desire to perform the act. "The evil I would not, that I do." This "law of reversed effect" is familiar to all. And in this form it makes freedom a cruel illusion. It is in man's image of his own growth, and not in a separate faculty of will, that we can most clearly define freedom.

The determinists are right in saying that the fabric of the world is structured and orderly. But they are wrong in believing that the fabric of a given life has reached its final, lawful form. The relative freedom of man lies in his seeking and utilizing knowledge that will enable him to discover the final shape of his life. The final shape will incorporate all dependencies, but will move toward the guiding image, the unfulfilled promise.

A Hindu Formulation

Curiosity concerning the nature of man is not confined to the West. It is inexcusable provincialism for scholars in the West to neglect the wisdom of the East. Although I cannot hope in this volume to redress the balance, I can, as a bare token of adequacy, call attention to one pertinent formulation in Hindu psychology.

Most men, the theory holds, have four central desires. To some extent, though only roughly, they correspond to earlier and later periods of life. *Pleasure* is the first desire. It is predominant in infancy, but remains throughout later ages. The desire for pleasure is soon supplemented by the need for *success*. Youth and the middle years are spent in the pursuit of occupational and social achievement. Some people never go beyond these two stages of desire. But as maturity sets in there is normally a strong orientation toward *duty*. One must provide for one's offspring and aging parents, and the ethics of social living take hold upon one's values. Finally, and especially toward the end of one's life, comes a desire for understanding—for philosophical or religious meaning—and with it a longing for *liberation* from the pleasure-success-duty stages of life.[11]

It is interesting to note that no major Western school of psychology includes this whole sequence of four stages within its view of human nature. Positivist psychology gives full and lavish attention to the first two stages—to pleasure, in its theories of tension-reduction, reinforcement, libido, and needs; and to success, in its studies of power, status, leadership, achievement, masculinity. But positivist psychology has little to say about the duty motive (except that it is a reaction to the internalized parent image), and still less to say about the desire for philosophical and religious meaning, except to hint that such desire is a defense mechanism, an escape device no different in kind from suicide, alcoholism, and neurosis. Existentialism, by contrast, gives full recognition to duty (responsibility) and to the will-to-meaning. Yet oddly, existentialism says little about pleasure and success as motives.

Therefore it seems that this Hindu formulation of the essential nature of man is more synoptic and complete than any one school of Western thought.

Style of Life

Many of the ideas we have surveyed in this chapter can be viewed under the inclusive concept of *life-style*. The individual, says Adler, adopts certain ways of attuning himself to life. In childhood there is merely a "style of departure," comprised of native equipment and temperament together with society's requirements for the child. Using these diverse ingredients, the child embarks on a process of self-styling and restyling so that he can meet, as suc-

11 See, e.g., H. Smith, *The religions of man* (New York: Harper, 1958).

cessfully as possible, the great problems of life, including the problematic nature of life itself.[12]

Not every style is mature. It is easy to slip into a self-defensive style whereby the growing individual merely wards off threats to his self-esteem. Prejudice, neurotic defenses, self-serving religion may be features of such a style. By contrast, a mature life-style allows fully for man's effort to cope with all the harshness of life in a realistic manner—to know the worst in life and to make the best of it —through the use of integrative rather than defensive mechanisms (page 154).

To view personality as a process of stylization has the merit of allowing for limitless individuality (although, of course, for purposes of comparison we may group similar styles into types). It has also the merit of bringing together the dynamics of striving with forms of action, including styles of expressive behavior discussed in Chapter 19. It allows for positivist principles so far as they are relevant, as well as for the basic formulations of existentialism. Thus as a synoptic concept it has value. However, to apply the concept of life-style in detail requires much borrowing from other schools of thought.

Links to Philosophy

Critics will say that an exclusively psychological conception of the human person is a vain dream. One must know also his metaphysical nature and his place in the cosmic design. Ancient wisdom, both philosophical and theological, should be consulted and incorporated lest we find ourselves dealing with elaborate trivialities. Psychology is a recent arrival on the scene, and its new insights are at best partial. Any science that pretends to be truly new cannot be wholly true.

The point is well taken. As a matter of fact, all the views we have considered have implicit ties with basic philosophical assumptions. The positivist and psychoanalytic views rest on physicalism or on a somewhat broader naturalism. The personalistic position in its vari-

---

12 Adlerian psychology, which centers in the concept of the life-style, is authoritatively reviewed by H. L. Ansbacher and R. R. Ansbacher (Eds.), *The individual psychology of Alfred Adler* (New York: Basic Books, 1956). Valuable likewise is the survey by A. R. Gilbert, The concept of life-style: its background and its psychological significance, *Jahrb. f. Psychol., Psychotherapie u. med. Anthrop.*, 1960, 7, 97–107. I concede here, as I did in Chapter 19, that "style" is a difficult concept to define. And yet it is highly relevant to the morphogenesis of personality, and as such will have to be dealt with by psychology in the future.

ous forms has ties with German idealism, with Protestant theology, or with Thomistic thought. Existentialism is itself a wide-ranging system of epistemology and value-theory. And so it goes with all the formulations that have been, or can be, considered. Our survey has been drawn only from the psychological surface of these doctrines. To know the human person as a whole we should have to place him in the cosmic context according to the tenets of philosophical theory. The philosophy of the person is inseparable from the psychology of the person. The student does well to keep this important warning in mind.

And yet the psychologist has his own special contribution to make. He hopes that his detailed search for facts will prevent erroneous philosophizing. For, after all, no philosophy of the person can be correct if it flatly contradicts known facts about human motivation, learning, cognition, stages of growth, pathology—provided, of course, that such facts are both firmly established and reasonably complete. As yet, however, psychology cannot provide full enough knowledge to warrant the final choice of one interpretation of man's nature and the rejection of all others. The best we can do at the present time is to seek the philosophical formulation that on the whole seems to be most coherent with available psychological evidence.

Personality as System

The best hope for discovering coherence would seem to lie in approaching personality as a total functioning structure, i.e., as a *system*. To be sure, it is an incomplete system, manifesting varying degrees of order and disorder. It has structure but also unstructure, function but also malfunction. As Murphy says, "all normal people have many loose ends."[13] And yet personality is well-enough knit to qualify as a system—which is defined merely as *a complex of elements in mutual interaction*.

Now systems may be classified as *closed* or *open*.[14] A closed system is defined as one that admits no matter from outside itself and therefore "runs down" (is subject to entropy according to the second law of thermodynamics). Although some outside energies, such as

[13] G. Murphy, *Personality: a biosocial approach to origins and structure* (New York. Harper, 1947), p. 661. The same author sets forth his views of personality as an emerging system in *Human potentialities* (New York: Basic Books, 1958).
[14] The analysis offered here is condensed from my paper entitled, The open system in personality theory. In *Personality and social encounter, op. cit.* Note 1.

change in temperature and wind, may play upon a closed system, it has no restorative properties and no transactions with its environment, and so, like a decaying barn, sinks into "thermodynamic equilibrium." No theory of personality holds to this view. Closed systems belong, if anywhere, to physics. All living systems belong to the class of open systems.

Open systems, we may say, are marked by four criteria: (1) There are intake and output of both matter and energy. (2) There are the achievement and maintenance of steady (homeostatic) states, so that the intrusion of outer energy will not seriously disrupt internal form and order. (3) There is generally an increase of order over time, owing to an increase in the complexity and differentiation of parts. (4) Finally, at least at the human level, there is extensive transactional commerce with the environment.[15]

Although all theories view personality as an open system, they do not agree on the emphasis to be placed on each of the criteria, nor on how many of the criteria to admit.

1. *Material and energy interchange.* Stimulus-response theory in its purest form concentrates on this criterion to the virtual exclusion of all others. It says, in effect, that a stimulus enters and a response is emitted. In between these poles there is, of course, machinery for summation, storage, and delay. But we need study only the two major poles in order to depict the functioning of personality. Some forms of methodological positivism would go one step further, and say that we can dispense with the concept of personality altogether if we focus attention on our measurements of stimulus input and of behavioral output.

2. *Homeostasis.* As we saw in earlier chapters, many prominent theories of motivation and of learning rest on the assumption that personality is a process of satisfying needs, reducing tension, and therefore of maintaining homeostatic equilibrium. Thus the whole course of man's development may be regarded as simply an extension of the principle involved in temperature regulation, balance of blood volume or sugar content, within the physical body. Personality is an endeavor to balance inner and outer pressures in order to

---

15 These criteria are drawn from various writings on systems theory. The four criteria correspond closely to what Charlotte Bühler has called "life's basic tendencies": Basic tendencies of human life: theoretical and clinical considerations. In R. Wisser (Ed.), *Sinn und Sein: ein philosophisches Symposion* (Tübingen: Niemeyer, 1960), pp. 475–494. By the same author, Theoretical observations about life's basic tendencies, *Amer. J. Psychother.*, 1959, **13**, 561–581.

achieve a state of rest or equilibrium. All need-theories and quasi-mechanical explanations of learning acknowledge this criterion.

Most current theories of personality take full account of these first two requirements of an open system. They allow for interchange of matter and energy, and for the tendency of organisms to maintain an orderly arrangement of elements in a steady state. Thus they emphasize stability rather than growth, "uncertainty reduction" (information theory) rather than creativity. In short, they emphasize *being* rather than *becoming*. These theories are biologistic in the sense that they ascribe to personality only the two features of an open system that are clearly present in all living organisms.

There are, however, two additional criteria, not stressed by positivist conceptions of the human person.

3. *Increased order over time.* Some theories correctly emphasize the tendency of human personality to go beyond steady states and to elaborate their internal order, even at the cost of disequilibrium. Theories of changing energies (Chapter 9) and of functional autonomy (Chapter 10) do so. These conceptions allow for a continual increase of men's purposes in life and for their morphogenic effect upon the system as a whole. Although homeostasis is a useful conception for short-run "target orientation," it is totally inadequate to account for the integrating tonus involved in "goal orientation."[16]

Many of the theories that we have considered in this chapter and in previous ones put weight on this criterion. Woodworth's principle of behavior primacy, as opposed to need primacy, does so. So, too, Goldstein's doctrine of self-actualization and Jung's individuation. One thinks of Maslow's growth motives, as opposed to deficit motives. Ego-psychology, with its allowance for autonomous and conflict-free motivation, belongs here. White's emphasis on competence, Lecky's self-consistency, Erikson's search for identity, Adler's style of life, McDougall's sentiment of self-regard—all are oriented to this criterion. Although these formulations differ among themselves, they all find the "go" of personality in some dynamic thrust that exceeds the pale function of homeostatic balance. They recognize increasing order over time, and view change within personality as a recentering, but not as abatement, of tension. Needless to add, existential thought moves in this same direction.

4. *Transaction with the environment.* The first three criteria

16 Cf. N. Bull, An introduction to attitude psychology, *J. clin. exp, Psychopath. & Quart. Rev. Psychiat. Neurol.,* 1960, **21,** 147–150.

view personality as a self-contained system—as it surely is. All writers acknowledge, of course, that the input and output of energies make for a certain interaction with the environment, but for the most part they focus upon the "inside" system.

Other writers point out that the personality system, more than any other living system, is wide open to the surrounding world. Countless objects are matters of interest and challenge. No other creature besides man attempts to mold the world, and even outer space, to his heart's content.

So vast is the outreach of the human person that some theories refuse to separate personality at all from its context. On page 114 we saw how even a temporary "sensory deprivation," isolating a person from the environment, will cause serious disturbances of personality. Some cultures, the Buddhist, for example, regard the individual, society, and nature as forming a single tripod of existence, a single system. Why has Western thought, Murphy asks, drawn a razor-sharp distinction between the person and all else? Perhaps the Judeo-Christian religion is a primary factor, enhanced by the growing role of the individual in the industrial revolution.[17] Whatever the reason, some writers insist that personality is an *interpersonal system;* it exists *only* in its social interactions with other people (cf. page 192).

Our view stops short of this point, for if we are not wary we shall find ourselves studying only the social and cultural systems which include the person. There is also emphatically a neuropsychic system "within the skin" that is the object of our study. It is the personality system proper. We can hold to this position without in the least denying that one important mark of this system is its continuous intercourse with, and dependence upon, larger systems of interaction. For all his elaborate transactions with the world, the individual remains a separate unit. It is well to consider the personality system as the special assignment of psychology, and the social and cultural systems, within which the individual is located, as the special assignment of sociology and anthropology.[18]

To view personality as a living system has the great merit of call-

---

17 G. Murphy, *Human potentialities, op. cit.,* p. 297. Note 13 above.

18 For a fuller treatment of this matter see T. Parsons's discussion of the two types of system in *The social system* (Glencoe, Ill.: Free Press, 1951). See also the distinction between "inside" and "outside" structures drawn by F. H. Allport, *Theories of perception and the concept of structure* (New York: Wiley, 1955).

ing our attention to the patterning of detailed facts from whatever source they are drawn. Thus biological knowledge and genetics can be fitted in; so too, nomothetic principles of growth; all valid portions of the quasi-mechanical laws of learning; the range of individual differences; homeostasis; principles of ego-defense; expressive behavior—everything that is validly established by positivist psychology. But since *system* is our focus of interest we must weave together with these data all our additional knowledge of individuality. Such knowledge comes from studies of propriate functions, of self-image, from configural understanding, from existential analysis, and from many other sources.

Within the framework of "system" one approach helps to correct the other. If positivism leans toward fragmentation and impersonality this bias can be tempered by emphasis on personal dispositions and unity. All that is valid in either approach must be fitted in. What is good in existentialism belongs to our study of system, although we cannot agree with its rash rejection of all methods other than phenomenology.

And so it goes. It is not fruitful to argue for one approach to personality at the expense of all others. Personality is many-sided, and needs many avenues of approach. It will not be difficult to reconcile them if we regard all data, from whatever source, as adding to our knowledge of a single organic system.

And we suspect that it is here the reconciliation of psychology and philosophy can occur. *System* is a concept congenial to most philosophy, for orderliness in nature has ever been the datum of philosophy. As psychology increasingly tells us how the personality system is patterned, we may call upon philosophy and theology to relate the findings as well as they can to cosmic order.

Perspective

This volume has reviewed research and theory concerning the psychological nature of human personality. In the course of our survey we have pressed for a limbering of the frame of psychological science so that it will no longer exclude the direct study of individuality.

On the opening page the reader was warned that he would have to shuttle back and forth between the nomothetic and idiographic points of view. We have done so, trying to discover not only why personality (in general) is an interesting topic for study, but why Walter (in particular) has a fascination of his own.

We do not deny the proposition that psychology seeks general laws, but we have drawn special attention to those laws and principles that tell how uniqueness comes about. It is also our argument that each single life is lawful, for it reveals its own orderly and necessary process of growth. Lawfulness does not depend upon frequency or upon uniformity, but upon inner necessity.

Personality for us is a pattern that exists "out there." We boldly ask what a person is like in his essential nature (not merely how he affects other people, or how he behaves in different situations). Of course, his behavior is variable, but always within the limits and ranges set by the structure itself.

The analysis of personality should proceed at significant levels; the elements we seek must be genuine *parts* of personality, not remote abstractions. The elements should not be too microscopic, for personality exists only at a high degree of complexity. Personal dispositions viewed as subsystems within the total organic system are the most significant units. Among these dispositions propriate interests and values are the most important. It is in the functionally autonomous motives of maturity that the mainsprings of adult personality are found.

Psychology, as we have seen, possesses many methods and many maps. This richness is remarkable in a science so young. It is inevitable that there should be discord. Whenever we have criticized a theory or a technique it has seldom been on the grounds of validity, but rather on the grounds that some one limited point of view is falsely pretending to cover the whole of the subject.

The personality system is a complex product of biological endowment, cultural shaping, cognitive style, and spiritual groping. Only if viewed in this way can all the diverse methods of inquiry be brought to a focus. Their separate contributions can best be blended if we regard personality as a system—incomplete but bent on growth and on becoming more than it is. Any other assumption falls short of the measure of man.

Most studies of personality are comparative; they employ the tools of differential psychology. And these tools are valuable. The danger is that they may lead to the dismemberment of personality in such a way that each fragment is related to corresponding fragments in other people, and not to the personal system within which they are embedded. Comparative studies are useful, but organic studies are more to the point.

Psychology is truly itself only when it can deal with individuality. It is vain to plead that other sciences do not do so, that they are allowed to brush off the bothersome issue of uniqueness. The truth is that psychology is *assigned* the task of being curious about human persons, and persons exist only in concrete and unique patterns.

Since psychology has this peculiar assignment it cannot be content with the dogma that understanding people is achieved merely by ordering the individual to a class. That inferential knowledge of this sort is important no one will deny. But, in addition, knowledge through direct perception, configural comprehension, "acquaintance with," needs to be sought. The full resources of our cognitive equipment are needed as tools of research.

We study the human person most fully when we take him as an individual. He is more than a bundle of habits, more than a point of intersection of abstract dimensions. He is more than a representative of his species, more than a citizen of the state, more than an incident in the movements of mankind. He transcends them all. The individual, striving ever for integrity and fulfillment, has existed under all forms of social life—forms as varied as the nomadic and feudal, capitalist and communist. No society holds together for long without the respect man shows to man. The individual today struggles on even under oppression, always hoping and planning for a more perfect democracy where the dignity and growth of each personality will be prized above all else.

Index of Subjects

Ability to judge, 503–06
Abnormality, 435; *see also* Neurosis, Normality
Abstract thinkers, 269
Acculturation, 169–71
Acquaintance with, 542f.
Active intellect, 96, 101–07, 524
Actuarial prediction, 19f., 369, 447f., 533
Addictions, 231f.
Adjective check list, 419
Adjustment, 29
Adolescence, 79, 124–26, 254, 383
Adult motives, 196–98, 203, 214
Affectation, 294
Aggression, 145
Aging, 295f., 306f.
Alienation, 558
American psychology, 318, 466, 525
Analogy, 525–33, 545
Andrew, case of, 103f.
Animal, 29f., 70, 230f., 525
Annoyances, 328f., 331
Anomie, 186–92
Anthropomorphism, 537f.
Anxiety, 556–60
Apperceptive tests, 439–42
Archetype, 149
Art and personality, 11f., 24–6, 39, 42–6, 54, 58, 396, 484

Ascendance–submission, 338f., 341f., 344, 425–27
Assessment; *see* Method
  Center, 333
Association method, 441
Associationism, 19, 524–33
Assumed similarity, 507
Asthenic type, 59
Athletic type, 59
Attention, 105f.
Attitudes, 177, 347f., 471
Aufgabe, 260
Autistic gestures, 470–72
  thinking, 133f.
Autobiography, 401–10; *see also* Life-history
  tory
Autonomic nervous system, 74f.
Autonomy, 118, 120, 152, 163; *see also* Ego, Functional
Authoritarian personality, 271–74, 433f.
Average, 532
Avoidance, 210, 246

Bar mitzvah, 125
Barnum effect, 452
Basic personality, 171–75, 194, 514
Becoming, 90, 376, 555, 563, 569
Behavior primacy, 207, 212, 251
Being-in-the-world, 556

Belongingness, 105
Bestimmung, 294–96
Biochemical factors, 5–7, 33, 39, 58, 399
Biography, 42–6
Biological theory of personality, 72–5
Birth, 76, 254
Blind analysis, 446
Bodily self, 113f., 137
Body and mind, 72f.
Body build, 39–42, 48, 58–63, 81
Brain, 47–9, 73, 143, 260, 482
     washing, 188–92, 282

California Psychological Inventory, 437
Canalization, 234f.
Cardinal dispositions, 16, 365, 374, 378
Case study, 367f., 401–10
Castration, 122
Catastrophic change, 186–92
Categorization, 502, 513f., 515, 525–33, 547
Cathexis, 202f.
Central dispositions, 365, 374, 412
Cerebrotonia, 61
Character, 30–3
     Education Inquiry, 415, 515–18
     reading, 39–52, 47–9, 393f., 475, 488
Characters, 42–6, 51, 54
Characteristic, 29, 32
Characterology, 31, 43–6, 48–50
Child training, 77, 136, 169–75, 181f., 194, 270, 274
Childhood, 97–9, 120–24
Circular mechanism, 232
Clinical psychology, 18–21, 369
Closure, 105, 233
Co-consciousness, 142, 175
Coding, 527f., 547; *see also* Inference
Cognition, 222, 258–74, 523–25, 527
Cognitive complexity, 508, 522
     cripple, 271–74
     dissonance, 217
     style, 267–74
Comic, 292–94
Common traits; *see* Traits
Compensation, 132–34
Competence, 213f., 216, 226, 251
Competition, 119
Compulsion, 151f.
Conatus, 379
Conceptualization; *see* Theory
Concrete thinkers, 269

Conditioning, 92–6, 100, 106, 209–12
Conduct sampling, 414–18
Configural comprehension, 538–44
Conformity, 430–33
Confrontation, 153
Congruence, 384–90, 474
Conscience, 134–37, 303f., 565
Consciousness, 139, 149f., 562; *see also* Self
Consistency, 81, 362, 384–90
Constitutional factor, 33–5, 39–42, 48, 58–63, 81, 238, 398–400
Convergence principle, 334, 377, 464, 476
Coping, 124, 156–58, 262, 445, 462–64, 473, 475, 493
Cornell Index, 425
Correlation, 61f.
Correspondence, 384–86
Cranioscopy, 47–9
Creativity, 305, 554, 559f.
Culture construct, 166f., 173
     defined, 167f.
     and expression, 467f.
     fallacy, 192
     memberships, 400
     and personality, 167–69, 194f.
     proception, 265f.
     real, 166f., 173, 195
     system, 171
     types, 352f.
     understanding, 544

DDD theory, 191
Defense mechanisms, 133, 155–63, 180
Deficit motives, 86–91, 215, 221, 569
Delayed gratification, 317
Delinquency, 20, 62
Democratic man, 286, 573
Depth analysis, 444f.; *see also* Psychoanalysis
Determining tendencies, 29; *see also* Mental set
Determinism, 560–64
Diagnostic Council, 416
Diary, 405
Differential psychology, 15f., 47, 572
Differentiation, 108, 141, 469
Direct action, 132f.
Directedness, 294–304, 306, 372
Disintegration, 188–92, 282, 378
Displacement, 161

Disposition; *see* Personal disposition
Doll play, 442
Draw-a-person, 442
Dreams, 147
Drive, 86–91, 108, 205f., 212, 238, 373
Duty, 200, 303f., 565
Dysplasia, 61

Economic maturity, 290, 295
  value, 297, 454–57
Ectomorph, 58–63
Effect, 95f.; *see also* Reinforcement
Effort after meaning; *see* Meaning
Ego; *see also* Self
  autonomy, 213
  defense, 155–63, 476
  Freudian, 144–50, 163
  involvement, 107f., 128, 383f.
  level, 119
  psychology, 148, 163, 213, 215–18, 552f.
  pure, 379
  relevance, 111, 138
  strata, 144, 163
  strength, 191, 438
  world, 266
Egotism, 118–20
Electrical processes, 73, 105, 398
Embarrassment, 120, 128, 130–32
Emotion, 38, 50, 198
Empathy, 488, 533–37, 547
Empiricism, 350–52, 436
Empty organism, 86, 345
Encaustics, 45
Endomorph, 59–63
Entropy, 567
Environmentalism, 31, 82
Equivalence, 322–24, 346f., 368, 373–75
Escapism, 153f.
Essentialist defined, 26, 28, 35
Esthetic value, 298, 454–57, 509
Ethnic differences, 175
Ethology, 49f., 54, 530
Evolution, 74f., 82
Existentialism, 217, 222, 282, 462, 555–64, 571
Expression, consistency, 472–75
  coping, 462–64
  defined, 461f.
  determinants, 464, 467–69
  face, 479–82
  gait, 487f.

genesis, 469–72
gesture, 120, 470–72, 475, 485f.
handwriting, 488–90
learning, 107
mouth, 481
posture, 485–87
psychodiagnosis, 475–79
speech, 482–85
style, 490–93
theory, 464–67
voice, 482–85
Expressive movement, 53, 445, 505
Extinction, 245f.
Extraversion–Introversion, 427–30
Eye-blink, 462f.

Face, 479–82
Face-validity, 476
Factors, 317, 324–30, 348, 429f., 436
Faculties, 47f., 51, 143, 258f., 311, 313
Familiarity, 233–35
Fantasy, 443
Father's role, 182
Fears, 288
Feedback, 246
Feral Child, 24
Field-dependence, 267–70, 416, 438
Field theory, 312
First impressions, 500–03, 521, 526
Fixation, 161, 239f., 267–70
Flexibility, 267–70, 274
Flicker fusion, 438
Form-quality, 492
Formal discipline, 321
Free association, 445
Freedom, 111, 560–64
Frequency, 96, 108
F-scale, 433f.
Functional autonomy, 155, 210, 217, 219–57, 283
  defined, 229, 244
  see also Motive
Futurity, 223–25, 249f.

Gait, 487f.
Gating, 248, 261, 371
Geist, 464f., 473, 475
Geisteswissenschaft, 543f.; *see also* Ver-stehen
Generalization, 94f., 346

Generalized other, 503f., 514, 521
Genes, 4, 67
Genesis of expression, 469–72
Genetics, 33, 57, 82
Genitality, 286f.
Genius, 16, 64f., 289
Genotype, 4f., 71, 364
Gestault psychology, 540
Gesture, 120, 470–72, 475, 485f.
Giton, 44f.
Glands, 5f., 33, 58
Graphic rating, 419
Graphology, 488–90, 534
Group norms, 13, 15; *see also* Role
Growth motives, 89f., 215, 221, 249f., 569
rates, 6f.
Guess Who technique, 446
Gynandromorphy, 61

Habit, 100f., 141, 238, 314–21, 331, 345–47
Halo effect, 420
Handedness, 69, 97
Handwriting, 53, 170, 465, 488–90
Health; *see* Maturity
Hedonism, 88, 95, 199–201
Heredity, 4–7, 57, 64–72, 81–3
Hindu theory, 564f.
Homeostasis, 88–91, 249f., 377, 558, 568f.
Homosexuality, 371f.
Honesty, 315–17
Hormic theory, 201f.
Hormones, 37, 58
Hospitalism, 78
Human demand, 537f.
Humor, 292–94, 301
Humoral psychology, 37, 39–42, 58
Hypothetical construct, 336f.

I–Thou, 537
Id, 52, 145–50, 163, 202
Ideal types, 17f., 297–300, 352, 454–57
Identical elements, 319–24, 492
twins, 5, 70f.
Identification, 92, 104f., 123, 171, 446, 536, 541
Identity, 114–18, 122–26, 137, 252, 273, 277f., 283, 304, 382
Idiodynamics, 12–5
Idiographic method, 9, 19, 21, 46, 456, 533, 557, 571f.
Imaginary companions, 121

Imitation, 103–05, 470, 533–37
Imprinting, 91f.
Individual, 30
differences, 15f., 47, 572
Individualistic fallacy, 192
Individuality and science, 8–21
biochemical, 5–7, 33, 39, 58, 399
patterned, 7f., 65, 252, 531–33, 545–48
Infancy, 75–81, 97–101, 111–21, 196–98, 203, 213
Inference, 19, 525–33, 545; *see also* Categorization
Inferiority feelings, 130–34
Information theory, 527
Innate knowledge, 541f.
Inner-directed, 430
Insight learning, 103f., 108
self, 290–92, 411, 443f., 508
Instantiation, 529, 547; *see also* Inference
Instinct, 50f., 87, 98, 149, 201–03, 222, 313
Integration, 99–101, 108, 154, 346, 377, 384
Intelligence, 7, 9, 13, 15, 33, 63–67, 248f., 507f.
Intention, 101f., 105f., 108, 222–25, 520
Interaction chronograph, 485
Interactionist, 73
Interest, 107, 235–37
Interpersonal sensitivity, 503f.
Interview, 416–18, 444
Intraceptiveness, 509–11, 521
Introversion, 58, 427–30
Intuition, 12, 536, 545; *see also* Configural comprehension
Isomorphism, 539f.

Jenny, case of, 368f.
Judeo–Christian ethics, 26
Judge of personality, 503–11, 521f.
Judgmental sets, 513

Karl, case of, 271–74
Knower, 128–30, 137f.
Knowledge about, 542f.
Knowledge of personality; *see* Understanding

Laboratory experimentation, 416
Ladder scale, 413f.
Law, meaning of, 10f., 226f., 272
of parsimony, 324

of participation, 106
Layers; *see* Strata
Leadership, 179
Learning, biographical, 105–09
  cognitive, 101–05, 108
  importance, 83
  interest, 107
  insight, 103f., 108
  opportunistic, 138
  propriate, 138
  quasi-mechanical, 91–101
  sets, 101, 104
  subsidiation, 105
Leveling, 269f.
Liberation, 559, 565
Libido; *see* Id
Life-history, 221, 367f., 401–10
Life-style, 266f., 386, 390
Literature, 24–26, 54, 396, 484
Localization in brain, 49
  self, 113f.
Love, 126, 151, 286, 380, 556
Lowe, case of, 66

McCarley, case of, 322
Matching, 81, 387f., 446f., 474, 483, 492
Maturity, 125, 328, 566
  criteria, 275–83, 307
  humor, 292–94
  insight, 291
  old age, 306f.
  philosophy, 294–304
  realism, 289f.
  security, 287f.
  self-extension, 283–85
  self-relating, 285–87
Meaning, 217, 222, 264
Measurement; *see* Method
Mental set, 259–61, 274, 345, 505, 529
Mesomorph, 59–63
Metabolism, 6, 34
Metaphor, 530f.
Method, case study, 401–10
  centered, 552
  classification, 396–98
  conduct sampling, 414–18
  constitutional, 398, 400
  depth, 444f.
  personal documents, 401–10
  precautions, 420f.

projective, 396f., 437–44
  safeguards, 452
  scales, 423–37
  synoptic, 445–48
  tests, 423–37
Mind-in-general, 3, 10
Miniature situations, 415f.
Minnesota Multiphasic Personality Inventory, 435–37, 451, 458
Modules, 529
Monopolistic concepts, 516, 518, 521f.
Monosymptomatic method, 469
Moral realist, 135
Morphogenesis, 356, 358, 361, 374, 386, 389
Mote-beam projection, 160, 519
Mothering, 77f.
Motives
  abstract, 225f.
  adult, 196–98, 203
  changing, 212–18, 226–28
  cognitive, 258f.
  concrete, 225f.
  contemporaneity, 220
  deficit, 86–91, 215, 221, 569
  dependable, 90f., 204
  growth, 89f., 215, 221, 249f., 569
  infant, 196–98, 203, 213
  personal dispositions, 369–72, 375
  personal documents, 401–04
  pluralism, 221
  theories, 84–91
  unchanging, 199–212
  see also Functional autonomy
Motor mimicry, 534, 536
Mouth, 481
Multidimensional scales, 435–37
Myokinetic diagnosis, 486f.

Names, trait, 333, 353–56
Narcosynthesis, 445
National character, 18, 171–75, 352
Nature of man, 84, 108, 245, 249; *see also* Person in psychology
Need integrate, 370
Need primacy, 207, 212, 251
Needs, 203f., 313, 370
Negativism, 118–20, 433
Neo-Freudianism; *see* Ego-psychology

Neural functions, 73–5, 98f., 231, 319, 360, 362
Neurasthenia, 161
Neurosis, 150–55, 228f., 239–41, 424f., 433, 481f., 566
Nominalism, 335f.
Nomothetic method, 8, 12, 14, 21, 550–52, 571f.
Normal distribution, 343–45, 351
Normality, 150–55, 399, 435; see also Maturity
Norms, 13, 19, 401

Office of Strategic Services, 333
Oral type, 17
Origins of personality, 24f., 76f.
Organization, 16, 28, 85, 108, 250, 360, 567–71
  hierarchical, 99–101, 109
Openness, 499f.
Operationism, 27
Other-directed, 430
Over-compensation, 133
Over-simplification, 518–20, 522

Parent–child, 136; see also Child Training
Parsimony, 324
Partial reinforcement, 246f.
Participation, 105–08, 284f.
Patterning, 7, 65, 252, 531–33, 545–48
Penurious Man, 43
Percept, 264f.
Perception, 262–65, 278–80, 437–39, 492, 498, 538, 540; see also Person perception
Perceptual accuracy, 262f., 271
Perceptual-motor regions, 141
Perseveration, 230–34, 247
Person, 57, 165
Person perception
  ability, 503–06
  accuracy, 512f.
  errors, 517–20
  first impression, 500–03
  focus, 520
  openness of other, 499f.
  processes, 512–16
  qualifications, 506–11
  sex differences, 511f.
Person in psychology
  existentialist, 555–64

Person in psychology existentialist (Cont.)
  Hindu, 564f.
  life-style, 565f.
  perspective, 571–73
  philosophy, 566f.
  positivist, 550–52, 571
  psychoanalytic, 552f.
  system, 567–71
Persona, 25, 31, 126
Personal constructs, 267, 407
Personal Data Sheet, 424f.
Personal disposition
  cardinal, 365
  central, 365
  consistency, 362–64
  focal, 362
  genotypical, 364
  interdependence, 361f.
  method, 367–69
  morphogenic, 358, 374
  motivational, 369–73
  number, 366f.
  phenotypical, 364
  pseudo, 364f.
  secondary, 365
  uniqueness, 358–61, 532
Personal documents, 401–10
  idiom, 491
  relevance, 107f.
  space, 554f.
  structure analysis, 368, 406
  time, 555
Person-in-world, 271–74
Personalistic view, 30, 65–67, 81, 553–55
Personality
  and art, 11f., 24–8, 39, 42–6, 54, 58, 396, 484
  assessment, 395–459
  authoritarian, 271–74
  basic, 171–75, 194, 514
  biological view, 72–75
  biosocial defined, 23
  and cognition, 258–74
  as constant, 27
  and culture, 167–69
  defined, 22–30
  disintegration, 190–92, 282, 378
  effect, 22, 24, 355
  essentialist, 26
  evolutionary view, 74f., 82

and heredity, 4–7, 57, 64–72, 81–3
hierarchy, 100f., 108
infancy, 75–81, 97–101, 111–21, 196–98, 203, 213
mature, 125, 275–307, 328, 566
methods, 395–459
neurotic, 150–55, 239–41, 424f., 433, 481f., 566
normal, 150–55, 399, 435
omnibus defined, 26
organization, 16, 28, 99–101, 108f., 567–71
origins, 24f., 76f.
perception of, 497–522
and perception, 262–65
popular defined, 22–4
positivist view, 22, 550–52
productive, 216
profile, 15f., 445f., 456
and self, 138
and situation, 120, 175–81
strata, 139–45
structural defined, 25f.
system, 192–94, 360, 567–70
in textbooks, 21
traits, 332–56
and unconscious, 145–63
understanding of, 523–48
units of, 311–31
unity of, 197, 252, 376–91, 475
variability in, 175–78, 333
Personalizing mental set, 537f.
Persuasibility, 430–33
Peter, case of, 66
Philo-phobe technique, 413
Phenomenology, 571
Phenotypical dispositions, 364
Philosophy, 378–80, 391, 506f.
of life, 294–304
see also Person in psychology
Phobia, 253
Phrenology, 47f., 54, 396
Physiognomic perception, 492, 540
Physiognomonica, 40
Physiognomy, 39–42, 54, 479–82
Physiological diagnosis, 398–400
Physique; see Constitutional factors
Pleasure, 88, 95, 199–201, 564f.
Political value, 299, 454–57
Popular personality defined, 23

Positivism, 27f., 550–52, 571
Posture, 485f.
Praise, 119
Preconscious, 142f., 152f.
Prediction, 19–21, 82
actuarial, 369, 389f., 447, 533
of development, 79–81
idiographic, 389f., 447, 533
Prejudice, 79, 94, 176f., 270, 434
Primacy, 96, 108
Primary abilities, 67, 504
process, 146
traits, 429
Proaction, 206, 550
Probabilistic functionalism, 527
Proception, 264–67, 499
Productive tests, 442
Profile, 15, 445f., 456
Projection, 160f., 510, 519
Projective methods, 396f., 437–44
Pronouns, 115f., 121
Propriate functions, 383f.
motives, 126–28, 137, 235–37, 520
trauma, 255f.
Proprium, 127f., 134, 136–38, 141f.
Proverbs, 50
Pseudo dispositions, 364
Psychiatric interview, 444f.
Psychoanalysis, 145–63, 207, 240f., 286f., 552f.
Psychodiagnosis, 475–79; see also Method
Psychodrama, 442
Psychograph, 15f., 445f., 456
Psychology
American, 31, 318, 466, 525
defined, 551
differential, 15f., 47, 572
ego, 148, 163, 213, 215–18, 552f.
European, 31
hormic, 201f.
morphogenic, 386, 390
positivist, 27f., 550–52, 571
stimulus-response, 87f., 92f., 108, 139, 209–11, 225, 245f., 248, 314–19, 345, 466
stratification, 139–45, 464f.
Psychoneurotic inventory, 424f.
Psychopathic personality, 134, 303
Psychophysical parallelism, 72
Psychotherapy, 7, 304f., 562.
Punctuality, 342f.

Pure ego, 129, 138
Pygmalion, 383
Pyknic type, 59

Q-sort, 412
Quasi-mechanical view, 86–101, 245–49
Quidikaka, 491

Radix, 365, 410
Range in personality, 166f., 169, 177, 181, 185f., 195, 333, 355f.
Ranking scale, 419f.
Rating, 410f., 418–20
Rationalization, 133f., 158–60
Raw materials, 57, 63, 80, 238
Reaction formation, 161f.
Reactivity, 206–12, 218, 251, 550–52
Recency, 96, 108
Reinforcement, 95f., 108, 208–11, 233f., 238f., 246f.
Reciprocity, 121
Regions, 141f.
Regression, 161
Reinforcement, 95f., 108, 208–11, 233f., 238f., 246f.
Reintegrations, 93f., 319–24, 492
Reliability, 319, 341, 384, 448f., 456
Religious value, 255, 299–303, 454–57, 542, 559
Repression, 52, 147–54, 156–58
Reputation, 24, 421
Response set, 428, 434, 450f., 456
Responsibility, 565
Reticular system, 89
Reversed effect, 564
Rhythm, 487
Role, 181–86, 536
Rorschach test, 438f., 445, 546
Rubricizing, 518; *see also* Inference

Safeguards in assessment, 448–52
Scales, 423–37; *see also* Method
Science, 8–21, 226, 396
Schemata, 259, 370
Schizophrenia, 59, 134
Scoring scales, 418f.
Secondary disposition, 365, 374
    process, 146
Security, 287f.; *see also* Trust
Seele, 464f., 467, 473, 475
Self
    acceptance, 117, 287f.
    actualization, 79, 85, 212, 215, 280f., 558

agent, 129f., 138, 252, 379
    anchoring scale, 413f.
    bodily, 113f., 137
    confrontation, 45f.
    consciousness, 111
    core, 110, 138
    defined, 110, 115, 138
    disclosure, 499f.
    early, 110–21
    and ego, 111
    esteem, 118–20, 132, 137, 154–63, 263, 479, 498
    extension, 122, 137, 283–85
    fighter, 127, 137f.
    identity, 114–18, 122–26, 137
    image, 81, 122–26, 137, 303, 381–83
    infancy, 111–21
    insight, 290–92, 411, 443f., 508
    Jamesian, 176
    judgment, 476–79
    knower, 128–30, 137f.
    localization, 113f., 479
    looking glass, 120
    objectification, 290–94
    presupposed, 553–55
    rating, 410f.
    rational, 124, 137
    recognition, 476–79
    regard, 51, 156, 237, 569
    solo-centered, 112
    system, 100f.
    transcendence, 560
    unity, 378, 381–83
    Wintu, 117
Sensorimotor behavior, 76, 112
Sensory deprivation, 114, 186
Sentence completion, 441
Sentiment, 50f., 54, 202, 300–03, 348
Sex differences, 182, 472, 511f., 516f.
Sexuality, 6, 52, 126, 145, 162, 225, 243, 283, 286f., 371f.
Sharpening, 269f.
Sigh, 462
Similarity, 321, 331, 507, 517, 522, 525, 531
Situation, 175–81, 468; *see also* Range
Small groups, 179f., 423
Smile, 497f., 530
Social change, 186–92
    class, 174
    desirability, 450

interaction, 120
status, 199
system, 171, 182, 185, 192–94
value, 298f., 454–57
Sociocultural assessment, 400
Somatotonia, 61
Somatotype, 59–63
Soul, 115
Soundness, 278–80; *see also* Maturity
Space, 554f.
Specificity, 314–24, 331, 335
Speech, 482–85
Spontaneity, 466
Stereotype, 480, 514, 519, 522
Stimulus generalization, 94f.
Stimulus-response, 27, 87, 92f., 96, 139, 209–11, 225, 245f., 248, 314–19, 345, 466
Stratification, 139–45, 464f.
Stress, 191
Striving, 126–28, 137, 235–37, 380f., 391, 520
Structure, 192–95; *see also* Organization
Study of Values, 299, 453–58
Style, 487, 490–93
of life, 349, 563, 565f., 569
Stylistic disposition, 370, 372, 375
Sublimation, 148, 162, 207, 242, 552
Subliminal process, 140, 526
Subsidiation, 105
Success, 565
Suffering, 189–92, 252, 282
Suggestibility, 430–33
Suicide, 559
Super-ego, 146–50; *see also* Conscience
Suppression, 158
Survival, 74
Syllogism, 525
Symmetrical face, 481f.
Sympathy, 541
Snyoptic methods, 445–48
System, 179, 360, 567–70
defined, 28
functional, 97
inside, 10
open, 89, 108, 567–70
personal, 15, 186, 192–94

Task-involvement, 106
Tautophone, 439

Teleology, 85
Television, 24, 107, 134, 292, 467
Temperament, 8, 33–9, 40f., 76, 80, 313, 326
Tension-reduction, 87–9, 199–213
Tests, 423–37; *see also* Method
Thematic Apperception Test, 439–41
Thematic productions, 441, 492
Theoretical value, 297, 454–57
Theory
configural understanding, 538–48
empathy, 533–37
expression, 464–67
hedonism, 199–201
hormic, 201
inference, 525–33
learning, 91–138
motivation, 84–91, 196–218, 219–57
need, 203f., 313, 370
need primacy, 207, 212, 251
psychoanalytic, 145–63, 207, 240f., 286f., 552f.
situationism, 175–81, 468
strata, 139–45, 464f.
tension-reduction, 87–9, 199–213
trait, 332–56
validity of, 408–10
Therapy, 7, 304f., 562f.
Time, personal, 555
sample, 414
Traces, 91f.
Trait, 44, 54, 176, 337–40
and attitude, 347
common, 532
defined, 340, 347, 349
denied, 314–20, 333f.
and disposition, 360f., 374
distribution, 343–45
established, 340–43
fictional, 334–39
generality, 322f.
and habit, 345f.
morphogenic, 100, 358, 375
names, 333, 353–56
and organization, 16
veridical, 334–39
Transaction, 569f.
Trauma, 186–92, 253–56
Trend structure, 359
Trust, 78f., 89, 102, 277, 288, 556

Types, 16–18, 349–53
  ideal, 297–300, 454–57
Type-token ratio, 484

Ultimate concern, 302
Unconscious, 140–63
  inference, 526, 531
  motives, 52, 145–50, 163, 202, 214
Understanding, 271–74; *see also* Person
    perception
  configural, 538–44
  demand, 537f.
  empathy, 533–37
  idiographic, 19
  inference, 525–33
  patterned, 545–48
  problem of, 523–25
Uniqueness, 4–11, 21, 226–29, 358–60, 373–
    75
Unitas multiplex, 376, 395
Units of personality, 311–31, 366f., 373–75
Unity, 252
  congruence, 384–86
  degrees of, 386, 475
  empirical, 386–90
  in perception, 541
  philosophical, 378–80

  propriate, 383f.
  of science, 86
  as self-image, 381–83
  as striving, 300f.
  thema, 365
Universal norms, 13f.

Validity, 449f., 456
Variability; *see* Range
Value, 25f., 31f., 169, 171, 237, 296–304,
    313f., 328, 453–57, 543
  vector, 370
Veridical cognition, 261–65
  nature of personality, 22–30, 289f.
  traits, 334–37
Verstehen, 12, 543f.
Viscerotonia, 61
Voice, 482–85

W-A-Y technique, 411f.
Waleula, 491
Wartegg Drawing Test, 443
Will; *see* Freedom
Wintu, 117
Word association, 441

Zen Buddhism, 382

Index of Names

Adams, D. K., 525
Adcock, C. J., 34
Adler, A., 132, 213, 238, 349, 486, 565, 569
Adorno, T. W., 433
Ainslie, D., 541
Aldington, R., 43, 45
Alexander, F., 156
Alimena, B. S., 452
Allen, R. M., 398, 404, 428, 441
Allport, F. H., 194, 232, 261, 263, 312, 338, 359, 368, 492, 534, 570
Allport, G. W., 31, 188, 270, 284, 291, 300, 338, 367, 426, 436, 455, 474, 525
Ames, L. B., 116, 121
Amundson, R., 90
Anastasi, A., 15, 70, 326, 330, 415, 442, 449
Anderson, G. L., 441, 443
Anderson, H. H., 441, 443
Andrews, T. G., 397, 406
Angel, E., 222, 557
Angyal, A., 240
Ansbacher, H. L., 132, 213, 556
Ansbacher, R. R., 132, 566
Anscombe, G. E. M., 224
Aquinas, St. Thomas, 225
Aristotle, 16, 31, 40, 42, 94, 457, 459
Arnheim, R., 539
Arnold, M., 89, 129, 198, 379, 553
Asch, S. E., 222, 259, 443, 516, 540

Atkinson, J. W., 203
Austin, G. A., 527
Ausubel, D. P., 102, 118
Azam, E., 12

Bach, S., 526
Bailey, D. E., 19, 369, 525, 527, 529, 531, 533
Bailey, S., 12
Bain, A., 51, 54
Bakan, D., 541
Baker, C. T., 64
Baldwin, A. L., 368, 406, 503
Barker, R. G., 414
Barnes, E., 282
Barron, F., 271, 279, 416
Bartholomew, E. S., 503
Bartlett, F. C., 105, 222, 259
Bass, B. M., 397, 434
Baumgarten, F., 335
Bayes, D., 435
Becker, H., 411
Beers, C., 403
Beier, E. G., 502
Bell, J. E., 443, 490
Belmont, L., 158
Beloff, H., 478
Beloff, J., 478
Bender, I. E., 303, 507, 519

Benedict, R., 255, 256
Bennett, C. E., 43
Bentham, J., 88, 156, 158, 199, 335
Bentley, M., 47
Berdyaev, N. A., 556
Berelson, B., 480
Berg, I. A., 397
Berger, C. Q., 415
Bergson, H., 12, 136, 524, 541
Berlyne, D. E., 76, 112, 213
Berman, A. B., 442
Bernard, L. L., 201, 313
Bernreuter, R. G., 436
Bertocci, P. A., 30, 129, 136, 229, 553
Bettelheim, B., 190–191
Bexton, W. A., 114
Bieri, J., 506
Binet, A., 424, 431
Bingham, W. V., 417
Binswanger, L., 556
Birch, C. M., 452
Birch, H. G., 158
Bismarck, O. von, 200
Blake, R. R., 431
Blake, R. W., 269
Blondel, C., 47
Bloom, R., 488
Blum, G. S., 490
Bogen, H., 386, 487, 488
Bond, N. A., Jr., 326
Bonner, H., 493
Boring, E. G., 47
Botter, J. B., 441
Bowers, A. M., 146
Bowlby, J., 78, 532
Bray, C. W., 425
Brengelmann, J. C., 433, 538
Brentano, F., 225, 229
Bridges, K. M. B., 99
Briggs, K. C., 429
Brightman, E. S., 378, 553
Bronfenbrenner, U., 503
Bronner, A. F., 146
Bruner, J. S., 188, 404, 416, 506, 514, 515, 527, 529
Brunswik, E., 481, 482
Buber, M., 537, 559
Buchler, J., 264, 265
Buck, J. N., 413
Bugental, J. F. T., 411
Bühler, C., 126, 213, 221, 251, 294, 568

Bull, N., 569
Bumstead, C. H., 46
Burks, B. S., 71
Buros, O. K., 423
Bush, R. R., 387

Cabot, R. C., 275, 276
Campbell, D. T., 397
Camus, A., 556
Canning, L., 236
Cannon, W. B., 250
Cantril, H., 46, 217, 222, 237, 384, 413, 483, 489, 490, 559
Carmichael, L., 26
Carrigan, P. M., 430
Casson, J. A., 379
Cattell, R. B., 326, 327, 330, 384, 429
Chance, J. E., 506
Chang, H. T., 246
Chapple, E. D., 485
Chesterfield, Lord, 290
Chesterton, G. K., 45, 197, 198
Chotlos, J. W., 484
Christensen, R. R., 326
Christie, R., 433, 434
Church, J., 77, 122
Claparède, E., 113
Clark, R. A., 203
Clark, W. H., 302, 303, 304
Cline, V. B., 505, 506, 511
Cole, L. B., 276
Collier, R. M., 149
Combs, A. W., 119
Confucius, 458
Conrad, H. S., 359, 360, 365, 367
Couch, A. S., 180, 434
Coutu, W., 177, 314
Cowles, J. T., 209
Craig, R. C., 323
Crawford, S. C., 230
Croce, B., 107, 541
Cronbach, L. J., 427, 437, 443, 450, 505, 507
Crook, M. N., 70
Crow, W. J., 502, 506

Dahlstrom, G. W., 435
Dailey, C. A., 410
Darwin, C., 68, 160, 222, 313, 461
David, H. P., 31, 266, 433, 525, 538, 557
Davids, A., 263, 444, 451
Davidson, M. A., 63

Dearborn, W. F., 7
De Grange, McQ., 47
De Silva, H. R., 307
Deutsch, F., 486
Dewey, J., 129, 138, 176, 233, 303, 349, 466
Diamond, S., 34, 38, 62, 76, 225, 328
Dilthey, W., 352, 524
Dobzhansky, T., 5
Dodson, J. D., 230
Dollard, J., 104, 211, 408
Donceel, J. F., 452
Donne, J., 44
Doob, L. W., 485
Dornbusch, S. M., 519
Dostoevski, F., 517
Douvan, E., 132
Drillis, R., 487
Dudycha, G. J., 342, 343, 420
Dunlap, K., 481
Dunn, L. C., 5
Dupertius, C. W., 59
Dymond, R., 175, 412, 536

Ebbinghaus, H., 39
Eccles, J. C., 231
Edwards, A. L., 450
Efron, D., 468, 486
Eisenberg, P., 488, 489
Eisler, R., 9
Eliot, C. W., 421
Eliot, G., 44
Ellis, A., 425
Ellenberger, H. F., 222, 557
Emerson, R. W., 159
Empedocles, 37
Engstrom, W. C., 237
Epictetus, 561
Ericksen, C. W., 269
Erikson, E. H., 78, 118, 124, 148, 277, 278, 286, 287, 304, 382, 569
Escalona, S., 80
Eysenck, H. J., 8, 19, 70, 351, 433, 489

Fährmann, R., 483
Farber, I. E., 191
Fechner, G., 379
Ferguson, L. W., 418
Ferster, C. B., 247
Festinger, L., 216, 222, 259
Fiske, D. W., 502
Flanagan, J. C., 436

Flemming, E. G., 23
Fluckiger, F. A., 488
Forster, E. S., 40
Forster, T., 47
Frank, L. K., 437
Franke, R., 386
Frankl, V., 217, 282, 304, 556, 557, 560
Freeman, F. N., 64, 70, 71
French, R. M., 128
Frenkel-Brunswik, E., 270, 271, 433
Freud, A., 78, 157
Freud, S., 52, 81, 105, 124, 135, 144, 145, 146, 148, 149, 150, 151, 155, 156, 158, 162, 163, 174, 201, 202, 204, 207, 208, 214, 215, 216, 217, 222, 238, 242, 259, 275, 290, 437, 536, 541, 559, 561
Freyd, M., 428, 429, 434
Friedman, M., 559
Frijda, N. H., 529
Fromm, E., 134, 216, 276, 304, 382, 467
Fuller, J. L., 68

Gage, N. L., 506, 514
Gahm, R. C., 476, 477
Galanter, E., 19
Galen, 37, 39
Gall, F. J., 47, 48, 50, 54, 313
Gallway, M. D., 503
Galton, F., 36, 52, 53, 54
Gandhi, M., 169
Garraty, J. A., 46, 408
Gasson, J. A., 129, 553
Gates, A. I., 106
Gerson, de J., 484
Gerth, H., 183
Getzels, J. W., 176, 444
Gibson, J. J., 101
Giese, F., 486
Gilbert, A. R., 143, 520, 566
Gillespie, J. M., 404
Glanville, A. D., 487
Glover, E., 146
Glueck, E., 62
Glueck, S., 62
Gobineau, H. de, 489
Goethe, 7, 25, 50, 97, 321, 363, 380, 534
Goldfarb, W., 78
Goldman-Eisler, F., 174
Goldstein, K., 212, 215, 269, 348, 498, 558, 569
Goodnow, J. J., 527

Gorer, G., 174
Gottschaldt, K., 268, 269
Gough, H. G., 419, 427, 437, 493
Gray, F. E., 425
Greene, E. B., 67, 423
Gross, N., 183
Gruen, A., 268
Grunes, W. F., 518
Griziwok, R., 293
Guilford, J. P., 326, 429, 435
Guthrie, E. R., 400

Haggard, E. A., 106
Hague, C., 229
Haire, M., 518
Hall, C. S., 27, 70, 146, 148, 149, 150, 162
Halmos, P., 282
Halsman, P., 486
Halstead, W. C., 438
Hamilton, W., 94, 524
Hammer, E. F., 442
Hammond, K. R., 506
Hammond, W. A., 43
Hanawalt, N. G., 481
Harding, J., 503
Harlow, H. F., 191
Harriman, P. L., 30
Harsh, C. M., 328, 329
Hartmann, H., 148, 213, 216, 217, 229
Hartshorne, H., 32, 314, 315, 446
Harvey, O. J., 159
Harvey, W., 39
Hastorf, A. H., 507, 519
Hathaway, S. R., 435
Havel, J., 434
Healy, W., 146
Heath, C. W., 295
Heath, P., 533
Hebb, D. O., 73, 231, 247, 248, 337, 371, 529
Hegel, G. W. F., 542
Heidbreder, E., 428, 429, 434
Heider, F., 224, 520, 538
Heider, G. M., 80
Heidigger, M., 556
Heinemann, F. H., 557
Hellersberg, E. F., 442
Helson. H., 431
Henderson, L. J., 85
Herbart, J. F., 39
Herman, P. S., 439

Heron, W., 114
Herrick, C. J., 5
Hertzman, M., 268
Hess, A., 78
Hewes, G. W., 486
Hill, J. P., 184
Hinkle, L. E., 186
Hippocrates, 37
Hobbes, T., 119, 156, 197
Hoch, P. H., 254, 453
Höffding, H., 39
Hollander, E. P., 433
Hollingworth, H. L., 94
Holt, E. B., 232
Holzinger, K. J., 64, 70, 71
Hoppe, F., 119
Horney, K., 304
Hovland, C. I., 432
Howells, T. H., 68
Hull, C. L., 53, 96, 210
Hulme, T. E., 541
Hume, D., 321, 379, 524
Hunt, J. McV., 73, 79, 400
Huntley, C. W., 478, 479
Hyman, H. H., 417

Ichheiser, G., 160, 518, 519
Inhelder, B., 92
Inkeles, A., 174
Irwin, J. R., 39

Jahoda, M., 276, 277, 433
James, H., 119
James, W., 100, 111, 119, 127, 129, 138, 176, 256, 263, 318, 323, 350, 366, 379, 404, 427, 542, 551, 554, 563
Jandorf, E. M., 188, 404
Janis, I. L., 432
Jasper, H. H., 556
Jebb, R. C., 43
Jenkin, N., 237, 263
Jenkins, C. I., 134
Jennings, H. S., 68, 69
Johnson, H. M., 486
Johnson, S., 44
Johnson, W. B., 473
Johnstone, J., 347, 348
Jones, E., 158, 208, 513
Jones, M. R., 267
Jonson, B., 44
Jourard, S. M., 132, 400, 499

Jung, C. G., 105, 148, 149, 363, 427, 428, 441, 517, 542, 569

Kamin, L. J., 210
Kant, E., 25, 39, 129, 138, 379, 524
Kaplan, B., 518
Kardiner, A., 172
Kašpárek, J., 489
Keats, J., 298
Keliner, R. J., 498
Kelley, E. L., 303, 502
Kelley, G. A., 267, 407, 410
Kelley, H. H., 159
Kempf, E. J., 74, 144, 222, 259
Kendig, I., 233
Keniston, K., 434
Kennedy, W. P., 463
Keyserling, E. von, 379
Kierkegaard, S., 381, 556
Kilpatrick, F. P., 413
Kinsey, A. C., 7, 286
Kipling, R., 96
Kirchhoff, P., 462
Klages, L., 39, 143, 464, 465, 466, 469, 490
Klein, G. S., 73, 240, 267, 269, 383, 384, 442, 526
Klineberg, O., 90, 91, 204, 205, 206, 213
Kluckhohn, C., 13, 79, 88, 168, 174, 182
Koch, K., 442
Koffka, K., 156, 349, 540
Kohler, W., 105, 524, 528, 540
Kolers, P. A., 140
Kotchen, T. A., 282
Kounin, J., 414
Krech, D., 73, 240
Kreezer, G., 487
Kretschmer, E., 39, 59
Kris, E., 148
Krout, M. H., 445, 471, 472, 473, 475
Kubie, L. S., 152, 153
Külpe, O., 39
Kusmin, A. A., 499
Kutner, B., 270

La Barre, W., 468
La Bruyère, J., 44
Lagerlöf, S., 402
Landis, C., 293
Lange, F., 480
Lasakow, P., 499
Lashley, K. S., 6

Lathers, E., 492
Lavater, J. K., 42, 54, 473
Leacock, S., 293
Learned, J., 121
Lecky, P., 26, 381, 569
Le Dantec, F., 119, 158
Lee, D., 117, 168
Leeper, R. W., 94
Lehmann, H. C., 314, 315
Leibnitz, F. W., 524
Leonard, W. E., 253
Lersch, P., 143
Levinson, D. J., 174, 433
Levy, D. M., 78, 118, 253
Lewin, K., 97, 141, 142, 221, 349, 364, 500
Lewis, H. B., 268
Lewis, S., 72
Lifton, R. J., 190, 191
Ligon, E. M., 32
Lindsley, D. B., 73
Lindsmith, A. R., 77, 232
Lindzey, G., 27, 104, 149, 158, 162, 174, 299, 312, 367, 387, 397, 437, 439, 454, 455, 482, 506, 514, 533
Linton, R., 26, 166
Lipmann, O., 386, 487, 488
Lippman, A., 442
Lipps, T., 533, 536, 537
Locke, J., 321, 421, 524, 530
Lorenz, K. Z., 92
Lorge, I., 65
Lotze, H., 159
Loveday, T., 40
Lowell, E. L., 203
Lundberg, G. W., 19
Luthe, W., 488
Lynn, D. R., 482
Lynn, J. G., 482
Lyons, J., 492

McCary, J. L., 433
McClelland, D., 27, 203, 229, 259, 370, 408, 439
McClosky, H., 427
Maccoby, E. E., 182
MacCorquodale, K., 336
McCulloch, W. S., 231
McDermott, E., 59
McDougall, W., 50, 51, 54, 98, 126, 156, 201, 202, 203, 222, 237, 313, 348, 569
McEachern, A. W., 183

McFarland, R. A., 306, 307
McGranahan, D. V., 158
McGregor, D., 467
Machover, K., 268, 442
McInnes, R. G., 63
McKee, J. P., 131
Macmurray, J., 129
McNeil, E. B., 490
Madison, P., 94
Malamud, W., 486
Maller, J. B., 317, 446
Mann, R. D., 179, 423
Mannheim, K., 158
Marcel, G., 556
Marquis, D., 76
Maslow, A. H., 79, 89, 90, 215, 221, 234,
    271, 279, 280, 281, 290, 349, 383, 427,
    463, 466, 518, 552, 558, 569
Mason, W. S., 183
Massarik, F., 536
Masserman, J. H., 253
Matarazzo, J. D., 485
Matarazzo, R. G., 485
May, M. A., 32, 314, 315, 335, 446
May, R., 222, 557
Mead, G. H., 120, 121
Mead, M., 119, 121, 187, 256, 500, 536
Meaders, W., 506
Mednick, S., 270
Meehl, P. E., 20, 336, 369, 390, 410, 427,
    435, 533
Meissner, P. B., 268
Mencken, H. L., 298
Meredith, G., 292
Metzner, R. G. H., 317
Meyer, E., 543
Michotte, A., 538
Mill, J. S., 48, 50, 51, 54, 199, 524
Miller, J. G., 101
Miller, N. E., 104, 211, 245, 248
Mills, C. W., 183
Mira, E., 486, 487
Mischel, W., 317
Moore, B. V., 417
Moore, R. C., 307
Moreno, J. L., 442
Morgan, C. D., 51, 204, 348
Morgan, C. T., 231
Morris, C. W., 296
Mosteller, F., 387
Moustakas, C. E., 137

Mouton, J. S., 431
Mowrer, O. H., 79, 249
Muhlhan, G., 406
Müller, F. M., 24
Murchison, C. C., 97, 348
Murphy, G., 154, 177, 213, 234, 533, 553,
    567, 570
Murray, H. A., 11, 13, 51, 88, 168, 174, 182,
    203, 204, 264, 313, 314, 348, 370, 416,
    439, 510
Mussen, P., 510
Myers, I. B., 429

Neilon, P., 81
Nelson, E. N. P., 303
Nelson, V. L., 64
Newbert, N., 425
Newman, H. H., 64, 70, 71
Nietzsche, F. W., 119, 156
Norman, R. D., 292
Nuttin, J., 132, 258, 266, 267, 557

Odbert, H., 353
Oden, M. H., 65, 289
Office of Strategic Services, 333, 415
Olds, J., 231
Olson, W. C., 231
Onqué, G. C., 81
Orlansky, H., 77
Osgood, C. E., 328
OSS Assessment Staff, 333, 415

Pareto, V., 158
Parnell, R. W., 63
Parsons, T., 171, 182, 229, 314, 370, 570
Pascal, G. R., 489
Pauleikhoff, B., 415
Pavlov, I., 37, 39
Payne, S. L., 417
Peck, R. F., 134
Penfield, W., 49
Pepys, S., 402
Perlmutter, H. V., 514
Perron, R., 489
Perry, R. B., 366
Petrullo, L., 480, 512, 513, 515
Piaget, J., 76, 112, 121, 135, 233, 248, 249
Pigors, P., 12, 297, 454
Pildner, H., 444
Plato, 51, 143, 258
Poincaré, H., 16

Ponder, E., 463
Ponsonby, A., 405
Postman, L., 267
Power, M. E., 237
Prell, D. B., 70
Prince, B., 482
Prince, M., 26
Prinzhorn, H., 465, 469

Rand, H. A., 489, 490
Rank, O., 254, 269, 557
Rapaport, D., 148, 216, 217
Rasmussen, T., 49
Razran, G., 101, 106, 107
Reichline, P. B., 488
Reid, T., 48
Reiter, L., 481, 482
Rethlingshaefer, D., 229
Revers, W. J., 170
Rhode, S., 177
Richards, J. M., 505
Richardson, S. A., 519
Richter, C. P., 230
Rickers-Ovsiankina, M. A., 499
Rickman, J., 174
Ricks, D. F., 473
Riesman, D., 430
Roback, A. A., 32
Robinson, D., 177
Robinson, J. H., 159
Roe, A., 67, 71
Rogers, C. R., 381, 412
Rohracher, H., 481
Rokeach, M., 434
Rorschach, H., 438
Rose, R. J., 106
Rosenberg, B. G., 419
Rosenzweig, S., 14, 181, 397, 439
Ross, J. W. H., 293
Ross, W. D., 40
Rothacker, E., 144
Rothney, J. W. M., 7
Rousseau, J. J., 402
Ruggles, R., 426
Ryan, T. A., 213

St. James, 380
St. Paul, 144
Sanford, R. N., 433
Sarbin, T. R., 137, 369, 419, 514, 525, 527, 529, 531, 533

Sargant, W., 191
Schanck, R. L., 177
Scheerer, M., 128, 269, 492
Schein, E., 191
Scheler, M., 533
Schmidtke, H., 438
Schneider, D. M., 13, 88, 168, 174, 182
Schoenfeld, W., 383, 384
Schopenhauer, A., 144, 222, 259, 468
Schweitzer, A., 378
Scodel, A., 293, 510
Scott, T. H., 114
Sears, R. R., 29, 292
Secord, P. F., 132, 400, 480
Seder, J., 270
Seeman, W., 19
Seidenberg, B., 434
Senn, M. J. E., 277
Sewell, W. H., 77
Shaffer, J., 270
Shaffer, L. F., 335
Shakespeare, W., 50, 58, 117, 441
Shakow, D., 439
Shand, A., 50, 54
Shapiro, D., 515
Shapiro, M. M., 159
Shaw, G. B., 50, 381, 383
Sheldon, W. H., 39, 59, 61, 62, 350
Sherif, M., 265
Sherriffs, A. C., 131
Sherrington, C. S., 39, 99, 371
Shils, E. A., 171, 182, 229, 314, 370
Shipley, W. C., 425
Shirley, M., 81
Shneidman, E. S., 442
Shoben, E. J., 282, 335
Shuttleworth, F. K., 32, 314, 315
Sinnott, E. W., 361
Skinner, B. F., 73, 247, 439
Smith, H. C., 511, 565
Smith, K. V., 488
Smith, M. B., 276, 416
Smith, M. W., 166
Snygg, D., 119
Socrates, 290
Solomon, R. L., 210, 246
Sontag, L. W., 64
Sorokin, P. A., 415
Spencer, H., 51, 339
Spinoza, B., 379
Spitz, R. A., 78, 113, 203, 498

Spoerl, H. D., 47, 229, 378, 553
Spranger, E., 12, 18, 296, 297, 300, 350, 352, 454, 457, 543
Spurzheim, J. G., 47, 49
Stagner, R., 88, 171, 249, 274, 337, 452
Stein-Lewinson, T., 489, 490
Stephenson, W., 412
Stevens, S. S., 59, 70
Stevenson, R. L., 100
Stern, W., 15, 25, 229, 372, 378, 438, 469, 544, 553, 554
Stewart, D., 48
Stirner, M., 119
Stone, A. A., 81
Stone, L. J., 77, 122
Stouffer, S. A., 183
Straus, E. W., 462, 485
Strauss, A. L., 77
Strong, E., 236
Strunk, O., 117
Stumpf, J., 502
Suci, G. J., 328
Sullivan, H. S., 434
Sundberg, N., 452
Super, D. E., 397
Sutton, M. A., 326
Suzuki, D. T., 382
Swan, T. H., 486
Symonds, P. M., 314, 319

Tabin, J. K., 445
Taft, R., 19, 506, 511, 525, 527, 529, 531, 533, 543
Tagiuri, R., 480, 506, 512, 513, 515, 538
Talmadge, M., 487
Tanner, J. M., 92
Taylor, W. S., 32
Terman, L. M., 65, 289, 410
Thackeray, W., 45
Theophrastus, 31, 42, 43, 44, 45, 51, 54
Thibaut, J. W., 513
Thomae, H., 144, 408
Thomas, W. I., 201, 213
Thomas à Kempis, 484
Thompson, W. R., 68
Thorndike, E. L., 70, 105, 201, 318, 485
Thurstone, L. L., 326
Tillich, P., 282, 556, 557
Titchener, E. B., 311, 533, 551
Toby, J., 183
Togawa, Y., 440

Tolman, E. C., 229
Tolstoy, L., 378
Toman, W., 171, 511
Toulouse, E., 16
Tripp, C. A., 488
Trumbo, D. A., 511
Tryon, R. C., 64
Tucker, W. B., 59
Twain, Mark, 499
Tyl, M. McI., 473

Veblen, T., 228
Vernon, P. E., 65, 292, 299, 387, 418, 443, 447, 454, 455, 474, 504, 508
Von Bracken, H., 31, 71, 266, 438, 525, 557
Von Herder, J. G., 376

Waehner, T. S., 447
Wahl, J., 557
Walker, L., 492
Walker, W. M., 132
Wallach, H., 105
Wallach, M. A., 476
Wallas, G., 216, 222
Walter, W. C., 73
Wapner, W., 268, 518
Warren, A. B., 307
Warren, H. C., 26, 115
Wartegg, E., 442
Watson, G. B., 318
Weider, A., 425
Weil, A., 121
Weinberg, G. H., 488
Wellek, A., 144, 532
Wells, H. G., 402
Welsh, G. S., 435
Werner, H., 117, 540
Weschler, I. R., 536
Wessman, A. E., 473
West, L. J., 191
White, R. K., 408
White, R. W., 213, 416, 453, 569
Whitehead, A. N., 266, 379
Whiting, J., 174
Whitman, W., 530
Wiegard, G. E., 486
Wikler, A., 232
Williams, R. J., 5, 70
Wilsmann, A. C., 487
Windelband, W., 9
Winthrop, H., 62

Wisser, R., 568
Witkin, H. A., 268
Witty, P. A., 315
Wolf, K. M., 78, 203
Wolfe, J. B., 209
Wolff, C., 48
Wolff, H. G., 186
Wolff, W., 388, 474, 478, 482, 488, 490
Wolman, B. B., 498, 524
Woodworth, D. G., 493
Woodworth, R. S., 207, 212, 213, 229, 249,
    424, 466, 569
Wright, H. F., 414, 482

Wright, R., 402
Wundt, W., 38, 39, 311, 551
Wyatt, F., 258
Wynne, L. C., 210, 246

Young, S., 45
Yule, G. U., 484

Zeigarnik, B., 233
Zelen, S. L., 411
Zimmerman, W. S., 326
Znaniecki, F., 183, 201
Zubin, J., 254, 453

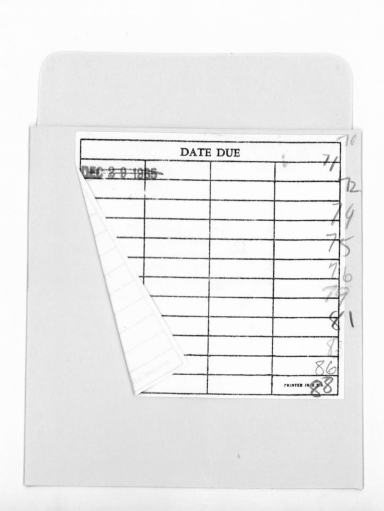